Internetworking With … /IP

Vol I:

Principles, Protocols, … …ure

Sixth Editio…

To Chris

Contents

Chapter 7 Internet Protocol: Connectionless Datagram Delivery (IPv4, IPv6) 119

Chapter 8 Internet Protocol: Forwarding IP Datagrams 147

Chapter 25 World Wide Web (HTTP) 525

Chapter 26 Voice And Video Over IP (RTP, RSVP, QoS) 539

Chapter 30 Connected Embedded Systems (The Internet of Things) 623

Appendix 1 Glossary Of Internetworking Terms And Abbreviations 639

Index 681

Foreword

It is a rare treat to be asked to write a foreword to the sixth edition of Doug Comer's now classic book on TCP/IP and the Internet. In 2012, there are nearly 3 billion people on line. Something like 6.5 billion mobile phones are in use and many of these are "smart phones" that have access to the Internet via the wireless telephone network and through Wi-Fi. In fact, the wireless systems are diverting traffic to Wi-Fi when this is possible in order to shed load. The most recent data from Telegeography is that 77 Tbps (terabits per second) flow across the Internet. A substantial component of the traffic is video, but increasingly, large data files are transferred that contain genetic sequence information, data from telescopes, sensor systems, the Large Hadron Collider, and other scientific instruments.

We have learned a lot about TCP/IP in many contexts, and this text collects much of the wisdom. We have learned that buffer memory may not be our friend if large amounts of it are located in a network device where there is a major drop in capacity. This is the so-called "buffer bloat" problem described in Chapter 11. Where a high-speed link meets a low-speed link, large buffers take a long time to empty going in the low-speed direction, which has the effect of increasing delay and affecting TCP flow control, generating serious congestion with all its negative side effects. We have also learned that there are conditions under which TCP/IP works poorly. Here I am thinking about highly disrupted and variably delayed environments. Examples include interplanetary communication and tactical communication (including mobile as well as military). For these conditions, new kinds of protocols called "delay and disruption tolerant networking" (DTN) are needed to supplement things like TCP. In fact, DTN can run over TCP or UDP or virtually any other transmission subsystem. The protocols that implement this type of networking are already in use on the International Space Station and on the rovers now on Mars!

New ideas such as Software Defined Networking and the OpenFlow protocol from Stanford University, described in Chapter 28, are also coloring the future of the Internet. While these systems can operate to support conventional Internet architectures, they are also able to go beyond the conventional notions of addressing to support content-based routing, among other things. Management of end-to-end flows works well with such systems. In addition to that, it seems timely to revisit wireless communication and to ask how broadcast modes could influence further evolution of the Internet. One imagines satellites "raining" IP or UDP packets down on hundreds of millions of receivers. In terrestrial contexts, the ability to radiate 360 degrees allows multiple receivers to receive one transmission. Advances in sharing of spectrum and in the use of beam-forming antennas make this an even more rich and intriguing area to explore.

The Internet continues to expand and change in unexpected ways. In addition to devices that humans use, a new wave of sensors, cameras, and actuators are being connected that will give us remote access and control of everything from scientific data to the lights in a building and manufacturing processes. We refer to the new devices as an *Internet of Things*; they are described in Chapter 30.

As I think this book amply demonstrates, the Internet is still exciting. There is still much research to be carried out in support of new and challenging applications. Opportunities for collaboration grow by the day.

Welcome to the 21st Century Internet where innovation is still the order of the day. This book provides the background you need to understand and participate.

Vint Cerf
Internet Evangelist, Google
President, ACM

March, 2013

Preface

Internetworking and TCP/IP now dominate all of networking — even telephone companies that were once the exclusive bastions of circuit switched networks have adopted IP technology. Two more revolutionary changes are occurring that rely on internetworking: the cloud computing paradigm and the Internet of Things. In the cloud model, computation and storage are performed in cloud data centers. Users rely on the Internet to upload, download, and access their information and to share data with others. The phrase *Internet of Things* is used to characterize an Internet of intelligent, embedded devices that act autonomously rather than devices, such as smart phones and laptops, that a human operates. Using Internet technology allows embedded devices to communicate with remote servers as well as with one another; the resulting cyber infrastructure already includes devices in homes, offices, and stores, as well as sensors that measure the environment and civil structures such as bridges and dams.

Many readers have requested that the text be updated to reflect recent changes; many have suggested specific topics and emphasis. Twenty years after its invention, IPv6 is finally gaining acceptance. Voice and video have replaced file transfer as major uses of the Internet. The sixth edition responds to readers suggestions by reorganizing and updating existing chapters and introducing new material. In particular, chapters on the early applications of Telnet and FTP have been eliminated to make space for newer material. A new chapter on the Internet of Things considers the use of TCP/IP in a wireless sensor network. A new chapter on Software Defined Networking examines the use of OpenFlow which, although is it not an IETF standard, has become an important part of network and Internet management.

To satisfy an oft-repeated request, the chapter on protocol layering has been moved earlier in the text. Instructors are warned, however, that layering is not a rigid architecture that explains all protocols. Students should see it as a basic but somewhat simplistic guideline that helps us understand protocols. In Chapter 30, for example, we learn that the protocols for a route-over mesh blur the boundaries between layers by adding shims and blending IP forwarding with Layer 2 reachability.

Each chapter has been updated to focus on ideas and technologies that are now being used in the Internet. The most significant change consists of integrating the IPv6 discussion with that of IPv4. Each chapter describes a principle, explains the general design, and then proceeds to explain how the principle applies to IPv4 and IPv6. Readers will see that the two versions of IP are closely interrelated and that it is impossible to understand the changes introduced by IPv6 without understanding IPv4.

Like earlier editions, which have been extremely popular, the entire text focuses on concepts and principles. Early chapters describe the motivation for internetworking and give the fundamentals of the TCP/IP internet technology. We will see that internetworking is a powerful abstraction that allows us to deal with the complexity of multiple underlying communication technologies by hiding the details of network hardware. We will understand the network level services that an internet provides and see how applications use the services. Later chapters fill in details. The text reviews both the architecture of network interconnections and the principles underlying protocols that make such interconnected networks function as a single, unified communication system.

After reading the book, you will understand how it is possible to interconnect multiple physical networks into a coordinated system, how internet protocols operate in that environment, and how application programs use the resulting system. As a specific example, you will learn the details of the global TCP/IP Internet, including the architecture of its router system and the application protocols it supports. In addition, you will understand some of the limitations of the internet approach and the TCP/IP protocols.

Designed as both a college text and as a professional reference, the book is written at an advanced undergraduate or graduate level. For professionals, the book provides a comprehensive introduction to the TCP/IP technology and the architecture of the Internet. Although it is not intended to replace protocol standards documents, the book is an excellent starting point for learning about internetworking because it provides a uniform overview that emphasizes principles. Moreover, it gives the reader perspective that can be extremely difficult to obtain from individual protocol documents.

When used in the classroom, the text provides more than sufficient material for a single semester network course at either the undergraduate or graduate level. In a graduate course, I urge professors to include significant design and implementation projects as well as readings from the literature that provide a basis for further exploration. Many of the exercises suggest such subtleties; solving them often requires students to read protocol standards and apply creative energy to comprehend consequences. For undergraduate courses, many of the details are unnecessary. Students should be expected to grasp the basic concepts described in the text, and they should be able to describe and use the fundamental protocols.

At all levels, hands-on experience sharpens the concepts and helps students gain intuition. Thus, I encourage instructors to invent projects that give students opportunities to use Internet services and protocols. In an undergraduate course, most of the projects will consist of writing applications that use the network. In my undergraduate course, I have students write a simplified network analyzer (i.e., given a packet in binary, print the value of each field). The semester project in my graduate Internetworking course at Purdue requires students to build significant IP protocol software; the traditional project involves implementing an IP router. We supply hardware and the source code for an operating system, including device drivers for network interfaces; students build a working router that interconnects three networks with different MTUs. The course is extremely rigorous, students work in teams, and the results have been impressive (many industries recruit graduates from the course). Although such experimentation is safest when the instructional laboratory network is isolated from production computing facilities, we have found that students exhibit the most enthusiasm, and benefit the most, when they have access to the global Internet and can test that their protocols interoperate with commercial versions.

The book is organized into five main parts. Chapters 1 and 2 form an introduction that provides an overview and discusses existing network technologies. In particular, Chapter 2 reviews physical network hardware. The intention is to provide basic intuition about the functionality the hardware supplies and what is possible, not to spend inordinate time on hardware details. Chapters 3–11 describe the TCP/IP Internet from the viewpoint of a single host, showing the protocols a host contains and how they operate. They cover the internet abstraction, the notion of protocol layering, the basics of Internet addressing and forwarding, and transport protocols. Chapters 12–14 consider the architecture of an internet when viewed globally. They explore routing architecture and the protocols routers use to exchange routing information. Chapters 15–19 consider variations and extensions of the basic technology, including multicasting, packet classification, network virtualization, and mobility. In particular, the chapter on mobility explains why mobility is difficult in an IP network. Finally, Chapters 20–30 discuss application level services available in the Internet (including network management), network security, and the Internet of Things. The chapters present the client-server model of interaction, give several examples of applications that use the client-server model, and show how client-server interaction applies to computer bootstrap and network management. Chapter 28 explains a new approach to network management known as Software Defined Networking (SDN) and the chief protocol, OpenFlow. Although not an official part of the TCP/IP standards, SDN technology has been included because it has generated considerable excitement.

The chapters have been organized bottom up. Instead of starting by viewing the Internet as a black box and learning how to use it, the text begins with an overview of hardware and continues to add the concepts and protocols needed to create the Internet. The bottom-up view will appeal to anyone who is interested in engineering because it follows the pattern one uses when building a system. In some classes, professors prefer to begin with Chapters 20 and 21 on client-server programming, which permits their students to start writing network applications early. Although writing applications that *use* the Internet is important, I urge professors to also include assignments that help students understand the underlying technology (i.e., protocols and packets). In one lab assignment, for example, I have students devise a very basic protocol to contact another endpoint and transfer two packets: one contains a file name and the other contains data for the file. Between the sender and receiver, an application randomly drops, duplicates, delays, and changes the contents of the packets. The experiment is carried out with UDP, making the implementation trivial. However, the students become keenly aware of how difficult it is to design protocols.

A modest background is required to understand the material. Readers do not need sophisticated mathematics, nor do they need to know information theory or theorems from data communications; the book describes the physical network as a black box around which an internetwork can be built. Readers are expected to have a basic understanding of computer systems and to be familiar with data structures like stacks, queues, and trees. In addition, a reader should have basic intuition about the services an operating system supplies and the notion that processes can execute concurrently. Prior understanding of Internet technology is not assumed: the text states all design principles clearly, and discusses motivations and consequences.

Many people deserve credit for contributing suggestions and ideas to various editions of the text over the years. For this edition, a set of reviewers commented on the organization, items that needed to be updated, and helped check technical details. I thank Anthony Barnard, Tom Calabrese, Ralph Droms, Tom Edmunds, Raymond Kelso, Lee Kirk, John Lin, Dave Roberts, Gustavo Rodriguez-Rivera, and Bhaskar Sharma who all reviewed a draft of the manuscript. John and Ralph were especially helpful. Barry Shein contributed the example client-server code in Chapter 21.

As always, my wife Christine provided the most help. She spent hours with the manuscript, identifying ambiguities, finding inconsistencies, and smoothing wording.

Douglas E. Comer

March, 2013

What Others Have Said About The Sixth Edition Of Internetworking With TCP/IP

"This is the book I go to for clear explanations of the basic principles and latest developments in TCP/IP technologies. It's a 'must have' reference for networking professionals."

Dr. Ralph Droms
Cisco Systems
Chair of the DHCP working group

"Excellent book! Thank you!"

Henrik Sundin
NTI Gymnasiet
Stockholm, Sweden

"The 6th Edition of Comer's classic *Internetworking* documents the ongoing and accelerating evolution of the Internet, while predicting the future with unmatched understanding and clarity."

Dr. Paul V. Mockapetris
Inventor of the Domain Name System

"... a true masterpiece."

Mr. Javier Sandino
Systems Engineer

"The best-written TCP/IP book I have ever read. Dr. Comer explains complex ideas clearly, with excellent diagrams and explanations. With this edition, Dr. Comer makes this classic textbook contemporary."

Dr. John Lin
Bell Laboratories

"This update to the definitive reference for the Internet's key technologies confirms Doug Comer's reputation for clear and accurate presentation of essential information; it should be the cornerstone of any Internet professional's library."

Dr. Lyman Chapin
Interisle Consulting Group
Former IAB Chair

"One of the greatest books I have read. True genius is when you are not only fluent in your field, but can get your point across simply. Thank you Dr. Comer for writing a great book!"

Marvin E. Miller
CIO, The ACS Corporation

"In a world of complexity, the ability to convey knowledge as opposed to information from a search engine is quite hard. Few make it seem as easy as Doug Comer, whose book *Internetworking Volume 1* continues to play a key role in teaching us about the role of protocols in the ever-changing Internet."

Dr. Balachander Krishnamurthy
AT&T Labs

"Rapid evolution of the Internet is happening as the entire world uses the Internet on a daily, hourly, or even continuous basis (as is the case with my grandchildren). Comer accurately tracks the relevant technological underpinnings for those building the Internet today."

Dan Lynch
Founder, INTEROP

About The Author

Dr. Douglas Comer, Distinguished Professor of Computer Science at Purdue University and former VP of Research at Cisco, is an internationally recognized expert on computer networking, the TCP/IP protocols, and the Internet. The author of numerous refereed articles and technical books, he is a pioneer in the development of curriculum and laboratories for research and education.

A prolific author, Comer's popular books have been translated into over 15 languages, and are used in industry as well as computer science, engineering, and business departments around the world. His landmark three-volume series *Internetworking With TCP/IP* revolutionized networking and network education. His textbooks and innovative laboratory manuals have and continue to shape graduate and undergraduate curricula.

The accuracy and insight of Dr. Comer's books reflect his extensive background in computer systems. His research spans both hardware and software. He has created a complete operating system, written device drivers, and implemented network protocol software for conventional computers as well as network processors. The resulting software has been used by industry in a variety of products.

Comer has created and teaches courses on network protocols and computer technologies for a variety of audiences, including courses for engineers as well as academic audiences. His innovative educational laboratories allow him and his students to design and implement working prototypes of large, complex systems, and measure the performance of the resulting prototypes. He continues to teach at industries, universities, and conferences around the world. In addition, Comer consults for industry on the design of computer networks and systems.

For over eighteen years, Professor Comer served as editor-in-chief of the research journal *Software — Practice and Experience.* He is a Fellow of the ACM, a Fellow of the Purdue Teaching Academy, and a recipient of numerous awards, including a Usenix Lifetime Achievement award.

Additional information can be found at:

www.cs.purdue.edu/people/comer

and information about Comer's books can be found at:

www.comerbooks.com

Internetworking With TCP/IP

Vol I:

Principles, Protocols, and Architecture

Sixth Edition

Chapter Contents

1

Introduction And Overview

1.1 The Motivation For Internetworking

Internet communication has become a fundamental part of life. Social networks, such as Facebook, provide connections among a group of friends and allow them to share interests. The World Wide Web contains information about such diverse subjects as politics, atmospheric conditions, stock prices, crop production, and airline fares. Family and friends use the Internet to share photos and keep in touch with VoIP telephone calls and live video chats. Consumers use the Internet to purchase goods and services and for personal banking. Companies take orders and make payments electronically. The move to cloud computing will put more information and services online.

Although it appears to operate as a unified network, the Internet is not engineered from a single networking technology because no technology suffices for all uses. Instead, networking hardware is designed for specific situations and budgets. Some groups need high-speed wired networks to connect computers in a single building. Others need a low-cost wireless network for a private home. Because low-cost hardware that works well inside a building cannot span large geographic distances, an alternative must be used to connect sites that are thousands of miles apart.

In the 1970s, a technology was created that makes it possible to interconnect many disparate individual networks and operate them as a coordinated unit. Known as *internetworking,* the technology forms the basis for the Internet by accommodating multiple, diverse underlying hardware technologies, providing a way to interconnect the networks, and defining a set of communication conventions that the networks use to interoperate. The internet technology hides the details of network hardware, and permits computers to communicate independent of their physical network connections.

Internet technology is an example of *open system interconnection*. It is called *open* because, unlike proprietary communication systems available from one specific vendor, the specifications are publicly available. Thus, any individual or company can build the hardware and software needed to communicate across the Internet. More important, the entire technology has been designed to foster communication among machines with diverse hardware architectures, to use almost any packet switched network hardware, to accommodate a wide variety of applications, and to accommodate arbitrary computer operating systems.

1.2 The TCP/IP Internet

In the 1970s and 1980s, U.S. government agencies realized the importance and potential of internet technology, and funded research that made possible a global Internet†. This book discusses principles and ideas that resulted from research funded by the *Defense Advanced Research Projects Agency* (*DARPA*‡). The DARPA technology includes a set of network standards that specify the details of how computers communicate, as well as a set of conventions for interconnecting networks and forwarding traffic. Officially named the *TCP/IP Internet Protocol Suite* and commonly referred to as *TCP/IP* (after the names of its two main standards), it can be used to communicate across any set of interconnected networks. For example, TCP/IP can be used to interconnect a set of networks within a single building, within a physical campus, or among a set of campuses.

Although the TCP/IP technology is noteworthy by itself, it is especially interesting because its viability has been demonstrated on a large scale. It forms the base technology for the global Internet that connects approximately two billion individuals in homes, schools, corporations, and governments in virtually all populated areas of the planet. An outstanding success, the Internet demonstrates the viability of the TCP/IP technology and shows how it can accommodate a wide variety of underlying hardware technologies.

1.3 Internet Services

One cannot appreciate the technical details underlying TCP/IP without understanding the services it provides. This section reviews internet services briefly, highlighting the services most users access, and leaves to later chapters the discussion of how computers connect to a TCP/IP internet and how the functionality is implemented.

Much of our discussion of services will focus on standards called *protocols*. Protocol specifications, such as those for TCP and IP, define the syntactic and semantic rules for communication. They give the details of message formats, describe how a computer responds when a message arrives, and specify how a computer handles errors or other abnormal conditions. Most important, protocols allow us to discuss computer communication independent of any particular vendor's network hardware. In a sense, protocols

†We will follow the usual convention of capitalizing *Internet* when referring specifically to the global Internet, and use lower case to refer to private internets that use TCP/IP technology.

‡At various times, *DARPA* has been called the *Advanced Research Projects Agency* (*ARPA*).

are to communication what algorithms are to computation. An algorithm allows one to specify or understand a computation without knowing the details of a particular programming language or CPU instruction set. Similarly, a communication protocol allows one to specify or understand data communication without depending on detailed knowledge of a particular vendor's network hardware.

Hiding the low-level details of communication helps improve productivity in several ways. First, because they can use higher-level protocol abstractions, programmers do not need to learn or remember as many details about a given hardware configuration. Thus, they can create new network applications quickly. Second, because software built using higher-level abstractions are not restricted to a particular computer architecture or a particular network hardware, the applications do not need to be changed when computers or networks are replaced or reconfigured. Third, because applications built using higher-level protocols are independent of the underlying hardware, they can be ported to arbitrary computers. That is, a programmer does not need to build a special version of an application for each type of computer or each type of network. Instead, applications that use high-level abstractions are more general-purpose — the same code can be compiled and run on an arbitrary computer.

We will see that the details of each service available on the Internet are given by a separate protocol. The next sections refer to protocols that specify some of the application-level services as well as those used to define network-level services. Later chapters explain each of the protocols in detail.

1.3.1 Application Level Internet Services

From a user's point of view, the Internet appears to consist of a set of application programs that use the underlying network to carry out useful tasks. We use the term *interoperability* to refer to the ability of diverse computing systems to cooperate in solving computational problems. Because the Internet was designed to accommodate heterogeneous networks and computers, interoperability was a key requirement. Consequently, Internet application programs usually exhibit a high degree of interoperability. In fact, most users access applications without understanding the types of computers or networks being used, the communication protocols, or even the path data travels from its source to its destination. Thus, a user might access a web page from a desktop system connected to a cable modem or from an iPad connected to a 4G wireless network.

The most popular and widespread Internet application services include:

- *World Wide Web.* The Web became the largest source of traffic on the global Internet between 1994 and 1995, and remains so. Many popular services, including Internet search (e.g., Google) and social networking (e.g., Facebook), use web technology. One estimate attributes approximately one quarter of all Internet traffic to Facebook. Although users distinguish among various web-based services, we will see that they all use the same application-level protocol.

- *Cloud Access And Remote Desktop.* Cloud computing places computation and storage facilities in *cloud data centers*, and arranges for users to access the services over the Internet. One access technology, known as a *remote desktop service*, allows a user to access a computer in a remote data center as if the computer is local. The user only needs an interface device with a screen, keyboard, mouse or touchpad, and a network connection. When the data center computer updates the video display, the remote desktop service captures the information, sends it across the Internet, and displays it on the user's screen. When the user moves the mouse or presses a key, the remote desktop service sends the information to the data center. Thus, the user has full access to a powerful PC, but only needs to carry a basic interface device such as a tablet.

- *File Transfer.* The file transfer protocol allows users to send or receive a copy of a data file. Many file downloads, including movie downloads, invoke a file transfer mechanism. Because they often invoke file transfer from a web page, users may not be aware that a file transfer application has run.

- *Electronic Mail (email).* Electronic mail, which once accounted for large amounts of Internet traffic, has largely been replaced by web applications. Many users now access email through a web application that allows a user to read messages in their mailbox, select a message for processing, and forward the message or send a reply. Once a user specifies sending a message, the underlying system uses an email transfer protocol to send the message to the recipient's mailbox.

- *Voice And Video Services.* Both streaming video and audio already account for a nontrivial fraction of bits transported across the global Internet, and the trend will continue. More important, a significant change is occurring; video upload is increasing, especially because users are using mobile devices to send video of live events.

We will return to a discussion of applications in later chapters and examine them in more detail. We will see exactly how applications use the underlying TCP/IP protocols, and why having standards for application protocols has helped ensure that they are widespread.

1.3.2 Network-Level Internet Services

A programmer who creates network applications has an entirely different view of the Internet than a user who merely runs applications such as web browsers. At the network level, the Internet provides two broad services that all application programs use. While it is unimportant at this time to understand the details of the services, they are fundamental to an overview of TCP/IP:

- *Connectionless Packet Delivery Service.* Packet delivery, explained in detail throughout the text, forms the basis for all internet services. Connectionless delivery is an abstraction of the service that most packet-switching networks offer. It means simply that a TCP/IP internet forwards small messages from one computer to another based on address information carried in the message. Because it forwards each packet independently, an internet does not guarantee reliable, in-order delivery. However, because it maps directly onto most of the underlying hardware technologies, a connectionless delivery service is extremely efficient. More important, because the design makes connectionless packet delivery the basis for all internet services, the TCP/IP protocols can accommodate a wide range of network hardware.

- *Reliable Stream Transport Service.* Most applications require the communication software to recover automatically from transmission errors, lost packets, or failures of intermediate switches along the path between sender and receiver. Consequently, most applications need a reliable transport service to handle problems. The Internet's reliable stream service allows an application on one computer to establish a "connection" to an application on another computer, and allows the applications to transfer arbitrarily large amounts of data across the connection as if it were a permanent, direct hardware link. Underneath, the communication protocols divide the stream of data into small packets and send them one at a time, waiting for the receiver to acknowledge reception.

Many networks provide basic services similar to those outlined above, so one might wonder what distinguishes TCP/IP services from others. The primary distinguishing features are:

- *Network Technology Independence.* Although it is based on conventional packet switching technology, TCP/IP is independent of any particular brand or type of hardware; the global Internet includes a variety of network technologies. TCP/IP protocols define the unit of data transmission, called a *datagram*, and specify how to transmit datagrams on a particular network, but nothing in a datagram is tied to specific hardware.

- *Universal Interconnection.* The Internet allows any arbitrary pair of computers to communicate. Each computer is assigned an *address* that is universally recognized throughout the Internet. Every datagram carries the addresses of its source and destination. Intermediate devices use the destination address to make forwarding decisions; a sender only needs to know the address of a recipient and the Internet takes care of forwarding datagrams.

- *End-to-End Acknowledgements.* The TCP/IP Internet protocols provide acknowledgements between the original source and ultimate destination instead of between successive machines along the path, even if the source and destination do not connect to a common physical network.

- *Application Protocol Standards.* In addition to the basic transport-level services (like reliable stream connections), the TCP/IP protocols include standards for many common applications, including protocols that specify how to access a web page, transfer a file, and send email. Thus, when designing applications that use TCP/IP, programmers often find that existing application protocols provide the communication services they need.

Later chapters discuss the details of the services provided to the programmer as well as examples of application protocol standards.

1.4 History And Scope Of The Internet

Part of what makes the TCP/IP technology so exciting is its universal adoption, as well as the size and growth rate of the global Internet. DARPA began working toward an internet technology in the mid 1970s, with the architecture and protocols taking their current form around 1977–79. At that time, DARPA was known as the primary funding agency for packet-switched network research, and pioneered many ideas in packet-switching with its well-known *ARPANET*. The ARPANET used conventional point-to-point leased line interconnections, but DARPA also funded exploration of packet-switching over radio networks and satellite communication channels. Indeed, the growing diversity of network hardware technologies helped force DARPA to study network interconnection, and pushed internetworking forward.

The availability of research funding from DARPA caught the attention and imagination of several research groups, especially those researchers who had previous experience using packet switching on the ARPANET. DARPA scheduled informal meetings of researchers to share ideas and discuss results of experiments. Informally, the group was known as the *Internet Research Group*. By 1979, so many researchers were involved in the TCP/IP effort that DARPA created an informal committee to coordinate and guide the design of the protocols and architecture of the emerging Internet. Called the *Internet Control and Configuration Board* (*ICCB*), the group met regularly until 1983, when it was reorganized.

The global Internet began around 1980 when DARPA started converting computers attached to its research networks to the new TCP/IP protocols. The ARPANET, already in place, quickly became the backbone of the new Internet and was used for many of the early experiments with TCP/IP. The transition to Internet technology became complete in January 1983 when the Office of the Secretary of Defense mandated that all computers connected to long-haul networks use TCP/IP. At the same time, the *Defense Communication Agency* (*DCA*) split the ARPANET into two separate networks, one for further research and one for military communication. The research part retained the name ARPANET; the military part, which was somewhat larger, became known as the *military network* (*MILNET*).

To encourage university researchers to adopt and use the new protocols, DARPA made an implementation available at low cost. At that time, most university computer science departments were running a version of the UNIX operating system available in the University of California's *Berkeley Software Distribution*, commonly called *BSD UNIX*. By funding Bolt Beranek and Newman, Incorporated (*BBN*) to implement its TCP/IP protocols for use with UNIX and funding Berkeley to integrate the protocols with its software distribution, DARPA was able to reach over 90% of university computer science departments. The new protocol software came at a particularly significant time because many departments were just acquiring second or third computers and connecting them together with local area networks. The departments needed communication protocols that provided application services such as file transfer.

Besides a set of utility programs, Berkeley UNIX created a new operating system abstraction known as a *socket* to allow applications to access the Internet protocols. A generalization of the UNIX mechanism for I/O, the socket interface has options for other network protocols besides TCP/IP. The introduction of the socket abstraction was important because it allowed programmers to use TCP/IP protocols with little effort. The socket interface has become a de facto standard, and is now used in most operating systems.

Realizing that network communication would soon be a crucial part of scientific research, the National Science Foundation (NSF) took an active role in expanding the TCP/IP Internet to reach as many scientists as possible. In the late 1970s, NSF funded a project known as the *Computer Science NETwork* (*CSNET*), which had as its goal connecting all computer scientists. Starting in 1985, NSF began a program to establish access networks centered around its six supercomputer centers, and in 1986 expanded networking efforts by funding a new wide area backbone network, known as the *NSFNET backbone*. NSF also provided seed money for regional networks, each of which connected major scientific research institutions in a given area.

By 1984, the Internet reached over 1,000 computers. In 1987, the size grew to over 10,000. By 1990, the size topped 100,000, and by 1993, exceeded 1,000,000. In 1997, more than 10,000,000 computers were permanently attached to the Internet, and in 2001, the size exceeded 100,000,000. In 2011, the Internet reached over 800,000,000 permanently-attached computers.

The early growth of the Internet did not occur merely because universities and government-funded groups adopted the protocols. Major computer corporations connected to the Internet, as did many other large corporations including oil companies, the auto industry, electronics firms, pharmaceutical companies, and telecommunications carriers. Medium and small companies began connecting in the 1990s. In addition, many companies experimented by using TCP/IP protocols on their internal corporate intranets before they chose to be part of the global Internet.

1.5 The Internet Architecture Board

Because the TCP/IP Internet protocol suite did not arise from a specific vendor or from a recognized professional society, it is natural to ask, "who set the technical direction and decided when protocols became standard?" The answer is a group known as the *Internet Architecture Board* (*IAB*†) that was formed in 1983 when DARPA reorganized the Internet Control and Configuration Board. The IAB provided the focus and coordination for much of the research and development underlying the TCP/IP protocols, and guided the evolution of the Internet. The IAB decided which protocols were a required part of the TCP/IP suite and set official policies.

†IAB originally stood for *Internet Activities Board.*

1.6 The IAB Reorganization

By the summer of 1989, both the TCP/IP technology and the Internet had grown beyond the initial research project into production facilities upon which thousands of people depended for daily business. It was no longer possible to introduce new ideas by changing a few installations overnight. To a large extent, the hundreds of commercial companies that offered TCP/IP products determined whether their products would interoperate by deciding when to incorporate protocol changes in their software. Researchers who drafted specifications and tested new ideas in laboratories could no longer expect instant acceptance and use of the ideas. It was ironic that the researchers who designed and watched TCP/IP develop found themselves overcome by the commercial success of their brainchild. In short, the TCP/IP protocols and the Internet became a successful production technology, and the marketplace began to dominate its evolution.

To reflect the political and commercial realities of both TCP/IP and the Internet, the IAB was reorganized in the summer of 1989. Researchers were moved from the IAB itself to a subsidiary group known as the *Internet Research Task Force* (*IRTF*), and a new IAB board was constituted to include representatives from the wider community. Responsibility for protocol standards and other technical aspects passed to a group known as the *Internet Engineering Task Force* (*IETF*).

The IETF existed in the original IAB structure, and its success provided part of the motivation for reorganization. Unlike most IAB task forces, which were limited to a few individuals who focused on one specific issue, the IETF was large — before the reorganization, it had grown to include dozens of active members who worked on many problems concurrently. Following the reorganization, the IETF was divided into over 20 *working groups*, each of which focused on a specific problem.

Because the IETF was too large for a single chairperson to manage, it has been divided into a set of approximately one dozen areas, each with its own manager. The IETF chairperson and the area managers constitute the *Internet Engineering Steering Group* (*IESG*), the individuals responsible for coordinating the efforts of IETF working groups. The name *IETF* now refers to the entire body, including the chairperson, area managers, and all members of working groups.

1.7 Internet Request For Comments (RFCs)

We have said that no vendor owns the TCP/IP technology, nor does any professional society or standards body. Thus, the documentation of protocols, standards, and policies cannot be obtained from a vendor. Instead, the IETF manages the standardization process. The resulting protocol documents are kept in an on-line repository and made available at no charge.

Documentation of work on the Internet, proposals for new or revised protocols, and TCP/IP protocol standards all appear in a series of technical reports called Internet *Requests For Comments*, or *RFC*s. RFCs can be short or long, can cover broad concepts or details, and can be standards or merely proposals for new protocols. There are references to RFCs throughout the text. While RFCs are not refereed in the same way as academic research papers, they are reviewed and edited. For many years, a single individual, the late Jon Postel, served as the RFC editor. The task of editing RFCs now falls to area managers of the IETF; the IESG as a whole approves new RFCs.

The RFC series is numbered sequentially in the chronological order RFCs are written. Each new or revised RFC is assigned a new number, so readers must be careful to obtain the highest numbered version of a document; an RFC index is available to help identify the correct version. In addition, preliminary versions of RFC documents, which are known as *Internet drafts*, are available.

RFCs and Internet Drafts can be obtained from:

www.ietf.org

1.8 Internet Growth

The Internet has grown rapidly and continues to evolve. New protocols are being proposed; old ones are being revised. The most significant demand on the underlying technology does not arise from added network connections, but from additional traffic. As new users connect to the Internet and new applications appear, traffic patterns change. For example, when the *World Wide Web* was introduced, it became incredibly popular, and Internet traffic increased dramatically. Later, when music sharing became popular, traffic patterns changed again. More changes are occurring as the Internet is used for telephone, video, and social networking.

Figure 1.1 summarizes expansion of the Internet, and illustrates an important component of growth: much of the change in complexity has arisen because multiple groups now manage various parts of the whole.

	Number of networks	Number of computers	Number of users	Number of managers
1980	10	10^2	10^2	10^0
1990	10^3	10^5	10^6	10^1
2000	10^5	10^7	10^8	10^2
2010	10^6	10^8	10^9	10^3

Figure 1.1 Growth of the Internet. In addition to increases in traffic, complexity has resulted from decentralized management.

The number of computers attached to the Internet helps illustrate the growth. Figure 1.2 contains a plot.

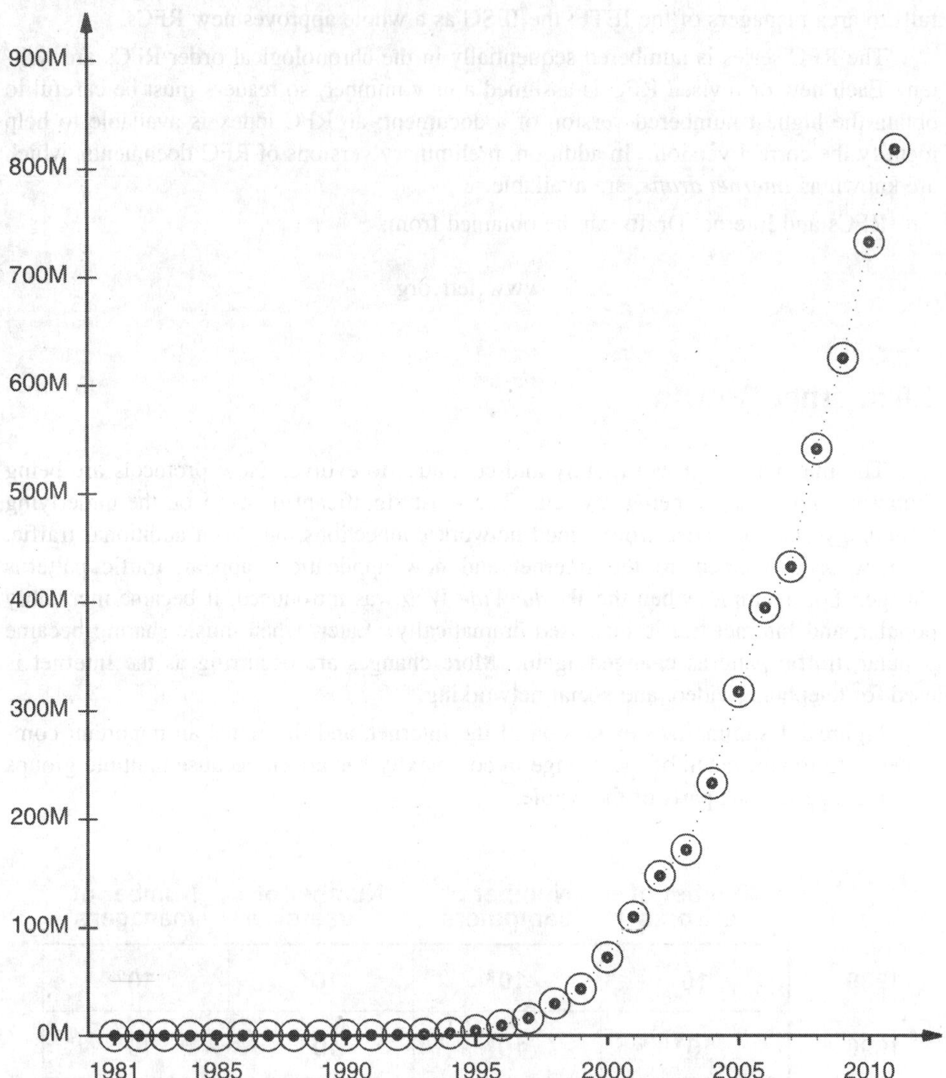

Figure 1.2 Computers on the Internet as a function of the year (linear scale).

The plot makes it appear that the Internet did not start to grow until the late 1990s. However, the linear scale hides an important point: even in the early Internet, the growth rate was high. Figure 1.3 shows the same data plotted on a log scale. The figure reveals that although the count of computers was much smaller, some of the most rapid growth occurred in the late 1980s when the Internet grew from 1,000 computers to over 10,000 computers.

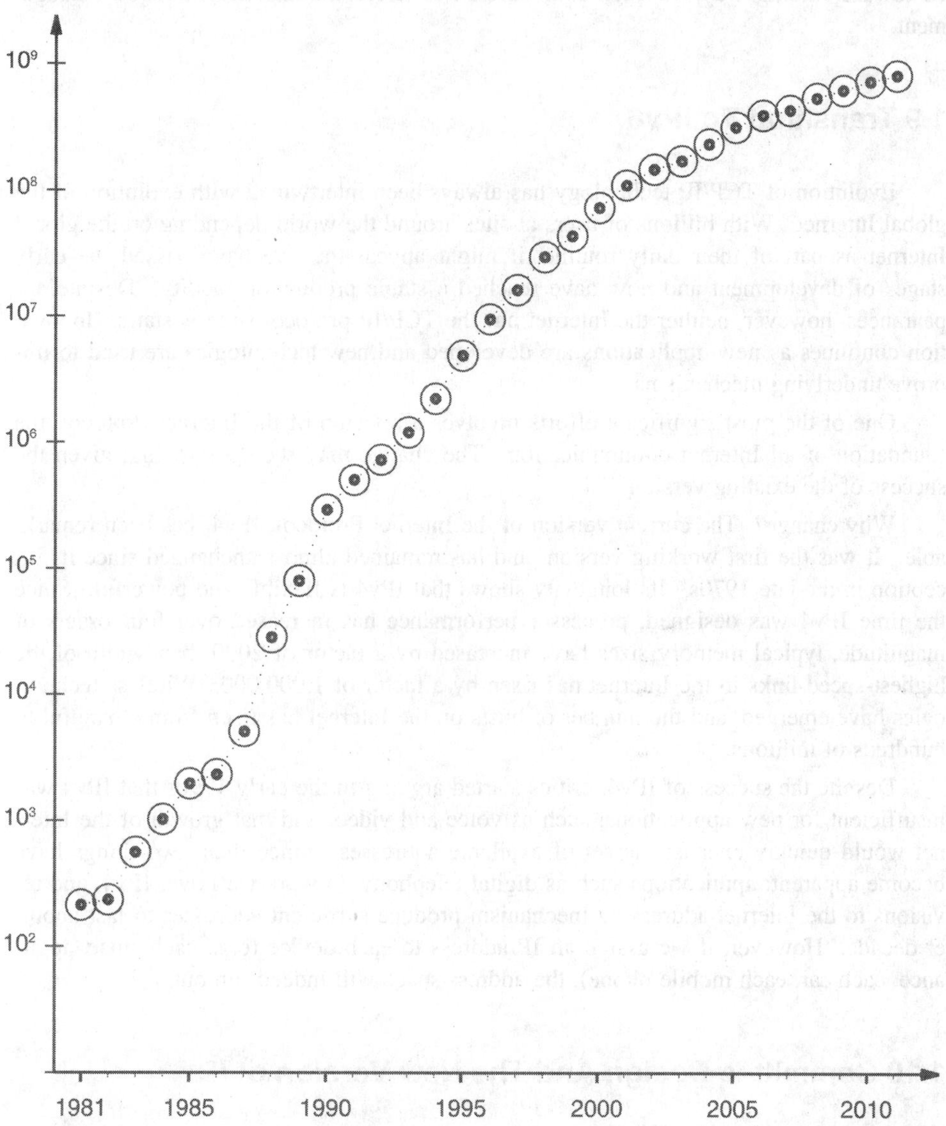

Figure 1.3 Computers on the Internet as a function of the year (log scale).

The count of computers is not the only significant change. Because the technology was developed when a single person at DARPA had control of all aspects of the Internet, the designs of many subsystems depended on centralized management and control.

As the Internet grew, responsibility and control were divided among multiple organizations. In particular, as the Internet became global, the operation and management needed to span multiple countries. Much of the effort since the early 1990s has been directed toward finding ways to extend the design to accommodate decentralized management.

1.9 Transition To IPv6

Evolution of TCP/IP technology has always been intertwined with evolution of the global Internet. With billions of users at sites around the world depending on the global Internet as part of their daily routine, it might appear that we have passed the early stages of development and now have reached a stable production facility. Despite appearances, however, neither the Internet nor the TCP/IP protocol suite is static. Innovation continues as new applications are developed and new technologies are used to improve underlying mechanisms.

One of the most significant efforts involves a revision of the Internet Protocol, the foundation of all Internet communication. The change may seem surprising, given the success of the existing version of IP.

Why change? The current version of the Internet Protocol, IPv4, has been remarkable. It was the first working version, and has remained almost unchanged since its inception in the late 1970s. Its longevity shows that IPv4 is flexible and powerful. Since the time IPv4 was designed, processor performance has increased over four orders of magnitude, typical memory sizes have increased by a factor of 2000, bandwidth of the highest-speed links in the Internet has risen by a factor of 1,000,000. Wireless technologies have emerged, and the number of hosts on the Internet has risen from a handful to hundreds of millions.

Despite the success of IPv4, critics started arguing in the early 1990s that IPv4 was insufficient for new applications, such as voice and video, and that growth of the Internet would quickly exhaust the set of available addresses. Since then, two things have become apparent: applications such as digital telephony do work well over IPv4, and revisions to the Internet addressing mechanism produce sufficient addresses to last another decade. However, if we assign an IP address to each device (e.g., each smart appliance, each car, each mobile phone), the address space will indeed run out.

1.10 Committee Design And The New Version of IP

It took several years for the IETF to formulate a new version of IP. Because the IETF produces *open* standards, representatives from the many communities were invited to participate in the process. Computer manufacturers, hardware and software vendors, users, managers, programmers, telephone companies, and the cable television industry all specified their requirements for the next version of IP, and all commented on specific proposals.

Many designs were proposed to serve a particular purpose or a particular community. In the end, the group produced an extended design that included ideas from several earlier proposals. The IETF assigned the revision of IP version number *6*, and named it *IPv6*†.

1.11 Relationship Between IPv4 And IPv6

Although proponents wanted to create a complete new Internet, IPv6 inherited many of the design principles and features of IPv4. Consequently, IPv6 cannot be understood in isolation — we need to review general principles, understand how they are implemented in IPv4, and then see how they are modified or extended in IPv6. For example, IPv6 uses a hierarchical design for addresses that is inherited directly from IPv4 classless addressing; the use of address masks and even some of the terminology has been derived from IPv4. In fact, IPv6 includes all the existing IPv4 addresses as one subset of the new set of addresses. Therefore, throughout the text, we will discuss principles and concepts, study their implementation in IPv4, and then look at IPv6 extensions and modifications.

How does IPv6 differ? The standards state that IPv6 retains many features that contributed to the success of IPv4. In fact, the designers characterize IPv6 as being basically the same as IPv4 with only minor modifications. For example, both IPv4 and IPv6 use a connectionless delivery paradigm, allow the sender to choose the size of data being sent, and require the sender to specify the maximum number of hops a datagram can make before being terminated. IPv6 retains many of the other IPv4 facilities, such as fragmentation. The important point is:

> *Because IPv6 inherits many of the concepts, principles, and mechanisms found in IPv4, we cannot understand IPv6 without understanding IPv4; both are presented throughout the text.*

Despite conceptual similarities, IPv6 changes most of the protocol details. IPv6 uses larger addresses and completely revises the format of packets. The changes introduced by IPv6 can be grouped into seven categories:

- *Larger Addresses.* The new address size is the most noticeable change. IPv6 quadruples the size of an IPv4 address from 32 bits to 128 bits.
- *Extended Address Hierarchy.* IPv6 uses the larger address space to create additional levels of addressing hierarchy (e.g., to allow an ISP to allocate blocks of addresses to each customer).
- *New Header Format.* IPv6 uses an entirely new and incompatible packet format that includes a set of optional headers.

†To avoid confusion and ambiguity, version number *5* was skipped; problems had arisen from a series of mistakes and misunderstandings.

- *Improved Options.* IPv6 allows a packet to include optional control information not available in IPv4.

- *Provision For Protocol Extension.* Instead of specifying all details, the IPv6 extension capability allows the IETF to adapt the protocol to new network hardware and new applications.

- *Support For Autoconfiguration And Renumbering.* IPv6 allows a site to change from one ISP to another by automating the requisite address changes.

- *Support For Resource Allocation.* IPv6 includes a flow abstraction and allows differentiated services

1.12 IPv6 Migration

How can the Internet change from IPv4 to IPv6? The designers considered the question carefully. By the 1990s, the Internet had already grown too large to simply take it offline, change every host and router, and then reboot. So, the designers planned to phase in the change gradually over time. We use the term *IPv6 migration* to capture the concept.

Many groups have proposed plans for IPv6 migration. The plans can be grouped into three major approaches as follows:

- A separate IPv6 Internet running in parallel
- IPv6 islands connected by IPv4 until ISPs install IPv6
- Gateways that translate between IPv4 and IPv6

Parallel Internets. Conceptually, the plan calls for ISPs to create a parallel Internet running IPv6. In practice, IPv6 and IPv4 can share many of the underlying wires and network devices (provided the devices are upgraded to handle IPv6). However, addressing and routing used by the two protocol versions will be completely independent. Proponents argue that because IPv6 offers so many advantages, everyone will switch to IPv6, meaning the IPv4 Internet will be decommissioned quickly.

IPv6 Islands. The plan allows individual organizations to start using IPv6 before all ISPs run IPv6. Each organization is an IPv6 island in the midst of an IPv4 ocean. To send a datagram between islands, the IPv6 datagram is wrapped inside an IPv4 datagram, sent across the Internet, and then unwrapped when it reaches the destination island. As ISPs adopt IPv6, sites can start sending IPv6 to more and more destinations until the entire Internet is using IPv6. Some IPv6 enthusiasts do not like the approach because it does not provide enough economic incentive for ISPs to adopt IPv6.

Gateways And Translation. The third approach uses network devices that translate between IPv4 and IPv6. For example, if a site chooses to use IPv6 but their ISP still uses IPv4, a gateway device can be placed between the site and the ISP to perform translation. The gateway will accept outgoing IPv6 packets, create equivalent IPv4 packets, and send the IPv4 packets to the ISP for delivery. Similarly, when an IPv4 packet arrives from the ISP, the gateway will create an equivalent IPv6 packet and send the IPv6 packet into the organization. Thus, computers in the organization can run IPv6 even if the ISP still uses IPv4. Alternatively, a site can use IPv4 even if the rest of the Internet has adopted IPv6.

Each strategy for migration has advantages and disadvantages. In the end, a central question arises: what economic incentive does a consumer, enterprise, or an ISP have to change? Surprisingly, there is little evidence that IPv6 offers much to the average consumer, organization, or provider. Of course there are exceptions. For example, a company whose business model involves the sale of information to advertisers will benefit greatly if each individual uses a separate IP address, because the company will be able to track individual habits much more accurately than when a family shares one computer or one address. In the end, each of the migration strategies has been used in some places, but none has emerged as a widely accepted consensus.

1.13 Dual Stack Systems

Many chapters in this text discuss protocol software, commonly known as a *protocol stack*. The impending change to IPv6 has affected the way protocol software is designed, especially for individual computers. Most operating systems (e.g., Linux, Windows, and OS-X) are already classified as *dual stack*. That is, in addition to all the software needed for IPv4, the system contains all the software needed for IPv6. In most systems, the two versions do not interact. That is, each side has an IP address and each side can send and receive packets. However, the addresses differ and neither side uses the other (or is even aware that the other side exists). The dual-stack idea is closely related to the parallel Internet approach discussed above.

Dual-stack systems allow applications to choose whether they will use IPv4, IPv6, or both. Older applications continue to use IPv4. However, a dual-stack mechanism allows an application to choose dynamically, making migration automatic. For example, consider a browser. If a given URL maps to both an IPv4 address and an IPv6 address, the browser might try to communicate using IPv6 first. If the attempt fails, the browser can try IPv4. If the computer is connected to an IPv6 network that reaches the destination, IPv6 communication will succeed. If not, the browser automatically falls back to using IPv4.

1.14 Organization Of The Text

The material on TCP/IP has been written in three volumes. This volume introduces the TCP/IP technology. It discusses the fundamentals of protocols like TCP and IP, presents packet formats, and shows how the protocols fit together in the Internet. In addition to examining individual protocols, the text highlights the general principles underlying network protocols, and explains why the TCP/IP protocols adapt easily to so many underlying physical network technologies. The text covers the architecture of the global Internet, and considers protocols that propagate routing information. Finally the text presents example network applications and explains how applications use the TCP/IP protocols.

The second and third volumes focus on implementation. Volume II examines the implementation of TCP/IP protocols themselves. The volume explains how protocol software is organized. It discusses data structures as well as facilities such as timer management. The volume presents algorithms and uses examples of code from a working system to illustrate the ideas. Volume III considers network applications and explains how they use TCP/IP for communication. It focuses on the client-server paradigm, the basis for all distributed programming. It discusses the interface between programs and protocols†, and shows how client and server programs are organized.

So far, we have talked about the TCP/IP technology and the Internet in general terms, summarizing the services provided and the history of their development. The next chapter provides a brief summary of the type of network hardware used throughout the Internet. Its purpose is not to illuminate nuances of a particular vendor's hardware, but to focus on the features of each technology that are of primary importance to an Internet architect. Later chapters delve into the protocols and the Internet, fulfilling three purposes: they explore general concepts and review the Internet architectural model, they examine the details of TCP/IP protocols, and they look at standards for application services. Later chapters describe services that span multiple machines, including the propagation of routing information, name resolution, and applications such as the Web.

An appendix that follows the main text contains an alphabetical list of terms and abbreviations used throughout the literature and the text. Because beginners often find the new terminology overwhelming and difficult to remember, they are encouraged to use the alphabetical list instead of scanning back through the text.

1.15 Summary

An internet consists of a set of connected networks that act as a coordinated whole. The chief advantage of an internet is that it provides universal interconnection while allowing individual groups to use whatever network hardware is best suited to their needs. We will examine principles underlying internet communication in general and the details of one internet protocol suite in particular. We will also discuss how internet protocols are used in an internet. Our example technology, called TCP/IP after its two main protocols, was developed by the Defense Advanced Research Projects Agency. It provides the basis for the global Internet, which now reaches over two billion people in countries around the world. The next version of the Internet Protocol (IPv6) draws heavily on concepts, terminology, and details in the current version (IPv4). Therefore, chapters throughout the text will examine both versions.

†Volume III is available in two versions: one that uses the Linux *socket interface*, and a second that uses the *Windows Sockets Interface* defined by Microsoft.

EXERCISES

1.1 Make a list of all the Internet applications that you use. How many are web-based?

1.2 Plot the growth of TCP/IP technology and Internet access at your organization. How many computers, users, and networks were connected each year?

1.3 Starting in 2000, major telephone companies began moving their networks from conventional telephone switching to IP-based networking. The major telephone networks will run only IP protocols. Why?

1.4 Find out when your site switched to IPv6 or when it plans to switch.

Chapter Contents

2

Overview Of Underlying Network Technologies

2.1 Introduction

The Internet introduced a key change in our thinking about computer networking. Earlier efforts all aimed at producing a new kind of networking. The Internet introduced a new method of interconnecting individual networks and a set of protocols that allowed computers to interact across many networks. While network hardware plays only a minor role in the overall design, understanding Internet technology requires one to distinguish between the low-level mechanisms provided by the hardware itself and the higher-level facilities that the TCP/IP protocols provide. It is also important to understand how the interfaces supplied by underlying packet-switched technology affect our choice of high-level abstractions.

This chapter introduces basic packet-switching concepts and terminology, and then reviews some of the underlying hardware technologies that have been used in TCP/IP internets. Later chapters describe how physical networks are interconnected and how the TCP/IP protocols accommodate vast differences in the hardware. While the list presented here is certainly not comprehensive, it clearly demonstrates the variety among physical networks over which TCP/IP operates. The reader can safely skip many of the technical details, but should try to grasp the idea of packet switching and try to imagine building a homogeneous communication system using such heterogeneous hardware. Most important, the reader should look closely at the details of the addressing schemes that various technologies use; later chapters will discuss in detail how high-level protocols use the hardware addresses.

2.2 Two Approaches To Network Communication

From a hardware perspective, networks are often classified by the forms of energy they use and the media over which the energy travels (e.g., electrical signals over copper wire, light pulses over optical fiber, and radio frequency waves transmitted through space). From a communication perspective, network technologies can be divided into two broad categories that depend on the interface they provide: *connection-oriented* (sometimes called *circuit-switched*) and *connectionless* (sometimes called *packet-switched*†). Connection-oriented networks operate by forming a dedicated *connection* or *circuit* between two points. Older telephone systems used a connection-oriented technology — a telephone call established a connection from the originating phone through the local switching office, across trunk lines, to a remote switching office, and finally to the destination telephone. While a connection was in place, the phone equipment sent voice signals from the microphone to the receiver. Because it dedicates one path in the network to each pair of communicating endpoints, a connection-oriented system can guarantee that communication is continuous and unbroken. That is, once a circuit is established, no other network activity will decrease the capacity of the circuit. One disadvantage of connection-oriented technology arises from cost: circuit costs are fixed, independent of use. For example, the rate charged for a phone call remained fixed, even during times when neither party was talking.

Connectionless networks, the type often used to connect computers, take an entirely different approach. In a connectionless system, data to be transferred across a network is divided into small pieces called *packets* that are multiplexed onto high capacity intermachine connections. A packet, which usually contains only a few hundred bytes of data, carries identification that enables the network hardware to know how to send it to the specified destination. For example, a large file to be transmitted between two machines must be broken into many packets that are sent across the network one at a time. The network hardware delivers the packets to the specified destination, where software reassembles them into a single file. The chief advantage of packet-switching is that multiple communications among computers can proceed concurrently, with intermachine connections shared by all pairs of computers that are communicating. The disadvantage, of course, is that as activity increases, a given pair of communicating computers receives less of the network capacity. That is, whenever a packet switched network becomes overloaded, computers using the network must wait before they can send additional packets.

Despite the potential drawback of not being able to guarantee network capacity, connectionless networks have become extremely popular. The chief motivations for adopting packet switching are cost and performance. Because multiple computers can share the underlying network channels, fewer connections are required and cost is kept low. Because engineers have been able to build high-speed packet switching hardware, capacity is not usually a problem. So many computer interconnections use connectionless networks that, throughout the remainder of this text, we will assume the term *network* refers to a connectionless network technology unless otherwise stated.

---

†Hybrid technologies are also possible, but such details are unimportant to our discussion.

2.3 WAN And LAN

Data networks that span large geographical distances (e.g., the continental U.S.) are fundamentally different from those that span short distances (e.g., a single room). To help characterize the differences in capacity and intended use, packet switched technologies are often divided into two broad categories: *Wide Area Networks* (*WAN*s) and *Local Area Networks* (*LAN*s). The two categories do not have formal definitions. Instead, vendors apply the terms loosely to help customers distinguish among technologies.

WAN technologies, sometimes called *long haul networks*, provide communication over long distances. Most WAN technologies do not limit the distance spanned; a WAN can allow the endpoints of a communication to be arbitrarily far apart. For example, a WAN can use optical fibers to span a continent or an ocean. Usually, WANs operate at slower speeds than LANs, and have much greater delay between connections. Typical speeds for a WAN range from 100 Mbps (million bits per second) to 10 Gbps (billion bits per second). Delays across a WAN can vary from a few milliseconds to several tenths of a second†.

LAN technologies provide the highest speed connections among computers, but sacrifice the ability to span long distances. For example, a typical LAN spans a small area like a single building or a small campus, and typically operates between 1 Gbps and 10 Gbps. Because LAN technologies cover short distances, they offer lower delays than WANs. The delay across a LAN can be as short as a few tenths of a millisecond or as long as 10 milliseconds.

2.4 Hardware Addressing Schemes

We will see that Internet protocols must handle one particular aspect of network hardware: heterogeneous addressing schemes. Each network hardware technology defines an *addressing mechanism* that computers use to specify the destination for a packet. Every computer attached to a network is assigned a unique *address*, which we can think of as an integer. A packet sent across a network includes two addresses: a *destination address* that specifies the intended recipient, and a *source address* that specifies the sender. The destination address is placed in the same position in each packet, making it possible for the network hardware to examine the destination address easily. A sender must know the address of the intended recipient, and must place the recipient's address in the destination address field of a packet before transmitting the packet.

The next sections examine four examples of network technologies that have been used in the Internet:

- Ethernet (IEEE 802.3)
- Wi-Fi (IEEE 802.11)
- ZigBee (IEEE 802.15.4)
- Wide Area Point-to-Point Networks (SONET)

†Exceptionally long delays can result from WANs that communicate by sending signals to a satellite orbiting the earth and back to another location on earth.

Our discussion of technologies will gloss over many of the hardware details because the purpose is to highlight ways in which the underlying hardware has influenced design choices in the protocols.

2.5 Ethernet (IEEE 802.3)

Ethernet is the name given to a popular packet-switched LAN technology invented at Xerox PARC in the early 1970s. Xerox Corporation, Intel Corporation, and Digital Equipment Corporation standardized Ethernet in 1978; the *Institute for Electrical and Electronic Engineers* (*IEEE*) released a compatible version of the standard using the standard number *802.3*. Ethernet has become the most popular LAN technology; it now appears in virtually all corporate and personal networks, and the Ethernet packet format is sometimes used across wide area networks. The current versions of Ethernet are known as *Gigabit Ethernet* (*GigE*) and *10 Gigabit Ethernet* (*10GigE*) because they transfer data at 1 Gbps and 10 Gbps, respectively. Next generation technologies operate at 40 and 100 gigabits per second. An Ethernet network consists of an *Ethernet switch* to which multiple computers attach†. A small switch can connect four computers; a large switch, such as the switches used in data centers, can connect hundreds of computers. Connections between a computer and a switch consist of copper wires for lower speeds or optical fibers for higher speeds. Figure 2.1 illustrates the topology of an Ethernet.

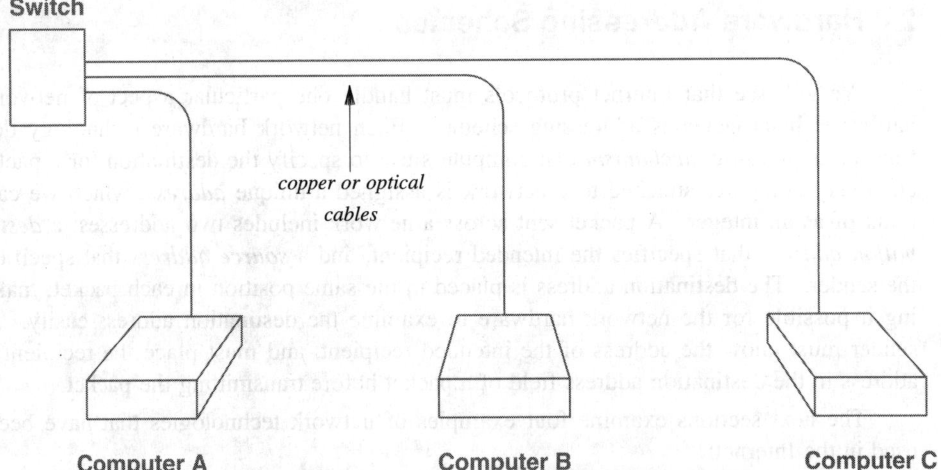

Figure 2.1 Illustration of the connections used with an Ethernet. Each computer connects to a central switch.

†We will describe networks as connecting computers, but they can also connect devices, such as printers, that have network connections.

An Ethernet switch is an electronic device that usually resides in a wiring closet. When using copper wire, the connection between a switch and a computer must be less than 100 meters long; optical connections can extend farther. Each computer must have a *Network Interface Card* (*NIC*) that operates as an I/O device that can send and receive packets.

2.5.1 Ethernet Capacity

We said that a *Gigabit Ethernet* transfers data at a gigabit per second (1000 megabits per second). Consequently, the formal name *1000Base-T* is applied to the version that uses twisted pair copper wiring. A related IEEE standard known as *1000Base-X* specifies Ethernet transmission over optical fiber. In essence, the optical version converts an Ethernet packet into pulses of light, which are then transferred across an optical fiber. The chief advantages of optical fiber are: higher capacity and immunity to electrical interference. The capacity of a fiber is sufficient to support bit rates much higher than 10 Gbps. Therefore, engineers are developing 40 and 100 Gbps Ethernet technologies that operate over optical fiber.

2.5.2 Automatic Negotiation

A modern Ethernet switch is not restricted to one speed. Instead, the switch can operate at 10, 100, 1000 or even 10000 Mbps. A set of speeds is available in most NICs as well as switches. The important aspect of multi-speed Ethernet lies in automated configuration. When a cable is plugged in, both ends enter a negotiation phase. The negotiation determines the type of cable (straight through or cross-over) and the maximum speed that the other side of the connection can support. The two sides agree to operate at the maximum speed that both sides can handle. Automatic negotiation provides backward compatibility — a computer with an old, slow NIC can attach to a Gigabit switch without any changes. Ethernet packet format does not depend on the link speed, which means that TCP/IP protocols can remain unaware of the negotiated link speed.

2.5.3 Important Properties Of An Ethernet

Broadcast Capability. Ethernet supports *broadcast*, which means a sender can specify that a given packet should be delivered to all computers that are attached to the network. In practice, switches usually implement broadcast by making one copy of the packet for each computer. We will see that TCP/IP depends on Ethernet broadcast.

Best-Effort Delivery Semantics. Ethernet uses *best-effort delivery semantics*, which means that the network tries to deliver packets, the hardware does not guarantee delivery and does not inform a sender if the packet cannot be delivered. If the destination machine happens to be powered down or its cable is unplugged, packets sent to the machine will be lost and the sender will not be notified. More important, if multiple computers attempt to send packets to a given computer at the same time, a switch can become overrun and start discarding packets. We will see later that best-effort semantics form a key concept in the design of TCP/IP protocols.

2.5.4 48-Bit Ethernet MAC (Hardware) Addresses

IEEE defines a 48-bit MAC addressing scheme that is used with Ethernet and other network technologies. The abbreviation MAC stands for *Media Access Control*, and is used to clarify the purpose of the address. A MAC address is assigned to each network interface card. To insure uniqueness, an Ethernet hardware manufacturer must purchase a block of MAC addresses from IEEE and must assign one address to each NIC that is manufactured. The assignment means that no two hardware interfaces have the same Ethernet address.

Because each address is assigned to a hardware device, we sometimes use the term *hardware address* or *physical address*. For our purposes, we will use the terms interchangeably.

Note the following important property of a MAC address:

> *An Ethernet address is assigned to a network interface card, not to a computer; moving the interface card to a new computer or replacing an interface card that has failed changes a computer's Ethernet address.*

Knowing that a change in hardware can change an Ethernet address explains why higher level protocols are designed to accommodate address changes.

The IEEE 48-bit MAC addressing scheme provides three types of addresses:

- *Unicast*
- *Broadcast*
- *Multicast*

A *unicast* address is a unique value assigned to a network interface card, as described above. If the destination address in a packet is a unicast address, the packet will be delivered to exactly one computer (or not delivered at all, if none of the computers on the network have the specified address).

A *broadcast* consists of all 1s, and is reserved for transmitting to all stations simultaneously. When a switch receives a packet with all 1s in the destination address field, the switch delivers a copy of the packet to each computer on the network except the sender.

A *multicast* address provides a limited form of broadcast in which a subset of the computers on a network agree to listen to a given multicast address. The set of participating computers is called a *multicast group*. The interface card on a computer must be configured to join a multicast group or the interface will ignore packets sent to the group. We will see that TCP/IP protocols use multicast and that IPv6 depends on multicast.

2.5.5 Ethernet Frame Format And Packet Size

Because the term *packet* is generic and can refer to any type of packet, we use the term *frame* to refer to a packet that is defined by hardware technologies†. Ethernet frames are variable length, with no frame smaller than 64 octets‡ or larger than 1514 octets (header and data). As expected, each Ethernet frame contains a field that holds the 48-bit address of a destination and another field that holds the 48-bit address of the sender. When transmitted, the frame also includes a 4-octet *Cyclic Redundancy Check* (*CRC*) that is used to check for transmission errors. Because the CRC field is added by the sending hardware and checked by the receiving hardware, the CRC is not visible to higher layers of protocol software. Figure 2.2 illustrates the pertinent parts of an Ethernet frame.

Destination Address	Source Address	Frame Type	Frame Payload (Data)
6 octets	6 octets	2 octets	46–1500 octets . . .

Figure 2.2 Ethernet frame format. Fields are not drawn to scale.

In the figure, the first three fields constitute a *header* for the frame, and the remaining field is the *payload*. The packets used in most network technologies follow the same pattern: the packet consists of a small header with fixed fields followed by a variable-size payload. The maximum size of the payload in an Ethernet frame is 1500 octets. Because Ethernet has been universally adopted, most ISPs have tuned their networks to accommodate the Ethernet payload. We can summarize:

> *The Ethernet payload size of 1500 octets has become a de facto standard; even if they use other networking technologies, ISPs try to design their networks so a packet can hold 1500 octets of data.*

In addition to fields that identify the source and destination of the frame, an Ethernet frame contains a 16-bit integer that identifies the type of data being carried in the frame. Most packet technologies include a type field. From the Internet's point of view, the frame type field is essential because it means Ethernet frames are *self-identifying*. When a frame arrives at a given machine, protocol software uses the frame type to determine which protocol module should process the frame. The chief advantages of self-identifying frames are that they allow multiple protocols to be used together on a single computer and they allow multiple protocols to be intermixed on the same physical network without interference. For example, one can have an application pro-

†The term *frame* derives from communication over serial lines in which the sender "frames" the data by adding special characters before and after the transmitted data.

‡Technically, the term *byte* refers to a hardware-dependent character size; networking professionals use the term *octet* because it refers to an 8-bit quantity on all computers.

gram on a computer using Internet protocols while another application on the same computer uses a local experimental protocol. The operating system examines the type field of each arriving frame to decide which module should process the contents. We will see that the type field can be used to define multiple protocols in the same family. For example, because the TCP/IP protocols include several protocols that can be sent over an Ethernet, TCP/IP defines several Ethernet types.

2.6 Wi-Fi (IEEE 802.11)

IEEE has developed a series of standards for wireless networks that are closely related to Ethernet. The most well-known have IEEE standard number *802.11* followed by a suffix (e.g., *802.11g* or *802.11n*). The set of standards can interoperate, which means a wireless device can include hardware for multiple standards, and can choose the standard that gives the maximum speed. A consortium of network equipment vendors has adopted the marketing term *Wi-Fi* to cover equipment that uses the IEEE wireless standards, and many Wi-Fi devices exist.

Each of the Wi-Fi standards can be used in two forms: as an access technology in which a single base station (called an *access point*) connects to multiple clients (e.g., users with laptops), or in a point-to-point configuration used to connect exactly two wireless radios. IEEE has also defined a higher-speed technology intended primarily for point-to-point interconnections. Marketed as *Wi-MAX* and assigned the standard number *802.16*, the technology is of most interest to network providers or corporations that need to connect two sites.

2.7 ZigBee (IEEE 802.15.4)

In addition to connecting conventional computers, an internet can be used by embedded devices. The concept of connecting devices is sometimes referred to as an *Internet of Things*. Of course, each device that connects to the Internet must have an embedded processor and must include a network interface. IEEE has created standard 802.15.4 for a low-power wireless network technology intended to support connections of small embedded devices. The low-power aspect makes 802.15.4 radios attractive for devices that run on battery power.

A consortium of vendors has chosen the term *ZigBee* to refer to products that use IEEE's 802.15.4 standard for radios and run a specific protocol stack that includes IPv6 plus protocols that allow a set of wireless nodes to organize themselves into a mesh that can forward packets to and from the Internet.

The IEEE 802.15.4 technology provides an interesting example of extremes for TCP/IP. The packet size is 127 octets, but only 102 octets are available for a payload. In addition, the standard defines two address formats, one uses 64-bit MAC addresses and the other uses 16-bit MAC addresses. The choice of addressing mode is handled at startup.

2.8 Optical Carrier And Packet Over SONET (OC, POS)

Phone companies originally designed digital circuits to carry digitized voice calls; only later did the phone company digital circuits become important for data networks. Consequently, the data rates of available circuits are not powers of ten. Instead, they have been chosen to carry multiples of 64 Kbps because a digitized voice call uses an encoding known as *Pulse Code Modulation* (*PCM*) which produces 8000 samples per second, where each sample is 8 bits.

The table in Figure 2.3 lists a few common data rates used in North America and Europe.

Name	Bit Rate	Voice Circuits	Location
–	0.064 Mbps	1	
T1	1.544 Mbps	24	North America
T2	6.312 Mbps	96	North America
T3	44.736 Mbps	672	North America
T4	274.760 Mbps	4032	North America
E1	2.048 Mbps	30	Europe
E2	8.448 Mbps	120	Europe
E3	34.368 Mbps	480	Europe
E4	139.264 Mbps	1920	Europe

Figure 2.3 Example data rates available on digital circuits leased from a telephone company.

Higher-rate digital circuits require the use of fiber. In addition to standards that specify the transmission of high data rates over copper, the phone companies have developed standards for transmission of the same rates over optical fiber. Figure 2.4 lists examples of *Optical Carrier* (*OC*) standards and the data rate of each. A suffix on "OC" denotes a capacity.

Optical Standard	Bit Rate	Voice Circuits
OC-1	51.840 Mbps	810
OC-3	155.520 Mbps	2430
OC-12	622.080 Mbps	9720
OC-24	1,244.160 Mbps	19440
OC-48	2.488 Gbps	38880
OC-96	4.976 Gbps	64512
OC-192	9.952 Gbps	129024
OC-256	13.271 Gbps	172032

Figure 2.4 Example data rates available on high-capacity digital circuits that use optical fiber.

The term *SONET* refers to a framing protocol that allows a carrier to multiplex multiple digital voice telephone calls onto a single connection. SONET is typically used across OC connections. Thus, if an ISP leases an OC-3 connection, the ISP may need to use SONET framing. The term *Packet Over SONET* (*POS*) refers to a technology used to send packets using SONET framing.

2.9 Point-To-Point Networks

From TCP/IP's point of view, any communication system used to pass packets is classified as a *network*. If the communication system connects exactly two endpoints, it is known as a *point-to-point network*. Thus, a leased data circuit is an example of a point-to-point network.

Purists object to using the term "network" to describe a point-to-point connection because they reserve the term for technologies that allow a set of computers to communicate. We will see, however, that classifying a connection as a network helps maintain consistency. For now, we only need to note that a point-to-point network differs from a conventional network in one significant way: because only two computers attach, no hardware addresses are needed. When we discuss internet address binding, the lack of hardware addresses will make point-to-point networks an exception.

Dialup provides an example of a point-to-point network. Early Internet access used dialup connections in which a dialup modem is used to place a phone call to another modem. Once the phone connection was in place, the two modems could use audio tones to send data. From the point of view of TCP/IP, dialing a telephone call is equivalent to running a wire. Once the call has been answered by a modem on the other end, there is a connection from one endpoint to another, and the connection stays in place as long as needed. Modern switched optical technology provides another form of point-to-point network. A network manager can request that an optical path be set up through a series of optical switches. From TCP/IP's point of view, the path is a high-capacity point-to-point network analogous to a leased circuit or a dialup connection. Later chapters discuss the concept of tunneling and overlay networks, which provide another form of point-to-point connections.

2.10 VLAN Technology And Broadcast Domains

We said that an Ethernet switch forms a single Local Area Network by connecting a set of computers. A more advanced form of switch, known as a *Virtual Local Area Network* (*VLAN*) switch, allows a manager to configure the switch to operate like several smaller switches. We say that the manager can create one or more *virtual networks* by specifying which computers attach to which VLAN.

A manager can use VLANs to separate computers according to policies. For example, a company can have a VLAN for employees and a separate VLAN for visitors.

Computers on the employee VLAN can be given more access privilege than computers on the visitor VLAN.

A key to understanding VLANs and their interaction with Internet protocols involves the way a VLAN switch handles broadcast and multicast. We say that each VLAN defines a *broadcast domain*, which means that when a computer sends a broadcast packet, the packet is only delivered to the set of computers in the same VLAN. The same definition holds for multicast. That is, VLAN technology emulates a set of independent physical networks. The computers in a given VLAN share broadcast and multicast access but, just as in separate physical networks, broadcast or multicast sent on a given VLAN does not spread to other VLANs.

How should Internet protocols handle VLANs? The answer is that Internet protocols do not distinguish between a VLAN and an independent physical network. We can summarize:

> *From the point of view of Internet protocols, a VLAN is treated exactly like a separate physical network.*

2.11 Bridging

We use the term *bridging* to refer to technologies that transport a copy of a frame from one network to another, and the term *bridge* to refer to a mechanism that implements bridging. The motivation for bridging is to form a single large network by using bridges to connect smaller networks.

A key idea is that when it transfers a copy of a frame, a bridge does not make any changes. Instead, the frame is merely replicated and transmitted over the other network. In particular, a bridge does not alter the source or destination addresses in the frame. Thus, computers on the two networks can communicate directly. Furthermore, computers use exactly the same hardware interface, frame format, and MAC addresses when communicating over a bridge as when communicating locally — the computers are completely unaware that bridging has occurred. To capture the concept, we say that the bridge is *transparent* (i.e., invisible) to computers using the network.

Originally, network equipment vendors sold bridges as separate physical devices. With the advent of modern switched networks, bridges were no longer feasible. Despite the change in technology, bridging is still used in many network systems. The difference is that bridging is now embedded in other devices. For example, ISPs that provide service to residences and businesses use bridging in equipment such as *cable modems* and *Digital Subscriber Line* (*DSL*) hardware. Ethernet frames transmitted over the Ethernet at a residence are bridged to the ISP, and vice versa. Computers at the house use the local Ethernet as if the ISP's router is connected directly; a router at the ISP communicates over the local Ethernet as if the customer's computers are local.

From our point of view, the most important point to understand about bridging arises from the resulting communication system:

> *Because bridging hides the details of interconnection, a set of bridged Ethernets acts like a single Ethernet.*

In fact, bridges do more than replicate frames from one network to another: a bridge makes intelligent decisions about which frames to forward. For example, if a user has a computer and printer at their residence, the bridge in a cable modem will not send copies of frames to the ISP if the frames are going from the user's computer to the user's printer or vice versa.

How does a bridge know whether to forward frames? Bridges are called *adaptive* or *learning* bridges because they use packet traffic to learn which computers are on each network. Recall that a frame contains the address of the sender as well as the address of a receiver. When it receives a frame, the bridge records the 48-bit source address. On a typical network, each computer (or device) will send at least one broadcast or multicast frame, which means the bridge will learn the computer's MAC address. Once it learns the addresses of computers, a bridge will examine each frame and check the list before forwarding a copy. If both the sender and receiver are on the same network, no forwarding is needed.

The advantages of adaptive bridging should be obvious. Because it uses addresses found in normal traffic, a bridging mechanism is both transparent and automatic — humans do not need to configure it. Because it does not forward traffic unnecessarily, a bridge helps improve performance. To summarize:

> *An adaptive Ethernet bridge connects two Ethernets, forwards frames from one to the other, and uses source addresses in packets to learn which computers are on which Ethernet. A bridge uses the location of computers to eliminate unnecessary forwarding.*

2.12 Congestion And Packet Loss

In practice, most networking technology works so well that it is easy to assume complete reliability. However, unless a packet system prereserves capacity before each use, the system is susceptible to *congestion* and *packet loss*. To understand why, consider a trivial example: an Ethernet switch with only three computers attached. Suppose two computers send data to a third as Figure 2.5 illustrates.

Assume each of the connections to the switch operates at 1 Gbps, and consider what happens if computers *A* and *B* send data to computer *C* continuously. *A* and *B* will forward data at an aggregate rate of 2 Gbps. Because the connection to *C* can only handle half that rate, the link to *C* will become *congested.*

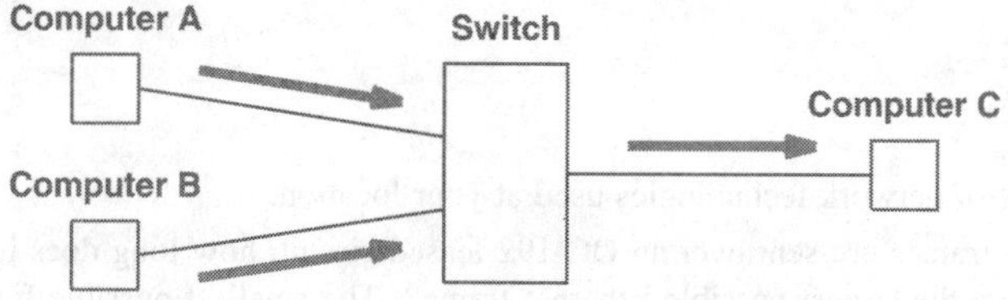

Figure 2.5 An Ethernet with arrows indicating the flow of traffic.

To understand what happens to traffic, recall that Ethernet uses best-effort delivery semantics. The switch has no way to inform *A* and *B* that an output link is congested, and no way to stop incoming traffic. Internally, a switch has a finite amount of buffer space. Once all buffers are used, the switch must discard additional frames that arrive. Thus, even with only three computers connected to an Ethernet, it is possible that packets will be dropped.

At this point, it is only important to understand that congestion and loss can indeed occur in packet networks. A later chapter examines TCP and the mechanisms that TCP uses to avoid congestion.

2.13 Summary

Internet protocols are designed to accommodate a wide variety of underlying hardware technologies. To understand some of the design decisions, it is necessary to be familiar with the basics of network hardware.

Packet switching technologies are broadly divided into connection-oriented and connectionless types. A packet switching network is further classified as a Wide Area Network or Local Area Network, depending on whether the hardware supports communication over long distances or is limited to short distances.

We reviewed several technologies used in the Internet, including Ethernet, Wi-Fi, ZigBee, and the leased digital circuits that can be used for long-distance. We also considered VLANs and bridged networks. While the details of specific network technologies are not important, a general idea has emerged:

> *The Internet protocols are extremely flexible; a wide variety of underlying hardware technologies has been used to transfer Internet traffic.*

Each hardware technology defines an addressing scheme known as MAC addresses. Differences are dramatic: Ethernet uses 48-bit MAC addresses, while 802.15.4 networks can use 16-bit or 64-bit MAC addresses. Because the goal is to interconnect arbitrary network hardware, the Internet must accommodate all types of MAC addresses.

EXERCISES

2.1 Make a list of network technologies used at your location.

2.2 If Ethernet frames are sent over an OC-192 leased circuit, how long does it take to transmit the bits from the largest possible Ethernet frame? The smallest possible frame? (Note: you may exclude the CRC from your calculations.)

2.3 Study Ethernet switch technology. What is the *spanning tree* algorithm, and why is it needed?

2.4 Read about IEEE 802.1Q. What does VLAN tagging accomplish?

2.5 What is the maximum packet size that can be sent over the 4G wireless networks used by cell phones?

2.6 If your site uses Ethernet, find the size of the largest and smallest switches (i.e., the number of ports to which computers can attach). How many switches are interconnected?

2.7 What is the maximum amount of data that can be transmitted in a Wi-Fi packet?

2.8 What is the maximum amount of data that can be transmitted in a ZigBee packet?

2.9 What characteristic of a satellite communication channel is most desirable? Least desirable?

2.10 Find a lower bound on the time it takes to transfer a gigabyte of data across a network that operates at: 100 Mbps, 1000 Mbps, and 10 Gbps.

2.11 Do the processor, disk, and internal bus on your computer operate fast enough to read data from a file on disk and send it across a network at 10 gigabits per second?

2.12 A wireless router that uses Wi-Fi technology to connect laptop computers to the Internet has an Ethernet connection and wireless connections to multiple laptops. Consider data flowing from the laptops to the Ethernet. If the Ethernet connection operates at 1 Gbps, how many laptops must be connected to cause congestion on the Ethernet? (Hint: what is the maximum data rate of a single Wi-Fi connection?)

Chapter Contents

3

Internetworking Concept And Architectural Model

3.1 Introduction

So far, we have looked at the low-level details of transmission across individual data networks, the foundation on which all computer communication is built. This chapter makes a giant conceptual leap by describing a scheme that allows us to collect the diverse network technologies into a coordinated whole. The primary goal is a system that hides the details of underlying network hardware, while providing universal communication services. The primary result is a high-level abstraction that provides the framework for all design decisions. Succeeding chapters show how we use the abstraction described here to build the necessary layers of internet communication software and how the software hides the underlying physical transport mechanisms. Later chapters show how applications use the resulting communication system.

3.2 Application-Level Interconnection

When faced with heterogeneous systems, early designers relied on special application programs, called *application gateways*, to hide the underlying differences and provide the appearance of uniformity. For example, one of the early incompatibilities arose from commercial email systems. Each vendor designed their own email system. The vendor chose a format for storing email, conventions for identifying a recipient, and a method for transferring an email message from the sender to the recipient. Unfortunately, the systems were completely incompatible.

When a connection between email systems was needed, an application gateway was used. The gateway software runs on a computer that connects to both email systems as Figure 3.1 illustrates.

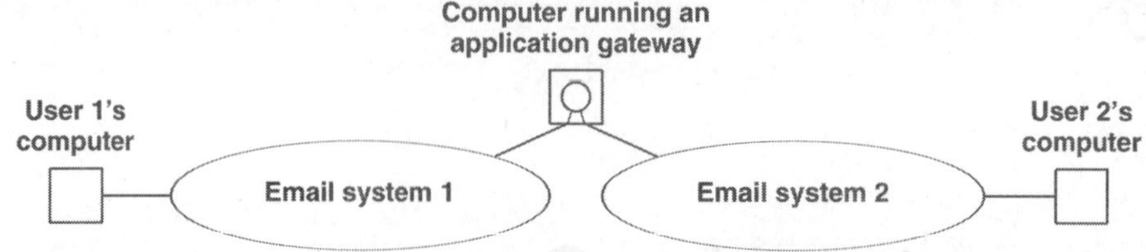

Figure 3.1 Illustration of an application gateway used to accommodate a pair of heterogeneous email systems.

The application gateway must understand the details of the network connections and the message protocols as well as the format of email messages used on the two email systems. When user 1 sends an email message to user 2, user 1's email is configured to send the message to the application gateway. The application gateway must translate the message and the email address to the form used by email system 2, and then forward the message to user 2.

Using application programs to hide network details may seem quite reasonable. Because everything can be handled by an application, no special hardware is needed. Furthermore, the original email systems on the users' computers remain unchanged. In fact, neither the users nor the email software on the users' computers can tell that the other user has a different email system.

Unfortunately, the application gateway approach is both cumbersome and limited. The primary disadvantage arises because a given application gateway can only handle one specific application. For example, even if an email gateway is in place, the gateway cannot be used to transfer files, connect chat sessions, or forward text messages. A second disadvantage arises when differences in functionality prevent interoperation. For example, if email system 1 permits a sender to attach a file to a message, but email system 2 does not, an application gateway will not be able to transfer messages that include files. A third disadvantage arises from the frequency of upgrades. Whenever either vendor changes their email software, the gateway must be updated to handle the change. Thus, application gateways must be updated frequently.

Our example only considers an application gateway that connects two systems. Users who are experienced with networking understand that once the size grows sufficient for a world-wide communication system and multiple vendors each create their own application software, it will be impossible to maintain a set of application gateways that interconnect all networks. Furthermore, to avoid building application gateways for all possible combinations, the system quickly evolves to use a step-at-a-time communication paradigm in which a message is sent to the first application gateway which translates and sends it to the second, and so on. Successful communication requires correct operation of all application gateways along the path. If any of them fail to perform the translation correctly, the message will not be delivered. Furthermore, the source and destination may remain unable to detect or control the problem. Thus, systems that use application gateways cannot guarantee reliable communication.

3.3 Network-Level Interconnection

The alternative to using application-level gateways is a system based on network-level interconnection. That is, we can devise a system that transfers packets from their original source to their ultimate destination without using intermediate application programs. Switching packets instead of files or large messages has several advantages. First, the scheme maps directly onto the underlying network hardware, making it extremely efficient. Second, network-level interconnection separates data communication activities from application programs, permitting intermediate computers to handle network traffic without understanding the applications that are sending or receiving messages. Third, using network-level communication keeps the entire system flexible, making it possible to build general purpose communication facilities that are not limited to specific uses. Fourth, we will see that the scheme allows network managers to add or change network technologies while application programs remain unchanged.

The key to designing universal network-level interconnection can be found in an abstract communication system concept known as *internetworking*. The *internet* concept is extremely powerful. It detaches the notions of communication from the details of network technologies and hides low-level details from users and applications. More important, it drives all software design decisions and explains how to handle physical addresses and routes. After reviewing basic motivations for internetworking, we will consider the properties of an internet in more detail.

We begin with two fundamental observations about the design of communication systems:

- No single network hardware technology can satisfy all constraints.
- Users desire universal interconnection.

The first observation is economic as well as technical. Inexpensive LAN technologies that provide high-speed communication only cover short distances; wide area networks that span long distances cannot supply local communication cheaply. It is possible to achieve any two of high speed, long distance, and low cost, but not possible to achieve all three. Therefore, because no single network technology satisfies all needs, we are forced to consider multiple underlying hardware technologies.

The second observation is self-evident. An arbitrary user would like to be able to communicate with an arbitrary endpoint, either another user or a computer system. Given the desire for mobile access, we can say that an arbitrary user would like to engage in communication from an arbitrary location. As a consequence, we desire a communication system that is not constrained by the boundaries of physical networks.

The goal is to build a unified, cooperative interconnection of networks that supports a universal communication service. Each computer will attach to a specific network, such as those described in Chapter 2, and will use the technology-dependent communication facilities of the underlying network. New software, inserted between the technology-dependent communication mechanisms and application programs, will hide all low-level details and make the collection of networks appear to be a single, large network. Such an interconnection scheme is called an *internetwork* or an *internet*.

The idea of building an internet follows a standard pattern of system design: researchers imagine a high-level facility and work from available underlying technologies to realize the imagined goal. In most cases, researchers build software that provides each of the needed mechanisms. The researchers continue until they produce a working system that implements the envisioned system efficiently. The next section shows the first step of the design process by defining the goal more precisely. Later sections explain the approach, and successive chapters explain principles and details.

3.4 Properties Of The Internet

The notion of universal service is important, but it alone does not capture all the ideas we have in mind for a unified internet. In fact, there can be many implementations of universal services. One of the first principles in our design focuses on encapsulation: we want to hide the underlying internet architecture from users, and permit communication without requiring knowledge of the internet's structure. That is, we do not want to require users or application programs to understand the details of underlying networks or hardware interconnections to use the internet. We also do not want to mandate a network interconnection topology. In particular, adding a new network to the internet should not mean connecting to a centralized switching point, nor should it mean adding direct physical connections between the new network and all existing networks. We want to be able to send data across intermediate networks even though they are not directly connected to the source or destination computers. We want all computers in the internet to share a universal set of machine identifiers (which can be thought of as *names* or *addresses*).

Our notion of a unified internet also includes the idea of network and computer independence. That is, we want the set of operations used to establish communication or to transfer data to remain independent of the underlying network technologies and the destination computer. A user should not need to know about networks or remote computers when invoking an application, and a programmer should not have to understand the network interconnection topology or the type of a remote computer when creating applications that communicate over our internet.

3.5 Internet Architecture

We have seen how computers connect to individual networks. The question arises: how are networks interconnected to form an internetwork? The answer has two parts. Physically, two networks cannot be plugged together directly. Instead, they can only be connected by a computer system that has the hardware needed to connect to each network. A physical attachment does not provide the interconnection we have in mind, however, because such a connection does not guarantee that a computer will cooperate with other machines that wish to communicate. To have a viable internet, we need special computers that are willing to transfer packets from one network to another. Computers that interconnect two networks and pass packets from one to the other are called *internet routers* or *IP routers*†.

To understand the interconnection, consider an example consisting of two physical networks and a router as shown in Figure 3.2.

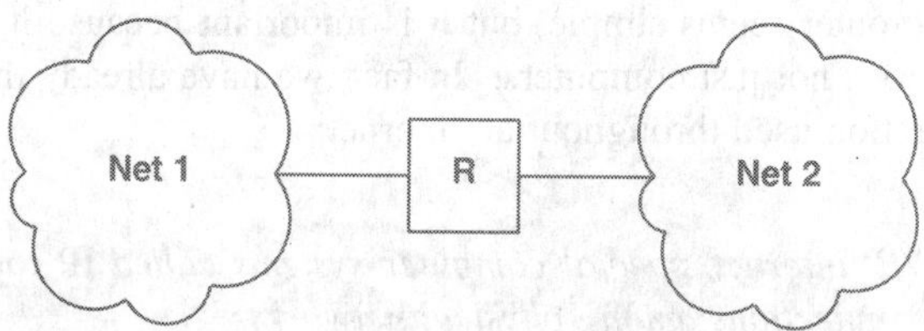

Figure 3.2 Two physical networks interconnected by an IP router, *R*.

In the figure, router *R* connects to both network *1* and network *2*. For *R* to act as a router, it must capture packets on network *1* that are bound for machines on network *2* and transfer them. Similarly, *R* must capture packets on network *2* that are destined for machines on network *1* and transfer them.

In the figure, clouds are used to denote physical networks because the exact hardware is unimportant. Each network can be a LAN or a WAN, and each may have many computers attached or a few computers attached. The use of clouds emphasizes an important difference between routers and bridges — a bridge can only connect two networks that use the same technology, but a router can connect arbitrary networks.

3.6 Interconnection Of Multiple Networks With IP Routers

Although it illustrates the basic connection strategy, Figure 3.2 is extremely simplistic. A realistic internet will include multiple networks and routers. In such a case, each router needs to know about networks beyond the networks to which it connects directly. For example, consider Figure 3.3 which shows three networks interconnected by two routers.

†The original literature used the term *IP gateway*. However, vendors have adopted the term *IP router*.

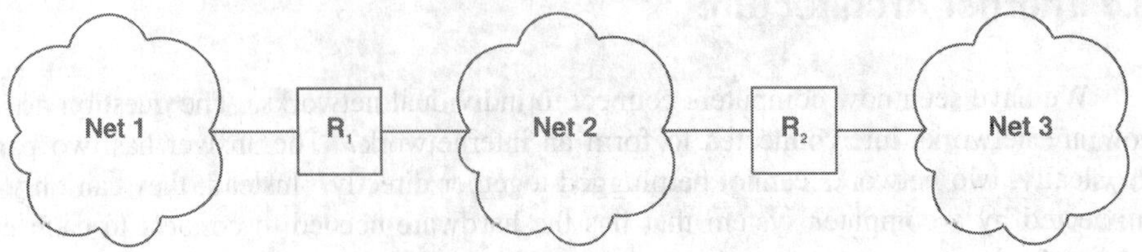

Figure 3.3 Three networks interconnected by two routers.

In the example, router R_1 must transfer from network *1* to network *2* all packets destined for computers on either network *2* or network *3*. Similarly, router R_2 must transfer packets from network *3* that are destined for either network *2* or network *1*. The important point is that a router must handle packets for networks to which the router does not attach. In a large internet composed of many networks, the router's task of making decisions about where to send packets becomes more complex.

The idea of a router seems simple, but it is important because it provides a way to interconnect networks, not just computers. In fact, we have already discovered the principle of interconnection used throughout an internet:

> *In a TCP/IP internet, special computer systems called* IP routers *provide interconnections among physical networks.*

You might suspect that routers, which must each know how to forward packets toward their destination, are large machines with enough primary or secondary memory to hold information about every computer in the internet to which they attach. In fact, routers used with TCP/IP internets can be modest computers similar to a desktop PC. They do not need especially large disk storage nor do they need a huge main memory. The trick that allows routers to be reasonable size lies in the following concept:

> *Routers use the destination network, not the destination computer, when forwarding a packet.*

Because packet forwarding is based on networks, the amount of information that a router needs to keep is proportional to the number of networks in the internet, not the number of computers. As we learned in Chapter 1, there are two orders of magnitude fewer networks in the Internet than computers.

Because they play a key role in internet communication, we will return to routers in later chapters to discuss the details of how they operate and how they learn about remote destinations. For now, we will assume that it is possible and practical for each router to have correct routes for all networks in an internet. We will also assume that only routers provide connections between physical networks in an internet.

3.7 The User's View

Recall that an internet is designed to provide a universal interconnection among computers independent of the particular networks to which they attach. We want a user to view an internet as a single, virtual network to which all machines connect despite their physical connections. Figure 3.4 illustrates the idea.

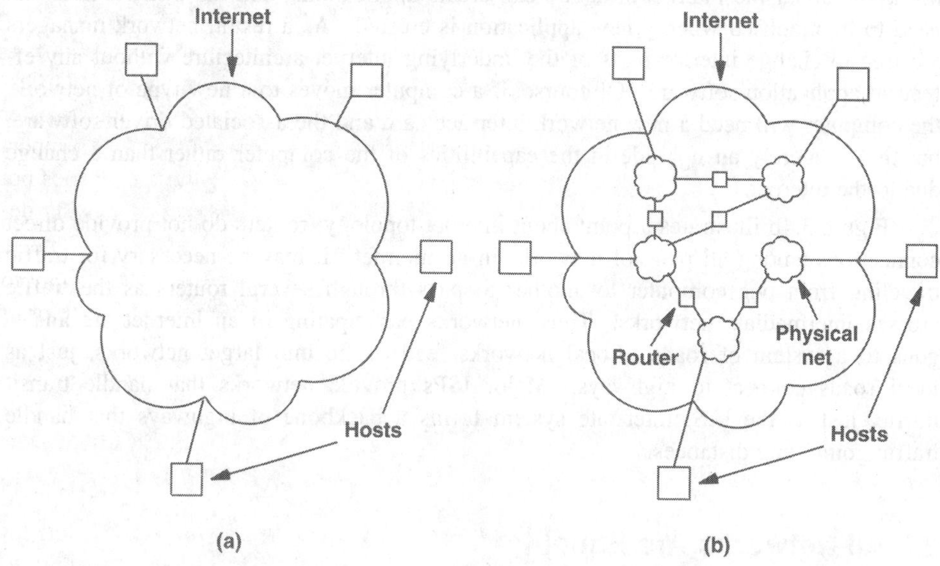

Figure 3.4 (a) The user's view of a TCP/IP internet in which each computer appears to attach to a single large network, and (b) the structure of physical networks and routers that provide interconnection.

In the figure, part (a) shows the view that user's have. They think of the internet as a unified communication system. The user's view simplifies the details and makes it easy to conceptualize communication. Part (b) illustrates the constituent networks and their interconnection with routers. Of course, each computer that connects to an internet must run software that enforces the view of a single, physical network. The software must hide details and allow application programs to send and receive packets to arbitrary locations as if the computer was connected to a single network.

The advantage of providing interconnection at the network level now becomes clear. Because application programs that communicate over the internet do not know the details of underlying connections, they can be run without change on any computer. Because the details of each machine's physical network connections are hidden in the internet software, only the internet software needs to react when new physical connections are added or existing connections are removed. For example, a portable device can connect to a Wi-Fi network in an airport, be turned off for a flight, and then connected to a Wi-Fi network in another airport without affecting the applications in any way. More important, it is possible to change the internal structure of the internet (e.g., by adding a network or a router) while application programs are executing.

A second advantage of having communication at the network level is more subtle: users do not have to understand, remember, or specify how networks connect, what traffic they carry, or what applications they support. In fact, internal networks do not know about applications — they merely transport packets. As a result, programmers who do not know about the internet structure can create applications, and the internet does not need to be modified when a new application is created. As a result, network managers are free to change interior parts of the underlying internet architecture without any effect on application software. Of course, if a computer moves to a new type of network, the computer will need a new network interface card and the associated driver software, but that is merely an upgrade in the capabilities of the computer rather than a change due to the internet.

Figure 3.4b illustrates a point about internet topology: routers do not provide direct connections among all pairs of networks in an internet. It may be necessary for traffic traveling from one computer to another to pass through several routers as the traffic crosses intermediate networks. Thus, networks participating in an internet are analogous to a system of roads. Local networks feed traffic into larger networks, just as local roads connect to highways. Major ISPs provide networks that handle transit traffic, just as the U.S. interstate system forms a backbone of highways that handle traffic going long distances.

3.8 All Networks Are Equal

Chapter 2 reviewed examples of the network hardware used to build TCP/IP internets, and illustrated the great diversity of technologies. We have described an internet as a collection of cooperative, interconnected networks. It is now important to understand a fundamental concept: from the internet point of view, any communication system capable of transferring packets counts as a single network, independent of its delay and throughput characteristics, maximum packet size, or geographic scale. In particular, Figure 3.4b uses the same small cloud shape to depict each physical network because TCP/IP treats them equally despite their differences. The point is:

> *The TCP/IP internet protocols treat all networks equally. A Local Area Network such as an Ethernet, a Wide Area Network used as a backbone, a wireless network such as a Wi-Fi hotspot, and a point-to-point link between two computers each count as one network.*

Readers unaccustomed to internet architecture may find it difficult to accept such a simplistic view of networks. In essence, TCP/IP defines an abstraction of "network" that hides the details of physical networks. In practice, network architects must choose a technology that is appropriate for each use. We will learn, however, that abstracting away from details helps make the TCP/IP protocols extremely flexible and powerful.

3.9 The Unanswered Questions

Our sketch of internets leaves many unanswered questions. For example, you might wonder about the exact form of internet addresses assigned to computers or how such addresses relate to the hardware addresses (e.g. 48-bit Ethernet MAC addresses) described in Chapter 2. Chapters 5 and 6 confront the question of addressing. They describe the format of IP addresses, and illustrate how software on a computer maps between internet addresses and physical addresses. You might also want to know exactly what a packet looks like when it travels through an internet, or what happens when packets arrive too fast for a computer or router to handle. Chapter 7 answers these questions. Finally, you might wonder how multiple application programs executing concurrently on a single computer can send and receive packets to multiple destinations without becoming entangled in each other's transmissions, or how internet routers learn about routes. All of the questions will be answered.

Although it may seem vague now, the direction we are following will let us learn about both the structure and use of internet protocol software. We will examine each part, looking at the concepts and principles as well as technical details. We began by describing the physical communication layer on which an internet is built. Each of the following chapters will explore one part of the internet software until we understand how all the pieces fit together.

3.10 Summary

An internet is more than a collection of networks interconnected by computers. Internetworking implies that the interconnected systems agree to conventions that allow each host to communicate with every other host. In particular, an internet will allow two host computers to communicate even if the communication path between them passes across a network to which neither connects directly. Such cooperation is only possible when host computers agree on a set of universal identifiers and a set of procedures for moving data to its final destination.

In an internet, interconnections among networks are formed by special-purpose computer systems called IP routers that attach to two or more networks. A router forwards packets between networks by receiving them from one network and sending them to another.

EXERCISES

3.1 Commercial vendors sell wireless routers for use in a home. Read about such routers. What processors are used? How many bits per second must such a router handle?

3.2 Approximately how many networks constitute the part of the Internet at your site? Approximately how many routers?

3.3 Find out about the largest router used in your company or organization. How many network connections does the router have?

3.4 Consider the internal structure of the example internet shown in Figure 3.4b. Which routers are most critical to correct operation of the internet? Why?

3.5 Changing the information in a router can be tricky because it is impossible to change all routers simultaneously. Investigate algorithms that guarantee to either install a change on a set of computers or install it on none.

3.6 In an internet, routers periodically exchange information from their routing tables, making it possible for a new router to appear and begin routing packets. Investigate the algorithms used to exchange routing information.

3.7 Compare the organization of a TCP/IP internet to the XNS style of internets designed by Xerox Corporation.

Chapter Contents

4

Protocol Layering

4.1 Introduction

The previous chapter reviews the architectural foundations of internetworking and describes the interconnection of networks with routers. This chapter considers the structure of the software found in hosts and routers that carries out network communication. It presents the general principle of layering, shows how layering makes protocol software easier to understand and build, and traces the path that packets take through the protocol software when they traverse a TCP/IP internet. Successive chapters fill in details by explaining protocols at each layer.

4.2 The Need For Multiple Protocols

We said that protocols allow one to specify or understand communication without knowing the details of a particular vendor's network hardware. They are to computer communication what programming languages are to computation. The analogy fits well. Like assembly language, some protocols describe communication across a physical network. For example, the details of the Ethernet frame format, the meaning of header fields, the order in which bits are transmitted on the wire, and the way CRC errors are handled constitute a protocol that describes communication on an Ethernet. We will see that the Internet Protocol is like a higher-level language that deals with abstractions, including Internet addresses, the format of Internet packets, and the way routers forward packets. Neither low-level nor high-level protocols are sufficient by themselves; both must be present.

Network communication is a complex problem with many aspects. To understand the complexity, think of some of the problems that can arise when computers communicate over a data network:

- *Hardware Failure.* A computer or router may fail either because the hardware fails or because the operating system crashes. A network transmission link may fail or accidentally become disconnected. Protocol software needs to detect such failures and recover from them if possible.
- *Network Congestion.* Even when all hardware and software operates correctly, networks have finite capacity that can be exceeded. Protocol software needs to arrange a way to detect congestion and suppress further traffic to avoid making the situation worse.
- *Packet Delay Or Packet Loss.* Sometimes, packets experience extremely long delays or are lost. Protocol software needs to learn about failures or adapt to long delays.
- *Data Corruption.* Electrical or magnetic interference or hardware failures can cause transmission errors that corrupt the contents of transmitted data; interference can be especially severe on wireless networks. Protocol software needs to detect and recover from such errors.
- *Data Duplication Or Inverted Arrivals.* Networks that offer multiple routes may deliver packets out of sequence or may deliver duplicates of packets. Protocol software needs to reorder packets and remove any duplicates.

Taken together, the problems seem overwhelming. It is impossible to write a single protocol specification that will handle them all. From the analogy with programming languages, we can see how to conquer the complexity. Program translation has been partitioned into four conceptual subproblems identified with the software that handles each subproblem: compiler, assembler, link editor, and loader. The division makes it possible for the designer to concentrate on one subproblem at a time, and for the implementer to build and test each piece of software independently. We will see that protocol software is partitioned similarly.

Two final observations from our programming language analogy will help clarify the organization of protocols. First, it should be clear that pieces of translation software must agree on the exact format of data passed between them. For example, the data passed from a compiler to an assembler consists of a program defined by the assembly programming language. The translation process involves multiple representations. The analogy holds for communication software because multiple protocols define the representations of data passed among communication software modules. Second, the four parts of the translator form a linear sequence in which output from the compiler becomes input to the assembler, and so on. Protocol software also uses a linear sequence.

4.3 The Conceptual Layers Of Protocol Software

We think of the modules of protocol software on each computer as being stacked vertically into *layers*, as Figure 4.1 illustrates. Each layer takes responsibility for handling one part of the problem.

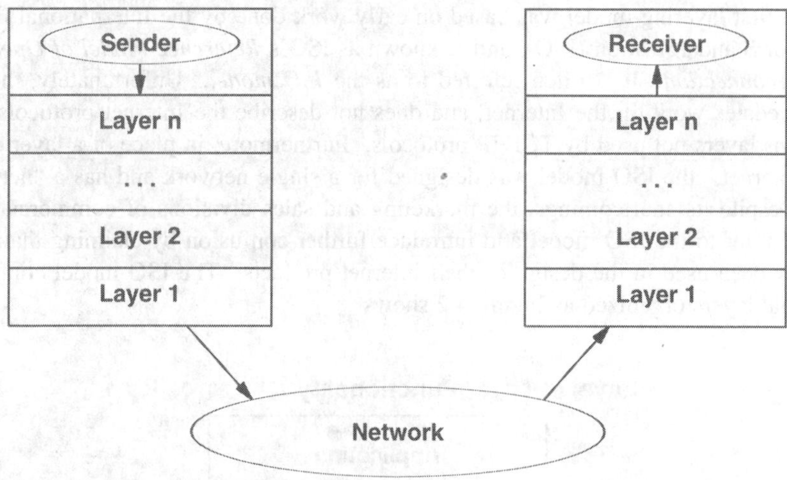

Figure 4.1 The conceptual organization of protocol software in layers.

Conceptually, sending a message from an application on one computer to an application on another means transferring the message down through successive layers of protocol software on the sender's machine, forwarding the message across the network, and transferring the message up through successive layers of protocol software on the receiver's machine.

4.4 Functionality Of The Layers

Once a decision has been made to partition the communication problem and organize the protocol software into layers that each handle one subproblem, two interrelated questions arise: how many layers should be created, and what functionality should reside in each layer? The questions are not easy to answer for several reasons. First, given a set of goals and constraints governing a particular communication problem, it is possible to choose an organization that will optimize protocol software for that problem. Second, even when considering general network-level services such as reliable transport, it is possible to choose from among fundamentally distinct approaches to solving the problem. Third, the design of network (or internet) architecture and the organization of the protocol software are interrelated; one cannot be designed without the other. Two approaches to protocol layering dominate the field, and the next two sections consider them.

4.5 ISO 7-Layer Reference Model

The first layering model was based on early work done by the International Organization for Standardization (ISO), and is known as ISO's *Reference Model of Open System Interconnection*. It is often referred to as the *ISO model*. Unfortunately, the ISO model predates work on the Internet, and does not describe the Internet protocols well. It contains layers not used by TCP/IP protocols. Furthermore, in place of a layer devoted to "internet," the ISO model was designed for a single network and has a "network" layer. Despite its shortcomings, the marketing and sales divisions of commercial vendors still refer to the ISO model and introduce further confusion by claiming that it has somehow been used in the design of their internet products. The ISO model contains 7 conceptual layers organized as Figure 4.2 shows.

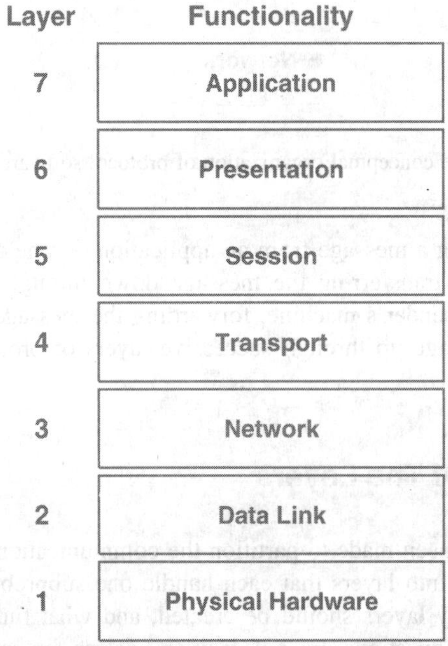

Layer	Functionality
7	Application
6	Presentation
5	Session
4	Transport
3	Network
2	Data Link
1	Physical Hardware

Figure 4.2 The ISO 7-layer reference model. Because it was designed to describe protocols in a single network, the model does not describe the organization of TCP/IP protocols well.

4.6 X.25 And Its Relation To The ISO Model

Although it was designed to provide a conceptual model and not an implementation guide, the ISO layering scheme was used as the basis for early protocol implementations. Among the protocols commonly associated with the ISO model, the suite of protocols known as X.25 was probably the most recognized and widely used. X.25 was established as a recommendation of the *International Telecommunications Union* (*ITU*†), an organization that recommends standards for international telephone services. X.25 was adopted by public data networks, and became especially popular in Europe. Considering X.25 will help explain ISO layering.

In the X.25 view, a network operates much like a telephone system. A network consists of packet switches that contain the intelligence needed to route packets. Computers do not attach directly to communication wires of the network. Instead, each computer attaches to one of the packet switches using a serial communication line. In one sense, the connection between a host and an X.25 packet switch is a miniature network consisting of one serial link. The host must follow a complicated procedure to transfer packets across the network. Layers of the protocol standard specify various aspects of the network as follows.

- *Physical Layer.* X.25 specifies a standard for the physical interconnection between computers and network packet switches. In the reference model, layer *1* specifies the physical interconnection including electrical characteristics of voltage and current.
- *Data Link Layer.* The layer *2* portion of the X.25 protocol specifies how data travels between a computer and the packet switch to which it connects. X.25 uses the term *frame* to refer to a unit of data as it transfers to a packet switch. Because the underlying hardware delivers only a stream of bits, the layer *2* protocol must define the format of frames and specify how the two machines recognize frame boundaries. Because transmission errors can destroy data, the layer *2* protocol includes error detection (e.g., a frame checksum) as well as a timeout mechanism that causes a computer to resend a frame until it has been transferred successfully. It is important to understand that successful transfer at layer *2* means a frame has been passed to the network packet switch; it does not mean that the packet switch was able to forward or deliver the packet.
- *Network Layer.* The ISO reference model specifies that the third layer contains functionality that completes the definition of the interaction between host and network. Called the *network* or *communication subnet* layer, the layer defines the basic unit of transfer across the network, and includes the concepts of destination addressing and forwarding. Because layer *2* and layer *3* are conceptually independent, the size of a layer *3* packet can be larger than the size of layer *2* frames (i.e., a computer can create a layer *3* packet and then layer *2* can divide the packet into smaller pieces for transfer to the packet switch).

†The ITU was formerly known as the *CCITT*.

- *Transport Layer.* Layer *4* provides end-to-end reliability by having the destination computer communicate with the source computer. The idea is that even though lower layers of protocols provide reliability checks at each transfer, the transport layer provides an extra check to insure that no machine in the middle failed.
- *Session Layer.* Higher layers of the ISO model describe how protocol software can be organized to handle all the functionality needed by application programs. When the ISO model was formed, networks were used to connect a terminal (i.e., a screen and keyboard) to a remote computer. In fact, the service offered by early public data networks focused on providing terminal access. Layer *5* handles the details.
- *Presentation Layer.* ISO layer *6* is intended to standardize the format of data that application programs send over a network. One of the disadvantages of standardizing data formats is that it stifles innovation — new applications cannot be deployed until their data format has been standardized. Another disadvantage arises because specific groups claim the right to standardize representations appropriate for their application domain (e.g., the data formats for digital video are specified by groups that handle standards for video rather than groups that standardize networks). Consequently, presentation standards are usually ignored.
- *Application Layer.* ISO layer *7* includes application programs that use the network. Examples include electronic mail and file transfer programs.

4.7 The TCP/IP 5-Layer Reference Model

The second major layering model did not arise from a formal standards body. Instead, the model arose from researchers who designed the Internet and the TCP/IP protocol suite. When the TCP/IP protocols became popular, proponents of the older ISO model attempted to stretch the ISO model to accommodate TCP/IP. However, the fact remains that the original ISO model did not provide an internet layer, and instead defined session and presentation layers that are not pertinent to TCP/IP protocols.

One of the major conceptual differences between the ISO and Internet layering models arises from the way in which they were defined. The ISO model was *prescriptive* — standards bodies convened a committee that wrote specifications for how protocols should be built. They then started to implement protocols. The important point is that the model predated the implementation. By contrast, the Internet model is *descriptive* — researchers spent years understanding how to structure the protocols, building prototype implementations, and documenting the results. After researchers were finally convinced that they understood the design, a model was constructed. The point can be summarized:

Unlike the ISO model, which was defined by committees before protocols were implemented, the Internet 5-layer reference model was formalized after protocols had been designed and tested.

TCP/IP protocols are organized into five conceptual layers — four layers define packet processing and a fifth layer defines conventional network hardware. Figure 4.3 shows the conceptual layers and lists the form of data that passes between each successive pair of layers.

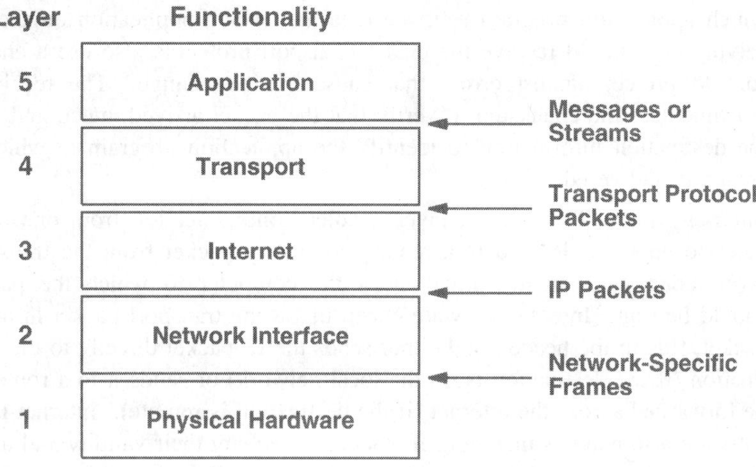

Figure 4.3 The 5-layer TCP/IP reference model showing the form of objects passed between layers.

The following paragraphs describe the general purpose of each layer. Later chapters fill in many details and examine specific protocols at each layer.

- *Application Layer.* At the highest layer, users invoke application programs that access services available across a TCP/IP internet. An application interacts with one of the transport layer protocols to send or receive data. Each application program chooses the style of transport needed, which can be either a sequence of individual messages or a continuous stream of bytes. The application program passes data in the required form to the transport layer for delivery.
- *Transport Layer.* The primary duty of the transport layer is to provide communication from one application program to another. Such communication is called *end-to-end*, because it involves applications on two endpoints rather than intermediate routers. A transport layer may regulate flow of information. It may also provide reliable transport, ensuring that data arrives

without error and in sequence. To do so, transport protocol software arranges to have the receiving side send back acknowledgements and the sending side retransmit lost packets. The transport software divides the stream of data being transmitted into small pieces (sometimes called *packets*) and passes each packet along with a destination address to the next layer for transmission.

As described below, a general purpose computer can have multiple applications accessing an internet at one time. The transport layer must accept data from several applications and send it to the next lower layer. To do so, it adds additional information to each packet, including values that identify which application program sent the data and which application on the receiving end should receive the data. Transport protocols also use a checksum to protect against errors that cause bits to change. The receiving machine uses the checksum to verify that the packet arrived intact, and uses the destination information to identify the application program to which it should be delivered.

- *Internet Layer.* The internet layer handles communication from one computer to another. It accepts a request to send a packet from the transport layer along with an identification of the computer to which the packet should be sent. Internet software encapsulates the transport packet in an IP packet, fills in the header, and either sends the IP packet directly to the destination (if the destination is on the local network) or sends it to a router to be forwarded across the internet (if the destination is remote). Internet layer software also handles incoming IP packets, checking their validity and using the forwarding algorithm to decide whether the packet should be processed locally or forwarded. For packets destined to the local machine, software in the internet layer chooses the transport protocol that will handle the packet.

- *Network Interface Layer.* The lowest-layer of TCP/IP software comprises a network interface layer, responsible for accepting IP packets and transmitting them over a specific network. A network interface may consist of a device driver (e.g., when the network is a local area network to which the computer attaches) or a complex subsystem that implements a data link protocol. Some networking professionals do not distinguish between the two types; they simply use the term *MAC layer* or *data link layer.*

In practice, TCP/IP Internet protocol software is much more complex than the simple model of Figure 4.3. Each layer makes decisions about the correctness of the message and chooses an appropriate action based on the message type or destination address. For example, the internet layer on the receiving machine must decide whether the message has indeed reached the correct destination. The transport layer must decide which application program should receive the message.

A primary difference between the simplistic model of layers illustrated in Figure 4.3 and the protocol software in a real system arises because a computer or a router can have multiple network interfaces and multiple protocols can occur at each layer. To understand some of the complexity, consider Figure 4.4, which shows a comparison between layers and software modules.

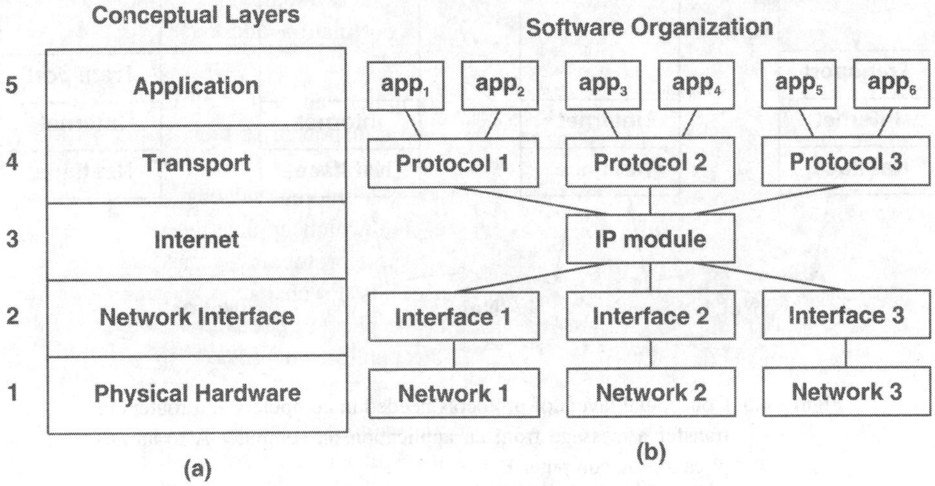

Figure 4.4 A comparison of (a) conceptual protocol layering and (b) a more realistic view of protocol software with multiple network interfaces and multiple protocols.

The conceptual diagram in Figure 4.4(a) shows five layers of protocols with a single box depicting each layer. The more realistic illustration of software in Figure 4.4(b) shows that there may indeed be a layer with one protocol (Layer *3*). However, there can be multiple applications at Layer *5*, and more than one application can use a given transport protocol. We will learn that the Internet protocols have multiple transport protocols at Layer *4*, multiple physical networks at Layer *1*, and multiple network interface modules at Layer *2*.

Networking professional use the terms *hour glass* and *narrow waist* to describe the role of the Internet Protocol in the TCP/IP suite. Figure 4.4(b) makes the terminology obvious — although multiple independent protocols can exist above IP and multiple networks can exist below IP, all outgoing or incoming traffic must pass through IP.

If a conceptual layering diagram does not accurately reflect the organization of software modules, why is it used? Although a layering model does not capture all details, it does help explain some general concepts. For example, even though it does not give the details about specific protocols, Figure 4.4(a) helps us understand that an outgoing message will traverse three intermediate protocol layers before being sent over a network. Furthermore, we can use the layering model to explain the difference between end systems (users' computers) and intermediate systems (routers). Figure 4.5 shows the layering used in an internet with three networks connected by two routers.

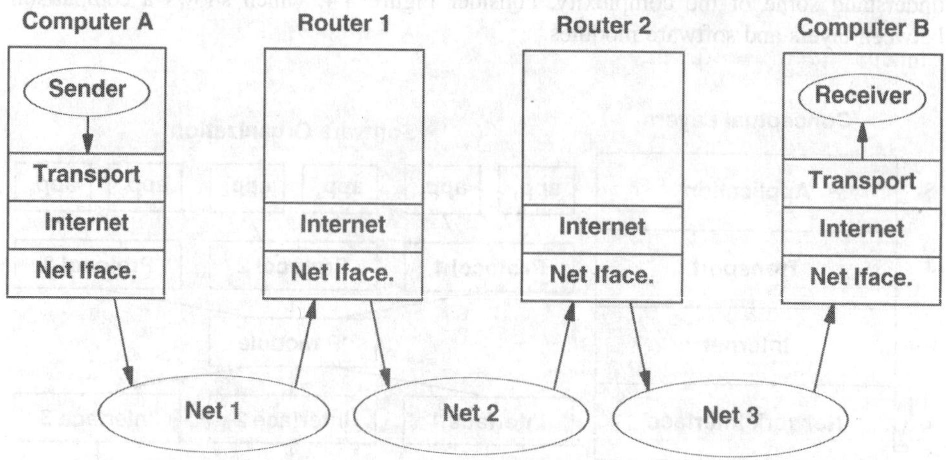

Figure 4.5 Conceptual layers of protocols needed in computers and routers to transfer a message from an application on computer A to an application on computer B.

In the figure, a sending application on computer *A* uses a transport protocol to send data to a receiving application on computer *B*. The message passes down the protocol stack on computer *A*, and is transmitted across network 1 to Router 1. When it reaches the first router, the packet passes up to the internet layer (Layer *3*), which forwards the packet over network 2 to Router 2. On Router 2, the message passes up to Layer *3*, and is forwarded over network 3 to the destination. When it reaches the final destination machine, the message passes up to the transport layer, which delivers the message to the receiving application. Later chapters explain how IP handles forwarding, and show why a transit packet does not use the transport protocol on a router.

4.8 Locus Of Intelligence

The Internet represents a significant departure from earlier network designs because much of the intelligence is placed outside of the network in the end systems (e.g., users' computers). The original voice telephone network illustrates the difference. In the analog telephone network, all the intelligence was located in phone switches; telephones only contained passive electronics (i.e., a microphone, earpiece, and a mechanism used to dial).

By contrast, the TCP/IP protocols require attached computers to run transport protocols and applications as well as Layer *3* and Layer *2* protocols. We have already mentioned that transport protocols implement end-to-end reliability by retransmitting lost packets. We will learn that transport protocols are complex, and that a computer attached to the Internet must also participate in forwarding because the computer must choose a router to use when sending packets. Thus, unlike the analog telephone system, a TCP/IP internet can be viewed as a relatively simple packet delivery system to which intelligent hosts attach. The concept is fundamental:

> *TCP/IP protocols place much of the intelligence in hosts — routers in the Internet forward Internet packets, but do not participate in higher-layer services.*

4.9 The Protocol Layering Principle

Independent of the particular layering scheme or the functions of the layers, the operation of layered protocols is based on a fundamental idea. The idea, called the *layering principle*, can be stated succinctly:

> *Layered protocols are designed so that layer* n *at the destination receives exactly the same object sent by layer* n *at the source.*

Although it may seem obvious or even trivial, the layering principle provides an important foundation that helps us design, implement, and understand protocols. Specifically, the layering principle offers:

- Protocol design independence
- Definition of the end-to-end property

Protocol Design Independence. By placing a guarantee on the items passing between each pair of layers, the layering principle allows protocol designers to work on one layer at a time. A protocol designer can focus on the message exchange for a given layer with the assurance that lower layers will not alter messages. For example, when creating a file transfer application, a designer only needs to imagine two copies of the file transfer application running on two computers. The interaction between the two copies can be planned without thinking about other protocols because the designer can assume each message will be delivered exactly as it was sent. The idea that the network should not change messages seems so obvious to application programmers that most of them cannot imagine building network applications without it.

Fortunately, the layering principle works for the design of lower layer protocols as well. At each layer, a designer can depend on the layering principle being enforced by lower layers; all a designer has to do is guarantee the layering principle to the next higher layer. For example, when a protocol designer works on a new transport protocol, the designer can assume the transport protocol module on the destination machine will receive whatever message is sent by the transport protocol module on the sending machine. The key idea is that a transport protocol can be designed independent of other protocols.

Definition Of The End-To-End Property. Informally, we classify a network technology as *end-to-end* if the technology provides communication from the original source to the ultimate destination. The informal definition is used with protocols as well. The layering principle allows us to be more precise: we say a protocol is *end-to-end* if and only if the layering principle applies between the original source and ultimate destination. Other protocols are classified as *machine-to-machine* because the layering principle only applies across one network hop. The next section explains how the layering principle applies to Internet protocols.

4.10 The Layering Principle Applied To A Network

To understand how the layering principle applies in practice, consider two computers connected to a network. Figure 4.6 illustrates the layers of protocol software running in each computer and the messages that pass between layers.

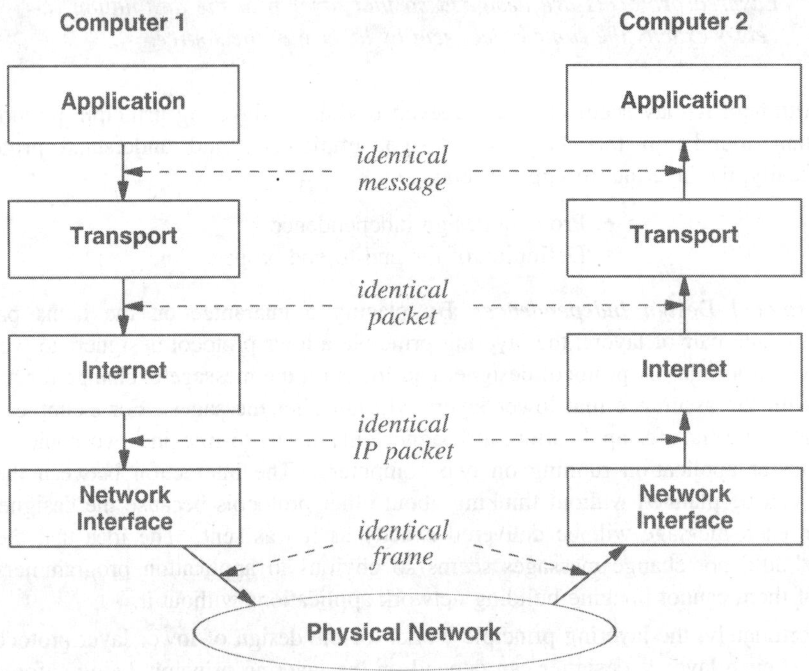

Figure 4.6 The layering principle when a message passes across a network from an application on one computer to an application on another.

4.10.1 Layering In A TCP/IP Internet Environment

Our illustration of the layering principle is incomplete because the diagram in Figure 4.6 only shows layering for two computers connected to a single network. How does the layering principle apply to an internet that can transfer messages across multiple networks? Figure 4.7 answers the question by showing an example where a message from an application program on one computer is sent to an application program on another computer through a router.

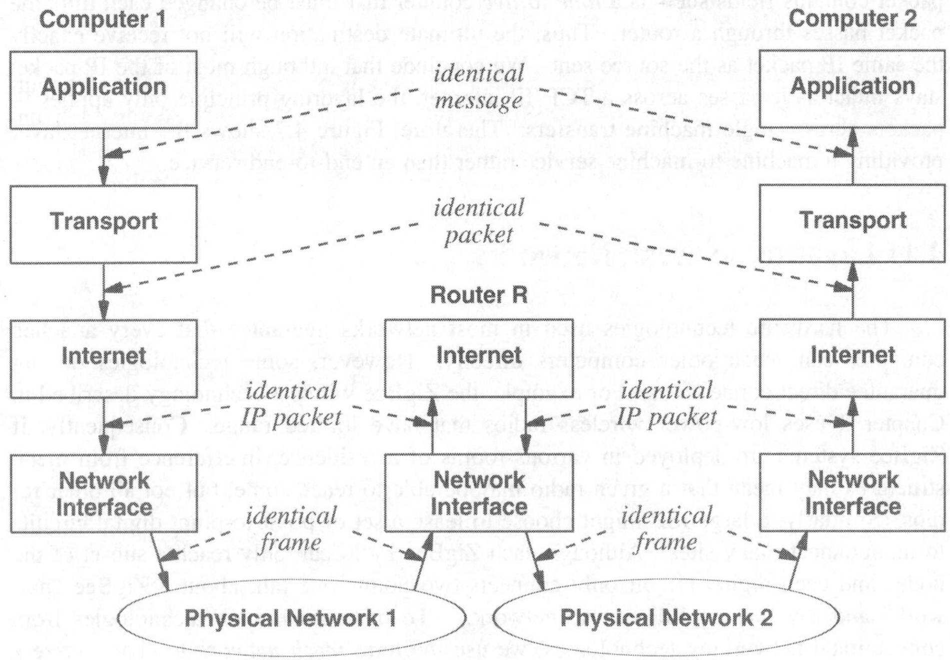

Figure 4.7 The layering principle when a message passes from an application on one computer, through a router, and is delivered to an application on another computer.

As the figure shows, message delivery uses two separate network frames, one for the transmission from computer 1 to router *R* and another from router *R* to computer 2. The network layering principle states that the frame delivered to *R* is identical to the frame sent by computer 1, and the frame delivered to computer 2 is identical to the frame sent by router *R*. However, the two frames will definitely differ. By contrast, for the application and transport protocols, the layering principle applies end-to-end. That is, the message delivered on computer 2 is exactly the same message that the peer protocol sent on computer 1.

It is easy to understand that for higher layers, the layering principle applies end-to-end, and that at the lowest layer, it applies to a single machine transfer. It is not as easy to see how the layering principle applies to the internet layer. On the one hand, the goal of the Internet design is to present a large, virtual network, with the internet layer sending packets across the virtual internet analogous to the way network hardware sends frames across a single network. Thus, it seems logical to imagine an IP packet being sent from the original source all the way to the ultimate destination, and to imagine the layering principle guaranteeing that the ultimate destination receives exactly the IP packet that the original source sent. On the other hand, we will learn that an IP packet contains fields such as a *time to live* counter that must be changed each time the packet passes through a router. Thus, the ultimate destination will not receive exactly the same IP packet as the source sent. We conclude that although most of the IP packet stays intact as it passes across a TCP/IP internet, the layering principle only applies to packets across single machine transfers. Therefore, Figure 4.7 shows the internet layer providing a machine-to-machine service rather than an end-to-end service.

4.11 Layering In Mesh Networks

The hardware technologies used in most networks guarantee that every attached computer can reach other computers directly. However, some technologies do not guarantee direct connections. For example, the ZigBee wireless technology described in Chapter 2 uses low-power wireless radios that have limited range. Consequently, if ZigBee systems are deployed in various rooms of a residence, interference from metal structures may mean that a given radio may be able to reach some, but not all other radios. Similarly, a large ISP might choose to lease a set of point-to-point digital circuits to interconnect many sites. Although each ZigBee radio can only reach a subset of the nodes and each digital circuit only connects two points, we talk about a ZigBee "network" and say that an ISP has a "network." To distinguish such technologies from conventional networking technologies, we use the term *mesh network* to characterize a communication system constructed from many individual links.

How does a mesh network fit into our layering model? The answer depends on how packets are forwarded across the links. On the one hand, if forwarding occurs at Layer 2, the entire mesh can be modeled as a single physical network. We use the term *mesh-under* to describe such a situation. On the other hand, if IP handles forwarding, the mesh must be modeled as individual networks. We use the term *IP route-over*, often shortened to *route-over*, to describe such cases.

Route-over. Most ISP networks use route-over. The ISP uses leased digital circuits to interconnect routers, and an individual router views the each circuit as a single network. IP handles all forwarding, and the router uses standard Internet routing protocols (described in later chapters) to construct the forwarding tables†.

Mesh-under. The IEEE 802.15.4 technology used in ZigBee networks can be configured to act as individual links or as a complete network. That is, they can organize themselves into a single mesh network by agreeing to discover neighbors and form a

†As Chapter 9 explains, it is possible to use an *anonymous link* mechanism that does not assign an IP prefix to each link; using unnumbered links does not change the layering.

Layer 2 mesh-under network that forwards packets without using IP, or they can form individual links and allow IP to handle forwarding. In terms of our layering model, the only change the mesh-under approach introduces is a software module added to the network interface to control forwarding on individual links. We say that the new software controls *intra-network forwarding*. The new software is sometimes referred to as an *intranet sublayer* as Figure 4.8 illustrates.

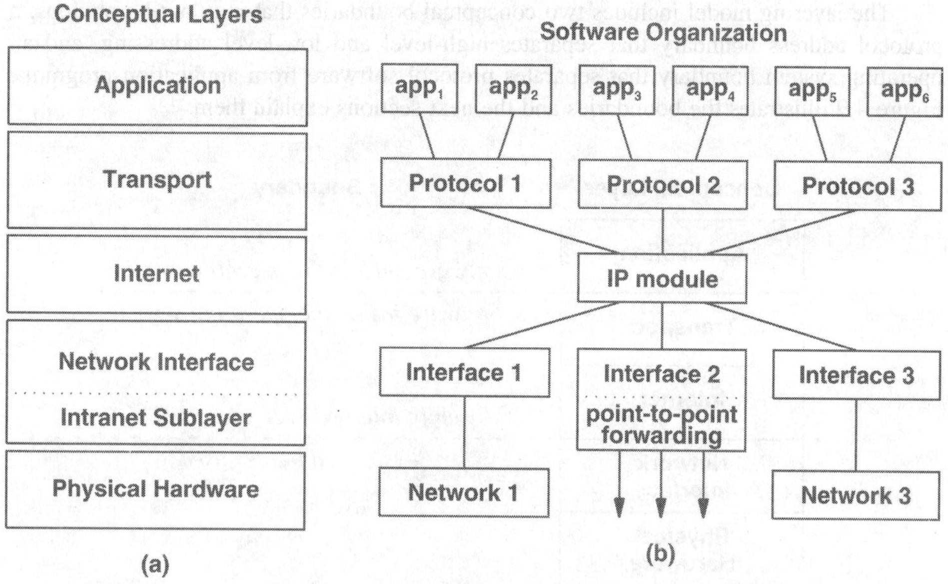

Figure 4.8 (a) Conceptual position of an intranet sublayer that handles forwarding using a mesh-under approach, and (b) the corresponding software organization.

Besides an intranet sublayer that handles forwarding across the set of individual links, no other changes are required to the overall layering scheme to accommodate the mesh-under approach. Interestingly, ZigBee uses a minor modification of the ideas described above. Although it recommends using the route-over approach, the ZigBee consortium does not recommend using standard IP routing protocols. Instead, the ZigBee stack uses a special routing protocol that learns about destinations in the ZigBee mesh and then configures IP forwarding across the individual links.

The main disadvantage of the route-over approach is that it proliferates many routes at the IP layer (one for each connection between two machines), causing IP forwarding tables to be larger than necessary. The main disadvantage of the mesh-under approach is that it uses a separate forwarding table and a separate routing protocol to update the forwarding table. The extra routing protocol means additional traffic, but because the mesh network is much smaller than the Internet and may be much more static, a special-purpose mesh routing protocol can be more efficient than a general-purpose IP routing protocol. A final disadvantage of the mesh-under approach is that intranet routing preempts IP routing which can make routing problems more difficult to diagnose and repair.

4.12 Two Important Boundaries In The TCP/IP Model

The layering model includes two conceptual boundaries that may not be obvious: a protocol address boundary that separates high-level and low-level addressing, and an operating system boundary that separates protocol software from application programs. Figure 4.9 illustrates the boundaries and the next sections explain them.

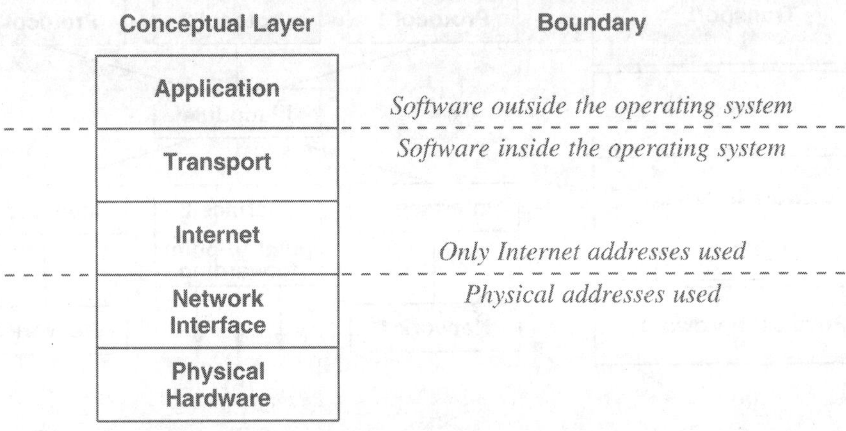

Figure 4.9 Two conceptual boundaries in the layering model.

4.12.1 High-Level Protocol Address Boundary

Chapter 2 describes the addresses used by various types of network hardware. Later chapters describe Internet protocols and Internet addressing. It is important to distinguish where the two forms of addressing are used, and the layering model makes it clear: there is a conceptual boundary between Layer *2* and Layer *3*. Hardware (MAC) addresses are used at Layers *1* and *2*, but not above. Internet addresses are used by Layers *3* through *5*, but not by the underlying hardware. We can summarize:

> *Application programs and all protocol software from the internet layer upward use only Internet addresses; addresses used by the network hardware are isolated at lower layers.*

4.12.2 Operating System Boundary

Figure 4.9 illustrates another important boundary: the division between protocol software that is implemented in an operating system and application software that is not. Although researchers have experimented by making TCP/IP part of an application, most implementations place the protocol software in the operating system where it can be shared by all applications. The boundary is important, because passing data among modules within the operating system is much less expensive than passing data between the operating system and an application. Furthermore, a special API is needed to permit an application to interact with protocol software. Chapter 21 discusses the boundary in more detail, and describes an example interface that an operating system provides to applications.

4.13 Cross-Layer Optimizations

We have said that layering is a fundamental idea that provides the basis for protocol design. It allows the designer to divide a complicated problem into subproblems and solve each one independently. Unfortunately, the software that results from strict layering can be extremely inefficient. As an example, consider the job of the transport layer. It must accept a stream of bytes from an application program, divide the stream into packets, and send each packet across the underlying internet. To optimize transfer, the transport layer should choose the largest packet size that will allow one packet to travel in one network frame. In particular, if the destination machine attaches directly to the same network as the source, only one physical network will be involved in the transfer and the sender can optimize packet size for that network. If protocol software preserves strict layering, however, the transport layer cannot know how the internet module will forward traffic or which networks attach directly. Furthermore, the transport layer will not understand the packet formats used by lower layers, nor will it be able to determine how many octets of header will be added to the message it sends. Thus, strict layering will prevent the transport layer from optimizing transfers.

Usually, implementers relax the strict layering scheme when building protocol software. They allow upper layers of a protocol stack to obtain information such as the maximum packet size or the route being used. When allocating packet buffers, transport layer protocols can use the information to optimize processing by leaving sufficient space for headers that will be added by lower-layer protocols. Similarly, lower-layer protocols often retain all the headers on an incoming frame when passing the frame to higher-layer protocols. Such optimizations can make dramatic improvements in efficiency while retaining the basic layered structure.

4.14 The Basic Idea Behind Multiplexing And Demultiplexing

Layered communication protocols use a pair of techniques known as *multiplexing* and *demultiplexing* throughout the layering hierarchy. When sending a message, the source computer includes extra bits that store meta-data, such as the message type, the identity of the application program that sent the data, and the set of protocols that have been used. At the receiving end, a destination computer uses the meta-data to guide processing.

Ethernet provides a basic example. Each Ethernet frame includes a *type* field that specifies what the frame carries. In later chapters, we will see that an Ethernet frame can contain an IP packet, an ARP packet, or a RARP packet. The sender sets the type field in the frame to indicate what is being sent. When the frame arrives, protocol software on the receiving computer uses the frame type to choose a protocol module to process the frame. We say that the software *demultiplexes* incoming frames. Figure 4.10 illustrates the concept.

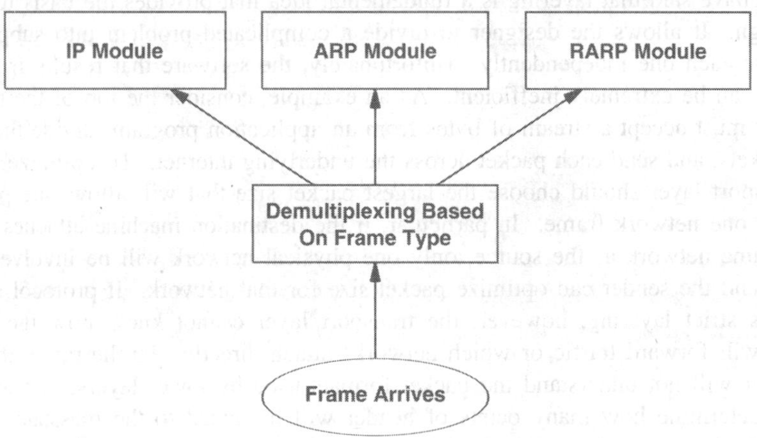

Figure 4.10 Illustration of frame demultiplexing that uses a type field in the frame header. Demultiplexing is used with most networks, including Ethernet and Wi-Fi.

Multiplexing and demultiplexing occur at each layer. The demultiplexing illustrated in Figure 4.10 occurs at the network interface layer, Layer *2*. To understand demultiplexing at Layer *3*, consider a frame that contains an IP packet. We have seen that frame demultiplexing will pass the packet to the IP module for processing. Once it has verified that the packet is valid (i.e., has indeed been delivered to the correct destination), IP will demultiplex further by passing the packet to the appropriate transport protocol module.

How can IP software know which transport protocol the sender used? Analogous to an Ethernet frame, each IP packet has a *type* field in the header. The sender sets the IP type field to indicate which transport protocol was used. In later chapters, we will learn about TCP, UDP, and ICMP, each of which can be sent in an IP packet. Figure 4.11 illustrates how IP demultiplexes among the three examples.

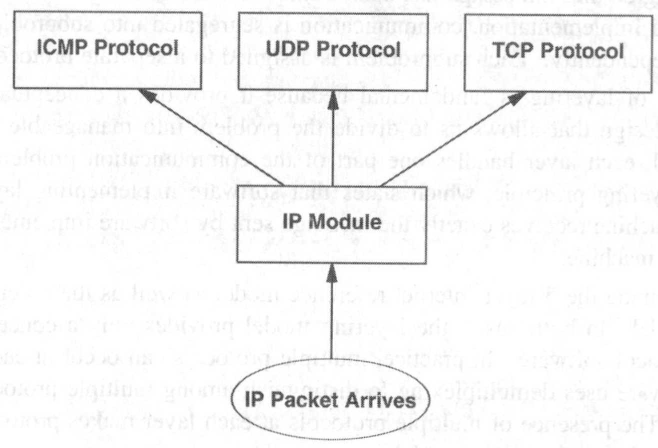

Figure 4.11 Illustration of demultiplexing incoming IP packets based on the type field in the IP header.

Our discussion of demultiplexing leaves many questions unanswered. How can we insure that the sender and receiver agree on the values used in a type field? What happens if an incoming packet contains a type other than the types the receiver can handle? Later chapters provide more information about demultiplexing, but we can give short answers to the above questions now. If a receiver does not understand the type in an arriving packet, the receiver discards the packet. To guarantee universal agreement on types, standards bodies specify values to be used (e.g., IEEE specifies the set of values for Ethernet types and the IETF specifies values for the Internet protocol). Provided senders and receivers each agree to follow the standards, no problems arise. Of course, researchers sometimes conduct experiments that use unassigned types. The rule that computers drop unknown packets helps — even if a researcher broadcasts a packet with an experimental type, no harm will occur because computers that do not understand the type will discard the packet.

4.15 Summary

Protocols are the standards that specify all aspects of communication across a computer network. Protocols specify both the syntax (e.g., the format of messages) as well as the semantics (e.g., how two computers exchange messages). Protocols include details such as voltages, how bits are sent, how errors are detected, and how the sender and receiver agree that a message has been transferred successfully. To simplify protocol design and implementation, communication is segregated into subproblems that can be solved independently. Each subproblem is assigned to a separate protocol.

The idea of layering is fundamental because it provides a conceptual framework for protocol design that allows us to divide the problem into manageable pieces. In a layered model, each layer handles one part of the communication problem. Protocols follow the layering principle, which states that software implementing layer *n* on the destination machine receives exactly the message sent by software implementing layer *n* on the source machine.

We examined the 5-layer Internet reference model as well as the older ISO 7-layer reference model. In both cases, the layering model provides only a conceptual framework for protocol software. In practice, multiple protocols can occur at each layer, and protocol software uses demultiplexing to distinguish among multiple protocols within a given layer. The presence of multiple protocols at each layer makes protocols software more complex than the layering models suggest.

EXERCISES

4.1 One of the main objections to layered protocols arises from the apparent overhead — copying occurs at each layer. How can copying be eliminated?

4.2 Layered protocols hide all underlying details from applications. Could application software be optimized if an application knew about the underlying networks being used? Explain.

4.3 Should the Internet protocols include a presentation layer that specifies standards for each data type (e.g., a graphic image type, a digital music type, etc)? Why or why not?

4.4 Build a case that TCP/IP is moving toward a six-layer protocol architecture that includes a presentation layer. (Hint: various programs use the XDR protocol, XML, and ASN.1.)

4.5 Find out how a UNIX system uses the *mbuf* structure to make layered protocol software efficient.

Chapter Contents

5

Internet Addressing

5.1 Introduction

Chapter 3 defines a TCP/IP internet as a virtual network built by interconnecting physical networks with routers. This chapter begins a discussion of addressing, an essential part of the design that helps TCP/IP software hide physical network details and makes the resulting internet appear to be a single, uniform entity.

In addition to discussing traditional Internet addressing, the chapter introduces IPv6 addresses. The traditional addressing scheme, which was introduced with version 4 of the Internet Protocol, is widely used. The next version of the Internet Protocol, version 6, has already started to appear, and will eventually replace IPv4.

5.2 Universal Host Identifiers

TCP/IP uses the term *host* to refer to an end system that attaches to the Internet. A host can be a large, powerful, general-purpose computer or a small, special-purpose system. A host may have an interface that humans use (e.g., a screen and keyboard) or may be an embedded device, such as a network printer. A host can use wired or wireless network technology. In short, the Internet divides all machines into two classes: routers and hosts. Any device that is not a router is classified as a host. We will use the terminology throughout the remainder of the text.

A communication system is said to supply *universal communication service* if the system allows an attached host to communicate with any other attached host. To make our communication system universal, it needs a globally accepted method of identifying each host that attaches to it.

Often, identifiers are classified as *names*, *addresses*, or *routes*. Shoch suggests that a name identifies *what* an object is, an address identifies *where* it is, and a route tells *how* to get there†. Although they are intuitively appealing, the definitions can be misleading. Names, addresses, and routes really refer to successively lower-level representations of host identifiers. In general, humans prefer to use pronounceable names to identify computers, while software works more efficiently with compact binary identifiers that we think of as addresses. Either could have been chosen as the TCP/IP host identifiers.

The decision was made to standardize on compact, binary addresses that make computations such as the selection of a next hop efficient. For now, we will only discuss binary addresses, postponing until later the questions of how to map between binary addresses and pronounceable names, and how to use addresses for forwarding packets.

We think of an internet as a large network like any other physical network. The difference, of course, is that an internet is a virtual structure, imagined by its designers and implemented by protocol software running on hosts and routers. Because an internet is virtual, its designers are free to choose packet formats and sizes, addresses, delivery techniques, and so on; nothing is dictated by hardware.

The designers of TCP/IP chose a scheme analogous to physical network addressing in which each host on an internet is assigned a unique integer address called its *Internet Protocol address* or *IP address*. The clever part of internet addressing is that the integers are carefully chosen to make forwarding efficient. Specifically, an IP address is divided into two parts: a prefix of the address identifies the network to which the host attaches and a suffix identifies a specific host on the network. That is, all hosts attached to the same network share a common prefix. We will see later why the division is important. For now, it is sufficient to remember:

> *Each host on an IPv4 internet is assigned a unique Internet address that is used in all communication with the host. To make forwarding efficient, a prefix of the address identifies a network and a suffix identifies a host on the network.*

The designers also decided to make IP addresses fixed size (32 bits was chosen for IPv4 and 128 bits for IPv6). Conceptually, each address is a pair (*netid*, *hostid*), where *netid* identifies a network and *hostid* identifies a host on that network. Once the decisions are made to use fixed-size IP addresses and divide each address into a network ID and host ID, a question arises: how large should each part be? The answer depends on the size of networks we expect in our internet. Allocating many bits to the network prefix allows our internet to contain many networks, but limits the size of each network. Allocating many bits to a host suffix means a given network can be large, but limits the number of networks in our internet.

†J. F. Shoch, "Internetwork Naming, Addressing, and Routing," *Proceedings of COMPCON 1978.*

5.3 The Original IPv4 Classful Addressing Scheme

This section describes the original IPv4 addressing mechanism. Although most of it is no longer used, we present it here because it explains how the IPv4 multicast address space was chosen. It also helps us understand subnet addressing, covered in the next section, which evolved to the current classless addressing scheme.

To understand addressing, observe that an internet allows arbitrary network technologies, which means it will contain a mixture of large and small networks. To accommodate the mixture, the designers did not choose a single division of the address. Instead, they invented a *classful* addressing scheme that allowed a given network to be large, medium, or small. Figure 5.1 illustrates how the original classful scheme divided each IPv4 address into two parts.

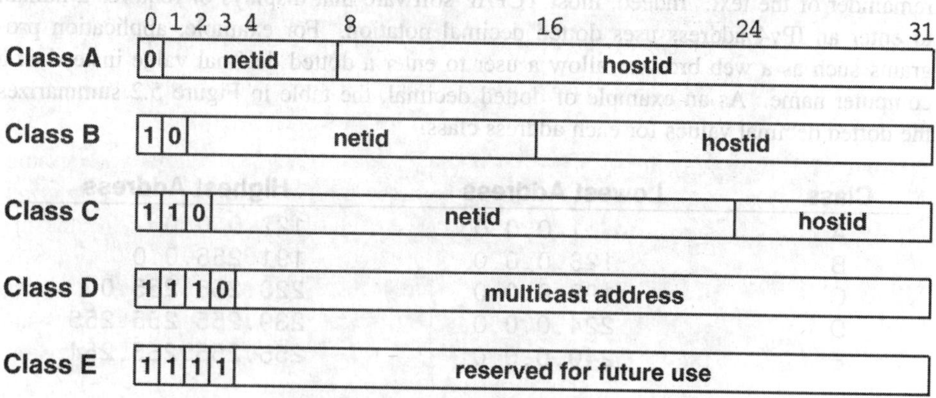

Figure 5.1 The five forms of Internet (IP) addresses used with the original IPv4 classful addressing scheme.

In the classful addressing scheme, each address is said to be *self-identifying* because the boundary between prefix and suffix can be computed from the address alone, without reference to external information. In particular, the class of an address can be determined from the three high-order bits, with two bits being sufficient to distinguish among the three primary classes. Class *A* addresses, used for the handful of large networks that have more than 2^{16} (i.e., 65,536) hosts, devote 7 bits to network ID and 24 bits to host ID. Class *B* addresses, used for medium size networks that have between 2^8 (i.e., 256) and 2^{16} hosts, allocate 14 bits to the network ID and 16 bits to the host ID. Finally, class *C* addresses, used for networks that have less than 2^8 hosts, allocate 21 bits to the network ID and only 8 bits to the host ID.

5.4 Dotted Decimal Notation Used With IPv4

When communicated to humans, either in technical documents or through application programs, IPv4 addresses are written as four decimal integers separated by decimal points, where each integer gives the value of one octet of the address†. Thus, the 32-bit internet address

10000000 00001010 00000010 00011110

is written

128.10.2.30

We will use dotted decimal notation when expressing IPv4 addresses throughout the remainder of the text. Indeed, most TCP/IP software that displays or requires a human to enter an IPv4 address uses dotted decimal notation. For example, application programs such as a web browser allow a user to enter a dotted decimal value instead of a computer name. As an example of dotted decimal, the table in Figure 5.2 summarizes the dotted decimal values for each address class.

Class	Lowest Address	Highest Address
A	1.0.0.0	127.0.0.0
B	128.0.0.0	191.255.0.0
C	192.0.0.0	223.255.255.0
D	224.0.0.0	239.255.255.255
E	240.0.0.0	255.255.255.254

Figure 5.2 The range of dotted decimal values that correspond to each of the original IPv4 address classes.

5.5 IPv4 Subnet Addressing

In the early 1980s, as Local Area Networks became widely available, it became apparent that the classful addressing scheme would have insufficient network addresses, especially class B prefixes. The question arose: how can the technology accommodate growth without abandoning the original classful addressing scheme? The first answer was a technique called *subnet addressing* or *subnetting*. Subnetting allows a single network prefix to be used for multiple physical networks. Although it appears to violate the addressing scheme, subnetting became part of the standard and was widely deployed.

To understand subnetting, it is important to think about individual sites connected to the Internet. Imagine, for example, that a university started with a single Local Area Network and obtained an IPv4 prefix. If the university adds another LAN, the original addressing scheme would require the university to obtain a second network ID for the second LAN. However, suppose the university only has a few computers. As long as

†A later section discusses colon hex notion used for IPv6 addresses.

the university hides the details from the rest of the Internet, the university can assign host addresses and arrange internal forwarding however it chooses. That is, a site can choose to assign and use IPv4 addresses in unusual ways internally as long as:

- All hosts and routers within the site agree to honor the site's addressing scheme.

- Other sites on the Internet can treat addresses as standard addresses with a network prefix that belongs to the site.

Subnet addressing takes advantage of the freedom by allowing a site to divide the host portion of their addresses among multiple networks. The easiest way to see how subnet addressing works is to consider an example. Suppose a site has been assigned a single class *B* prefix, 128.10.0.0. The rest of the Internet assumes each address at the site has one physical network with the 16-bit network ID 128.10. If the site obtains a second physical network, the site can use subnet addressing by using a portion of the host ID field to identify which physical network to use. Only hosts and routers at the site will know that there are multiple physical networks and how to forward traffic among them; routers and hosts in the rest of the Internet will assume there is a single physical network at the site with hosts attached. Figure 5.3 shows an example using the third octet of each address to identify a subnet.

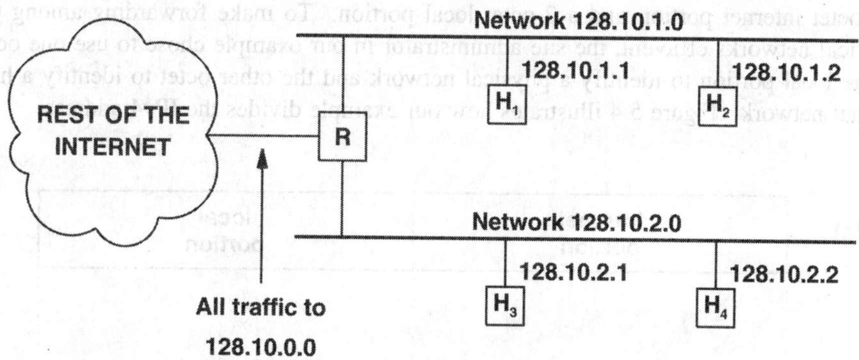

Figure 5.3 Illustration of IPv4 subnet addressing using the third octet of an address to specify a physical network.

In the figure, the site has decided to assign its two networks the subnet numbers 1 and 2. All hosts on the first network have addresses of the form:

128.10.1.*

where an asterisk denotes a host ID. For example, the figure shows two hosts on network 1 with addresses 128.10.1.1 and 128.10.1.2. Similarly, hosts on network 2 have addresses of the form:

128.10.2.*

When router *R* receives a packet, it checks the destination address. If the address starts with 128.10.1, the router delivers the packet to a host on network 1; if the address starts with 128.10.2, the router delivers the packet to a host on network 2. We will learn more about how routers forward packets; at present, it is sufficient to understand that a router at the site can use the third octet of the address to choose between the two networks.

Conceptually, adding subnets only changes the interpretation of IPv4 addresses slightly. Instead of dividing the 32-bit IPv4 address into a network prefix and a host suffix, subnetting divides the address into an *internet portion* and a *local portion*. The interpretation of the internet portion remains the same as for networks that do not use subnetting (i.e., it contains a network ID). However, interpretation of the local portion of an address is left up to the site (within the constraints of the formal standard for subnet addressing). To summarize:

> *When using subnet addressing, we think of a 32-bit IPv4 address as having an internet portion and a local portion, where the internet portion identifies a site, possibly with multiple physical networks, and the local portion identifies a physical network and host at that site.*

The example in Figure 5.3 shows subnet addressing with a class *B* address that has a 2-octet internet portion and a 2-octet local portion. To make forwarding among the physical networks efficient, the site administrator in our example chose to use one octet of the local portion to identify a physical network and the other octet to identify a host on that network. Figure 5.4 illustrates how our example divides the IPv4 address.

(a)	Internet portion	local portion	
(b)	Internet portion	physical network	host

Figure 5.4 (a) The interpretation of a 32-bit IPv4 address from Figure 5.3 when subnetting is used, and (b) the local portion divided into two fields that identify a physical network at the site and a host on that network.

Subnetting imposes a form of *hierarchical addressing* that leads to *hierarchical routing*. Routers throughout the Internet use the top level of the hierarchy to forward a packet to the correct site. Once the packet enters the site, local routers use the physical network octet to select the correct network. When the packet reaches the correct network, a router uses the host portion to identify a particular host.

Hierarchical addressing is not new; many systems have used it before. For example, the U.S. telephone system divides a 10-digit phone number into a 3-digit area code, 3-digit exchange, and 4-digit connection. The advantage of using hierarchical addressing is that it accommodates large growth without requiring routers to understand details about distant destinations. One disadvantage is that choosing a hierarchical structure is complicated, and it often becomes difficult to change once a hierarchy has been established.

5.6 Fixed Length IPv4 Subnets

In the example above, a site was assigned a 16-bit network prefix and used the third octet of the address to identify a physical network at the site. The TCP/IP standard for subnet addressing recognizes that not every site will have a 16-bit prefix and not every site will have the same needs for an address hierarchy. Consequently, the standard allows sites flexibility in choosing how to assign subnets. To understand why such flexibility is desirable, consider two examples. Figure 5.3 represents one example, a site that only has two physical networks. As another example, imagine a company that owns twenty large buildings and has deployed twenty LANs in each building. Suppose the second site has a single 16-bit network prefix and it wants to use subnetting for all its networks. How should the 16-bit local portion of the address be divided into fields for a physical network and host?

The division shown in Figure 5.4 results in an 8-bit physical network identifier and an 8-bit host identifier. Using eight bits to identify a physical network means a manager can generate up to 256 unique physical network numbers. Similarly, with eight bits for a host ID, a manager can generate up to 256 host IDs for each network†. Unfortunately, the division does not suffice for the company in our second example because the company has 400 networks, which exceeds the 254 possible numbers.

To permit flexibility, the subnet standard does not specify that a site must always use the third octet to specify a physical network. Instead, a site can choose how many bits of the local portion to dedicate to the physical network and how many to dedicate to the host ID. Our example company with 400 networks might choose the division that Figure 5.5 illustrates because a 10-bit field allows up to 1022 networks.

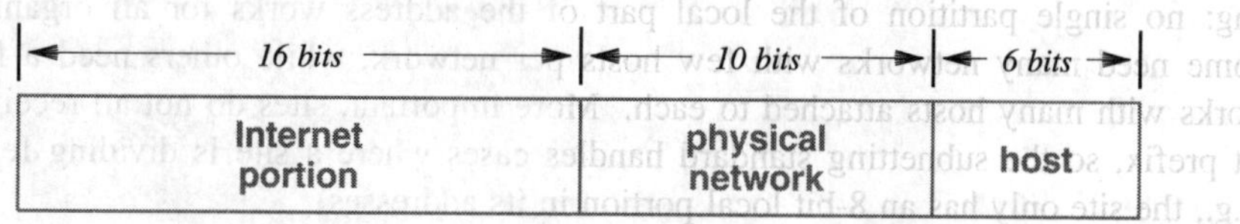

Figure 5.5 A division of a 16-bit local portion that accommodates 400 networks.

†In practice, the limit is 254 subnets of 254 hosts per subnet because the standard reserves the all 1s and all 0s subnet and host addresses.

The idea of allowing a site to choose a division for the local portion of its address and then using the division throughout the site is known as *fixed-length subnetting*. Fixed-length subnetting is easy to understand because it partitions the local portion of an address between networks and hosts. In essence, as a manager chooses how many networks the site can have, the manager also determines the maximum number of hosts on a given network. Figure 5.6 illustrates the possible choices if a site uses fixed-length subnetting with a 16-bit local portion.

Network Bits	Number of Networks	Hosts per Network
0	1	65534
2	2	16382
3	6	8190
4	14	4094
5	30	2046
6	62	1022
7	126	510
8	254	254
9	510	126
10	1022	62
11	2046	30
12	4094	14
13	8190	6
14	16382	2

Figure 5.6 The possible ways to divide a 16-bit local portion of an IPv4 address when using fixed-length subnetting. A site must choose one line in the table.

As the figure illustrates, an organization that adopts fixed-length subnetting must choose a compromise. If the organization opts for a large number of physical networks, none of the networks can contain many hosts; if the organization expects to connect many hosts to a network, the number of physical networks must be small. For example, allocating 3 bits to identify a physical network results in up to 6 networks that each support up to 8190 hosts. Allocating 12 bits results in up to 4094 networks, but restricts the size of each to 14 hosts.

It should be clear why the designers did not choose a specific division for subnetting: no single partition of the local part of the address works for all organizations. Some need many networks with few hosts per network, while others need a few networks with many hosts attached to each. More important, sites do not all receive a 16-bit prefix, so the subnetting standard handles cases where a site is dividing fewer bits (e.g., the site only has an 8-bit local portion in its addresses).

5.7 Variable-Length IPv4 Subnets

Most sites use fixed-length subnetting because it is straightforward to understand and administer. However, the compromise described above makes fixed-length subnetting unattractive if a site expects a mixture of large and small networks. When they invented subnetting, the designers realized that fixed-length subnetting would not suffice for all sites and created a standard that provides more flexibility. The standard specifies that an organization can select a subnet partition on a per-network basis. Although the technique is known as *variable-length subnetting*, the name is slightly misleading because the partition does not vary over time — once a partition has been selected for a particular network, the partition never changes. All hosts and routers attached to that network must follow the decision; if they do not, datagrams can be lost or misrouted. We can summarize:

> *To allow maximum flexibility in choosing how to partition subnet addresses, the TCP/IP subnet standard permits variable-length subnetting in which a partition can be chosen independently for each physical network. Once a subnet partition has been selected, all machines on that network must honor it.*

The chief advantage of variable-length subnetting is flexibility: an organization can have a mixture of large and small networks, and can achieve higher utilization of the address space. However, variable-length subnetting has serious disadvantages. The most severe disadvantage arises because the scheme can be difficult to administer. The partition for each subnet and the values chosen for subnet numbers must be assigned carefully to avoid *address ambiguity*, a situation in which an address is interpreted differently on two physical networks. In particular, because the network field used on one physical network can be larger than the network field used on another network, some of the host bits on the second network will be interpreted as network bits on the first network. As a result, invalid variable-length subnets may make it impossible for all pairs of hosts at the site to communicate. Furthermore, the ambiguity cannot be resolved except by renumbering. Thus, network managers are discouraged from using variable-length subnetting.

5.8 Implementation Of IPv4 Subnets With Masks

The subnet technology makes configuration of either fixed or variable length subnets easy. The standard specifies that a 32-bit *mask* is used to specify the division. Thus, a site using subnet addressing must choose a 32-bit *subnet mask* for each network. The mask covers the internet portion of the address as well as the physical network part of the local portion. That is, bits in the subnet mask are set to *1* if machines on the network treat the corresponding bit in the IP address as part of the subnet prefix, and *0* if they treat the bit as part of the host identifier.

As an example, the following 32-bit subnet mask:

11111111 11111111 11111111 00000000

specifies that the first three octets identify the network and the fourth octet identifies a host on that network. Similarly, the mask:

11111111 11111111 11111111 11000000

corresponds to the partition that Figure 5.5 illustrates where the physical network portion occupies 10 bits.

An interesting twist in subnet addressing arises because the original standard did not restrict subnet masks to select contiguous bits of the address. For example, a network might be assigned the mask:

11111111 11111111 00011000 01000000

which selects the first two octets, two bits from the third octet, and one bit from the fourth. Although the standard allows one to arrange interesting assignments of addresses, doing so makes network management almost impossible. Therefore, it is now recommended that sites only use contiguous subnet masks.

5.9 IPv4 Subnet Mask Representation And Slash Notation

Specifying subnet masks in binary is both awkward and prone to errors. Therefore, most software allows alternative representations. For example, most software allows managers to use dotted decimal representation when specifying IPv4 subnet masks. Dotted decimal has the advantage of being familiar, but the disadvantage of making it difficult to understand bit patterns. Dotted decimal works well if a site can align the subnet boundary on octet boundaries. The example in Figure 5.4b shows how easy it is to understand subnetting when the third octet of an address is used to identify a physical network and the fourth octet is used to identify a host. In such cases, the subnet mask has dotted decimal representation *255.255.255.0*, making it easy to write and understand.

The literature also contains examples of subnet addresses and subnet masks represented in braces as a 3-tuple:

{ <network number>, <subnet number>, <host number> }

In this representation, each section can be represented in dotted decimal, and the value *–1* means "all ones." For example, if the subnet mask for a class *B* network is *255.255.255.0*, it can be written *{–1, –1, 0}*.

The chief advantage is that it abstracts away from the details of bit fields and emphasizes the values of the three parts of the address. The chief disadvantage is that it does not accurately specify how many bits are used for each part of the address. For example, the 3-tuple:

{ 128.10 , –1, 0 }

denotes an address with a network number *128.10*, all ones in the subnet field, and all zeroes in the host field. The address could correspond to a subnet where the boundary occurs after the third octet or could correspond to a situation like the one shown in Figure 5.5 where the boundary allocates 10 bits to the network and 6 bits to the host.

To make it easy for humans to express and understand address masks, the IETF invented a syntactic form that is both convenient and unambiguous. Known informally as *slash notation*, the form specifies writing a slash followed by a decimal number that gives the number of 1s in the mask. For example, instead of writing the dotted decimal value 255.255.255.0, a manager can write /24. Figure 5.7 lists each possible slash value and the dotted decimal equivalent. The next section explains how variable-length subnetting has been generalized and how slash notation is used in all routers.

5.10 The Current Classless IPv4 Addressing Scheme

We said that subnet addressing arose in an attempt to conserve the IPv4 address space. By 1993, it became apparent that subnetting alone would not prevent Internet growth from quickly exhausting the address space, and preliminary work began on defining an entirely new version of IP with larger addresses. To accommodate growth until the new version of IP could be standardized and adopted, a temporary solution was invented.

Known as *classless addressing*, the temporary address scheme does away with class A, B, and C addresses†. In place of the three classes, the new scheme extends the idea used in subnet addressing to permit a network prefix to be an arbitrary length. Later chapters explain that in addition to a new addressing model, the designers modified forwarding and route propagation techniques to handle classless addresses. As a result, the entire technology has become known as *Classless Inter-Domain Routing* (*CIDR*).

To understand the impact of CIDR, one needs to know three facts. First, the classful scheme did not divide network addresses into equal size classes — although fewer than seventeen thousand class B numbers were created, more than two million class C network numbers were created. Second, because class C prefixes only suffice for small networks and are not amenable to subnetting, demand for class C prefixes was much smaller than demand for class B prefixes. Third, studies showed that at the rate class B numbers were being assigned, class B prefixes would be exhausted quickly.

†Classless addressing preserves class D addresses, which are used for IPv4 multicast.

Slash Notation	Dotted Decimal Equivalent
/0	0 . 0 . 0 . 0
/1	128 . 0 . 0 . 0
/2	192 . 0 . 0 . 0
/3	224 . 0 . 0 . 0
/4	240 . 0 . 0 . 0
/5	248 . 0 . 0 . 0
/6	252 . 0 . 0 . 0
/7	254 . 0 . 0 . 0
/8	255 . 0 . 0 . 0
/9	255 . 128 . 0 . 0
/10	255 . 192 . 0 . 0
/11	255 . 224 . 0 . 0
/12	255 . 240 . 0 . 0
/13	255 . 248 . 0 . 0
/14	255 . 252 . 0 . 0
/15	255 . 254 . 0 . 0
/16	255 . 255 . 0 . 0
/17	255 . 255 . 128 . 0
/18	255 . 255 . 192 . 0
/19	255 . 255 . 224 . 0
/20	255 . 255 . 240 . 0
/21	255 . 255 . 248 . 0
/22	255 . 255 . 252 . 0
/23	255 . 255 . 254 . 0
/24	255 . 255 . 255 . 0
/25	255 . 255 . 255 . 128
/26	255 . 255 . 255 . 192
/27	255 . 255 . 255 . 224
/28	255 . 255 . 255 . 240
/29	255 . 255 . 255 . 248
/30	255 . 255 . 255 . 252
/31	255 . 255 . 255 . 254
/32	255 . 255 . 255 . 255

Figure 5.7 Address masks expressed in slash notation along with the dotted decimal equivalent of each.

One of the first uses of classless addressing was known as *supernetting*. The intent was to group together a set of contiguous class C addresses to be used instead of a class B address. To understand how supernetting works, consider a medium-sized organization that joins the Internet. Under the classful scheme, such an organization would request a class B prefix. The supernetting scheme allows an ISP to assign the organization a block of class C addresses instead of a single class B number. The block must be large enough to number all the networks in the organization and (as we will see) must lie on a boundary that is a power of 2. For example, suppose the organization expects to have 200 networks. Supernetting can assign the organization a block of 256 contiguous class C numbers.

Although the first intended use of CIDR involved blocks of class C addresses, the designers realized that CIDR could be applied in a much broader context. They envisioned a hierarchical addressing model in which each commercial *Internet Service Provider* (*ISP*) could be given a large block of Internet addresses that the ISP could then allocate to subscribers. Because it permits the network prefix to occur on an arbitrary bit boundary, CIDR allows an ISP to assign each subscriber a block of addresses appropriate to the subscriber's needs.

Like subnet addressing, CIDR uses a 32-bit *address mask* to specify the boundary between prefix and suffix. Contiguous 1 bits in the mask specify the size of the prefix, and 0 bits in the mask correspond to the suffix. At first glance, a CIDR mask appears to be identical to a subnet mask. The major difference is that a CIDR mask is not merely known within a site. Instead, a CIDR mask specifies the size of a network prefix, and the prefix is known globally. For example, suppose an organization is assigned a block of 2048 contiguous addresses starting at address 128.211.168.0. The table in Figure 5.8 lists the binary values of addresses in the range.

	Dotted Decimal	32-bit Binary Equivalent
Lowest	128.211.168.0	10000000 11010011 10101000 00000000
Highest	128.211.175.255	10000000 11010011 10101111 11111111

Figure 5.8 An example IPv4 CIDR block that contains 2048 host addresses. The table shows the lowest and highest addresses in the range expressed as dotted decimal and binary values.

Because 2048 is 2^{11}, eleven bits are needed for the host portion of an address. That means the CIDR address mask will have 21 bits set (i.e., the division between network prefix and host suffix occurs after the 21st bit). In binary, the address mask is:

11111111 11111111 11111000 00000000

5.11 IPv4 Address Blocks And CIDR Slash Notation

Unlike the original classless scheme, CIDR addresses are not self-identifying. For example, if a router encounters address 128.211.168.1, which is one of the addresses in the example block, a router cannot know the position where the boundary lies unless external information is present. Thus, when configuring a CIDR block, a network manager must supply two pieces of information: the starting address and an address mask that tells which bits are in the prefix.

As noted above, using binary or dotted decimal for a mask is both inconvenient and error prone. Therefore, CIDR specifies that a manager should use slash notation to specify the mask. Syntactically, the format, which is sometimes called *CIDR notation*, consists of a starting address in dotted decimal followed by a mask size in slash notation. Thus, in CIDR notation, the block of addresses in Figure 5.8 is expressed:

128.211.168.0 / 21

where */21* denotes an address mask with 21 bits set to 1†.

5.12 A Classless IPv4 Addressing Example

The table in Figure 5.8 illustrates one of the chief advantages of classless addressing: complete flexibility in allocating blocks of various sizes. When using CIDR, the ISP can choose to assign each customer an address block of an appropriate size (i.e., the size the customer needs rounded to the nearest power of 2). Observe that a CIDR mask of N bits defines an address block of $32-N$ host addresses. Therefore, a smaller address block has a longer mask. If the ISP owns a CIDR block of N bits, the ISP can choose to assign a customer any piece of its address space by using a mask longer than N bits. For example, if the ISP is assigned 128.211.0.0 / 16, the ISP may choose to give one of its customers the 2048 address in the / 21 range that Figure 5.8 specifies. If the same ISP also has a small customer with only two computers, the ISP might choose to assign another block 128.211.176.212 / 30, which covers the address range that Figure 5.9 specifics.

	Dotted Decimal	32-bit Binary Equivalent
Lowest	128.211.176.212	10000000 11010011 10110000 11010100
Highest	128.211.176.215	10000000 11010011 10110000 11010111

Figure 5.9 An example IPv4 CIDR block, 128.211.176.212 / 30.

One way to think about classless addresses is as if each customer of an ISP obtains a (variable-length) subnet of the ISP's CIDR block. Thus, a given block of addresses can be subdivided on an arbitrary bit boundary, and a router at the ISP can be configured to forward correctly to each subdivision. As a result, the group of computers on a

†The table in Figure 5.7 on page 80 summarizes all possible values used in slash notation.

given network will be assigned addresses in a contiguous range, but the range does not need to correspond to the old class A, B, and C boundaries. Instead, the scheme makes subdivision flexible by allowing one to specify the exact number of bits that correspond to a prefix. To summarize:

> *Classless IPv4 addressing, which is now used throughout the Internet, assigns each ISP a CIDR block and allows the ISP to partition addresses into contiguous subblocks, where the lowest address in a subblock starts at a power of two and the subblock contains a power of two addresses.*

5.13 IPv4 CIDR Blocks Reserved For Private Networks

How should addresses be assigned on a private intranet (i.e., on an internet that does not connect to the global Internet)? In theory, arbitrary addresses can be used. For example, on the global Internet, the IPv4 address block 9.0.0.0/8 has been assigned to IBM Corporation. Although private intranets could use IBM's address blocks, experience has shown that doing so is dangerous because packets tend to leak out onto the global Internet, and will appear to come from valid sources. To avoid conflicts between addresses used on private intranets and addresses used on the global Internet, the IETF reserved several address prefixes and recommends using them on private intranets. Collectively, the reserved prefixes are known as *private addresses* or *nonroutable addresses*. The latter term is used because the IETF prohibits packets that use private addresses from appearing on the global Internet. If a packet containing one of the private addresses is accidentally forwarded onto the global Internet, a router will detect the problem and discard the packet.

When classless addressing was invented, the set of reserved IPv4 prefixes was redefined and extended. Figure 5.10 lists the values of private addresses using CIDR notation as well as the dotted decimal value of the lowest and highest addresses in the block. The last address block in the list, *169.254.0.0/16*, is unusual because it is used by systems that *autoconfigure* IP addresses. Although autoconfiguration is seldom used with IPv4, a later chapter explains how it has become an integral part of IPv6.

Prefix	Lowest Address	Highest Address
10.0.0.0/8	10.0.0.0	10.255.255.255
172.16.0.0/12	172.16.0.0	172.31.255.255
192.168.0.0/16	192.168.0.0	192.168.255.255
169.254.0.0/16	169.254.0.0	169.254.255.255

Figure 5.10 The prefixes reserved for use with private intranets not connected to the global Internet. If a datagram sent to one of these addresses accidentally reaches the Internet, an error will result.

5.14 The IPv6 Addressing Scheme

We said that each IPv6 address occupies 128 bits (16 octets). The large address space guarantees that IPv6 can tolerate any reasonable address assignment scheme. In fact, if the community decides to change the addressing scheme later, the address space is sufficiently large to accommodate a reassignment.

It is difficult to comprehend the size of the IPv6 address space. One way to look at it relates the magnitude to the size of the population: the address space is so large that every person on the planet can have sufficient addresses to have their own internet three times as large as the current Internet. A second way to think of IPv6 addressing relates it to the physical space available: the earth's surface has approximately 5.1×10^8 square kilometers, meaning that there are over 10^{24} addresses per square meter of the earth's surface. Another way to understand the size relates it to address exhaustion. For example, consider how long it would take to assign all possible addresses. A 16-octet integer can hold 2^{128} values. Thus, the address space is greater than 3.4×10^{38}. If addresses are assigned at the rate of one million addresses every microsecond, it would take over 10^{20} years to assign all possible addresses.

5.15 IPv6 Colon Hexadecimal Notation

Although it solves the problem of having insufficient capacity, the large address size poses an interesting new problem: humans who manage the Internet must read, enter, and manipulate such addresses. Obviously, binary notation is untenable. The dotted decimal notation used for IPv4 does not make IPv6 addresses sufficiently compact either. To understand why, consider an example 128-bit number expressed in dotted decimal notation:

```
104.230.140.100.255.255.255.255.0.0.17.128.150.10.255.255
```

To help make addresses slightly more compact and easier to enter, the IPv6 designers created *colon hexadecimal notation* (abbreviated *colon hex*) in which the value of each 16-bit quantity is represented in hexadecimal separated by colons. For example, when the value shown above in dotted decimal notation is translated to colon hex notation and printed using the same spacing, it becomes:

```
68E6:8C64:FFFF:FFFF:0:1180:96A:FFFF
```

Colon hex notation has the obvious advantage of requiring fewer digits and fewer separator characters than dotted decimal. In addition, colon hex notation includes two techniques that make it extremely useful. First, colon hex notation allows *zero compression* in which a string of repeated zeros is replaced by a pair of colons. For example, the address:

```
FF05:0:0:0:0:0:0:B3
```

can be written:

FF05::B3

To ensure that zero compression produces an unambiguous interpretation, the standards specify that it can be applied only once in any address. Zero compression is especially useful because the IPv6 assignments will create many addresses that contain contiguous strings of zeros. Second, colon hex notation incorporates dotted decimal suffixes; such combinations are intended to be used during the transition from IPv4 to IPv6. For example, the following string is a valid colon hex notation:

0:0:0:0:0:0:128.10.2.1

Note that although the numbers separated by colons each specify the value of a 16-bit quantity, numbers in the dotted decimal portion each specify the value of one octet. Of course, zero compression can be used with the number above to produce an equivalent colon hex string that looks quite similar to an IPv4 address:

::128.10.2.1

Finally, IPv6 extends CIDR-like notation by allowing an address to be followed by a slash and an integer that specifies a number of bits. For example,

12AB::CD30:0:0:0:0 / 60

specifies the first 60 bits of the address which is 12AB00000000CD3 in hexadecimal.

5.16 IPv6 Address Space Assignment

The question of how to partition the IPv6 address space has generated much discussion. There are two central issues: how humans manage address assignment and how routers handle the necessary forwarding tables. The first issue focuses on the practical problem of devising a hierarchy of authority. Unlike the current Internet, which uses a two-level hierarchy of network prefix (assigned by an ISP) and host suffix (assigned by an organization), the large address space in IPv6 permits a multi-level hierarchy or multiple hierarchies. Large ISPs can start with large blocks of addresses and assign subblocks to second-level ISPs, which can each assign subblocks from their allocation to third-level ISPs, and so on. The second issue focuses on router efficiency, and will be explained later. For now, it is sufficient to understand that a router must examine each datagram, so the choice of assignment can affect the way routers handle forwarding.

The IPv6 address space has been divided into blocks of addresses analogous to the original classful scheme used with IPv4. The first 8 bits of an address are sufficient to identify the basic types. Like IPv4 classful addressing, IPv6 does not partition the address space into equal-size sections. Figure 5.11 lists the IPv6 prefixes and their meanings.

Binary Prefix	Type Of Address	Fraction Of Address Space
0000 0000	Reserved (IPv4 compatibility)	1/256
0000 0001	Unassigned	1/256
0000 001	NSAP Addresses	1/128
0000 01	Unassigned	1/64
0000 1	Unassigned	1/32
0001	Unassigned	1/16
001	Global Unicast	1/8
010	Unassigned	1/8
011	Unassigned	1/8
100	Unassigned	1/8
101	Unassigned	1/8
110	Unassigned	1/8
1110	Unassigned	1/16
1111 0	Unassigned	1/32
1111 10	Unassigned	1/64
1111 110	Unassigned	1/128
1111 1110 0	Unassigned	1/512
1111 1110 10	Link-Local Unicast Addresses	1/1024
1111 1110 11	IANA - Reserved	1/1024
1111 1111	Multicast Addresses	1/256

Figure 5.11 Prefixes used to divide the IPv6 address space into blocks and the purpose of each block.

As the figure shows, only 15% of the address space has been assigned. The IETF will use the remaining portions as demand grows. Despite the sparse assignment, addresses have been chosen to make processing more efficient. For example, the high-order octet of an address distinguishes between multicast (all 1 bits) and unicast (a mixture of 0's and 1's).

5.17 Embedding IPv4 Addresses In IPv6 For Transition

To enable transition from IPv4 to IPv6, the designers have allocated a small fraction of addresses in the IPv6 space to encode IPv4 addresses. For example, any address that begins with 80 zero bits followed by 16 bits of all ones contains an IPv4 address in the low-order 32 bits. In addition, a set of addresses are reserved for use with the *Stateless IP/ICMP Translation* protocol (*SIIT*). Figure 5.12 illustrates the two forms.

Embedding an IPv4 address in an IPv6 address will be used during the transition from IPv4 to IPv6 for two reasons. First, a computer may choose to upgrade from IPv4 to IPv6 software before it has been assigned a valid IPv6 address. Second, a computer running IPv6 software may need to communicate with a computer that runs only IPv4 software.

← 64 zero bits →	16 bits	16 bits	← 32 bits →
0000 0000	0000	FFFF	IPv4 Address
0000 0000	FFFF	0000	IPv4 Address

Figure 5.12 Two ways to embed an IPv4 address in an IPv6 address. The second form is used for Stateless IP/ICMP Translation.

Having a way to embed an IPv4 address in an IPv6 address does not solve the problem of making the two versions interoperate. In addition to address embedding, packet translation is needed to convert between IPv4 and IPv6 packet formats. We will understand the conversion after later chapters explain the two packet formats.

It may seem that translating protocol addresses could fail because higher layer protocols verify address integrity. In particular, we will see that TCP and UDP checksum computations use a *pseudo-header* that includes the IP source and destination addresses. As a result, it would seem that translating an address would invalidate the checksum. However, the designers planned carefully to allow TCP or UDP on an IPv4 machine to communicate with the corresponding transport protocol on an IPv6 machine. To avoid checksum mismatch, the IPv6 encoding of an IPv4 address has been chosen so that the 16-bit one's complement checksum for both an IPv4 address and the IPv6 embedded version of the address are identical. The point is:

> *In addition to choosing technical details of a new Internet Protocol, the IETF work on IPv6 has focused on finding a way to transition from the current protocol to the new protocol. In particular, IPv6 provides a way to embed an IPv4 address in an IPv6 address such that changing between the two forms does not affect the pseudo-header checksum used by transport protocols.*

5.18 IPv6 Unicast Addresses And /64

The IPv6 scheme for assigning each host computer an address extends the IPv4 scheme. Instead of dividing an address into two parts (a network ID and a host ID), an IPv6 address is divided into three conceptual parts: a globally-unique prefix used to identify a site, a subnet ID used to distinguish among multiple physical networks at the destination site, and an interface ID used to identify a particular computer connected to the subnet. Figure 5.13 illustrates the partitioning.

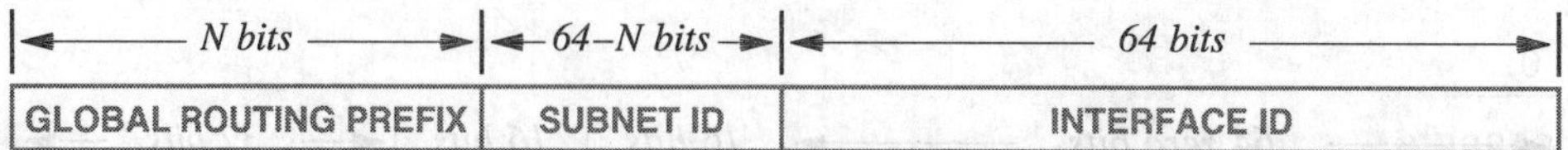

Figure 5.13 The division of an IPv6 unicast address into three conceptual parts. The interface ID always occupies 64 bits.

Note that the three-level hierarchy formalizes the idea of subnet addressing from IPv4. Unlike subnetting, however, the IPv6 address structure is not restricted to a single site. Instead, the address structure is recognized globally.

5.19 IPv6 Interface Identifiers And MAC Addresses

IPv6 uses the term *interface identifier* (*interface ID*) rather than *host identifier* to emphasize that a host can have multiple interfaces and multiple IDs. As the next section shows, IPv4 and IPv6 share the concept; only the terminology differs.

In Figure 5.13, the low-order 64 bits of an IPv6 unicast address identifies a specific network interface. The IPv6 suffix was chosen to be large enough to allow a hardware (MAC) address to be used as the unique ID. As we will see later, embedding a hardware address in an IPv6 address makes finding the hardware address of a computer trivial. Of course, to guarantee interoperability, all computers on a network must agree to use the same representation for a hardware address. Consequently, the IPv6 standards specify exactly how to represent various forms of hardware addresses. In the simplest case, the hardware address is placed directly in the low-order bits of an IPv6 address; some formats use more complex transformations.

Two examples will help clarify the concept. IEEE defines a standard 64-bit globally unique MAC address format known as *EUI-64*. The only change needed when using an EUI-64 address in an IPv6 address consists of inverting bit 6 in the high-order octet of the address. Bit 6 indicates whether the address is known to be globally unique. A more complex change is required for a conventional 48-bit Ethernet address as Figure 5.14 illustrates.

As the figure shows, bits from the original MAC address are not contiguous in an IPv6 address. Instead, 16 bits with hexadecimal value $FFFE_{16}$ are inserted in the middle. In addition, bit 6, which indicates whether the address has global scope, is changed from *0* to *1*. Remaining bits of the address, including the group bit (labeled *g*), the ID of the company that manufactured the interface (labeled *c*), and the manufacturer's extension are copied as shown.

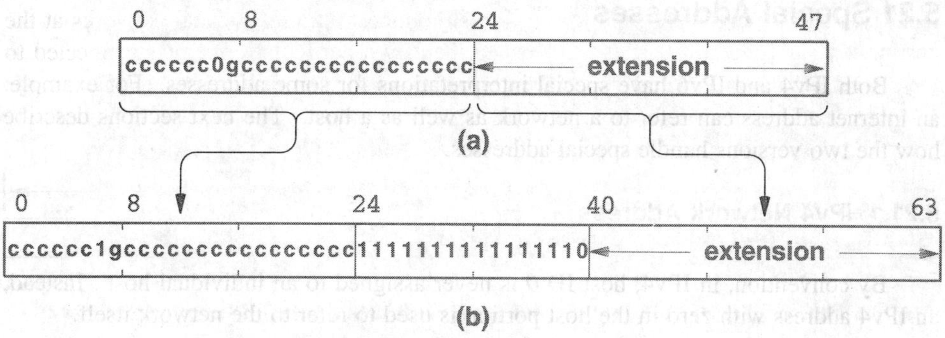

Figure 5.14 (a) The format of a 48-bit Ethernet address, with bits that identify a manufacturer and extension, and (b) the address when placed in the low-order 64 bits of an IPv6 unicast address.

5.20 IP Addresses, Hosts, And Network Connections

To simplify the discussion earlier in the chapter, we said that an IPv4 address identifies a host. However, the description is not strictly accurate. Consider a router that attaches to two physical networks. How can we assign a single IP address if every address includes a network identifier as well as a host identifier? In fact, we cannot. A similar situation exists for a conventional computer that has two or more physical network connections (such computers are known as *multi-homed hosts*). Each of the computer's network connections must be assigned an address that identifies a network. The idea is fundamental in both IPv4 and IPv6 addressing:

> *Because an IP address identifies a network as well as a host on the network, an address does not specify an individual computer. Instead, an address identifies a connection to a network.*

A router that connects to n networks has n distinct IP addresses; one for each network connection. IPv6 makes the distinction clear by using the term *interface address* (i.e., an address is assigned to the interface from a computer to a network). For IPv6 the situation is even more complex than multiple network connections: to handle migration from one ISP to another, IPv6 specifies that a given interface can have multiple addresses at the same time. For now, we only need to keep in mind that each address specifies a network connection. Chapter 18 will consider the issue further.

5.21 Special Addresses

Both IPv4 and IPv6 have special interpretations for some addresses. For example, an internet address can refer to a network as well as a host. The next sections describe how the two versions handle special addresses.

5.21.1 IPv4 Network Address

By convention, in IPv4, host ID *0* is never assigned to an individual host. Instead, an IPv4 address with zero in the host portion is used to refer to the network itself.

> *An IPv4 address that has a host ID of* 0 *is reserved to refer to the network.*

5.21.2 IPv4 Directed Broadcast Address

IPv4 includes a *directed broadcast address* that is sometimes called a *network broadcast address*. When used as a destination address, it refers to all computers on a network. The standard specifies that a hostid of all *1s* is reserved for directed broadcast†.

When a packet is sent to such an address, a single copy of the packet is transferred across the internet from the source to the destination. Routers along the path use the network portion of the address without looking at the host portion. Once the packet reaches a router attached to the final network, the router examines the host portion of the address and if it finds all *1s*, the router broadcasts the packet to all machines on the network.

On some network technologies (e.g., Ethernet), the underlying hardware supports broadcasting. On other technologies, software implements broadcast by sending an individual copy to each host on the network. The point is that having an IP directed broadcast address does not guarantee that delivery will be efficient. In summary,

> *IPv4 supports directed broadcast in which a packet is sent to all computers on a specific network; hardware broadcast is used if available. A directed broadcast address has a valid network portion and a hostid of all 1s.*

Directed broadcast addresses provide a powerful and dangerous mechanism because an arbitrary sender can transmit a single packet that will be broadcast on the specified network. To avoid potential problems, many sites configure routers to reject all directed broadcast packets.

---

†An early release of TCP/IP code that accompanied Berkeley UNIX incorrectly used a hostid of all zeroes for broadcast. Because the error still survives, TCP/IP software often includes an option that allows a site to use a hostid of all zeroes for directed broadcast.

5.21.3 IPv4 Limited (Local Network) Broadcast Address

In addition to network-specific broadcast addresses described above, IPv4 supports *limited broadcasting*, sometimes called local network broadcast. A limited broadcast means a packet is broadcast across the local network. The local broadcast address consists of thirty-two *1*s (hence, it is sometimes called the "all *1*s" broadcast address). As we will see, a host can use the limited broadcast address at startup before the host learns its IP address or the IP address of the network. Once the host learns the correct IP address for the local network, directed broadcast is preferred.

To summarize:

> *An IPv4 limited broadcast address consists of thirty-two 1 bits. A packet sent to the limited broadcast address will be broadcast across the local network, and can be used at startup before a computer learns its IP address.*

5.21.4 IPv4 Subnet Broadcast Address

If a site uses subnetting, IPv4 defines a corresponding *subnet broadcast address*. A subnet broadcast address consists of a network prefix, a subnet number, and all 1s in the host field.

> *A subnet broadcast address is used to broadcast on a single network within a site that uses subnetting. The address contains a network and subnet prefix and has all 1s in the host field.*

5.21.5 IPv4 All-0s Source Address

An address that consists of thirty-two zero bits is reserved for cases where a host needs to communicate, but does not yet know its own IP address (i.e., at startup). In particular, we will see that to obtain an IP address, a host sends a datagram to the limited broadcast address and uses address *0* to identify itself. The receiver understands that the host does not yet have an IP address, and the receiver uses a special method to send a reply.

> *In IPv4, an address with thirty-two 0 bits is used as a temporary source address at startup before a host learns its IP address.*

5.21.6 IPv4 Multicast Addresses

In addition to *unicast delivery*, in which a packet is delivered to a single computer, and *broadcast delivery*, in which a packet is delivered to all computers on a given network, the IPv4 addressing scheme supports a special form of multipoint delivery known as *multicasting*, in which a packet is delivered to a specific subset of hosts. Chapter 15 discusses multicast addressing and delivery in detail. For now, it is sufficient to understand that any IPv4 address that begins with three 1 bits is used for multicasting.

5.21.7 IPv4 Loopback Address

The network prefix 127.0.0.0/8 (a value from the original class A range) is reserved for *loopback*, and is intended for use in testing TCP/IP and for inter-process communication on the local computer. By convention, programmers use 127.0.0.1 for testing, but any host value can be used because TCP/IP software does not examine the host portion.

When an application sends a packet to a 127 address, the protocol software in the computer accepts the outgoing packet and immediately feeds the packet back to the module that handles incoming packets, as if the packet just arrived. Loopback is restricted to a local operating system; no packet with a 127 address should ever appear in the Internet.

> *IPv4 reserves 127.0.0.0/8 for loopback testing; a packet destined to any host with prefix 127 stays within the computer and does not travel across a network.*

5.21.8 Summary Of IPv4 Special Address Conventions

Figure 5.15 summarizes the special addresses used in IPv4. As the notes in the figure mention, the all *0*s address is never used as a destination, and can only be used as a source address during initial startup. Once a computer learns its IP address, the machine must not use all *0*s as a source.

5.21.9 IPv6 Multicast And Anycast Addresses

In theory, the choice between multicast and broadcast is irrelevant because one can be simulated with the other. That is, broadcasting and multicasting are duals of one another that provide the same functionality. To understand why, consider how to simulate one with the other. If broadcast is available, a packet can be delivered to a group by broadcasting to all machines and arranging for software on each machine to decide whether to accept or discard the incoming packet. If multicast is available, a packet can be delivered to all machines by arranging for all machines to listen to the *all nodes* multicast group.

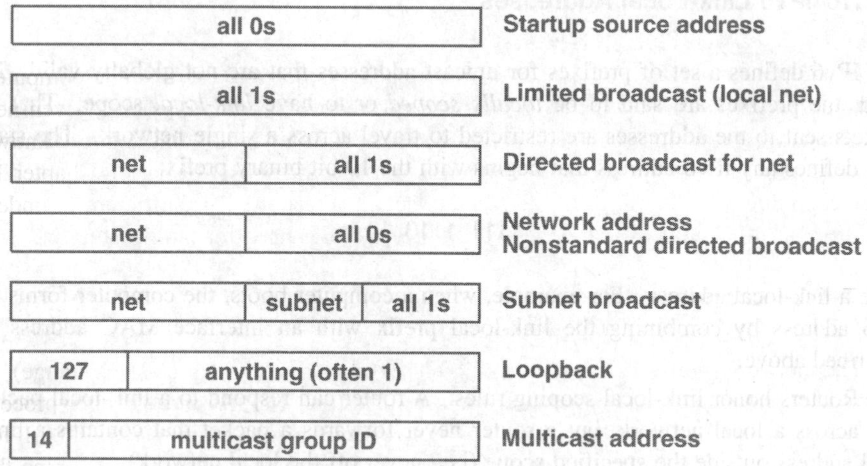

Figure 5.15 Summary of IPv4 special addresses.

Knowing that broadcasting and multicasting are theoretical duals of one another does not help choose between them. IPv6 designers decided to avoid broadcast and use only multicast. Therefore, IPv6 defines several reserved sets of multicast groups. For example, if an IPv6 host wants to broadcast a packet that will reach routers on the local network, the host sends the packet to the *all routers* multicast group. IPv6 also defines an *all hosts* multicast group (the packet is delivered to all hosts on the local network) and an *all nodes* multicast group (the packet is delivered to all hosts and all routers).

To understand why the designers of IPv6 chose multicasting as the central abstraction instead of broadcasting, consider applications instead of looking at the underlying hardware. An application either needs to communicate with a single application or with a group of applications. Direct communication is handled best via unicast; group communication can be handled either by multicast or broadcast. In an Internet, group membership is not related to (or restricted to) a single network — group members can reside at arbitrary locations. Using broadcast for all group communication does not scale across the global Internet, so multicast is the only option. Ironically, even efforts to implement multicast on the global Internet have failed so far. Thus, little has been accomplished by IPv6 multicast.

In addition to multicast, IPv6 introduces a new type of address known as an *anycast* address†. Anycast addressing is designed to handle server replication. A provider can deploy a set of identical servers at arbitrary locations in the Internet. All servers in the set must offer exactly the same service, and all are assigned the same anycast address. Forwarding is set up so that a packet sent to the anycast address goes to the nearest server.

†Anycast addresses were originally known as *cluster* addresses.

5.21.10 IPv6 Link-Local Addresses

IPv6 defines a set of prefixes for unicast addresses that are not globally valid. Instead, the prefixes are said to be *locally scoped* or to have *link-local* scope. That is, packets sent to the addresses are restricted to travel across a single network. The standard defines any IPv6 address that begins with the 10-bit binary prefix:

1111 1110 10

to be a link-local address. For example, when a computer boots, the computer forms an IPv6 address by combining the link-local prefix with an interface MAC address as described above.

Routers honor link-local scoping rules. A router can respond to a link-local packet sent across a local network, but a router never forwards a packet that contains a link-local address outside the specified scope (i.e., never off the local network).

Link-local addresses provide a way for a computer to talk to its neighbors (e.g., at startup) without danger of packets being forwarded across the Internet. We will see, for example, that an IPv6 node uses a link-local address at startup to discover its neighbors, including the address of a router. Computers connected to an *isolated network* (i.e., a network that does not have routers attached) can use link-local addresses to communicate.

5.22 Weaknesses In Internet Addressing

Embedding network information in an internet address does have some disadvantages. The most obvious disadvantage is that addresses refer to network connections, not to the host computer:

> *If a host computer moves from one network to another, its internet address must change.*

IPv6 tries to alleviate the problem by making it easier to change an address. However, the basic problem remains. Chapter 18 discusses how the addressing scheme makes *mobility* difficult.

A weakness of the IPv4 scheme arises from early binding — once a prefix size is chosen, the maximum number of hosts on the network is fixed. If the network grows beyond the original bound, a new prefix must be selected and all hosts on the network must be renumbered. While *renumbering* may seem like a minor problem, changing network addresses can be incredibly time-consuming and difficult to debug. IPv6 solves the problem of network growth by allocating an absurd number of bits (64) to a suffix that identifies a host (or to be precise, a network interface).

The most important flaw in the internet addressing scheme will become apparent when we examine forwarding. However, its importance warrants a brief introduction here. We have suggested that forwarding will be based on destination Internet addresses. Specifically, a router will use a prefix of the address that identifies a destination network. Now consider a host that has two network connections. We know that such a host must have two IP addresses, one for each interface. The following is true:

> *Because forwarding uses the network portion of the IP address, the path taken by packets traveling to a host with multiple IP addresses depends on the address used.*

The implications are surprising. Humans think of each host as a single entity and want to use a single name. They are often surprised to find that they must learn more than one name and even more surprised to find that packets sent using multiple names can behave differently.

Another surprising consequence of the internet addressing scheme is that merely knowing one IP address for a destination may not be sufficient. If a network is down, it may be impossible to reach the destination using a specific address.

To understand, consider the example in Figure 5.16.

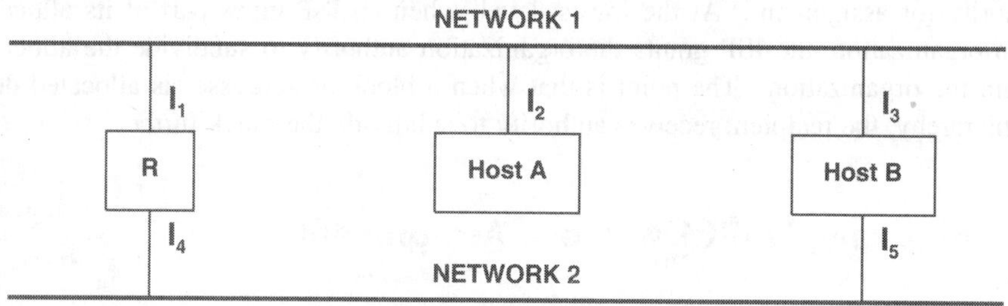

Figure 5.16 An example of two networks with connections to a router, *R*, conventional host, *A*, and a multi-homed host, *B*.

In the figure, hosts *A* and *B* both attach to network 1. Thus, we would normally expect *A* to send to *B*'s address on network 1. Suppose, however, that *B*'s connection to network 1 breaks (i.e., interface I_3 becomes disconnected). If *A* tries to use *B*'s network 1 address (i.e., the address for interface I_3, *A* will conclude that *B* is down because no packets go through. Surprisingly, if *A* sends to the address for interface I_5, packets will be forwarded through router *R*, and will reach *B*. That is, an alternate path exists from *A* to *B*, but the path will not be used unless the alternate address is specified. We will discuss the problem in later chapters when we consider forwarding and name binding.

5.23 Internet Address Assignment And Delegation Of Authority

Each network prefix used in the global Internet must be unique. To ensure uniqueness, all prefixes are assigned by a central authority. Originally, the *Internet Assigned Numbers Authority* (*IANA*) had control over numbers assigned, and set the policy. From the time the Internet began until the fall of 1998, a single individual, the late Jon Postel, ran the IANA and assigned addresses. In late 1998, after Jon's untimely death, a new organization was created to handle address assignment. Named the *Internet Corporation for Assigned Names and Numbers* (*ICANN*), the organization sets policy and assigns values for names and other constants used in protocols as well as addresses.

Most sites that need an Internet prefix never interact with the central authority directly. Instead, an organization usually contracts with a local *Internet Service Provider* (*ISP*). In addition to providing physical network connections, ISPs obtain a valid address prefix for each of their customers' networks. Many local ISPs are, in fact, customers of larger ISPs — when a customer requests an address prefix, the local ISP merely obtains a prefix from a larger ISP. Thus, only the largest ISPs need to contact one of the regional *address registries* that ICANN has authorized to administer blocks of addresses (*ARIN*, *RIPE*, *APNIC*, *LACNIC*, or *AFRINIC*).

Note how delegation authority passes down the ISP hierarchy as addresses are assigned. By giving a block of addresses to a regional registry, ICANN delegates authority for their assignment. When it gives a subblock to a major ISP, a registry delegates authority for assignment. At the lowest level, when an ISP gives part of its allocation to an organization, the ISP grants the organization authority to subdivide the allocation within the organization. The point is that when a block of addresses is allocated down the hierarchy, the recipient receives authority to subdivide the block further.

5.24 An Example IPv4 Address Assignment

To clarify the IPv4 addressing scheme, consider an example of two networks at a site. Figure 5.17 shows the conceptual architecture: two networks connected to an ISP.

The example shows three networks and the classless network numbers they have been assigned. The Internet Service Provider's network has been assigned 9.0.0.0/8. An Ethernet at the site has been assigned 128.10.0.0/16, and a Wi-Fi network at the site has been assigned 128.210.0.0/16.

Figure 5.18 shows the same networks with host computers attached to the networks and an Internet address assigned to each network connection. The figure shows three hosts which are labeled *Merlin*, *Lancelot*, and *Guenevere*. The figure also shows two routers: R_1 connects the Ethernet and Wi-Fi networks, and R_2 connects the site to an ISP.

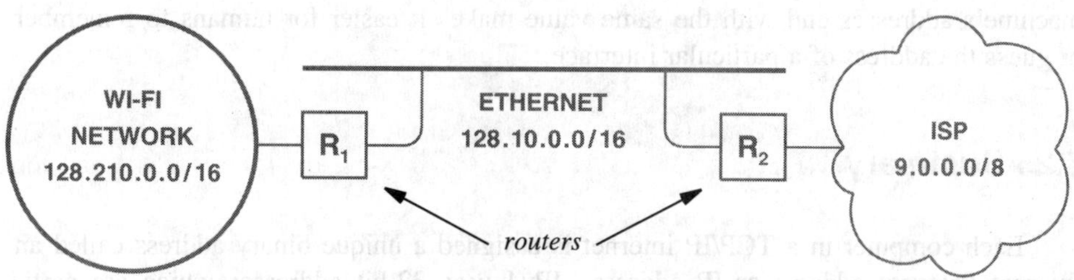

Figure 5.17 Example architecture of a site with IPv4 address prefixes assigned to two networks.

Host *Merlin* has connections to both the Ethernet and the Wi-Fi network, so it can reach destinations on either network directly. The distinction between a router (e.g., R_1) and a multi-homed host (e.g., *Merlin*) arises from the configuration: a router is configured to forward packets between the two networks; a host can use either network, but does not forward packets.

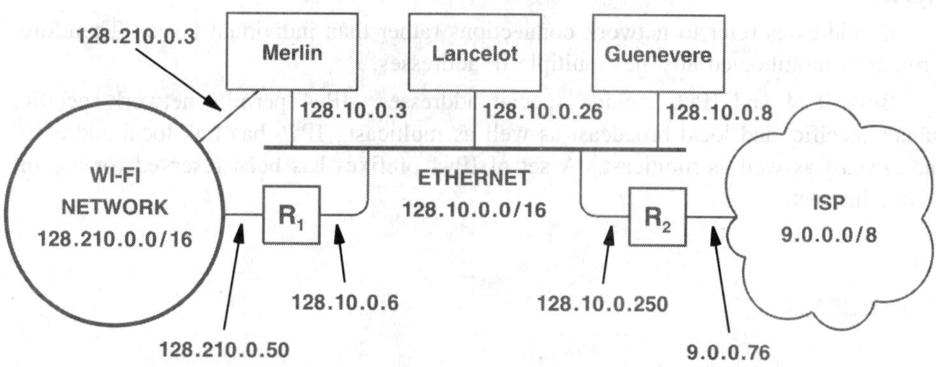

Figure 5.18 The example network from Figure 5.17 with IPv4 addresses assigned to hosts and routers.

As the figure shows, an IP address is assigned to each network interface. *Lancelot*, which connects only to the Ethernet, has been assigned 128.10.0.26 as its only IP address. Because it is a dual-homed host, *Merlin* has been assigned address 128.10.0.3 for its connection to the Ethernet and 128.210.0.3 for its connection to the Wi-Fi network. Whoever made the address assignment chose the same value for the host number in each address. Router R_1 also has two addresses: 128.10.0.6 and 128.210.0.50. Note that the host portion of the two addresses are unrelated. IP protocols do not care whether any of the bytes in the dotted decimal form of a computer's addresses are the same or different. However, network technicians, managers, and administrators need to enter addresses for maintenance, testing, and debugging. Choosing to make all of a machine's addresses end with the same value makes it easier for humans to remember or guess the address of a particular interface.

5.25 Summary

Each computer in a TCP/IP internet is assigned a unique binary address called an Internet Protocol address or IP address. IPv4 uses 32-bit addresses which are partitioned into two main pieces: a prefix identifies the network to which the computer attaches, and the suffix provides a unique identifier for a computer on that network. The original IPv4 addressing scheme is known as classful; a prefix belongs to one of three primary classes. Later variations extended the IPv4 addressing mechanism with subnet addressing and classless addressing. Classless IPv4 addressing uses a bit mask to specify how many bits correspond to a prefix.

To make addresses easier for humans to understand, syntactic forms have been invented. IPv4 addresses are written in dotted decimal notation in which each octet is written in decimal, with the values separated by decimal points. IPv6 addresses are written in colon hex notation, with octets represented in hexadecimal separated by colons.

IP addresses refer to network connections rather than individual hosts. Therefore, a router or multihomed host has multiple IP addresses.

Both IPv4 and IPv6 include special addresses. IPv4 permits network-specific, subnet-specific, and local broadcast as well as multicast. IPv6 has link-local addresses and anycast as well as multicast. A set of IPv4 prefixes has been reserved for use on private intranets.

EXERCISES

5.1 How many class *A*, *B*, and *C* networks can exist? How many hosts can a network in each class have? Be careful to allow for broadcast as well as class *D* and *E* addresses.

5.2 If your site uses IPv4, find out what size address mask is used. How many hosts does it permit your site to have?

5.3 Does your site permit IPv4 directed broadcast packets? (Think of a way to test by using ping.)

5.4 If your site uses IPv6, try sending a ping to the all-nodes multicast address. How many responses are received?

5.5 If your site uses IPv6, find out when IPv6 was first deployed.

5.6 What is the chief difference between the IP addressing scheme and the U.S. telephone numbering scheme?

5.7 The address registries around the world cooperate to hand out blocks of IP addresses. Find out how they ensure no ISP is given addresses that overlap with those given to another ISP.

5.8 How many IPv6 addresses would be needed to assign a unique address to every house in your country? The world? Is the IPv6 address space sufficient?

5.9 Suppose each person on the planet had a smart phone, laptop computer, and ten other devices that each had an IPv6 address. What percentage of the IPv6 address space would be required?

Chapter Contents

6

Mapping Internet Addresses To Physical Addresses (ARP)

6.1 Introduction

The previous chapter describes the IPv4 and IPv6 addressing schemes and states that an internet behaves like a virtual network, using only the assigned addresses when sending and receiving packets. Chapter 2 reviews several network hardware technologies, and notes that two machines on a given physical network can communicate *only if they know each other's physical network address*. What we have not mentioned is how a host or a router maps an IP address to the correct physical address when it needs to send a packet across a physical network. This chapter considers the mapping, showing how it is implemented in IPv4 and IPv6.

6.2 The Address Resolution Problem

Consider two machines *A* and *B* that connect to the same physical network. Each machine has an assigned IP address, I_A and I_B, and a hardware (MAC) address, H_A and H_B. Ultimately, communication must be carried out by sending frames across the underlying network using the hardware addresses that the network equipment recognizes. Our goal, however, is to allow applications and higher-level protocols to work only with Internet addresses. That is, we want to devise software that hides the hardware addresses at a low level of the protocol stack. For example, assume machine *A* needs to send an IP packet to machine *B* across the network to which they both attach, but *A* only knows *B*'s Internet address, I_B. The question arises: how does *A* map *B*'s Internet address to *B*'s hardware address, H_B? There are two answers, IPv4 usually uses one and IPv6 usually uses the other. We will consider each.

It is important to note that address mapping must be performed at each step along a path from the original source to the ultimate destination. In particular, two cases arise. First, at the last step of delivering an IP packet, the packet must be sent across a physical network to the ultimate destination. The machine sending the datagram (usually a router) must map the final destination's Internet address to the destination's hardware address before transmission is possible. Second, at any point along the path from the source to the destination other than the final step, the packet must be sent to an intermediate router. We will see that the protocol software always uses an IP address to identify the next router along the path. Thus, a sender must map the router's Internet address to a hardware address.

The problem of mapping high-level addresses to physical addresses is known as the *address resolution problem*, and has been solved in several ways. Some protocol suites keep tables in each machine that contain pairs of high-level and physical addresses. Other protocols solve the problem by embedding a hardware address in high-level addresses. Using either approach exclusively makes high-level addressing awkward at best. This chapter discusses two techniques for address resolution used by TCP/IP protocols, and shows when each is appropriate.

6.3 Two Types Of Hardware Addresses

There are two basic types of hardware addresses: those that are larger than the host portion of an IP address and those that are smaller. Because it dedicates 64 bits to the host portion of an address, IPv6 accommodates all types of hardware addresses. Therefore, the distinction is only important for IPv4. We will start by considering the technique used for IPv6 and for IPv4 when addresses are small enough. We will then consider a technique that IPv4 uses when addresses are large.

6.4 Resolution Through Direct Mapping

IPv6 uses a technique known as *direct mapping*. The basic idea is straightforward: use a computer's hardware address as the host portion of the computer's Internet address. IPv4 can use direct mapping when addresses are sufficiently small. Figure 6.1 illustrates the concept.

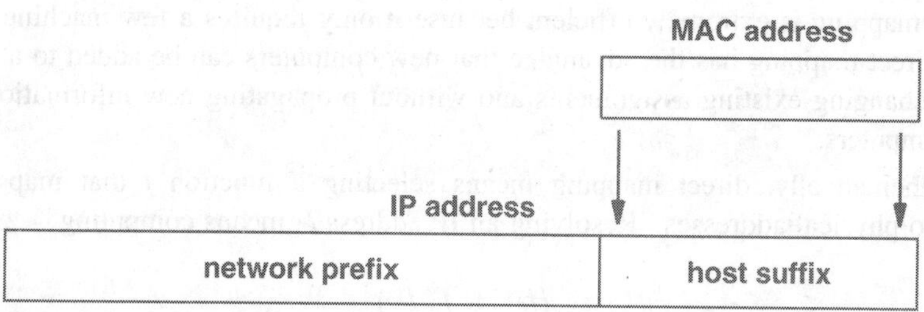

Figure 6.1 An illustration of a direct mapping scheme in which a computer's hardware address is embedded in the computer's IP address.

To see how direct mapping works with IPv4, it is important to know that some hardware uses small, configurable integers as hardware addresses. Whenever a new computer is added to such a network, the system administrator chooses a hardware address and configures the computer's network interface card. The only important rule is that no two computers can have the same address. To make assignment easy and safe, an administrator typically assigns addresses sequentially: the first computer connected to the network is assigned address 1, the second computer is assigned address 2, and so on.

As long as a manager has the freedom to choose both an IP address and a hardware address, the pair of addresses can be selected such that the hardware address and the host portion of the IP address are identical. IPv6 makes such an assignment trivial — the hardware address always fits into the area of the address used for an interface ID. For IPv4, consider an example where a network has been assigned the IPv4 prefix:

192.5.48.0/24

The network prefix occupies the first three octets, leaving one octet for the host ID. The first computer on the network is assigned hardware address 1 and IP address 192.5.48.1, the second computer is assigned hardware address 2 and IP address 192.5.48.2, and so on. That is, the network is configured such that the low-order octet of each IP address is the same as the computer's hardware address. Of course, the example only works if the hardware addresses are between 1 and 254.

6.5 Resolution In A Direct-Mapped Network

If a computer's IP address includes the computer's hardware address, address resolution is trivial. Given an IP address, the computer's hardware address can be extracted from the host portion. In the example above, if protocol software is given the IP address of a computer on the network (e.g., 192.5.48.3), the corresponding hardware address can be computed merely by extracting the low-order octet, 3. As the name *direct mapping* implies, the mapping can be performed without reference to external data. In fact, the mapping is extremely efficient because it only requires a few machine instructions. Direct mapping has the advantage that new computers can be added to a network without changing existing assignments and without propagating new information to existing computers.

Mathematically, direct mapping means selecting a function f that maps IP addresses to physical addresses. Resolving an IP address I_A means computing

$$H_A = f(I_A)$$

Although it is possible to choose mappings other than the one described in the example above, we want the computation of f to be efficient, and we want choices to be easy for a human to understand. Thus, a scheme is preferred in which the relationship between the IP address and hardware address is obvious.

6.6 IPv4 Address Resolution Through Dynamic Binding

Although it is efficient, direct mapping cannot be used with IPv4 if a hardware addresses is larger than an IPv4 address. Specifically, an Ethernet MAC address cannot be directly mapped into an IPv4 address because a MAC address is 48 bits long and an IPv4 address is only 32 bits long. Furthermore, because it is assigned when a device is manufactured, an Ethernet MAC address cannot be changed.

Designers of TCP/IP protocols found a creative solution to the address resolution problem for networks like Ethernet that have broadcast capability. The solution allows new hosts or routers to be added to a network without recompiling code, and does not require maintenance of a centralized database. To avoid maintaining a centralized database, the designers chose to use a low-level protocol that resolves addresses dynamically. Named the *Address Resolution Protocol* (*ARP*), the protocol provides a mechanism that is reasonably efficient and does not require an administrator to configure tables manually.

The idea behind dynamic resolution with ARP is straightforward: when it wants to resolve IP address I_B, a host broadcasts an ARP request packet that asks the host with IP address I_B to respond with its hardware address H_B. All hosts, including B, receive the request, but only host B recognizes its IP address and sends a reply that contains its hardware address. ARP is only used when a host needs to send an IP packet. Therefore, when it receives a reply to its request, the host that made the request will use the information to send an IP packet directly to B. We can summarize:

> *The Address Resolution Protocol, ARP, allows a host to find the physical address of a target host on the same physical network, given only the target's IP address.*

Figure 6.2 illustrates the ARP protocol by showing host *A* broadcasting a request for *B*, and *B* responding. Note that although the request is broadcast; the reply is not.

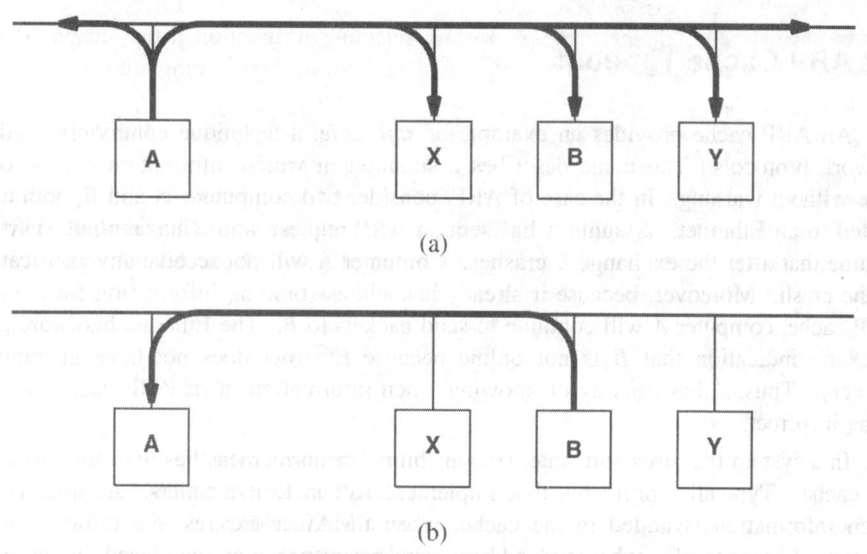

Figure 6.2 Illustration of ARP where (a) host *A* broadcasts an ARP request containing I_B, and (b) host *B* responds with an ARP reply that specifies its hardware address H_B.

6.7 The ARP Cache

It may seem silly that before *A* can send an Internet packet to *B* it must send a broadcast that consumes time on every host. Or it may seem even sillier that *A* broadcasts the question, "how can I reach you?," instead of just broadcasting the packet it wants to deliver. But there is an important reason for the exchange. Broadcasting is far too expensive to be used every time one machine needs to transmit a packet to another, because every machine on the network must receive and process the broadcast packet. So, ARP software in *A* uses an optimization: it records the answer and reuses the information for successive transmissions.

The standard specifies that ARP software must maintain a *cache* of recently acquired IP-to-hardware address bindings. That is, whenever a computer sends an ARP request and receives an ARP reply, it saves the IP address and corresponding hardware address information in its cache temporarily. Doing so reduces overall communication costs dramatically. When transmitting a packet, a computer always looks in its cache before sending an ARP request. If it finds the desired binding in its ARP cache, the computer does not need to broadcast a request. Thus, when two computers on a network communicate, they begin with an ARP request and response, and then repeatedly transfer packets without using ARP for each packet. Experience shows that because most network communication involves more than one packet transfer, even a small cache is worthwhile.

6.8 ARP Cache Timeout

An ARP cache provides an example of *soft state*, a technique commonly used in network protocols. The name describes a situation in which information can become stale without warning. In the case of ARP, consider two computers, *A* and *B*, both connected to an Ethernet. Assume *A* has sent an ARP request, and *B* has replied. Further assume that after the exchange *B* crashes. Computer *A* will not receive any notification of the crash. Moreover, because it already has address binding information for *B* in its ARP cache, computer *A* will continue to send packets to *B*. The Ethernet hardware provides no indication that *B* is not online because Ethernet does not have guaranteed delivery. Thus, *A* has no way of knowing when information in its ARP cache has become incorrect.

In a system that uses soft state, responsibility for correctness lies with the owner of the cache. Typically, protocols that implement soft state use timers. A timer is set when information is added to the cache; when the timer expires, the information is deleted. For example, whenever address binding information is placed in an ARP cache, the protocol requires a timer to be set, with a typical timeout being 20 minutes. When the timer expires, the information must be removed. After removal there are two possibilities. If no further packets are sent to the destination, nothing occurs. If a packet must be sent to the destination and there is no binding present in the cache, the computer follows the normal procedure of broadcasting an ARP request and obtaining the binding. If the destination is still reachable, the new binding will be placed in the ARP cache. If not, the sender will discover that the destination is not reachable.

The use of soft state in ARP has advantages and disadvantages. The chief advantage arises from autonomy. First, a computer can determine when information in its ARP cache should be revalidated independent of other computers. Second, a sender does not need successful communication with the receiver or a third party to determine that a binding has become invalid; if a target does not respond to an ARP request, the sender will declare the target to be down. Third, the scheme does not rely on network hardware to provide reliable transfer or inform a computer whether another computer is online. The chief disadvantage of soft state arises from delay — if the timer interval is *N* minutes, a sender may not detect that a receiver has crashed until *N* minutes elapse.

6.9 ARP Refinements

Several refinements of ARP have been included in the protocol that reduce the amount of network traffic and automate recovery after a hardware address changes:

- First, observe that host *A* only broadcasts an ARP request for *B* when it has an Internet packet ready to send to *B*. Because most Internet protocols involve a two-way exchange, there is a high probability that host *B* will send an Internet packet back to *A* in the near future. To anticipate *B*'s need and avoid extra network traffic, ARP requires *A* to include its IP-to-hardware address binding when sending *B* a request. *B* extracts *A*'s binding from the request and saves the binding in its ARP cache. Thus, when sending an Internet packet to *A*, *B* will find the binding is already in its cache.

- Second, notice that because requests are broadcast, all machines on the network receive a copy of the request. The protocol specifies that each machine extract the sender's IP-to-hardware address binding from the request, and use the information to *update* the binding in their cache. For example, if *A* broadcasts a request, machines on the network will update their information for *A*. Machines that do not already have an entry for *A* in their cache do not add *A*'s information; the standard only specifies updating the hardware address on existing entries. The idea is that if a machine has been communicating with *A*, its cache should have the latest information, but if a machine has not been communicating with *A*, its cache should not be clogged with a useless entry.

- Third, when a computer has its host interface replaced, (e.g., because the hardware has failed), its physical address changes. Other computers on the net that have stored a binding in their ARP cache need to be informed so they can change the entry. The computer can notify others of a new address by broadcasting a *gratuitous ARP request*. Changing a MAC address requires replacing a NIC, which occurs when a computer is down. Because a computer does not know whether its MAC address has changed, most computers broadcast a gratuitous ARP during system initialization. Gratuitous ARP has a secondary purpose: to see if any other machine is using the same IP address. The booting machine sends an ARP request for its own IP address; if it receives a reply, there must be a misconfiguration or a security problem where a computer is intentionally spoofing.

The following summarizes the key idea of automatic cache updates.

> *The sender's IP-to-hardware address binding is included in every ARP broadcast; receivers use the information to update their address binding information. The intended recipient uses the information to create a new cache entry in anticipation of a reply.*

6.10 Relationship Of ARP To Other Protocols

As we have seen, because it uses direct mapping, IPv6 does not need ARP. Thus, ARP merely provides one possible mechanism to map an IP address to a hardware address. Interestingly, ARP and other address binding mechanisms would be completely unnecessary if we could redesign all network hardware to recognize IP addresses. Thus, from our point of view, address binding is only needed to hide the underlying hardware addresses. Conceptually, we impose our new IP addressing scheme on top of whatever low-level address mechanism the hardware uses. Therefore, we view ARP as a low-level protocol associated with the hardware rather than a key part of the TCP/IP protocols which run above the hardware. The idea can be summarized:

> *ARP is a low-level protocol that hides the underlying addressing used by network hardware, permitting us to assign an arbitrary IP address to every machine. We think of ARP as associated with the physical network system rather than as part of the Internet protocols.*

6.11 ARP Implementation

Functionally, ARP software is divided into two parts. The first part provides address resolution for outgoing packets: given the IP address of a computer on the network, it finds the hardware address of the computer. If an address is not in the cache, it sends a request. The second part handles incoming ARP packets. It updates the cache, answers requests from other computers on the network, and checks whether a reply matches an outstanding request.

Address resolution for outgoing packets seems straightforward, but small details complicate an implementation. Given the IP address of a computer to which a packet must be sent, the software consults its ARP cache to see if the cache already contains the mapping from the IP address to a hardware address. If the answer is found, the software extracts the hardware address, fills in the destination address on the outgoing frame, and sends the frame. If the mapping is not in cache, two things must happen. First, the host must store the outgoing packet so it can be sent once the address has been resolved. Second, ARP software must broadcast an ARP request.

Coordination between the part of ARP that sends requests and the part that receives replies can become complicated. If a target machine is down or too busy to accept the request, no reply will be received (or the reply may be delayed). Furthermore, because Ethernet is a best-effort delivery system, the initial ARP broadcast request or the reply can be lost. Therefore, a sender should retransmit the request at least once, which means a timer must be used and the input side must cancel the timer if a reply arrives. More important, the question arises: while ARP is resolving a given IP address, what happens if another application attempts to send to the same address? ARP may choose to create a queue of outgoing packets, or simply may choose to discard successive packets. In any case, the key design decisions involve concurrent access: can other applications proceed while ARP resolves an address? If another application attempts to send to the same address, should the application be blocked or should ARP merely create a queue of outgoing packets? How can ARP software be designed to prevent it from unnecessarily broadcasting a second request to a computer?

One final detail distinguishes ARP cache management from the management of a typical cache. In a typical cache, timeouts are used to eliminate inactive entries. Thus, the timestamp on an entry is reset each time the entry is used. When space must be reclaimed, the entry with the oldest timestamp is removed from the cache. For an ARP cache, however, the time at which an entry was last referenced is irrelevant — ARP can continue to use the entry even if the destination computer has crashed. Thus, it is important to timeout an entry even if the entry is still being used.

We said that the second part of the ARP software handles ARP packets that arrive from the network. When an ARP packet arrives, the software first extracts the sender's IP address and hardware address pair, and examines the local cache to see if it already has an entry for the sender. If a cache entry exists for the given IP address, the handler updates that entry by overwriting the physical address with the physical address obtained from the packet. After updating the cache, a receiver processes the rest of the ARP packet.

To process the rest of an ARP packet, the receiver checks the operation. If the incoming packet is an ARP request, the receiving machine checks to see whether it is the target of the request (i.e., some other machine has broadcast a request and "I" am the target of the request). If so, the ARP software adds the sender's address pair to its cache (if the pair is not already present), forms a reply, and sends the reply directly back to the requester. If the IP address mentioned in a request does not match the local IP address (i.e., the request is for another computer), the incoming ARP packet is discarded.

If the incoming packet is an ARP reply, the receiver tries to match the reply with a previously issued request. If the reply does not match a request, the packet is discarded. Otherwise, the address binding is known (the entry in the cache will already have been updated in the first step above). Therefore, the ARP software examines the queue of outgoing IP packets (packets that have been waiting for the response). ARP software places each IP packet in a frame, uses the address binding information from the cache to fill in the destination address in the frame, and sends the packet.

6.12 ARP Encapsulation And Identification

When ARP messages travel from one computer to another, they must be carried in a network frame. As Figure 6.3 illustrates, an ARP message is carried in the payload area of a frame (i.e., is treated as data).

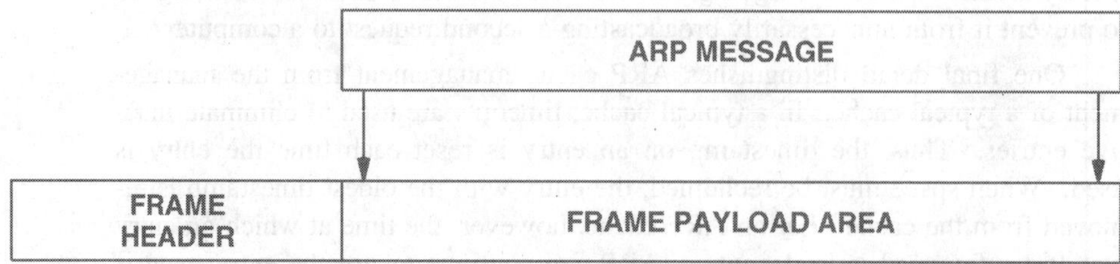

Figure 6.3 An ARP message encapsulated in a physical network frame.

To identify the frame as carrying an ARP message, the sender assigns a special value to the type field in the frame header. When a frame arrives at a computer, the network software uses the frame type to determine its contents. In most technologies, a single type value is used for all frames that carry an ARP message — network software in the receiver must further examine the ARP message to distinguish between ARP requests and ARP replies. For example, on an Ethernet, frames carrying ARP messages have a type field of 0x0806, where the prefix *0x* indicates a hexadecimal value. The frame type for ARP has been standardized by IEEE (which owns the Ethernet standards). Thus, when ARP travels over any Ethernet, the type is always 0x0806. Other hardware technologies may use other values.

6.13 ARP Message Format

Unlike most of the TCP/IP protocols, an ARP message does not have a fixed-format header. Instead, to allow ARP to be used on a variety of network technologies, the designers chose to make the length of hardware address fields depend on the addresses used by the underlying network. In fact, the designers did not restrict ARP to IPv4 addresses. Instead, the size of protocol address fields in an ARP message depends on the type of high-level protocol address being used. Ironically, with only a few exceptions such as research experiments, ARP is always used with 32-bit IPv4 protocol addresses and 48-bit Ethernet hardware addresses. The point is:

> *The design allows ARP to map an arbitrary high-level protocol address to an arbitrary network hardware address. In practice, ARP is only used to map 32-bit IPv4 addresses to 48-bit Ethernet addresses.*

The example in Figure 6.4 shows the format of a 28-octet ARP message when used with an IPv4 protocol address and an Ethernet hardware address. The protocol address is 32 bits (4 octets) long, and the hardware address is 48-bits (6 octets) long.

0	8	16	24 31
HARDWARE TYPE		PROTOCOL TYPE	
HLEN	PLEN	OPERATION	
SENDER HARD (octets 0-3)			
SENDER HARD (octets 4-5)		SENDER IPv4 (octets 0-1)	
SENDER IPv4 (octets 2-3)		TARGET HARD (octets 0-1)	
TARGET HARD (octets 2-5)			
TARGET IPv4 (octets 0-3)			

Figure 6.4 The ARP message format when used to map an IPv4 address to an Ethernet address.

The figure shows an ARP message with 4 octets per line, a format that is standard throughout this text and the TCP/IP standards. Unfortunately, the 48-bit Ethernet address means that fields in the ARP message do not all align neatly on 32-bit boundaries. Thus, the diagram can be difficult to read. For example, the sender's hardware address, labeled *SENDER HARD*, occupies 6 contiguous octets, so it spans two lines in the diagram, the third line and half of the fourth line.

Field *HARDWARE TYPE* specifies a hardware interface type for which the sender seeks an answer; it contains the value *1* to specify that the hardware address is an Ethernet MAC address. Similarly, field *PROTOCOL TYPE* specifies the type of high-level protocol address the sender has supplied; it contains 0x0800 (hexadecimal) to specify that the protocol address is IPv4. The ARP message format makes it possible for a computer to interpret any ARP message, even if the computer does not recognize the protocol address type or hardware address type. Interpretation is possible because the fixed fields near the beginning of a message labeled *HLEN* and *PLEN* specify the length of a hardware address and the length of a protocol address.

Field *OPERATION* specifies an ARP request (*1*), ARP response (*2*), RARP† request (*3*), or RARP response (*4*). When sending an ARP packet, a sender places its hardware address in fields *SENDER HARD* and its IPv4 address, if known, in *SENDER IPv4*.

Fields *TARGET HARD* and *TARGET IPv4* give the hardware address and protocol address of the target machine, if known. For a response message (i.e., a reply), the target information can be extracted from the request message. When sending an ARP request, a sender knows the target's IPv4 address, but does not know the target's

†A later section describes RARP, a protocol that uses the same message format as ARP.

hardware address. Therefore, in a request, the target hardware address field contains zeroes. To summarize:

> *An ARP reply carries the IPv4 address and hardware address of the original requester as well as the IPv4 address and hardware address of the sender. In a request, the target hardware address is set to zero because it is unknown.*

6.14 Automatic ARP Cache Revalidation

It is possible to use a technique that avoids introducing *jitter* (i.e., variance in packet transfer times). To understand how jitter can occur, think of one computer sending a steady stream of packets to another computer. Whenever the sender's ARP timer expires, ARP will remove the cache entry. The next outgoing packet will trigger ARP. The packet will be delayed until ARP can send a request and receive a response. The delay lasts approximately twice as long as it takes to transmit a packet. Although such delays may seem negligible, they do introduce jitter, especially for real-time data such as a voice phone call.

The key to avoiding jitter arises from *early revalidation.* That is, the implementation associates two counters with each entry in the ARP cache: the traditional timer and a revalidation timer. The revalidation timer is set to a slightly smaller value than the traditional timer. When the revalidation timer expires, the software examines the entry. If datagrams have recently used the entry, the software sends an ARP request and continues to use the entry. When it receives a reply, both timers are reset. Of course, if no reply arrives, the traditional timer will expire, and ARP will again try to obtain a response. In normal cases, however, revalidation will reset the cache timer without interrupting the flow of packets.

6.15 Reverse Address Resolution (RARP)

We saw above that the operation field in an ARP packet can specify a *Reverse Address Resolution* (*RARP*) message. RARP was once an essential protocol used to bootstrap systems that did not have stable storage (i.e., diskless devices). The paradigm is straightforward: at startup, a system broadcasts a RARP request to obtain an IP address. The request contains the sender's Ethernet address. A server on the network receives the request, looks up the Ethernet address in a database, extracts the corresponding IPv4 address from the database, and sends a RARP reply with the information. Once the reply arrives, the diskless system continues to boot, and uses the IPv4 address for all communication. Interestingly, RARP uses the same packet format as ARP†. The only difference is that RARP uses Ethernet type 0x8035.

---

†The ARP packet format can be found on page 111.

RARP is no longer important for diskless devices, but has an interesting use in cloud data centers. In a data center, when a Virtual Machine migrates from one PC to another, the VM retains the same Ethernet address it was using before. To let the underlying Ethernet switch know that the move has occurred, the VM must send a frame (the source address in the frame will cause the switch to update its tables). Which frame should a VM send? Apparently, RARP was chosen because it has the advantage of updating the MAC address table in the switch without causing further processing. In fact, after updating the address table, the switch will simply drop the RARP packet.

6.16 ARP Caches In Layer 3 Switches

An Ethernet switch is classified as a *Layer 3 switch* if the switch understands IP packets and can examine IP headers when deciding how to process a packet. Some Layer 3 switches have an unusual implementation of ARP that can be confusing to someone who is trying to understand the protocol.

The implementation arises from a desire to reduce ARP traffic. To see why optimization is helpful, think about the traffic generated by ARP. Suppose a switch has 192 ports that connect to computers. If each computer implements ARP cache timeouts, the computer will periodically timeout cache entries and then broadcast an ARP request. Even if the computer uses automatic revalidation, the switch will receive periodic broadcasts that must be sent to all computers.

How can a switch reduce broadcast traffic to computers? We observe three things. First, a switch can watch ARP traffic and keep a record of bindings between IP addresses and Ethernet addresses. Second, if it has the necessary information, a switch can respond to an ARP request without broadcasting the request. Third, an Ethernet address can only change if a computer is powered down, and a switch can tell whether a computer has been powered down. Therefore, a switch can create its own cache of ARP information and can answer requests. For example, if computer *A* sends an ARP request for computer *B*, the switch can intercept the request, look in its cache, and create an ARP reply *as if the reply came from B.*

For a production environment, the optimization described above works well. Computer *A* appears to broadcast an ARP request for *B*, and *A* receives a valid reply. It reduces extra traffic, and does not require any modifications to the software running on the computers. For anyone testing network protocols, however, it can be confusing. A computer broadcasts a request that is not received by any other computer on the network! Furthermore, the computer that sent the request receives a phantom reply that was never sent by the source!

6.17 Proxy ARP

Intranets sometimes use a technique known as *proxy ARP* to implement a form of security. We will first examine proxy ARP, and then see how it can be used.

Early in the history of the Internet a technique was developed that allowed a single IPv4 prefix to be used across two networks. Originally called *The ARP Hack*, the technique became known by the more formal term *proxy ARP*. Proxy ARP relies on a computer that has two network connections and runs special-purpose ARP software. Figure 6.5 shows an example configuration in which proxy ARP can be used.

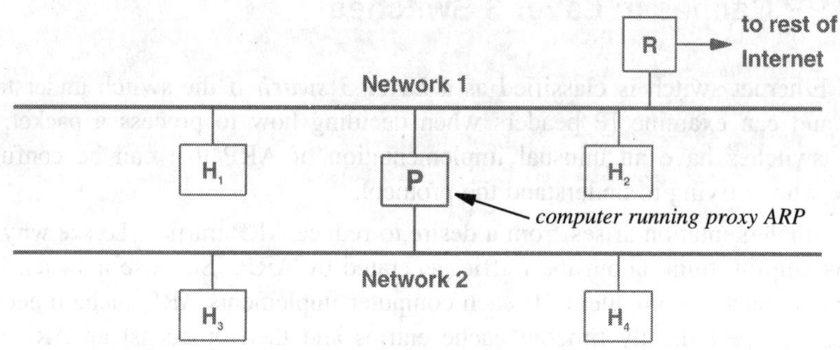

Figure 6.5 Illustration of two networks using proxy ARP.

In the figure, the computer labeled *P* runs proxy ARP software. Computer *P* has a database that contains the IPv4 address and the Ethernet MAC address of each other machine on network 1 and network 2. The router and all the other hosts run standard ARP; they are unaware that proxy ARP is being used. More important, all the other hosts and the router are configured as if they are on a single network.

To understand proxy ARP interaction, consider what happens when router *R* receives a packet from the Internet that is destined for the IPv4 address being used. Before it can deliver the incoming packet, *R* must use ARP to find the hardware address of the computer. *R* broadcasts an ARP request. There are two cases to consider: the destination is on network 1 or the destination is on network 2. Consider the first case (e.g., suppose the destination is host H_1). All machines on network 1 receive a copy of *R*'s request. Computer *P* looks in its database, discovers that H_1 is on network 1, and ignores the request. Host H_1 also receives a copy of the request and responds normally (i.e., sends an ARP reply).

Now consider the second case where *R* broadcasts a request for a machine on network 2 (e.g., host H_4). ARP was only intended to be used on a single network, so broadcasting for a computer on another network seems like a violation of the protocol. However, *R* is behaving correctly because it does not know there are two networks. All computers on network 1 will receive a copy of the broadcast, including *P*. Computer *P* consults its database, discovers that H_4 is on network 2, and sends an ARP reply that specifies R's Ethernet address as the hardware address. R will receive the reply, place it in the ARP cache, and send an IP packet to P (because P has impersonated H_4). When it receives an Internet packet, P examines the destination address in the packet, and forwards the packet to H_4.

Proxy ARP also handles impersonation and forwarding when a computer on network 2 sends to a computer on network 1. For example, when H_4 forms an Internet packet and needs to send the packet to router R, H_4 will broadcast an ARP request for R. P will receive a copy of the request, consult its database, and send an ARP reply that impersonates R.

How can proxy ARP be used for security? Proxy ARP can be used for a firewall or on a VPN connection. The idea is that because a proxy ARP machine impersonates machines on the second network, all packets must travel though the proxy ARP machine where they can be checked. In Figure 6.4, for example, a site could place all hosts on network 2 and put firewall software in machine P. Whenever a packet arrives from the Internet, the packet will go through P (where the packet can be examined and firewall can be rules applied) on its way to the destination host.

6.18 IPv6 Neighbor Discovery

IPv6 uses the term *neighbor* to describe another computer on the same network. IPv6's *Neighbor Discovery Protocol* (*NDP*) replaces ARP and allows a host to map between an IPv6 address and a hardware address†. However, NDP includes many other functions. It allows a host to find the set of routers on a network, determine whether a given neighbor is still reachable, learn the network prefix being used, determine characteristics of the network hardware (e.g., the maximum packet size), configure an address for each interface and verify that no other host on the network is using the address, and find the best router to use for a given destination.

Instead of creating a protocol analogous to ARP to handle neighbor discovery, the designers of IPv6 chose to use ICMPv6‡. Thus, ICMPv6 includes messages that a computer uses to find its neighbors at startup and to check the status of a neighbor periodically.

A key difference between ARP and NDP arises from the way each handles the status of neighbors. ARP uses a late-binding approach with soft state. That is, ARP waits until a datagram must be sent to a neighbor before taking any action. After it performs an exchange, ARP stores the binding in its cache, and then sends IP packets to the neighbor without checking the neighbor's status until the ARP cache timer expires. The delay can last many minutes. NDP uses early binding and takes a proactive approach to state maintenance. Instead of waiting until a datagram must be sent, an IPv6 node uses NDP to discover neighbors at startup. Furthermore, an IPv6 node continually checks the status of neighbors. Thus, transmission of an IPv6 datagram to a neighbor can proceed without delay and does not involve broadcast.

†See Chapter 22 for a discussion of NDP.

‡See Chapter 9 for a discussion of ICMPv6.

6.19 Summary

Internet protocol software uses IP addresses. To send a packet across a network, however, hardware addresses must be used. Therefore, protocol software must map the Internet address of a computer to a hardware address. If hardware addresses are smaller than IP addresses, a direct mapping can be established by having the machine's hardware address embedded in its IP address. Because IPv6 has large addresses, it always uses direct mapping. IPv4 uses dynamic mapping when the hardware address is larger than the host portion of an IPv4 address. The Address Resolution Protocol (ARP) performs dynamic address resolution, using only the low-level network communication system. ARP permits a computer to resolve addresses without using a database of bindings and without requiring a manager to configure software.

To find the hardware address of another computer on the same network, a machine broadcasts an ARP request. The request contains the IPv4 address of the target machine. All machines on a network receive an ARP request, and only the target machine responds. The ARP reply contains the sender's IPv4 address and hardware address. Replies are sent unicast; they are not broadcast.

To make ARP efficient, each machine caches IP-to-hardware address bindings. Using a cache avoids unnecessary broadcast traffic; early revalidation can be used to eliminate jitter.

An older protocol related to ARP, RARP, is being used in cloud data centers. The proxy ARP technique can be used in security systems, such as a VPN or a firewall that is transparent to routers and hosts. IPv6 has replaced ARP with a Neighbor Discovery Protocol (NDP). Unlike ARP, NDP continually checks neighbor status to determine whether a neighbor has remained reachable.

EXERCISES

6.1 Given a small set of hardware addresses (positive integers), can you find a function *f* and an assignment of IP addresses such that *f* maps the IP addresses 1-to-1 onto the physical addresses and computing *f* is efficient? (Hint: look at the literature on perfect hashing.)

6.2 In what special cases does a host connected to an Ethernet not need to use ARP or an ARP cache before transmitting an IP datagram? (Hint: what about multicast?)

6.3 One common algorithm for managing the ARP cache replaces the least recently used entry when adding a new one. Under what circumstances can this algorithm produce unnecessary network traffic?

6.4 Should ARP software modify the cache even when it receives information without specifically requesting it? Why or why not?

6.5 Any implementation of ARP that uses a fixed-size cache can fail when used on a network that has many hosts and heavy ARP traffic. Explain how.

6.6 ARP is often cited as a security weakness. Explain why.

6.7 Suppose machine *C* receives an ARP request sent from *A* looking for target *B*, and suppose *C* has the binding from I_B to H_B in its cache. Should *C* answer the request? Explain.

6.8 ARP can prebuild a cache for all possible hosts on an Ethernet by iterating through the set of possible IP addresses and sending an ARP request for each. Is doing so a good idea? Why or why not?

6.9 Should early revalidation send a request for all possible IP address on the local network, all entries in the ARP cache, or only for destinations that have experienced traffic recently? Explain.

6.10 How can a computer use ARP at boot time to find out if any other machine on the network is impersonating it? What are the disadvantages of the scheme?

6.11 Explain how sending IPv4 packets to nonexistent addresses on a remote Ethernet can generate broadcast traffic on that network.

6.12 Suppose a given Ethernet switch connects 4095 hosts and a router. If 99% of all traffic is sent between individual hosts and the router, does ARP or NDP incur more overhead?

6.13 Answer the previous question for the case where traffic is uniformly distributed among random pairs of hosts.

Chapter Contents

7

Internet Protocol: Connectionless Datagram Delivery (IPv4, IPv6)

7.1 Introduction

Previous chapters review pieces of network hardware and software that make internet communication possible, explaining the underlying network technologies and address resolution. This chapter explains the fundamental principle of connectionless delivery, and discusses how it is provided by the *Internet Protocol* (*IP*), which is one of the two major protocols used in internetworking (TCP being the other). We will study the format of packets used for both IPv4 and IPv6, and will see how such packets form the basis for all internet communication. The next two chapters continue our examination of the Internet Protocol by discussing packet forwarding and error handling.

7.2 A Virtual Network

Chapter 3 discusses internet architecture in which routers connect multiple physical networks. Looking at the architecture may be misleading, because the focus of internet technology is on the abstraction that an internet provides to applications and users, not on the underlying interconnection technology.

> *Internet technology presents the abstraction of a single virtual network that interconnects all hosts, and through which communication is possible. The underlying architecture is both hidden and irrelevant.*

In a sense, an internet is an abstraction of a large physical network. At the lowest level, internet technology provides the same basic functionality as a physical network: it accepts packets and delivers them. Higher levels of internet software and network applications add most of the rich functionality that users perceive.

7.3 Internet Architecture And Philosophy

Conceptually, a TCP/IP internet provides three sets of services. Figure 7.1 lists the three categories and illustrates dependencies among them.

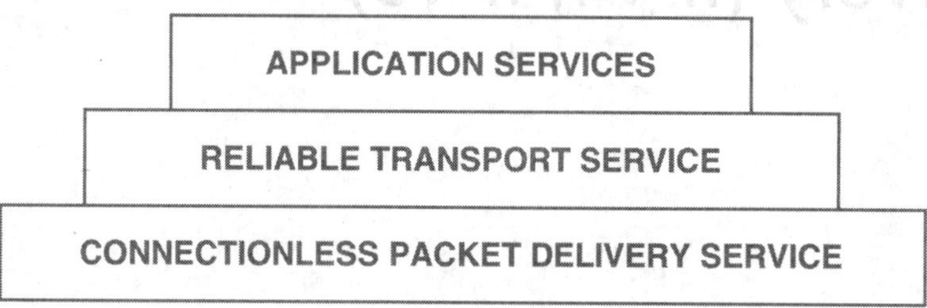

Figure 7.1 The three conceptual levels of internet services.

At the lowest level, a connectionless delivery service provides a foundation on which everything rests. At the next level, a reliable transport service provides a higher-level platform on which applications depend. We will explore each of the services, understand the functionality they provide, the mechanisms they use, and the specific protocols associated with them.

7.4 Principles Behind The Structure

Although we can associate protocol software with each of the levels in Figure 7.1, the reason for identifying them as conceptual parts of the TCP/IP Internet technology is that they clearly point out two philosophical underpinnings of the design. First, the figure shows that the design builds reliable service on top of an unreliable, connectionless base. Second, it shows why the design has been so widely accepted: the lowest level service exactly matches the facilities provided by underlying hardware networks and the second level provides the service that applications expect.

The three-level concept accounts for much of the Internet's success; as a consequence of the basic design, the Internet technology has been surprisingly robust and adaptable. The connectionless service runs over arbitrary network hardware, and the reliable transport service has been sufficient for a wide variety of applications. We can summarize:

> *Internet protocols are designed around three conceptual levels of service. A connectionless service at the lowest level matches underlying hardware well, a reliable transport service provides service to applications, and a variety of applications provide the services users expect.*

The design in Figure 7.1 is significant because it represents a dramatic departure from previous thinking about data communication. Early networks followed the approach of building reliability at each level. The Internet protocols are organized to start with a basic packet delivery service and then add reliability. When the design was first proposed, many professionals doubted that it could work.

An advantage of the conceptual separation is that it enables one service to be enhanced or replaced without disturbing others. In the early Internet, research and development proceeded concurrently on all three levels. The separation will be especially important during the transition from IPv4 to IPv6 because it allows higher layer protocols and applications to remain unchanged.

7.5 Connectionless Delivery System Characteristics

The most fundamental Internet service consists of a packet delivery system. Technically, the service is defined as an unreliable, best-effort, connectionless packet delivery system. The service is analogous to the service provided by most network hardware because packet-switching technologies such as Ethernet operate on a best-effort delivery paradigm. We use the technical term *unreliable* to mean that delivery is not guaranteed. A packet may be lost, duplicated, delayed, or delivered out of order. The connectionless service will not detect such conditions, nor will it inform the sender or receiver. The basic service is classified as *connectionless* because each packet is treated independently from all others. A sequence of packets sent from one computer to another may travel over different paths, or some may be lost while others are delivered. Finally, the service is said to use *best-effort delivery* because the Internet software makes an earnest attempt to deliver packets. That is, the Internet does not discard packets capriciously; unreliability arises only when resources are exhausted or underlying networks fail.

7.6 Purpose And Importance Of The Internet Protocol

The protocol that defines the unreliable, connectionless delivery mechanism is called the *Internet Protocol* (*IP*). We will follow the convention used in standards documents by using the terms *Internet Protocol* and *IP* when statements apply broadly, and only using *IPv4* or *IPv6* when a particular detail is applied to one version but not the other.

The Internet Protocol provides three important specifications. First, IP defines the basic unit of data transfer used throughout a TCP/IP internet. Thus, it specifies the exact packet format used by all data as the data passes across an internet. Second, IP software performs the *forwarding* function, choosing a path over which a packet will be sent. The standards specify how forwarding is performed. Third, in addition to the precise, formal specification of data formats and forwarding, IP includes a set of rules that embody the basis of unreliable delivery. The rules characterize how hosts and routers should process packets, how and when error messages should be generated, and the conditions under which packets can be discarded. The Internet Protocol is such a fundamental part of the design that the Internet is sometimes called an *IP-based technology.*

We begin our consideration of IP by looking at the packet format it specifies. The chapter first examines the IPv4 packet format, and then considers the format used with IPv6. We leave until later chapters the topics of packet forwarding and error handling.

7.7 The IP Datagram

On a physical network, the unit of transfer is a frame that contains a header and data, where the header gives information such as the (physical) source and destination addresses. The Internet calls its basic transfer unit an *Internet datagram*, usually abbreviated *IP datagram*†. In fact, TCP/IP technology has become so successful that when someone uses the term *datagram* without any qualification, it is generally accepted to mean *IP datagram.*

The analogy between a datagram and a network packet is strong. As Figure 7.2 illustrates, a datagram is divided into a header and payload just like a typical network frame. Also like a frame, the datagram header contains metadata such as the source and destination addresses and a type field that identifies the contents of the datagram. The difference, of course, is that the datagram header contains IP addresses, whereas the frame header contains hardware addresses.

Figure 7.2 General form of an IP datagram, the Internet analogy of a network frame.

†Networking professionals sometimes refer to "Internet packets" to refer to a datagram as it travels over a network; the distinction will become clear when we talk about encapsulation.

7.7.1 IPv4 Datagram Format

Now that we have described the general layout of an IP datagram, we can look at the contents in more detail. Figure 7.3 shows the arrangement of fields in an IPv4 datagram. The next paragraphs discuss some of the header fields; later sections on fragmentation and options cover remaining fields.

0	4	8	16	19	24 — 31
VERS	HLEN	SERVICE TYPE	TOTAL LENGTH		
IDENTIFICATION			FLAGS	FRAGMENT OFFSET	
TIME TO LIVE		PROTOCOL	HEADER CHECKSUM		
SOURCE IP ADDRESS					
DESTINATION IP ADDRESS					
IP OPTIONS (IF ANY)					PADDING
PAYLOAD ...					

Figure 7.3 Format of an IPv4 datagram, the basic unit of transfer in a TCP/IP internet.

Because an internet is virtual, the contents and format are not constrained by network hardware. For example, the first 4-bit field in a datagram (*VERS*) contains the version of the IP protocol that was used to create the datagram. Thus, for IPv4, the version field contains the value *4*. The field is used to verify that the sender, receiver, and any routers in between them agree on the format of the datagram. All IP software is required to check the version field before processing a datagram to ensure it matches the format the software expects. We will see that although the IPv6 datagram header differs from the IPv4 header, IPv6 also uses the first four bits for a version number, making it possible for a router or host computer to distinguish between the two versions. In general, a computer will reject any datagram if the computer does not have software to handle the version specified in the datagram. Doing so prevents computers from misinterpreting datagram contents or applying an outdated format.

The header length field (*HLEN*), also 4 bits, gives the datagram header length measured in 32-bit words. As we will see, all fields in the header have fixed length except for the *IP OPTIONS* and corresponding *PADDING* fields. The most common datagram header, which contains no options and no padding, measures 20 octets and has a header length field equal to *5*.

The *TOTAL LENGTH* field gives the length of the IP datagram measured in octets, including octets in the header and payload. The size of the payload area can be computed by subtracting the length of the header (thirty two times *HLEN*) from the *TOTAL LENGTH*. Because the *TOTAL LENGTH* field is 16 bits long, the maximum possible size of an IP datagram is 2^{16} or 65,535 octets. For most applications the limit does not present a problem. In fact, most underlying network technologies use much smaller frame sizes; we will discuss the relationship between datagram size and frame size later.

Field *PROTOCOL* is analogous to the type field in a network frame; the value specifies which high-level protocol was used to create the message carried in the *PAYLOAD* area of the datagram. In essence, the value of *PROTOCOL* specifies the format of the *PAYLOAD* area. The mapping between a high-level protocol and the integer value used in the *PROTOCOL* field must be administered by a central authority to guarantee agreement across the entire Internet.

Field *HEADER CHECKSUM* ensures integrity of header values. The IP checksum is formed by treating the header as a sequence of 16-bit integers (in network byte order), adding them together using one's complement arithmetic, and then taking the one's complement of the result. For purposes of computing the checksum, field *HEADER CHECKSUM* is assumed to contain zero.

It is important to note that the checksum only applies to values in the IP header and not to the payload. Separating the checksums for headers and payloads has advantages and disadvantages. Because the header usually occupies fewer octets than the payload, having a separate checksum reduces processing time at routers which only need to compute header checksums. The separation also allows higher-level protocols to choose their own checksum scheme for the messages they send. The chief disadvantage is that higher-level protocols are forced to add their own checksum or risk having a corrupted payload go undetected.

Fields *SOURCE IP ADDRESS* and *DESTINATION IP ADDRESS* contain the 32-bit IP addresses of the datagram's sender and intended recipient. Although the datagram may be forwarded through many intermediate routers, the source and destination fields never change; they specify the IP addresses of the original source and ultimate destination†. Note that intermediate router addresses do not appear in the datagram. The idea is fundamental to the overall design:

> *The source address field in a datagram always refers to the original source and the destination address field refers to the ultimate destination.*

The field labeled *PAYLOAD* in Figure 7.3 only shows the beginning of the area of the datagram that carries the data. The length of the payload depends, of course, on what is being sent in the datagram. The *IP OPTIONS* field, discussed below, is variable length. The field labeled *PADDING*, depends on the options selected. It represents bits containing zero that may be needed to ensure the datagram header extends to an exact multiple of 32 bits (recall that the header length field is specified in units of 32-bit words).

†An exception is made when the datagram includes the source route options listed below.

7.7.2 IPv6 Datagram Format

IPv6 completely revises the datagram format by replacing the IPv4 datagram header. Instead of trying to specify all details in a single header, IPv6 uses an extension capability that allows the IETF to adapt the protocol. Figure 7.4 illustrates the concept: an IPv6 datagram begins with a fixed-size *base header* followed by zero or more *extension headers*, followed by a payload.

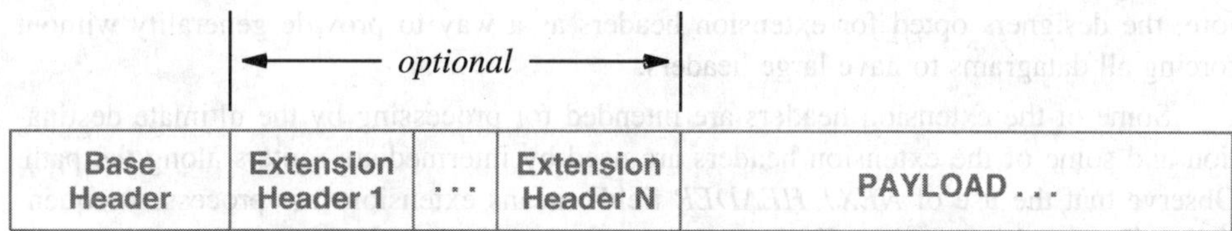

Figure 7.4 The general form of an IPv6 datagram with a base header followed by optional extension headers.

How can a receiver know which extension headers have been included in a given datagram? Each IPv6 header contains a *NEXT HEADER* field that specifies the type of the header that follows. The final header uses the *NEXT HEADER* field to specify the type of the payload. Figure 7.5 illustrates the use of *NEXT HEADER* fields.

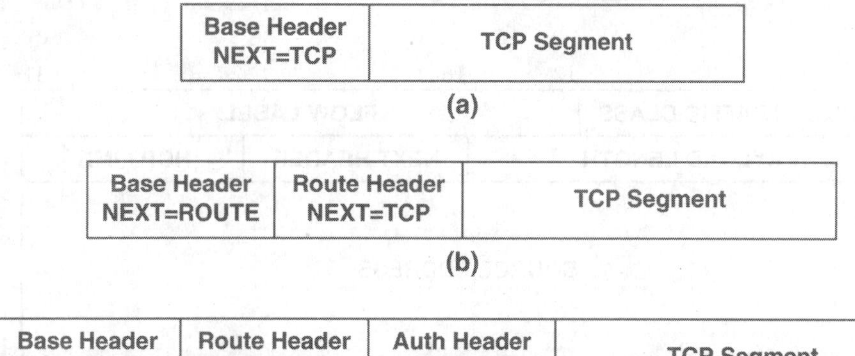

Figure 7.5 Illustration of the *NEXT HEADER* fields in IPv6 datagrams with (a) only a base header, (b) a base header and one extension, and (c) a base header and two extension headers.

The paradigm of a fixed base header followed by a set of optional extension headers was chosen as a compromise between generality and efficiency. To be totally general, IPv6 needs to include mechanisms to support functions such as fragmentation, source routing, and authentication. However, choosing to allocate fixed fields in the datagram header for all mechanisms is inefficient because most datagrams do not use all mechanisms; the large IPv6 address size exacerbates the inefficiency. For example, when sending a datagram across a single local area network, a header that contains unused address fields can occupy a substantial fraction of each frame. More important, the designers realized that no one can predict which facilities will be needed. Therefore, the designers opted for extension headers as a way to provide generality without forcing all datagrams to have large headers.

Some of the extension headers are intended for processing by the ultimate destination and some of the extension headers are used by intermediate routers along the path. Observe that the use of *NEXT HEADER* fields means extensions are processed sequentially. To speed processing, IPv6 requires extension headers that are used by intermediate routers to precede extension headers used by the final destination. We use the term *hop-by-hop header* to refer to an extension header that an intermediate router must process. Thus, hop-by-hop headers precede end-to-end headers.

7.7.3 IPv6 Base Header Format

Each IPv6 datagram begins with a 40-octet base header as Figure 7.6 illustrates. Although it is twice as large as a typical IPv4 datagram header, the IPv6 base header contains less information because fragmentation information has been moved to extension headers. In addition, IPv6 changes the alignment from 32-bit to 64-bit multiples.

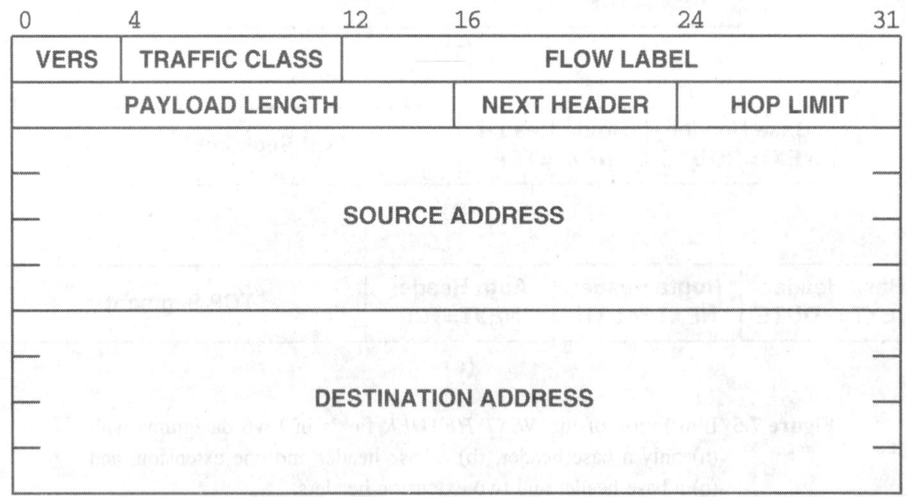

Figure 7.6 The IPv6 base header format; the size is fixed at 40 octets.

As in IPv4, the initial 4-bit *VERS* field specifies the version of the protocol; *6* specifies an IPv6 datagram. As described below, the *TRAFFIC CLASS* field is interpreted exactly the same as IPv4's *TYPE OF SERVICE* field. Field *FLOW LABEL* is intended to allow IPv6 to be used with technologies that support resource reservation. The underlying abstraction, a *flow*, consists of a path through an internet. Intermediate routers along the path guarantee a specific quality of service for packets on the flow. The *FLOW LABEL* holds an ID that allows a router to identify the flow, which is used instead of the destination address when forwarding a datagram. Chapter 16 explains the potential uses of a flow label in more detail. IPv6 uses a *PAYLOAD LENGTH* field rather than a datagram length field; the difference is that the *PAYLOAD LENGTH* refers only to the data being carried and does not include the size of the base header or extension header(s). To allow a payload to exceed 2^{16} octets, IPv6 defines an extension header that specifies a datagram to be a *jumbogram*. A *NEXT HEADER* field appears in all headers (the base header as shown and each extension header); the field specifies the type of the next extension header, and in the final header, gives the type of the payload. The *HOP LIMIT* field specifies the maximum number of networks the datagram can traverse before being discarded. Finally, the *SOURCE ADDRESS* and *DESTINATION ADDRESS* fields specify the IPv6 addresses of the original sender and ultimate destination.

7.8 Datagram Type Of Service And Differentiated Services

Informally called *Type Of Service* (*TOS*), the 8-bit *SERVICE TYPE* field in an IPv4 header and the *TRAFFIC CLASS* field in an IPv6 header specify how the datagram should be handled. In IPv4, the field was originally divided into subfields that specified the datagram's precedence and desired path characteristics (low delay or high throughput). In the late 1990s, the IETF redefined the meaning of the field to accommodate a set of *differentiated services* (*DiffServ*). Figure 7.7 illustrates the resulting definition which applies to IPv6 as well as IPv4.

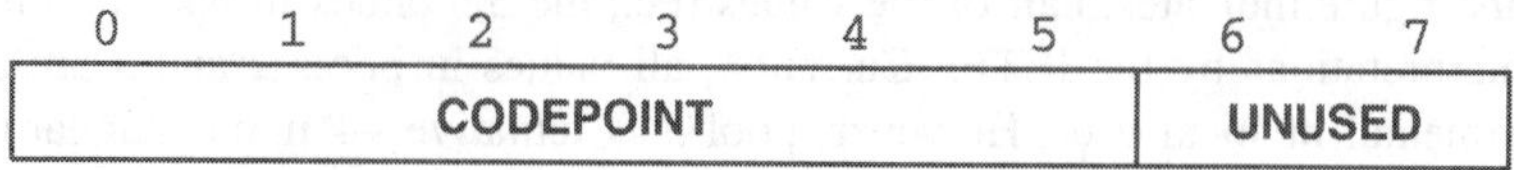

Figure 7.7 The differentiated services (DiffServ) interpretation of bits in the IPv4 *SERVICE TYPE* and IPv6 *TRAFFIC CLASS* header fields.

Under DiffServ, the first six bits of the field constitute a *codepoint*, which is sometimes abbreviated *DSCP*, and the last two bits are left unused. A codepoint value maps to an underlying service definition, typically through an array of pointers. Although it is possible to define 64 separate services, the designers suggest that a given router will only need a few services, and multiple codepoints will map to each service. For example, a router might be configured with a *voice* service, a *video* service, a *network management* service, and a *normal data* service. To maintain backward compatibility with the original definition, the standard distinguishes between the first three bits of the codepoint (bits that were formerly used for precedence) and the last three bits. When the last three bits contain zero, the precedence bits define eight broad classes of service that adhere to the same guidelines as the original definition: datagrams with a higher number in their precedence field are given preferential treatment over datagrams with a lower number. That is, the eight ordered classes are defined by codepoint values of the form:

xxx000

where x denotes either a zero or a one.

The differentiated services design also accommodates another existing practice — the widespread use of precedence 6 or 7 to give highest priority to routing traffic. The standard includes a special case to handle the two precedence values. A router is required to implement at least two priority schemes: one for normal traffic and one for high-priority traffic. When the last three bits of the *CODEPOINT* field are zero, the router must map a codepoint with precedence 6 or 7 into the higher-priority class and other codepoint values into the lower-priority class. Thus, if a datagram arrives that was sent using the original TOS scheme, a router using the differentiated services scheme will honor precedence 6 and 7 as the datagram sender expects.

Figure 7.8 illustrates how the 64 codepoint values are divided into three administrative pools.

Pool	Codepoint	Assigned By
1	xxxxx0	Standards organization
2	xxxx11	Local or experimental
3	xxxx01	Local or experimental

Figure 7.8 The three administrative pools of DiffServ codepoint values.

As the figure indicates, half of the values (i.e., the 32 values in pool *1*) must be assigned interpretations by the IETF. Currently, all values in pools *2* and *3* are available for experimental or local use. However, pool *3* is tentative — if the standards bodies exhaust all values in pool *1*, they will leave pool *2* alone, but may also choose to assign values in pool *3*.

The division into pools may seem unusual because it relies on the low-order bits of the value to distinguish pools. Thus, rather than a contiguous set of values, pool *1* contains every other codepoint value (i.e., the even numbers between 2 and 64). The division was chosen to keep the eight codepoints corresponding to values xxx000 in the same pool.

Whether the original TOS interpretation or the revised differentiated services interpretation is used, it is important to realize that forwarding software must choose from among the underlying physical network technologies at hand and must adhere to local policies. Thus, specifying a level of service in a datagram does not guarantee that routers along the path will agree to honor the request. To summarize:

> *We regard the service type specification as a hint to the forwarding algorithm that helps it choose among various paths to a destination based on local policies and its knowledge of the hardware technologies available on those paths. An internet does not guarantee to provide any particular type of service.*

7.9 Datagram Encapsulation

Before we can understand the other fields in an IPv4 datagram, it is important to consider how datagrams relate to physical network frames. We start with a question: how large can a datagram be? Unlike physical network frames that must be recognized by hardware, datagrams are handled by software. They can be of any length the protocol designers choose. We have seen that the IPv4 datagram format allots 16 bits to the total length field, limiting the datagram to at most 65,535 octets.

More fundamental limits on datagram size arise in practice. We know that as datagrams move from one machine to another, they must be transported by the underlying network hardware. To make internet transportation efficient, we would like to guarantee that each datagram travels in a distinct network frame. That is, we want our abstraction of a network packet to map directly onto a real packet if possible.

The idea of carrying one datagram in one network frame is called *encapsulation*, and is used with both IPv4 and IPv6. To the underlying network, a datagram is like any other message sent from one machine to another — the network hardware does not recognize the datagram format, nor does it understand the IP destination address. Instead, the network treats a datagram as bytes of data to be transferred. Figure 7.9 illustrates the idea: when it travels across a network from one machine to another, the entire datagram travels in the payload area of the network frame.

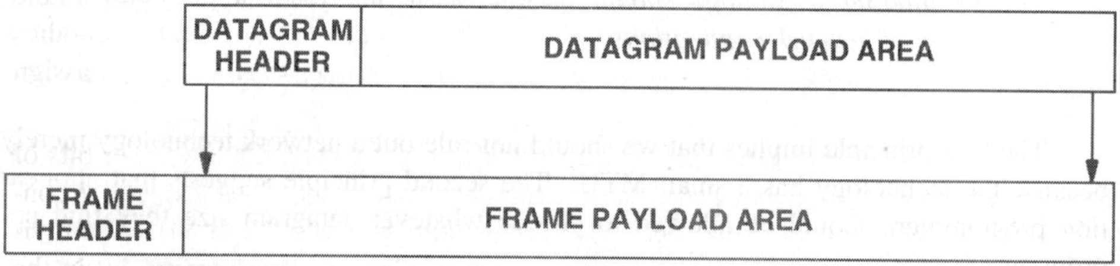

Figure 7.9 The encapsulation of an IP datagram in a frame. The underlying network treats the entire datagram, including the header, as data.

How does a receiver know that the payload area in a frame contains an IP datagram? The type field in the frame header identifies the data being carried. For example, Ethernet uses the type value 0x0800 to specify that the payload contains an encapsulated IPv4 datagram and 0x86DD to specify that the payload contains an IPv6 datagram.

7.10 Datagram Size, Network MTU, and Fragmentation

In the ideal case, an entire IP datagram fits into one physical frame, making transmission across the underlying network efficient. To guarantee such efficiency, the designers of IP might have selected a maximum datagram size such that a datagram would always fit into one frame. But which frame size should be chosen? After all, a datagram may travel across many types of networks as it moves across an internet from its source to its final destination.

To understand the problem, we need a fact about network hardware: each packet-switching technology places a fixed upper bound on the amount of data that can be transferred in one frame. For example, Ethernet limits transfers to 1500 octets of data†. We refer to the size limit as the network's *maximum transfer unit*, *maximum transmission unit* or *MTU*. MTU sizes can be larger than 1500 or smaller: technologies like IEEE 802.15.4 limit a transfer to 128 octets. Limiting datagrams to fit the smallest possible MTU in the internet makes transfers inefficient. The inefficiency is especially severe because most paths in the Internet can carry much larger datagrams. However, choosing a large size causes another problem. Because the hardware will not permit packets larger than the MTU, we will not be able to send large datagrams in a single network frame.

Two overarching internet design principles help us understand the dilemma:

> *The internet technology should accommodate the greatest possible variety of network hardware.*
>
> *The internet technology should accommodate the greatest possible variety of network applications.*

The first principle implies that we should not rule out a network technology merely because the technology has a small MTU. The second principle suggests that application programmers should be allowed to choose whatever datagram size they find appropriate.

To satisfy both principles, TCP/IP protocols use a compromise. Instead of restricting datagram size a priori, the standards allow each application to choose a datagram size that is best suited to the application. Then when transferring a datagram, check the size to see if the datagram is less than the MTU. If the datagram does not fit into a frame, divide the datagram into smaller pieces called *fragments*. Choose the fragment

†The limit of 1500 octets has become important because many networks in the global Internet use Ethernet technology.

size such that each fragment can be sent in a network frame. The process of dividing a datagram is known as *fragmentation*.

To understand fragmentation, consider three networks interconnected by two routers as Figure 7.10 illustrates.

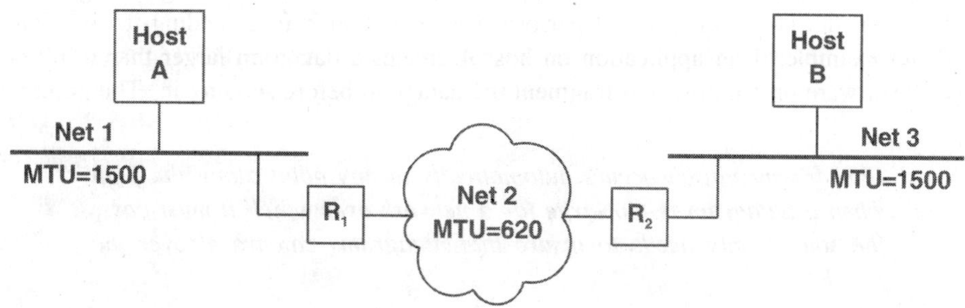

Figure 7.10 An illustration of IPv4 fragmentation. Each router may need to fragment datagrams before sending across network 2.

In the figure, each host attaches directly to an Ethernet, which has an MTU of 1500 octets. The standard requires routers to accept datagrams up to the maximum of the MTUs of networks to which they attach. Thus, either host can create and send a datagram up to 1500 octets, the MTU of the directly-connected network. If an application running on host *A* sends a 1500-octet datagram to *B*, the datagram can travel across network 1 in a single frame. However, because network 2 has an MTU of 620, fragmentation is required for the datagram to travel across network 2.

In addition to defining the MTU of each individual network, it will be important to consider the MTU along a path through an internet. The *path MTU* is defined to be the minimum of the MTUs on networks along the path. In the figure, the path from *A* to *B* has a *path MTU* of 620.

Although they each provide datagram fragmentation, IPv4 and IPv6 take completely different approaches. IPv4 allows any router along a path to fragment a datagram. In fact, if a later router along the path finds that a fragment is too large, the router can divide the fragment into fragments that are even smaller. IPv6 requires the original source to learn the path MTU and perform fragmentation; routers are forbidden from performing fragmentation. The next sections consider the two approaches and give the details for IPv4 and IPv6

7.10.1 IPv4 Datagram Fragmentation

In IPv4, fragmentation is delayed and only performed when necessary. Whether a datagram will be fragmented depends on the path a datagram follows through an internet. That is, a source only insures that a datagram can fit into a frame on the first network it must traverse. Each router along the path looks at the MTU of next network over which the datagram must pass, and fragments the datagram if necessary. In Figure 7.10, for example, router R_1 will fragment a 1500-octet datagram before sending it over network 2.

We said that a host must insure a datagram can fit into a frame on the first network. Applications often try to choose a message size that is compatible with the underlying network. However, if an application chooses to send a large datagram, IP software on the host software can perform fragmentation before sending it. In Figure 7.10, for example, if an application on host *A* creates a datagram larger than 1500 octets, IP software on the host will fragment the datagram before sending it. The point is:

> *IPv4 fragmentation occurs automatically at any point along the path when a datagram is too large for a network over which it must pass; the source only needs to insure that datagrams can travel over the first hop.*

How large should each fragment be? We said that each fragment must be small enough to fit in a single frame. In the example, a fragment must be 620 octets or smaller. A router could divide the datagram into fragments of approximately equal size. Most IPv4 software simply extracts a series of fragments that each fill the MTU, and then sends a final fragment of whatever size remains.

You may be surprised to learn that an IPv4 fragment uses the same format as a complete IPv4 datagram. The *FLAGS* field in the datagram header contains a bit that specifies whether the datagram is a complete datagram or a fragment. Another bit in the *FLAGS* field specifies whether more fragments occur (i.e., whether a particular fragment occupies the tail end of the original datagram). Finally, the *OFFSET* field in the datagram header specifies where in the original datagram the data in the fragment belongs. An interesting fragmentation detail arises because the *OFFSET* field stores a position in multiples of eight octets. That is, an octet offset is computed by multiplying the *OFFSET* field by eight. As a consequence, the size of each fragment must be chosen to be a multiple of eight. Therefore, when performing fragmentation, IP chooses the fragment size to be the largest multiple of eight that is less than or equal to the size of the MTU. Figure 7.11 illustrates IPv4 fragmentation.

Fragmentation starts by replicating the original datagram header and then modifying the *FLAGS* and *OFFSET* fields. The headers in fragments 1 and 2 have the *more fragments* bit set in the *FLAGS* field; the header in fragment 3 has zero in the *more fragments* bit. Note: in the figure, data offsets are shown as octet offsets in decimal; they must be divided by eight to get the value stored in the fragment headers.

Each fragment contains a datagram header that duplicates most of the original datagram header (except for bits in the *FLAGS* field that specify fragmentation), followed by as much data as can be carried in the fragment while keeping the total length smaller than the MTU of the network over which it must travel and the size of the data a multiple of eight octets.

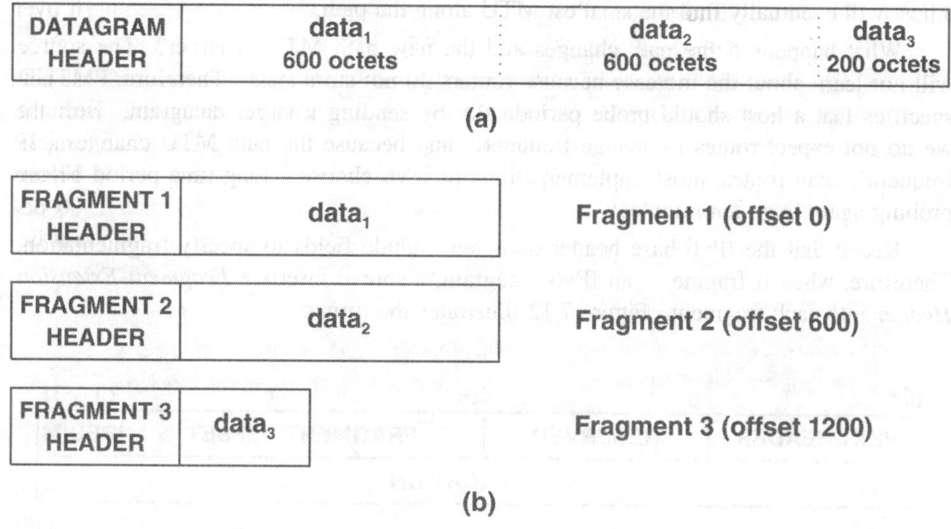

Figure 7.11 (a) An original IPv4 datagram carrying 1400 octets of data and (b) three fragments for an MTU of 620.

7.10.2 IPv6 Fragmentation And Path MTU Discovery (PMTUD)

Instead of delayed fragmentation, IPv6 uses a form of early binding: the original source host is required to find the minimum MTU along the path to the destination and fragment each datagram according to the path it will take. IP routers along the path are not permitted to fragment IPv6 datagrams; if a datagram does not fit into the MTU of a network, the router sends an error message to the original source and drops the datagram.

In many ways, the IPv6 approach to fragmentation is the opposite of the IPv4 approach, which is puzzling. Why change? When IPv6 was being defined, phone companies were pushing Asynchronous Transfer Mode (*ATM*) technologies, and the IPv6 designers assumed ATM would become widely used. ATM is a connection-oriented technology, meaning that a sender must pre-establish a path to the destination and then send along the path. Thus, the designers assumed that a source computer would learn path characteristics (including the path MTU) when the path was established and the path would not change.

Because networking technologies used in the Internet do not inform a host about the path MTU, a host must engage in a trial-and-error mechanism to determine the path MTU. Known as *Path MTU Discovery* (*PMTUD*), the mechanism consists of sending an IPv6 datagram that fits in the MTU of the directly-connected network. If a network along the path has a smaller MTU, a router will send an ICMP error message to the original source that specifies the smaller MTU. The host fragments datagrams according to the new path MTU and tries again. If a later network along the path has an MTU that is even smaller, another router will send an error message. By repeatedly probing, a host will eventually find the smallest MTU along the path.

What happens if the path changes and the new path MTU is larger? The source will not learn about the increase because routers do not store state. Therefore, PMTUD specifies that a host should probe periodically by sending a larger datagram. Because we do not expect routes to change frequently and because the path MTU changes less frequently than routes, most implementations of IPv6 choose a long time period before probing again (e.g., ten minutes).

Recall that the IPv6 base header does not include fields to specify fragmentation. Therefore, when it fragments an IPv6 datagram, a source inserts a *Fragment Extension Header* into each fragment. Figure 7.12 illustrates the format.

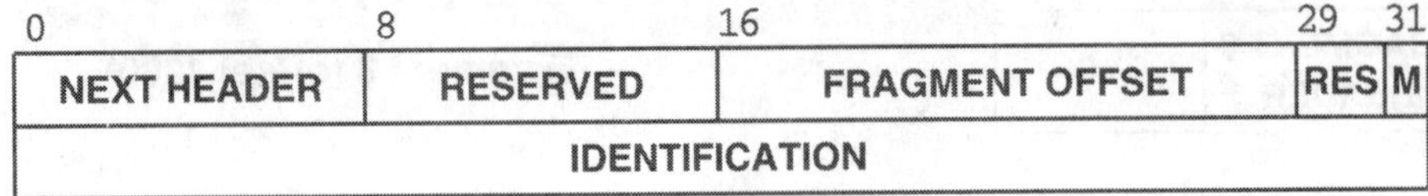

Figure 7.12 The format of an IPv6 *Fragmentation Extension Header.*

As the figure shows, the extension header includes the required *NEXT HEADER* field. It also includes two fields that are reserved for future use. The remaining three fields have the same meaning as IPv4 fragmentation control fields. A 13-bit *FRAGMENT OFFSET* field specifies where in the original datagram this fragment belongs, the *M* bits is a *more fragments* bit that specifies whether a fragment is the final (rightmost) fragment of the original datagram, and the *IDENTIFICATION* field contains a unique datagram ID that is shared by all the fragments of a datagram.

7.11 Datagram Reassembly

Eventually, fragments must be *reassembled* to produce a complete copy of the original datagram. The question arises: where should fragments be reassembled? That is, should a datagram be reassembled when it reaches a network with a larger MTU, or should the datagram remain fragmented and the fragments be transported to the ultimate destination? We will see that the answer reveals another design decision.

In a TCP/IP internet, once a datagram has been fragmented, the fragments travel as separate datagrams all the way to the ultimate destination where they are reassembled. Preserving fragments all the way to the ultimate destination may seem odd because the approach has two disadvantages. First, if only one network along the path has a small MTU, sending small fragments over the other networks is inefficient, because transporting small packets means more overhead than transporting large packets. Thus, even if networks encountered after the point of fragmentation have very large MTUs, IP will send small fragments across them. Second, if any fragments are lost, the datagram cannot be reassembled. The mechanism used to handle fragment loss consists of a *reassembly timer*. The ultimate destination starts a timer when a fragment arrives for a given datagram. If the timer expires before all fragments arrive, the receiving machine discards the surviving fragments. The source must retransmit the entire datagram; there is no way for the receiver to request individual fragments. Thus, the probability of datagram loss increases when fragmentation occurs because the loss of a single fragment results in loss of the entire datagram.

Despite the minor disadvantages, performing reassembly at the ultimate destination works well. It allows each fragment to be forwarded independently. More important, it does not require intermediate routers to store or reassemble fragments. The decision to reassemble at the ultimate destination is derived from an important principle in Internet design: the state in routers should be minimized.

> *In the Internet, the ultimate destination reassembles fragments. The design means that routers do not need to store fragments or keep other information about packets.*

7.12 Header Fields Used For Datagram Reassembly

Three fields in an IPv4 datagram header or an IPv6 Fragment Extension Header control reassembly of datagrams: *IDENTIFICATION*, *FLAGS* (*M* in IPv6), and *FRAGMENT OFFSET*. Field *IDENTIFICATION* contains a unique integer that identifies the datagram. That is, each datagram sent by a given source has a unique ID. A typical implementation uses a sequence number — a computer sends a datagram with identification *S*, the next datagram will have identification $S + 1$. Assigning a unique identification to each datagram is important because fragmentation starts by copying the identification number into each fragment. Thus, each fragment has exactly the same *IDENTIFICATION* number as the original datagram. A destination uses the *IDENTIFICATION* field in fragments along with the datagram source address to group all the fragments of a given datagram. The value in the *FRAGMENT OFFSET* field specifies the offset in the original datagram of the payload being carried in the fragment, measured in units of 8 octets†, starting at offset zero. To reassemble the datagram, the destination must obtain all fragments starting with the fragment that has offset *0* through the fragment with the highest offset. Fragments do not necessarily arrive in order, and there is no communication between the system that fragmented the datagram (a router in IPv4 or the sender in IPv6) and the destination trying to reassemble it.

In IPv4, the low-order two bits of the 3-bit *FLAGS* field control fragmentation. Usually, applications using TCP/IP do not care about fragmentation because both fragmentation and reassembly are automatic procedures that occur at lower levels of the protocol stack, invisible to applications. However, to test network software or debug operational problems, it may be important to determine the size of datagrams for which fragmentation occurs. The first control bit aids in such testing by specifying whether the datagram may be fragmented. It is called the *do not fragment* bit because setting

†Offsets are specified in multiples of 8 octets to save space in the header.

the bit to *1* specifies that the datagram should not be fragmented. Whenever a router needs to fragment a datagram that has the *do not fragment* bit set, the router discards the datagram and sends an error message back to the source.

The low order bit in the *FLAGS* field in IPv4 or the *M* bit in IPv6 specifies whether the payload in the fragment belongs somewhere in the middle of the original datagram or at the tail end. It is known as a *more fragments* bit because the value *1* means the payload in the fragment is not the tail of the datagram. Because fragments may arrive out-of-order, the destination needs to know when all fragments for a datagram have arrived. A given fragment does not specify the size of the original datagram, so a receiver must compute the datagram size. The *more fragments* bit solves the problem: once a fragment arrives with the *more fragments* bit turned off, the destination knows the fragment carries data from the tail of the original datagram. From the *FRAGMENT OFFSET* field and the size of the fragment, the destination can compute the length of the original datagram. Thus, once the tail of the original datagram arrives, the destination can tell when all other fragments have arrived.

7.13 Time To Live (IPv4) And Hop Limit (IPv6)

Originally, the IPv4 *TIME TO LIVE* (*TTL*) header field specified how long, in seconds, a datagram was allowed to remain in an internet — a sender set a maximum time that each datagram should survive, and routers that processed the datagram decremented the TTL as time passed. When a TTL reached zero, the datagram was discarded.

Unfortunately, computing an exact time is impossible because routers do not know the transit time for underlying networks. Furthermore, the notion of datagrams spending many seconds in transit became outdated (current routers and networks are designed to forward each datagram within a few milliseconds). However, a mechanism was still needed to handle a case where an internet has a forwarding problem when routers forward datagrams in a circle. To prevent a datagram from traveling around a circle forever, a rule was added as a fail-safe mechanism. The rule requires each router along the path from source to destination to decrement the TTL by *1*. In essence, each network that a datagram traverses counts as one *network hop*. Thus, in practice, the TTL field is now used to specify how many hops a datagram may traverse before being discarded. IPv6 includes the exact same concept. To clarify the meaning, IPv6 uses the name *HOP LIMIT*† in place of *TIME-TO-LIVE*.

> *IP software in each machine along a path from source to destination decrements the field known as TIME-TO-LIVE (IPv4) or HOP LIMIT (IPv6). When the field reaches zero the datagram is discarded.*

A router does more than merely discard a datagram when the TTL reaches zero — the router sends an error message back to the source. Chapter 9 describes error handling.

†Most networking professionals use the term *hop count* instead of *hop limit*.

7.14 Optional IP Items

Both IPv4 and IPv6 define optional items that can be included in a datagram. In IPv4, the *IP OPTIONS* field that follows the destination address is used to send optional items. In IPv6, each of the extension headers is optional, and a given datagram may include multiple extensions.

In practice, few datagrams in the global Internet include optional items. Many of the options in the standards are intended for special control or for network testing and debugging. Options processing is an integral part of the IP protocol; all standard implementations must include it.

The next sections discuss options in IPv4 and IPv6. Because our purpose is to provide a conceptual overview rather than a catalog of all details, the text highlights examples and discusses how each example might be used.

7.14.1 IPv4 Options

If an IPv4 datagram contains options, the options follow the *DESTINATION IP ADDRESS* field in the datagram header. The length of the options field depends on which options have been included. Some options are one octet long and other options are variable length. Each option starts with a single octet *option code* that identifies the option. An option code may be followed by a single octet length and a set of data octets for that option. When multiple options are present, they appear contiguously, with no special separators between them. That is, the options area of the header is treated as an array of octets, and options are placed in the array one after another. The high-order bit of an option code octet specifies whether the option should be copied into all fragments or only the first fragment; a later section that discusses option processing explains copying.

Figure 7.13 lists examples of options that can accompany an IPv4 datagram. As the list shows, most options are used for control purposes. The route and timestamp options are the most interesting because they provide a way to monitor or control how routers forward datagrams.

Record Route Option. The *record route* option allows the source to create an empty list of IPv4 addresses and request that each router along the path add its IPv4 address to the list. The list begins with a header that specifies the type of the option, a length field, and a pointer. The length field specifies the number of octets in the list, and the pointer specifies the offset of the next free item. Each router that forwards the datagram compares the pointer to the length. If the pointer equals or exceeds the length, the list is full. Otherwise, the router places its IP address in the next four octets of the option, increments the pointer by four, and forwards the datagram.

Number	Length	Description
0	1	End of option list, used if options do not end at end of header (see header padding field)
1	1	No operation. Used to align octets in a list
2	11	Security and handling restrictions for military apps.
3	var	Loose source route. Used to request routing through a set of specified routers
4	var	Internet timestamp. Used to record a timestamp at each hop along the path across an internet
7	var	Record route. Causes each router along the path to record its IP address in the options of the datagram
9	var	Strict source route. Used to specify an exact path through a set of routers
11	4	MTU Probe. Used by a host during IPv4 Path MTU Discovery
12	4	MTU Reply. Returned by router during IPv4 Path MTU Discovery
18	var	Traceroute. Used by the traceroute program to find the routers along a path
20	4	Router Alert. Causes each router along a path to examine the datagram, even if a router is not the ultimate destination

Figure 7.13 Examples of IPv4 options along with their length and a brief description of each.

Source Route Options. Two options, *Strict Source Route* and *Loose Source Route*, provide a way for a sender to control forwarding along a path through an internet. For example, to test a particular network, a system administrator could use source route options to force IP datagrams to traverse the network, even if normal forwarding uses another path.

The ability to source route packets is especially important as a tool for testing in a production environment. It gives the network manager freedom to test a new experimental network while simultaneously allowing users' traffic to proceed along a path that only includes production networks. Of course, source routing is only useful to someone who understands the network topology; an average user has neither a motivation to consider source routing nor the knowledge required to use it.

Strict Source Route. Strict source routing specifies a complete path through an internet (i.e., the path the datagram must follow to reach its destination). The path consists of IPv4 addresses that each correspond to a router (or to the ultimate destination). The word *strict* means that each pair of routers along the path must be directly connected by a network; an error results if a router cannot reach the next router specified in the list.

Loose Source Route. Loose source routing specifies a path through an internet, and the option includes a sequence of IP addresses. Unlike strict source routing, a loose source route specifies that the datagram must visit the sequence of IP addresses, but allows multiple network hops between successive addresses on the list.

Both source route options require routers along the path to overwrite items in the address list with their local network addresses. Thus, when the datagram arrives at its destination, it contains a list of all addresses visited, exactly like the list produced by the record route option.

Internet Timestamp Option. The timestamp option works like the record route option: the option field starts with an initially empty list, and each router along the path from source to destination fills in one entry. Unlike the record route option, each entry in a timestamp list contains two 32-bit values that are set to the IPv4 address of the router that filled the entry and a 32-bit integer timestamp. Timestamps give the time and date at which a router handles the datagram, expressed as milliseconds since midnight, Universal Time†.

7.14.2 IPv6 Optional Extensions

IPv6 uses the mechanism of extension headers in place of IPv4 options. Figure 7.14 lists examples of IPv6 options headers and explains their purpose.

Next Hdr	Length	Description
0	var	Hop-by-Hop Options. A set of options that must be examined at each hop
60	var	Destination Options. A set of options passed to the first hop router and each intermediate router
43	var	Route Header. A header that allows various types of routing information to be enclosed
44	8	Fragment Header. Present in a fragment to specify the fields used for reassembly
51	var	Authentication Header. Specifies the type of authentication used and data for the receiver
50	var	Encapsulation Security Payload Header. Specifies the encryption used
60	var	Destination Options. A set of options passed to the ultimate destination
135	var	Mobility Header. Used to specify forwarding information for a mobile host

Figure 7.14 Example options headers used with IPv6 and the *NEXT HEADER* value assigned to each.

†Universal Time was formerly called Greenwich Mean Time; it is the time of day at the prime meridian.

Some IPv6 options use a fixed-size extension header. For example, a fragment header contains exactly eight octets†. However, many of the IPv6 extension headers, such as examples listed in Figure 7.14, are variable size; the size depends on the contents. For example, the *Authentication Header* specifies the form of authentication being used and contains an authentication message in the specified form.

The format of variable-length extension headers is not fixed. A header may contain a single item (e.g., the *Authentication Header* contains an authentication message) or a set of items. As an example, consider the *Hop-By-Hop* extension header. The standard specifies a general format that allows multiple options to be enclosed. Figure 7.15 illustrates the format.

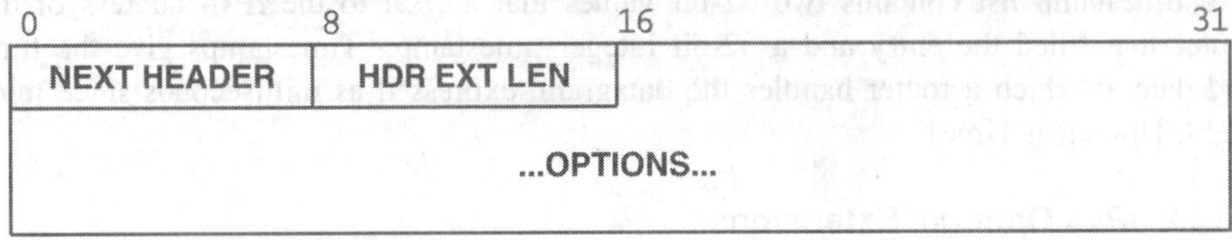

Figure 7.15 The IPv6 Hop-By-Hop extension header that encloses multiple options.

As the figure indicates, only the first two octets are specified: a *NEXT HEADER* field and a *Header Extension Length* field (*HDR EXT LEN*). The length field specifies the length of the extension header in octets. The body of the extension header follows a *Type-Length-Value* (*TLV*) approach. The body consists of options that each begin with a 2-octet header. The first octet specifies the type of the option, the second octet specifies the length, and the next octets contain the value. As in IPv4, the options in the extension header are contiguous.

IPv6 requires datagram headers to be aligned to a multiple of eight octets. Variable-size options mean that the *Hop-By-Hop header* may not align correctly. In such cases, IPv6 defines two padding options that a sender can use to align the headers. One of the two consists of a single octet of padding; the other uses two octets to specify a padding length.

Initially, IPv6 included many of the same options as IPv4. For example, one of the IPv6 extension headers is designated to be a *Route Header*, and the initial definition provided strict source route and loose source route variants. The general format of the route header was also taken from IPv4 — a list of addresses, a field that specified the length of the list in octets, and a field that pointed to the next address. However, an assessment of security concluded that giving users the ability to specify a source route through an arbitrary list of addresses would allow an attacker to send a datagram around a set of routers many times, consuming bandwidth. Therefore, the source route options are now deprecated (i.e., the IETF discourages their use). They have instead been replaced by a source route that includes one intermediate site because a single intermediate site is needed for Mobile IPv6‡.

†Figure 7.12 on page 134 illustrates fields in the fragment header.

‡Chapter 18 describes mobile IP.

7.15 Options Processing During Fragmentation

Both IPv4 and IPv6 use the same conceptual approach to handle options during fragmentation. When creating fragments, the IP code examines each of the options in the original datagram. If an option must be processed by intermediate routers, the option is copied into each fragment. However, if the option is only used at the ultimate destination, the option is copied into the header of the first fragment but not the rest. Omitting unnecessary options from later fragments reduces the total number of bits transmitted. Interestingly, omitting options may also reduce the number of fragments needed (i.e., a smaller header means a fragment can hold more data from the payload).

Although they use the same concept, IPv4 and IPv6 differ in most details. The next sections describe how each handles options.

7.15.1 IPv4 Processing Options During Fragmentation

Recall that in IPv4, each option begins with a code octet. Each code octet contains a *copy bit* that specifies whether the option should be replicated in all fragments or in only one fragment. As an example, consider the record route option. Because each fragment is treated as an independent datagram, there is no guarantee that all fragments follow the same path to the destination. It may be interesting to learn a set of paths that each of the fragments took, but the designers decided that a destination will have no way to arbitrate among multiple paths. Therefore, the IP standard specifies that the record route option should only be copied into one of the fragments.

Source route options provide an example of options that must be copied into each fragment. When a sender specifies a source route, the sender intends for the datagram to follow the specified path through an internet. If the datagram is fragmented at some point along the path, all fragments should follow the remainder of the path that the sender specified, which means that source routing information must be replicated in all fragment headers. Therefore, the standard specifies that a source route option must be copied into all fragments.

7.15.2 IPv6 Processing Options During Fragmentation

IPv6 divides a datagram into two conceptual pieces: an initial piece that is classified as *unfragmentable* and the remainder, which is classified as *fragmentable*. The base header lies in the unfragmentable piece and the payload lies in the fragmentable piece. Therefore, the only question is about the extension headers: how should each be classified? As with IPv4, extension headers that are only processed by the ultimate destination do not need to be present in each fragment. The IPv6 standards specify whether a header is fragmentable. In particular, the *Hop-By-Hop Header* and *Route Header* are not fragmentable; other extension headers are fragmentable. Therefore, the fragmentable part of the datagram begins after the non-fragmentable extension headers. To clarify the idea, consider the example in Figure 7.16, which illustrates the fragmentation of an IPv6 datagram that has a base header, four extension headers, and 1400 octets of payload.

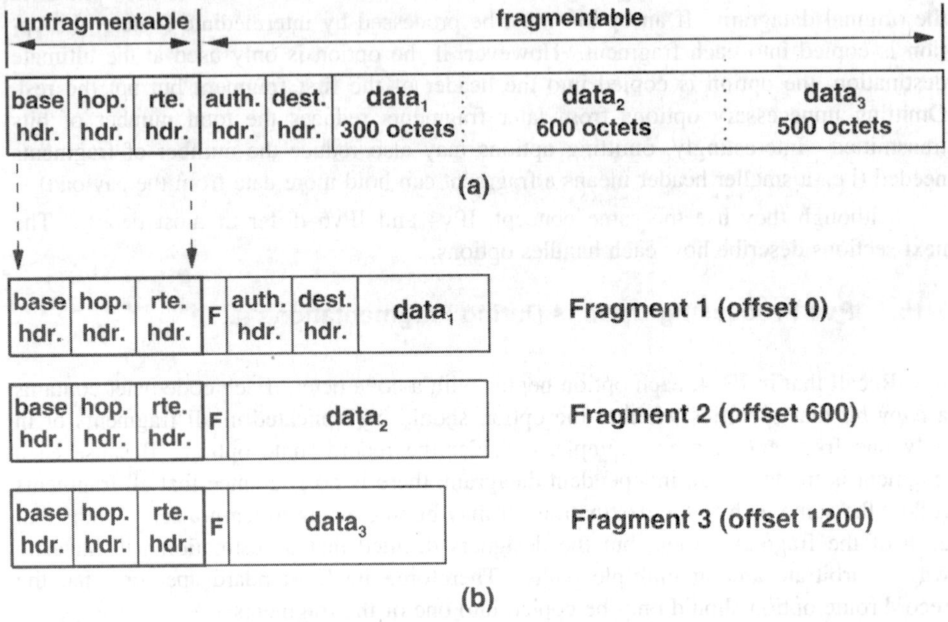

Figure 7.16 IPv6 fragmentation with (a) an IPv6 datagram with extension headers divided into fragmentable and unfragmentable pieces, and (b) a set of fragments.

As the figure indicates, each fragment starts with a copy of the unfragmentable piece of the original datagram. In the figure, the unfragmentable piece includes a *Base Header*, a *Hop-By-Hop Header*, and a *Route Header*. Following the unfragmentable piece, a fragment has a *Fragment Header* labeled *F* in the figure.

IPv6 treats the fragmentable piece of the datagram as an array of octets to be divided into fragments. In the example, the first fragment carries an *Authentication Header*, a *Destination Header*, and 300 octets of data from the original payload. The second fragment carries the next 600 octets of payload from the original datagram, and the third fragment carries the remainder of the payload. We can conclude from the figure that in this particular instance the *Authentication Header* and *Destination Header* occupy exactly 300 octets.

7.16 Network Byte Order

Our discussion of header fields omits a fundamental idea: protocols must specify enough detail to insure that both sides interpret data the same way. In particular, to keep internetworking independent of any particular vendor's machine architecture or network hardware, we must specify a standard representation for data. Consider what happens, for example, when software on one computer sends a 32-bit binary integer to another computer. We can assume that the underlying network hardware will move the sequence of bits from the first machine to the second without changing the order. However, not all computers store 32-bit integers in the same way. On some (called *little endian*), the lowest memory address contains the low-order byte of the integer. On others (called *big endian*), the lowest memory address holds the high-order byte of the integer. Still others store integers in groups of 16-bit words, with the lowest addresses holding the low-order word, but with bytes swapped. Thus, direct copying of bytes from one machine to another may change the value of the integer.

Standardizing byte-order for integers is especially important for protocol headers because a header usually contains binary values that specify information such as the packet length or a type field that specifies the type of data in the payload area. Such quantities must be understood by both the sender and receiver.

The TCP/IP protocols solve the byte-order problem by defining a *network standard byte order* that all machines must use for binary fields in headers. Each host or router converts binary items from the local representation to network standard byte order before sending a packet, and converts from network byte order to the host-specific order when a packet arrives. Naturally, the payload field in a packet is exempt from the byte-order standard because the TCP/IP protocols do not know what data is being carried — application programmers are free to format their own data representation and translation. When sending integer values, many application programmers choose to follow the TCP/IP byte-order standards, but the choice is often made merely as a convenience (i.e., use an existing standard rather than choose one just for an application). In any case, the issue of byte order is only relevant to application programmers; users seldom deal with byte order problems directly.

The Internet standard for byte order specifies that integers are sent with the most significant byte first (i.e., big endian style). If one considers the successive bytes in a packet as it travels from one machine to another, a binary integer in that packet has its most significant byte nearest the beginning of the packet and its least significant byte nearest the end of the packet.

> *The Internet protocols define* network byte order *to be big endian. A sender must convert all integer fields in packet headers to network byte order before sending a packet, and a receiver must convert all integer fields in packet headers to local byte order before processing a packet.*

Many arguments have been offered about which data representation should be used, and the Internet standard still comes under attack from time to time. In particular, proponents of change argue that although most computers were big endian when the standard was defined, most are now little endian. However, everyone agrees that having a standard is crucial, and the exact form of the standard is far less important.

7.17 Summary

The fundamental service provided by TCP/IP Internet software consists of a connectionless, unreliable, best-effort packet delivery system. The Internet Protocol (IP) formally specifies the format of internet packets, called *datagrams*, and informally embodies the ideas of connectionless delivery. This chapter concentrated on datagram formats; later chapters will discuss IP forwarding and error handling.

Analogous to a physical frame, the IP datagram is divided into header and data areas. Among other information, the datagram header contains the source and destination Internet addresses and the type of the item that follows the header. Version 6 of the Internet Protocol changes the format from a single header with several fields to a base header plus a series of extension headers.

A large datagram can be divided into fragments for transmission across a network that has a small MTU. Each fragment travels as an independent datagram; the ultimate destination reassembles fragments. In IPv4, a router performs fragmentation when a datagram must be sent over a network and the datagram does not fit into the network frame. In IPv6, the original source performs all fragmentation; a host must probe to find the path MTU. Options that must be processed by intermediate routers are copied into each fragment; options that are handled by the ultimate destination are sent in the first fragment.

EXERCISES

7.1 What is the single greatest advantage of having a checksum cover only the datagram header and not the payload? What is the disadvantage?

7.2 Is it necessary to use an IP checksum when sending packets over an Ethernet? Why or why not?

7.3 What is the MTU of an 802.11 network? Fibre Channel? 802.15.4?

7.4 Do you expect a high-speed local area network to have larger or smaller MTU than a wide area network? Why?

7.5 Argue that a fragment should *not* resemble a datagram.

7.6 Ethernet assigns a new type value for IPv6, which means the frame type can be used to distinguish between arriving IPv6 and IPv4 datagrams. Why is it necessary to have a version number in the first four bits of each datagram?

7.7 In the previous exercise, estimate how many total bits are transmitted around the world each year just to carry the 4-bit version number.

7.8 What is the advantage of using a one's complement checksum for IP instead of a Cyclic Redundancy Check?

7.9 Suppose the Internet design was changed to allow routers along a path to reassemble datagrams. How would the change affect security?

7.10 What is the minimum network MTU required to send an IPv4 datagram that contains at least one octet of data? An IPv6 datagram?

7.11 Suppose you are hired to implement IP datagram processing in hardware. Is there any rearrangement of fields in the header that would make your hardware more efficient? Easier to build?

7.12 When a minimum-size IP datagram travels across an Ethernet, how large is the frame? Explain.

7.13 The differentiated services interpretation of the *SERVICE TYPE* field allows up to 64 separate service levels. Argue that fewer levels are needed (i.e., make a list of all possible services that a user might access).

Chapter Contents

8

Internet Protocol: Forwarding IP Datagrams

8.1 Introduction

We have seen that all internet services use an underlying, connectionless packet delivery system and the basic unit of transfer in a TCP/IP internet is the IP datagram. This chapter adds to the description of connectionless service by describing how routers forward IP datagrams and deliver them to their final destinations. We think of the datagram format from Chapter 7 as characterizing the static aspects of the Internet Protocol. The description of forwarding in this chapter characterizes the operational aspects. The next chapter completes our basic presentation of IP by describing how errors are handled. Later chapters show how other protocols use IP to provide higher-level services.

8.2 Forwarding In An Internet

Traditionally, the term *routing* was used with packet switching systems such as the Internet to refer to the process of choosing a path over which to send packets, and the term *router* was used to describe the packet switching device that makes such a choice. Approximately twenty years after the inception of the Internet, networking professionals started using the term *forwarding* to refer to the process of choosing the path for a packet. Interestingly, they retained the term *router* to refer to the system that performs forwarding. We will follow popular usage, and use the term *forwarding*.

Forwarding occurs at several levels. For example, within a switched Ethernet that spans multiple physical chassis, the switches are responsible for forwarding Ethernet frames among computers. The frame enters the switch through a port that connects to the sending computer, and the switch transmits the frame out the port that leads to the destination host. Such internal forwarding is completely self-contained inside a single Ethernet network. Machines on the outside do not participate in Ethernet forwarding; they merely view the network as an entity that accepts and delivers packets.

Remember that the goal of IP is to provide a virtual network that encompasses multiple physical networks, and offers a connectionless datagram delivery service that is an abstract version of the service provided by an Ethernet switch. That is, we want the Internet to accept an Internet packet and deliver the packet to the intended recipient (i.e., operate as if the Internet worked like a giant Ethernet switch). The major differences are that in place of frames the Internet accepts and delivers IP datagrams, and in place of Ethernet addresses, the Internet uses IP addresses. Therefore, throughout the chapter, we will restrict the discussion to *IP forwarding*.

The information IP software uses to make forwarding decisions is known as a *Forwarding Information Base* (*FIB*). Each IP module has its own FIB, and each has to make forwarding decisions. The basic idea is straightforward: given a datagram, IP chooses how to send the datagram on toward its destination. Unlike forwarding within a single network, however, the IP forwarding algorithm does not simply choose among a local set of destination computers. Instead, IP must be configured to send a datagram across multiple physical networks.

Forwarding in an internet can be difficult, especially among computers that have multiple physical network connections. You might imagine that forwarding software would choose a path according to the current load on all the networks, the datagram size, the type of data being carried, the type of service requested in the datagram header, and (perhaps) the economic cost of various paths. We will see that most internet forwarding software is much less sophisticated, however, and selects routes based on fixed assumptions about shortest paths.

To understand IP forwarding completely, we must think about the architecture of a TCP/IP internet. First, recall that an internet is composed of multiple physical networks interconnected by routers. Each router has direct connections to two or more networks. By contrast, a host computer usually connects directly to one physical network. We know that it is possible to have a multi-homed host directly connected to multiple networks, but we will defer thinking about multi-homed hosts for now.

Both hosts and routers participate in forwarding an IP datagram to its destination. When an application program on a host communicates with a remote application, protocol software on the host begins to generate IP datagrams. When it receives an outgoing datagram, the IP software on the host makes a forwarding decision: it chooses where to send the datagram. Even if a host only connects to a single network, the host may need to make routing decisions. Figure 8.1 shows an example architecture where a host with one network connection must make forwarding decisions.

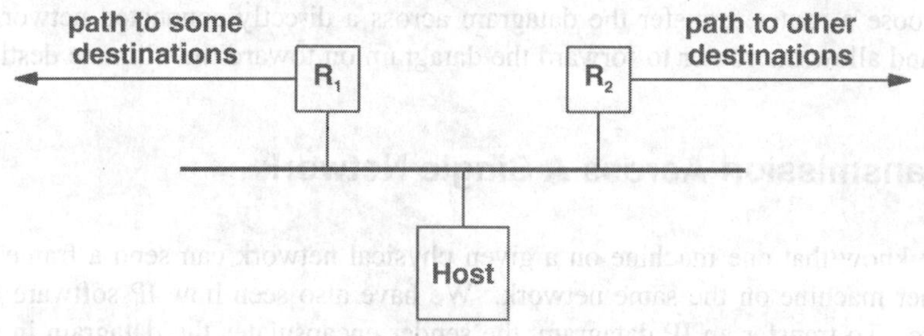

Figure 8.1 An example of a singly-homed host that must make a choice between router R_1 and router R_2 when sending a datagram.

In the figure, two routers connect to the same network as the host. Some internet destinations lie beyond router R_1 and other destinations lie beyond R_2. The host must decide which router to use for a given datagram.

A router performs *transit forwarding*, which means the router will accept incoming datagrams from any of the networks to which the router attaches, and will forward each datagram on toward its destination. A question arises for multi-homed hosts. Suppose, for example, that a computer has both Wi-Fi and 4G cellular network connections. Should the computer act like a router and provide transit forwarding between the networks? We will see that any computer running TCP/IP has all the software needed to forward datagrams. Thus, in theory, any computer with multiple network connections can act as a router. However, the TCP/IP standards draw a sharp distinction between the functions of a host and those of a router. Anyone who tries to mix host and router functions on a single machine by configuring a host to provide transit forwarding discovers that the machine may not perform as expected. For now, we will distinguish hosts from routers, and assume that hosts do not perform the router's function of transferring packets from one network to another.

> *The Internet design distinguishes between hosts and routers. Although a host with multiple network connections can be configured to act as a router, the resulting system may not perform as expected.*

8.3 Direct And Indirect Delivery

Loosely speaking, we can divide forwarding into two forms: *direct delivery* and *indirect delivery*. Direct delivery, the transmission of a datagram from one machine across a single physical network directly to another, is the basis on which all internet communication rests. Two machines can engage in direct delivery only if they both attach directly to the same underlying physical transmission system (e.g., a single Ethernet). *Indirect delivery* occurs when the destination of a datagram is not on a directly attached network. Because the ultimate destination cannot be reached directly, the sender must choose a router, transfer the datagram across a directly-connected network to the router, and allow the router to forward the datagram on toward the ultimate destination.

8.4 Transmission Across A Single Network

We know that one machine on a given physical network can send a frame directly to another machine on the same network. We have also seen how IP software uses the hardware. To transfer an IP datagram, the sender encapsulates the datagram in a physical frame as described in Chapter 7, maps the next-hop IP address to a hardware address, places the hardware address in the frame, and uses the network hardware to transfer the frame. As Chapter 6 describes, IPv4 typically uses ARP to map an IP address into a hardware address, and IPv6 uses Neighbor Discovery to learn the hardware addresses of neighboring nodes. Therefore, previous chapters examine all the pieces needed to understand direct delivery. To summarize:

> *Transmission of an IP datagram between two machines on a single physical network does not involve routers. The sender encapsulates the datagram in a physical frame, binds the next-hop address to a physical hardware address, and sends the resulting frame directly to the destination.*

The idea of sending datagrams directly across a single network may seem obvious, but originally it was not. Before TCP/IP was invented, several network technologies required the equivalent of a router to be attached to each network. When two computers on the network needed to communicate, they did so through the local router. Proponents argued that having all communication go through a router meant all communication used the same paradigm and allowed security to be implemented easily. The TCP/IP design showed that direct communication reduced the network traffic by a factor of two.

Suppose the IP software on a machine is given an IP datagram. How does the software know whether the destination lies on a directly connected network? The test is straightforward and helps explain the IP addressing scheme. Recall that each IP address is divided into a prefix that identifies the network and a suffix that identifies a host. To determine if a destination lies on one of the directly connected networks, IP software extracts the network portion of the destination IP address and compares the network ID to the network ID of its own IP address(es). A match means the destination lies on a directly-connected network and the datagram can be delivered directly to the destination. The test is computationally efficient, which highlights why the Internet address scheme works well:

Because the internet addresses of all machines on a single network include a common network prefix and extracting that prefix requires only a few machine instructions, testing whether a destination can be reached directly is efficient.

From an internet perspective, it is easiest to think of direct delivery as the final step in any datagram transmission. A datagram may traverse many networks and intermediate routers as it travels from source to destination. The final router along the path will connect directly to the same physical network as the destination. Thus, the final router will deliver the datagram using direct delivery. In essence, a path through an internet involves zero or more intermediate routers plus one step of direct delivery. The special case arises when there are no routers in the path — the sending host must perform the direct delivery step.

8.5 Indirect Delivery

Indirect delivery is more difficult than direct delivery because the sending machine must identify an initial router to handle the datagram. The router must then forward the datagram on toward the destination network.

To visualize how indirect forwarding works, imagine a large internet with many networks interconnected by routers, but with only two hosts at the far ends. When a host has a datagram to send, the host encapsulates the datagram in a frame and sends the frame to the nearest router. We know that the host can reach a router because all physical networks are interconnected, so there must be a router attached to each network. Thus, the originating host can reach a router using a single physical network. Once the frame reaches the router, software extracts the encapsulated datagram, and the IP software selects the next router along the path toward the destination. The datagram is again placed in a frame and sent over the next physical network to a second router, and so on, until it can be delivered directly. The concept can be summarized:

Routers in a TCP/IP internet form a cooperative, interconnected structure. Datagrams pass from router to router until they reach a router that can deliver the datagram directly.

The internet design concentrates forwarding knowledge in routers and insures that a router can forward an arbitrary datagram. Hosts rely on routers for all indirect delivery. We can summarize:

- A host only knows about directly-connected networks; a host relies on routers to transfer datagrams to remote destinations.
- Each router knows how to reach all possible destinations in the internet; given a datagram, a router can forward it correctly.

How can a router know how to reach a remote destination? How can a host know which router to use for a given destination? The two questions are related because they both involve IP forwarding. We will answer the questions in two stages by considering a basic table-driven forwarding algorithm in this chapter and postponing a discussion of how routers learn about remote destinations until Chapters 12–14.

8.6 Table-Driven IP Forwarding

IP performs datagram forwarding. The IP forwarding algorithm employs a data structure that stores information about possible destinations and how to reach them. The data structure is known formally as an *Internet Protocol forwarding table* or *IP forwarding table*, and informally as simply a *forwarding table*†.

Because they each must forward datagrams, both hosts and routers have a forwarding table. We will see that the forwarding table on a typical host is much smaller than the forwarding table on a router, but the advantage of using a table is that a single forwarding mechanism handles both cases. Whenever it needs to transmit a datagram, IP forwarding software consults the forwarding table to decide where to send the datagram.

What information should be kept in a forwarding table? If every forwarding table contained information about every possible destination in an internet, it would be impossible to keep the tables current. Furthermore, because the number of possible destinations is large, small special-purpose systems could not run IP because they would not have sufficient space to store the forwarding information.

Conceptually, it is desirable to use the principle of information hiding and allow machines to make forwarding decisions with minimal information. For example, we would like to isolate information about specific hosts to the local environment in which they exist, and arrange for machines that are far away to forward packets to them without knowing such details. Fortunately, the IP address scheme helps achieve the goal. Recall that IP addresses are assigned to make all machines connected to a given physical network share a common prefix (the network portion of the address). We have already seen that such an assignment makes the test for direct delivery efficient. It also means that routing tables only need to contain network prefixes and not full IP addresses. The distinction is critical: the global Internet has over 800,000,000 individual computers, but only 400,000 unique IPv4 prefixes. Thus, the forwarding information needed for prefixes is three orders of magnitude smaller than the forwarding information for individual computers. The point is:

> *Because it allows forwarding to be based on network prefixes, the IP addressing scheme controls the size of forwarding tables.*

When we discuss route propagation, we will see that the IP forwarding scheme also has another advantage: we are only required to propagate information about networks, not about individual hosts. In fact, a host can attach to a network (e.g., Wi-Fi

†Originally, the table was known as a *routing table*; some networking professionals use the original terminology.

hot spot) and begin using the network without any changes in the forwarding tables in routers.

8.7 Next-Hop Forwarding

We said that using the network portion of a destination IP address instead of the complete address keeps forwarding tables small. It also makes forwarding efficient. More important, it helps hide information, keeping the details of specific hosts confined to the local environment in which the hosts operate. Conceptually, a forwarding table contains a set of pairs (*N*, *R*), where *N* is the *network prefix* for a network in the internet and *R* is the IP address of the "next" router along the path to network *N*. Router *R* is called the *next hop*, and the idea of using a forwarding table to store a next hop for each destination is called *next-hop forwarding*. Thus, the forwarding table in a router *R* only specifies one step along the path from *R* to each destination network — the router does not know the complete path to a destination.

It is important to understand that each entry in a forwarding table points to a router that can be reached across a single network. That is, all routers listed in machine *M*'s forwarding table must lie on networks to which *M* connects directly. When a datagram is ready to leave *M*, IP software locates the destination IP address and extracts the network portion. *M* then looks up the network portion in its forwarding table, selecting one of the entries. The selected entry in the table will specify a next-hop router that can be reached directly.

In practice, we apply the principle of information hiding to hosts as well. We insist that although hosts have IP forwarding tables, they must keep minimal information in their tables. The idea is to force hosts to rely on routers for most forwarding.

Figure 8.2 shows a concrete example that helps explain forwarding tables. The example internet consists of four networks connected by three routers. The table in the figure corresponds to the forwarding table for router *R*. Although the example uses IPv4 addresses, the concept applies equally to IPv6.

In the figure, each network has been assigned a slash-8 prefix and each network interface has been assigned a 32-bit IPv4 address. The network administrator who assigned IP addresses has chosen the same host suffix for both interfaces of a router. For example, the interfaces on router *Q* have addresses 10.0.0.5 and 20.0.0.5. Although IP allows arbitrary suffixes, choosing the same value for both interfaces makes addressing easier for humans to remember.

Because router *R* connects directly to networks 20.0.0.0 and 30.0.0.0, it can use direct delivery to send to a host on either of those networks. The router uses ARP (IPv4) or direct mapping (IPv6) to find the physical address of a computer on those networks. Given a datagram destined for a host on network 40.0.0.0, however, *R* cannot deliver directly. Instead, *R* forwards the datagram to router *S* (address 30.0.0.7). *S* will then deliver the datagram directly. *R* can reach address 30.0.0.7 because both *R* and *S* attach directly to network 30.0.0.0.

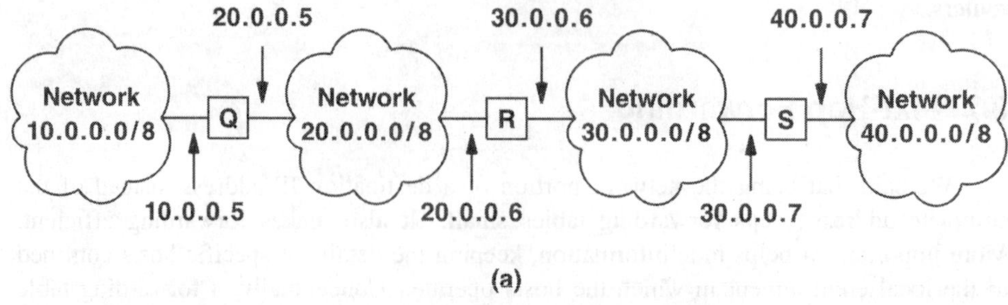

(a)

TO REACH HOSTS ON THIS NETWORK	FORWARD TO THIS ADDRESS
20.0.0.0/8	DELIVER DIRECTLY
30.0.0.0/8	DELIVER DIRECTLY
10.0.0.0/8	20.0.0.5
40.0.0.0/8	30.0.0.7

(b)

Figure 8.2 (a) An example internet with 4 networks and 3 routers, and (b) the forwarding table in *R*.

As Figure 8.2 demonstrates, the size of the forwarding table depends on the number of networks in the internet; the table only grows when new networks are added. That is, the table size and contents are independent of the number of individual hosts connected to the networks. We can summarize the underlying principle:

To hide information, keep forwarding tables small, and make forwarding decisions efficient, IP forwarding software only keeps information about destination network addresses, not about individual host addresses.

Choosing routes based on the destination network prefix alone has several consequences. First, in most implementations, it means that all traffic destined for a given network takes the same path. As a result, even when multiple paths exist, they may not be used concurrently. Also, in the simplest case, all traffic follows the same path without regard to the delay or throughput of physical networks. Second, because only the final router along the path attempts to communicate with the destination host, only the final router can determine if the host exists or is operational. Thus, we need to arrange a way for the final router to send reports of delivery problems back to the original source. Third, because each router forwards traffic independently, datagrams traveling from host *A* to host *B* may follow an entirely different path than datagrams traveling from host *B* back to host A. Moreover, the path in one direction can be down (e.g., if a network or router fails) even if the path in the other direction remains available. We need to ensure that routers cooperate to guarantee that two-way communication is always possible.

8.8 Default Routes And A Host Example

The IP design includes an interesting optimization that further hides information and reduces the size of forwarding tables: consolidation of multiple entries into a single *default* case. Conceptually, a default case introduces a two-step algorithm. In the first step, IP forwarding software looks in the forwarding table to find a next-hop. If no entry in the table matches the destination address, the forwarding software takes a second step of checking for a default route. We say that the next hop specified in a default route is a *default router*.

In practice, we will see that default routing does not require two separate steps. Instead, a default route can be incorporated into a forwarding table. That is, an extra entry can be added to a forwarding table that specifies a default router as the next hop. The lookup algorithm can be arranged to match other table entries first and only examine the default entry if none of the other entries match. A later section explains the forwarding algorithm that accommodates default routes.

A default route is especially useful when many destinations lie beyond a single router. For example, consider a company that uses a router to connect two small department networks to the company intranet. The router has a connection to each department network and a connection to the rest of the company intranet. Forwarding is straightforward because the router only needs three entries in its forwarding table: one for each of the two departmental networks and a default route for all other destinations.

Default routing works especially well for typical host computers that obtain service from an ISP. For example, when a user acquires service over a DSL line or cable modem, the hardware connects the computer to a network at the ISP. The host uses a router on the ISP's network to reach an arbitrary destination in the global Internet. In such cases, the forwarding table in the host table only needs two entries: one for the local net at the ISP and a default entry that points to the ISP's router. Figure 8.3 illustrates the idea.

Although the example in the figure uses IPv4 addresses, the same principle works for IPv6: a host only needs to know about the local network plus have a default route that is used to reach the rest of the Internet. Of course, an IPv6 address is four times as large as an IPv4 address, which means that each entry in the forwarding table is four times larger. The consequence for lookup times is more significant: on modern computers, an IPv4 address fits into a single integer, which means a computer can use a single integer comparison to compare two IPv4 addresses. When comparing two IPv6 addresses, multiple comparisons are needed.

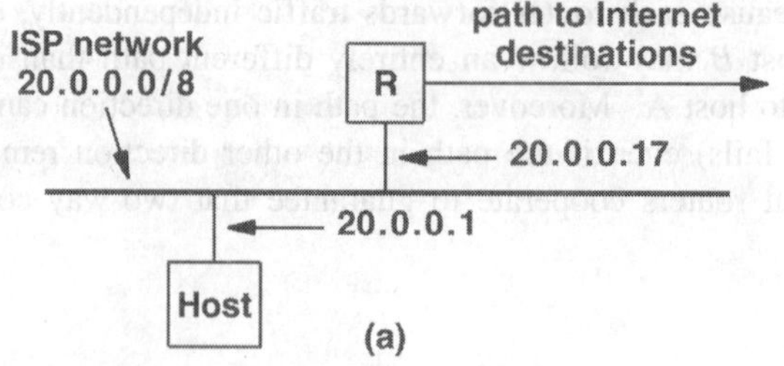

TO REACH HOSTS ON THIS NETWORK	FORWARD TO THIS ADDRESS
20.0.0.0/8	DELIVER DIRECTLY
DEFAULT	20.0.0.17

(b)

Figure 8.3 (a) An example Internet connection using IPv4 addresses, and (b) the forwarding table used in the host.

8.9 Host-Specific Routes

Although we said that all forwarding is based on networks and not on individual hosts, most IP forwarding software allows a *host-specific* route to be specified as a special case. Having host-specific routes gives a network administrator more control. The ability to specify a route for individual machines turns out to have several possible uses:

- Control over network use. An administrator can send traffic for certain hosts along one path and traffic for remaining hosts along another path. For example, an administrator can separate traffic destined to the company's web server from other traffic.
- Testing a new network. A new, parallel network can be installed and tested by sending traffic for specific hosts over the new network while leaving all other traffic on the old network.
- Security. An administrator can use host-specific routes to direct traffic through security systems. For example, traffic destined to the company's financial department may need to traverse a secure network that has special filters in place.

Although concepts like default routes and host-specific routes seem to be special cases that require special handing, the next section explains how all forwarding information can be combined into a single table and handled by a single, uniform lookup algorithm.

8.10 The IP Forwarding Algorithm

Taking all the special cases described above into account, it may seem that IP software should take the following steps when deciding how to forward a datagram:

1. Extract the destination IP address, D, from the datagram
2. If the forwarding table contains a host-specific entry for destination D,

   Forward the datagram to the next hop specified in the entry
3. If the network prefix of D matches the prefix of any directly connected network,

   Send the datagram directly over the network to D
4. If the forwarding table contains an entry that matches the network prefix of D,

   Forward the datagram to the next hop specified in the entry
5. If the forwarding table contains a default route,

   Forward the datagram to the next hop specified in the default route
6. If none of the above cases has forwarded the datagram,

   Declare a forwarding error

Thinking of the six steps individually helps us understand all the cases to be considered. In terms of implementation, however, programming six separate steps makes the code clumsy and filled with special cases (e.g., checking whether a default route has been specified). Early in the history of the Internet, designers found a way to unify all the cases into a single lookup mechanism that is now used in most commercial IP software. We will explain the conceptual algorithm, examine a straightforward implementation using a table, and then consider a version that scales to handle forwarding in routers near the center of the Internet that have large forwarding tables.

The unified lookup scheme requires four items to be specified for each entry in the forwarding table:

- The IP address, *A*, that gives the destination for the entry
- An address mask, *M*, that specifies how many bits of *A* to examine
- The IP address of a next-hop router, *R*, or "deliver direct"
- A network interface, *I*, to use when sending

The four items define a route unambiguously. It should be clear that each entry in a forwarding table needs the third item, a next-hop router address. The fourth item is needed because a router that attaches to multiple networks has multiple internal network interfaces. When it forwards a datagram, IP must specify which internal interface to use when sending the datagram. The first two items define a network prefix — the mask specifies which bits of the destination address to use during comparison and the IP address, *A*, gives a value against which to compare. That is, the algorithm computes the bit-wise *logical and* of the mask, *M*, with the destination address and then compares the result to *A*, the first item in the entry.

We define the *length* of an address mask to be the number of 1 bits in the mask. In slash notation, the length of a mask is given explicitly (e.g., /28 denotes a mask with length 28). The length of an address mask is important because the unified forwarding algorithm includes more than traditional network prefixes. The mask, which determines how many bits to examine during comparisons, also allows us to handle host-specific and default cases. For example, consider an IPv6 destination. A /64 mask means that a comparison will consider the first 64 bits of the address (i.e., the network prefix). A /128 mask means that all 128 bits of address *A* in the entry will be compared to the destination (i.e., the entry specifies a host-specific route).

As another example of how the four items suffice for arbitrary forwarding, consider a default route. To create an entry for a default route, the mask, *M*, is set to zero (all zero bits), and the address field, *A*, is set to zero. No matter what destination address is in a datagram, using a mask of all zeroes results in a value of zero, which is equal to the value of *A* in the entry. In other words, the entry always matches (i.e., it provides a *default* route). Algorithm 8.1 summarizes steps taken to forward a datagram.

In essence, the algorithm iterates through entries in the forwarding table until it finds a match. The algorithm assumes entries are arranged in longest-prefix order (i.e., the entries with the longest mask occur first). Therefore, as soon as the destination matches an entry, the algorithm can send the datagram to the specified next hop. There are two cases: direct or indirect delivery. For direct delivery, the datagram destination is used as the next hop. For indirect delivery, the forwarding table contains the address of a router, *R*, to use as the next hop. Once a next hop has been determined, the algorithm maps the next-hop address to a hardware address, creates a frame, fills in the hardware address in the frame, and sends the frame carrying the datagram to the next hop.

The algorithm assumes that the forwarding table contains a default route. Thus, even if no other entries match a given destination, the default entry will match. Of course, a manager could make a mistake and inadvertently remove the default route. In such cases, our algorithm will iterate through the entire table without finding a match, and will then reach the point at which it declares a forwarding error has occurred.

8.11 Longest-Prefix Match Paradigm

To make the algorithm work correctly, entries in the table must be examined in an order that guarantees entries with a longer mask are checked before entries with a shorter mask. For example, suppose the table contains a host-specific route for a host X and also contains a network-specific route for the network portion of X. Both entries will match X, but forwarding should choose the most specific match (i.e., the host-specific route).

Algorithm 8.1

```
ForwardIPDatagram ( Datagram , ForwardingTable )  {

  Insure forwarding table is ordered with longest-prefix first

  Extract the destination, D, from the datagram

  For each table entry {

    Compute the logical and of D with mask to obtain a prefix, P

    If prefix P matches A, the address in entry {

      /* Found a matching entry -- forward as specified */

      if (next hop in entry is "deliver direct") {

         Set NextHop to the destination address, D

      } otherwise {

         Set NextHop to the router address in the entry, R

      }

      Resolve address NextHop to a hardware address, H

      Encapsulate the datagram in a frame using address H

      Send the datagram over network using interface I

      Stop because the datagram has been sent successfully

    }

  }

  Stop and declare that a forwarding error has occurred

}
```

Algorithm 8.1 Unified IP Forwarding Algorithm in which each table entry contains an address, A, a mask, M, a next-hop router, R (or "direct delivery"), and a network interface, I.

We use the term *longest-prefix match* to describe the idea of examining the most-specific routes first. If we imagine the forwarding table to be an array, the longest-prefix match rule means entries in the array must be sorted in descending order according to the length of their mask.

8.12 Forwarding Tables And IP Addresses

It is important to understand that except for decrementing the hop limit (TTL in IPv4) and recomputing the checksum, IP forwarding does not alter the original datagram. In particular, the datagram source and destination addresses remain unaltered; they specify the IP address of the original source and the IP address of the ultimate destination†. When it executes the forwarding algorithm, IP computes a new address, the IP address of the machine to which the datagram should be sent next. The new address is most likely the address of a router. If the datagram can be delivered directly, the new address is the same as the address of the ultimate destination.

In the algorithm, the IP address selected by the IP forwarding algorithm is called a *next-hop address* because it tells where the datagram must be sent next. Where does IP store the next-hop address? Not in the datagram; no place is reserved for it. In fact, IP does not store the next-hop address at all. After it executes the forwarding algorithm, the IP module passes the datagram and the next-hop address to the network interface responsible for the network over which the datagram must be sent. In essence, IP requests that the datagram be sent to the specified next-hop address.

When it receives a datagram and a next-hop address from IP, the network interface must map the next-hop address to a hardware address, create a frame, place the hardware address in the destination address field of the frame, encapsulate the datagram in the payload area of the frame, and transmit the result. Once it has obtained a hardware address, the network interface software discards the next-hop address.

It may seem odd that a forwarding table stores the IP address of each next hop instead of the hardware address of the next hop. An IP address must be translated into a corresponding hardware address before the datagram can be sent, so an extra step is required to map a next-hop IP address to an equivalent hardware address. If we imagine a host sending a sequence of many datagrams to a single destination, the use of IP addresses for forwarding can seem incredibly inefficient. Each time an application generates a datagram, IP extracts the destination address and searches the forwarding table to produce a next-hop address. IP then passes the datagram and next-hop address to the network interface, which recomputes the binding to a hardware address. If the forwarding table stored hardware addresses, the binding between the next hop's IP address and hardware address could be performed once, saving unnecessary computation.

Why does IP software avoid using hardware addresses in a forwarding table? Figure 8.4 helps illustrates the two important reasons. First, a forwarding table provides an especially clean interface between IP software that forwards datagrams and management tools and high-level software that manipulate routes. Second, the goal of internetworking is to hide the details of underlying networks. Using only IP addresses in forwarding tables allows network managers to work at a higher level of abstraction. A manager can examine or change forwarding rules and debug forwarding problems while only using IP addresses. Thus, a manager does not need to worry about or understand the underlying hardware addresses.

†The only exception occurs when a datagram contains a source route option.

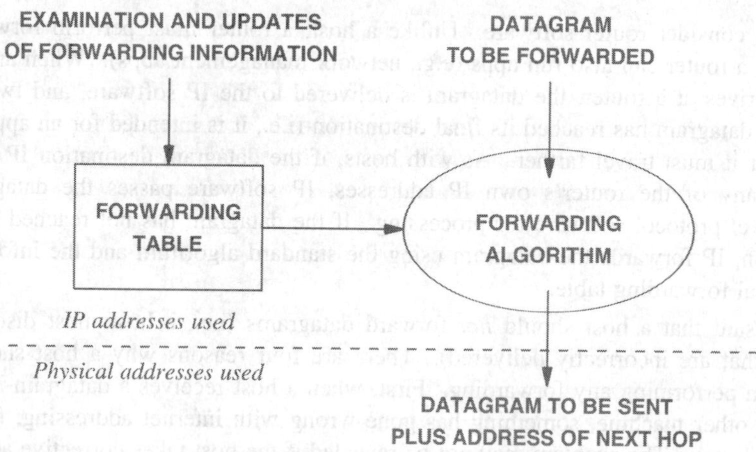

Figure 8.4 Illustration of the forwarding algorithm using a forwarding table while entries are being examined or changed.

The figure illustrates an interesting idea: concurrent access to forwarding information. Datagram forwarding, which happens millisecond-to-millisecond, can continue to use the forwarding table while a manager examines entries or makes changes. A change takes effect immediately because the forwarding continues concurrently (unless the manager manually disables network interfaces).

Figure 8.4 also illustrates the *address boundary*, an important conceptual division between low-level software that understands hardware addresses and internet software that only uses high-level addresses. Above the boundary, all software can be written to use internet addresses; knowledge of hardware addresses is relegated to a few small, low-level functions that transmit a datagram. We will see that observing the address boundary also helps keep the implementation of higher-level protocols, such as TCP, easy to understand, test, and modify.

8.13 Handling Incoming Datagrams

So far, we have discussed IP forwarding by describing how forwarding decisions are made about outgoing datagrams. It should be clear, however, that IP software must process incoming datagrams as well.

First consider host software. When an IP datagram arrives at a host, the network interface software delivers the datagram to the IP module for processing. If the datagram's destination address matches the host's IP address (or one of the host's addresses), IP software on the host accepts the datagram and passes it to the appropriate higher-level protocol software for further processing. If the destination IP address does not match one of host's addresses, the host is required to discard the datagram (i.e., hosts are forbidden from attempting to forward datagrams that are accidentally forwarded to the wrong machine).

Now consider router software. Unlike a host, a router must perform forwarding. However, a router can also run apps (e.g., network management apps). When an IP datagram arrives at a router, the datagram is delivered to the IP software, and two cases arise: the datagram has reached its final destination (i.e., it is intended for an app on the router), or it must travel farther. As with hosts, if the datagram destination IP address matches any of the router's own IP addresses, IP software passes the datagram to higher-level protocol software for processing. If the datagram has not reached its final destination, IP forwards the datagram using the standard algorithm and the information in the local forwarding table.

We said that a host should *not* forward datagrams (i.e., a host must discard datagrams that are incorrectly delivered). There are four reasons why a host should refrain from performing any forwarding. First, when a host receives a datagram intended for some other machine, something has gone wrong with internet addressing, forwarding, or delivery. The problem may not be revealed if the host takes corrective action by forwarding the datagram. Second, forwarding will cause unnecessary network traffic (and may steal CPU time from legitimate uses of the host). Third, simple errors can cause chaos. Suppose that hosts are permitted to forward traffic, and imagine what happens if a computer accidentally broadcasts a datagram that is destined for a host, *H*. Because it has been broadcast, a copy of the datagram will be delivered to every host on the network. Each host examines the datagram and forwards the copy to *H*, which will be bombarded with many copies. Fourth, as later chapters show, routers do more than merely forward traffic. The next chapter explains that routers use a special protocol to report errors, while hosts do not (again, to avoid having multiple error reports bombard a source). Routers also propagate information to ensure that their forwarding tables are consistent and correct. If hosts forward datagrams without participating fully in all router protocols, unexpected anomalies can arise.

8.14 Forwarding In The Presence Of Broadcast And Multicast

Determining whether an IP datagram has reached its final destination is not quite as trivial as described above. We said that when a datagram arrives, the receiving machine must compare the destination address in the datagram to the IP address of each network interface. Of course, if the destination matches, the machine keeps the datagram and processes it. However, a machine must also handle datagrams that are broadcast (IPv4) or multicast (IPv4 and IPv6) across one of the networks to which the machine attaches. If the machine is participating in the multicast group† or an IPv4 datagram has been broadcast across a local network, a copy of the datagram must be passed to the local protocol stack for processing. A router may also need to forward a copy on one or more of the other networks. For IPv4, directed broadcast introduces several possibilities. If a directed broadcast is addressed to a network N and the datagram arrives over network N, a router only needs to keep a copy for the local protocol stack. However, if a directed broadcast for network N arrives over another network, the router must keep a copy and also broadcast a copy over network N.

†Chapter 15 describes IP multicast.

8.15 Software Routers And Sequential Lookup

Our description of the forwarding algorithm implies that IP searches a forwarding table sequentially. For low-end routers, sequential search is indeed used. Low-end routers are often called *software routers* to emphasize that the router does not have special-purpose hardware to assist in forwarding. Instead, a software router consists of a general-purpose computer with a processor, memory, and network interface cards. All the IP forwarding is performed by software.

Software routers can use sequential table search because the tables are small. For example, consider a typical host. We expect the forwarding table to contain two entries as Figure 8.3 illustrates. In such a situation, sequential search works fine. In fact, more sophisticated search techniques only pay off for larger tables — the overhead of starting a search means that sequential lookup wins for small tables.

Despite being useful in software routers, sequential search does not suffice for all cases. A high-end router near the center of the IPv4 Internet has approximately 400,000 entries in its forwarding table. In such cases, sequential table search takes too long. The most common data structure used for high-end forwarding tables consists of a *trie*†. It is not important to know the details of a trie data structure and the lookup algorithm used to search a trie, but we should be aware that high-end routers use more sophisticated mechanisms than the ones described in this chapter.

8.16 Establishing Forwarding Tables

We have discussed the IP forwarding algorithm and described how forwarding uses a table. However, we have not specified how hosts or routers initialize their forwarding tables, nor have we described how the contents of forwarding tables are updated as the network changes. Later chapters deal with the questions and discuss protocols that allow routers to keep forwarding tables consistent. For now, it is important to understand that IP software uses a forwarding table whenever it decides how to forward a datagram. The consequence is that changing the values in a forwarding table will change the paths that datagrams follow.

8.17 Summary

IP software forwards datagrams; the computation consists of using the destination IP address and forwarding information. Direct delivery is possible if the destination machine lies on a network to which the sending machine attaches. If the sender cannot reach the destination directly, the sender must forward the datagram to a router. The general paradigm is that hosts send an indirectly forwarded datagram to the nearest router; the datagram travels through the internet from router to router until the last router along the path can deliver the datagram directly to the ultimate destination.

†Pronounced "try."

IP keeps information needed for forwarding in a table known as a forwarding table. When IP forwards a datagram, the forwarding algorithm produces the IP address of the next machine (i.e., the address of the next hop) to which the datagram should be sent. IP passes the datagram and next-hop address to network interface software. The interface software encapsulates the datagram in a network frame, maps the next-hop internet address to a hardware address, uses the hardware address as the frame destination, and sends the frame across the underlying hardware network.

Internet forwarding only uses IP addresses; the binding between an IP address and a hardware address is not part of the IP forwarding function. Because each forwarding table entry includes an address mask, a single unified forwarding algorithm can handle network-specific routes, host-specific routes, and a default route.

EXERCISES

8.1 Create forwarding tables for all the routers in Figure 8.2. Which router or routers will benefit most from using a default route?

8.2 Examine the forwarding algorithm used on your local operating system. Are all forwarding cases mentioned in the chapter covered? Does the algorithm allow entries that are not described in the chapter?

8.3 When does a router modify the *hop limit* (or *time-to-live*) field in a datagram header?

8.4 Consider a machine with two physical network connections and two IP addresses I_1 and I_2. Is it possible for that machine to receive a datagram destined for I_2 over the network with address I_1? Explain.

8.5 In the above exercise, what is the appropriate response if such a situation arises?

8.6 Consider two hosts, *A* and *B*, that both attach to a common physical network, *N*. What happens if another host on the network sends *A* a datagram that has IP destination *B*?

8.7 Modify Algorithm 8.1 to accommodate the IPv4 source route options discussed in Chapter 7.

8.8 When it forwards a datagram, a router performs a computation that takes time proportional to the length of the datagram header. Explain the computation.

8.9 In the above question, can you find an optimization that performs the computation in a few machine instructions?

8.10 A network administrator wants to monitor traffic destined for host *H*, and has purchased a router *R* with monitoring software. The manager only wants traffic destined for *H* to pass through *R*. Explain how to arrange forwarding to satisfy the manager.

8.11 Does Algorithm 8.1 allow a manager to specify forwarding for a multicast address? Explain.

8.12 Does Algorithm 8.1 apply to fragments or only to complete datagrams? Explain.

Chapter Contents

9

Internet Protocol: Error And Control Messages (ICMP)

9.1 Introduction

The previous chapter describes IP as a best-effort mechanism that makes an attempt to deliver datagrams but does not guarantee delivery. The chapter shows how the Internet Protocol arranges for each router to forward datagrams toward their destination. A datagram travels through an internet from router to router until it reaches a router that can deliver the datagram directly to its final destination. Best effort means that IP does not discard datagrams capriciously. If a router does not know how to forward a datagram, cannot contact the destination host when delivering a datagram, or the router detects an unusual condition that affects its ability to transfer the datagram (e.g., network failure), the router informs the original source about the problem. This chapter discusses the mechanism that routers and hosts use to communicate such control or error information. We will see that routers use the mechanism to report problems and hosts use the mechanism to find neighbors and to test whether destinations are reachable.

9.2 The Internet Control Message Protocol

In the connectionless system we have described so far, each router operates autonomously. When a datagram arrives, a router forwards or delivers the datagram and then goes on to the next datagram; the router does not coordinate with the original sender of a datagram. Such a system works well if all hosts and routers have been configured correctly because they agree on routes to each destination. Unfortunately, no large communication system works correctly all the time. Besides failures of network and processor hardware, IP cannot deliver a datagram if the destination machine is temporarily or permanently disconnected from the network, if the hop limit expires before a datagram reaches its destination, or if an intermediate router becomes so overloaded that it must discard a datagram. The important difference between having a single network implemented with homogeneous, dedicated hardware and an internet implemented with multiple, independent systems is that in the former, the designer can arrange for the underlying hardware to inform attached hosts when problems arise. In an internet, which has no such hardware mechanism, a sender cannot tell whether a delivery failure resulted from a malfunction of the local network or a failure of a system somewhere along the path to a destination. Debugging in such an environment becomes extremely difficult. The IP protocol itself contains nothing to help the sender test connectivity or learn about failures. Although we said that IP is unreliable, we want our internet to detect and recover from errors whenever possible. Therefore, an additional mechanism is needed.

To allow routers in an internet to report errors or provide information about unexpected circumstances, the designers added a special-purpose mechanism to the TCP/IP protocols. Known as the *Internet Control Message Protocol* (*ICMP*), the mechanism is considered a required part of IP and must be included in every IP implementation†.

ICMP is primarily intended to inform a source when a datagram sent by the source experiences problems. However, the ultimate destination of an ICMP message is not an application program running on the source computer or the user who launched the application. Instead, ICMP messages are sent to Internet Protocol software on the source computer. That is, when an ICMP error message arrives on a computer, the ICMP software module on the computer handles the message. Of course, ICMP may take further action in response to the incoming message. For example, ICMP might inform an application or a higher-level protocol about an incoming message. We can summarize:

> *The Internet Control Message Protocol allows routers to send error or control messages back to the source of a datagram that caused a problem. ICMP messages are not usually delivered to applications. We think of ICMP as providing communication between an ICMP module on one machine and an ICMP module on another.*

ICMP was initially designed to allow routers to report the cause of delivery errors to hosts, but ICMP is not restricted exclusively to routers. Although guidelines specify that some ICMP messages should only be sent by routers, an arbitrary machine can send an ICMP message to any other machine. Thus, a host can use ICMP to correspond with a router or another host. The chief advantage of allowing hosts to use ICMP is that it provides a single mechanism used for all control and information messages.

†When referring specifically to the version of ICMP that accompanies IPv4, we will write *ICMPv4*, and when referring to the version that accompanies IPv6, we will write *ICMPv6*.

9.3 Error Reporting Vs. Error Correction

Technically, ICMP is an *error reporting mechanism.* It provides a way for routers that encounter an error to report the error to the original source, but ICMP does not interact with the host nor does ICMP attempt to correct the error. The idea of reporting problems rather than working to correct problems arises from the fundamental design principle discussed earlier: routers are to be as stateless as possible. We note that the idea of error reporting rather than error correction helps improve security. If a router tried to maintain state when an error occurred, an attacker could simply flood the router with incorrect packets and either not respond or respond very slowly when the router attempted to correct the problem. Such an attack could exhaust router resources. Thus, the idea of only reporting errors can prevent certain security attacks.

Although the protocol specification outlines intended uses of ICMP and suggests possible actions to take in response to error reports, ICMP does not fully specify the action to be taken for each possible error. Thus, hosts have flexibility in how they relate error reports to applications. In short:

> *When a datagram causes an error, ICMP can only report the error condition back to the original source of the datagram; the source must relate the error to an individual application program or take other action to correct the problem.*

Most errors stem from the original source, but some do not. Because ICMP reports problems to the original source, it cannot be used to inform intermediate routers about problems. For example, suppose a datagram follows a path through a sequence of routers, R_1, R_2, ..., R_k. If R_k has incorrect routing information and mistakenly forwards the datagram to router R_E, R_E cannot use ICMP to report the error back to router R_k; ICMP can only send a report back to the original source. Unfortunately, the original source has no responsibility for the problem and cannot control the misbehaving router. In fact, the source may not be able to determine which router caused the problem.

Why restrict ICMP to communication with the original source? The answer should be clear from our discussion of datagram formats and forwarding in the previous chapters. A datagram only contains fields that specify the original source and the ultimate destination; it does not contain a complete record of its trip through the internet (except for unusual cases when the record route option is used). Furthermore, because routers can establish and change their own routing tables, there is no global knowledge of routes. Thus, when a datagram reaches a given router, it is impossible to know the path it has taken to arrive. If the router detects a problem, IP cannot know the set of intermediate machines that processed the datagram, so it cannot inform them of the problem. Instead of silently discarding the datagram, the router uses ICMP to inform the original source that a problem has occurred, and trusts that host administrators will cooperate with network administrators to locate and repair the problem.

9.4 ICMP Message Delivery

The designers of ICMP took a novel approach to error reporting: instead of using a lower-level communications system to handle errors, they chose to use IP to carry ICMP messages. That is, like all other traffic, ICMP messages travel across the internet in the payload area of IP datagrams. The choice reflects an important assumption: errors are rare. In particular, we assume that datagram forwarding will remain intact at most times (i.e., error messages will be delivered). In practice, the assumption has turned out to be valid — errors are indeed rare.

Because each ICMP message travels in an IP datagram, two levels of encapsulation are required. Figure 9.1 illustrates the concept.

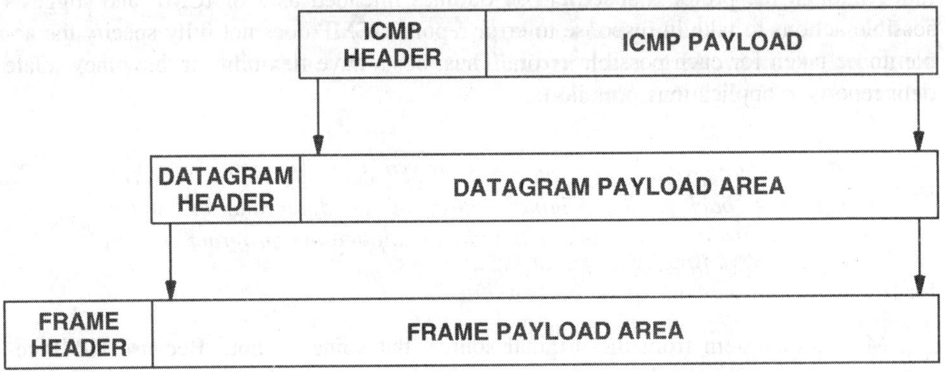

Figure 9.1 The two levels of encapsulation used when an ICMP message is sent across a network.

As the figure shows, each ICMP message travels across an internet in the payload portion of an IP datagram, which itself travels across an underlying network in the payload portion of a frame. Although both IPv4 and IPv6 use a datagram to carry an ICMP message, the details differ. IPv4 uses the *PROTOCOL* field in the datagram header as a type field. When an ICMP message is carried in the payload area of an IPv4 datagram, the *PROTOCOL* field is set to 1. IPv6 uses the *NEXT HEADER* field to specify the type of the item being carried. When an ICMP message is carried in the payload area of an IPv6 datagram, the *NEXT HEADER* field of the header that is previous to the ICMP message contains 58.

In terms of processing, a datagram that carries an ICMP message is forwarded exactly like a datagram that carries information for users; there is no additional reliability or priority. Thus, error messages themselves may be lost, duplicated, or discarded. Furthermore, in an already congested network, the error message may increase congestion. An exception is made to the error handling procedures if an IP datagram carrying an ICMP message causes an error. The exception, established to avoid the problem of having error messages about error messages, specifies that ICMP messages are not generated for errors that result from datagrams carrying ICMP error messages.

9.5 Conceptual Layering

Usually, encapsulation and layering go hand-in-hand. For example, consider IP and Ethernet. When it travels across an Ethernet, an IP datagram is encapsulated in an Ethernet frame. The encapsulation follows the layering scheme presented in Chapter 4 because IP is a Layer 3 protocol and Ethernet is a Layer 2 technology. The Ethernet type field allows a variety of higher-layer packets to be encapsulated in Ethernet frames with no ambiguity.

ICMP represents an important exception. Although each ICMP message is encapsulated in an IP datagram, ICMP is not considered a higher-level protocol. Instead, ICMP is a required part of IP, which means ICMP is classified as a Layer 3 protocol. We can think of the encapsulation as using the existing IP-based forwarding scheme rather than creating a parallel forwarding mechanism for ICMP messages. ICMP must send error reports to the original source, so an ICMP message must travel across multiple underlying networks to reach its final destination. Thus, ICMP messages cannot be delivered by a Layer 2 transport alone.

9.6 ICMP Message Format

The standards define two sets of ICMP messages: a set for IPv4 and a larger set for IPv6. In both versions of IP, each ICMP message has its own format. However, all ICMP messages begin with the same three fields. Figure 9.2 illustrates the general format of an ICMP message.

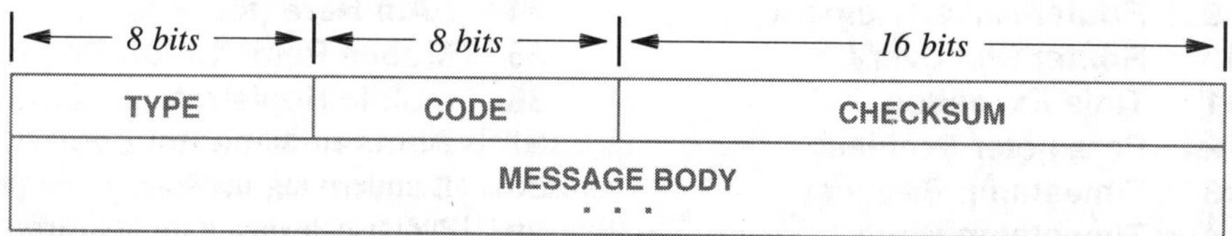

Figure 9.2 The first three fields in each ICMP message.

As the figure shows, an ICMP message begins with an 8-bit integer ICMP message *TYPE* field. The *TYPE* field identifies the specific ICMP message that follows. Because the format of a message is defined by the message type, a receiver uses the value in the *TYPE* field to know how to parse the remainder of the message.

An 8-bit *CODE* field in an ICMP message provides further information about the message type. For example, an ICMP *TIME EXCEEDED* message can have a code value to indicate that the hop count (TTL) of the datagram reached zero or that reassembly timed out before all fragments arrived.

The third field in each ICMP message consists of a 16-bit *CHECKSUM* that is computed over the entire ICMP message. ICMP uses the same 16-bit one's complement checksum as IP.

The message body in an ICMP message depends entirely on the ICMP type. However, for ICMP messages that report an error, the message body always includes the header plus additional octets from the datagram that caused the problem†.

The reason ICMP returns more than the datagram header alone is to allow the receiver to determine more precisely which protocol(s) and which application program were responsible for the datagram. As we will see later, higher-level protocols in the TCP/IP suite are designed so that crucial information is encoded in the first few octets beyond the IP header‡.

9.7 Example ICMP Message Types Used With IPv4 And IPv6

Figure 9.3 lists example ICMP message types used with IPv4. Later sections describe the meanings in more detail and give examples of message formats.

Type	Meaning	Type	Meaning
0	Echo Reply	17	Address Mask Request
3	Destination Unreachable	18	Address Mask Reply
4	Source Quench	30	Traceroute
5	Redirect (change a route)	31	Datagram Conversion Error
6	Alternate Host Address	32	Mobile Host Redirect
8	Echo Request	33	Where-Are-You (for IPv6)
9	Router Advertisement	34	I-Am-Here (for IPv6)
10	Router Discovery	35	Mobile Registration Request
11	Time Exceeded	36	Mobile Registration Reply
12	Parameter Problem	37	Domain Name Request
13	Timestamp Request	38	Domain Name Reply
14	Timestamp Reply	39	SKIP (Simple Key Mgmt)
15	Information Request	40	Photuris
16	Information Reply	41	Experimental Mobility

Figure 9.3 Example ICMPv4 message types and the meaning of each. Values not listed are unassigned or reserved.

As the figure shows, many of the original ICMP messages were designed to carry information rather than error messages (e.g., a host uses type 17 to request the address mask being used on a network and a router responds with type 18 to report the address mask). IPv6 distinguishes between error messages and informational messages by dividing the type values into two sets: types less than 128 are used for error messages, and types between 128 and 255 are used for information message. Figure 9.4 lists ex-

†ICMP only returns part of the datagram that caused the problem to avoid having ICMP messages fragmented.

‡Both TCP and UDP store protocol port numbers in the first 32 bits.

ample ICMP message types used with IPv6 and shows that although only four error messages have been defined, IPv6 defines many informational messages.

Type	Meaning	Type	Meaning
1	Destination Unreachable	138	Router Renumbering
2	Packet Too Big	139	ICMP Node Info. Query
3	Time Exceeded	140	ICMP Node Info. Response
4	Parameter Problem	141	Inverse Neighbor Solicitation
128	Echo Request	142	Inverse Neighbor Advertise.
129	Echo Reply	143	Multicast Listener Reports
130	Multicast Listener Query	144	Home Agent Request
131	Multicast Listener Report	145	Home Agent Reply
132	Multicast Listener Done	146	Mobile Prefix Solicitation
133	Router Solicitation (NDP)	147	Mobile Prefix Advertisement
134	Router Advertise. (NDP)	148	Certification Path Solicitation
135	Neighbor Solicitation (NDP)	149	Certification Path Advertise.
136	Neighbor Advertise. (NDP)	151	Multicast Router Advertise.
137	Redirect Message		

Figure 9.4 Example ICMPv6 message types and the meaning of each.

As the figure shows, IPv6 incorporates three major subsystems into ICMP: the *Neighbor Discovery Protocol* mentioned in Chapter 6, Multicast support described in Chapter 15, and IP mobility described in Chapter 18. ICMP messages have been defined for each of the subsystems. For example, when using Neighbor Discovery, an IPv6 node can broadcast a *Neighbor Solicitation Message* (type 135) to discover directly-reachable neighbors or a *Router Solicitation Message* (type 133) to discover directly-reachable routers.

9.8 Testing Destination Reachability And Status (Ping)

The *ping*† program is perhaps the most widely used internet diagnostic tool. Originally created for IPv4, ping has been extended to accommodate IPv6. In either case, ping sends an ICMP *Echo Request* message to a remote computer. Any computer that receives an ICMP Echo Request creates an ICMP *Echo Reply* and returns the reply to the original sender. Thus, the ping program receives an the Echo Reply from the remote machine. The request message contains an optional section for data, and the reply contains a copy of the data that was sent in the request.

How can a simple message exchange help diagnose internet problems? When sending an echo request, a user must specify a destination. The straightforward answer is that an echo request and associated reply can be used to test whether a destination is reachable and responding. Because both the request and reply travel in IP datagrams,

†Dave Mills once suggested that *PING* is an acronym for *Packet InterNet Groper*.

receiving a reply from a remote machine verifies that major pieces of the IP transport system are working correctly. First, IP software on the source computer must have an entry in its forwarding table for the destination. Second, the source computer has created a correct datagram. Third, the source was able to reach a router, which means ARP (IPv4) or Neighbor Discovery (IPv6) is working. Third, intermediate routers between the source and destination must be operating, and must forward datagrams correctly in both directions between the source and destination. Finally, the destination machine must be running, the device driver must be able to receive and send packets, and both ICMP and IP software modules must be working.

Several versions of ping exist. Most include options that allow a user to specify whether to send a request and wait for a reply, send several requests and then wait for a reply, or send requests periodically (e.g., every second) and display all replies. If ping sends a series of requests, it displays statistics about message loss. The advantage of sending a continuous series of requests arises from an ability to discover intermittent problems. For example, consider a wireless network where electrical interference causes loss but the interference occurs randomly (e.g., when a printer starts).

Most versions of ping also allow a user to specify the amount of data being sent in each request. Sending a large ping packet is useful for testing fragmentation and reassembly. Large packets also force IPv6 to engage in path MTU discovery. Thus, a seemingly trivial application has several uses.

9.9 Echo Request And Reply Message Format

Both IPv4 and IPv6 use a single format for all ICMP Echo Request and Echo Reply messages. Figure 9.5 illustrates the message format.

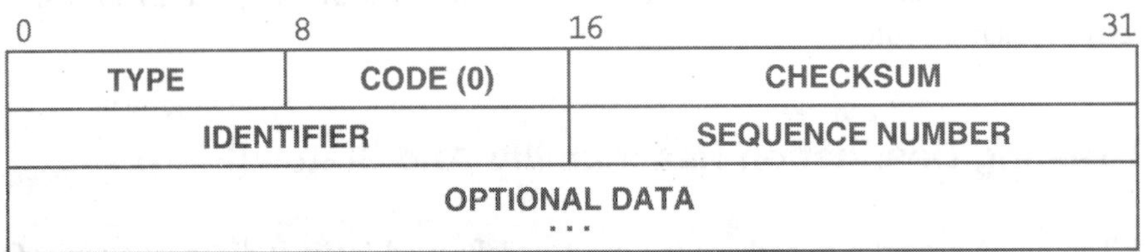

Figure 9.5 ICMP echo request or reply message format.

Although the same message format is used for echo requests and replies, the value of the *TYPE* differs. For IPv4, the *TYPE* is *8* in a request and *0* in a reply. For IPv6, the *TYPE* is *128* in a request and *129* in a reply. For any value in the *TYPE* field, the *CODE* is zero (i.e., echo requests and replies do not use the code field).

Fields *IDENTIFIER* and *SEQUENCE NUMBER* are used by the sender to match replies to requests. A receiving ICMP does not interpret the two fields, but does return the same values in the reply that were found in the request. Therefore, a machine that sends a request can set the *IDENTIFIER* field to a value that identifies an application, and can use the *SEQUENCE NUMBER* field to number successive requests sent by the application. For example, the *IDENTIFIER* might be the process ID of the sending application, which allows ICMP software to match incoming replies with the application that sent a request.

The field labeled *OPTIONAL DATA* is a variable length field that contains data to be returned to the sender. An echo reply always returns exactly the same data as was received in the request. Although arbitrary data can be sent, typical ping programs store sequential values in octets of the data area, making it easy to verify that the data returned is exactly the same as the data sent without needing to store copies of packets. As mentioned above, the variable size allows a manager to test fragmentation.

9.10 Checksum Computation And The IPv6 Pseudo-Header

Both IPv4 and IPv6 use the *CHECKSUM* field in an ICMP message, and both require a sender to compute a 16-bit one's complement checksum of the complete message. Furthermore, both versions require a receiver to validate the checksum and to discard ICMP messages that have an invalid checksum. However, the details of the checksum computation differ because IPv6 adds an additional requirement: the checksum used with IPv6 also covers fields from the IP base header. Conceptually, the designated header fields are arranged into a *pseudo-header* as Figure 9.6 illustrates.

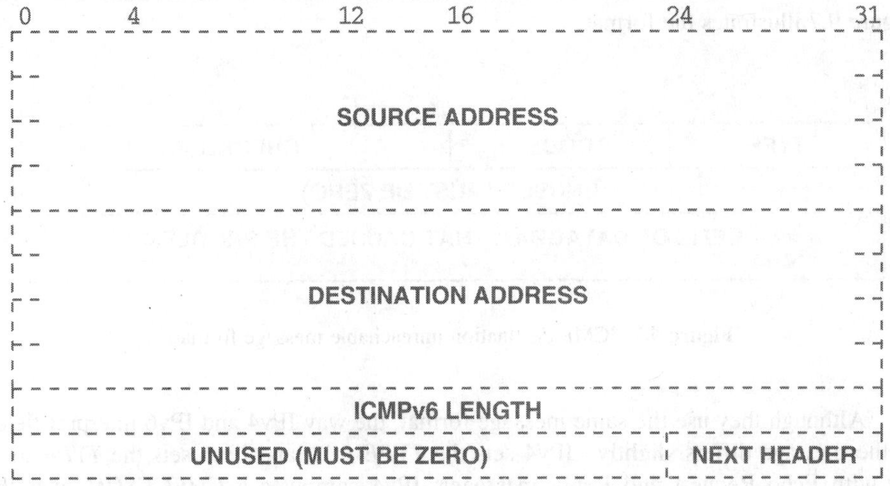

Figure 9.6 The IPv6 pseudo-header used for the checksum computation with ICMPv6.

The term *pseudo-header* and the use of dashed lines in the figure indicate that the arrangement of extra fields is merely used for the checksum computation and is never placed in a packet. We can imagine, for example, that the checksum code creates a pseudo-header in memory by copying fields from the base header, appends a copy of the ICMP message to the pseudo-header, and then computes a checksum across both the pseudo-header and the message†.

Why did IPv6 include a pseudo-header in the checksum? The designers of IPv6 were conscious of possible security weaknesses, and wanted to insure that a computer would not mistakenly process an ICMP message that was not intended for the computer. Including a pseudo-header in the checksum adds an additional verification that the message was delivered properly. The pseudo-header does not guarantee correctness — if stronger security is needed, the datagram must be encrypted.

9.11 Reports Of Unreachable Destinations

Although IP implements a best-effort delivery mechanism, discarding datagrams should not be taken lightly. Whenever an error prevents a router from forwarding or delivering a datagram, the router sends an ICMP *destination unreachable* message back to the source and then *drops* (i.e., discards) the datagram. Network unreachable errors imply forwarding failures at intermediate points; host unreachable errors imply delivery failures across the final hop‡.

Both IPv4 and IPv6 use the same format for destination unreachable messages. Figure 9.7 illustrates the format.

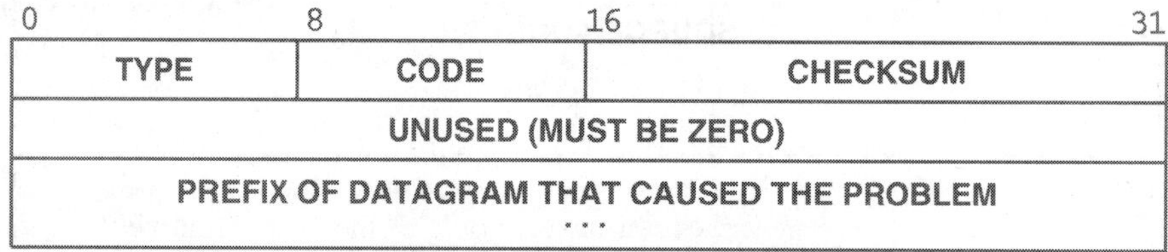

Figure 9.7 ICMP destination unreachable message format.

Although they use the same message format, the way IPv4 and IPv6 interpret fields in the message differs slightly. IPv4 sets the *TYPE* to *3*, and IPv6 sets the *TYPE* to *1*. As with Echo Request and Reply messages, IPv4 computes a *CHECKSUM* over the ICMP message only and IPv6 includes a pseudo-header in the checksum.

The *CODE* field contains an integer that further describes the problem; codes for IPv4 and IPv6 differ. Figure 9.8 lists the meaning of *CODE* values.

†In practice, it is possible to compute a checksum over the pseudo-header fields without copying them.

‡The IETF recommends only reporting host unreachable messages to the original source, and using routing protocols to handle other forwarding problems.

IPv4 interpretation

Code	Meaning	Code	Meaning
0	Network unreachable	8	Source host isolated
1	Host unreachable	9	Comm. with net prohibited
2	Protocol unreachable	10	Comm. with host prohibited
3	Port unreachable	11	Net unreachable for TOS
4	Fragmentation needed	12	Host unreachable for TOS
5	Source route failed	13	Communication prohibited
6	Dest. net unknown	14	Host precedence violation
7	Dest. host unknown	15	Precedence cutoff

IPv6 interpretation

Code	Meaning	Code	Meaning
0	No route to dest.	4	Port unreachable
1	Comm. prohibited	5	Source addr. failed policy
2	Beyond src. scope	6	Reject route to dest.
3	Address unreachable	7	Source route error

Figure 9.8 The CODE values for an ICMP destination unreachable message.

The two versions of IP also differ in the way they select a prefix of the datagram that caused the problem. IPv4 sends the datagram header plus the first 64 bits of the datagram payload. IPv6 allows the datagram carrying the ICMP message to be up to 1280 octets long (the IPv6 minimum MTU), and chooses a maximum prefix size accordingly. Because the ICMP error message contains a short prefix of the datagram that caused the problem, the source will know exactly which address is unreachable.

Destinations may be unreachable because hardware is temporarily out of service, because the sender specified a nonexistent destination address, or (in rare circumstances) because the router does not have a route to the destination network. Note that although routers report failures they encounter, they may not detect all delivery failures. For example, if the destination machine connects to an Ethernet network, the network hardware does not provide acknowledgements. Therefore, a router can continue to send packets to a destination after the destination is powered down without receiving any indication that the packets are not being delivered. To summarize:

> *Although a router sends a destination unreachable message when it encounters a datagram that cannot be forwarded or delivered, a router cannot detect all such errors.*

The meaning of port unreachable messages will become clear when we study how higher-level protocols use abstract destination points called *ports*. Many of the remaining codes are self explanatory. For example, a site may choose to restrict certain incoming or outgoing datagrams for administrative reasons. In IPv6, some addresses are classified as *site-local*, meaning that the address cannot be used on the global Internet. Attempting to send a datagram that has a site-local source address will trigger an error that the datagram has been sent beyond the valid scope of the source address.

9.12 ICMP Error Reports Regarding Fragmentation

Both IPv4 and IPv6 allow a router to report an error when a datagram is too large for a network over which it must travel and cannot be fragmented. However, the details differ. IPv4 sends a *destination unreachable* message with the *CODE* field set to *4* and IPv6 sends a *packet too big* message, which has a *TYPE* field of *2*. It may seem that no fragmentation reports are needed for IPv4 because a router can fragment an IPv4 datagram. Recall that an IPv4 header includes a "do not fragment" bit. When the bit is set, a router is prohibited from performing fragmentation, which causes the router to send an ICMPv4 *destination unreachable* message with *CODE 4*.

The reason IPv6 defines a separate ICMP message to report fragmentation problems arises from the design. Routers are always prohibited from fragmenting an IPv6 datagram, which means a source must perform path MTU discovery. A key part of path MTU discovery involves receiving information about the MTU of remote networks. Therefore, the *packet too big* message contains a field that a router uses to inform the source about the MTU of the network that caused the problem. Figure 9.9 illustrates the message format.

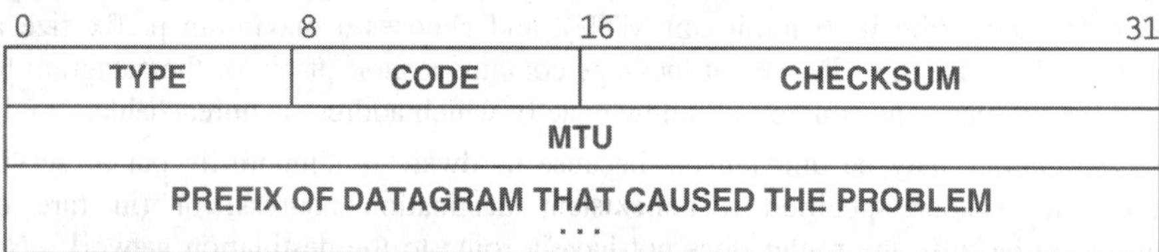

Figure 9.9 The format of an ICMPv6 *packet too big* message.

9.13 Route Change Requests From Routers

Host forwarding tables usually remain static over long periods of time. A host initializes its forwarding table at system startup, and system administrators seldom change the table during normal operation. As we will see in later chapters, routers are more dynamic — they exchange routing information periodically to accommodate network changes and keep their forwarding tables up-to-date. Thus, as a general rule:

Routers are assumed to know correct routes; hosts begin with minimal routing information and learn new routes from routers.

To follow the rule and to avoid sending forwarding information when configuring a host, the initial host configuration usually specifies the minimum possible forwarding information needed to communicate (e.g., the address of a single default router). Thus, a host may begin with incomplete information and rely on routers to update its forwarding table as needed. When a router detects a host using a nonoptimal first hop, the router sends the host an ICMP *redirect* message that instructs the host to change its forwarding table. The router also forwards the original datagram on to its destination.

The advantage of the ICMP redirect scheme is simplicity: a host boots without any need to download a forwarding table and can immediately communicate with any destination. A router only sends a redirect message if the host sends a datagram along a non-preferred route. Thus, the host forwarding table remains small, but will have optimal routes for all destinations in use.

Because they are limited to interactions between a router and a host on a directly connected network, redirect messages do not solve the problem of propagating routing information in a general way. To understand why, consider Figure 9.10 which illustrates a set of networks connected by routers.

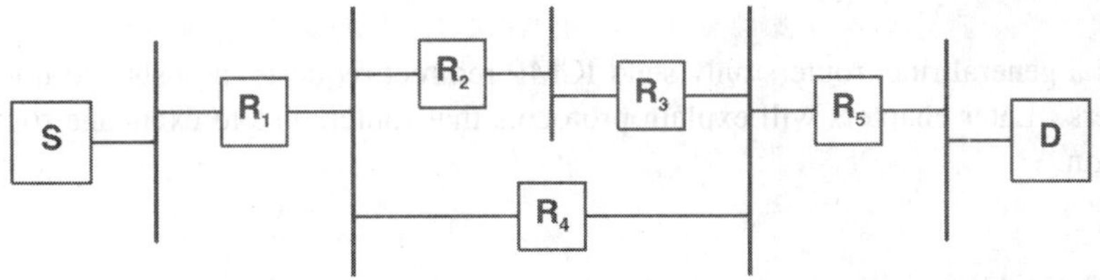

Figure 9.10 Example topology showing why ICMP *redirect* messages do not handle all routing problems.

In the figure, host *S* sends a datagram to destination *D*. If router R_1 incorrectly forwards the datagram through router R_2 instead of through router R_4 (i.e., R_1 incorrectly chooses a longer path than necessary), the datagram will arrive at router R_5. However, R_5 cannot send an ICMP redirect message to R_1 because R_5 does not know R_1's address. Later chapters explore the problem of how to propagate routing information across multiple networks.

As with several other ICMP message types, IPv4 and IPv6 use the same general format for *redirect* messages. The message begins with the requisite *TYPE, CODE*, and *CHECKSUM* fields. The message further contains two pieces of information: the IP address of a router to use as a first hop and the destination address that caused the problem. The message formats differ. An IPv4 redirect message contains the 32-bit IPv4 address of a router followed by the prefix of the datagram that was incorrectly forwarded. An IPv6 redirect message contains the IPv6 address of a router and the IPv6 destination address that should be forwarded through the router. Figure 9.11 illustrates the format used with IPv6.

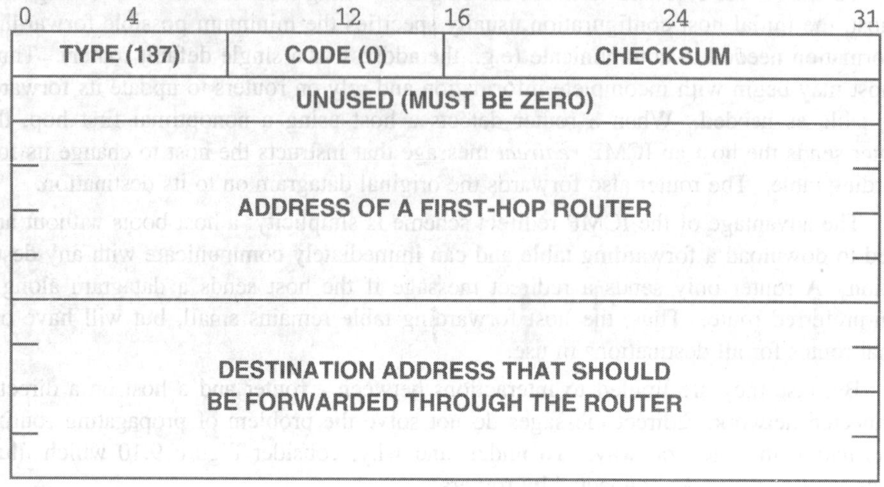

Figure 9.11 The ICMPv6 *redirect* message format.

As a general rule, routers only send ICMP redirect requests to hosts and not to other routers. Later chapters will explain protocols that routers use to exchange routing information.

9.14 Detecting Circular Or Excessively Long Routes

Because internet routers each use local information when forwarding datagrams, errors or inconsistencies in forwarding information can produce a cycle known as a *routing loop* for a given destination, *D*. A routing loop can consist of two routers that each forward a given datagram to the other, or it can consist of multiple routers that each forward a datagram to the next router in the cycle. If a datagram enters a routing loop, it will pass around the loop endlessly. As mentioned previously, to prevent datagrams from circling forever in a TCP/IP internet, each IP datagram contains a *hop limit*. Whenever it processes a datagram, a router decrements the hop limit and discards the datagram when the count reaches zero. A router does not merely discard a datagram that has exceed its hop limit. Instead, a router takes the further action of sending the source an ICMP *time exceeded* message.

Both IPv4 and IPv6 send a *time exceeded* message, and both use the same format as Figure 9.12 illustrates. IPv4 sets the *TYPE* to *11*, and IPv6 sets the *TYPE* to *3*.

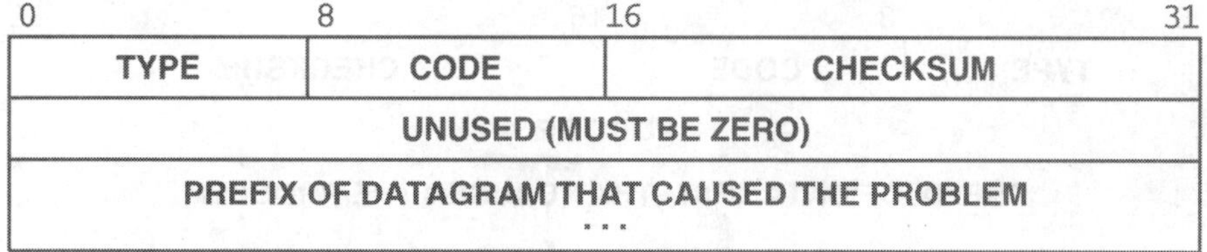

Figure 9.12 ICMP time exceeded message format.

It may seem odd that the message refers to time when the error being reported is a hop limit. The name is derived from IPv4, which originally interpreted the hop limit as a *time to live* (*TTL*) counter. Thus, it made sense to interpret TTL expiration as exceeding a time limit. Although the interpretation of the field has changed, the name persists.

The *time exceeded* message is also used to report another time expiration: timeout during the reassembly of a fragmented datagram. Recall that IP software on a destination host must gather fragments and construct a complete datagram. When a fragment arrives for a new datagram, the host sets a timer. If one or more fragments do not arrive before the timer expires, the fragments are discarded and the receiving host sends an ICMP *time exceeded* message back to the source. ICMP uses the *CODE* field in a *time exceeded* message to explain the nature of the timeout being reported as Figure 9.13 shows.

Code Value	Meaning
0	Hop limit exceeded
1	Fragment reassembly time exceeded

Figure 9.13 Interpretation of the *CODE* field in an ICMP *time exceeded* message. Both IPv4 and IPv6 use the same interpretation.

9.15 Reporting Other Problems

When a router or host finds problems with a datagram not covered by previous ICMP error messages (e.g., an incorrect datagram header), it sends a *parameter problem* message to the original source. In IPv4, a possible cause of such problems occurs when arguments to an option are incorrect. In IPv6, parameter problems can arise if the value in a header field is out of range, the *NEXT HEADER* type is not recognized, or one of the options is not recognized. In such cases, a router sends a *parameter problem* message and uses the *CODE* field to distinguish among subproblems. Figure 9.14 illustrates the format of a *parameter problem* message. Such messages are only sent when a problem is so severe that the datagram must be discarded.

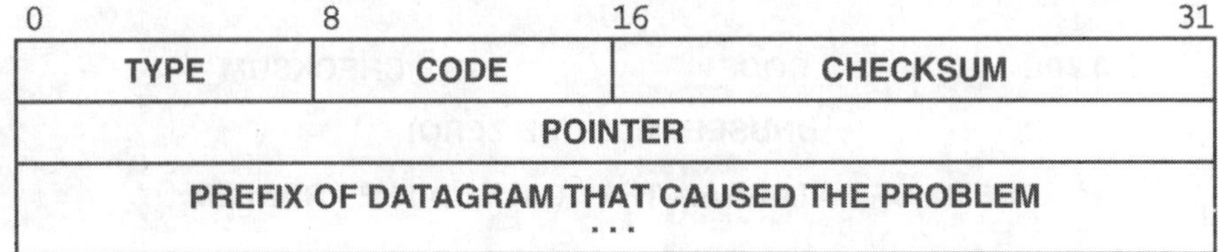

Figure 9.14 ICMP parameter problem message format.

To make the message unambiguous, the sender uses the *POINTER* field in the message header to identify the octet in the datagram that caused the problem.

9.16 Older ICMP Messages Used At Startup

Originally, ICMP defined a set of messages that a host used at startup to determine its IP address, the address of a router, and the address mask used on the network. Eventually, a protocol known as *DHCP*† was introduced that provides an IPv4 host with all the necessary information in a single exchange. In addition, ICMP defined messages that a host or router could use to obtain the current time. Protocols to exchange time information have also been devised, making the ICMP version obsolete. As a consequence, IPv4 no longer uses ICMP messages that were designed to obtain information at startup.

Interestingly, ICMPv6 has returned to one of the ideas that was originally part of ICMPv4: router discovery. At startup, an IPv6 host multicasts an ICMPv6 *Router Discovery* message to learn about routers on the local network. There are two conceptual differences between router discovery and DHCP that make it attractive for IPv6. First, because the information is obtained directly from the router itself, there is never a third-party error. With DHCP, such errors are possible because a DHCP server must be configured with information to hand out. If a network manager fails to update the DHCP configuration after a network changes, hosts may be given out-of-date information. Second, ICMP router discovery uses a *soft state* technique with timers to prevent hosts from retaining a forwarding table entry after a router crashes — routers advertise their information periodically, and a host discards a route if the timer for the route expires.

9.17 Summary

The Internet Control Message Protocol is a required and integral part of IP that is used to report errors and to send control information. In most cases, ICMP error messages originate from a router in the Internet. An ICMP message always goes back to the original source of the datagram that caused the error.

†Chapter 22 examines DHCP as well as the protocols IPv6 uses at startup.

ICMP includes *destination unreachable* messages that report when a datagram cannot be forwarded to its destination, *packet too big* messages that specify a datagram cannot fit in the MTU of a network, *redirect* messages that request a host to change the first-hop in its forwarding table, *time exceeded* messages that report when a hop limit expires or reassembly times out, and *parameter problem* messages for other header problems. In addition, ICMP *echo request/reply* messages can be used to test whether a destination is reachable. A set of older ICMPv4 messages that were intended to supply information to a host that booted are no longer used.

An ICMP message travels in the data area of an IP datagram and has three fixed-length fields at the beginning of the message: an ICMP message *type* field, a *code* field, and an ICMP *checksum* field. The message type determines the format of the rest of the message as well as its meaning.

EXERCISES

9.1 Devise an experiment to record how many of each ICMP message type arrive at your host during a day.

9.2 Examine the *ping* application on your computer. Try using *ping* with an IPv4 network broadcast address or an IPv6 *All Nodes* address. How many computers answer? Read the protocol documents to determine whether answering a broadcast request is required, recommended, not recommended, or prohibited.

9.3 Explain how a *traceroute* application can use ICMP.

9.4 Should a router give ICMP messages priority over normal traffic? Why or why not?

9.5 Consider an Ethernet that has one conventional host, *H*, and 12 routers connected to it. Find a single (slightly illegal) frame carrying an IP packet that when sent by host *H* causes *H* to receive exactly 24 packets.

9.6 There is no ICMP message that allows a machine to inform the source that transmission errors are causing datagrams to arrive with an incorrect checksum. Explain why.

9.7 In the previous question, under what circumstances might such a message be useful?

9.8 Should ICMP error messages contain a timestamp that specifies when they are sent? Why or why not?

9.9 If routers at your site participate in ICMP router discovery, find out how many addresses each router advertises on each interface.

9.10 Try to reach a server on a nonexistent host on your local network. Also try to communicate with a nonexistent host on a remote network. In which case(s) do you receive an ICMP error message, and which message(s) do you receive? Why?

Chapter Contents

10

User Datagram Protocol (UDP)

10.1 Introduction

Previous chapters describe an abstract internet capable of transferring IP datagrams among host computers, where each datagram is forwarded through the internet based on the destination's IP address. At the internet layer, a destination address identifies a host computer; no further distinction is made regarding which user or which application on the computer will receive the datagram. This chapter extends the TCP/IP protocol suite by adding a mechanism that distinguishes among destinations within a given host, allowing multiple application programs executing on a given computer to send and receive datagrams independently.

10.2 Using A Protocol Port As An Ultimate Destination

The operating systems in most computers permit multiple applications to execute simultaneously. Using operating system jargon, we refer to each executing application as a *process*. It may seem natural to say that an application is the ultimate destination for a message. However, specifying a particular process on a particular machine as the ultimate destination for a datagram is somewhat misleading. First, because a process is created whenever an application is launched and destroyed when the application exits, a sender seldom has enough knowledge about which process on a remote machine is running a given application. Second, we would like a scheme that allows TCP/IP to be used on an arbitrary operating system, and the mechanisms used to identify a process vary among operating systems. Third, rebooting a computer can change the process associated with each application, but senders should not be required to know about such changes. Fourth, we seek a mechanism that can identify a service the computer offers without knowing how the service is implemented (e.g., to allow a sender to contact a web server without knowing which process on the destination machine implements the server function).

Instead of thinking of a running application as the ultimate destination, we will imagine that each machine contains a set of abstract destination points called *protocol ports*. Each protocol port is identified by a positive integer. The local operating system provides an interface mechanism that processes use to specify a port or access it.

Most operating systems provide synchronous access to ports. From an application's point of view, synchronous access means the computation stops when the application accesses the port. For example, if an application attempts to extract data from a port before any data arrives, the operating system temporarily stops (blocks) the application until data arrives. Once the data arrives, the operating system passes the data to the application and restarts execution. In general, ports are *buffered* — if data arrives before an application is ready to accept the data, the protocol software will hold the data so it will not be lost. To achieve buffering, the protocol software located inside the operating system places packets that arrive for a particular protocol port in a (finite) queue until the application extracts them.

To communicate with a remote port, a sender needs to know both the IP address of the destination machine and a protocol port number within that machine. Each message carries two protocol port numbers: a *destination port* number specifies a port on the destination computer to which the message has been sent, and a *source port* number specifies a port on the sending machine from which the message has been sent. Because a message contains the port number the sending application has used, the application on the destination machine has enough information to generate a reply and forward the reply back to the sender.

10.3 The User Datagram Protocol

In the TCP/IP protocol suite, the *User Datagram Protocol* (*UDP*) provides the primary mechanism that application programs use to send datagrams to other application programs. UDP messages contain protocol port numbers that are used to distinguish among multiple applications executing on a single computer. That is, in addition to the data sent, each UDP message contains both a destination port number and a source port number, making it possible for the UDP software at the destination to deliver an incoming message to the correct recipient and for the recipient to send a reply.

UDP uses the underlying Internet Protocol to transport a message from one machine to another. Surprisingly, UDP provides applications with the same best-effort, connectionless datagram delivery semantics as IP. That is, UDP does not guarantee that messages arrive, does not guarantee messages arrive in the same order they are sent, and does not provide any mechanisms to control the rate at which information flows between a pair of communicating hosts. Thus, UDP messages can be lost, duplicated, or arrive out of order. Furthermore, packets can arrive faster than the recipient can process them. We can summarize:

> *The User Datagram Protocol (UDP) provides an unreliable, best-effort, connectionless delivery service using IP to transport messages between machines. UDP uses IP to carry messages, but adds the ability to distinguish among multiple destinations within a given host computer.*

An important consequence arises from UDP semantics: an application that uses UDP must take full responsibility for handling the problems of reliability, including message loss, duplication, delay, out-of-order delivery, and loss of connectivity. Unfortunately, application programmers sometimes choose UDP without understanding the liability. Moreover, because network software is usually tested across Local Area Networks that have high reliability, high capacity, low delay, and no packet loss, testing may not expose potential failures. Thus, applications that rely on UDP that work well in a local environment can fail in dramatic ways when used across the global Internet.

10.4 UDP Message Format

We use the term *user datagram* to describe a UDP message; the emphasis on *user* is meant to distinguish UDP datagrams from IP datagrams. Conceptually, a user datagram consists of two parts: a header that contains meta-information, such as source and destination protocol port numbers, and a payload area that contains the data being sent. Figure 10.1 illustrates the organization.

Figure 10.1 The conceptual organization of a UDP message.

The header on a user datagram is extremely small: it consists of four fields that specify the protocol port from which the message was sent, the protocol port to which the message is destined, the message length, and a UDP checksum. Each field is sixteen bits long, which means the entire header occupies a total of only eight octets. Figure 10.2 illustrates the header format.

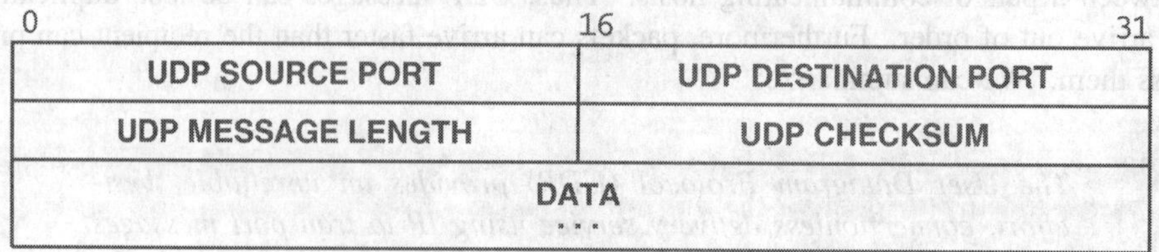

Figure 10.2 The format of fields in a UDP datagram.

The *UDP SOURCE PORT* field contains a 16-bit protocol port number used by the sending application, and the *UDP DESTINATION PORT* field contains the 16-bit UDP protocol port number of the receiving application. In essence, protocol software uses the port numbers to demultiplex datagrams among the applications waiting to receive them. Interestingly, the *UDP SOURCE PORT* is optional. We think of it as identifying the port to which a reply should be sent. In a one-way transfer where the receiver does not send a reply, the source port is not needed and can be set to zero.

The *UDP MESSAGE LENGTH* field contains a count of octets in the UDP datagram, including the UDP header and the user data. Thus, the minimum value is eight, the length of the header alone. The *UDP MESSAGE LENGTH* field consists of sixteen bits, which means the maximum value that can be represented is 65,535. As a practical matter, however, we will see that a UDP message must fit into the payload area of an IP datagram. Therefore, the maximum size permitted depends on the size of the IP header(s), which are considerably larger in an IPv6 datagram than in an IPv4 datagram.

10.5 Interpretation Of the UDP Checksum

IPv4 and IPv6 differ in their interpretation of the *UDP CHECKSUM* field. For IPv6, the UDP checksum is required. For IPv4, the UDP checksum is optional and need not be used at all; a value of zero in the *CHECKSUM* field means that no checksum has been computed (i.e., a receiver should not verify the checksum). The IPv4 designers chose to make the checksum optional to allow implementations to operate with little computational overhead when using UDP across a highly reliable local area network. Recall, however, that IP does not compute a checksum on the data portion of an IP datagram. Thus, the UDP checksum provides the only way to guarantee that data has arrived intact and should be used†.

Beginners often wonder what happens to UDP messages for which the computed checksum is zero. A computed value of zero is possible because UDP uses the same checksum algorithm as IP: it divides the data into 16-bit quantities and computes the one's complement of their one's complement sum. Surprisingly, zero is not a problem because one's complement arithmetic has two representations for zero: all bits set to zero or all bits set to one. When the computed checksum is zero, UDP uses the representation with all bits set to one.

†The author once experienced a problem in which a file copied across an Ethernet was corrupted because the Ethernet NIC had failed and the application (NFS) used UDP without checksums.

10.6 UDP Checksum Computation And The Pseudo-Header

The UDP checksum covers more information than is present in the UDP datagram alone. Information is extracted from the IP header and the checksum covers the extra information as well as the UDP header and UDP payload. As with ICMPv6, we use the term *pseudo-header* to refer to the extra information. We can imagine that the UDP checksum software extracts the pseudo-header fields, places them in memory, appends a copy of the UDP message, and computes a checksum over the entire object.

It is important to understand that a pseudo-header is only used for the checksum computation. It is not part of the UDP message, is not placed in a packet, and is never sent over a network. To emphasize the difference between a pseudo-header and other header formats shown throughout the text, we use dashed lines in figures that illustrate a pseudo-header.

The purpose of using a pseudo-header is to verify that a UDP datagram has reached its correct destination. The key to understanding the pseudo-header lies in realizing that the correct destination consists of a specific machine and a specific protocol port within that machine. The UDP header itself specifies only the protocol port number. Thus, to verify the destination, UDP includes the destination IP address in the checksum as well as the UDP header. At the ultimate destination, UDP software verifies the checksum using the destination IP address obtained from the header of the IP datagram that carried the UDP message. If the checksums agree, then it must be true that the datagram has reached the intended destination host as well as the correct protocol port within that host.

10.7 IPv4 UDP Pseudo-Header Format

The pseudo-header used in the UDP checksum computation for IPv4 consists of 12 octets of data arranged as Figure 10.3 illustrates.

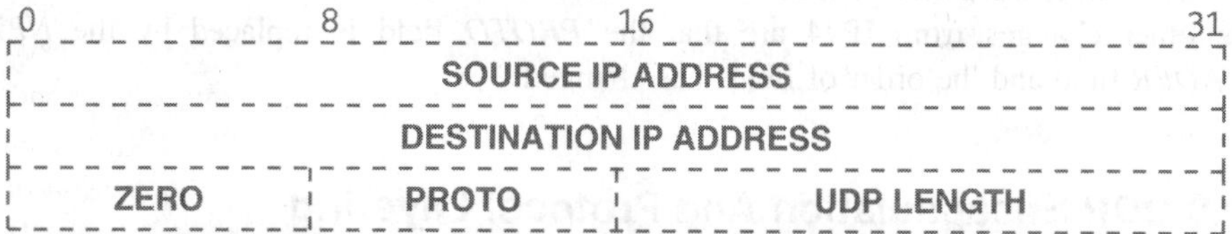

Figure 10.3 The 12 octets of the IPv4 pseudo-header used during UDP checksum computation.

The fields of the pseudo-header labeled *SOURCE IP ADDRESS* and *DESTINATION IP ADDRESS* contain the source and destination IPv4 addresses that will be placed in an IPv4 datagram when sending the UDP message. Field *PROTO* contains the IPv4 protocol type code (*17* for UDP), and the field labeled *UDP LENGTH* contains the length of the UDP datagram (not including the pseudo-header). To verify the checksum, the receiver must extract these fields from the IPv4 header, assemble them into the pseudo-header format, and compute the checksum†.

10.8 IPv6 UDP Pseudo-Header Format

The pseudo-header used in the UDP checksum computation for IPv6 consists of 40 octets of data arranged as Figure 10.4 illustrates.

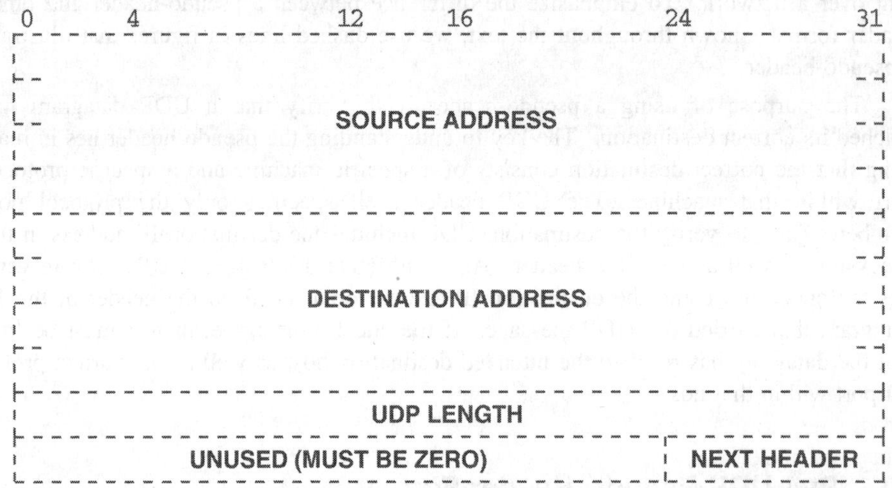

Figure 10.4 The 40 octets of the IPv6 pseudo-header used during UDP checksum computation.

Of course, the pseudo-header for IPv6 uses IPv6 source and destination addresses. The other changes from IPv4 are that the *PROTO* field is replaced by the *NEXT HEADER* field and the order of fields has changed.

10.9 UDP Encapsulation And Protocol Layering

UDP provides our first example of a transport protocol. In the 5-layer TCP/IP reference model in Chapter 4, UDP lies in the transport layer above the internet layer. Conceptually, applications access UDP, which uses IP to send and receive datagrams. Figure 10.5 illustrates the conceptual layering.

†In practice, it is possible to build checksum software that performs the correct computation without copying fields into a pseudo-header.

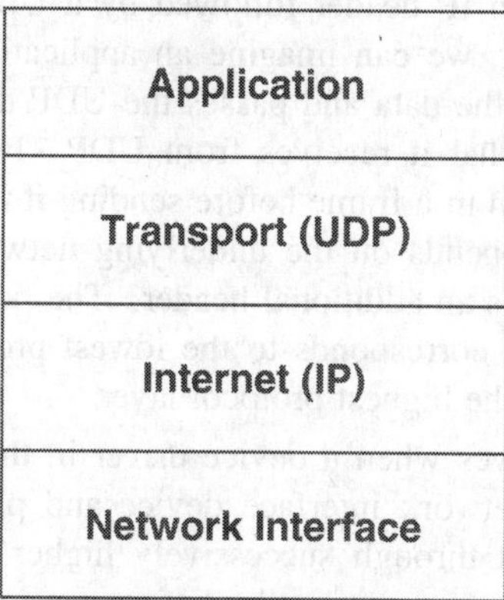

Figure 10.5 The conceptual layering of UDP between application programs and IP.

In the case of UDP, the conceptual layering in the figure also implies encapsulation. That is, because UDP is layered above IP, a complete UDP message, including the UDP header and payload, is encapsulated in an IP datagram as it travels across an internet. Of course, the datagram is encapsulated in a network frame as it travels across an underlying network, which means there are two levels of encapsulation. Figure 10.6 illustrates the encapsulation.

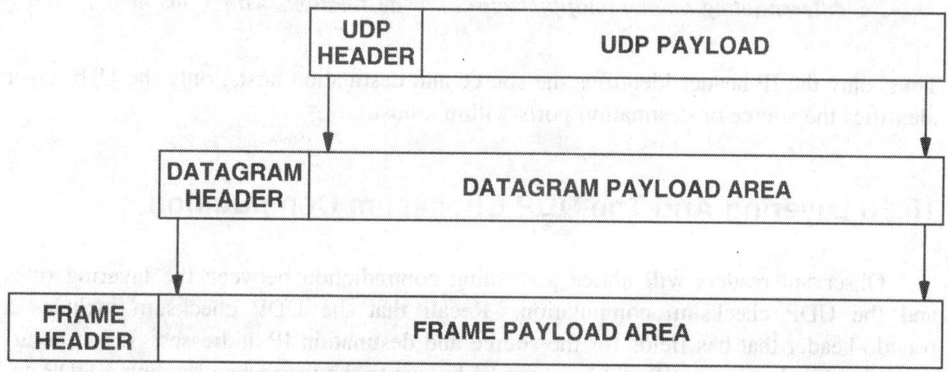

Figure 10.6 Two levels of encapsulation used when a UDP message travels in an IP datagram, which travels in a network frame.

As the figure indicates, encapsulation will result in a linear sequence of headers. Therefore, if one captured a frame that contained UDP, the frame would start with a frame header followed by an IP header followed by a UDP header. In terms of constructing an outgoing packet, we can imagine an application specifies data to be sent. UDP prepends its header to the data and passes the UDP datagram to IP. The IP layer prepends an IP header to what it receives from UDP. Finally, the network interface layer embeds the IP datagram in a frame before sending it from one machine to another. The format of the frame depends on the underlying network technology, but in most technologies a frame includes an additional header. The point is that when looking at a frame, the outermost header corresponds to the lowest protocol layer, while the innermost header corresponds to the highest protocol layer.

On input, a packet arrives when a device driver in the network interface layer receives a packet from the network interface device and places the packet in memory. Processing begins an ascent through successively higher layers of protocol software. Conceptually, each layer removes one header before passing the message up to the next layer. By the time the transport layer passes data to the receiving process, all headers have been removed. When considering how headers are inserted and removed, it is important to keep in mind the layering principle. In particular, observe that the layering principle applies to UDP, which means that the UDP datagram received from IP on the destination machine is identical to the datagram that UDP passed to IP on the source machine. Also, the data that UDP delivers to an application on the receiving machine will be exactly the data that an application passed to UDP on the sending machine.

The division of duties among various protocol layers is rigid and clear:

> *The IP layer is responsible only for transferring data between a pair of hosts on an internet, while the UDP layer is responsible only for differentiating among multiple sources or destinations within one host.*

Thus, only the IP header identifies the source and destination hosts; only the UDP layer identifies the source or destination ports within a host.

10.10 Layering And The UDP Checksum Computation

Observant readers will notice a seeming contradiction between the layering rules and the UDP checksum computation. Recall that the UDP checksum includes a pseudo-header that has fields for the source and destination IP addresses. It can be argued that the destination IP address must be known to the user when sending a UDP datagram, and the user must pass the address to the UDP layer. Thus, the UDP layer can obtain the destination IP address without interacting with the IP layer. However, the source IP address depends on the route IP chooses for the datagram because the IP source address identifies the network interface over which a datagram is transmitted. Thus, unless it interacts with the IP layer, UDP cannot know the IP source address.

We assume that UDP software asks the IP layer to compute the source and (possibly) destination IP addresses, uses them to construct a pseudo-header, computes the checksum, discards the pseudo-header, and then passes the UDP datagram to IP for transmission. An alternative approach that produces greater efficiency arranges to have the UDP layer encapsulate the UDP datagram in an IP datagram, obtain the source address from IP, store the source and destination addresses in the appropriate fields of the datagram header, compute the UDP checksum, and then pass the IP datagram to the IP layer, which only needs to fill in the remaining IP header fields.

Does the strong interaction between UDP and IP violate our basic premise that layering reflects separation of functionality? Yes. UDP has been tightly integrated with the IP protocol. It is clearly a compromise of the layering rules, made for entirely practical reasons. We are willing to overlook the layering violation because it is impossible to identify a destination application program fully without specifying the destination machine, and the goal is to make the mapping between addresses used by UDP and those used by IP efficient. One of the exercises examines this issue from a different point of view, asking the reader to consider whether UDP should be separated from IP.

10.11 UDP Multiplexing, Demultiplexing, And Protocol Ports

We have seen in Chapter 4 that software throughout the layers of a protocol hierarchy must multiplex or demultiplex among multiple objects at the next layer. UDP software provides another example of multiplexing and demultiplexing.

- Multiplexing occurs on output. On a given host computer, multiple applications can use UDP simultaneously. Thus, we can envision UDP software accepting outgoing messages from a set of applications, placing each in a UDP datagram, and passing the datagrams to IP for transmission.

- Demultiplexing occurs on input. We can envision UDP accepting incoming UDP datagrams from IP, choosing the application to which the datagram has been sent, and passing the data to the application.

Conceptually, all multiplexing and demultiplexing between UDP software and applications occur through the port mechanism. In practice, each application program must negotiate with the operating system to obtain a local protocol port number and create the resources needed to send and receive UDP messages†. Once the operating system has created the necessary resources, the application can send data; UDP code in the operating system will create an outgoing UDP datagram and place the local port number in the *UDP SOURCE PORT* field.

Conceptually, only the destination port number is needed to handle demultiplexing. When it processes an incoming datagram, UDP accepts the datagram from the IP software, extracts the *UDP DESTINATION PORT* from the header, and passes the data to the application. Figure 10.7 illustrates demultiplexing.

†For now, we describe the mechanisms abstractly; Chapter 21 provides an example of the socket primitives that many operating systems use to create and use ports.

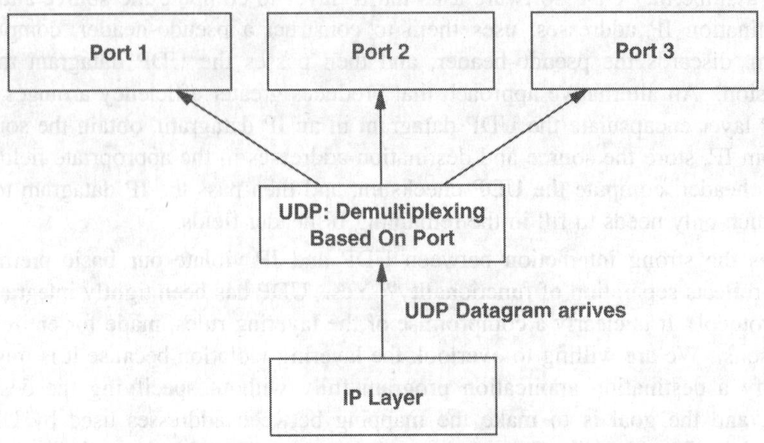

Figure 10.7 Conceptual view of UDP demultiplexing incoming datagrams.

The easiest way to think of a UDP port is as a queue of incoming datagrams. In most implementations, when an application negotiates with the operating system to allocate a port, the operating system creates the internal queue needed to hold arriving datagrams. The application can specify or change the queue size. When UDP receives a datagram, it checks to see that the destination port number matches one of the ports currently in use†. If it finds a match, UDP enqueues the new datagram at the port where the application program can access it. If none of the allocated ports match the incoming datagram, UDP sends an ICMP message to inform the source that the port was unreachable and discards the datagram. Of course, an error also occurs if the port is full. In such cases, UDP discards the incoming datagram and sends an ICMP message.

10.12 Reserved And Available UDP Port Numbers

How should protocol port numbers be assigned? The problem is important because applications running on two computers need to agree on port numbers before they can interoperate. For example, when a user on computer *A* decides to place a VoIP phone call to a user on computer *B*, the application software needs to know which protocol port number the application on computer *B* is using. There are two fundamental approaches to port assignment. The first approach uses a central authority. Everyone agrees to allow a central authority to assign port numbers as needed and to publish the list of all assignments. Software is built according to the list. The approach is sometimes called *universal assignment*, and the port assignments specified by the authority are called *well-known port assignments*.

†In practice, UDP demultiplexing allows an application to specify matching on a source port as well as a destination port.

The second approach to port assignment uses dynamic binding. In the dynamic binding approach, ports are not globally known. Instead, whenever an application program needs a protocol port number, protocol software in the operating system chooses an unused number and assigns it to the application. When an application needs to learn the current protocol port assignments on another computer, the application must send a request that asks for a port assignment (e.g., "What port is the VoIP phone service using?"). The target machine replies by giving the port number to use.

The TCP/IP designers adopted a hybrid scheme that assigns some port numbers a priori, but leaves others available for local sites or application programs to assign dynamically. The well-known port numbers assigned by the central authority begin at low values and extend upward, leaving larger integer values available for dynamic assignment. The table in Figure 10.8 lists examples of well-known UDP protocol port numbers.

Port	Keyword	Description
0	-	Reserved
7	echo	Echo
9	discard	Discard
11	systat	Active Users
13	daytime	Daytime
15	netstat	Network Status Program
17	qotd	Quote of the Day
19	chargen	Character Generator
37	time	Time
42	name	Host Name Server
43	whois	Who Is
53	nameserver	Domain Name Server
67	bootps	BOOTP or DHCP Server
68	bootpc	BOOTP or DHCP Client
69	tftp	Trivial File Transfer
88	kerberos	Kerberos Security Service
111	sunrpc	ONC Remote Procedure Call (Sun RPC)
123	ntp	Network Time Protocol
161	snmp	Simple Network Management Protocol
162	snmp-trap	SNMP traps
264	bgmp	Border Gateway Multicast Protocol (BGMP)
389	ldap	Lightweight Directory Access Protocol (LDAP)
512	biff	UNIX comsat
514	syslog	System Log
520	rip	Routing Information Protocol (RIP)
525	timed	Time Daemon
546	dhcpv6-c	DHCPv6 client
547	dhcpv6-s	DHCPv6 server
944	nsf	Network File System (NFS) service
973	nfsv6	Network File System (NFS) over IPv6

Figure 10.8 Examples of well-known UDP protocol port numbers.

10.13 Summary

Modern operating systems permit multiple application programs to execute concurrently. The User Datagram Protocol, UDP, distinguishes among multiple applications on a given machine by allowing senders and receivers to assign a 16-bit protocol port number to each application. A UDP message includes two protocol port numbers that identify an application on the sending computer and an application on the destination computer. Some of the UDP port numbers are *well known* in the sense that they are permanently assigned by a central authority and honored throughout the Internet. Other port numbers are available for arbitrary application programs to use.

UDP is a thin protocol in the sense that it does not add significantly to the semantics of IP. It merely provides application programs with the ability to communicate using IP's unreliable connectionless packet delivery service. Thus, UDP messages can be lost, duplicated, delayed, or delivered out of order; a pair of application programs that use UDP must be prepared to handle the errors. If a UDP application does not handle the errors, the application may work correctly over a highly reliable Local Area Network but not over a Wide Area internet where problems of delay and loss are more common.

In the protocol layering scheme, UDP resides at Layer 4, the transport layer, above Layer 3, the internet layer, and below Layer 5, the application layer. Conceptually, the transport layer is independent of the internet layer, but in practice they interact strongly. The UDP checksum includes a pseudo-header with the IP source and destination addresses in it, meaning that UDP software must interact with IP software to find IP addresses before sending datagrams.

EXERCISES

10.1 Build two programs that use UDP and measure the average transfer speed with messages of 256, 512, 1024, 2048, 4096, and 8192 octets. Can you explain the results. (Hint: what is the MTU of the network you are using?)

10.2 Why is the UDP checksum separate from the IP checksum? Would you object to a protocol that used a single checksum for the complete IP datagram including the UDP message?

10.3 Not using checksums can be dangerous. Explain how a single corrupted ARP packet broadcast by machine P can make it impossible to reach another machine, Q.

10.4 Should the notion of multiple destinations identified by protocol ports have been built into IP? Why, or why not?

10.5 What is the chief advantage of using preassigned UDP port numbers? The chief disadvantage?

10.6 What is the chief advantage of using protocol ports instead of process identifiers to specify the destination within a machine?

10.7 UDP provides unreliable datagram communication because it does not guarantee delivery of the message. Devise a reliable datagram protocol that uses timeouts and acknowledgements to guarantee delivery. How much network overhead and delay does reliability introduce?

10.8 *Name Registry.* Suppose you want to allow arbitrary pairs of application programs to establish communication with UDP, but you do not wish to assign either of them a fixed UDP port number. Instead, you would like potential correspondents to be identified by a character string of 64 or fewer characters. Thus, an application on machine *A* might want to communicate with the "special-long-id" application on machine *B*. Meanwhile, suppose an application on machine *C* wants to communicate with an application on machine *A* that has chosen an ID "my-own-private-id." Show that you only need to assign one UDP port to make such communication possible by designing software on each machine that allows (a) a local application to pick an unused UDP port number over which it will communicate, (b) a local application to register the 64-character name to which it responds, and (c) a remote application to use UDP to establish communication using only the 64-character name and destination internet address.

10.9 Implement the name registry software from the previous exercise.

10.10 Send UDP datagrams across a wide area network and measure the percentage lost and the percentage reordered. Does the result depend on the time of day? The network load?

10.11 The standard defines UDP port 7 to be an echo port — a datagram sent to the echo port is simply sent back to the sender. What can a UDP echo service tell a manager that an ICMP echo service cannot?

10.12 Consider a protocol design in which UDP and IPv4 are merged, and an address consists of 48 bits that include a conventional 32-bit IPv4 address and a 16-bit port number. What is the chief disadvantage of such a scheme?

Chapter Contents

11

Reliable Stream Transport Service (TCP)

11.1 Introduction

Previous chapters explore the unreliable connectionless packet delivery service, which forms the basis for all Internet communication, and the IP protocol that defines it. This chapter introduces a second key piece of the Internet protocol suite, a reliable stream service implemented by the *Transmission Control Protocol* (*TCP*). We will see that TCP adds substantial functionality to the protocols already discussed, and we will see that it is substantially more complex than UDP.

11.2 The Need For Reliable Service

At the lowest level, computer communication networks provide unreliable packet delivery. Packets can be lost when transmission errors interfere with data or when network hardware fails. They can be delayed when networks become overloaded. Packet switching systems change routes dynamically, which means they can deliver packets out of order, deliver them after a substantial delay, or deliver duplicates.

At the highest level, application programs often need to send large volumes of data from one computer to another. Using an unreliable connectionless delivery system for large transfers becomes tedious and annoying; programmers must incorporate error detection and recovery into each application. Because it is difficult to design, understand, and implement software that correctly provides reliability, networking researchers have worked to create a general purpose solution — a single reliable transfer protocol that all applications can use. Having a single general purpose protocol means that application programmers do not need to incorporate a reliable transfer protocol into each application.

11.3 Properties Of The Reliable Delivery Service

The reliable transfer service that TCP provides to applications can be characterized by five features that are discussed below:

- Stream Orientation
- Virtual Circuit Connection
- Buffered Transfer
- Unstructured Stream
- Full Duplex Communication

Stream Orientation. When two application programs use TCP to transfer large volumes of data, the data is viewed as a *stream* of *octets*. The application on the destination host receives exactly the same sequence of octets that was sent by the application on the source host.

Virtual Circuit Connection. Before data transfer starts, both the sending and receiving applications must agree to establish a *TCP connection.* One application contacts the other to initiate a connection. TCP software on the two hosts communicate by sending messages across the underlying internet. They verify that the transfer is authorized and both sides are ready. Once all details have been settled, the protocol modules inform the application programs on each end that a connection has been established and that transfer can begin. TCP monitors data transfer; if communication fails for any reason (e.g., because network hardware along the path fails), the application programs are informed. We use the term *virtual circuit* to describe a TCP connection, because a connection acts like a dedicated hardware circuit, even though all communication is performed with packets.

Buffered Transfer. Application programs send a data stream across a TCP connection, repeatedly passing data octets to the protocol software. When transferring data, an application uses whatever size pieces it finds convenient; the pieces can be as small as a single octet. TCP places data in packets and sends the packets to the destination. On the receiving host, TCP insures data is placed in the original order so the application receives octets in exactly the same order they were sent.

TCP is free to divide the stream into packets independent of the pieces the application program transfers. To make transfer more efficient and to minimize network traffic, implementations usually collect enough data from a stream to fill a reasonably large datagram before transmitting it across an internet. Thus, even if the application program generates the stream one octet at a time, transfer across an internet can be efficient. Similarly, if the application program chooses to generate extremely large blocks of data, the protocol software can choose to divide each block into pieces that each fit into a single packet.

For applications where data must be transferred without waiting to fill a buffer, the stream service provides a *push* mechanism that applications use to force immediate transfer. At the sending side, a push forces protocol software to transfer all data that has been generated without waiting to fill a buffer. On the receiving side, the push causes TCP to make the data available to the application without delay. The push function only guarantees that all data will be transferred; it does not provide any boundaries. Thus, even when delivery is forced, the protocol software may choose to divide the stream in unexpected ways or if a receiving application is slow, data from several pushed packets may be delivered to the application all at once.

Unstructured Stream. The TCP/IP stream service does not provide structured data streams. For example, there is no way for a payroll application to identify the contents of the stream as being payroll data, nor can stream service mark boundaries between employee records. Application programs using the stream service must understand stream content and agree on a stream format before they initiate a connection.

Full Duplex Communication. Connections provided by the TCP/IP stream service allow concurrent transfer in both directions. Such connections are called *full duplex.* Conceptually, a full duplex connection consists of two independent data streams flowing in opposite directions; from an application's point of view, there is no apparent interaction between the two. TCP allows an application to terminate flow in one direction while data continues to flow in the other direction, making the connection *half duplex.* The advantage of a full duplex connection is that the underlying protocol software can send control information for one stream back to the source in datagrams carrying data in the opposite direction. Such *piggybacking* reduces network traffic.

11.4 Reliability: Acknowledgements And Retransmission

We said that the reliable stream delivery service guarantees delivery of a stream of data sent from one computer to another without duplication or data loss. The question arises: how can protocol software provide reliable transfer if the underlying communication system offers only unreliable packet delivery? The answer is complicated, but reliable protocols rely on a fundamental technique known as *positive acknowledgement with retransmission* (*PAR*). The technique requires a recipient to communicate with the source, sending back an *acknowledgement* (*ACK*) each time data arrives successfully. When it sends a packet, the sending software starts a timer. If an acknowledgement arrives before the timer expires, the sender cancels the timer and prepares to send more data. If the timer expires before an acknowledgement arrives, the sender *retransmits* the packet.

Before we can understand the TCP retransmission mechanism, we must consider a few basics. The simplest possible retransmission scheme waits for a given packet to be acknowledged before it sends the next packet. Known as *send-and-wait*, the approach can only send one packet at a time. Figure 11.1 illustrates the packet exchange when using send-and-wait.

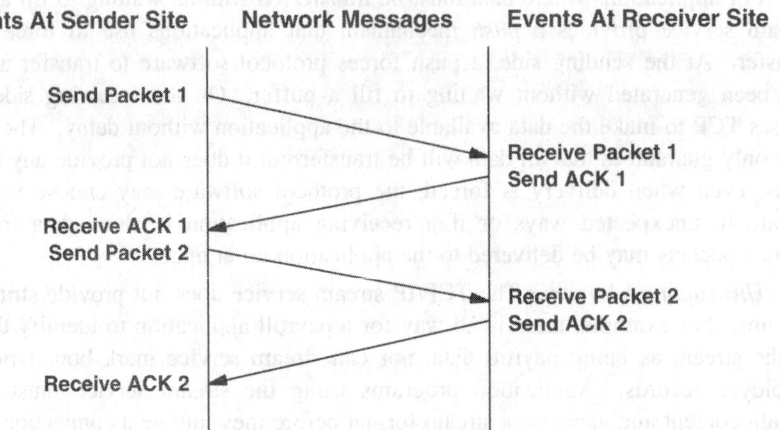

Figure 11.1 The packet exchange for a basic send-and-wait protocol. Time proceeds down the figure.

The left side of the figure lists events at the sending host, and the right side of the figure lists events at the receiving host. Each diagonal line crossing the middle shows the transfer of one packet or one ACK.

Figure 11.2 uses the same format as Figure 11.1 to show what happens when a packet is lost. The sender transmits a packet and starts a timer. The packet is lost, which means no ACK will arrive. When the timer expires, the sender retransmits the lost packet. The sender must start a timer after retransmission in case the second copy is also lost. In the figure, the second copy arrives intact, which means the receiver sends an ACK. When the ACK reaches the sending side, the sender cancels the timer.

In our description above, a sender must retain a copy of a packet that has been transmitted in case the packet must be retransmitted. In practice, a sender only needs to retain the data that goes in the packet along with sufficient information to allow the sender to reconstruct the packet headers. The idea of keeping *unacknowledged data* is important in TCP.

Although it handles packet loss or excessive delay, the acknowledgement mechanism described above does not solve all problems: a packet can be duplicated. Duplicates can arise if an excessive delay causes a sender to retransmit unnecessarily. Solving duplication requires careful thought because both packets and acknowledgements can be duplicated. Usually, reliable protocols detect duplicate packets by assigning each packet a sequence number and requiring the receiver to remember which sequence numbers it has received. To avoid ambiguity, positive acknowledgement protocols arrange for each acknowledgement to contain the sequence number of the packet that arrived. Thus, when an acknowledgment arrives, the acknowledgement is easily associated with a particular packet.

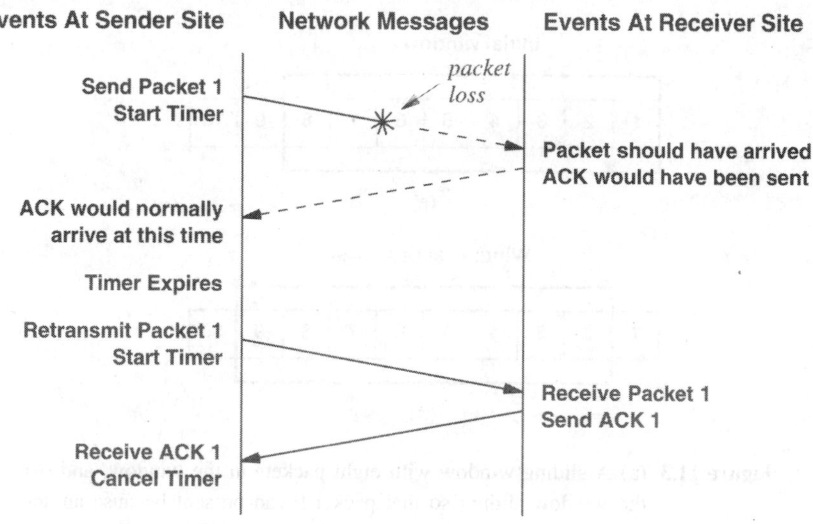

Figure 11.2 Illustration of timeout and retransmission when a packet is lost.

11.5 The Sliding Window Paradigm

Before examining the TCP stream service, we need to explore an additional mechanism that underlies reliable transmission. Known as a *sliding window*, the mechanism improves overall throughput. To understand the motivation for sliding windows, recall the sequence of events in Figure 11.1. To achieve reliability, the sender transmits a packet and then waits for an acknowledgement before transmitting another. As the figure shows, data flows between the machines one packet at a time. The network will remain completely idle until the acknowledgement returns. If we imagine a network with high transmission delays, the problem becomes clear:

> *A simple positive acknowledgement protocol wastes a substantial amount of network capacity because it must delay sending a new packet until it receives an acknowledgement for the previous packet.*

The sliding window technique uses a more complex form of positive acknowledgement and retransmission. The key idea is that a sliding window allows a sender to transmit multiple packets before waiting for an acknowledgement. The easiest way to envision a sliding window in action is to think of a sequence of packets to be transmitted as Figure 11.3 shows. The protocol places a small, fixed-size *window* on the sequence and transmits all packets that lie inside the window.

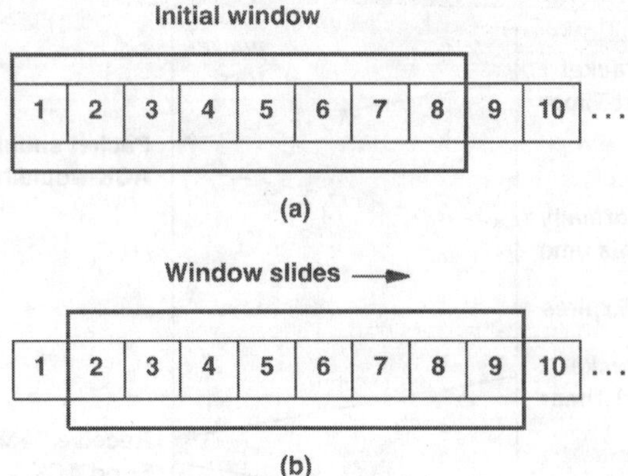

Figure 11.3 (a) A sliding window with eight packets in the window, and (b) the window sliding so that packet *9* can be sent because an acknowledgement has been received for packet *1*.

We say that a packet is *unacknowledged* if it has been transmitted but no acknowledgement has been received. Technically, the number of packets that can be unacknowledged at any given time is constrained by the *window size*, which is limited to a small, fixed number. For example, in a sliding window protocol with window size *8*, the sender is permitted to transmit *8* packets before it receives an acknowledgement.

As Figure 11.3 shows, once the sender receives an acknowledgement for the first packet inside the window, it "slides" the window along and sends the next packet. The window slides forward each time an acknowledgement arrives.

The performance of sliding window protocols depends on the window size and the speed at which the network accepts packets. Figure 11.4 shows an example of the operation of a sliding window protocol for a window size of three packets. Note that the sender transmits all three packets before receiving any acknowledgements.

With a window size of *1*, a sliding window protocol is exactly the same as our simple positive acknowledgement protocol. By increasing the window size, it is possible to eliminate network idle time completely. That is, in the steady state, the sender can transmit packets as fast as the network can transfer them. To see the advantage of sliding window, compare the rate at which data is transferred in Figures 11.1 and 11.4. The main point is:

> *Because a well-tuned sliding window protocol keeps the network completely saturated with packets, it can obtain substantially higher throughput than a simple positive acknowledgement protocol.*

Conceptually, a sliding window protocol always remembers which packets have been acknowledged and keeps a separate timer for each unacknowledged packet. If a packet is lost, the timer expires and the sender retransmits that packet. When the sender slides its window, it moves past all acknowledged packets. At the receiving end, the protocol software keeps an analogous window, accepting and acknowledging packets as they arrive. Thus, the window partitions the sequence of packets into three sets: those packets to the left of the window have been successfully transmitted, received, and acknowledged; those packets to the right have not yet been transmitted; and those packets that lie in the window are being transmitted. The lowest numbered packet in the window is the first packet in the sequence that has not been acknowledged.

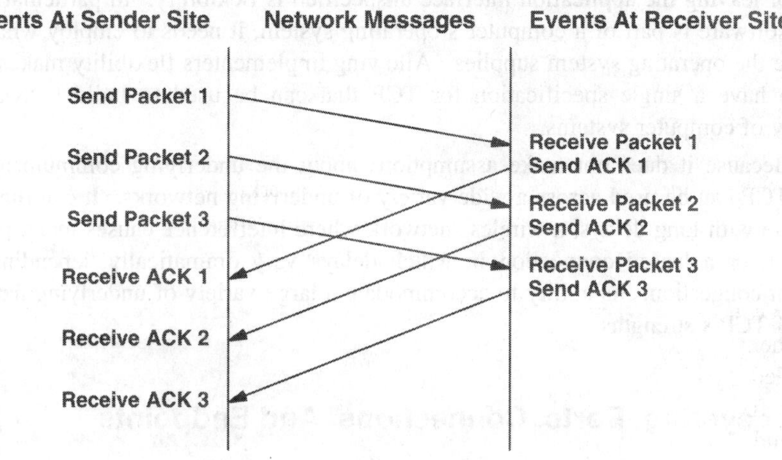

Figure 11.4 An example of sliding window with a window size of three.

11.6 The Transmission Control Protocol

Now that we understand the principle of sliding windows, we can examine the *Transmission Control Protocol* (*TCP*), the protocol that provides reliable stream service. The stream service is so significant that the entire Internet protocol suite is referred to as TCP/IP.

We will make a key distinction between the TCP protocol and the software that implements TCP. The TCP protocol provides a specification analogous to a blueprint; TCP software implements the specification. Although it is sometimes convenient to think of TCP as a piece of software, readers should recognize the distinction:

> *TCP is a communication protocol, not a piece of software.*

Exactly what does TCP provide? TCP is complex, so there is no simple answer. The protocol specifies the format of the data and acknowledgements that two computers exchange to achieve a reliable transfer, as well as the procedures the computers use to ensure that the data arrives correctly. It specifies how TCP software distinguishes among multiple destinations on a given machine, and how communicating machines recover from errors like lost or duplicated packets. The protocol also specifies how two computers initiate a TCP connection and how they agree when it is complete.

It is also important to understand what the protocol does not include. Although the TCP specification describes how application programs use TCP in general terms, it does not dictate the details of the interface between an application program and TCP. That is, the protocol documentation only discusses the operations TCP supplies; it does not specify the exact procedures that applications invoke to access the operations. The reason for leaving the application interface unspecified is flexibility. In particular, because TCP software is part of a computer's operating system, it needs to employ whatever interface the operating system supplies. Allowing implementers flexibility makes it possible to have a single specification for TCP that can be used to build software for a variety of computer systems.

Because it does not make assumptions about the underlying communication system, TCP can be used across a wide variety of underlying networks. It can run across a satellite with long delays, a wireless network where interference causes many packets to be lost, or a leased connection in which delays vary dramatically depending on the current congestion. Its ability to accommodate a large variety of underlying networks is one of TCP's strengths.

11.7 Layering, Ports, Connections, And Endpoints

TCP, which resides in the transport layer just above IP, allows multiple application programs on a given computer to communicate concurrently, and it demultiplexes incoming TCP traffic among the applications. Thus, in terms of the layering model, TCP is a conceptual peer of UDP, as Figure 11.5 shows:

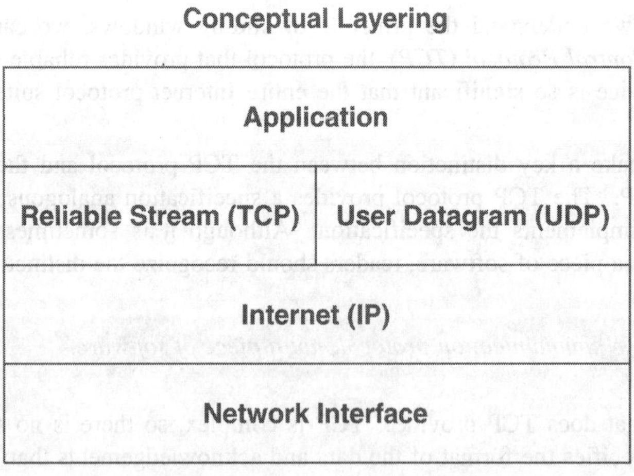

Conceptual Layering

Application	
Reliable Stream (TCP)	User Datagram (UDP)
Internet (IP)	
Network Interface	

Figure 11.5 The conceptual layering of UDP and TCP above IP.

Although they are at the same conceptual layer, TCP and UDP provide completely different services. We will understand many of the differences as the chapter proceeds.

Like the User Datagram Protocol, TCP uses *protocol port* numbers to identify application programs. Also like UDP, a TCP port number is sixteen bits long. Each TCP port is assigned a small integer used to identify it. It is important to understand that TCP ports are conceptually independent of UDP ports — one application can use UDP port 30,000 while another application uses TCP port 30,000.

We said that a UDP port consists of a queue that holds incoming datagrams. TCP ports are much more complex because a single port number does not identify an application. Instead, TCP has been designed on a *connection abstraction* in which the objects to be identified are TCP connections, not individual ports. Each TCP connection is specified by a pair of endpoints that correspond to the pair of communicating applications. Understanding that TCP uses the notion of connections is crucial because it helps explain the meaning and use of TCP port numbers:

> *TCP uses the connection, not the protocol port, as its fundamental abstraction; connections are identified by a pair of endpoints.*

Exactly what are the "endpoints" of a TCP connection? We have said that a connection consists of a virtual circuit between two application programs, so it might be natural to assume that an application program serves as the connection endpoint. It is not. Instead, TCP defines an *endpoint* to be a pair of integers (*host, port*), where *host* is the IP address for a host and *port* is a TCP port on that host. For example, an IPv4 endpoint (*128.10.2.3, 25*) specifies TCP port *25* on the machine with IPv4 address *128.10.2.3*.

Now that we have defined endpoints, it is easy to understand TCP connections. Recall that a connection is defined by its two endpoints. Thus, if there is a connection from machine (*18.26.0.36*) at MIT to machine (*128.10.2.3*) at Purdue University, it might be defined by the endpoints:

(*18.26.0.36, 1069*) and (*128.10.2.3, 25*).

Meanwhile, another connection might be in progress from machine (*128.9.0.32*) at the Information Sciences Institute to the same machine at Purdue, identified by its endpoints:

(*128.9.0.32, 1184*) and (*128.10.2.3, 53*).

So far, our examples of connections have been straightforward because the ports used at all endpoints have been unique. However, the connection abstraction allows multiple connections to share an endpoint. For example, we could add another connection to the two listed above from machine (*128.2.254.139*) at CMU to the machine at Purdue using endpoints:

(*128.2.254.139, 1184*) and (*128.10.2.3, 53*).

It might seem strange that two connections can use the TCP port *53* on machine 128.10.2.3 simultaneously, but there is no ambiguity. Because TCP associates incoming messages with a connection instead of a protocol port, it uses both endpoints to identify the appropriate connection. The important idea to remember is:

> *Because TCP identifies a connection by a pair of endpoints, a given TCP port number can be shared by multiple connections on the same machine.*

From a programmer's point of view, the connection abstraction is significant. It means a programmer can devise a program that provides concurrent service to multiple connections simultaneously, without needing unique local port numbers for each connection. For example, most systems provide concurrent access to their electronic mail service, allowing multiple computers to send them electronic mail simultaneously. Because it uses TCP to communicate, the application that accepts incoming mail only needs to use one local TCP port, even though multiple connections can proceed concurrently.

11.8 Passive And Active Opens

Unlike UDP, TCP is a connection-oriented protocol that requires both endpoints to agree to participate. That is, before TCP traffic can pass across an internet, application programs at both ends of the connection must agree that the connection is desired. To do so, the application program on one end performs a *passive open* by contacting the local operating system and indicating that it will accept an incoming connection for a specific port number. The protocol software prepares to accept a connection at the port. The application program on the other end can then perform an *active open* by requesting that a TCP connection be established. The two TCP software modules communicate to establish and verify a connection. Once a connection has been created, application programs can begin to pass data; the TCP software modules at each end exchange messages that guarantee reliable delivery. We will return to the details of establishing connections after examining the TCP message format.

11.9 Segments, Streams, And Sequence Numbers

TCP views the data stream as a sequence of octets that it divides into *segments* for transmission. Usually, each segment travels across the underlying internet in a single IP datagram. TCP uses a specialized sliding window mechanism that optimizes throughput and handles flow control. Like the sliding window protocol described earlier, the TCP window mechanism makes it possible to send multiple segments before an acknowledgement arrives. Doing so increases total throughput because it keeps the network busy. We will see that the TCP form of a sliding window protocol also solves the end-to-end *flow control* problem by allowing the receiver to restrict transmission until it has sufficient buffer space to accommodate more data.

The TCP sliding window mechanism operates at the octet level, not at the segment or packet level. Octets of the data stream are numbered sequentially, and a sender keeps three pointers associated with every connection. The pointers define a sliding window as Figure 11.6 illustrates. The first pointer marks the left of the sliding window, separating octets that have been sent and acknowledged from octets yet to be acknowledged. A second pointer marks the right of the sliding window and defines the highest octet in the sequence that can be sent before more acknowledgements are received. The third pointer marks the boundary inside the window that separates those octets that have already been sent from those octets that have not been sent. The protocol software sends all octets in the window without delay, so the boundary inside the window usually moves from left to right quickly.

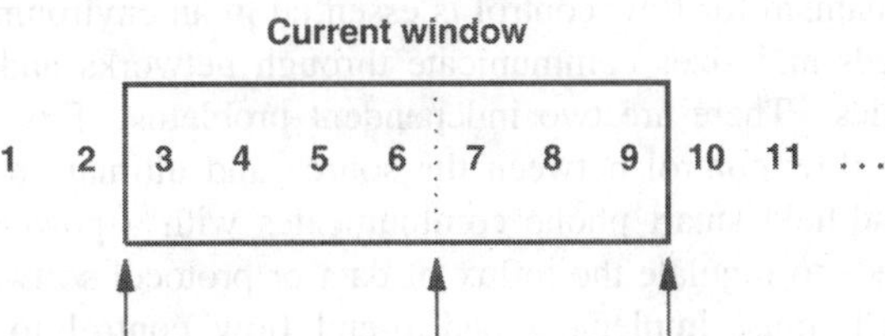

Figure 11.6 An example of TCP's sliding window where octets through 2 have been sent and acknowledged, octets 3 through 6 have been sent but not acknowledged, octets 7 though 9 have not been sent but will be sent without delay, and octets 10 and higher cannot be sent until the window moves.

We have described how the sender's TCP window slides along and mentioned that the receiver must maintain a similar window to recreate the stream. It is important to understand, however, that because TCP connections are full duplex, two transfers proceed simultaneously over each connection, one in each direction. We think of the transfers as completely independent because at any time data can flow across the connection in one direction, or in both directions. Thus, TCP software on a computer maintains two windows per connection: one window slides along as the data stream is sent, while the other slides along as data is received.

11.10 Variable Window Size And Flow Control

One difference between the TCP sliding window protocol and the simplified sliding window protocol presented in Figure 11.4† arises because TCP allows the window size to vary over time. Each acknowledgement, which specifies how many octets have been received, contains a *window advertisement* that specifies how many additional octets of data the receiver is prepared to accept beyond the data being acknowledged. We think of the window advertisement as specifying the receiver's current buffer size. In response to an increased window advertisement, the sender increases the size of its slid-

†Figure 11.4 can be found on page 205.

ing window and proceeds to send octets that have not been acknowledged. In response to a decreased window advertisement, the sender decreases the size of its window and stops sending octets beyond the boundary. TCP software must not contradict previous advertisements by shrinking the window past previously acceptable positions in the octet stream. Instead, smaller advertisements accompany acknowledgements, so the window size only changes at the time it slides forward.

The advantage of using a variable size window is that it provides the ability to handle flow control. To avoid receiving more data than it can store, the receiver sends smaller window advertisements as its buffer fills. In the extreme case, the receiver advertises a window size of zero to stop all transmissions. Later, when buffer space becomes available, the receiver advertises a nonzero window size to trigger the flow of data again†.

Having a mechanism for flow control is essential in an environment where computers of various speeds and sizes communicate through networks and routers of various speeds and capacities. There are two independent problems. First, protocols need to provide end-to-end flow control between the source and ultimate destination. For example, when a hand-held smart phone communicates with a powerful supercomputer, the smartphone needs to regulate the influx of data or protocol software will be overrun quickly. Thus, TCP must implement end-to-end flow control to guarantee reliable delivery. Second, a mechanism is needed that allows intermediate systems (i.e., routers) to control a source that sends more traffic than the machine can tolerate.

When intermediate machines become overloaded, the condition is called *congestion*, and mechanisms to solve the problem are called *congestion control mechanisms*. TCP uses its sliding window scheme to solve the end-to-end flow control problem. We will discuss congestion control later, but it should be noted that a well-designed protocol can detect and recover from congestion, while a poorly-designed protocol will make congestion worse. In particular, a carefully chosen retransmission scheme can help avoid congestion, but a poorly chosen scheme can exacerbate it by aggressively retransmitting.

11.11 TCP Segment Format

The unit of transfer between the TCP software on two machines is called a *segment*. Segments are exchanged to establish a connection, transfer data, send acknowledgements, advertise window sizes, and close connections. Because TCP allows *piggybacking*, an acknowledgement traveling from computer *A* to computer *B* may travel in the same segment as data traveling from computer *A* to computer *B*, even though the acknowledgement refers to data sent from *B* to *A*‡.

†There are two exceptions to transmission when the window size is zero: a sender transmits a segment with the urgent bit set when urgent data is available, and a sender probes a zero-sized window periodically in case a nonzero advertisement is lost.

‡In practice, piggybacking does not usually occur because most applications do not send data in both directions simultaneously.

Like most protocols, a message is divided into two conceptual parts: a header that contains meta-data and a payload area that carries data. Figure 11.7 shows the TCP segment format.

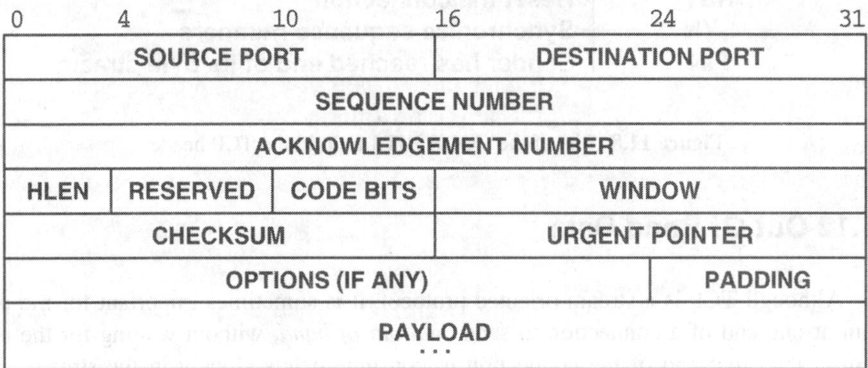

Figure 11.7 TCP segment format with a TCP header followed by a payload.

The header, known as the *TCP header*, consists of at least 20 octets and may contain more if the segment carries options. The header has the expected identification and control information. Fields *SOURCE PORT* and *DESTINATION PORT* contain the TCP port numbers that identify the application programs at the ends of the connection. The *SEQUENCE NUMBER* field identifies the position in the sender's octet stream of the data in the segment. The *ACKNOWLEDGEMENT NUMBER* field identifies the number of the octet that the source expects to receive next. Note that the sequence number refers to the stream flowing in the same direction as the segment, while the acknowledgement number refers to the stream flowing in the opposite direction from the segment.

The *HLEN*† field contains an integer that specifies the length of the segment header measured in 32-bit multiples. It is needed because the *OPTIONS* field varies in length, depending on which options are included. Thus, the size of the TCP header varies depending on the options selected. The 6-bit field marked *RESERVED* is reserved for future use (a later section describes a proposed use).

Some segments carry only an acknowledgement, while some carry data. Others carry requests to establish or close a connection. TCP software uses the 6-bit field labeled *CODE BITS* to determine the purpose and contents of the segment. The six bits tell how to interpret other fields in the header according to the table in Figure 11.8.

TCP software advertises how much data it is willing to accept every time it sends a segment by specifying its buffer size in the *WINDOW* field. The field contains a 16-bit unsigned integer in network-standard byte order. Window advertisements provide an example of piggybacking because they accompany all segments, including those carrying data as well as those carrying only an acknowledgement.

†The TCP specification says the *HLEN* field is the *offset* of the data area within the segment.

Bit (left to right)	Meaning if bit set to 1
URG	Urgent pointer field is valid
ACK	Acknowledgement field is valid
PSH	This segment requests a push
RST	Reset the connection
SYN	Synchronize sequence numbers
FIN	Sender has reached end of its byte stream

Figure 11.8 Bits of the CODE BITS field in the TCP header.

11.12 Out Of Band Data

Although TCP is a stream-oriented protocol, it is sometimes important for the program at one end of a connection to send data *out of band*, without waiting for the program at the other end of the connection to consume octets already in the stream. For example, when TCP is used for a remote desktop application, the user may decide to send a keyboard sequence that *interrupts* or *aborts* the currently running program. Such signals are most often needed when an application on the remote machine freezes and fails to respond to mouse clicks or normal keystrokes. The interrupt signal must be sent without waiting for the remote program to read octets already in the TCP stream (or one would not be able to abort programs that stop reading input).

To accommodate out-of-band signaling, TCP allows the sender to specify data as *urgent*, meaning that the receiving application should be notified of its arrival as quickly as possible, regardless of its position in the stream. The protocol specifies that when urgent data is found, the receiving TCP should notify the application program associated with the connection to go into "urgent mode." After all urgent data has been consumed, TCP tells the application program to return to normal operation.

The exact details of how TCP informs an application about urgent data depend on the computer's operating system. The mechanism used to mark urgent data when transmitting it in a segment consists of the URG code bit and the *URGENT POINTER* field in the segment header. When the URG bit is set, the *URGENT POINTER* field specifies the position in the segment where urgent data ends.

11.13 TCP Options

As Figure 11.7 indicates, a TCP header can contain zero or more *options*; the next sections explain the available options. Each option begins with a 1-octet field that specifies the option *type* followed by a 1-octet length field that specifies the size of the option in octets. Recall that the header length is specified in 32-bit multiples. If the options do not occupy an exact multiple of 32 bits, *PADDING* is added to the end of the header.

11.13.1 Maximum Segment Size Option

A sender can choose the amount of data that is placed in each segment. However, both ends of a TCP connection need to agree on a maximum segment they will transfer. TCP uses a *maximum segment size* (*MSS*) option to allow a receiver to specify the maximum size segment that it is willing to receive. An embedded system that only has a few hundred bytes of buffer space can specify an MSS that restricts segments so they fit in the buffer. MSS negotiation is especially significant because it permits heterogeneous systems to communicate — a supercomputer can communicate with a small wireless sensor node. To maximize throughput, when two computers attach to the same physical network, TCP usually computes a maximum segment size such that the resulting IP datagrams will match the network MTU. If the endpoints do not lie on the same physical network, they can attempt to discover the minimum MTU along the path between them, or choose a maximum segment size equal to the minimum datagram payload size.

In a general internet environment, choosing a good maximum segment size can be difficult, because performance can be poor for either extremely large segment sizes or extremely small segment sizes. On the one hand, when the segment size is small, network utilization remains low. To see why, recall that TCP segments travel encapsulated in IP datagrams which are encapsulated in physical network frames. Thus, each frame carries at least 20 octets of TCP header plus 20 octets of IP header (IPv6 is larger). Therefore, datagrams carrying only one octet of data use at most 1/41 of the underlying network bandwidth for the data being transferred (less for IPv6).

On the other hand, extremely large segment sizes can also produce poor performance. Large segments result in large IP datagrams. When such datagrams travel across a path with small MTU, IP must fragment them. Unlike a TCP segment, a fragment cannot be acknowledged or retransmitted independently; all fragments must arrive or the entire datagram must be retransmitted. If the probability of losing a given fragment is nonzero, increasing the segment size above the fragmentation threshold decreases the probability the datagram will arrive, which decreases throughput.

In theory, the optimum segment size, *S*, occurs when the IP datagrams carrying the segments are as large as possible without requiring fragmentation anywhere along the path, from the source to the destination. In practice, finding *S* means finding the path MTU, which involves probing. For a short-lived TCP connection (e.g., where only a few packets are exchanged), probing can introduce delay. Second, because routers in an internet can change routes dynamically, the path datagrams follow between a pair of communicating computers can change dynamically and so can the size at which datagrams must be fragmented. Third, the optimum size depends on lower-level protocol headers (e.g., the TCP segment size will be smaller if the IP datagram includes IPv4 options or IPv6 extension headers).

11.13.2 Window Scaling Option

Because the *WINDOW* field in the TCP header is 16 bits long, the maximum size window is 64 Kbytes. Although the window was sufficient for early networks, a larger window size is needed to obtain high throughput on a network, such as a satellite channel, that has a large delay-bandwidth product (informally called a *long fat pipe*).

To accommodate larger window sizes, a *window scaling option* was created for TCP. The option consists of three octets: a type, a length, and a *shift* value, *S*. In essence, the shift value specifies a binary scaling factor to be applied to the window value. When window scaling is in effect, a receiver extracts the value from the *WINDOW* field, *W*, and shifts *W* left *S* bits to obtain the actual window size.

Several details complicate the design. The option can be negotiated when the connection is initially established, in which case all successive window advertisements are assumed to use the negotiated scale, or the option can be specified on each segment, in which case the scaling factor can vary from one segment to another. Furthermore, if either side of a connection implements window scaling but does not need to scale its window, the side sends the option set to zero, which makes the scaling factor 1.

11.13.3 Timestamp Option

The TCP *timestamp option* was invented to help TCP compute the delay on the underlying network. It can also handle the case where TCP sequence numbers exceed 2^{32} (known as *Protect Against Wrapped Sequence* numbers, *PAWS*). In addition to the required type and length fields, a timestamp option includes two values: a timestamp value and an echo reply timestamp value. A sender places the time from its current clock in the timestamp field when sending a packet; a receiver copies the timestamp field into the echo reply field before returning an acknowledgement for the packet. Thus, when an acknowledgement arrives, the sender can accurately compute the total elapsed time since the segment was sent.

11.14 TCP Checksum Computation

The *CHECKSUM* field in the TCP header is a 16-bit one's complement checksum used to verify the integrity of the data as well as the TCP header. As with other checksums, TCP uses 16-bit arithmetic and takes the one's complement of the one's complement sum. To compute the checksum, TCP software on the sending machine follows a procedure similar to the one described in Chapter 10 for UDP. Conceptually, TCP prepends a *pseudo-header* to the TCP segment, appends enough zero bits to make the segment a multiple of 16 bits, and computes the 16-bit checksum over the entire result. As with UDP, the pseudo-header is not part of the segment, and is never transmitted in a packet. At the receiving site, TCP software extracts fields from the IP header, reconstructs a pseudo-header, and performs the same checksum computation to verify that the segment arrived intact.

The purpose of using a TCP pseudo-header is exactly the same as in UDP. It allows the receiver to verify that the segment has reached the correct endpoint, which includes both an IP address and a protocol port number. Both the source and destination IP addresses are important to TCP because it must use them to identify the connection to which the segment belongs. Therefore, whenever a datagram arrives carrying a TCP segment, IP must pass to TCP the source and destination IP addresses from the datagram as well as the segment itself. Figure 11.9 shows the format of the pseudo-header used in the checksum computation for IPv4 and Figure 11.10 shows the format for an IPv6 pseudo-header.

Figure 11.9 The 12 octets of the IPv4 pseudo-header used in TCP checksum computations.

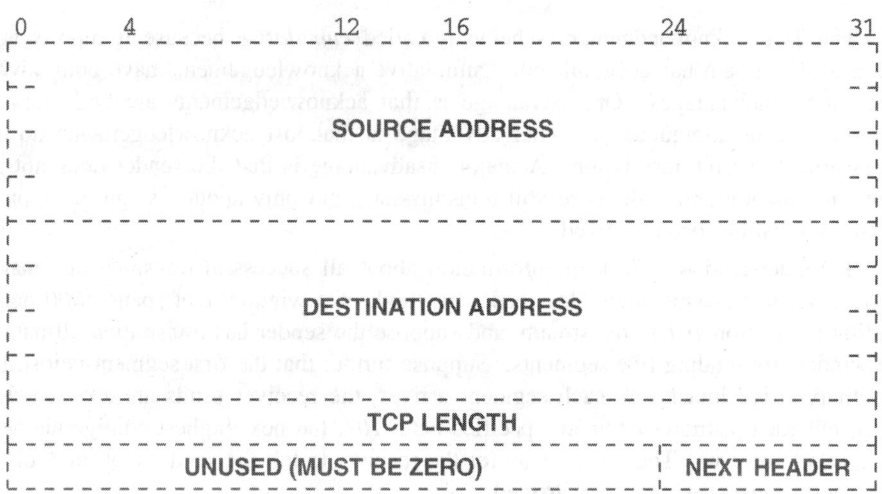

Figure 11.10 The 40 octets of the IPv6 pseudo-header used in TCP checksum computations.

Of course, the IPv4 pseudo-header uses IPv4 source and destination addresses and the IPv6 pseudo-header uses IPv6 addresses. The *PROTOCOL* field (IPv4) or the *NEXT HEADER* field (IPv6) is assigned the value *6*, the value for datagrams carrying TCP. The *TCP LENGTH* field specifies the total length of the TCP segment including the TCP header.

11.15 Acknowledgements, Retransmission, And Timeouts

Because TCP sends data in variable length segments and because retransmitted segments can include more data than the original, an acknowledgement cannot easily refer to a datagram or a segment. Instead, an acknowledgement refers to a position in the stream using the stream sequence numbers. The receiver collects data octets from arriving segments and reconstructs an exact copy of the stream being sent. Because segments travel in IP datagrams, they can be lost or delivered out of order; the receiver uses the sequence number in each segment to know where the data in the segment fits into the stream. At any time, a receiver will have reconstructed zero or more octets contiguously from the beginning of the stream, but may also have additional pieces of the stream from segments that arrived out of order. The receiver always acknowledges the longest contiguous prefix of the stream that has been received correctly. Each acknowledgement specifies a sequence value one greater than the highest octet position in the contiguous prefix it received. Thus, the sender receives continuous feedback from the receiver as it progresses through the stream. We can summarize this important idea:

> *A TCP acknowledgement specifies the sequence number of the next octet that the receiver expects to receive.*

The TCP acknowledgement scheme is called *cumulative* because it reports how much of the stream has accumulated. Cumulative acknowledgements have both advantages and disadvantages. One advantage is that acknowledgements are both easy to generate and unambiguous. Another advantage is that lost acknowledgements do not necessarily force retransmission. A major disadvantage is that the sender does not receive information about all successful transmissions, but only about a single position in the stream that has been received.

To understand why lack of information about all successful transmissions makes cumulative acknowledgements less efficient, think of a window that spans *5000* octets starting at position *101* in the stream, and suppose the sender has transmitted all data in the window by sending five segments. Suppose further that the first segment is lost, but all others arrive intact. As each segment arrives, the receiver sends an acknowledgement, but each acknowledgement specifies octet *101*, the next highest contiguous octet it expects to receive. There is no way for the receiver to tell the sender that most of the data for the current window has arrived.

In our example, when a timeout occurs at the sender's side, a sender must choose between two potentially inefficient schemes. It may choose to retransmit one segment or all five segments. Retransmitting all five segments is inefficient. When the first segment arrives, the receiver will have all the data in the window and will acknowledge *5101*. If the sender follows the accepted standard and retransmits only the first unacknowledged segment, it must wait for the acknowledgement before it can decide what and how much to send. Thus, retransmission reverts to a send-and-wait paradigm, which loses the advantages of having a large window.

One of the most important and complex ideas in TCP is embedded in the way it handles timeout and retransmission. Like other reliable protocols, TCP expects the destination to send acknowledgements whenever it successfully receives new octets from the data stream. Every time it sends a segment, TCP starts a timer and waits for an acknowledgement. If the timer expires before data in the segment has been acknowledged, TCP assumes that the segment was lost or corrupted and retransmits it.

To understand why the TCP retransmission algorithm differs from the algorithm used in many network protocols, we need to remember that TCP is intended for use in an internet environment. In an internet, a segment traveling between a pair of machines may traverse a single Local Area Network (e.g., a high-speed Ethernet), or it may travel across multiple intermediate networks through multiple routers. Thus, it is impossible to know *a priori* how quickly acknowledgements will return to the source. Furthermore, the delay at each router depends on traffic, so the total time required for a segment to travel to the destination and an acknowledgement to return to the source can vary dramatically from one instant to another. To understand, consider the world for which TCP was designed. Figure 11.11 illustrates the situation by showing measurements of *round trip times* (RTTs) for 100 consecutive packets sent across the global Internet of the 1980s.

Although most modern networks do not behave quite as badly, the plot illustrates the situations that TCP is designed to accommodate: incredibly long delays and changes in the round trip delay on a given connection. To handle the situation, TCP uses an *adaptive retransmission algorithm*. That is, TCP monitors the round trip time on each connection and computes reasonable values for timeouts. As the performance of a connection changes, TCP revises its timeout value (i.e., it adapts to the change).

To collect the data needed for an adaptive algorithm, TCP records the time at which each segment is sent and the time at which an acknowledgement arrives for the data in that segment. From the two times, TCP computes an elapsed time known as a *round trip sample*. Whenever it obtains a new round trip sample, TCP must adjust its notion of the average round trip time for the connection. To do so, TCP uses a weighted average to estimate the round trip time and uses each new round trip sample to update the average. The original averaging technique used a constant weighting factor, α, where $0 \leq \alpha < 1$, to weight the old average against the latest round trip sample†:

$$\text{RTT} = \alpha \times \text{RTT} + (1-\alpha) \times \text{New\_Round\_Trip\_Sample}$$

The idea is that choosing a value for α close to *1* makes the weighted average immune to changes that last a short time (e.g., a single segment that encounters long delay). Choosing a value for α close to *0* makes the weighted average respond to changes in delay very quickly.

When it sends a segment, TCP computes a timeout value as a function of the current round trip estimate. Early implementations of TCP used a constant weighting factor, β ($\beta > 1$), and made the timeout greater than the current round trip average:

$$\text{Timeout} = \beta \times \text{RTT}$$

†A later section explains how the computation has been modified in subsequent versions of TCP. The simplistic formula used in early TCP implementations makes it easy to understand the basic concept of a round-trip estimate that changes over time.

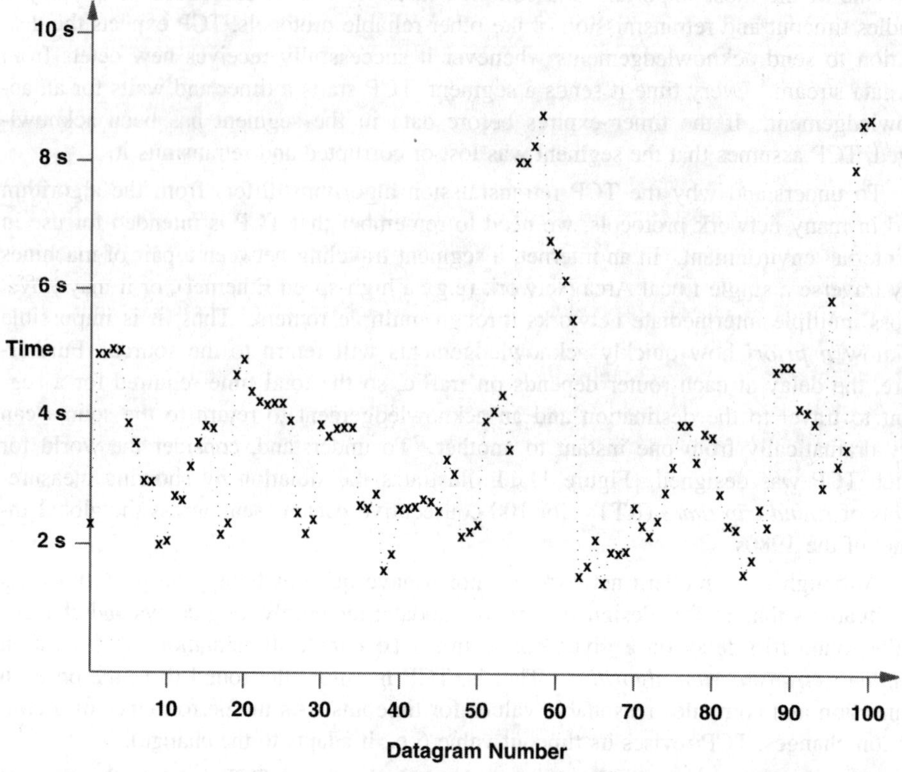

Figure 11.11 An extreme case for TCP: a plot of Internet round trip times from the 1980s. Although the Internet now operates with much lower delay, delays still vary over time.

We can summarize the ideas presented so far:

> *To accommodate the varying delays encountered in an internet environment, TCP uses an adaptive retransmission algorithm that monitors delays on each connection and adjusts its timeout parameter accordingly.*

11.16 Accurate Measurement Of Round Trip Samples

In theory, measuring a round trip sample is trivial — it consists of subtracting the time at which the segment is sent from the time at which the acknowledgement arrives. However, complications arise because TCP uses a cumulative acknowledgement scheme in which an acknowledgement refers to data received, and not to the instance of a specific datagram that carried the data. Consider a retransmission. TCP forms a segment, places it in a datagram and sends it, the timer expires, and TCP sends the segment again in a second datagram. Because both datagrams carry exactly the same segment data, the sender has no way of knowing whether an acknowledgement corresponds to the original or retransmitted datagram. This phenomenon has been called *acknowledgement ambiguity*.

Should TCP assume an acknowledgement belongs with the earliest (i.e., original) transmission or the latest (i.e., the most recent retransmission)? Surprisingly, neither assumption works. Associating the acknowledgement with the original transmission can make the estimated round trip time grow without bound in cases where an internet loses datagrams†. If an acknowledgement arrives after one or more retransmissions, TCP will measure the round trip sample from the original transmission, and compute a new RTT using the excessively long sample. Thus, RTT will grow slightly. The next time TCP sends a segment, the larger RTT will result in slightly longer timeouts, so if an acknowledgement arrives after one or more retransmissions, the next sample round trip time will be even larger, and so on.

Associating the acknowledgement with the most recent retransmission can also fail. Consider what happens when the end-to-end delay suddenly increases. When TCP sends a segment, it uses the old round trip estimate to compute a timeout, which is now too small. The segment arrives and an acknowledgement starts back, but the increase in delay means the timer expires before the acknowledgement arrives, and TCP retransmits the segment. Shortly after TCP retransmits, the first acknowledgement arrives and is associated with the retransmission. The round trip sample will be much too small and will result in a slight decrease of the estimated round trip time, RTT. Unfortunately, lowering the estimated round trip time guarantees that TCP will set the timeout too small for the next segment. Ultimately, the estimated round trip time can stabilize at a value, *T*, such that the correct round trip time is slightly longer than some multiple of *T*. Implementations of TCP that associate acknowledgements with the most recent retransmission were observed in a stable state with RTT slightly less than one-half of the correct value (i.e., TCP sends each segment exactly twice even though no loss occurs).

11.17 Karn's Algorithm And Timer Backoff

If the original transmission and the most recent transmission both fail to provide accurate round trip times, what should TCP do? The accepted answer is simple: TCP should not update the round trip estimate for retransmitted segments. The idea, known as *Karn's Algorithm*, avoids the problem of ambiguous acknowledgements altogether by only adjusting the estimated round trip for unambiguous acknowledgements (acknowledgements that arrive for segments that have only been transmitted once).

Of course, a simplistic implementation of Karn's algorithm, one that merely ignores times from retransmitted segments, can lead to failure as well. Consider what happens when TCP sends a segment after a sharp increase in delay. TCP computes a timeout using the existing round trip estimate. The timeout will be too small for the

†The estimate can only grow arbitrarily large if every segment is lost at least once.

new delay and will force retransmission. If TCP ignores acknowledgements from retransmitted segments, it will never update the estimate and the cycle will continue.

To accommodate such failures, Karn's algorithm requires the sender to combine retransmission timeouts with a *timer backoff* strategy. The backoff technique computes an initial timeout using a formula like the one shown above. However, if the timer expires and causes a retransmission, TCP increases the timeout. In fact, each time it must retransmit a segment, TCP increases the timeout (to keep timeouts from becoming ridiculously long, most implementations limit increases to an upper bound that is larger than the delay along any path in the internet).

Implementations use a variety of techniques to compute backoff. Most choose a multiplicative factor, γ, and set the new value to:

$$\text{new\_timeout} = \gamma \times \text{timeout}$$

Typically, γ is *2*. (It has been argued that values of γ less than 2 lead to instabilities.) Other implementations use a table of multiplicative factors, allowing arbitrary backoff at each step†.

Karn's algorithm combines the backoff technique with round trip estimation to solve the problem of never increasing round trip estimates:

> *Karn's algorithm: when computing the round trip estimate, ignore samples that correspond to retransmitted segments, but use a backoff strategy and retain the timeout value from a retransmitted packet for subsequent packets until a valid sample is obtained.*

Generally speaking, when an internet misbehaves, Karn's algorithm separates computation of the timeout value from the current round trip estimate. It uses the round trip estimate to compute an initial timeout value, but then backs off the timeout on each retransmission until it can successfully transfer a segment. When it sends subsequent segments, TCP retains the timeout value that results from backoff. Finally, when an acknowledgement arrives corresponding to a segment that did not require retransmission, TCP recomputes the round trip estimate and resets the timeout accordingly. Experience shows that Karn's algorithm works well even in networks with high packet loss‡.

11.18 Responding To High Variance In Delay

Research into round trip estimation has shown that the computations described above do not adapt to a wide range of variation in delay. Queueing theory suggests that the round trip time increases proportional to $1/(1-L)$, where L is the current network load, $0 \leq L < 1$, and the variation in round trip time, σ, is proportional to $1/(1-L)^2$. If an internet is running at 50% of capacity, we expect the round trip delay to vary by a factor of *4* from the mean round trip time. When the load reaches 80%, we expect a variation by a factor of *25*. The original TCP standard specified the technique for estimating

†BSD UNIX uses a table of factors, but values in the table are equivalent to using γ=2.

‡Phil Karn developed the algorithm for TCP communication across a high-loss amateur radio connection.

round trip time that we described earlier. Using that technique and limiting β to the suggested value of *2* means the round trip estimation can adapt to loads of at most 30%.

The 1989 specification for TCP requires implementations to estimate both the average round trip time and the variance and to use the estimated variance in place of the constant β. As a result, new implementations of TCP can adapt to a wider range of variation in delay and yield substantially higher throughput. Fortunately, the approximations require little computation; extremely efficient programs can be derived from the following simple equations:

$$\text{DIFF} = \text{SAMPLE} - \text{Old\_RTT}$$

$$\text{Smoothed\_RTT} = \text{Old\_RTT} + \delta \times \text{DIFF}$$

$$\text{DEV} = \text{Old\_DEV} + \rho \times (\,|\text{DIFF}| - \text{Old\_DEV}\,)$$

$$\text{Timeout} = \text{Smoothed\_RTT} + \eta \times \text{DEV}$$

where *DEV* is the estimated mean deviation, δ is a fraction between *0* and *1* that controls how quickly the new sample affects the weighted average, ρ is a fraction between *0* and *1* that controls how quickly the new sample affects the mean deviation, and η is a factor that controls how much the deviation affects the round trip timeout.

To make the computation efficient, TCP chooses δ and ρ to each be an inverse of a power of *2*, scales the computation by 2^n for an appropriate *n*, and uses integer arithmetic. Research suggests using values of:

$$\delta = 1/2^3$$

$$\rho = 1/2^2$$

$$\eta = 4$$

The original value for η in 4.3BSD UNIX was *2*. After experience and measurements it was changed to *4* in 4.4 BSD UNIX.

To illustrate how current versions of TCP adapt to changes in delay, we used a random-number generator to produce a set of round-trip times and fed the set into the round-trip estimate described above. Figure 11.12 illustrates the result. The plot shows individual round-trip times plotted as individual points and the computed timeout plotted as a solid line. Note how the retransmission timer varies as the round-trip time changes. Although the round-trip times are artificial, they follow a pattern observed in practice: successive packets show small variations in delay as the overall average rises or falls.

Note that frequent change in the round-trip time, including a cycle of increase and decrease, can produce an increase in the retransmission timer. Furthermore, although the timer tends to increase quickly when delay rises, it does not decrease as rapidly when delay falls.

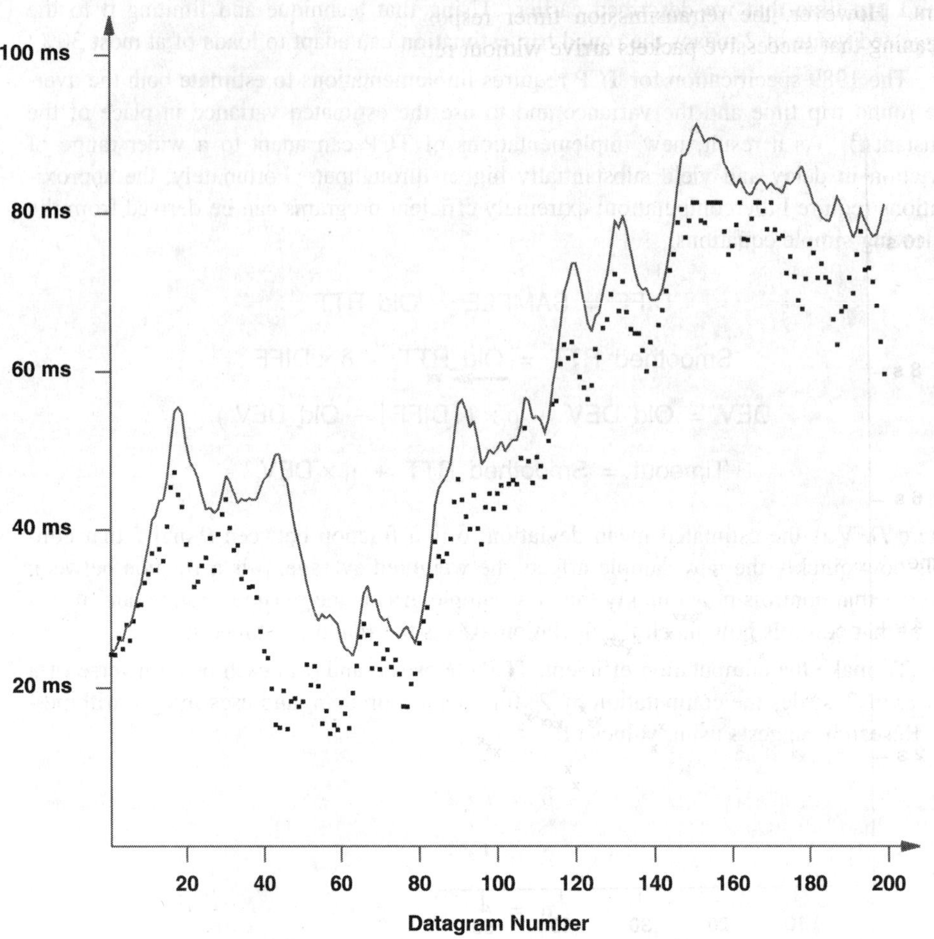

Figure 11.12 A set of 200 (randomly generated) round-trip times shown as dots, and the TCP retransmission timer shown as a solid line.

Although the randomly-generated data illustrates the algorithm, it is important to see how TCP performs on worst case data. Figure 11.13 uses the measurements from Figure 11.11 to show how TCP responds to an extreme case of variance in delay. Recall that the goal is to have the retransmission timer estimate the actual round-trip time as closely as possible without underestimating. The figure shows that although the timer responds quickly, it can underestimate. For example, between the two successive datagrams marked with arrows, the delay doubles from less than 4 seconds to more than 8. More important, the abrupt change follows a period of relative stability in which the variation in delay is small, making it impossible for any algorithm to anticipate the change. In the case of the TCP algorithm, because the timeout (approximately 5 seconds) substantially underestimates the large delay, an unnecessary retransmission occurs. However, the retransmission timer responds quickly to the increase in delay, meaning that successive packets arrive without retransmission.

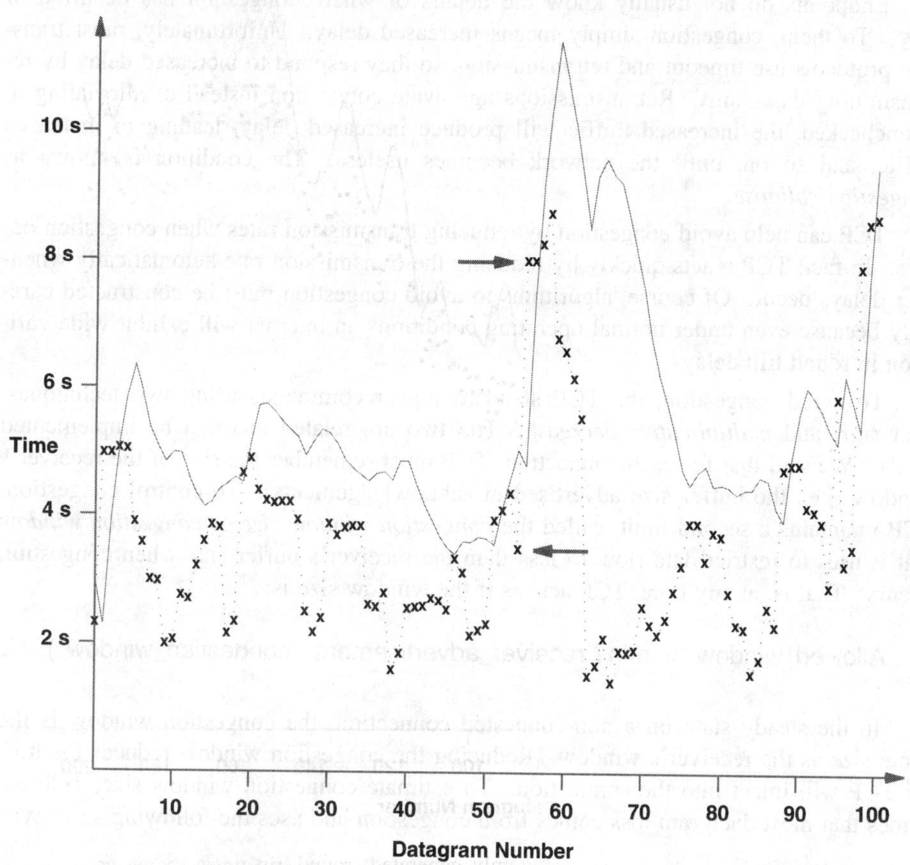

Figure 11.13 The value of TCP's retransmission timer for the extreme data in Figure 11.11. Arrows mark two successive datagrams where the delay doubles.

11.19 Response To Congestion

It may seem that TCP software could be designed by considering the interaction between the two endpoints of a connection and the communication delays between those endpoints. In practice, however, TCP must also react to *congestion* in an internet. Congestion is a condition of severe delay caused by an overload of datagrams at one or more switching points (e.g., at routers). When congestion occurs, delays increase and the router begins to enqueue datagrams until it can forward them. We must remember that each router has finite storage capacity and that datagrams compete for that storage (i.e., in a datagram-based internet, there is no preallocation of resources to individual TCP connections). In the worst case, the total number of datagrams arriving at the congested router grows until the router reaches capacity and starts to drop datagrams.

Endpoints do not usually know the details of where congestion has occurred or why. To them, congestion simply means increased delay. Unfortunately, most transport protocols use timeout and retransmission, so they respond to increased delay by retransmitting datagrams. Retransmissions aggravate congestion instead of alleviating it. If unchecked, the increased traffic will produce increased delay, leading to increased traffic, and so on, until the network becomes useless. The condition is known as *congestion collapse*.

TCP can help avoid congestion by reducing transmission rates when congestion occurs. In fact, TCP reacts quickly by reducing the transmission rate automatically whenever delays occur. Of course, algorithms to avoid congestion must be constructed carefully because even under normal operating conditions an internet will exhibit wide variation in round trip delays.

To avoid congestion, the TCP standard now recommends using two techniques: *slow-start* and *multiplicative decrease*. The two are related and can be implemented easily. We said that for each connection, TCP must remember the size of the receiver's window (i.e., the buffer size advertised in acknowledgements). To control congestion, TCP maintains a second limit, called the *congestion window size* or *congestion window* that it uses to restrict data flow to less than the receiver's buffer size when congestion occurs. That is, at any time, TCP acts as if the window size is:

Allowed_window = min (receiver_advertisement, congestion_window)

In the steady state on a non-congested connection, the congestion window is the same size as the receiver's window. Reducing the congestion window reduces the traffic TCP will inject into the connection. To estimate congestion window size, TCP assumes that most datagram loss comes from congestion and uses the following strategy:

> *Multiplicative Decrease Congestion Avoidance: upon loss of a segment, reduce the congestion window by half (but never reduce the window to less than one segment). When transmitting segments that remain in the allowed window, backoff the retransmission timer exponentially.*

Because TCP reduces the congestion window by half for *every* loss, it decreases the window exponentially if loss continues. In other words, if congestion is likely, TCP reduces the volume of traffic exponentially and the rate of retransmission exponentially. If loss continues, TCP eventually limits transmission to a single datagram and continues to double timeout values before retransmitting. The idea is to provide quick and significant traffic reduction to allow routers enough time to clear the datagrams already in their queues.

How can TCP recover when congestion ends? You might suspect that TCP should reverse the multiplicative decrease and double the congestion window when traffic begins to flow again. However, doing so produces an unstable system that oscillates wildly between no traffic and congestion. Instead, TCP uses a technique named *slow-start*† to scale up transmission.

> *Slow-Start (Additive) Recovery: whenever starting traffic on a new connection or increasing traffic after a period of congestion, start the congestion window at the size of a single segment and increase the congestion window by one segment each time an acknowledgement arrives.*

Slow-start avoids swamping the underlying internet with additional traffic immediately after congestion clears as well as when a new connection starts.

The term *slow-start* may be a misnomer because under ideal conditions, the start is not very slow. TCP initializes the congestion window to *1*, sends an initial segment, and waits. When the acknowledgement arrives, it increases the congestion window to *2*, sends two segments, and waits. When the two acknowledgements arrive they each increase the congestion window by *1*, so TCP can send *4* segments. Acknowledgements for those segments will increase the congestion window to *8*. Within four round trip times, TCP can send *16* segments, often enough to reach the receiver's window limit. Even for extremely large windows, it takes only $\log_2 N$ round trips before TCP can send N segments.

To avoid increasing the window size too quickly and causing additional congestion, TCP adds one additional restriction. Once the congestion window reaches one half of its original size before congestion, TCP enters a *congestion avoidance* phase and slows down the rate of increment. During congestion avoidance, it increases the congestion window by *1* only if all segments in the window have been acknowledged. The overall approach is known as *Additive Increase Multiplicative Decrease* (*AIMD*).

Taken together, slow-start, additive increase, multiplicative decrease, measurement of variation, and exponential timer backoff improve the performance of TCP dramatically without adding any significant computational overhead to the protocol software. Versions of TCP that use these techniques have improved the performance of previous versions significantly.

11.20 Fast Recovery And Other Response Modifications

Minor modifications have been made to TCP over many years. An early version of TCP, sometimes referred to as *Tahoe*, used the retransmission scheme described above, waiting for a timer to expire before retransmitting. In 1990, the *Reno* version of TCP appeared that introduced several changes, including a heuristic known as *fast recovery* or *fast retransmit* that has higher throughput in cases where only occasional loss occurs. Following the *Reno* version, researchers explored a *Vegas* version.

†The term *slow-start* is attributed to John Nagle; the technique was originally called *soft-start*.

The trick used in fast recovery arises from TCP's cumulative acknowledgement scheme: loss of a single segment means that the arrival of subsequent segments will cause the receiver to generate an ACK for the point in the stream where the missing segment begins. From a sender's point of view, a lost packet means multiple acknowledgements will arrive that each carry the same sequence number. The fast retransmit heuristic uses a series of three *duplicate acknowledgements* (i.e., an original plus three identical copies) to trigger a retransmission without waiting for the timer to expire.

In a case where only one segment is lost, waiting for the retransmitted segment to be acknowledged also reduces throughput. Therefore, to maintain higher throughput, the fast retransmit heuristic continues to send data from the window while awaiting acknowledgement of the retransmitted segment. Furthermore, the congestion window is artificially inflated: the congestion window is halved for the retransmission, but then the congestion window is increased by one maximum size segment for each duplicate ACK that previously arrived or arrives after the retransmission occurs. As a result, while fast retransmit occurs, TCP keeps many segments "in flight" between the sender and receiver.

A further optimization of the fast retransmit hueristic was incorporated in a later modification of TCP known as the *NewReno* version. The optimization handles a case where two segments are lost within a single window. In essence, when fast retransmit occurs, NewReno records information about the current window and retransmits as described above. When the ACK arrives, for the retransmitted segment, there are two possibilities: the ACK specifies the sequence number at the end of the window (in which case the retransmitted segment was the only segment missing from the window), or the ACK specifies a sequence number higher than the missing segment, but less than the end of the window (in which case a second segment from the window has also been lost). In the latter case, NewReno proceeds to retransmit the second missing segment.

Minor modifications to the AIMD scheme† have been proposed and used in later versions of TCP. To understand, consider how AIMD changes the sender's congestion window, w, in response to segment loss or the arrival of an acknowledgement:

$$w \leftarrow w - aw \quad \text{when loss is detected}$$

$$w \leftarrow w + \frac{b}{w} \quad \text{when an ACK arrives}$$

In the original scheme, a is .5 and b is 1. In thinking about protocols like *STCP*, which is used in sensor networks, researchers proposed setting a to 0.125 and b to 0.01 to prevent the congestion window from oscillating and increase throughput slightly. Other proposals for modifications (e.g. a protocol known as *HSTCP*) suggest making a and b functions of w (i.e., $a(w)$ and $b(w)$). Finally, proposals for TCP congestion control such as *Vegas* and *FAST* use increasing RTT as a measure of congestion instead of packet loss, and define the congestion window size to be a function of the measured RTT. Typically, the modifications only lead to performance improvements in special cases (e.g., networks with high bandwidth and low loss rates); the AIMD congestion control in NewReno is used for general cases.

†AIMD is defined in the previous section.

A final proposal related to TCP congestion control concerns UDP. Observe that although TCP reduces transmission when congestion occurs, UDP does not, which means that as TCP flows continue to back off, UDP flows consume more of the bandwidth. A solution known as *TCP Friendly Rate Control* (*TFRC*) was proposed. TFRC attempts to emulate TCP behavior by having a UDP receiver report datagram loss back to the sender and by having the sender use the reported loss to compute a rate at which UDP datagrams should be sent; TFRC has only been adopted for special cases.

11.21 Explicit Feedback Mechanisms (SACK and ECN)

Most versions of TCP use *implicit* techniques to detect loss and congestion. That is, TCP uses timeout and duplicate ACKs to detect loss, and changes in round trip times to detect congestion. Researchers have observed that slight improvements are possible if TCP includes mechanisms that provide such information *explicitly*. The next two sections describe two explicit techniques that have been proposed.

11.21.1 Selective Acknowledgement (SACK)

The alternative to TCP's cumulative acknowledgement mechanism is known as a *selective acknowledgement* mechanism. In essence, selective acknowledgements allow a receiver to specify exactly which data has been received and which is still missing. The chief advantage of selective acknowledgements arises in situations where occasional loss occurs: selective acknowledgements allow a sender to know exactly which segments to retransmit.

The *Selective ACKnowledgement* (*SACK*) mechanism proposed for TCP does not completely replace the cumulative acknowledgement mechanism, nor is it mandatory. Instead, TCP includes two options for SACK. The first option is used when the connection is established to allow a sender to specify that SACK is permitted. The second option is used by a receiver when sending an acknowledgement to include information about specific blocks of data that were received. The information for each block includes the first sequence number in a block (called the *left edge*) and the sequence number immediately beyond the block (called the *right edge*). Because the maximum size of a segment header is fixed, an acknowledgement can contain at most four SACK blocks. Interestingly, the SACK documents do not specify exactly how a sender responds to SACK; most implementations retransmit all missing blocks.

11.21.2 Explicit Congestion Notification

A second proposed technique to avoid implicit measurement is intended to handle congestion in the network. Known as *Explicit Congestion Notification* (*ECN*), the mechanism requires routers throughout an internet to notify TCP as congestion occurs. The mechanism is conceptually straightforward: as a TCP segment passes through the internet, routers along the path use a pair of bits in the IP header to record congestion.

Thus, when a segment arrives, the receiver knows whether the segment experienced congestion at any point. Unfortunately, the sender, not the receiver, needs to learn about congestion. Therefore, the receiver uses the next ACK to inform the sender that congestion occurred. The sender then responds by reducing its congestion window.

ECN uses two bits in the IP header to allow routers to record congestion, and uses two bits in the TCP header (taken from the reserved area) to allow the sending and receiving TCP to communicate. One of the TCP header bits is used by a receiver to send congestion information back to a sender; the other bit allows a sender to inform the receiver that the congestion notification has been received. Bits in the IP header are taken from unused bits in the TYPE OF SERVICE field. A router can choose to set either bit to specify that congestion occurred (two bits are used to make the mechanism more robust).

11.22 Congestion, Tail Drop, And TCP

We said that communication protocols are divided into layers to make it possible for designers to focus on a single problem at a time. The separation of functionality into layers is both necessary and useful — it means that one layer can be changed without affecting other layers, but it means that layers operate in isolation. For example, because it operates end-to-end, TCP remains unchanged when the path between the endpoints changes (e.g., routes change or additional networks routers are added). However, the isolation of layers restricts inter-layer communication. In particular, although TCP on the original source interacts with TCP on the ultimate destination, it cannot interact with lower-layer elements along the path†. Thus, neither the sending nor receiving TCP receives reports about conditions in the network, nor does either end inform lower layers along the path before transferring data.

Researchers have observed that the lack of communication between layers means that the choice of policy or implementation at one layer can have a dramatic effect on the performance of higher layers. In the case of TCP, policies that routers use to handle datagrams can have a significant effect on both the performance of a single TCP connection and the aggregate throughput of all connections. For example, if a router delays some datagrams more than others‡, TCP will back off its retransmission timer. If the delay exceeds the retransmission timeout, TCP will assume congestion has occurred. Thus, although each layer is defined independently, researchers try to devise mechanisms and implementations that work well with protocols in other layers.

The most important interaction between IP implementation policies and TCP occurs when a router becomes overrun and drops datagrams. Because a router places each incoming datagram in a queue in memory until it can be processed, the policy focuses on queue management. When datagrams arrive faster than they can be forwarded, the queue grows; when datagrams arrive slower than they can be forwarded, the queue shrinks. However, because memory is finite, the queue cannot grow without bound. Early routers used a *tail-drop* policy to manage queue overflow:

† The Explicit Congestion Notification scheme mentioned above has not yet been adopted.

‡Variance in delay is referred to as *jitter*.

> *Tail-Drop Policy For Routers: if a packet queue is filled when a datagram must be placed on the queue, discard the datagram.*

The name *tail-drop* arises from the effect of the policy on an arriving sequence of datagrams. Once the queue fills, the router begins discarding all additional datagrams. That is, the router discards the "tail" of the sequence.

Tail-drop has an interesting effect on TCP. In the simple case where datagrams traveling through a router carry segments from a single TCP connection, the loss causes TCP to enter slow-start, which reduces throughput until TCP begins receiving ACKs and increases the congestion window. A more severe problem can occur, however, when the datagrams traveling through a router carry segments from many TCP connections because tail-drop can cause global synchronization. To see why, observe that datagrams are typically multiplexed, with successive datagrams each coming from a different source. Thus, a tail-drop policy makes it likely that the router will discard one segment from N connections rather than N segments from one connection. The simultaneous loss causes all N instances of TCP to enter slow-start at the same time†.

11.23 Random Early Detection (RED)

How can a router avoid global synchronization? The answer lies in a clever scheme that avoids tail-drop whenever possible. Known as *Random Early Detection*, *Random Early Drop*, or *Random Early Discard*, the scheme is more frequently referred to by its acronym, *RED*. The general idea behind RED lies in randomization: instead of waiting until a queue fills completely, a router monitors the queue size. As the queue begins to fill, the router chooses datagrams at random to drop.

A router that implements RED runs the algorithm on each queue (e.g., each network connection). To simplify our description, we will only discuss a single queue and assume the reader realizes that the same technique must be applied to other queues.

A router uses two threshold values to mark positions in the queue: T_{min} and T_{max}. The general operation of RED can be described by three rules that determine the disposition of a datagram that must be placed in the queue:

- If the queue currently contains fewer than T_{min} datagrams, add the new datagram to the queue.
- If the queue contains more than T_{max} datagrams, discard the new datagram.
- If the queue contains between T_{min} and T_{max} datagrams, randomly discard the datagram with a probability, p, that depends on the current queue size.

†Interestingly, global synchronization does not occur if the number of TCP connections sharing a link is sufficiently large (>500) and the RTTs vary.

The randomness of RED means that instead of waiting until the queue overflows and then driving many TCP connections into slow-start, a router slowly and randomly drops datagrams as congestion increases. We can summarize:

> *RED Policy For Routers: if the input queue is full when a datagram arrives, discard the datagram; if the input queue is below a minimum threshold, add the datagram to the queue; otherwise, discard the datagram with a probability that depends on the queue size.*

The key to making RED work well lies in the choice of the thresholds T_{min} and T_{max} and the discard probability p. T_{min} must be large enough to ensure that the queue has sufficiently high throughput. For example, if the queue is connected to an output link, the queue should drive the network at high utilization. Furthermore, because RED operates like tail-drop when the queue size exceeds T_{max}, the value of T_{max} must be greater than T_{min} by more than the typical increase in queue size during one TCP round trip time (e.g., set T_{max} at least twice as large as T_{min}). Otherwise, RED can cause the same global oscillations as tail-drop (e.g., T_{min} can be set to one-half of T_{max}).

Computation of the discard probability, p, is the most complex aspect of RED. Instead of using a constant, a new value of p is computed for each datagram; the value depends on the relationship between the current queue size and the thresholds. To understand the scheme, observe that all RED processing can be viewed probabilistically. When the queue size is less than T_{min}, RED does not discard any datagrams, making the discard probability *0*. Similarly, when the queue size is greater than T_{max}, RED discards all datagrams, making the discard probability *1*. For intermediate values of queue size, (i.e., those between T_{min} and T_{max}), the probability can vary from *0* to *1* linearly.

Although the linear scheme forms the basis of RED's probability computation, a change must be made to avoid overreacting. The need for the change arises because network traffic is bursty, which results in rapid fluctuations of a router's queue. If RED used a simplistic linear scheme, later datagrams in each burst would be assigned high probability of being dropped (because they arrive when the queue has more entries). However, a router should not drop datagrams unnecessarily, because doing so has a negative impact on TCP throughput. Thus, if a burst is short, it is unwise to drop datagrams because the queue will never overflow. Of course, RED cannot postpone discard indefinitely because a long-term burst will overflow the queue, resulting in a tail-drop policy which has the potential to cause global synchronization problems.

How can RED assign a higher discard probability as the queue fills without discarding datagrams from each burst? The answer lies in a technique borrowed from TCP: instead of using the actual queue size at any instant, RED computes a weighted average queue size, *avg*, and uses the average size to determine the probability. The value of *avg* is an exponential weighted average, updated each time a datagram arrives according to the equation:

$$\text{avg} = (1-\gamma) \times \text{Old\_avg} + \gamma \times \text{Current\_queue\_size}$$

where γ denotes a value between *0* and *1*. If γ is small enough, the average will track long term trends, but will remain immune to short bursts†

In addition to equations that determine γ, RED contains other details that we have glossed over. For example, RED computations can be made extremely efficient by choosing constants as powers of two and using integer arithmetic. Another important detail concerns the measurement of queue size, which affects both the RED computation and its overall effect on TCP. In particular, because the time required to forward a datagram is proportional to its size, it makes sense to measure the queue in octets rather than in datagrams; doing so requires only minor changes to the equations for p and γ. Measuring queue size in octets affects the type of traffic dropped because it makes the discard probability proportional to the amount of data a sender puts in the stream, rather than the number of segments. Small datagrams (e.g., those that carry remote login traffic or requests to servers) have lower probability of being dropped than large datagrams (e.g., those that carry file transfer traffic). One positive consequence of using datagram size is that when acknowledgements travel over a congested path, they have a lower probability of being dropped. As a result, if a (large) data segment does arrive, the sending TCP will receive the ACK and will avoid unnecessary retransmission.

Both analysis and simulations show that RED works well. It handles congestion, avoids the synchronization that results from tail-drop, and allows short bursts without dropping datagrams unnecessarily. Consequently, the IETF now recommends that routers implement RED.

11.24 Establishing A TCP Connection

To establish a connection, TCP uses a *three-way handshake*. That is, three messages are exchanged that allow each side to agree to form a connection and know that the other side has agreed. The first segment of a handshake can be identified because it has the SYN‡ bit set in the code field. The second message has both the SYN and ACK bits set to indicate that it acknowledges the first SYN segment and continues the handshake. The final handshake message is only an acknowledgement and is merely used to inform the destination that both sides agree that a connection has been established.

Usually, the TCP software on one machine waits passively for the handshake, and the TCP software on another machine initiates it. However, the handshake is carefully designed to work even if both machines attempt to initiate a connection simultaneously. Thus, a connection can be established from either end or from both ends simultaneously. Once the connection has been established, data can flow in both directions equally well (i.e., the connection is symmetric). That is, there is no master or slave, and the side that initiates the connection has no special abilities or privileges. In the simplest case, the handshake proceeds as Figure 11.14 illustrates.

---

†An example value suggested for γ is .002.

‡SYN stands for *synchronization*, and is pronounced "sin"; the segment carrying the SYN is called the "sin segment."

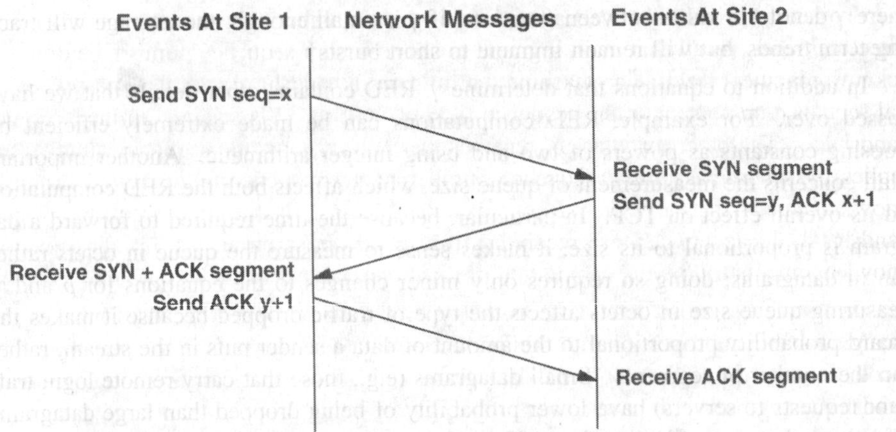

Figure 11.14 The sequence of messages in a three-way handshake. Time proceeds down the page; diagonal lines represent segments sent between sites.

It may seem that a two-message exchange would suffice to establish a connection. However, the three-way handshake is both necessary and sufficient for correct synchronization between the two ends of the connection given internet delivery semantics. To understand the reason that connection establishment is difficult, remember that TCP uses an unreliable packet delivery service. Therefore, messages can be lost, delayed, duplicated, or delivered out of order. To accommodate loss, TCP must retransmit requests. However, trouble can arise if excessive delay causes retransmission, which means both the original and retransmitted copy arrive while the connection is being established. Retransmitted requests can also be delayed until after a connection has been established, used, and terminated! The three-way handshake and rules that prevent restarting a connection after it has terminated are carefully designed to compensate for all possible situations.

11.25 Initial Sequence Numbers

The three-way handshake accomplishes two important functions. It guarantees that both sides are ready to transfer data (and that they know they are both ready) and it allows both sides to agree on initial sequence numbers. Sequence numbers are sent and acknowledged during the handshake. Each machine must choose an initial sequence number at random that it will use to identify octets in the stream it is sending. Sequence numbers cannot always start at the same value. In particular, TCP cannot merely choose sequence *1* every time it creates a connection (one of the exercises examines problems that can arise if it does). Of course, it is important that both sides agree on an initial number, so octet numbers used in acknowledgements agree with those used in data segments.

To see how machines can agree on sequence numbers for two streams after only three messages, recall that each segment contains both a sequence number field and an acknowledgement field. The machine that initiates a handshake, call it *A*, passes its initial sequence number, *x*, in the sequence field of the first SYN segment in the three-way handshake. The other machine, *B*, receives the SYN, records the sequence number, and replies by sending its initial sequence number in the sequence field as well as an acknowledgement that specifies *B* expects octet *x+1*. In the final message of the handshake, *A* "acknowledges" receiving from *B* all octets through *y*. In all cases, acknowledgements follow the convention of using the number of the *next* octet expected.

We have described how TCP usually carries out the three-way handshake by exchanging segments that contain a minimum amount of information. Because of the protocol design, it is possible to send data along with the initial sequence numbers in the handshake segments. In such cases, the TCP software must hold the data until the handshake completes. Once a connection has been established, the TCP software can release data being held and deliver it to a waiting application program quickly. The reader is referred to the protocol specification for the details.

11.26 Closing a TCP Connection

Two applications that use TCP to communicate can terminate the conversation gracefully using the *close* operation. Once again, it is important that both sides agree to close a connection and both sides know the connection is closed. Therefore, TCP uses a three-way handshake to close connections. To understand the handshake used to close a connection, recall that TCP connections are full duplex and that we view them as containing two independent stream transfers, one going in each direction. When an application program tells TCP that it has no more data to send, TCP will close the connection *in one direction*. To close its half of a connection, the sending TCP finishes transmitting the remaining data, waits for the receiver to acknowledge it, and then sends a segment with the *FIN* bit set†. Upon receipt of a FIN, TCP sends an acknowledgement and then informs the application that the other side has finished sending data. The details depend on the operating system, but most systems use the "end-of-file" mechanism.

Once a connection has been closed in a given direction, TCP refuses to accept more data for that direction. Meanwhile, data can continue to flow in the opposite direction until the sender closes it. Of course, a TCP endpoint that is still receiving data must send acknowledgements, even if the data transmission in the reverse direction has terminated. When both directions have been closed, the TCP software at each endpoint deletes its record of the connection.

The details of closing a connection are even more subtle than suggested above because TCP uses a modified three-way handshake to close a connection. Figure 11.15 illustrates the messages that are exchanged for the typical case where all communication has finished and the connection is closed in both directions.

†A segment with the FIN bit set is called a "fin segment."

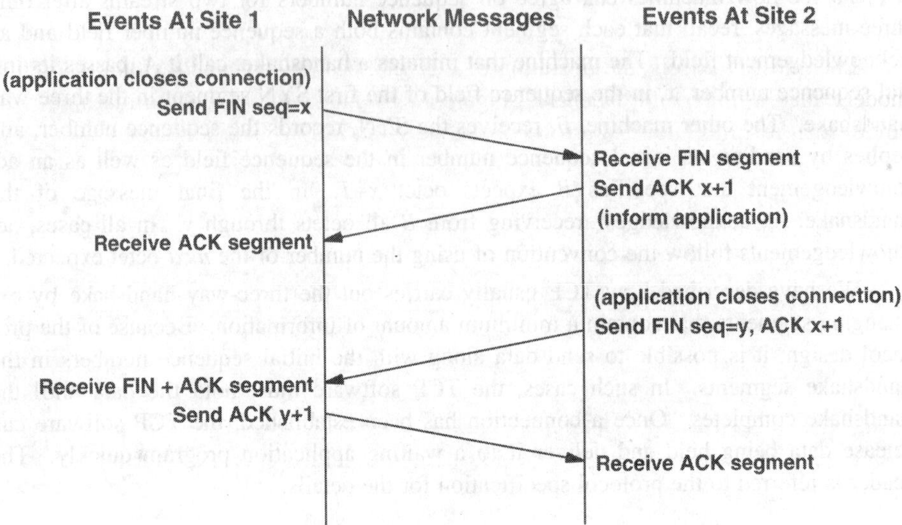

Figure 11.15 The three-way handshake used to close a connection with an extra ACK sent immediately upon receipt of a FIN.

The difference between three-way handshakes used to establish and close connections occurs after a machine receives the initial FIN segment. Instead of generating a second FIN segment immediately, TCP sends an acknowledgement and then informs the application of the request to shut down. Informing the application program of the request and obtaining a response may take considerable time (e.g., it may involve human interaction). The acknowledgement prevents retransmission of the initial FIN segment during the delay. Finally, when the application program instructs TCP to shut down the connection completely, TCP sends the second FIN segment and the original site replies with the third message, an ACK.

11.27 TCP Connection Reset

Normally, an application program uses the *close* operation to shut down a connection when it finishes sending data. Thus, closing connections is considered a normal part of use, analogous to closing files. We say that the connection terminated *gracefully*. However, sometimes abnormal conditions arise that force an application or the network software to break a connection without a graceful shutdown. TCP provides a reset facility to handle abnormal disconnections.

To reset a connection, one side initiates termination by sending a segment with the *RST* (*RESET*) bit in the *CODE* field set. The other side responds to a reset segment immediately by aborting the connection. When a reset occurs, TCP informs any local application that was using the connection. Note that a reset occurs immediately and cannot be undone. We think of it as an instantaneous abort that terminates transfer in both directions and releases resources, such as buffers.

11.28 TCP State Machine

Like most protocols, the operation of TCP can best be explained with a theoretical model called a *finite state machine*. Figure 11.16 shows the TCP state machine, with circles representing states and arrows representing transitions between them.

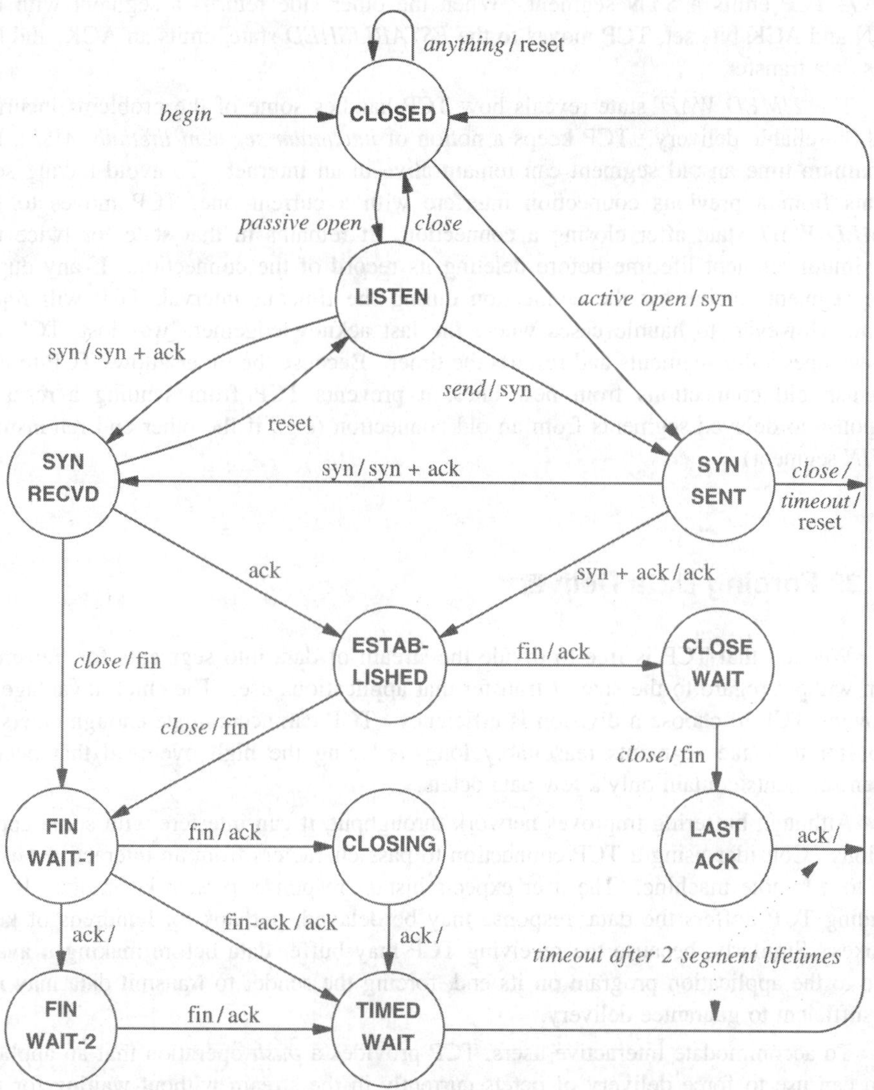

Figure 11.16 The finite state machine for TCP. Labels on state transitions show the input that caused the transition followed by the output if any.

In the figure, the label on each state transition shows what causes the transition and what TCP sends when it performs the transition. For example, the TCP software at each endpoint begins in the *CLOSED* state. Application programs must issue either a *passive open* command to wait for a connection from another machine, or an *active open* command to initiate a connection. An active open command forces a transition from the *CLOSED* state to the *SYN SENT* state. When it follows the transition to *SYN SENT*, TCP emits a SYN segment. When the other side returns a segment with the SYN and ACK bits set, TCP moves to the *ESTABLISHED* state, emits an ACK, and begins data transfer.

The *TIMED WAIT* state reveals how TCP handles some of the problems incurred with unreliable delivery. TCP keeps a notion of *maximum segment lifetime* (*MSL*), the maximum time an old segment can remain alive in an internet. To avoid having segments from a previous connection interfere with a current one, TCP moves to the *TIMED WAIT* state after closing a connection. It remains in that state for twice the maximum segment lifetime before deleting its record of the connection. If any duplicate segments arrive for the connection during the timeout interval, TCP will reject them. However, to handle cases where the last acknowledgement was lost, TCP acknowledges valid segments and restarts the timer. Because the timer allows TCP to distinguish old connections from new ones, it prevents TCP from sending a reset in response to delayed segments from an old connection (e.g., if the other end retransmits a *FIN* segment).

11.29 Forcing Data Delivery

We said that TCP is free to divide the stream of data into segments for transmission without regard to the size of transfer that applications use. The chief advantage of allowing TCP to choose a division is efficiency. TCP can accumulate enough octets in a buffer to make segments reasonably long, reducing the high overhead that occurs when segments contain only a few data octets.

Although buffering improves network throughput, it can interfere with some applications. Consider using a TCP connection to pass characters from an interactive terminal to a remote machine. The user expects instant response to each keystroke. If the sending TCP buffers the data, response may be delayed, perhaps for hundreds of keystrokes. Similarly, because the receiving TCP may buffer data before making it available to the application program on its end, forcing the sender to transmit data may not be sufficient to guarantee delivery.

To accommodate interactive users, TCP provides a *push* operation that an application can use to force delivery of octets currently in the stream without waiting for the buffer to fill. The *push* operation does more than force the local TCP to send a segment. It also requests TCP to set the *PSH* bit in the segment code field, so the data will be delivered to the application program on the receiving end. Thus, an interactive application uses the *push* function after each keystroke. Similarly, applications that control a remote display can use the *push* function to insure that the data is sent across the connection promptly and passed to the application on the other side immediately.

11.30 Reserved TCP Port Numbers

Like UDP, TCP uses a combination of statically and dynamically assigned protocol port numbers. A set of *well-known ports* have been assigned by a central authority for commonly invoked services (e.g., web servers and electronic mail servers). Other port numbers are available for an operating system to allocate to local applications as needed. Many well-known TCP ports now exist. Figure 11.17 lists some of the currently assigned TCP ports.

Port	Keyword	Description
0		Reserved
7	echo	Echo
9	discard	Discard
13	daytime	Daytime
19	chargen	Character Generator
20	ftp-data	File Transfer Protocol (data)
21	ftp	File Transfer Protocol
22	ssh	Secure Shell
23	telnet	Terminal connection
25	smtp	Simple Mail Transport Protocol
37	time	Time
53	domain	Domain name server
80	www	World Wide Web
88	kerberos	Kerberos security service
110	pop3	Post Office Protocol vers. 3
123	ntp	Network Time Protocol
161	snmp	Simple Network Management Protocol
179	bgp	Border Gateway Protocol
443	https	Secure HTTP
860	iscsi	iSCSI (SCSI over IP)
993	imaps	Secure IMAP
995	pop3s	Secure POP3
30301	bittorrent	BitTorrent service

Figure 11.17 Examples of currently assigned TCP port numbers.

We should point out that although TCP and UDP port numbers are independent, the designers have chosen to use the same integer port numbers for any service that is accessible from both UDP and TCP. For example, a domain name server can be accessed either with TCP or with UDP. When using either protocol, a client application can use the same port number, *53*, because IANA assigned *53* as the domain name service port for both TCP and UDP.

11.31 Silly Window Syndrome And Small Packets

Researchers who developed TCP observed a serious performance problem that can result when the sending and receiving applications operate at different speeds. To understand the problem, remember that TCP buffers incoming data, and consider what can happen if a receiving application chooses to read incoming data one octet at a time. When a connection is first established, the receiving TCP allocates a buffer of K bytes, and uses the *WINDOW* field in acknowledgement segments to advertise the available buffer size to the sender. If the sending application generates data quickly, the sending TCP will transmit segments with data for the entire window. Eventually, the sender will receive an acknowledgement that specifies the entire window has been filled and no additional space remains in the receiver's buffer.

When the receiving application reads an octet of data from a full buffer, one octet of space becomes available. We said that when space becomes available in its buffer, TCP on the receiving machine generates an acknowledgement that uses the *WINDOW* field to inform the sender. In the example, the receiver will advertise a window of *1* octet. When it learns that space is available, the sending TCP responds by transmitting a segment that contains one octet of data.

Although single-octet window advertisements work correctly to keep the receiver's buffer filled, they result in a series of small data segments. The sending TCP must compose a segment that contains one octet of data, place the segment in an IP datagram, and transmit the result. When the receiving application reads another octet, TCP generates another acknowledgement, which causes the sender to transmit another segment that contains one octet of data. The resulting interaction can reach a steady state in which TCP sends a separate segment for each octet of data.

Transferring small segments unnecessarily consumes network bandwidth and introduces computational overhead. Small segments consume more network bandwidth per octet of data than large segments because each datagram has a header. If the datagram only carries one octet of data; the ratio of header to data is large. Computational overhead arises because TCP on both the sending and receiving computers must process each segment. The sending TCP software must allocate buffer space, form a segment header, and compute a checksum for the segment. Similarly, IP software on the sending machine must encapsulate the segment in a datagram, compute a header checksum, forward the datagram, and transfer it to the appropriate network interface. On the receiving machine, IP must verify the IP header checksum and pass the segment to TCP. TCP must verify the segment checksum, examine the sequence number, extract the data, and place it in a buffer.

Although we have described how small segments result when a receiver advertises a small available window, a sender can also cause each segment to contain a small amount of data. For example, imagine a TCP implementation that aggressively sends data whenever it is available, and consider what happens if a sending application generates data one octet at a time. After the application generates an octet of data, TCP creates and transmits a segment. TCP can also send a small segment if an application generates data in fixed-sized blocks of B octets, and the sending TCP extracts data from the buffer in maximum segment sized blocks, M, where $M \neq B$, because the last block in a buffer can be small.

The problem of TCP sending small segments became known as the *silly window syndrome* (*SWS*). Early TCP implementations were plagued by SWS. To summarize,

> *Early TCP implementations exhibited a problem known as* silly window syndrome, *in which each acknowledgement advertises a small amount of space available and each segment carries a small amount of data.*

11.32 Avoiding Silly Window Syndrome

TCP specifications now include heuristics that prevent silly window syndrome. A heuristic used on the sending machine avoids transmitting a small amount of data in each segment. Another heuristic used on the receiving machine avoids sending small increments in window advertisements that can trigger small data packets. Although the heuristics work well together, having both the sender and receiver avoid silly window helps ensure good performance in the case that one end of a connection fails to correctly implement silly window avoidance.

In practice, TCP software must contain both sender and receiver silly window avoidance code. To understand why, recall that a TCP connection is full duplex — data can flow in either direction. Thus, an implementation of TCP includes code to send data as well as code to receive it.

11.32.1 Receive-Side Silly Window Avoidance

The heuristic a receiver uses to avoid silly window is straightforward and easier to understand. In general, a receiver maintains an internal record of the currently available window, but delays advertising an increase in window size to the sender until the window can advance a significant amount. The definition of "significant" depends on the receiver's buffer size and the maximum segment size. TCP defines it to be the minimum of one half of the receiver's buffer or the number of data octets in a maximum-sized segment.

Receive-side silly window prevents small window advertisements in the case where a receiving application extracts data octets slowly. For example, when a receiver's buffer fills completely, it sends an acknowledgement that contains a zero window advertisement. As the receiving application extracts octets from the buffer, the receiving TCP computes the newly available space in the buffer. Instead of sending a window advertisement immediately, however, the receiver waits until the available space reaches one half of the total buffer size or a maximum sized segment. Thus, the sender always receives large increments in the current window, allowing it to transfer large segments. The heuristic can be summarized as follows:

> *Receive-Side Silly Window Avoidance: before sending an updated window advertisement after advertising a zero window, wait for space to become available that is either at least 50% of the total buffer size or equal to a maximum sized segment.*

11.32.2 Delayed Acknowledgements

Two approaches have been taken to implement silly window avoidance on the receive side. In the first approach, TCP acknowledges each segment that arrives, but does not advertise an increase in its window until the window reaches the limits specified by the silly window avoidance heuristic. In the second approach, TCP delays sending an acknowledgement when silly window avoidance specifies that the window is not sufficiently large to advertise. The standards recommend delaying acknowledgements.

Delayed acknowledgements have both advantages and disadvantages. The chief advantage arises because delayed acknowledgements can decrease traffic and thereby increase throughput. For example, if additional data arrives during the delay period, a single acknowledgement will acknowledge all data received. If the receiving application generates a response immediately after data arrives (e.g., a character echo for an interactive session), a short delay may permit the acknowledgement to piggyback on a data segment. Furthermore, TCP cannot move its window until the receiving application extracts data from the buffer. In cases where the receiving application reads data as soon as it arrives, a short delay allows TCP to send a single segment that acknowledges the data and advertises an updated window. Without delayed acknowledgements, TCP will acknowledge the arrival of data immediately, and later send an additional acknowledgement to update the window size.

The disadvantages of delayed acknowledgements should be clear. Most important, if a receiver delays acknowledgements too long, the sending TCP will retransmit the segment. Unnecessary retransmissions lower throughput because they waste network bandwidth. In addition, retransmissions require computational overhead on the sending and receiving machines. Furthermore, TCP uses the arrival of acknowledgements to estimate round trip times; delaying acknowledgements can confuse the estimate and make retransmission times too long.

To avoid potential problems, the TCP standards place a limit on the time TCP delays an acknowledgement. Implementations cannot delay an acknowledgement for more than 500 milliseconds. Furthermore, to guarantee that TCP receives a sufficient number of round trip estimates, the standard recommends that a receiver should acknowledge at least every other data segment.

11.32.3 Send-Side Silly Window Avoidance

The heuristic a sending TCP uses to avoid silly window syndrome is both surprising and elegant. Recall that the goal is to avoid sending small segments. Also recall that a sending application can generate data in arbitrarily small blocks (e.g., one octet at a time). Thus, to achieve the goal, a sending TCP must allow the sending application to make multiple calls to *write* (or *send*) and must collect the data transferred in each call before transmitting it in a single, large segment. That is, a sending TCP must delay sending a segment until it can accumulate a reasonable amount of data. The technique is known as *clumping*.

The question arises, how long should TCP wait before transmitting data? On one hand, if TCP waits too long, the application experiences large delays. More important, TCP cannot know whether to wait because it cannot know whether the application will generate more data in the near future. On the other hand, if TCP does not wait long enough, segments will be small and throughput will be low.

Protocols designed prior to TCP confronted the same problem and used techniques to clump data into larger packets. For example, to achieve efficient transfer across a network, early remote terminal protocols delayed transmitting each keystroke for a few hundred milliseconds to determine whether the user would continue to press keys. Because TCP is designed to be general, however, it can be used by a diverse set of applications. Characters may travel across a TCP connection because a user is typing on a keyboard or because a program is transferring a file. A fixed delay is not optimal for all applications.

Like the algorithm TCP uses for retransmission and the slow-start algorithm used to avoid congestion, the technique a sending TCP uses to avoid sending small packets is adaptive — the delay depends on the current performance of the underlying internet. Like slow-start, send-side silly window avoidance is called *self clocking* because it does not compute delays. Instead, TCP uses the arrival of an acknowledgement to trigger the transmission of additional packets. The heuristic can be summarized:

> *Send-Side Silly Window Avoidance: when a sending application generates additional data to be sent over a connection for which previous data has been transmitted but not acknowledged, place the new data in the output buffer as usual, but do not send additional segments until there is sufficient data to fill a maximum-sized segment. If still waiting to send when an acknowledgement arrives, send all data that has accumulated in the buffer. Apply the rule even when the user requests a* push *operation.*

If an application generates data one octet at a time, TCP will send the first octet immediately. However, until the ACK arrives, TCP will accumulate additional octets in its buffer. Thus, if the application is reasonably fast compared to the network (i.e., a file transfer), successive segments will each contain many octets. If the application is slow compared to the network (e.g., a user typing on a keyboard), small segments will be sent without long delay.

Known as the *Nagle algorithm* after its inventor, the technique is especially elegant because it requires little computational overhead. A host does not need to keep separate timers for each connection, nor does the host need to examine a clock when an application generates data. More important, although the technique adapts to arbitrary combinations of network delay, maximum segment size, and application speed, it does not lower throughput in conventional cases.

To understand why throughput remains high for conventional communication, observe that applications optimized for high throughput do not generate data one octet at a time (doing so would incur unnecessary operating system overhead). Instead, such applications write large blocks of data with each call. Thus, the outgoing TCP buffer begins with sufficient data for at least one maximum size segment. Furthermore, because the application produces data faster than TCP can transfer data, the sending buffer remains nearly full and TCP does not delay transmission. As a result, TCP continues to send segments at whatever rate the underlying internet can tolerate, while the application continues to fill the buffer. To summarize:

> *TCP now requires the sender and receiver to implement heuristics that avoid the silly window syndrome. A receiver avoids advertising a small window, and a sender uses an adaptive scheme to delay transmission so it can clump data into large segments.*

11.33 Buffer Bloat And Its Effect On Latency

TCP is designed to maximize throughput by adapting to conditions in the network. As a result, TCP keeps buffers in network devices nearly full. Over several decades, the price of memory has dropped and vendors have increased the amount of memory in network devices. Even a small home Wi-Fi router has orders of magnitude more memory than the largest routers of the 1980s.

It may seem that adding memory to a network device will always improve performance because the device can accommodate packet bursts with fewer packets being dropped. However, a serious problem can arise when network devices have large memories and send packets across slow links: long latency. Increased latency means that real-time communication, such as VoIP phone calls, becomes unusable.

To appreciate the problem, consider a Wi-Fi router in a home. Assume two users are using the Internet: one is downloading a movie and the other is using Skype to make a phone call. Assume the router uses only 4 MB of memory as a packet buffer (a conservative estimate). Because it uses TCP and always has data to send, the movie download will keep the buffer nearly full. The Skype conversation sends data at a much lower rate than the download. When a Skype packet arrives, the packet will be placed in the back of the buffer, and will not be delivered until all the packets that were waiting in the buffer have been sent. How long does it take to empty a buffer? A Wi-

Fi connection using 802.11g has an effective delivery rate of approximately 20 Mbps. A megabyte of memory contains 8,388,608 bits, so a 4 megabyte buffer holds 33,554,432 bits. We know that the receiver will transmit ACKs, which means the router cannot send data from the buffer continuously. For purposes of analysis, assume a best case where the network has no other traffic and there is no delay between packets. Even under the idealized conditions, the time to transmit a buffer of data is:

$$\textit{Buffer delay} \quad = \quad \frac{3.36 \times 10^7 \ \textit{bits}}{2.0 \times 10^7 \ \textit{bits / second}} \quad = \quad 1.68 \ \textit{seconds}$$

In other words, the user who is attempting to conduct a Skype call will experience an intolerable delay. The delay is noticeable even if a user is only browsing the Web.

We use the term *buffer bloat* to describe the use of very large buffers in network devices. The most surprising aspect of buffer bloat is that increasing the network bandwidth before the bottleneck link will not improve performance and may make latency worse. That is, paying for a higher-speed Internet connection will not solve the problem. For more information on the subject, see the following video:

http://www.youtube.com/watch?v=-D-cJNtKwuw

11.34 Summary

The Transmission Control Protocol, TCP, defines a key service for internet communication, namely, reliable stream delivery. TCP provides a full duplex connection between two machines, allowing them to exchange large volumes of data efficiently.

Because it uses a sliding window protocol, TCP can make efficient use of a network. Because it makes few assumptions about the underlying delivery system, TCP is flexible enough to operate over a large variety of delivery systems. Because it provides flow control, TCP allows systems of widely varying speeds to communicate.

The basic unit of transfer used by TCP is a segment. Segments are used to pass data or control information (e.g., to allow TCP software on two machines to establish connections or break them). The segment format permits a machine to piggyback acknowledgements for data flowing in one direction by including them in the segment headers of data flowing in the opposite direction.

TCP implements flow control by having the receiver advertise the amount of data it is willing to accept. It also supports out-of-band messages using an urgent data facility, and forces delivery using a push mechanism.

The current TCP standard specifies exponential backoff for retransmission timers and congestion avoidance algorithms like slow-start, additive increase, and multiplicative decrease. In addition, TCP uses heuristics to avoid transferring small packets. Finally, the IETF recommends that routers use RED instead of tail-drop because doing so avoids TCP synchronization and improves throughput.

EXERCISES

11.1 TCP uses a finite field to contain stream sequence numbers. Study the protocol specification to find out how it allows an arbitrary length stream to pass from one machine to another.

11.2 The text notes that one of the TCP options permits a receiver to specify the maximum segment size it is willing to accept. Why does TCP support an option to specify maximum segment size when it also has a window advertisement mechanism?

11.3 Under what conditions of delay, bandwidth, load, and packet loss will TCP retransmit significant volumes of data unnecessarily?

11.4 A single lost TCP acknowledgement does not necessarily force a retransmission. Explain why.

11.5 Experiment with local machines to determine how TCP handles computer reboots. Establish a connection from machine *X* to machine *Y* and leave the connection idle. Reboot machine *Y* and then force the application on machine *X* to send a segment. What happens?

11.6 Imagine an implementation of TCP that discards segments that arrive out of order, even if they fall in the current window. That is, the imagined version only accepts segments that extend the byte stream it has already received. Does it work? How does it compare to a standard TCP implementation?

11.7 Consider computation of a TCP checksum. Assume that although the checksum field in the segment has *not* been set to zero, the result of computing the checksum *is* zero. What can you conclude?

11.8 What are the arguments for and against automatically closing idle TCP connections?

11.9 If two application programs use TCP to send data but only send one character per segment (e.g., by using the *push* operation), what is the maximum percent of the network bandwidth they will have for their data with IPv4? With IPv6?

11.10 Suppose an implementation of TCP uses initial sequence number *1* when it creates a connection. Explain how a system crash and restart can confuse a remote system into believing that the old connection remained open.

11.11 Find out how implementations of TCP solve the *overlapping segment problem*. The problem arises because the receiver must accept only one copy of all bytes from the data stream even if the sender transmits two segments that partially overlap one another (e.g., the first segment carries bytes 100 through 200 and the second carries bytes 150 through 250).

11.12 Trace the TCP finite state machine transitions for two ends of a connection. Assume one side executes a passive open and the other side executes an active open, and step through the three-way handshake.

11.13 Read the TCP specification to find out the exact conditions under which TCP can make the transition from *FIN WAIT-1* to *TIMED WAIT*.

11.14 Trace the TCP state transitions for two machines that agree to close a connection gracefully.

11.15 Assume TCP is sending segments using a maximum window size of 64 Kbytes on a channel that has infinite bandwidth and an average round-trip time of 20 milliseconds. What is the maximum throughput? How does throughput change if the round-trip time increases to 40 milliseconds (while bandwidth remains infinite)? Did you need to assume IPv4 or IPv6 to answer the question? Why or why not?

11.16 Can you derive an equation that expresses the maximum possible TCP throughput as a function of the network bandwidth, the network delay, and the time to process a segment and generate an acknowledgement. (Hint: consider the previous exercise.)

11.17 Describe (abnormal) circumstances that can leave one end of a connection in state *FIN WAIT-2* indefinitely. (Hint: think of datagram loss and system crashes.)

11.18 Show that when a router implements RED, the probability a packet will be discarded from a particular TCP connection is proportional to the percentage of traffic that the connection generates.

11.19 Argue that fast retransmit could be even faster if it used one duplicate ACK as a trigger. Why does the standard require multiple duplicate ACKs?

11.20 To see if a SACK scheme is needed in the modern Internet, measure the datagram loss on a long-lived TCP connection (e.g., a video streaming application). How many segments are lost? What can you conclude?

11.21 Consider a wireless router with a 3 Mbps connection to the Internet and a (bloated) buffer of 256 MB. If two users are downloading movies and a third user tries to contact *google.com*, what is the minimum time before the third user receives a response?

11.22 In the previous exercise, does your answer change if the connection between the router and the Internet is 10 Mbps? Why or why not?

Chapter Contents

12

Routing Architecture: Cores, Peers, And Algorithms

12.1 Introduction

Previous chapters concentrate on the communication services TCP/IP offers to applications and the details of the protocols in hosts and routers that provide the services. In the discussion, we assumed that routers always contain correct routes, and saw that a router can use the ICMP redirect mechanism to instruct a directly-connected host to change a route.

This chapter considers two broad questions: what values should each forwarding table contain, and how can those values be obtained? To answer the first question, we will consider the relationship between internet architecture and routing. In particular, we will discuss internets structured around a backbone and those composed of multiple peer networks, and consider the consequences for routing. The former is typical of a corporate intranet; the latter applies to the global Internet. To answer the second question, we will consider the two basic types of route propagation algorithms and see how each supplies routing information automatically.

We begin by discussing forwarding in general. Later sections concentrate on internet architecture and describe the algorithms routers use to exchange routing information. Chapters 13 and 14 continue to expand our discussion of routing. They explore protocols that routers owned by two independent administrative groups use to exchange information, and protocols that a single group uses among all its routers.

12.2 The Origin Of Forwarding Tables

Recall from Chapter 3 that IP routers provide active interconnections among networks. Each router attaches to two or more physical networks and forwards IP datagrams among them, accepting datagrams that arrive over one network interface and sending them out over another interface. Except for destinations on directly attached networks, hosts pass all IP traffic to routers which forward datagrams on toward their final destinations. In the general case, a datagram travels from router to router until it reaches a router that attaches directly to the same network as the final destination. Thus, the router system forms the architectural basis of an internet and handles all traffic except for direct delivery from one host to another.

Chapter 8 describes the algorithm that hosts and routers follow when they forward datagrams, and shows how the algorithm uses a table to make decisions. Each entry in the forwarding table uses an address and a mask to specify the network prefix for a particular destination and gives the address of the next router along a path used to reach that network. In practice, each entry also specifies a local network interface that should be used to reach the next hop.

We have not said how hosts or routers obtain the information for their forwarding tables. The issue has two aspects: *what* values should be placed in the tables, and *how* routers obtain the values. Both choices depend on the architectural complexity and size of the internet as well as administrative policies.

In general, establishing routes involves two steps: initialization and update. A host or router must establish an initial table of routes when it starts, and it must update the table as routes change (e.g., when hardware fails, making a particular network unusable). This chapter will focus on routers; Chapter 22 describes how hosts use DHCP to obtain initial entries for a forwarding table.

Initialization depends on the hardware and operating system. In some systems, the router reads an initial forwarding table from secondary storage at startup, either a disk or flash memory. In others, the router begins with an empty table that is filled in by executing a startup script when the router boots. Among other things, the startup script contains commands that initialize the network hardware and configure an IP address for each network interface. Finally, some systems start by broadcasting (or multicasting) a message that discovers neighbors and requests the neighbors to supply information about network addresses being used.

Once an initial forwarding table has been built, a router must accommodate changes in routes. In small, slowly changing internets, managers can establish and modify routes by hand. In large, rapidly changing environments, however, manual update is impossibly slow and prone to human errors. Automated methods are needed. Before we can understand the automatic protocols used to exchange routing information, we need to review several underlying ideas. The next sections do so, providing the necessary conceptual foundation for routing.

12.3 Forwarding With Partial Information

The principal difference between routers and typical hosts is that hosts usually know little about the structure of the internet to which they connect. Hosts do not have complete knowledge of all possible destination addresses, or even of all possible destination networks. In fact, many hosts have only two entries in their forwarding table: an entry for the local network, and a default entry for a directly-connected router. The host sends all nonlocal datagrams to the local router for delivery. The point is:

> *A host can forward datagrams successfully even if it only has partial forwarding information because it can rely on a router.*

Can routers also forward datagrams with only partial information? Yes, but only under certain circumstances. To understand the criteria, imagine an internet to be a foreign country crisscrossed with dirt roads that have directional signs posted at intersections. Imagine that you have no map, cannot ask directions because you cannot speak the local language, and have no knowledge about visible landmarks, but you need to travel to a village named *Sussex*. You leave on your journey, following the only road out of town, and begin to look for directional signs. The first sign reads:

Norfolk to the left; Hammond to the right; others straight ahead.†

Because the destination you seek is not listed explicitly, you continue straight ahead. In routing jargon, we say you follow a *default route*. After several more signs, you finally find one that reads:

Essex to the left; Sussex to the right; others straight ahead.

You turn to the right, follow several more signs, and emerge on a road that leads to Sussex.

Our imagined travel is analogous to a datagram traversing an internet, and the road signs are analogous to forwarding tables in routers along the path. Without a map or other navigational aids, travel is completely dependent on road signs, just as datagram forwarding in an internet depends entirely on forwarding tables. Clearly, it is possible to navigate even though each road sign contains only partial information.

A central question concerns correctness. As a traveler, you might ask: "How can I be sure that following the signs will lead to my destination?" You also might ask: "How can I be sure that following the signs will lead me to my destination along a shortest path?" These questions may seem especially troublesome if you pass many signs without finding your destination listed explicitly. Of course, the answers depend on the topology of the road system and the contents of the signs, but the fundamental idea is that when taken as a whole, the information on the signs should be both consistent and complete. Looking at this another way, we see that it is not necessary for each intersection to have a sign for every destination. The signs can list default paths as long as all

†Fortunately, signs are printed in a language you can read.

explicit signs point along a shortest path, and the turns for shortest paths to all destinations are marked. A few examples will explain some ways that consistency can be achieved.

At one extreme, consider a simple star-shaped topology of roads in which each town has exactly one road leading to it, and all the roads meet at a central point. Figure 12.1 illustrates the topology.

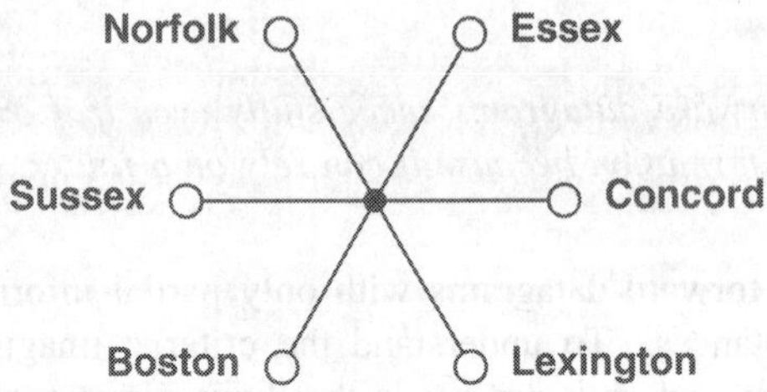

Figure 12.1 An example star-shaped topology of roads connecting towns.

We imagine a sign at the central intersection that lists each possible town and the road to reach that town. In other words, only the central intersection has information about each possible destination; a traveler always proceeds to the central intersection on the way to any destination.

At another extreme, we can imagine an arbitrary set of connected roads and a sign at each intersection listing all possible destinations. To guarantee that the signs lead travelers along the best route, it must be true that at any intersection if the sign for destination *D* points to road *R*, no road other than *R* leads to a shorter path to *D*.

Neither of the architectural extremes works well for a larger internet routing system. On one hand, the central intersection approach fails because no equipment is fast enough to serve as a central switch through which all traffic passes. On the other hand, having information about all possible destinations in all routers is impractical because it requires propagating large volumes of information whenever a change occurs in the internet. Therefore, we seek a solution that allows groups to manage local routers autonomously, adding new network interconnections and routes without changing the forwarding information in distant routers.

To understand the routing architecture used in the Internet, consider a third topology in which half of the cities lie in the eastern part of the country and half lie in the western part. Suppose a single bridge spans the river that separates east from west. Assume that people living in the eastern part do not like westerners, so they are unwilling to allow any road sign in the east to list destinations in the west. Assume that people living in the west do the opposite. Routing will be consistent if every road sign in the east lists all eastern destinations explicitly and points the default path to the bridge, and every road sign in the west lists all western destinations explicitly and points the default path to the bridge. However, there is a catch: if a tourist arrives who has accidentally written down the name of a non-existent town, the tourist could cross the bridge one way and then find that the default path points back to the bridge.

12.4 Original Internet Architecture And Cores

Much of our knowledge of forwarding and route propagation protocols has been derived from experience with the Internet. When TCP/IP was first developed, participating research sites were connected to the ARPANET, which served as a backbone network connecting all sites on the Internet. During initial experiments, each site managed forwarding tables and installed routes to other destinations by hand. As the fledgling Internet began to grow, it became apparent that manual maintenance of routes was impractical; automated mechanisms were needed. The concept of a backbone network continues to be used: many large enterprises have a backbone that connects sites on the enterprise's intranet.

The Internet designers selected a router architecture that followed the star-shaped topology described above. The original design used a small, central set of routers that kept complete information about all possible destinations, and a larger set of outlying routers that kept partial information. In terms of our analogy, it is like designating a small set of centrally located intersections that have signs listing all destinations, and allowing the outlying intersections to list only local destinations. As long as the default route at each outlying intersection points to one of the central intersections, travelers will eventually reach their destination.

The central set of routers that maintained complete information was known as the *core* of the Internet. Because each core router stores a route for each possible destination, a core router does not need a default route. Therefore, the set of core routers is sometimes referred to as the *default-free zone*. The advantage of partitioning Internet routing into a two-tier system is that it permits local administrators to manage local changes in outlying routers without affecting other parts of the Internet. The disadvantage is that it introduces the potential for inconsistency. In the worst case, an error in an outlying router can make distant routes unreachable.

We can summarize the ideas:

> *The advantage of a core routing architecture lies in autonomy: the manager of a noncore router can make changes locally. The chief disadvantage is inconsistency: an outlying site can introduce errors that make some destinations unreachable.*

Inconsistencies among forwarding tables can arise from errors in the algorithms that compute forwarding tables, incorrect data supplied to those algorithms, or errors that occur while transmitting the results to other routers. Protocol designers look for ways to limit the impact of errors, with the objective being to keep all routes consistent at all times. If routes become inconsistent, the routing protocols should be robust enough to detect and correct the errors quickly. Most important, the protocols should be designed to constrain the effect of errors.

The early Internet architecture is easy to understand if one remembers that the Internet evolved with a wide-area backbone, the ARPANET, already in place. A major motivation for the core router system came from the desire to connect local networks to the backbone. Figure 12.2 illustrates the idea.

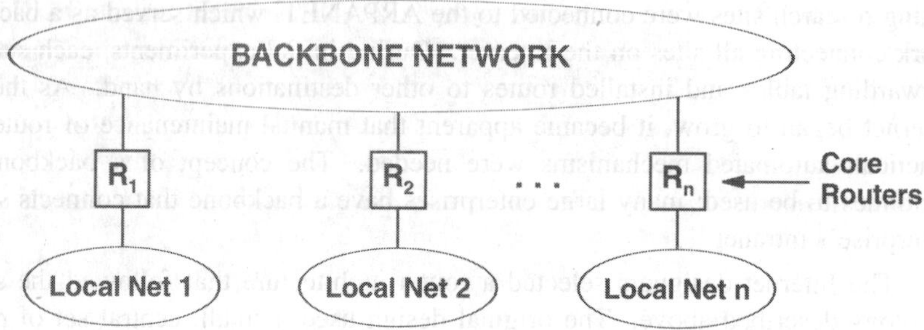

Figure 12.2 The early Internet core router system viewed as a set of routers that connect local area networks to the backbone. The architecture is now used in enterprise networks.

To understand why routers in Figure 12.2 cannot use partial information, consider the path a datagram follows if a set of routers use a default route. At the source site, the local router checks to see if it has an explicit route to the destination, and if not, sends the datagram along the path specified by its default route. All datagrams for which the router has no explicit route follow the same default path regardless of their ultimate destination. The next router along the path diverts datagrams for which it has an explicit route, and sends the rest along its default route. To ensure global consistency, the chain of default routes must reach every router in a giant cycle. Thus, the architecture requires all local sites to coordinate their default routes.

There are two problems with a routing architecture that involves a set of default routes. First, suppose a computer accidentally generates a datagram to a nonexistent destination (i.e., to an IP address that has not been assigned). The host sends the datagram to the local router, the local router follows the default path to the next router, and so on. Unfortunately, because default routes form a cycle, the datagram will go around the cycle until the hop limit expires. Second, if we ignore the problem of nonexistent addresses, forwarding is inefficient. A datagram that follows the default routes may pass through $n - 1$ routers before it reaches a router that connects to the local network of the destination.

To avoid the inefficiencies and potential routing loops that default routes can cause, the early Internet prohibited default routes in core routers. Instead of using default routes, the designers arranged for routers to communicate with one another and exchange routing information so that each router learned how to forward datagrams directly. Arranging for core routers to exchange routing information is easy — the routers all attach to the backbone network, which means they can communicate directly.

12.5 Beyond The Core Architecture To Peer Backbones

The introduction of the NSFNET backbone into the Internet added new complexity to the routing structure and forced designers to invent a new routing architecture. More important, the change in architecture foreshadowed the current Internet in which a set of *Tier-1 ISPs* each have a wide-area backbone to which customer sites connect. In many ways, the work on NSFNET and the routing architecture that was created to support it was key in moving away from the original Internet architecture to the current Internet architecture.

The primary change that occurred with the NSFNET backbone was the evolution from a single, central backbone to a set of *peer backbone networks*, often called *peers* or *routing peers*. Although the global Internet now has several Tier-1 peers, we can understand the routing situation by considering only two. Figure 12.3 illustrates an Internet topology with a pair of backbone networks.

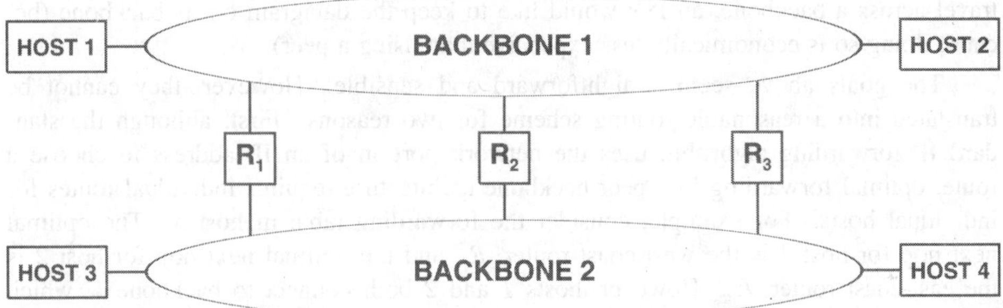

Figure 12.3 An example of two peer backbones interconnected by multiple routers similar to the two peer backbones in the Internet in 1989.

To help us understand the difficulties of IP routing among peer backbones, the figure shows four hosts directly connected to the backbones. Although such direct connection may seem unrealistic, it simplifies the example. Look at the figure and consider routes from host *3* to host *2*. Assume for the moment that the figure shows geographic orientation: host *3* is on the West Coast attached to backbone 2, while host *2* is on the East Coast attached to backbone 1. When establishing routes between hosts *3* and *2*, the managers must decide among three options:

(a) Route the traffic from host *3* through the West Coast router, R_1, and then across backbone 1.

(b) Forward the traffic from host *3* across backbone 2, through the Midwest router, R_2, and then across backbone 1 to host *2*.

(c) Forward the traffic across backbone 2, through the East Coast router, R_3, and then to host *2*.

A more circuitous route is possible as well: traffic could flow from host *3* through the West Coast router, across backbone 1 to the Midwest router, back onto backbone 2 to the East Coast router, and finally across backbone 1 to host *2*. Such a route may or may not be advisable, depending on the policies for network use and the capacity of various routers and backbones. Nevertheless, we will concentrate on routing in which a datagram never traverses a network twice (i.e., never moves to a network, moves off the network, and then moves back to the network again).

Intuitively, we would like all traffic to take a shortest path. That is, we would like traffic between a pair of geographically close hosts to take a short path independent of the routes chosen for long-distance traffic. For example, it is desirable for traffic from host *3* to host *1* to flow through the West Coast router, R_1, because such a path minimizes the total distance that the datagram travels. More important, if a datagram must travel across a backbone, an ISP would like to keep the datagram on its backbone (because doing so is economically less expensive than using a peer).

The goals above seem straightforward and sensible. However, they cannot be translated into a reasonable routing scheme for two reasons. First, although the standard IP forwarding algorithm uses the network portion of an IP address to choose a route, optimal forwarding in a peer backbone architecture requires individual routes for individual hosts. For example, consider the forwarding table in host *3*. The optimal next hop for host *1* is the west-coast router, R_1, and the optimal next hop for host *2* is the east-coast router, R_3. However, hosts *1* and *2* both connect to backbone 1, which means they have the same network prefix. Therefore, instead of using network prefixes, the host forwarding table must contain host-specific routes. Second, managers of the two backbones must agree to keep routes consistent among all routers or a *forwarding loop* (*routing loop*) can develop in which a set of the routers forward to each other in a cycle.

12.6 Automatic Route Propagation And A FIB

We said that the original Internet core system avoided default routes because it propagated complete information about all possible destinations to every core router. Many corporate intranets now use a similar approach — they propagate information about each destination in the corporation to all routers in their intranet. The next sections discuss two basic types of algorithms that compute and propagate routing information; later chapters discuss protocols that use the algorithms.

Routing protocols serve two important functions. First, they compute a set of shortest paths. Second, they respond to network failures or topology changes by continually updating the routing information. Thus, when we think about route propagation, it is important to consider the dynamic behavior of protocols and algorithms.

Conceptually, routing protocols operate independently from the forwarding mechanism. That is, routing protocol software runs as a separate process that uses IP to exchange messages with routing protocol software on other routers. Routing protocols learn about destinations, compute a shortest path to each destination, and pass information to the routing protocol software on other routers.

Although a routing protocol computes shortest paths, the routing protocol software does not store information directly in the router's forwarding table. Instead, routing software creates a *Forwarding Information Base* (*FIB*). A FIB may contain extra information not found in a forwarding table, such as the source of the routing information, how old the information is (i.e., the last time a routing protocol on another router sent a message about the route), and whether a manager has temporarily overridden a specific route.

When the FIB changes, routing software recomputes a forwarding table for the router and installs the new forwarding table. A crucial step occurs between items being placed in a FIB and the items being propagated to the forwarding table: policy rules are applied. Policies allow a manager to control which items are automatically installed in the forwarding table. Therefore, even if routing software finds a shorter path to a particular destination and places the information in the FIB, policies may prevent the path from being injected into the forwarding table.

12.7 Distance-Vector (Bellman-Ford) Routing

The term *distance-vector*‡ refers to a class of algorithms used to propagate routing information. The idea behind distance-vector algorithms is quite simple. Each router keeps a list of all known destinations in its FIB. When it boots, a router initializes its FIB to contain an entry for each directly connected network. Each entry in the FIB identifies a destination network, a next-hop router used to reach the destination, and the "distance" to the network (according to some measure of distance). For example, some distance-vector protocols use the number of network hops as a measure of distance. A directly-connected network is zero hops away; if a datagram must travel through N routers to reach a destination, the destination is N hops away. Figure 12.4 illustrates the initial contents of a FIB on a router that attaches to two networks. In the figure, each entry corresponds to a directly-connected network (zero hops away).

‡The terms *vector-distance*, *Ford-Fulkerson*, *Bellman-Ford*, and *Bellman* are synonymous with *distance-vector*; the last three are taken from the names of researchers who published the idea.

Destination	Distance	Route
Net 1	0	direct
Net 2	0	direct

Figure 12.4 An initial FIB used with a distance-vector algorithm. Each entry contains the IP address of a directly connected network and an integer distance to the network.

When using distance-vector, routing software on each router sends a copy of its FIB to any other router it can reach directly. When a report arrives at router *K* from router *J*, *K* examines the set of destinations reported and the distance to each and applies three rules:

- If *J* lists a destination that *K* does not have in its FIB, *K* adds a new entry to its FIB with the next hop of *J*.
- If *J* knows a shorter way to reach a destination *D*, *K* replaces the next hop in its FIB entry for *D* with *J*.
- If *K*'s FIB entry for destination *D* already lists *J* as the next hop and *J*'s distance to the destination has changed, *K* replaces the distance in its FIB entry.

The first rule can be interpreted, "If my neighbor knows a way to reach a destination that I don't know, I can use the neighbor as a next hop." The second rule can be interpreted, "If my neighbor has a shorter route to a destination, I can use the neighbor as a next hop." The third rule can be interpreted, "If I am using my neighbor as the next hop for a destination and the neighbor's cost to reach the destination changes, my cost must change."

Figure 12.5 shows an existing FIB in a router, *K*, and a distance-vector update message from another router, *J*. Three items in the message cause changes in the FIB. Note that if *J* reports a distance *N* hops to a given destination and *K* uses *J* as a next hop, the distance stored in *K*'s FIB will have distance $N + 1$ (i.e., the distance from *J* to the destination plus the distance to reach *J*). The third column in our example FIB is labeled *Route*. In practice, the column contains the IP address of a next-hop router. To make it easy to understand, the figure simply lists a symbolic name (e.g., *Router J*).

The term *distance-vector* comes from the information sent in the periodic messages. A message contains a list of pairs (D, V), where *D* is a distance to a destination and *V* identifies the destination (called the *vector*). Note that distance-vector algorithms report routes in the first person (i.e., we think of a router advertising, "I can reach destination *V* at distance *D*"). In such a design, all routers must participate in the distance-vector exchange for the routes to be efficient and consistent.

Destination	Distance	Route
Net 1	0	direct
Net 2	0	direct
Net 4	8	Router L
Net 17	5	Router M
Net 24	6	Router J
Net 30	2	Router Q
Net 42	2	Router J

(a)

	Destination	Distance
	Net 1	2
→	Net 4	3
	Net 17	6
→	Net 21	4
	Net 24	5
	Net 30	10
→	Net 42	3

(b)

Figure 12.5 (a) An existing FIB in router *K*, and (b) an incoming routing update message from router *J* that will cause changes.

Although they are easy to implement, distance-vector algorithms have several disadvantages. In a completely static environment, distance-vector algorithms do indeed compute shortest paths and correctly propagate routes to all destinations. When routes change rapidly, however, the computations may not stabilize. When a route changes (i.e, a new connection appears or an old one fails), the information propagates slowly from one router to another. Meanwhile, some routers may have incorrect routing information.

12.8 Reliability And Routing Protocols

Most routing protocols use connectionless transport — early protocols encapsulated messages directly in IP; modern routing protocols usually encapsulate in UDP†. Unfortunately, UDP offers the same semantics as IP: messages can be lost, delayed, duplicated, corrupted, or delivered out of order. Thus, a routing protocol that uses them must compensate for failures.

Routing protocols use several techniques to handle reliability. First, checksums are used to handle corruption. Loss is either handled by *soft state*‡ or through acknowledgements and retransmission. *Sequence numbers* are used to handle two problems. First, sequence numbers allow a receiver to handle out-of-order delivery by placing incoming messages back in the correct order. Second, sequence numbers can be used to handle *replay*, a condition that can occur if a duplicate of a message is delayed and arrives long after newer updates have been processed. Chapter 14 illustrates how distance-vector protocols can exhibit slow convergence, and discusses additional techniques that distance-vector protocols use to avoid problems. In particular, the chapter covers split horizon and poison reverse techniques.

†The next chapter discusses an exception — a routing protocol that uses TCP.
‡Recall that soft state relies on timeouts to remove old information.

12.9 Link-State (SPF) Routing

The main disadvantage of the distance-vector algorithm is that it does not scale well. Besides the problem of slow response to change mentioned earlier, the algorithm requires the exchange of large messages — because each routing update contains an entry for every possible network, message size is proportional to the total number of networks in an internet. Furthermore, because a distance-vector protocol requires every router to participate, the volume of information exchanged can be enormous.

The primary alternative to distance-vector algorithms is a class of algorithms known as *link state*, *link status*, or *Shortest Path First*† (*SPF*). The SPF algorithm requires each participating router to compute topology information. The easiest way to think of topology information is to imagine that every router has a map that shows all other routers and the networks to which they connect. In abstract terms, the routers correspond to nodes in a graph, and networks that connect routers correspond to edges. There is an edge (link) between two nodes in the topology graph if and only if the corresponding routers can communicate directly.

Instead of sending messages that contain a list of destinations that a router can reach, each router participating in an SPF algorithm performs two tasks:

- Actively test the status of each neighboring router. Two routers are considered neighbors if they attach to a common network.
- Periodically broadcast link-state messages of the form, "The link between me and router X is up" or "The link between me and router X is down."

To test the status of a directly connected neighbor, the two neighbors exchange short messages that verify that the neighbor is alive and reachable. If the neighbor replies, the link between them is said to be *up*. Otherwise, the link is said to be *down*‡. To inform all other routers, each router periodically broadcasts a message that lists the status (state) of each of its links. A status message does not specify routes — it simply reports whether communication is possible between pairs of routers. When using a link-state algorithm, the protocol software must find a way to deliver each link-state message to all routers, even if the underlying network does not support broadcast. Thus, individual copies of each message may be forwarded point-to-point.

Whenever a link-state message arrives, software running on the router uses the information to update its map of the internet. First, it extracts the pair of routers mentioned in the message and makes sure that the local graph contains an edge between the two. Second, it uses the status reported in the message to mark the link as up or down. Whenever an incoming message causes a change in the local topology graph, the link-state algorithm recomputes routes by applying Dijkstra's algorithm. The algorithm computes the shortest path from the local router to each destination. The resulting information is placed in the FIB, and if policies permit, used to change the forwarding table.

†Dijkstra, the inventor of the algorithm, coined the name "shortest path first," but it is misleading because all routing algorithms compute shortest paths.

‡In practice, to prevent oscillations between the up and down states, many protocols use a *k-out-of-n rule* to test liveness, meaning that the link remains up until a significant percentage of requests have no reply, and then it remains down until a significant percentage of messages receive a reply.

One of the chief advantages of SPF algorithms is that each router computes routes independently using the same original status data; they do not depend on the computation of intermediate routers. Compare the approach to a distance-vector algorithm in which each router updates its FIB and then sends the updated information to neighbors — if the software in any router along the path is incorrect, all successive routers will receive incorrect information. With a link-state algorithm, routers do not depend on intermediate computation — the link-status messages propagate throughout the network unchanged, making it is easier to debug problems. Because each router performs the shortest path computation locally, the computation is guaranteed to converge. Finally, because each link-status message only carries information about the direct connection between a pair of routers, the size does not depend on the number of networks in the underlying internet. Therefore, SPF algorithms scale better than distance-vector algorithms.

12.10 Summary

To ensure that all networks remain reachable with high reliability, an internet must provide globally consistent forwarding. Hosts and most routers contain only partial routing information; they depend on default routes to send datagrams to distant destinations. Originally, the global Internet solved the routing problem by using a core router architecture in which a set of core routers each contained complete information about all networks.

When additional backbone networks were added to the Internet, a new routing architecture arose to match the extended topology. Currently, a set of separately managed peer backbone networks exist that interconnect at multiple places.

When they exchange routing information, routers usually use one of two basic algorithms; distance-vector or link-state (also called SPF). The chief disadvantage of distance-vector algorithms is that they perform a distributed shortest path computation that may not converge if the status of network connections changes continually. Thus, for large internets or internets where the underlying topology changes quickly, SPF algorithms are superior.

EXERCISES

12.1 Suppose a router discovers it is about to forward an IP datagram back over the same network interface on which the datagram arrived. What should it do? Why?

12.2 After reading RFC 823 and RFC 1812, explain what an Internet core router (i.e., one with complete routing information) should do in the situation described in the previous question.

12.3 How can routers in a core system use default routes to send all illegal datagrams to a specific machine?

12.4 Imagine that a manager accidentally misconfigures a router to advertise that it has direct connections to six specific networks when it does not. How can other routers that receive the advertisement protect themselves from invalid advertisements while still accepting other updates from "untrusted" routers?

12.5 Which ICMP messages does a router generate?

12.6 Assume a router is using unreliable transport for delivery. How can the router determine whether a designated neighbor's status is *up* or *down*? (Hint: consult RFC 823 to find out how the original core system solved the problem.)

12.7 Suppose two routers each advertise the same cost, k, to reach a given network, N. Describe the circumstances under which forwarding through one of them may take fewer total hops than forwarding through the other one.

12.8 How does a router know whether an incoming datagram carries a routing update message?

12.9 Consider the distance-vector update shown in Figure 12.5 carefully. For each item updated in the table, give the reason why the router will perform the update.

12.10 Consider the use of sequence numbers to ensure that two routers do not become confused when datagrams are duplicated, delayed, or delivered out of order. How should initial sequence numbers be selected? Why?

Chapter Contents

13

Routing Among Autonomous Systems (BGP)

13.1 Introduction

The previous chapter introduces the idea of route propagation. This chapter extends our understanding of internet routing architectures and discusses the concept of autonomous systems. We will see that autonomous systems correspond to large ISPs or large enterprises, and that each autonomous system comprises a group of networks and routers operating under one administrative authority.

The central topic of the chapter is a routing protocol named BGP that is used to provide routing among autonomous systems. BGP is the key routing protocol used at the center of the Internet to allow each major ISP to inform other peers about destinations that it can reach.

13.2 The Scope Of A Routing Update Protocol

A fundamental principle guides the design of a routing architecture: no routing update protocol can scale to allow all routers in the global Internet to exchange routing information. Instead, routers must be divided into separate groups, and routing protocols designed to operate within a group. There are three reasons that routers must be divided:

- *Traffic.* Even if each site only has a single network, no routing protocol can accommodate an arbitrary number of sites, because adding sites increases routing traffic — if the set of routers is sufficiently large, the routing traffic becomes overwhelming. Distance-vector protocols require routers to exchange the entire set of networks (i.e., the size of each update is proportional to the size of a forwarding table). Link-state protocols periodically broadcast announcements of connectivity between pairs of routers (i.e., broadcasts would travel throughout the Internet).

- *Indirect Communication.* Because they do not share a common network, routers in the global Internet cannot communicate directly. In many cases, a router is far from the center of the Internet, meaning that the only path the router can use to reach all other routers goes through many intermediate hops.

- *Administrative Boundaries.* In the Internet, the networks and routers are not all owned and managed by a single entity. More important, shortest paths are not always used! Instead, large ISPs route traffic along paths that generate revenue or have lower financial cost. Therefore, a routing architecture must provide a way for each administrative group to control routing and access independently.

The consequences of limiting router interaction are significant. The idea provides the motivation for much of the routing architecture used in the Internet, and explains some of the mechanisms we will study. To summarize this important principle:

> *Although it is desirable for routers to exchange routing information, it is impractical for all routers in an arbitrarily large internet, such as the global Internet, to participate in a single routing update protocol.*

13.3 Determining A Practical Limit On Group Size

The above discussion leaves many questions open. For example, what internet size is considered large? If only a limited set of routers can participate in an exchange of routing information, what happens to routers that are excluded? Do they function correctly? Can a router that is not participating ever forward a datagram to a router that is participating? Can a participating router forward a datagram to a non-participating router?

The answer to the question of size involves understanding the traffic a specific protocol will generate, the capacity of the networks that connect the routers, and other requirements, such as whether the protocol requires broadcast. There are two issues: delay and overhead.

Delay. The main delay of interest is not how long it takes a single routing update message to propagate. Instead, the question concerns convergence time, the maximum delay until all routers are informed about a change. When routers use a distance-vector protocol, each router must receive the new information, update its FIB, and then forward the information to its neighbors. In an internet with N routers arranged in a linear topology, N steps are required. Thus, N must be limited to guarantee rapid distribution of information.

Overhead. The issue of overhead is also easy to understand. Because each router that participates in a routing protocol must send messages, a larger set of participating routers means more routing traffic. Furthermore, if routing messages contain a list of possible destinations, the size of each message grows as the number of routers and networks increase. To ensure that routing traffic remains a small percentage of the total traffic on the underlying networks, the size of routing messages must be limited.

In fact, few network managers have sufficient information about routing protocols to perform detailed analysis of the delay or overhead. Instead, they follow a simple heuristic guideline:

> *It is safe to allow up to a dozen routers to participate in a single routing information protocol across a wide area network; approximately five times as many can safely participate across a set of local area networks.*

Of course, the rule only gives general advice and there are many exceptions. For example, if the underlying networks have especially low delay and high capacity, the number of participating routers can be larger. Similarly, if the underlying networks have unusually low capacity or a high amount of traffic, the number of participating routers must be smaller to avoid overloading the networks with routing traffic.

Because an internet is not static, it can be difficult to estimate how much traffic routing protocols will generate or what percentage of the underlying bandwidth the routing traffic will consume. For example, as the number of hosts on a network grows over time, increases in the traffic generated consume more of the spare network capacity. In addition, increased traffic can arise from new applications. Therefore, network managers cannot rely solely on the guideline above when choosing a routing architecture. Instead, they usually implement a *traffic monitoring* scheme. In essence, a traffic monitor listens passively to a network and records statistics about the traffic. In particular, a monitor can compute both the network utilization (i.e., percentage of the underlying bandwidth being used) and the percentage of packets carrying routing protocol messages. A manager can observe traffic trends by taking measurements over long periods (e.g., weeks or months), and can use the output to determine whether too many routers are participating in a single routing protocol.

13.4 A Fundamental Idea: Extra Hops

Although the number of routers that participate in a single routing protocol must be limited, doing so has an important consequence because it means that some routers will be outside the group. For example, consider a corporate intranet with a backbone and a set of routers that all participate in a routing update protocol. Suppose a new department is added to the network and the new department acquires a router. It might seem that the new router would not need to participate in the routing update protocol — the "outsider" could merely use a member of the group as a default.

The same situation occurred in the early Internet. As new sites were added, the core system functioned as a central routing mechanism to which noncore routers sent datagrams for delivery. Researchers uncovered an important lesson: if a router outside of a group uses a member of the group as a default route, routing will be suboptimal. More important, one does not need a large number of routers or a wide area network — the problem can occur even in a small corporate network in which a nonparticipating router uses a participating router for delivery.

To understand how nonoptimal forwarding occurs, consider the example network configuration in Figure 13.1.

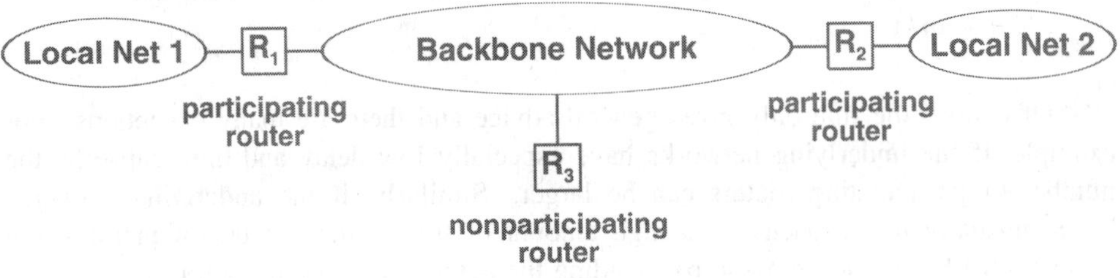

Figure 13.1 An example architecture that can cause the extra hop problem if a nonparticipating router uses a participating router as a default next hop.

In the figure, routers R_1 and R_2 connect to local area networks *1* and *2*, respectively. Each router participates in a routing protocol, and knows how to reach both networks. A new router, R_3 is added. Instead of configuring R_3 to participate in the routing update protocol, the manager configures it to use one of the existing routers, say R_1, as a default.

If R_1 has a datagram destined for a host on local network *1*, no problem occurs. However, if R_3 has a datagram destined for local network 2, it will send the datagram across the backbone to R_1, which must then forward the datagram back across the backbone to router R_2. The optimal route, of course, requires R_3 to send datagrams destined for network *2* directly to R_2. Notice that the choice of a participating router makes no difference: only destinations that lie beyond the chosen router have optimal routes. For all other destinations, a datagram will make a second, unnecessary trip across the backbone network. Also recall that routers cannot use ICMP redirect messages to inform R_3 that it has nonoptimal routes, because ICMP redirect messages can only be sent to the original source and not to intermediate routers.

We call the anomaly illustrated in Figure 13.1 the *extra hop problem*. The problem is insidious because everything appears to work correctly — datagrams do indeed reach their destination. However, because routing is not optimal, the system is extremely inefficient. Each datagram that takes an extra hop consumes resources on the intermediate router as well as twice as much of the backbone capacity as it should. The extra hop problem was first discovered in the early Internet. Solving the problem required us to change our view of routing architecture:

> *Treating a group of routers that participate in a routing update protocol as a default delivery system can introduce an extra hop for datagram traffic; a mechanism is needed that allows nonparticipating routers to learn routes from participating routers so they can choose optimal routes.*

13.5 Autonomous System Concept

How should the Internet be divided into sets of routers that can each run a routing update protocol? The key to the answer lies in realizing that the Internet does not consist of independent networks. Instead, networks and routers are owned by organizations and individuals. Because the networks and routers owned by a given entity fall under a single administrative authority, the authority can guarantee that internal routes remain consistent and viable. Furthermore, the administrative authority can choose one or more of its routers to apprise the outside world of networks within the organization and to learn about networks that are outside the organization.

For purposes of routing, a group of networks and routers controlled by a single administrative authority is called an *Autonomous System* (*AS*). The idea is that we will let each autonomous system choose its own mechanisms for discovering, propagating, validating, and checking the consistency of routes (the next chapter reviews some of the protocols that autonomous systems use to propagate routing information internally). Then, we will arrange ways for an autonomous system to summarize routing information and send the summary to neighboring autonomous systems.

Is an autonomous system an ISP? It can be, but an autonomous system can also be a large enterprise (e.g., a major corporation or university). Although the definition of an autonomous system may seem vague, the definition is intended to include almost any group that runs a large network. Of course, the boundaries between autonomous systems must be defined precisely to allow automated algorithms to make routing decisions, and to prevent the routing update protocols used in one autonomous system from accidentally spilling over into another. Furthermore, each autonomous system defines a set of policies. For example, an autonomous system may prefer to avoid routing packets through a competitor's autonomous system, even if such a path exists. To make it possible for automated routing algorithms to distinguish among autonomous systems, each is assigned an *autonomous system number* by the central authority that is charged with assigning all Internet numbers. When routers in two autonomous systems exchange routing information, the protocol arranges for each router to learn the other's autonomous system number.

We can summarize the idea:

> *The Internet is divided into autonomous systems that are each owned and operated by a single administrative authority. An autonomous system is free to choose an internal routing architecture and protocols.*

In practice, although some large organizations have obtained autonomous system numbers to allow them to connect to multiple ISPs, it is easiest to think of each autonomous system as corresponding to a large ISP. The point is:

> *In the current Internet, each large ISP is an autonomous system. During informal discussions, engineers often refer to routing among major ISPs when they mean routing among autonomous systems.*

13.6 Exterior Gateway Protocols And Reachability

We said that an autonomous system must summarize information from its routing update protocols and propagate that information to other autonomous systems. To do so, an autonomous system configures one or more of its routers to communicate with routers in other autonomous systems. Information flows in two directions. First, the router must collect information about networks inside its autonomous system and pass the information out. Second, the router must accept information about networks in other autonomous system(s) and disseminate the information inside. Technically, we say that the autonomous system advertises *network reachability* to the outside, and we use the term *Exterior Gateway Protocol*† (*EGP*) to denote any protocol used to pass network reachability information between two autonomous systems. Strictly speaking, an EGP is not a routing protocol because advertising reachability is not the same as propagating routing information. In practice, however, most networking professionals do not make a distinction — one is likely to hear exterior gateway protocols referred to as routing protocols.

Currently, a single EGP is used to exchange reachability information in the Internet. Known as the *Border Gateway Protocol* (*BGP*), it has evolved through four (quite different) versions. Each version is numbered, which gives rise to the formal name of the current version, *BGP-4*. Following standard practice in the networking industry, we will use the term *BGP* in place of *BGP-4*.

†The terminology was coined at a time when a router was called a *gateway*, and has persisted.

When a pair of autonomous systems agree to use BGP to exchange routing information, each must designate a router† that will speak BGP on its behalf; the two routers are said to become *BGP peers* of one another. Because a router speaking BGP must communicate with a peer in another autonomous system, it makes sense to select a machine that is near the border (i.e., the edge) of the autonomous system. Hence, BGP terminology calls the router a *border gateway* or *border router*. Figure 13.2 illustrates the idea.

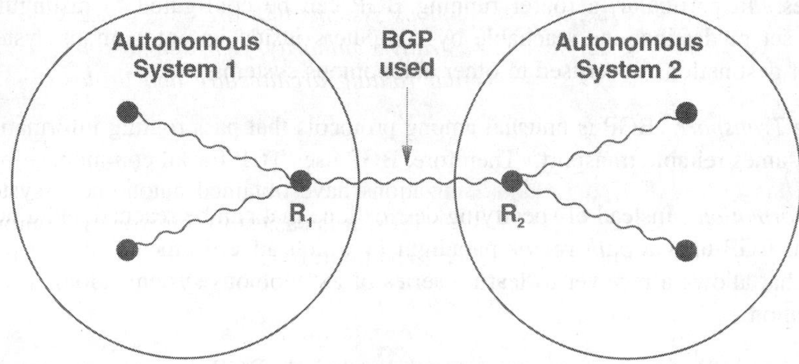

Figure 13.2 Conceptual illustration of BGP used between router R_1 in one autonomous system and router R_2 in another autonomous system.

In the figure, information flows in both directions. Router R_1 gathers information about networks in autonomous system *1* and uses BGP to report the information to router R_2, while router R_2 gathers information about networks in autonomous system *2* and uses BGP to report the information to router R_1.

13.7 BGP Characteristics

BGP is unusual in several ways. Most important, because it advertises reachability instead of routing information, BGP does not use either the distance-vector algorithm or the link-state algorithm. Instead, BGP uses a modification known as a *path-vector* algorithm. BGP is characterized by the following:

Inter-Autonomous System Communication. Because BGP is designed as an exterior gateway protocol, its primary role is to allow one autonomous system to communicate with another.

Coordination Among Multiple BGP Speakers. If an autonomous system has multiple routers each communicating with a peer in an outside autonomous system, a form of BGP known as *iBGP* can be used to coordinate among routers inside the system to guarantee that they all propagate consistent information.

†Although it is possible to run BGP on a system other than a router, most autonomous systems choose to run BGP on a router that has a direct connection to another autonomous system.

Propagation Of Reachability Information. BGP allows an autonomous system to advertise destinations that are reachable either in or through it, and to learn such information from another autonomous system.

Next-Hop Paradigm. Like distance-vector routing protocols, BGP supplies *next hop* information for each destination.

Policy Support. Unlike most distance-vector protocols that advertise exactly the routes in the local forwarding table, BGP can implement policies that the local administrator chooses. In particular, a router running BGP can be configured to distinguish between the set of destinations reachable by computers inside its autonomous system and the set of destinations advertised to other autonomous systems.

Reliable Transport. BGP is unusual among protocols that pass routing information because it assumes reliable transport. Therefore, BGP uses TCP for all communication.

Path Information. Instead of specifying destinations that can be reached and a next hop for each, BGP uses a *path-vector* paradigm in which advertisements specify path information that allows a receiver to learn a series of autonomous systems along a path to the destination.

Incremental Updates. To conserve network bandwidth, BGP does not pass full information in each update message. Instead, full information is exchanged once, and then successive messages carry incremental changes called *deltas*.

Support For IPv4 and IPv6. BGP supports IPv4 classless addresses and IPv6 addresses. That is, BGP sends a prefix length along with each address.

Route Aggregation. BGP conserves network bandwidth by allowing a sender to aggregate route information and send a single entry to represent multiple, related destinations (e.g., many networks owned by a single AS).

Authentication. BGP allows a receiver to authenticate messages (i.e., verify the identity of a sender).

13.8 BGP Functionality And Message Types

BGP peers perform three basic functions. The first function consists of initial peer acquisition and authentication. The two peers establish a TCP connection and perform a message exchange that guarantees both sides have agreed to communicate. The second function forms the primary focus of the protocol — each side sends positive or negative reachability information. That is, a sender can advertise that one or more destinations are reachable by giving a next hop for each, or the sender can declare that one or more previously advertised destinations are no longer reachable. The third function provides ongoing verification that the peers and the network connections between them are functioning correctly.

To handle the three functions described above, BGP defines five basic message types. Figure 13.3 contains a summary.

Type Code	Message Type	Description
1	OPEN	Initialize communication
2	UPDATE	Advertise or withdraw routes
3	NOTIFICATION	Response to an incorrect message
4	KEEPALIVE	Actively test peer connectivity
5	REFRESH	Request readvertisement from peer

Figure 13.3 The five basic message types in BGP.

13.9 BGP Message Header

Each BGP message begins with a fixed header that identifies the message type. Figure 13.4 illustrates the header format.

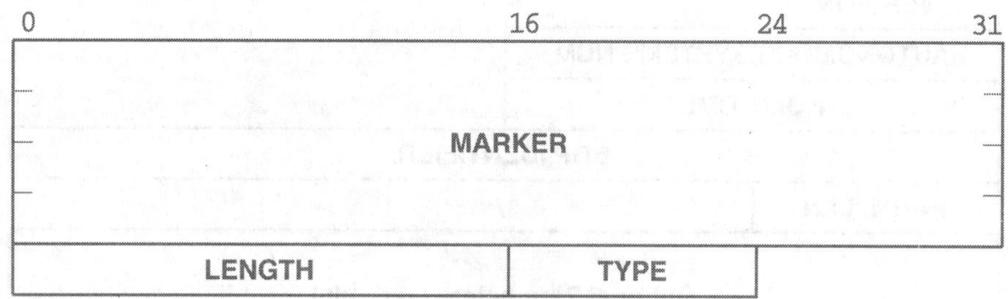

Figure 13.4 The format of the header that precedes every BGP message.

In the figure, the 16-octet *MARKER* field contains a value that both sides agree to use to mark the beginning of a message. The 2-octet *LENGTH* field specifies the total message length measured in octets. The minimum message size is *19* octets (for a message type that has only a header and no data following the header), and the maximum allowable length is *4096* octets. Finally, the 1-octet *TYPE* field contains one of the five values for the message type listed in Figure 13.3.

The *MARKER* field may seem unusual. In the initial message, the marker consists of all 1s; if the peers agree to use an authentication mechanism, the marker can contain authentication information. In any case, both sides must agree on the value so it can be used for *synchronization*. To understand why synchronization is necessary, recall that all BGP messages are exchanged across a stream transport (i.e., TCP), which does not identify the boundary between one message and the next. In such an environment, a simple error on either side can have dramatic consequences. In particular, if either the sender or receiver software miscounts the octets in a message, a *synchronization error* will occur in which a receiver incorrectly reads items in the stream as a header. More important, because the transport protocol does not specify message boundaries, the transport protocol will not alert the receiver to the error. Thus, to ensure that the sender and receiver remain synchronized, BGP places a well-known sequence value at the beginning of each message, and requires a receiver to verify that the value is intact before processing the message.

13.10 BGP OPEN Message

As soon as two BGP peers establish a TCP connection, they each send an *OPEN* message to declare their autonomous system number and establish other operating parameters. In addition to the standard header, an *OPEN* message contains a value for a *hold timer* that is used to specify the maximum number of seconds which may elapse between the receipt of two successive messages. Figure 13.5 illustrates the format.

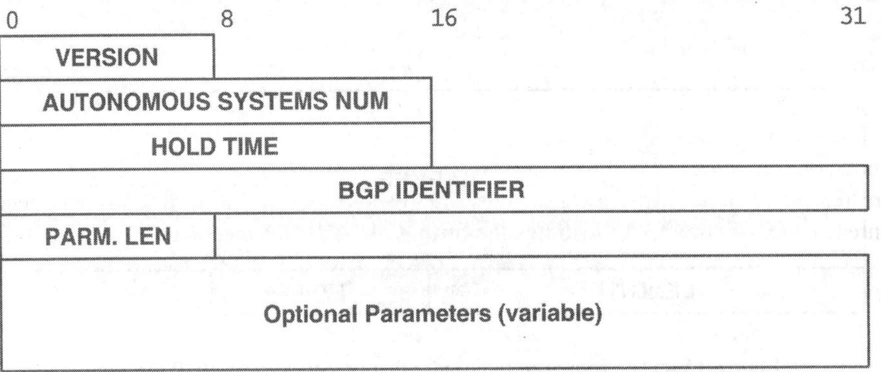

Figure 13.5 The format of the IPv4 BGP OPEN message that is sent at start-up. Octets shown in the figure follow the standard message header.

Most fields in the figure are straightforward. The *VERSION* field identifies the protocol version used (the version for the format shown is version 4; a later section discusses BGP extensions for IPv6). Recall that each autonomous system is assigned a unique number. Field *AUTONOMOUS SYSTEMS NUM* gives the autonomous system number of the sender's system. The *HOLD TIME* field specifies a maximum time that the receiver should wait for a message from the sender. The receiver is required to implement a timer using the specified value. The timer is reset each time a message arrives; if the timer expires, the receiver assumes the sender is no longer available (and stops forwarding datagrams along routes learned from the sender).

Field *BGP IDENTIFIER* contains a 32-bit integer value that uniquely identifies the sender. If a machine has multiple peers (e.g., perhaps in multiple autonomous systems), the machine must use the same identifier in all communication. The protocol specifies that the identifier is an IP address. Thus, a border router must choose one of its IPv4 addresses to use with all BGP peers.

The last field of an *OPEN* message is optional. If present, field *PARM. LEN* specifies the length measured in octets, and the field labeled *Optional Parameters* contains a list of parameters. The parameter list has been labeled *variable* to indicate that the size varies from message to message. When parameters are present, each parameter in the list is preceded by a 2-octet header, with the first octet specifying the type of the parameter and the second octet specifying the length. If there are no parameters, the value of *PARM. LEN* is zero and the message ends with no further data.

When it accepts an incoming *OPEN* message, a border router speaking BGP responds by sending a *KEEPALIVE* message (discussed below). Each peer must send an *OPEN* and receive a *KEEPALIVE* message before they can exchange routing information. Thus, a *KEEPALIVE* message functions as the acknowledgement for an *OPEN*.

13.11 BGP UPDATE Message

Once BGP peers have created a TCP connection, sent *OPEN* messages, and acknowledged them, the peers use *UPDATE* messages to advertise new destinations that are reachable or to withdraw previous advertisements when a destination has become unreachable. Figure 13.6 illustrates the format of *UPDATE* messages.

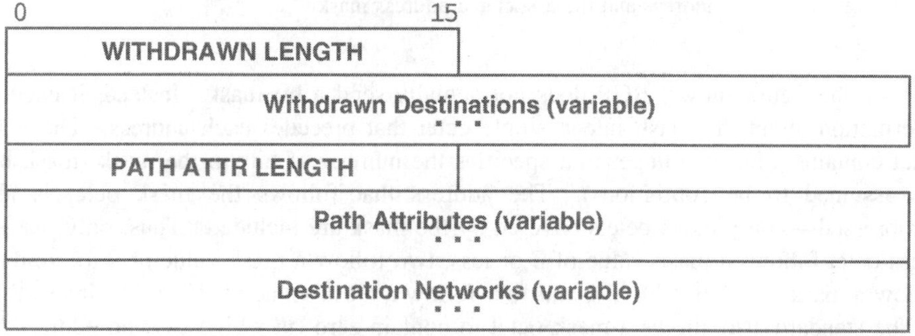

Figure 13.6 BGP UPDATE message format in which variable size areas of the message may be omitted. These octets follow the standard message header.

As the figure shows, each *UPDATE* message is divided into two parts: the first part lists previously advertised destinations that are being withdrawn, and the second part specifies new destinations being advertised. The second part lists path attributes followed by a set of destination networks that use the attributes. Fields labeled *variable* do not have a fixed size. In fact, variable-size fields do not need to be present — if the information is not needed for a particular *UPDATE*, the corresponding field is omitted from the message. Field *WITHDRAWN LENGTH* is a 2-octet field that specifies the size of the *Withdrawn Destinations* field that follows. If no destinations are being withdrawn, *WITHDRAWN LENGTH* contains zero. Similarly, the *PATH ATTR LENGTH* field specifies the size of the *Path Attributes* that are associated with new destinations being advertised. If there are no new destinations, the *PATH ATTR LENGTH* field contains zero.

13.12 Compressed IPv4 Mask-Address Pairs

Both the *Withdrawn Destinations* and the *Destination Networks* fields can contain a list of IPv4 network addresses. Conceptually, BGP should send an address mask with each IPv4 address. Instead of sending an address and a mask as separate 32-bit quantities, BGP uses a compressed representation to reduce message size. Figure 13.7 illustrates the format:

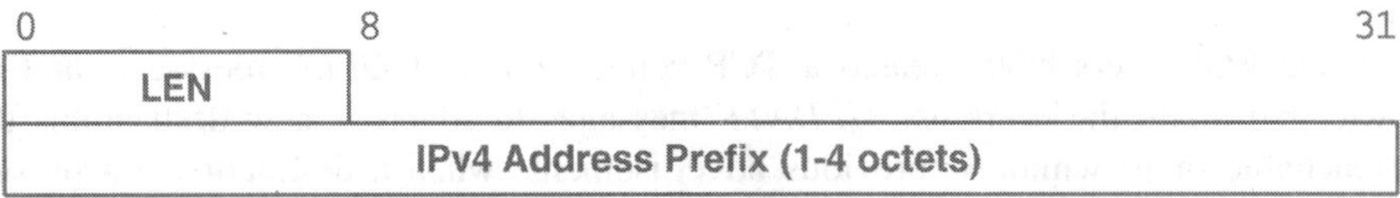

Figure 13.7 The compressed format BGP uses to store an IPv4 destination address and the associated address mask.

As the figure shows, BGP does not actually send a bit mask. Instead, it encodes information about the mask into a single octet that precedes each address. The mask octet contains a binary integer that specifies the number of bits in the mask (mask bits are assumed to be contiguous). The address that follows the mask octet is also compressed — only those octets covered by the mask are included. Thus, only one address octet follows a mask value of *8* or less, two follow a mask value of *9* to *16*, three follow a mask value of *17* to *24*, and four follow a mask value of *25* to *32*. Interestingly, the standard also allows a mask octet to contain zero (in which case no address octets follow it). A zero length mask is useful because it corresponds to a default route.

13.13 BGP Path Attributes

We said that BGP is not a traditional distance-vector protocol. Instead of merely advertising a distance to each destination, BGP advertises additional information, including a path. The additional information is contained in the *Path Attributes* field of an update message. A sender can use the path attributes to specify: a next hop for the advertised destinations, a list of autonomous systems along the path to the destinations, and whether the path information was learned from another autonomous system or derived from within the sender's autonomous system.

It is important to note that the path attributes are factored to reduce the size of the UPDATE message, meaning that the attributes apply to all destinations advertised in the message. Thus, if a BGP sender intends to advertise paths to several sets of destinations that each have their own path attributes, BGP must send multiple UPDATE messages.

Path attributes are important in BGP for three reasons. First, path information allows a receiver to check for forwarding loops. The sender specifies an exact path of autonomous systems that will be used to reach the destination. If the receiver's autonomous system appears on the list, the advertisement must be rejected or there will be a forwarding loop. Second, path information allows a receiver to implement policy constraints (e.g., reject a path that includes a competitor's autonomous system). Third, path information allows a receiver to know the source of all routes. In addition to allowing a sender to specify whether the information came from inside its autonomous system or from another system, the path attributes allow the sender to declare whether the information was collected with an exterior gateway protocol such as BGP or an interior gateway protocol†. Thus, each receiver can decide whether to accept or reject routes that originate in autonomous systems beyond its peers.

Conceptually, the *Path Attributes* field contains a list of items, where each item consists of a triple:

(type, length, value)

Instead of using fixed-size fields for the three items, the designers chose a flexible encoding scheme that minimizes the space each item occupies. The *type* field has a fixed size of two octets, the *length* field is one or two octets, and size of the *value* field depends on the length. Figure 13.8 illustrates that the type field is divided into two octets.

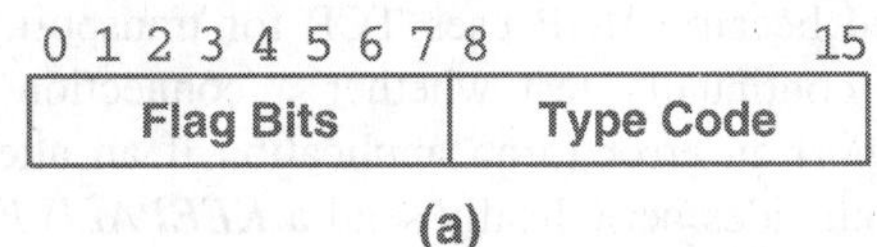

(a)

Flag Bits	Description
0	0 for required attribute, 1 if optional
1	1 for transitive, 0 for nontransitive
2	0 for complete, 1 for partial
3	0 if length field is one octet, 1 if two
5-7	unused (must be zero)

(b)

Figure 13.8 (a) The two-octet type field that appears before each BGP attribute path item, and (b) the meaning of each flag bit.

†The next chapter describes interior gateway protocols.

Each item in the *Path attributes* field can have one of eight possible type codes. Figure 13.9 summarizes the possibilities.

Type Code	Meaning
1	ID of the origin of the path information
2	List of autonomous systems on path to destination
3	Next hop to use for destination
4	Discriminator used for multiple AS exit points
5	Preference used within an autonomous system
6	Indication that routes have been aggregated
7	ID of autonomous system that aggregated routes
8	ID of community for advertised destinations

Figure 13.9 The BGP attribute type codes and the meaning of each.

For each item in the *Path Attributes* list, a length field follows the 2-octet type field, and is either one or two octets long. As Figure 13.8 shows, flag bit *3* specifies the size of the length field. A receiver uses the type field to determine the size of the length field, and then uses the contents of the length field to compute the size of the value field.

13.14 BGP KEEPALIVE Message

Two BGP peers periodically exchange *KEEPALIVE* messages to test network connectivity and to verify that both peers continue to function. A *KEEPALIVE* message consists of the standard message header with no additional data. Thus, the total message size is *19* octets (the minimum BGP message size).

There are two reasons why BGP uses *KEEPALIVE* messages. First, periodic message exchange is needed because BGP uses TCP for transport, and TCP does not include a mechanism to continually test whether a connection endpoint is reachable. However, TCP does report an error to an application if an attempt to send data fails. Therefore, as long as both sides periodically send a *KEEPALIVE*, they will be informed if the TCP connection fails. Second, *KEEPALIVE* messages conserve bandwidth compared to other messages. Many early routing protocols relied on periodic exchange of routing information to test connectivity. However, because routing information changes infrequently, the message content seldom changes. Unfortunately, because routing messages are often large, resending the same message wastes network bandwidth. To avoid the inefficiency, BGP separates the functionality of route update from connectivity testing, allowing BGP to send small *KEEPALIVE* messages frequently and reserving larger *UPDATE* messages for situations when reachability information changes.

Recall that a BGP speaker specifies a *hold timer* when it opens a connection; the hold timer defines a maximum time that BGP is to wait without receiving a message. As a special case, the hold timer can be zero to specify that no *KEEPALIVE* messages are used. If the hold timer is greater than zero, the standard recommends setting the *KEEPALIVE* interval to one third of the hold timer. In no case can a BGP peer make the *KEEPALIVE* interval less than one second (which agrees with the requirement that a nonzero hold timer cannot be less than three seconds).

13.15 Information From The Receiver's Perspective

An Exterior Gateway Protocol, such as BGP, differs from traditional routing protocols in a significant way: a peer that uses an exterior protocol does not merely report information from its own FIB. Instead, exterior protocols provide information that is correct from the outsider's perspective. We say that an exterior protocol supplies *third-party routing information*. There are two issues: policies and optimal routes. The policy issue is obvious: a router inside an autonomous system may be allowed to reach some destinations that outsiders are prohibited from reaching. The routing issue means that a peer must advertise a next hop that is optimal from the outsider's perspective. The architecture in Figure 13.10 can be used to illustrate the idea.

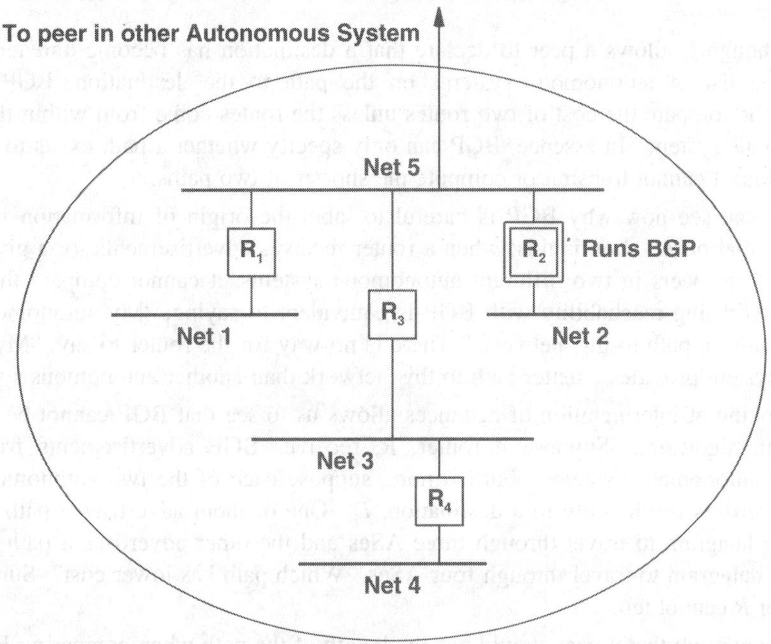

Figure 13.10 Example of an autonomous system where R_2 runs BGP and reports information from the outsider's perspective, not from its own forwarding table.

In the figure, router R_2 has been designated to speak BGP on behalf of the autonomous system. It must report reachability to networks *1* through *4*. However, when giving a next hop, it should report network *1* as reachable through router R_1, networks *3* and *4* as reachable through router R_3, and network *2* as reachable through R_2. The key point is that if R_2 lists itself as the next hop for all destinations in the autonomous system, routing will be suboptimal. The peer would send all traffic to R_2. In particular, when a datagram arrives from the peer destined for networks *1*, *3*, or *4*, the peer would send to R_2 and the datagram would then take an extra hop across network *5*.

13.16 The Key Restriction Of Exterior Gateway Protocols

We have already seen that because exterior protocols follow policy restrictions, the networks they advertise may be a subset of the networks they can reach. However, there is a more fundamental limitation imposed on exterior routing:

> *An exterior gateway protocol does not communicate or interpret distance metrics, even if metrics are available.*

Although it allows a peer to declare that a destination has become unreachable or to give a list of autonomous systems on the path to the destination, BGP cannot transmit or compare the cost of two routes unless the routes come from within the same autonomous system. In essence, BGP can only specify whether a path exists to a given destination; it cannot transmit or compute the shorter of two paths.

We can see now why BGP is careful to label the origin of information it sends. The essential observation is this: when a router receives advertisements for a given destination from peers in two different autonomous systems, it cannot compare the costs. Thus, advertising reachability with BGP is equivalent to saying, "My autonomous system provides a path to this network." There is no way for the router to say, "My autonomous system provides a better path to this network than another autonomous system."

Looking at interpretation of distances allows us to see that BGP cannot be used as a routing algorithm. Suppose a router, *R*, receives BGP advertisements from two separate autonomous systems. Furthermore, suppose each of the two autonomous systems advertises reachability to a destination, *D*. One of them advertises a path that requires a datagram to travel through three ASes and the other advertises a path that requires a datagram to travel through four ASes. Which path has lower cost? Surprisingly, router *R* cannot tell.

It may seem that a peer should use the length of the path when comparing BGP advertisements. After all, if one path lists autonomous systems *F*, *G*, *H*, and *I*, and another path lists autonomous systems *X*, *Y*, and *Z*, intuition tells us that the latter path is shorter. However, a given autonomous system can be large or small. Once a datagram reaches the autonomous system, the datagram may need to traverse multiple networks. How many? What are the network characteristics of delay and throughput? A border router cannot answer the questions because:

The internal structure of an autonomous system is hidden, and no information about the cost of paths inside the system is provided by BGP.

The consequence is that a peer has no way of comparing the real cost of two paths if all the peer receives is a list of autonomous systems. It could turn out that a path with four ASes involves much faster networks than a path with three ASes.

Because BGP does not allow an autonomous system to specify a metric with each route, the autonomous system must be careful to advertise only routes that traffic should follow. We can summarize:

Because an Exterior Gateway Protocol like BGP only propagates reachability information, a receiver can implement policy constraints, but cannot choose a least cost route. Therefore, BGP should only be used to advertise paths that traffic should follow.

The key point here is: an autonomous system that uses BGP to provide exterior routing information must either rely on policies or assume that every autonomous system transit is equally expensive. Although it may seem innocuous, the restriction has some surprising consequences:

1. Although BGP can advertise multiple paths to a given network, it does not provide a way for an autonomous system to request that traffic be forwarded over multiple paths. That is, at any given instant, all traffic sent from a computer in one autonomous system to a network in another will traverse one path, even if multiple physical connections are present. Also note that an outside autonomous system will only use one return path, even if the source system divides outgoing traffic among two or more paths. As a result, delay and throughput between a pair of hosts can be asymmetric, making traffic difficult to monitor or debug and errors difficult to report.

2. BGP does not support load sharing on peers between arbitrary autonomous systems. If two autonomous systems have multiple routers connecting them, one would like to balance the traffic equally among all routers. BGP allows autonomous systems to divide the load by network (e.g., to partition themselves into multiple subsets and have multiple routers advertise partitions), but it does not support more general load sharing.

3. As a special case of point 2, BGP alone is inadequate for optimal routing in an architecture that has two or more wide area networks interconnected at multiple points. Instead, managers must manually configure which networks are advertised by each exterior router.

4. To have rationalized routing, all autonomous systems in the Internet must agree on a consistent scheme for advertising reachability. That is, BGP alone will not guarantee global consistency.

13.17 The Internet Routing Architecture And Registries

For the Internet to operate flawlessly, routing information must be globally consistent. Individual protocols such as BGP that handle the exchange between a pair of routers, do not guarantee global consistency. Thus, further effort is needed to rationalize routing information globally. In the original Internet routing architecture, the core system guaranteed globally consistent routing information because at any time the core had exactly one path to each destination. However, the core system and its successor (called the routing arbiter system) have been removed. Ironically, no single mechanism has been devised as a replacement to handle the task of routing rationalization — the current Internet does not have a central mechanism to validate routes and guarantee global consistency.

To understand the current routing architecture, we need to examine the physical topology. A pair of ISPs can interconnect privately (e.g., by agreeing to lease a circuit between two routers), or can interconnect at *Internet Exchange Points* (*IXPs*), which are also known as *Network Access Points* (*NAPs*). We say that the ISPs engage in *private peering* or that they enter into a *peering agreement*. In terms of routing, a private peering represents the boundary between the two autonomous systems. The two ISPs define their relationship, which can be viewed as *upstream* (a large ISP agrees to take traffic from a smaller ISP), *downstream*, (a large ISP passes traffic to a smaller ISP), or *transit* (an ISP agrees to accept and forward traffic to other ISPs).

To assist in assuring that routes are valid, ISPs use services known as *Routing Registries*. In essence, a Routing Registry maintains information about which ISPs own which blocks of addresses. Thus, if ISP *A* sends an advertisement to ISP *B* claiming to have reachability to network *N*, ISP *B* can use information from a Routing Registry to verify that address *N* has been assign to ISP *A*. Unfortunately, many Routing Registries exist, and there is no mechanism in place to validate the data in a registry. Thus, temporary routing problems occur, such as *black holes*, in which a given address is not reachable from all parts of the Internet. Of course, ISPs and most Routing Registries attempt to find and repair such problems quickly, but without a centralized, authoritative registry, Internet routing is not flawless.

13.18 BGP NOTIFICATION Message

In addition to the OPEN and UPDATE message types described above, BGP supports a *NOTIFICATION* message type used for control or when an error occurs. Errors are permanent — once it detects a problem, BGP sends a notification message and then closes the TCP connection. Figure 13.11 illustrates the message format.

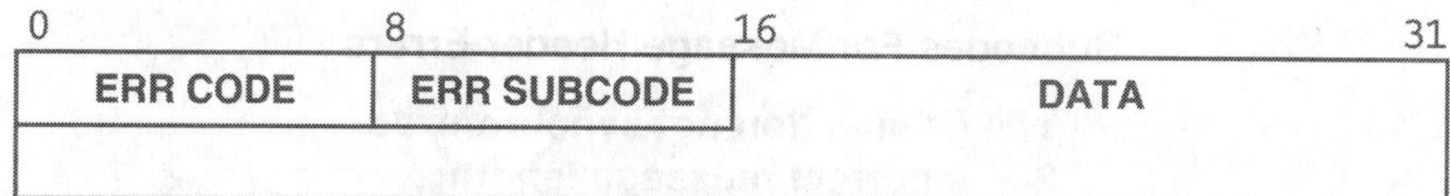

Figure 13.11 BGP NOTIFICATION message format. These octets follow the standard message header.

The 8-bit field labeled *ERR CODE* specifies one of the possible reasons listed in Figure 13.12.

ERR CODE	Meaning
1	Error in message header
2	Error in OPEN message
3	Error in UPDATE message
4	Hold timer expired
5	Finite state machine error
6	Cease (terminate connection)

Figure 13.12 The possible values of the *ERR CODE* field in a BGP NOTIFICATION message.

For each possible *ERR CODE*, the *ERR SUBCODE* field contains a further explanation. Figure 13.13 lists the possible values.

13.19 BGP Multiprotocol Extensions For IPv6

BGP was originally designed to convey IPv4 routing information. By 2000, it had become apparent that autonomous systems needed to exchange additional types of routing information. At the time, the two most pressing needs were IPv6 and MPLS, which is described in Chapter 16. Rather than create one version of BGP for IPv6 and another version for MPLS, a group in the IETF created *multiprotocol extensions*. The idea is that when advertising destinations, a sender can specify that the destination addresses are of a particular *address family*. To send IPv6 information a sender specifies the IPv6 address family, and to send MPLS information a sender specifies the MPLS address family.

Only three items carried in BGP messages use IPv4 addresses: the address of a *destination* that is advertised, the address of a *next hop* used to reach the destination, and the address of an *aggregator* that has aggregated prefixes. The extensions are designed to allow any of the three items to use an arbitrary address family rather than IPv4.

Subcodes For Message Header Errors

1	Connection not synchronized
2	Incorrect message length
3	Incorrect message type

Subcodes For OPEN Message Errors

1	Version number unsupported
2	Peer AS invalid
3	BGP identifier invalid
4	Unsupported optional parameter
5	Deprecated (no longer used)
6	Hold time unacceptable

Subcodes For UPDATE Message Errors

1	Attribute list malformed
2	Unrecognized attribute
3	Missing attribute
4	Attribute flags error
5	Attribute length error
6	Invalid ORIGIN attribute
7	Deprecated (no longer used)
8	Next hop invalid
9	Error in optional attribute
10	Invalid network field
11	Malformed AS path

Figure 13.13 The meaning of the *ERR SUBCODE* field in a BGP NOTIFICATION message.

The designers chose two key properties for the multiprotocol extensions:

- *Optional.* Multiprotocol extensions are not required.
- *Non-transitive.* A router may not pass the extensions to other ASes.

The decisions are important for two reasons. Making the extensions optional guarantees backward compatibility (i.e., old BGP software will continue to function). If an implementation of BGP does not understand the extensions, it will simply ignore the extensions and the routes they advertise. The prohibition on forwarding extensions keeps Internet routing from being vulnerable to attack. If blind forwarding were permitted, an AS that did not understand the extensions might inadvertently forward incorrect information, which the next AS would trust.

The multiprotocol extensions are carried in BGP's *Path Attributes*. Two new attribute types were created to allow a sender to specify a list of non-IPv4 destinations that are reachable and a list of non-IPv4 destinations that are unreachable. Rather than use the term *reachable destinations*, the extensions use the term *Network Layer Reachability Information* (*NLRI*). Consequently, the two attributes types are:

- Multiprotocol Reachable NLRI (Type 14)
- Multiprotocol Unreachable NLRI (Type 15)

13.20 Multiprotocol Reachable NLRI Attribute

A router uses the *Multiprotocol Reachable NLRI* attribute to advertise reachable destinations, either within its autonomous system or destinations reachable through the autonomous system. Each destination in the attribute is called a *Subnetwork Protocol Address* (*SNPA*). Figure 13.14 lists the fields in the attribute:

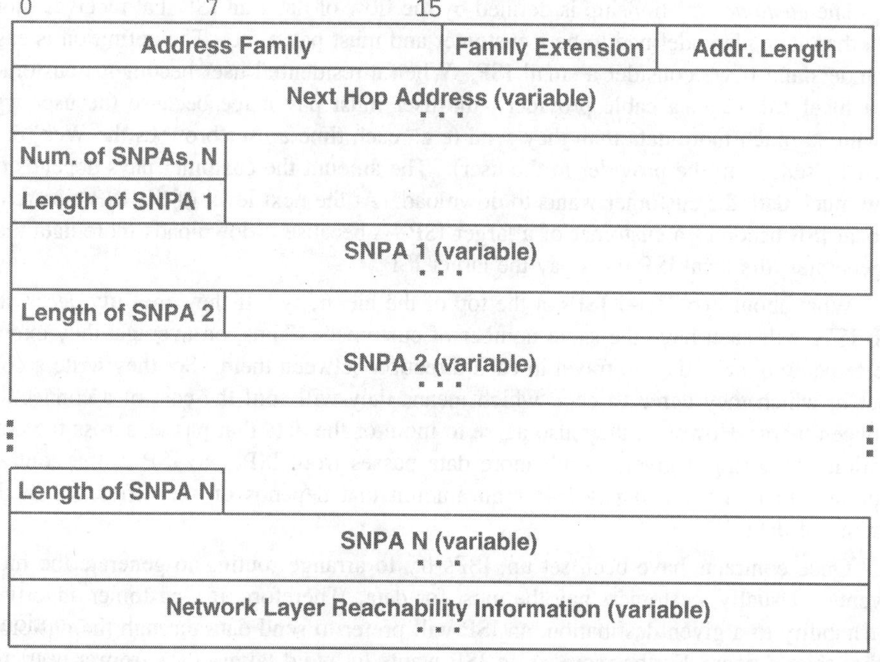

Figure 13.14 The format of a BGP *Multiprotocol Reachable NLRI* attribute used for IPv6 and other non-IPv4 destination addresses.

As the figure shows, the attribute starts with fields that give the address family and address length. The attribute then specifies a next-hop address and a set of destinations (SNPAs) reachable through the next hop. Each destination is preceded by a 1-octet length.

13.21 Internet Routing And Economics

Although research on routing focuses on finding mechanisms that compute shortest paths, shortest paths are not the primary concern of Tier-1 ISPs; economics is. Before they interconnect their networks and begin passing traffic, a pair of ISPs negotiates a business contract. Typical contacts specify one of three possibilities:

- ISP 1 is a *customer* of ISP 2.
- ISP 2 is a *customer* of ISP 1.
- The two ISPs are *peers*.

The *customer* relationship is defined by the flow of data: an ISP that receives more data than it sends is defined to be a customer and must pay a fee. The definition is easy to understand if we consider a small ISP. When a residential user becomes a customer of a local ISP (e.g., a cable provider), the user must pay a fee because the user will download much more data than they send (e.g., each time a user browses the Web, data must be sent from the provider to the user). The amount the customer pays depends on how much data the customer wants to download. At the next level of the ISP hierarchy, a local ISP becomes a customer of a larger ISP — because it downloads more data than it generates, the local ISP must pay the larger ISP.

What about two Tier-1 ISPs at the top of the hierarchy? If they are truly *peers*, the two ISPs will each have the same number of customers. Thus, on average, they expect the same amount of data to travel in each direction between them. So, they write a contract in which they agree to peer, which means they will split the cost of a connection between them. However, they also agree to monitor the data that passes across the connection. If during a given month more data passes from ISP 1 to ISP 2, the contract stipulates that ISP 2 will pay ISP 1 an amount that depends on the difference in the amount of data.

Once contracts have been set up, ISPs try to arrange routing to generate the most revenue. Usually, customers pay the most for data. Therefore, if a customer advertises reachability to a given destination, an ISP will prefer to send data through the customer rather than a peer. Furthermore, if an ISP wants to avoid taking data from a peer, the ISP can arrange BGP messages that cause the peer to stop sending (e.g., if an ISP puts the peer's AS number on the path in an advertisement, the peer will reject the path as having a routing loop). The point is:

At the center of the Internet, routing is based largely on economics rather than shortest paths. Major ISPs arrange policies, preferences, and BGP advertisements to force datagrams along routes that generate the most revenue, independent of whether the route is shortest.

13.22 Summary

In a large internet, routers must be partitioned into groups or the volume of routing traffic would be intolerable. The global Internet is composed of a set of autonomous systems, where each autonomous system consists of routers and networks under one administrative authority. An autonomous system uses an Exterior Gateway Protocol to advertise routes to other autonomous systems. Specifically, an autonomous system must advertise reachability of its networks to another system before its networks are reachable from sources within the other system.

The Border Gateway Protocol, BGP, is the most widely used Exterior Gateway Protocol. BGP contains five message types that are used to initiate communication (OPEN), send reachability information (UPDATE), report an error condition (NOTIFICATION), revalidate information (REFRESH), and ensure peers remain in communication (KEEPALIVE). Each message starts with a standard header. BGP uses TCP for communication.

Although originally created for IPv4, BGP has been extended to handle other protocols. In particular, a set of multiprotocol extensions allow BGP to pass information about MPLS as well as IPv6.

In the global Internet, each large ISP is a separate autonomous system, and the boundary between autonomous systems consists of a peering agreement between two ISPs. Physically, peering can occur in an Internet Exchange Point or over a private leased circuit. An ISP uses BGP to communicate with its peer, both to advertise networks (i.e., address prefixes) that can be reached through it and to learn about networks that can be reached by forwarding to the peer. Although services known as Routing Registries exist that aid ISPs in validating advertisements, problems can occur because the Internet does not currently have an authoritative, centralized registry.

At the center of the Internet, routing is based on economics rather than shortest paths. Major ISPs choose routes that will maximize their revenue and minimize their costs.

EXERCISES

13.1 If your site runs an Exterior Gateway Protocol such as BGP, how many routes do you advertise? How many routes do you import from an ISP?

13.2 Some implementations of BGP use a *hold down* mechanism that causes the protocol to delay accepting an *OPEN* from a peer for a fixed time following the receipt of a *cease request* message from that neighbor. Find out what problem a hold down helps solve.

13.3 The formal specification of BGP includes a finite state machine that explains how BGP operates. Draw a diagram of the state machine and label transitions.

13.4 What happens if a router in an autonomous system sends BGP routing update messages to a router in another autonomous system, claiming to have reachability for every possible Internet destination?

13.5 Can two autonomous systems establish a forwarding loop by sending BGP update messages to one another? Why or why not?

13.6 Should a router that uses BGP to advertise routes treat the set of routes advertised differently than the set of routes in the local forwarding table? For example, should a router ever advertise reachability if it has not installed a route to that network in its forwarding table? Why or why not? (Hint: read RFC 1771.)

13.7 With regard to the previous question, examine the BGP-4 specification carefully. Is it legal to advertise reachability to a destination that is not listed in the local forwarding table?

13.8 If you work for a large corporation, find out whether it includes more than one autonomous system. If so, how do they exchange routing information?

13.9 What is the chief advantage of dividing a large, multi-national corporation into multiple autonomous systems? What is the chief disadvantage?

13.10 Corporations *A* and *B* use BGP to exchange routing information. The network administrator at Corporation *A* configures BGP to omit network *N* from advertisements sent to *B*, which is intended to prevent computers in *B* from reaching machines on network *N*. Is network *N* secure? Why or why not?

13.11 Because BGP uses a reliable transport protocol, KEEPALIVE messages cannot be lost. Does it make sense to specify a keepalive interval as one-third of the hold timer value? Why or why not?

13.12 Consult the RFCs for details of the *Path Attributes* field. What is the minimum size of a BGP UPDATE message?

Chapter Contents

14

Routing Within An Autonomous System (RIP, RIPng, OSPF, IS-IS)

14.1 Introduction

The previous chapter introduces the autonomous system concept and examines BGP, an Exterior Gateway Protocol that a router uses to advertise networks within its system to other autonomous systems. This chapter completes our overview of internet routing by examining how a router in an autonomous system learns about other networks within its autonomous system.

14.2 Static Vs. Dynamic Interior Routes

Two routers within an autonomous system are said to be *interior* to one another. For example, two routers on a university campus are considered interior to one another as long as machines on the campus are collected into a single autonomous system.

How can routers in an autonomous system learn about networks within the autonomous system? In the smallest intranets, network managers can establish and modify routes manually. The manager keeps a list of networks and updates the forwarding tables whenever a new network is added to, or deleted from, the autonomous system. For example, consider the small corporate intranet shown in Figure 14.1.

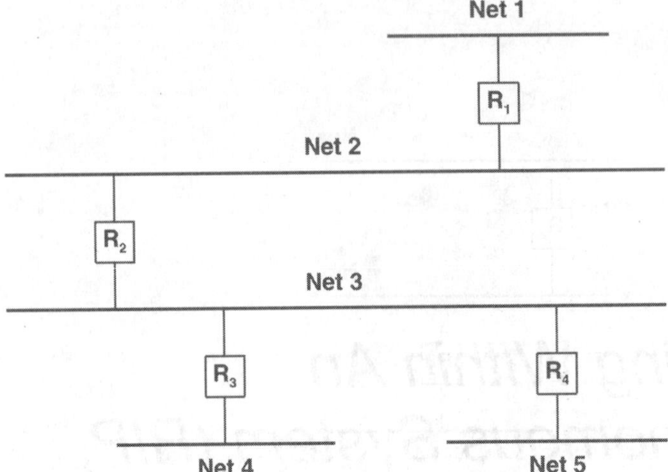

Figure 14.1 An example of a small intranet consisting of five networks and four routers. Only one possible route exists between any two hosts in the example.

Routing for the intranet in the figure is trivial because only one path exists between any two points. If a network or router fails, the intranet will be disconnected because there are no redundant paths. Therefore, a manager can configure routes in all hosts and routers manually, and never needs to change the routes. Of course, if the intranet changes (e.g., a new network is added), the manager must reconfigure the routes accordingly.

The disadvantages of a manual system are obvious: manual systems cannot accommodate rapid growth and rely on humans to change routes whenever a network failure occurs. In most intranets, humans simply cannot respond to changes fast enough to handle problems; automated methods must be used. To understand how automated routing can increase reliability, consider what happens if we add one additional router to the intranet in Figure 14.1, producing the intranet shown in Figure 14.2.

In the figure, multiple paths exist between some hosts. In such cases, a manager usually chooses one path to be a *primary path* (i.e., the path that will be used for all traffic). If a router or network along the primary path fails, routes must be changed to send traffic along an alternate path. Automated route changes help in two ways. First, because computers can respond to failures much faster than humans, automated route changes are less time consuming. Second, because humans can make small errors when entering network addresses, automated routing is less error-prone. Thus, even in small internets, an automated system is used to change routes quickly and reliably.

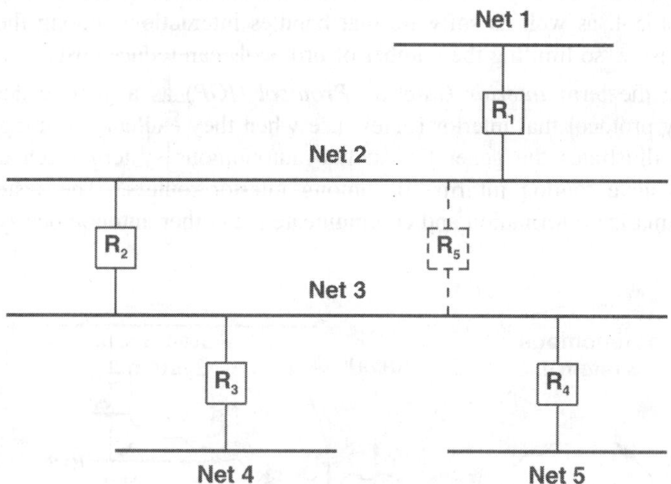

Figure 14.2 The addition of router R_5 introduces an alternate path between networks *2* and *3*. Routing software can quickly adapt to a failure and automatically switch routes to the alternate path.

To automate the task of keeping routing information accurate, interior routers periodically communicate with one another to exchange routing information. Unlike exterior router communication, for which BGP provides a widely accepted standard, no single protocol has emerged for use within an autonomous system or a site. Part of the reason for diversity arises from the diversity in autonomous systems. Some autonomous systems correspond to a large enterprise (e.g., a corporation) at a single site, while others correspond to an organization with many sites connected by a wide area network. Even if we consider individual Internet sites, the network topologies (e.g., degree of redundancy), sizes, and network technologies vary widely. Another reason for diversity of interior routing protocols stems from the tradeoffs between ease of configuration, functionality, and traffic the protocols impose on the underlying networks — protocols that are easy to install and configure may not provide the functionality needed or may impose intolerable load on the networks. As a result, a handful of protocols have become popular, but no single protocol is always optimal.

Although multiple interior protocols are used, a given autonomous system often chooses to limit the number of protocols that are deployed. A small AS tends to choose a single protocol and use it exclusively to propagate routing information internally. Even larger autonomous systems tend to choose a small set. There are two reasons. First, one of the most complex aspects of routing arises from the interaction of protocols. If protocol A is used on some routers and protocol B is used on other routers, at least one router between the two sets must communicate using both protocols and must have a way to transfer information between them. Such interactions are complex, and care must be taken or differences in protocols can lead to unexpected consequences. Second, because routing protocols are difficult to understand and configure, each autonomous system must have a staff that is trained to install, configure, and support each individual protocol, as well as software that handles interactions among them. Training can be expensive, so limiting the number of protocols can reduce costs.

We use the term *Interior Gateway Protocol* (*IGP*) as a generic description that refers to any protocol that interior routers use when they exchange routing information. Figure 14.3 illustrates the general idea: two autonomous systems each use a specific IGP to propagate routing information among interior routers. The systems then use BGP to summarize information and communicate it to other autonomous systems.

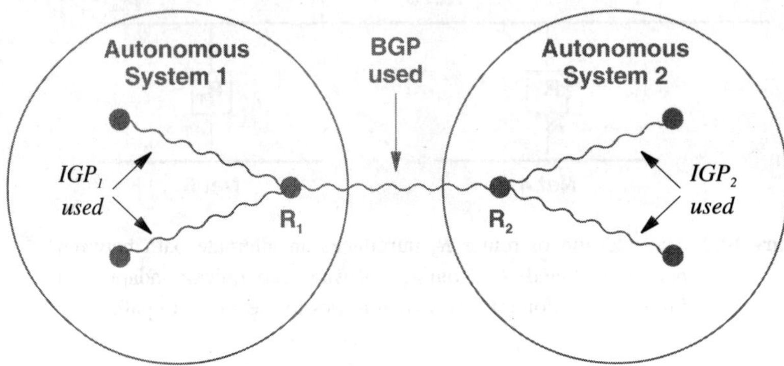

Figure 14.3 Conceptual view of two autonomous systems, each using its own IGP internally, and then using BGP to communicate routes to another system.

In the figure, IGP_1 refers to the interior routing protocol used within autonomous system *1*, and IGP_2 refers to the protocol used within autonomous system *2*. Router R_1 will use IGP_1 to obtain routes internally, summarize the information, apply policies, and then use BGP to export the resulting information. Similarly, router R_2 will use IGP_2 to obtain information that it exports. We can summarize the key concept:

> *If multiple routing protocols are used, a single router may run two or more routing protocols simultaneously.*

In particular, routers that run BGP to advertise reachability usually also need to run an IGP to obtain information from within their autonomous system. The next sections describe specific interior gateway protocols; later sections consider some consequences of using multiple protocols.

14.3 Routing Information Protocol (RIP)

14.3.1 History of RIP

The *Routing Information Protocol* (*RIP*) has remained in widespread use since early in the Internet. Originally, RIP was known by the name of an application that implements it, *routed*†. The *routed* software was designed at the University of California at Berkeley to provide consistent routing information among machines on local networks. The protocol was based on earlier research done at Xerox Corporation's Palo Alto Research Center (PARC). The Berkeley version of RIP generalized the PARC version to cover multiple families of networks. RIP relies on physical network broadcast to make routing exchanges quickly, and was not originally designed to be used on large, wide area networks. Vendors later developed versions of RIP suitable for use on WANs.

Despite minor improvements over its predecessors, the popularity of RIP as an IGP does not arise from its technical merits alone. Instead, it is the result of Berkeley distributing *routed* software along with their popular 4BSD UNIX systems. Many early TCP/IP sites adopted and installed RIP without considering its technical merits or limitations. Once installed and running, it became the basis for local routing, and vendors began offering products compatible with RIP.

14.3.2 RIP Operation

The underlying RIP protocol is a straightforward implementation of distance-vector routing for local networks. RIP supports two type of participants: *active* and *passive*. Active participants advertise their routes to others; passive participants listen to RIP messages and use them to update their forwarding table, but do not advertise. Only a router can run RIP in active mode; if a host runs RIP, the host must use passive mode.

A router running RIP in active mode broadcasts a routing update message every 30 seconds. The update contains information taken from the router's current FIB. Each update contains a set of pairs, where each pair specifies an IP network address and an integer distance to that network. RIP uses a *hop count metric* to measure distances. In the RIP metric, a router is defined to be one hop from a directly connected network‡, two hops from a network that is reachable through one other router, and so on. Thus, the *number of hops* or the *hop count* along a path from a given source to a given destination refers to the number of networks that a datagram encounters along that path. It should be obvious that using hop counts to calculate shortest paths does not always produce optimal results. For example, a path with hop count *3* that crosses three Ethernets may be substantially faster than a path with hop count *2* that crosses two satellite connections. To compensate for differences in technologies, many RIP implementations allow managers to configure artificially high hop counts when advertising connections to slow networks.

Both active and passive RIP participants listen to all broadcast messages and update their forwarding tables according to the distance-vector algorithm described in

---

†The name comes from the UNIX convention of attaching "d" to the names of daemon processes; it is pronounced "route-d".

‡Other routing protocols define a direct connection to be zero hops; we say that RIP uses 1-origin hop counts.

Chapter 12. For example, if the routers in the intranet of Figure 14.2 on page 291 use RIP, router R_1 will broadcast a message on network *2* that contains the pair *(1, 1)*, meaning that it can reach network *1* at distance (i.e., cost) *1*. Routers R_2 and R_5 will receive the broadcast and install a route to network *1* through R_1 (at cost 2). Later, routers R_2 and R_5 will include the pair *(1, 2)* when they broadcast their RIP messages on network *3*. Eventually, all routers will install a route to network *1*.

RIP specifies a few rules to improve performance and reliability. For example, once a router learns a route from another router, it must apply *hysteresis*, meaning that it does not replace the route with an equal cost route. In our example, if routers R_2 and R_5 both advertise network *1* at cost *2*, routers R_3 and R_4 will install a route through the one that happens to advertise first. We can summarize:

> *To prevent oscillation among equal cost paths, RIP specifies that existing routes should be retained until a new route has strictly lower cost.*

What happens if a router fails (e.g., the router crashes)? RIP specifies that when a router receives and installs a route in its forwarding table, the router must start a timer for the entry. The timer is reset whenever the router receives another RIP message advertising the same route. The route becomes invalid if 180 seconds pass without the route being advertised again.

RIP must handle three kinds of errors caused by the underlying algorithm. First, because the algorithm does not explicitly detect forwarding loops, RIP must either assume participants can be trusted or take precautions to prevent such loops. Second, to prevent instabilities, RIP must use a low value for the maximum possible distance (RIP uses *16*). Thus, for intranets in which legitimate hop counts approach *16*, managers must divide the intranet into sections or use an alternative protocol†. Third, the distance-vector algorithm used by RIP can create a problem known as *slow convergence* or *count to infinity* in which inconsistencies arise because routing update messages propagate slowly across the network. Choosing a small infinity (*16*) helps limit slow convergence, but does not eliminate it.

14.4 Slow Convergence Problem

Forwarding table inconsistencies and the slow convergence problem are not unique to RIP. They are fundamental problems that can occur with any distance-vector protocol in which update messages carry only pairs of destination network and distance to that network. To understand the problem, consider using a distance-vector protocol on the routers in Figure 14.2 (page 291). To simply the example, we will only consider three routers, R_1, R_2, and R_3, and only consider the routes they have for network *1*. To reach network *1*, R_3 forwards to R_2, and R_2 forwards to R_1. Part (a) of Figure 14.4 illustrates the forwarding.

†Note that the hop count used in RIP measures the *span* of the intranet — the longest distance between two routers — rather than the total number of networks or routers. Most corporate intranets have a span that is much smaller than 16.

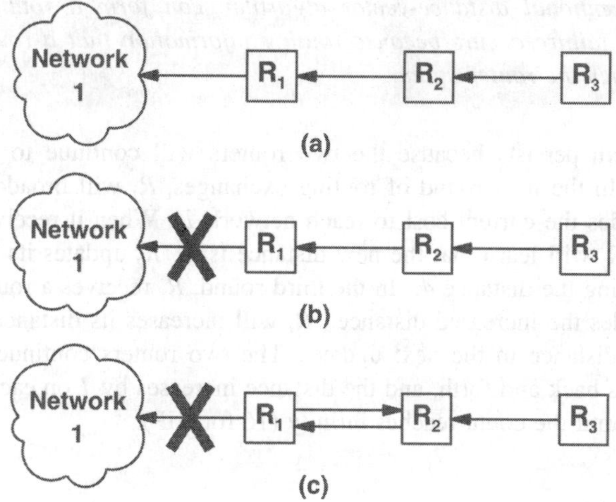

Figure 14.4 Illustration of the slow convergence problem with (a) three routers that have a route to network *1*, (b) the connection to network *1* has failed and R_1 has lost its router, and (c) a routing loop caused because R_2 advertises a route to network 1.

In part (a), we assume all routers are running a distance-vector protocol. We will assume RIP, but the idea applies to any distance-vector protocol. Router R_1 has a direct connection to network *1*. Therefore, when it broadcasts the set of destinations from its FIB, R_1 includes an entry for network *1* at distance *1*. Router R_2 has learned the route from R_1, installed the route in its forwarding table, and advertises the route at distance *2*. Finally, R_3 has learned the route from R_2 and advertises the route at distance *3*.

In part (b) of the figure, we assume a failure has occurred and disconnected R_1 from network 1. Perhaps the connection between router R_1 and network *1* was unplugged or network 1 lost power. The network interface in R_1 will detect the loss of connectivity, and IP will remove the route to network *1* from the forwarding table (or leave the entry, but set the distance to infinity so the route will not be used).

Remember that R_2 broadcasts its routing information periodically. Suppose that immediately after R_1 detects the failure and removes the route from its table, R_2 broadcasts its routing information. Among other items in the broadcast, R_2 will announce a route to network *1* at distance *2*. However, unless the protocol includes extra mechanisms to prevent it, the rules for distance-vector routing mean that R_1 will examine the broadcast from R_2, find a route to network *1*, and add a new route to its table with distance *3* (the distance R_2 advertised plus 1) and R_2 as the next hop.

Unfortunately, part (c) of the figure shows what has happened: R_1 has installed a route for network *1* that goes through R_2, and R_2 has a route that goes through R_1. At this point, if either R_1 or R_2 receives a datagram destined for network *1*, they will route the datagram back and forth until the datagram's hop limit is reached. In other words:

> *A conventional distance-vector algorithm can form a routing loop after a failure occurs because routing information that a router sent can reach the router again.*

The problem persists because the two routers will continue to remain confused about routing. In the next round of routing exchanges, R_1 will broadcast an advertisement that includes the current cost to reach network *1*. When it receives the advertisement from R_1, R_2 will learn that the new distance is *3*. R_2 updates its distance to reach network *1*, making the distance *4*. In the third round, R_1 receives a routing update from R_2 which includes the increased distance. R_1 will increases its distance to *5* and advertise the higher distance in the next update. The two routers continue sending routing update messages back and forth, and the distance increases by *1* on each exchange. Updates continue until the count reaches infinity (16 for RIP).

14.5 Solving The Slow Convergence Problem

A technique known as *split horizon update* has been invented that allows distance-vector protocols, such as RIP, to solve the slow convergence problem. When using split horizon, a router does not propagate information about a route back over the same interface from which the route arrived. In our example, split horizon prevents router R_2 from advertising a route to network *1* back to router R_1, so if R_1 loses connectivity to network *1*, it will stop advertising a route. With split horizon, no forwarding loop appears in the example network. Instead, after a few rounds of routing updates, all routers will agree that the network is unreachable. However, the split horizon heuristic does not prevent forwarding loops in all possible topologies as one of the exercises suggests.

Another way to think of the slow convergence problem is in terms of information flow. If a router advertises a short route to some network, all receiving routers respond quickly to install that route. If a router stops advertising a route, the protocol must depend on a timeout mechanism before it considers the route unreachable. Once the timeout occurs, the router finds an alternative route and starts propagating that information. Unfortunately, a router cannot know if the alternate route depended on the route that just disappeared. Thus, negative information does not always propagate quickly. A short epigram captures the idea and explains the phenomenon:

> *In routing protocols, good news travels quickly; bad news travels slowly.*

Another technique used to solve the slow convergence problem employs *hold down*. Hold down forces a participating router to ignore information about a network for a fixed period of time following receipt of a message that claims the network is unreachable. For RIP, the hold down period is set to 60 seconds, twice as long as a normal update period. The idea is to wait long enough to ensure that all machines receive the bad news and not mistakenly accept a message that is out of date. It should be noted that all machines participating in a RIP exchange need to use identical notions of hold down, or forwarding loops can occur. The disadvantage of a hold down technique is that if forwarding loops occur, they will be preserved for the duration of the hold down period. More important, the hold down technique preserves all incorrect routes during the hold down period, even when alternatives exist.

A final technique that helps solve the slow convergence problem is called *poison reverse*. Once a connection disappears, the router advertising the connection retains the entry for several update periods, and includes an infinite cost route in its broadcasts. To make poison reverse most effective, it must be combined with *triggered updates*. The triggered update mechanism forces a router to broadcast routing information immediately after receiving bad news. That is, the router does not wait until its next periodic broadcast. By sending an update immediately, a router minimizes the time it is vulnerable (i.e., the time during which neighbors might advertise short routes because they have not received the bad news).

Unfortunately, while triggered updates, poison reverse, hold down, and split horizon techniques all solve some problems, they introduce others. For example, consider what happens with triggered updates when many routers share a common network. A single broadcast may change all their forwarding tables, triggering a new round of broadcasts. If the second round of broadcasts changes tables, it will trigger even more broadcasts. A broadcast avalanche can result†.

The use of broadcast, potential for forwarding loops, and use of hold down to prevent slow convergence can make RIP extremely inefficient in a wide area network. Broadcasting always takes substantial bandwidth. Even if no avalanche problems occur, having all machines broadcast periodically means that the traffic increases as the number of routers increases. The potential for forwarding loops can also be deadly when line capacity is limited. Once lines become saturated by looping packets, it may be difficult or impossible for routers to exchange the routing messages needed to break the cycle. Also, in a wide area network, hold down periods are so long that the timers used by higher-level protocols can expire and lead to broken connections.

14.6 RIP Message Format (IPv4)

RIP messages can be broadly classified into two types: routing information messages and messages used to request information. Both use the same format, which consists of a fixed header followed by an optional list of network and distance pairs. Figure 14.5 shows the message format used with RIP version 2 (*RIP2*), the current version.

In the figure, field *COMMAND* specifies an operation; only five commands are defined. Figure 14.6 lists the commands and the meaning of each.

†To help avoid an avalanche, RIP requires each router to wait a small random time before sending a triggered update.

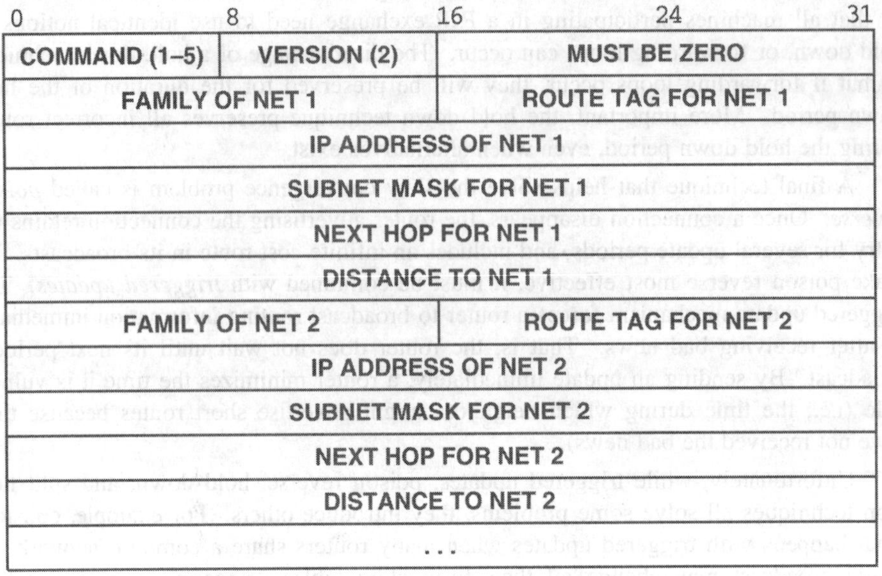

Figure 14.5 The format of an IPv4 version 2 RIP message. After the 32-bit header, the message contains a sequence of pairs, where each pair specifies an IPv4 prefix, next hop, and distance to the destination.

Command	Meaning
1	Request for partial or full routing information
2	Response containing network-distance pairs from sender's forwarding information base
9	Update Request (used with demand circuits)
10	Update Response (used with demand circuits)
11	Update Acknowledge (used with demand circuits)

Figure 14.6 The commands used with RIP. In typical implementations, only command 2 is used.

Although we have described RIP as sending routing updates periodically, the protocol includes commands that permit queries to be sent. For example, a host or router can send a *request* command to request routing information. Routers can use the *response* command to reply to requests. In most cases, a router periodically broadcasts unsolicited response messages. Field *VERSION* in Figure 14.5 contains the protocol version number (*2* in this case), and is used by the receiver to verify it will interpret the message correctly.

14.7 Fields In A RIP Message

Because it was initially used with addresses other than IPv4, RIP uses a 16-bit *FAMILY OF NET* field to specify the type of the address that follows. Values for the field were adopted values from 4.3 BSD Unix; IPv4 addresses are assigned family *2*. Two fields in each entry specify an IPv4 prefix: *IP ADDRESS OF NET* and *SUBNET MASK FOR NET*. As expected, the mask specifies which bits in the address correspond to the prefix. The *NEXT HOP FOR NET* field specifies the address of a router that is the next hop for the route. The last field of each entry in a RIP message, *DISTANCE TO NET*, contains an integer count of the distance to the specified network. As discussed above, RIP uses 1-origin routes, which means a directly connected network is one hop away. Furthermore, because RIP interprets *16* as infinity (i.e., no route exists), all distances are limited to the range *1* through *16*. Surprisingly, the distance is assigned a 32-bit field, even though only the low-order five bits are used.

RIP2 attaches a 16-bit *ROUTE TAG FOR NET* field to each entry. A router must send the same tag it receives when it transmits the route. Thus, the route tag provides a way to propagate additional information such as the origin of the route. In particular, if RIP2 learns a route from another autonomous system, it can use the route tag to propagate the autonomous system's number.

In addition to unicast IPv4 addresses, RIP uses the convention that a zero address (e.g., *0.0.0.0*), denotes a *default route*. RIP attaches a distance metric to every route it advertises, including the default route. Thus, it is possible to arrange for two routers to advertise a default route (e.g., a route to the rest of the internet) at different metrics, making one of them a primary path and the other a backup.

To prevent RIP from increasing the CPU load of hosts unnecessarily, the designers allow RIP2 to multicast updates instead of broadcasting them. Furthermore, RIP2 is assigned a fixed multicast address, 224.0.0.9, which means that machines using RIP2 do not need to run IGMP†. Finally, RIP2 multicast is restricted to a single network.

Note that a RIP message does not contain an explicit length field or an explicit count of entries. Instead, RIP assumes that the underlying delivery mechanism will tell the receiver the length of an incoming message. In particular, when used with TCP/IP, RIP messages rely on UDP to tell the receiver the message length. RIP operates on UDP port *520*. Although a RIP request can originate at other UDP ports, the destination UDP port for requests is always *520*, as is the source port from which RIP broadcast messages originate.

14.8 RIP For IPv6 (RIPng)

It may seem that the *FAMILY OF NET* field in the original design permits arbitrary protocol addresses to be used. However, instead of merely using the existing design, a new version of RIP was created for IPv6. Called *RIPng*‡, the new protocol has an entirely new message format and even operates on a different UDP port than RIP (port *521* as opposed to port *520*). Figure 14.7 illustrates the format.

†Chapter 15 describes the *Internet Group Management Protocol*.

‡The suffix *ng* stands for "next generation"; IPv6 was initially named *IPng*.

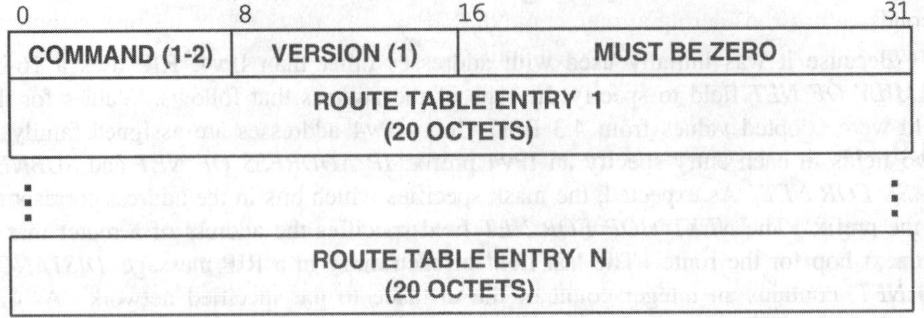

Figure 14.7 The overall format of a RIPng message used to carry IPv6 routing information.

Like RIP2, a RIPng message does not include a size field, nor does it include a count of items that follow; a receiver computes the number of route table entries from the size of the packet (which is obtained from UDP). As the figure indicates, each *ROUTE TABLE ENTRY* occupies 20 octets (i.e., the figure is not drawn to scale). Figure 14.8 illustrates the format of an individual route table entry.

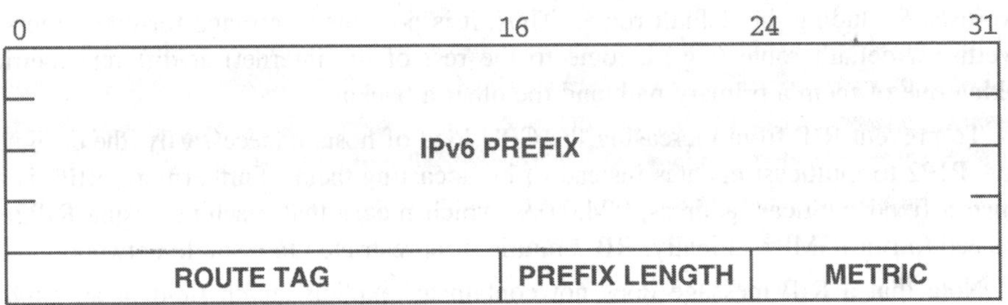

Figure 14.8 The format of each ROUTE TABLE ENTRY in a RIPng message

Observant readers may have noticed that RIPng does not include a field that stores the next hop for a route. The designers were aware that including a next hop in each route table entry would make the message size extremely large. Therefore, they chose an alternative: a route table entry with a metric field of 0xFF specifies a next hop rather than a destination. The next hop applies to all the route table entries that follow until another next hop entry or the end of the message.

Other than the new message format, the use of IPv6 addresses, and the special provision for a next hop, RIPng resembles RIP. Messages are still sent via UDP, and

RIPng still transmits a routing update every 30 seconds and uses a timeout of 180 seconds before considering a route expired. RIPng also preserves the techniques of split horizon, poison reverse, and triggered updates.

14.9 The Disadvantage Of Using Hop Counts

Using RIP or RIPng as an interior gateway protocol restricts routing to a hop-count metric. Even in the best cases, hop counts provide only a crude measure of network capacity or responsiveness. We know that using hop counts does not always yield routes with least delay or highest capacity. Furthermore, computing routes on the basis of minimum hop counts has the severe disadvantage that it makes routing relatively static because routes cannot respond to changes in network load. Therefore, it may seem odd that a protocol would be designed to use a hop-count metric. The next sections consider an alternative metric and explain why hop count metrics remain popular despite their limitations.

14.10 Delay Metric (HELLO)

Although now obsolete, the HELLO protocol provides an example of an IGP that was once deployed in the Internet and uses a routing metric other than hop count. Each HELLO message carried timestamp information as well as routing information, which allowed routers using HELLO to synchronize their clocks. Interestingly, HELLO used the synchronized clocks to find the delay on the link between each pair of routers so that each router could compute shortest delay paths to all destinations.

The basic idea behind HELLO is simple: use a distance-vector algorithm to propagate routing information. Instead of having routers report a hop count, however, HELLO reports an estimate of the delay to the destination. Having synchronized clocks allows a router to estimate delay by placing a timestamp on each packet. Before sending a packet, the sender places the current clock value in the packet as a timestamp, and the receiver subtracts the value from the current clock value. Having synchronized clocks allows delay to be computed without relying on round-trip samples, which means the delay in each direction can be estimated independently (i.e., congestion in one direction will not affect the estimated delay in the other direction).

HELLO uses the standard distance-vector approach for updates. When a message arrives from machine *X*, the receiver examines each entry in the message and changes the next hop to *X* if the route through *X* is less expensive than the current route (i.e., the delay to *X* plus the delay from *X* to the destination is less than the current delay to the destination).

14.11 Delay Metrics, Oscillation, And Route Flapping

It may seem that using delay as a routing metric would produce better routes than using a hop count and that all routing protocols should adopt a delay metric. In fact, HELLO worked well in the early Internet backbone. However, there is an important reason why delay is not used as a metric in current protocols: instability.

Even if two paths have identical characteristics, any protocol that changes routes quickly can become unstable. Instability arises because delay, unlike hop counts, is not static. Minor variations in delay measurements occur because of hardware clock drift, CPU load during measurement, or bit delays caused by link-level synchronization. Thus, if a routing protocol reacts quickly to slight differences in delay, it can produce a two-stage oscillation effect in which traffic switches back and forth between the alternate paths. In the first stage, the router finds the delay on path *1* slightly less and abruptly switches traffic onto it. In the next round, the router finds that changing the load to path *1* has increased the delay and that path *2* now has slightly less delay. So, the router switches traffic back to path *2* and the situation repeats.

To help avoid oscillation, protocols that use delay implement several heuristics. First, they employ the *hold down* technique discussed previously to prevent routes from changing rapidly. Second, instead of measuring as accurately as possible and comparing the values directly, the protocols round measurements to large multiples or implement a minimum *threshold* by ignoring differences less than the threshold. Third, instead of comparing each individual delay measurement, they keep a running *average* of recent values or alternatively apply a *K-out-of-N* rule that requires at least *K* of the most recent *N* delay measurements be less than the current delay before the route can be changed.

Even with heuristics, protocols that use delay can become unstable when comparing delays on paths that do not have identical characteristics. To understand why, it is necessary to know that traffic can have a dramatic effect on delay. With no traffic, the network delay is simply the time required for the hardware to transfer bits from one point to another. As the traffic load imposed on the network increases, delays begin to rise because routers in the system need to enqueue packets that are waiting for transmission. If the load is even slightly more than 100% of the network capacity, the queue becomes unbounded, meaning that the effective delay becomes infinite. To summarize:

> *The effective delay across a network depends on traffic; as the load approaches 100% of the network capacity, delay grows rapidly.*

Because delays are extremely sensitive to changes in load, protocols that use delay as a metric can easily fall into a *positive feedback cycle.* The cycle is triggered by a small external change in load (e.g., one computer injecting a burst of additional traffic). The increased traffic raises the delay, which causes the protocol to change routes. However, because a route change affects the load, it can produce an even larger change in delays, which means the protocol will again recompute routes. As a result, protocols that use delay must contain mechanisms to dampen oscillation.

We described heuristics that can solve simple cases of route oscillation when paths have identical throughput characteristics and the load is not excessive. The heuristics can become ineffective, however, when alternative paths have different delay and throughput characteristics. As an example consider the delay on two paths: one over a satellite and the other over a low-capacity digital circuit (e.g., a fractional T1 circuit). In the first stage of the protocol when both paths are idle, the digital circuit will appear to have significantly lower delay than the satellite, and will be chosen for traffic. Because the circuit has low capacity, it will quickly become overloaded, and the delay will rise sharply. In the second stage, the delay on the circuit will be much greater than that of the satellite, so the protocol will switch traffic away from the overloaded path. Because the satellite path has large capacity, traffic which overloaded the serial line does not impose a significant load on the satellite, meaning that the delay on the satellite path does not change with traffic. In the next round, the delay on the unloaded digital circuit will once again appear to be much smaller than the delay on the satellite path. The protocol will reverse the routing, and the cycle will continue. We say that the routes *flap* back and forth. Such oscillations do, in fact, occur in practice. As the example shows, they are difficult to manage because traffic which has little effect on one network can overload another. The point is:

> *Although intuition suggests that routing should use paths with lowest delay, doing so makes routing subject to oscillations known as route flapping.*

14.12 The Open SPF Protocol (OSPF)

In Chapter 12, we said that a link-state approach to routing, which employs an SPF graph algorithm to compute shortest paths, scales better than a distance-vector algorithm. To encourage the adoption of link-state technology, a working group of the IETF designed an interior gateway protocol that uses the link-state algorithm. Named *Open SPF* (*OSPF*), the protocol tackles several ambitious goals.

- *Open Standard.* As the name implies, the specification is available in the published literature. Making it an open standard that anyone can implement without paying license fees has encouraged many vendors to support OSPF.

- *Type Of Service Routing.* Managers can install multiple routes to a given destination, one for each priority or type of service. A router running OSPF can use both the destination address and type of service when choosing a route.

- *Load Balancing.* If a manager specifies multiple routes to a given destination at the same cost, OSPF distributes traffic over all routes equally.

- *Hierarchical Subdivision Into Areas.* To handle large intranets and limit routing overhead, OSPF allows a site to partition its networks and routers into subsets called *areas*. Each area is self-contained; knowledge of an area's topology remains hidden from other areas. Thus, multiple groups within a given site can cooperate in the use of OSPF for routing even though each group retains the ability to change its internal network topology independently.

- *Support For Authentication.* OSPF allows all exchanges between routers to be *authenticated*. OSPF supports a variety of authentication schemes, and allows one area to choose a different scheme than another area.

- *Arbitrary Granularity.* OSPF includes support for host-specific, subnet-specific, network-specific, and default routes.

- *Support For Multi-Access Networks.* To accommodate networks such as Ethernet, OSPF extends the SPF algorithm. Normally, SPF requires each pair of routers to broadcast messages about the link between them. If K routers attach to an Ethernet, they will broadcast K^2 status messages. Instead of a graph that uses point-to-point connections, OSPF reduces broadcasts by allowing a more complex graph topology in which each node represents either a router or a network. A *designated gateway* (i.e., a *designated router*) sends link-status messages on behalf of all routers attached to the network.

- *Multicast Delivery.* To reduce the load on nonparticipating systems, OSPF uses hardware multicast capabilities, where they exist, to deliver link-status messages. OSPF sends messages via IP multicast, and allows the IP multicast mechanism to map the multicast into the underlying network; two IPv4 multicast addresses are preassigned to OSPF 224.0.0.5 for all routers and 224.0.0.6 for all nodes.

- *Virtual Topology.* A manager can create a virtual network topology. For example, a manager can configure a virtual link between two routers in the routing graph even if the physical connection between the two routers requires communication across multiple transit networks.

- *Route Importation.* OSPF can import and disseminate routing information learned from external sites (i.e., from routers that do not use OSPF). OSPF messages distinguish between information acquired from external sources and information acquired from routers interior to the site.

- *Direct Use Of IP.* Unlike RIP and RIPng, OSPF messages are encapsulated directly in IP datagrams. The value *89* is used in the *PROTO* field (IPv4) or the *NEXT HOP* field (IPv6) in the header to identify the datagram is carrying OSPF.

14.13 OSPFv2 Message Formats (IPv4)

Currently, the standard version of OSPF is version 2. Version 2 was created for IPv4 and cannot handle IPv6. Unlike RIP, where the IETF chose to create an entirely new protocol for IPv6, an IETF working group has proposed that the changes in OSPFv2 for IPv6 merely be incorporated in a new version of OSPF, version 3. We will first examine the version 2 message formats used with IPv4, and then consider the version 3 message formats used with IPv6. To distinguish between them, we will write *OSPFv2* and *OSPFv3*.

Each OSPFv2 message begins with a fixed, 24-octet header. Figure 14.9 illustrates the format.

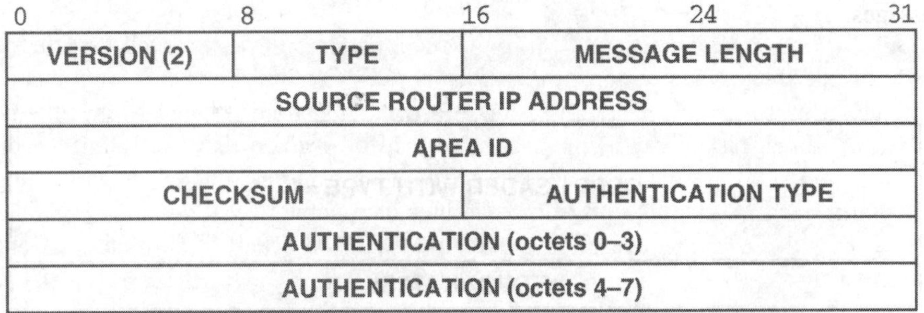

Figure 14.9 The fixed 24-octet OSPFv2 header that appears in each message.

Field *VERSION* specifies the version of the protocol as *2*. Field *TYPE* identifies the message type as one of the following types (which are explained in the next sections):

Type	Meaning
1	Hello (used to test reachability)
2	Database description (topology)
3	Link-status request
4	Link-status update
5	Link-status acknowledgement

The field labeled *SOURCE ROUTER IP ADDRESS* gives the address of the sender, and the field labeled *AREA ID* gives the 32-bit identification number of the area. By convention, Area 0 is the backbone area. Because each message can include authentication, field *AUTHENTICATION TYPE* specifies which authentication scheme is used (e.g., *0* means no authentication and *1* means a simple password is used).

14.13.1 OSPFv2 Hello Message Format

OSPFv2 sends *hello* messages on each link periodically to establish and test neighbor reachability. Figure 14.10 shows the message format. Field *NETWORK MASK* contains an address mask for the network over which the message has been sent. Field *ROUTER DEAD INTERVAL* gives a time in seconds after which a nonresponding neighbor is considered dead. Field *HELLO INTERVAL* is the normal period, in seconds, between hello messages. Field *GWAY PRIO* is the integer priority of this router, and is used in selecting a backup designated router. The fields labeled *DESIGNATED ROUTER* and *BACKUP DESIGNATED ROUTER* contain IP addresses that give the sender's view of the designated router and backup designated router for the network over which the message is sent. Finally, fields labeled *NEIGHBOR IP ADDRESS* give the IP addresses of all neighbors from which the sender has recently received hello messages.

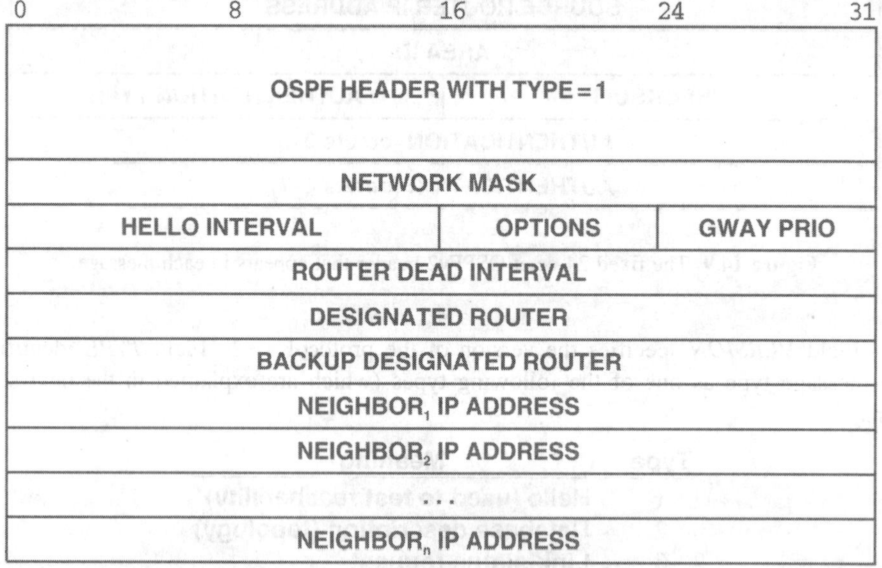

Figure 14.10 The OSPFv2 *hello* message format. A pair of neighbor routers exchanges hello messages periodically to test reachability.

14.13.2 OSPFv2 Database Description Message Format

Routers exchange OSPFv2 *database description* messages to initialize their network topology database. In the exchange, one router serves as a master, while the other is a slave. The slave acknowledges each database description message with a response. Figure 14.11 shows the format.

Because it can be large, a topology database may be divided into multiple messages using the *I* and *M* bits. Bit *I* is set to 1 in the initial message; bit *M* is set to 1 if additional messages follow. Bit *S* indicates whether a message was sent by a master (1) or by a slave (0). Field *DATABASE SEQUENCE NUMBER* numbers messages sequentially so the receiver can tell if one is missing. The initial message contains a random integer *R*; subsequent messages contain sequential integers starting at *R*.

Field *INTERFACE MTU* gives the size of the largest IP datagram that can be transmitted over the interface without fragmentation. The fields from *LS AGE* through *LS LENGTH* describe one link in the network topology; they are repeated for each link.

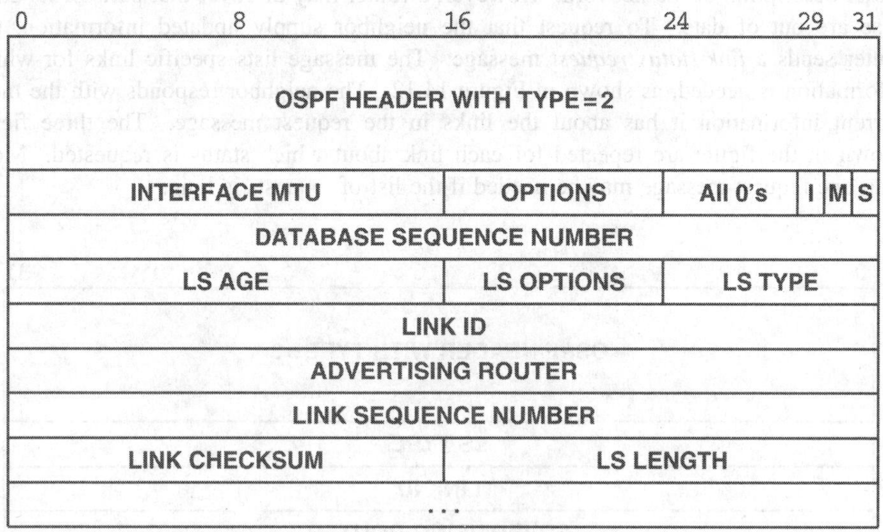

Figure 14.11 OSPFv2 *database description* message format. The fields starting at *LS AGE* are repeated for each link being specified.

Field *LS TYPE* describes the type of a link. The possible values are given by the following table.

LS Type	Meaning
1	Router link
2	Network link
3	Summary link (IP network)
4	Summary link (link to border router)
5	External link (link to another site)

Field *LINK ID* gives an identification for the link (which can be the IP address of a router or a network, depending on the link type).

Field *LS AGE* helps order messages — it gives the time in seconds since the link was established. Field *ADVERTISING ROUTER* specifies the address of the router advertising this link, and *LINK SEQUENCE NUMBER* contains an integer generated by that router to ensure that messages are not missed or received out of order. Field *LINK CHECKSUM* provides further assurance that the link information has not been corrupted.

14.13.3 OSPFv2 Link-Status Request Message Format

After exchanging database description messages with a neighbor, a router has an initial description of the network. However, a router may discover that parts of its database are out of date. To request that the neighbor supply updated information, the router sends a *link-status request* message. The message lists specific links for which information is needed, as shown in Figure 14.12. The neighbor responds with the most current information it has about the links in the request message. The three fields shown in the figure are repeated for each link about which status is requested. More than one request message may be needed if the list of requests is long.

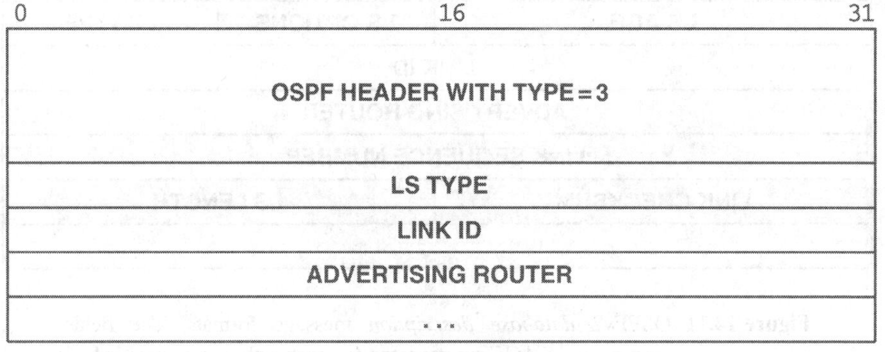

Figure 14.12 OSPFv2 *link-status request* message format. A router sends the message to a neighbor to request current information about a specific set of links.

14.13.4 OSPFv2 Link-Status Update Message Format

Because OSPF uses a link-state algorithm, routers must periodically broadcast messages that specify the status of directly-connected links. To do so, routers use a type *4* OSPFv2 message that is named a *link-status update*. Each update message consists of a count of advertisements followed by a list of advertisements. Figure 14.13 shows the format of link-status update messages.

In the figure, each *link-status advertisement* (*LSA*) has a format that specifies information about the network being advertised. Figure 14.14 shows the format of the link-status advertisement. The values used in each field are the same as in the database description message.

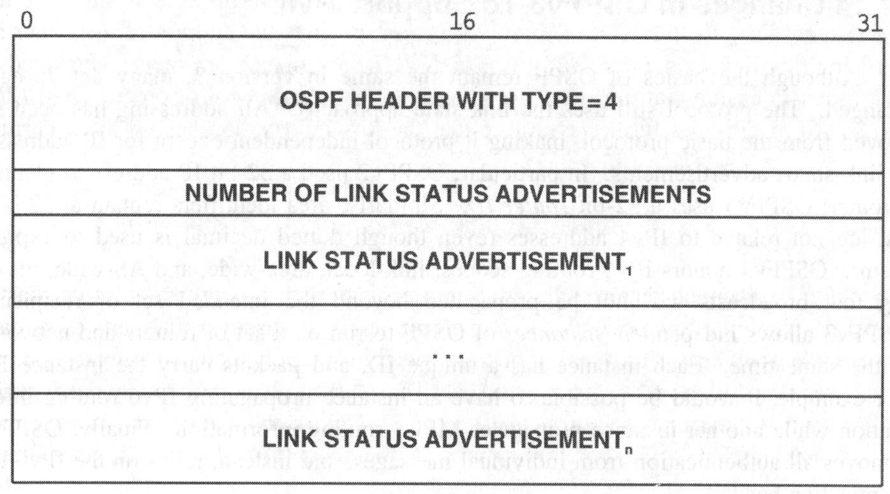

Figure 14.13 OSPFv2 *link-status update* message format. A router sends such a message to broadcast information about its directly connected links to all other routers.

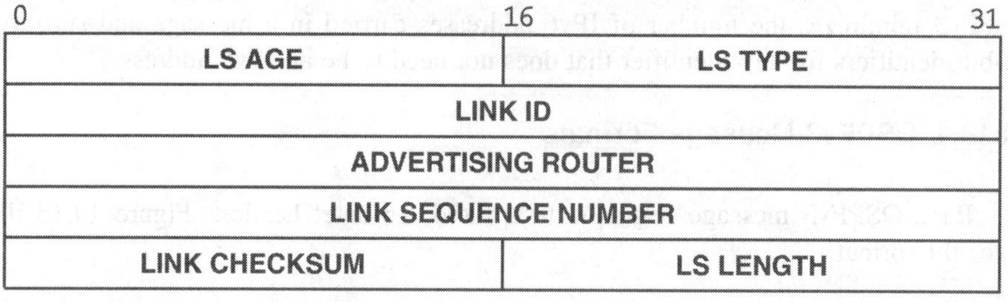

Figure 14.14 The format of an OSPFv2 *link-status advertisement* used in a link-status message.

Following the link-status header comes one of four possible formats to describe the links from a router to a given area, the links from a router to a specific network, the links from a router to the physical networks that constitute a single, subnetted IP network (see Chapter 5), or the links from a router to networks at other sites. In all cases, the *LS TYPE* field in the link-status header specifies which of the formats has been used. Thus, a router that receives a link-status update message knows exactly which of the described destinations lie inside the site and which are external.

14.14 Changes In OSPFv3 To Support IPv6

Although the basics of OSPF remain the same in version 3, many details have changed. The protocol still uses the link-state approach†. All addressing has been removed from the basic protocol, making it protocol-independent except for IP addresses in link-status advertisements. In particular, OSPFv2 used a 32-bit IP address to identify a router; OSPFv3 uses a 32-bit *router ID*. Similarly, area identifiers remain at 32 bits, but are not related to IPv4 addresses (even though dotted decimal is used to express them). OSPFv3 honors IPv6 routing scopes: link-local, area-wide, and AS-wide, meaning that broadcasts will not be propagated beyond the intended set of recipients. OSPFv3 allows independent *instances* of OSPF to run on a set of routers and networks at the same time. Each instance has a unique ID, and packets carry the instance ID. For example, it would be possible to have an instance propagating IPv6 routing information while another instance propagates MPLS routing information. Finally, OSPFv3 removes all authentication from individual messages, and instead, relies on the IPv6 authentication header.

The most significant change between OSPFv2 and OSPFv3 arises from the message formats, which all change. There are two motivations. First, messages must be changed to accommodate IPv6 addresses. Second, because IPv6 addresses are much larger, the designers decided that merely replacing each occurrence of an IPv4 address with an IPv6 address would make messages too large. Therefore, whenever possible, OSPFv3 minimizes the number of IPv6 addresses carried in a message and substitutes 32-bit identifiers for any identifier that does not need to be an IPv6 address.

14.14.1 OSPFv3 Message Formats

Each OSPFv3 message begins with a fixed, 16-octet header. Figure 14.15 illustrates the format.

0	8	16	24 31
VERSION (3)	TYPE	MESSAGE LENGTH	
SOURCE ROUTER ID			
AREA ID			
CHECKSUM		INSTANCE ID	0

Figure 14.15 The fixed 16-octet OSPFv3 header that appears in each message.

Note that the version number occupies the first octet, exactly as in OSPFv2. Therefore, OSPFv3 messages can be sent using the same *NEXT HEADER* value as

†Unfortunately, the terminology has become somewhat ambiguous because IPv6 uses the term *link* in place of *IP subnet* (to permit multiple IPv6 prefixes to be assigned to a given network). In most cases, the IPv6 concept and OSPFv3 concept align, but the distinction can be important in special cases.

OSPFv2 with no ambiguity. Also note that the fixed header is smaller than the OSPFv2 header because authentication information has been removed.

14.14.2 OSPFv3 Hello Message Format

The OSPFv3 *hello* message helps illustrate the basic change from IPv4 addressing to 32-bit identifiers. The goal is to keep the packet size small while separating the protocol from IPv4. As Figure 14.16 illustrates, readers should compare the version 3 format to the version 2 format shown on page 306.

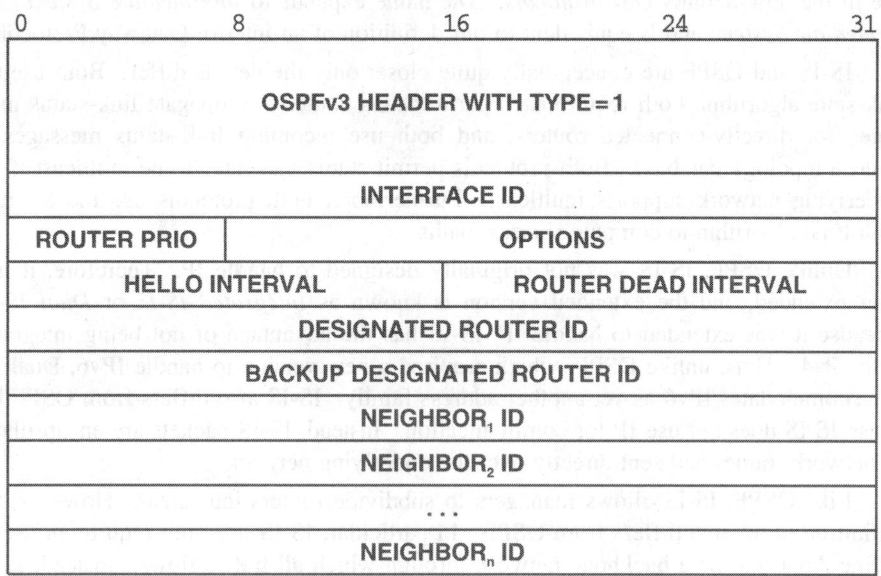

Figure 14.16 The OSPFv3 *hello* message format. All IPv4 addresses have been replaced by 32-bit identifiers.

14.14.3 Other OSPFv3 Features And Messages

OSPFv3 combines and generalizes many of the facilities and features that have been defined for OSPFv2. Consequently, OSPFv3 defines several types of link-status advertisement (LSA). For example, OSPFv3 supports router LSAs, link LSAs, inter-area prefix LSAs, inter-area router LSAs, AS-external LSAa, intra-area prefix LSAs, and *Not So Stubby Area* (*NSSA*) LSAs. Each link-status message begins with a header that is the same as the OSPFv2 header illustrated in Figure 14.14 on page 309, and uses the type field to identify the remaining contents.

The point of providing multiple LSA types is to support large autonomous systems that have a complex topology and complex rules for areas. In particular, Tier-1 providers use OSPF as an IGP across an intranet that includes a backbone, many regional networks, and many attached networks.

14.15 IS-IS Route Propagation Protocol

About the same time the IETF defined OSPF, Digital Equipment Corporation developed an interior route propagation protocol named *IS-IS*†. IS-IS was part of Digital's *DECnet Phase V* protocol suite, and was later standardized by ISO in 1992 for use in the now-defunct *OSI protocols*. The name expands to *Intermediate System - Intermediate System*, and is equivalent to our definition of an Interior Gateway Protocol.

IS-IS and OSPF are conceptually quite close; only the details differ. Both use the link-state algorithm, both require each participating router to propagate link-status messages for directly-connected routers, and both use incoming link-status messages to build a topology database. Both protocols permit status messages to be multicast if the underlying network supports multicast. Furthermore, both protocols use the Shortest Path First algorithm to compute shortest paths.

Unlike OSPF, IS-IS was not originally designed to handle IP. Therefore, it was later extended, and the extended version is known as *Integrated IS-IS* or *Dual IS-IS*. Because it was extended to handle IP, IS-IS has the advantage of not being integrated with IPv4. Thus, unlike OSPF, which required a new version to handle IPv6, Dual IS-IS accommodates IPv6 as yet another address family. IS-IS also differs from OSPF because IS-IS does *not* use IP for communication. Instead, IS-IS packets are encapsulated in network frames and sent directly over the underlying network.

Like OSPF, IS-IS allows managers to subdivide routers into areas. However, the definition of an area differs from OSPF. In particular, IS-IS does not require an ISP to define Area 0 to be a backbone network through which all traffic flows. Instead, IS-IS defines a router as *Level 1* (intra-area), *Level 2* (inter-area), or *Level 1-2* (both intra-area and inter-area). A Level 1 router only communicates with other Level 1 routers in the same area. A Level 2 router only communicates with Level 2 routers in other areas. A Level 1-2 router connects the other two sets. Thus, unlike OSPF which imposes a star-shaped topology, IS-IS allows the center to be a set of Level 2 networks.

Proponents of OSPF point out that OSPF has been extended to handle many special cases that arise in a large ISP. For example, OSPF has mechanisms to deal with stub networks, not-so-stubby networks, and communication with other IETF protocols. Proponents of IS-IS point out that IS-IS is less "chatty" (i.e., sends fewer messages per unit time), and can handle larger areas (i.e., areas with more routers). Thus, IS-IS is considered a suitable alternative to OSPF for special cases.

†The name is spelled out "I-S-I-S".

14.16 Trust And Route Hijacking

We have already observed that a single router may use an Interior Gateway Protocol to gather routing information within its autonomous system and an Exterior Gateway Protocol to advertise routes to other autonomous systems. In principle, it should be easy to construct a single piece of software that combines information from the two protocols, making it possible to gather routes and advertise them without human intervention. In practice, technical and political obstacles make doing so complex.

Technically, IGP protocols, like RIP and Hello, are routing protocols. A router uses such protocols to update its forwarding table based on information it acquires from other routers inside its autonomous system. Thus, RIP or OSPF software changes the local forwarding table when new routing updates arrive carrying new information. IGPs trust routers within the same autonomous system to pass correct data.

In contrast, exterior protocols such as BGP do not trust arbitrary routers and do not reveal all information from the local forwarding table. Instead, exterior protocols keep a database of network reachability, and apply policy constraints when sending or receiving information. Ignoring such policy constraints can affect routing in a larger sense — some parts of the Internet can be become unreachable. For example, if a router in an autonomous system that is running an IGP happens to propagate a low-cost route to a network at Purdue University when it has no such route, other routers that receive the advertisement accept and install the route. Consequently, routers within the AS where the mistake occurred will forward Purdue traffic incorrectly; Purdue may become unreachable from networks within the AS. The problem becomes more serious if Exterior Gateway Protocols propagate incorrect information — if an AS incorrectly claims to have route to a given destination, the destination may become unreachable throughout the Internet. We say that the destination address has been *hijacked.*

14.17 Gated: A Routing Gateway Daemon

A mechanism has been created to provide an interface among a large set of routing protocols, such as RIP, RIPng, BGP, HELLO, and OSPF. The mechanism also includes routing information learned via ICMP and ICMPv6. Known as *gated*†, the mechanism understands multiple protocols (both interior and exterior gateway protocols, including BGP), and ensures that policy constraints are honored. For example, *gated* can accept RIP messages and modify the local computer's forwarding table. It can also advertise routes from within its autonomous system using BGP. The rules *gated* follows allow a system administrator to specify exactly which networks *gated* may and may not advertise and how to report distances to those networks. Thus, although *gated* is not an IGP, it plays an important role in routing because it demonstrates that it is feasible to build an automated mechanism linking an IGP with BGP without sacrificing protection.

Gated has an interesting history. It was originally created by Mark Fedor at Cornell, and was adopted by MERIT for use with the NSFNET backbone. Academic

†The name is short for *gateway daemon,* and is pronounced "gate d."

researchers contributed new ideas, an industry consortium was formed, and eventually, MERIT sold *gated* to Nexthop.

14.18 Artificial Metrics And Metric Transformation

The previous chapter said that ISPs often choose routes for economic rather than technical reasons. To do so, network managers configure routing protocols manually, and assign artificial weights or distances, which the protocol software uses in place of actual weights or distances. Consider a network using RIP. If a manager wants to direct traffic over a path that has more hops than the optimal path, the manager can configure a router to specify that the optimal path is several hops longer. For example, one router can be configured to advertise a directly-connected network as distance *5*. Similarly, when using OSPF, each link must be assigned a weight. Rather than base the weight on the capacity of the underlying network, a manager can choose artificial weights that make the protocol software prefer one path over another. In the largest ISPs, the assignment of artificial weights is important because it has a direct and significant relationship to revenue. Therefore, large ISPs often hire talented individuals whose entire job is to analyze routing and choose weights that will optimize revenue.

Software like *gated* helps network managers control routing by offering metric transformations. A manager can place such software between two groups of routers that each use an IGP and configure the software to transform metrics so routing proceeds as desired. For example, there may be a low-cost route used within one group that is reserved for internal use. To avoid having outsiders use the reserved route, software on the border between groups artificially inflates the cost of the route before advertising it externally. Thus, outsiders think the route is expensive and choose an alternative. The point is:

> *Although we have described routing protocols as finding shortest paths, protocol software usually includes configuration options that allow a network manager to override actual costs and use artificial values that will cause traffic to follow routes the manager prefers.*

Of course, a manager could achieve the same result by manually configuring the forwarding tables in all routers. Using artificial metrics has a significant advantage: if a network fails, the software will automatically select an alternate route. Therefore, managers focus on configuring metrics rather than on configuring forwarding tables.

14.19 Routing With Partial Information

We began our discussion of internet router architecture and routing by discussing the concept of partial information. Hosts can route with only partial information because they rely on routers. It should be clear now that not all routers have complete information. Most autonomous systems have a single router that connects the autonomous system to other autonomous systems. For example, if the site connects to the global Internet, at least one router must have a connection that leads from the site to an ISP. Routers within the autonomous system know about destinations within that autonomous system, but they use a default route to send all other traffic to the ISP.

How to do routing with partial information becomes obvious if we examine a router's forwarding tables. Routers at the center of the Internet have a complete set of routes to all possible destinations; such routers do not use default routing. Routers beyond those in ISPs at the center of the Internet do not usually have a complete set of routes; they rely on a default route to handle network addresses they do not understand.

Using default routes for most routers has two consequences. First, it means that local routing errors can go undetected. For example, if a machine in an autonomous system incorrectly routes a packet to an external autonomous system instead of to a local router, the external system may send it back (perhaps to a different entry point). Thus, connectivity may appear to be preserved even if routing is incorrect. The problem may not seem severe for small autonomous systems that have high-speed local area networks. However, in a wide area network, incorrect routes can be disastrous because the path packets take may involve multiple ISPs, which incurs a long delay, and ISPs along the path may charge for transit, which results in needless loss of revenue. Second, on the positive side, using default routes whenever possible means that the routing update messages exchanged by most routers will be much smaller than they would be if complete information were included.

14.20 Summary

The owner of an autonomous system (AS) is free to choose protocols that pass routing information among routers within the AS. Manual maintenance of routing information suffices only for small, slowly changing internets that have minimal interconnection; most require automated procedures that discover and update routes automatically. We use the term *Interior Gateway Protocol* (*IGP*) to refer to a protocol that is used to exchange routing information within an AS.

An IGP implements either the distance-vector algorithm or the link-state algorithm, which is known by the name Shortest Path First (SPF). We examined three IGPs: RIP, HELLO, and OSPF. RIP is a distance-vector protocol that uses split horizon, hold-down, and poison reverse techniques to help eliminate forwarding loops and the problem of counting to infinity. Although it is obsolete, Hello is interesting because it illustrates a distance-vector protocol that uses delay instead of hop counts as a distance metric. We discussed the disadvantages of using delay as a routing metric, and pointed out that although heuristics can prevent instabilities from arising when paths have equal throughput characteristics, long-term instabilities arise when paths have different characteristics. OSPF implements the link-status algorithm and comes in two versions: OSPFv2 for IPv4 and OSPFv3 for IPv6. IS-IS is an alternative that handles some special cases better than OSPF.

Although routing protocols are described as computing shortest paths, protocol software includes configuration options that allow managers to inflate costs artificially. By configuring costs carefully, a manager can direct traffic along paths that implement corporate policy or generate the most revenue, while still having the ability to route along alternative paths automatically when network equipment fails.

EXERCISES

14.1 What network families does RIP support? Why?

14.2 Consider a large autonomous system using an IGP that bases routes on delay. What difficulty does the autonomous system have if a subgroup decides to use RIP on its routers? Explain.

14.3 Within a RIP message, each IP address is aligned on a 32-bit boundary. Will such addresses be aligned on a 32-bit boundary if the IP datagram carrying the message starts on a 32-bit boundary? Why or why not?

14.4 An autonomous system can be as small as a single local area network or as large as multiple wide area networks. Why does the variation in size make it difficult to define a single IGP that works well in all situations?

14.5 Characterize the circumstances under which the split horizon technique will prevent slow convergence.

14.6 Consider an internet composed of many local area networks running RIP as an IGP. Find an example that shows how a forwarding loop can result even if the code uses "hold down" after receiving information that a network is unreachable.

14.7 Should a host ever run RIP in active mode? Why or why not?

14.8 Under what circumstances will a hop count metric produce better routes than a metric that uses delay?

14.9 Can you imagine a situation in which an autonomous system chooses *not* to advertise all its networks? (Hint: think of a university.)

14.10 In broad terms, we could say that an IGP distributes the local forwarding table, while BGP distributes a table of networks and routers used to reach them (i.e., a router can send a BGP advertisement that does not exactly match items in its own forwarding table). What are the advantages of each approach?

14.11 Consider a function used to convert between delay and hop-count metrics. Can you find properties of such functions that are sufficient to prevent forwarding loops? Are the properties necessary as well?

14.12 Are there circumstances under which an SPF protocol can form forwarding loops? (Hint: think of best-effort delivery.)

14.13 Build an application program that sends a request to a router running RIP and displays the routes returned.

14.14 Read the RIP specification carefully. Can routes reported in a response to a query differ from the routes reported by a routing update message? If so how?

14.15 Read the OSPFv2 specification carefully. How can a manager use OSPF's virtual link facility?

14.16 OSPFv2 allows managers to assign many of their own identifiers, possibly leading to duplication of values at multiple sites. Which identifier(s) may need to change if two sites running OSPFv2 decide to merge?

14.17 Can you use ICMP redirect messages to pass routing information among *interior* routers? Why or why not?

14.18 Read the specification for OSPFv3. What is a *stub area*, and what is a *not so stubby area* (*NSSA*)? Why are the two important?

14.19 What timeout does the OSPFv3 standard recommend for a Hello interval?

14.20 Write a program that takes as input a description of your organization's internet, uses SNMP to obtain forwarding tables from all the routers, and reports any inconsistencies.

14.21 If your organization runs software such as *gated* or *Zebra* that manages multiple TCP/IP routing protocols, obtain a copy of the configuration files and explain the meaning of each item.

Chapter Contents

15

Internet Multicasting

15.1 Introduction

Earlier chapters define the mechanisms IP uses to forward and deliver unicast datagrams. This chapter explores another feature of IP: multipoint datagram delivery. We begin with a brief review of the underlying hardware support. Later sections describe IP addressing for multipoint delivery and the protocols that routers use to propagate necessary routing information.

15.2 Hardware Broadcast

Many hardware technologies contain mechanisms to send packets to multiple destinations simultaneously (or nearly simultaneously). In Chapter 2, we review several technologies and discuss the most common form of multipoint delivery: *hardware broadcast*. Broadcast delivery means that the network delivers one copy of a packet to each destination. The details of hardware broadcast vary. On some technologies, the hardware sends a single copy of a packet and arranges for each attached computer to receive a copy. On other networks, the networking equipment implements broadcast by forwarding an independent copy of a broadcast packet to each individual computer.

Most hardware technologies provide a special, reserved destination address called a *broadcast address*. To specify broadcast delivery, all a sender needs to do is create a frame where the destination address field contains the broadcast address. For example, Ethernet uses the all 1s hardware address as a broadcast address; each computer attached to an Ethernet network accepts frames sent to the broadcast address as well as packets sent to the computer's unicast MAC address.

The chief disadvantage of hardware broadcast arises from its demand on resources — in addition to using network bandwidth, each broadcast consumes computational resources on the computers attached to the network. In principle, it might be possible to design internet software that used broadcast for all datagrams sent across a network. Every computer would receive a copy of each datagram, and IP software on the computer could examine the IP destination address and discard datagrams intended for other machines. In practice, however, such a scheme is nonsense because each computer would spend CPU cycles to discard most of the datagrams that arrived. Thus, the designers of TCP/IP devised address binding mechanisms that allow datagrams to be delivered via unicast.

15.3 Hardware Multicast

Some hardware technologies support a second form of multi-point delivery called hardware multicast. Unlike hardware broadcast, hardware multicast allows each computer to choose whether it will participate in receiving a given multicast. Typically, a hardware technology reserves a large set of addresses for use with multicast. When a group of applications want to use hardware multicast, they choose one particular *multicast address* to use for communication. The application running on a computer must ask the operating system to configure the network interface card to recognize the multicast address that has been selected. After the hardware has been configured, the computer will receive a copy of any packet sent to the multicast address.

We use the term *multicast group* to denote the set of computers that are listening to a particular multicast address. If applications on six computers are listening to a particular multicast address, the multicast group is said to have six *members*. In many hardware technologies, a multicast group is defined only by the set of listeners — an arbitrary computer can send a packet to a given multicast address (i.e., the sender does not need to be a member of the multicast group).

At a conceptual level, multicast addressing can be viewed as sufficiently general to include all other forms of addressing. For example, we can imagine a conventional *unicast address* to be a multicast address to which exactly one computer is listening. Similarly, we can think of a broadcast address as a multicast address to which all computers on a particular network are listening. Other multicast addresses can correspond to arbitrary subsets of computers on the network, possibly the empty set.

Despite its apparent generality, multicast addressing will not replace conventional forms of addressing because there is a fundamental difference in the way the underlying hardware mechanisms implement packet forwarding and delivery. Instead of a single computer or all computers, a multicast address identifies an arbitrary subset of computers, and members of the group can change at any time. Therefore, hardware cannot determine exactly where a given computer connects to the network, and must flood packets to all computers and let them choose whether to accept the packet. Flooding is expensive because it prevents packet transfers in parallel. Therefore, we can conclude:

> *Although it is interesting to think of multicast addressing as a generalization that subsumes unicast and broadcast addresses, the underlying forwarding and delivery mechanisms can make multicast less efficient.*

15.4 Ethernet Multicast

Ethernet provides an example of hardware multicasting, and is especially pertinent to IP multicasting because Ethernet is widely deployed in the global Internet. One-half of the Ethernet address space is reserved for multicast — the low-order bit of the high-order octet distinguishes conventional unicast addresses (*0*) from multicast addresses (*1*). In dashed hexadecimal notation†, the multicast bit is given by:

$$01\text{-}00\text{-}00\text{-}00\text{-}00\text{-}00_{16}$$

When an Ethernet interface board is initialized, it begins accepting packets destined for either the unicast hardware address or the Ethernet broadcast address. However, device driver software can reconfigure the device to allow it to also recognize one or more multicast addresses. For example, suppose the driver configures the Ethernet multicast address:

$$01\text{-}5E\text{-}00\text{-}00\text{-}00\text{-}01_{16}$$

After configuration, the interface hardware will accept any packet sent to the computer's unicast MAC address, the broadcast MAC address, or the example multicast MAC address (the hardware will continue to ignore packets sent to other multicast addresses). The next sections explain IP multicast semantics and how IP uses basic multicast hardware.

15.5 The Conceptual Building Blocks Of Internet Multicast

Three conceptual building blocks are required for a general purpose internet multicasting system:

- A multicast addressing scheme
- An effective notification and delivery mechanism
- An efficient internetwork forwarding facility

Many details and constraints present challenges for an overall design. For example, in addition to providing sufficient addresses for many groups, the multicast *addressing scheme* must accommodate two conflicting goals: allow local autonomy in assigning addresses while defining addresses that have meaning globally. Similarly, hosts

†Dashed hexadecimal notation represents each octet as two hexadecimal digits with octets separated by a dash; the subscript *16* can be omitted only when the context is unambiguous.

need a *notification mechanism* to inform routers about multicast groups in which they are participating, and routers need a *delivery mechanism* to transfer multicast packets to hosts. Again there are two possibilities: internet multicast should make effective use of hardware multicast when it is available, but it should also allow delivery over networks that do not have hardware support for multicast. Finally, a multicast *forwarding facility* presents the biggest design challenge of the three: the goal is a scheme that is both efficient and dynamic — it should forward multicast packets along shortest paths, should not send a copy of a datagram along a path if the path does not lead to a member of the group, and should allow hosts to join and leave groups at any time.

We will see that the IP multicasting mechanism includes all three building blocks. It defines multicast addressing for both IPv4 and IPv6, provides a mechanism that allows hosts to join and leave IP multicast groups, specifies how multicast datagrams are transferred across individual hardware networks, and provides a set of protocols routers can use to exchange multicast routing information and construct forwarding tables for multicast groups. The next section lists properties of the IP multicast scheme, and the remainder of the chapter considers each aspect in more detail, beginning with addressing.

15.6 The IP Multicast Scheme

IP multicasting is an abstraction of hardware multicasting. It follows the paradigm of allowing transmission to a subset of host computers, but generalizes the concept to allow the subset to spread across arbitrary physical networks throughout an internet. The idea is that whenever possible, a single copy of a multicast datagram is transmitted until a router must forward the datagram along multiple paths. At that point, one copy of the datagram is sent down each path. Thus, the goal is to avoid unnecessary duplication.

In IP terminology, a subset of computers listening to a given IP multicast address is known as an *IP multicast group*. IP multicasting is available for both IPv4 and IPv6. The definition is incredibly ambitious, and has the following general characteristics:

- *One IP Multicast Address Per Group*. Each IP multicast group is assigned a unique IP multicast address. A few IP multicast addresses are permanently assigned by the Internet authority, and correspond to groups that always exist even if they have no current members. Other addresses are temporary, and are available for private use.

- *Number Of Groups*. IPv4 provides addresses for up to 2^{28} simultaneous multicast groups; IPv6 provides many more. In a practical sense, the limit on addresses does not pose a restriction on IP multicast. Instead, practical restrictions on the number of simultaneous multicast groups arise from constraints on forwarding table size and the network traffic needed to propagate routes as group membership changes.

- *Dynamic Group Membership.* An arbitrary host can join or leave an IP multicast group at any time. Furthermore, a host may be a member of an arbitrary number of multicast groups simultaneously.
- *Use Of Hardware.* If the underlying network hardware supports multicast, IP uses hardware multicast to deliver an IP multicast datagram on the network. If the hardware does not support multicast, IP uses broadcast or unicast to deliver IP multicast datagrams.
- *Internetwork Forwarding.* Because members of an IP multicast group can attach to arbitrary networks throughout an internet, special *multicast routers* are required to forward IP multicast datagrams. In most cases, instead of using separate routers, multicast capability is added to conventional routers.
- *Delivery Semantics.* IP multicast uses the same best-effort delivery semantics as other IP datagram delivery, meaning that multicast datagrams can be lost, delayed, duplicated, or delivered out of order.
- *Membership And Transmission.* An arbitrary host may send datagrams to any multicast group; group membership is only used to determine whether the host receives datagrams sent to the group.

15.7 IPv4 And IPv6 Multicast Addresses

We said that IP multicast addresses are divided into two types: those that are permanently assigned and those that are available for temporary use. Permanent addresses are called *well-known*; they are defined for major services on the global Internet as well as for infrastructure maintenance (e.g., we saw that RIP and RIPng use a well-known multicast address). Other multicast addresses correspond to *transient multicast groups* that are created when needed and discarded when the count of group members reaches zero.

Like hardware multicasting, IP multicasting uses the datagram's destination address to specify that a particular datagram must be delivered via multicast. IPv4 reserves class *D* addresses for multicast: the first *4* bits contain *1110* and identify the address as a multicast address. In IPv6, a multicast address has the first *8* bits set to *1* as Figure 15.1 illustrates.

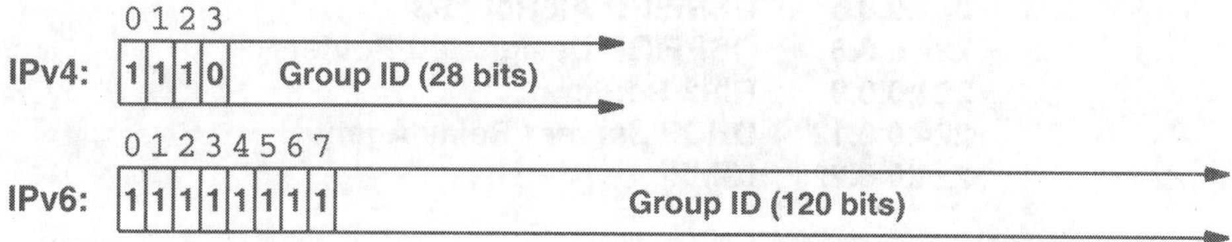

Figure 15.1 The format of IPv4 and IPv6 multicast addresses. A prefix identifies the address as multicast.

In each case, the remainder of an address following the prefix consists of an identifier for a particular multicast group. IPv4 allocates 28 bits to multicast group IDs, which means 10^8 groups are possible. IPv6 allocates 120 bits for group IDs, giving 10^{36} possible groups! The multicast group ID is *not* partitioned into bits that identify the origin or owner of the group.

15.7.1 IPv4 Multicast Address Space

When expressed in dotted decimal notation, IPv4 multicast addresses range from

224.0.0.0 through 239.255.255.255

Many parts of the address space have been assigned special meaning. For example, the lowest address, 224.0.0.0, is reserved; it cannot be assigned to any group. Addresses up through 224.0.0.255 are restricted to a single network (i.e., a router is prohibited from forwarding a datagram sent to any address in the range, and a sender is supposed to set the TTL to 1), and addresses 239.0.0.0 through 239.255.255.255 are restricted to one organization (i.e., routers should not forward them across external links). Figure 15.2 shows how the IPv4 multicast address space is divided.

Address Range	Meaning
224.0.0.0	Base Address (Reserved)
224.0.0.1 – 224.0.0.255	Scope restricted to one network
224.0.1.0 – 238.255.255.255	Scope is global across the Internet
239.0.0.0 – 239.255.255.255	Scope restricted to one organization

Figure 15.2 The division of the IPv4 multicast address space according to scope.

Figure 15.3 lists a few examples of specific IPv4 multicast address assignments. Many other addresses have been assigned, and some vendors have chosen addresses to use with their systems.

Address	Assigned Purpose
224.0.0.1	All Systems on this Subnet
224.0.0.2	All Routers on this Subnet
224.0.0.5	OSPFIGP All Routers
224.0.0.6	OSPFIGP Designated Routers
224.0.0.9	RIP2 Routers
224.0.0.12	DHCP Server / Relay Agent
224.0.0.22	IGMP

Figure 15.3 Examples of IPv4 multicast address assignments. All the examples have a scope restricted to one network.

In Figure 15.3, address 224.0.0.1 is permanently assigned to the *all systems group*, and address 224.0.0.2 is permanently assigned to the *all routers group*. The *all systems* group includes all hosts and routers on a network that are participating in IP multicast, whereas the *all routers* group includes only the routers that are participating. Both of these groups are used for control protocols and must be on the same local network as the sender; there are no IP multicast addresses that refer to all systems in the Internet or all routers in the Internet.

15.7.2 IPv6 Multicast Address Space

Like IPv4, IPv6 specifies the scope associated with multicast addresses. Recall that the first octet of an IPv6 multicast address contains all 1s. IPv6 uses the second octet of the address to specify the scope. Figure 15.4 lists the assignments.

Second Octet	Meaning
0x?0	Reserved
0x?1	Scope is restricted to a computer (loopback)
0x?2	Scope is restricted to the local network
0x?3	Scope is equivalent to IPv4 local scope
0x?4	Scope is administratively configured
0x?5	Scope is restricted to a single site
0x?8	Scope is restricted to a single organization
0x?E	Scope is global across the Internet

Figure 15.4 The use of the second octet in an address to specify the scope of an IPv6 multicast address.

In the figure, constants starting with *0x* are hexadecimal. The question mark denotes an arbitrary nibble. Thus, 0x?1 refers to 0x01, 0x11, 0x21... 0xF1.

Using an octet to specify the scope allows a service to be accessed with a variety of scopes. For example, the *Network Time Protocol* (*NTP*) has been assigned the multicast group ID 0x101. The scope of the assignment is unrestricted, meaning that a sender can choose the scope of a multicast. For example, it is possible to send a multicast datagram to all NTP servers on a single link (address FF02::101) or all NTP servers in an organization (address FF08::101). Only the second octet of the address differs.

Some services are assigned a specific scope or a specific set of scopes, because the IETF can foresee no reason to send a multicast to the group globally. For example, the *All Nodes* multicast group is limited — one cannot specify a multicast datagram for all nodes throughout the Internet. Most routing protocols are also limited to a single link because the intended communication is between routers on the same underlying network. Figure 15.5 lists a few examples of permanently assigned IPv6 multicast addresses.

Address	Assigned Purpose
FF02::1	All nodes on the local network segment
FF02::2	All routers on the local network segment
FF02::5	OSPFv3 AllSPF routers
FF02::6	OSPFv3 AllDR routers
FF02::9	RIP routers
FF02::a	EIGRP routers
FF02::d	PIM routers
FF02::1:2	DHCP servers and relay agents on the local network
FF05::1:3	DHCP servers on the local network site
FF0x::FB	Multicast DNS
FF0x::101	Network Time Protocol
FF0x::108	Network Information Service
FF0x::114	Available for experiments

Figure 15.5 Examples of a few permanent IPv6 multicast address assignments using colon hex notation and abbreviating zeroes with double colons. Many other addresses have specific meanings.

As with IPv4, vendors have chosen certain IPv6 multicast addresses for use with their products. Although not all choices are officially registered with the Internet authority that controls addressing, they are generally honored.

15.8 Multicast Address Semantics

The rules IP follows when forwarding a multicast datagram differ dramatically from the rules used to forward unicast datagrams. For example, a multicast address can only be used as a destination address. Thus, if a router finds a multicast address in the source address field of a datagram or in an option (e.g., source route), the router drops the datagram. Furthermore, no ICMP error messages can be generated about multicast datagrams. The restriction applies to ICMP echo (i.e., ping requests) as well as conventional errors such as destination unreachable. Therefore, a ping sent to a multicast address will go unanswered.

The rule prohibiting ICMP errors is somewhat surprising, because IP routers do honor the hop limit field in the header of a multicast datagram. As usual, each router decrements the count, and discards the datagram if the count reaches zero. The only distinction is that a router does not send an ICMP message for a multicast datagram. We will see that some multicast protocols use the hop limit as a way to limit datagram propagation.

15.9 Mapping IP Multicast To Ethernet Multicast

Although they do not cover all types of network hardware, the IP multicast standards do specify how to map an IP multicast address to an Ethernet multicast address. For IPv4, the mapping is efficient and easy to understand: IANA owns the Ethernet address prefix *0x01005E*†. A mapping has been defined as follows:

> *To map an IPv4 multicast address to the corresponding Ethernet multicast address, place the low-order 23 bits of the IPv4 multicast address into the low-order 23 bits of the special Ethernet multicast address 01-00-5E-00-00-00*$_{16}$.

For example, the IPv4 multicast address 224.0.0.2 becomes Ethernet multicast address 01-00-5E-00-00-02$_{16}$.

IPv6 does not use the same mapping as IPv4. In fact, the two versions do not even share the same MAC prefix. Instead, IPv6 uses the Ethernet prefix *0x3333* and selects 32 bits of the IP multicast group ID:

> *To map an IPv6 multicast address to the corresponding Ethernet multicast address, place the low-order 32 bits of the IPv6 multicast address into the low-order 32 bits of the special Ethernet multicast address 33-33-00-00-00-00*$_{16}$.

For example, IPv6 multicast address FF02:09:09:1949::DC:1 would map to the Ethernet MAC address 33-33-00-DC-00-01.

Interestingly, neither the IPv4 nor IPv6 mappings are unique. Because IPv4 multicast addresses have 28 significant bits that identify the multicast group, more than one multicast group may map onto the same Ethernet multicast address at the same time. Similarly, many IPv6 multicast group IDs map to the same Ethernet multicast. The designers chose the scheme as a compromise. On one hand, using 23 (IPv4) or 32 (IPv6) of the group ID bits for a hardware address means most of the multicast address is included. The set of addresses is large enough so the chances of two groups choosing addresses with the low-order bits identical is small. On the other hand, arranging for IP to use a fixed part of the Ethernet multicast address space makes debugging much easier and eliminates interference between Internet protocols and other protocols that share an Ethernet. The consequence of the design is that some multicast datagrams may be received at a host that are not destined for that host. Thus, the IP software must carefully check addresses on all incoming datagrams, and discard any unwanted multicast datagrams.

†The IEEE assigns an *Organizational Unique Identifier* (*OUI*) prefix to each organization that creates Ethernet addresses.

15.10 Hosts And Multicast Delivery

We said that IP multicasting can be used on a single physical network or throughout an internet. In the former case, a host can send directly to a destination host merely by placing the datagram in a frame and using a hardware multicast address to which the receiver is listening. In the latter case, *multicast routers* are needed to forward copies of multicast datagrams across multiple networks to all hosts participating in a multicast group. Thus, if a host has a datagram with scope other than the local network, the host must send the datagram to a multicast router. Surprisingly, a host does not need to install a route to a multicast router, nor does IP software use a default route to reach a multicast router. Instead, the technique a host uses to forward a multicast datagram to a router is unlike the forwarding for unicast and broadcast datagrams — a host merely uses the local network hardware's multicast capability to transmit the datagram. Multicast routers listen for *all* IP multicast transmissions; if a multicast router is present on the network, it will receive the datagram and forward it on to another network if necessary†. Thus, the primary difference between local and nonlocal multicast lies in multicast routers, not in hosts.

15.11 Multicast Scope

The term *multicast scope* is used for two concepts. We use the term to clarify the set of hosts that are listening to a given multicast group or to specify a property of a multicast address. In the case of specifying how hosts are located, we use the term to clarify whether the current members of the group are on one network, multiple networks within a site, multiple networks at multiple sites within an organization, multiple networks within an administratively-defined boundary, or arbitrary networks in the global Internet. In the second case, we know that the standards specify how far a datagram sent to a specific address will propagate (i.e., the set of networks over which a datagram sent to the address will be forwarded). Informally, we sometimes use the term *range* in place of scope.

IP uses two techniques to control multicast scope. The first technique relies on the datagram's *hop limit* field to control its range. By setting the hop limit to a small value, a host can limit the distance the datagram will be forwarded. For example, the standard specifies that control messages, which are used for communication between a host and a router on the same network, must have a hop limit of 1. As a consequence, a router never forwards any datagram carrying control information because the hop limit has reached zero. Similarly, if two applications running on a single host want to use IP multicast for interprocess communication (e.g., for testing software), they can choose a TTL value of 0 to prevent the datagram from leaving the host. It is possible to use successively larger values of the TTL field to further extend the notion of scope. For example, some router vendors suggest configuring routers at a site to restrict multicast datagrams from leaving the site unless the datagram has a hop limit greater than 15. The point is: the hop limit in a datagram header provides coarse-grain control over the datagram's scope.

†In practice, sites that use IP multicast usually configure conventional routers to handle multicast forwarding as well as unicast forwarding.

The second technique, which is known as *administrative scoping*, consists of choosing multicast addresses that have limited scope. According to the standard, routers in the Internet are forbidden from forwarding any datagram that has an address chosen from the restricted space. Thus, to prevent multicast communication among group members from accidentally reaching outsiders, an organization can assign the group an address that has local scope (e.g., restricted to a site or restricted to an organization).

15.12 Host Participation In IP Multicasting

A host can participate in IP multicast at one of three levels as Figure 15.6 shows:

Level	Meaning
0	Host can neither send nor receive IP multicast
1	Host can send but not receive IP multicast
2	Host can both send and receive IP multicast

Figure 15.6 The three levels of host participation in IP multicast.

Extending IP software to allow a host to send IP multicast is not difficult; providing host software that can receive IP multicast datagrams is more complex. To send a multicast datagram, an application must be able to supply a multicast address as a destination. To receive multicast, an application must be able to declare that it wants to join or leave a particular multicast group, and protocol software must forward a copy of an arriving datagram to each application that joined the group. Furthermore, multicast datagrams do not arrive at a host automatically: later sections explain that when it joins a multicast group, a host must use a special protocol to inform a local multicast router of its membership status. Much of the software complexity arises from an IP multicast design decision:

A host joins specific IP multicast groups on specific networks.

That is, a host with multiple network connections may join a particular multicast group on one network and not on another. To understand the reason for keeping group membership associated with networks, remember that it is possible to use IP multicasting among local sets of machines. The host may want to use a multicast application to interact with machines on one network, but not with machines on another.

Because group membership is associated with particular networks, the software must keep separate lists of multicast addresses for each network to which the host attaches. Furthermore, an application program must specify a particular network when it asks to join or leave a multicast group. Of course, most applications do not know (or care) about the networks to which a host attaches, which means they do not know which network to specify when they need to join a multicast group.

15.13 IPv4 Internet Group Management Protocol (IGMP)

We said that to send or receive in IPv4 multicast across a single local network, a host only needs software that allows it to use the underlying network to transmit and receive IP multicast datagrams. However, to participate in a multicast that spans multiple networks, the host must inform at least one local multicast router. The local router contacts other multicast routers, passing on the membership information and establishing routes. We will see that the concept is similar to conventional route propagation among Internet routers.

Multicast routers do not act until at least one host on a given network joins a multicast group. When it decides to join a multicast group, a host informs a local multicast router. An IPv4 host uses the *Internet Group Management Protocol* (*IGMP*). Because the current version is *3*, the protocol described here is officially known as *IGMPv3*.

IGMP is a standard for IPv4; it is required on all machines that receive IPv4 multicast (i.e., all hosts and routers that participate at level *2*). IGMP uses IP datagrams to carry messages. Furthermore, we consider IGMP to be a service that is integrated with IP, analogous to ICMP. Therefore, we should not think of IGMP as a protocol used by arbitrary applications:

> *Although it uses IP datagrams to carry messages, we think of IGMP as an integral part of IPv4, not an independent protocol.*

Conceptually, IGMP has two phases. Phase 1: When it joins a new multicast group, a host sends an IGMP message to the group's multicast address declaring its membership. Local multicast routers receive the message, and establish necessary routing by propagating the group membership information to other multicast routers throughout the Internet. Phase 2: Because membership is dynamic, local multicast routers periodically poll hosts on the local network to determine whether any hosts still remain members of each group. If any host responds for a given group, the router keeps the group active. If no host reports membership in a group after several polls, the multicast router assumes that none of the hosts on the network remain in the group, and stops advertising group membership to other multicast routers.

To further complicate group membership, IGMP permits an application on a host to install a *source address filter* that specifies whether the host should include or exclude multicast traffic from a given source address. Thus, it is possible to join a multicast group, but to exclude datagrams sent to the group by a given source. The presence of filters is important because IGMP allows a host to pass the set of filter specifications to the local multicast router along with group membership information. In the case where two applications disagree (i.e., one application excludes a given source and another includes the source), software on the host must rationalize the two specifications and then handle the decision about which applications receive a given datagram locally.

15.14 IGMP Details

IGMP is carefully designed to avoid adding overhead that can congest networks. In particular, because a given network can include multiple multicast routers as well as multiple hosts that participate in multicasting, IGMP must avoid having participants generate unnecessary control traffic. There are several ways IGMP minimizes its effect on the network:

- All communication between hosts and multicast routers uses IP multicast. That is, when sending messages, IGMP always uses IPv4 multicast. Therefore, datagrams carrying IGMP messages are transmitted using hardware multicast if it is available, meaning that a host which is not participating in IP multicast never receives IGMP messages.

- When polling to determine group membership, a multicast router sends a single query to request information about all groups instead of sending a separate message to each. The default polling rate is 125 seconds, which means that IGMP does not generate much traffic.

- If multiple multicast routers attach to the same network, they quickly and efficiently choose a single router to poll host membership, which means the IGMP traffic on a network does not increase when more multicast routers are added.

- Hosts do not respond to a router's IGMP query simultaneously. Instead, each query contains a value, *N*, that specifies a maximum response time (the default is 10 seconds). When a query arrives, a host chooses a random delay between *0* and *N* that it waits before sending a response. If a host is a member of multiple groups, the host chooses a different random number for each. Thus, a host's response to a router's query will be spaced over *10* seconds.

- If a host is a member of multiple multicast groups, the host can send reports for multiple group memberships in a single packet to minimize traffic.

Although such careful attention to detail may seem unnecessary, the dynamic nature of IP multicast means that the messages exchanged over a given network depend on applications. So, unlike routing protocols where the traffic depends on the protocol, IGMP traffic depends on the number of multicast groups to which applications are listening.

15.15 IGMP Group Membership State Transitions

On a host, IGMP must remember the status of each multicast group to which the host belongs along with the source filters associated with each group†. We think of a host as keeping a table in which it records group membership information. Initially, all entries in the table are unused. Whenever an application program on the host joins a new group, IGMP software allocates an entry and fills in information about the group, including address filters that the application has specified. When an application leaves a group, the corresponding entry is removed from the table. When forming a report, the software consults the table, rationalizes all filters for a group, and forms a single report.

The actions IGMP software takes in response to various events can best be explained by the state transition diagram in Figure 15.7.

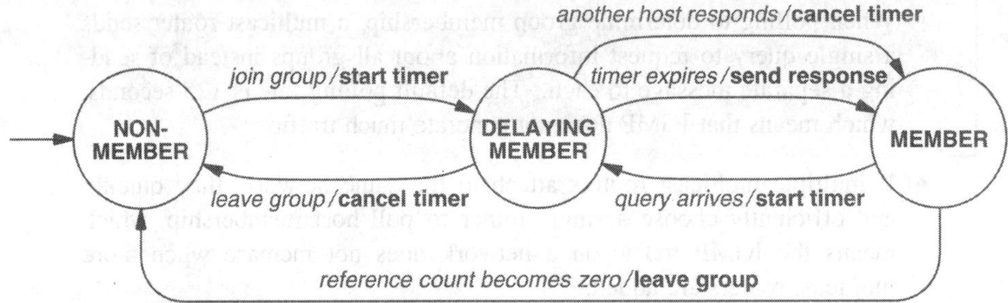

Figure 15.7 The three possible states of an entry in a host's multicast group table and transitions among them, where each transition is labeled with an event and an action. The state transitions do not show messages sent when joining and leaving a group.

A host maintains an independent table entry for each group of which it is currently a member. As the figure shows, when a host first joins the group or when a query arrives from a multicast router, the host moves the entry to the *DELAYING MEMBER* state and chooses a random delay. If another host in the group responds to the router's query before the timer expires, the host cancels its timer and moves to the *MEMBER* state. If the timer expires, the host sends a response message before moving to the *MEMBER* state. Because a router only generates a query every 125 seconds, one expects a host to remain in the *MEMBER* state most of the time.

The diagram in Figure 15.7 omits a few details. For example, if a query arrives while the host is in the *DELAYING MEMBER* state, the protocol requires the host to reset its timer.

†The *all systems group*, 224.0.0.1, is an exception — a host never reports membership in that group.

15.16 IGMP Membership Query Message Format

IGMPv3 defines two message types: a *membership query* message that a router sends to probe for group members, and a *membership report* message that a host generates to report the groups that applications on the host are currently using. Figure 15.8 illustrates the membership query message format.

0			8	16	31
TYPE (0x11)			RESP CODE	CHECKSUM	
GROUP ADDRESS					
RES	S	QRV	QQIC	NUM SOURCES	
SOURCE ADDRESS 1					
SOURCE ADDRESS 2					
⋮					
SOURCE ADDRESS N					

Figure 15.8 The format of an IGMP *membership query* message.

As the figure shows, a membership query message begins with a fixed-size header of twelve octets. Field *TYPE* identifies the type of message, with the types for various versions of IGMP listed in Figure 15.9.

Type	Protocol Vers.	Meaning
0x11	3	Membership query
0x22	3	Membership report
0x12	1	Membership report
0x16	2	Membership report
0x17	2	Leave group

Figure 15.9 IGMP message types. For backward compatibility, version 3 of the protocol includes version 1 and 2 message types.

When a router polls for group membership, the field labeled *RESP CODE* specifies a maximum interval for the random delay that group members compute. If the field starts with a 0 bit, the value is taken to be an integer measured in tenths of seconds; if the field begins with a 1, the value is a floating point number with three bits of exponent and four bits of mantissa. Each host in the group delays a random time between zero and the specified value before responding. As we said, the default value is 10 seconds, which means all hosts in a group choose a random value between 0 and 10. IGMP allows routers to set a maximum value in each query message to give managers control over IGMP traffic. If a network contains many hosts, a higher delay value further spreads out response times, and thereby lowers the probability of having more than one host respond to the query. The *CHECKSUM* field contains a checksum for the message (IGMP checksums are computed over the IGMP message only, and use the same 16-bit one's complement algorithm as IP). The *GROUP ADDRESS* field is either used to specify a particular group or contains zero for a general query. That is, when it sends a query to a specific group or a specific group and source combination, a router fills in the *GROUP ADDRESS* field. The *S* field indicates whether a router should suppress the normal timer updates that are performed when an update arrives; the bit does not apply to hosts. Field *QRV* controls robustness by allowing IGMP to send a packet multiple times on a lossy network. The default value is 2; a sender transmits the message *QRV–1* times. Field *QQIC* specifies the Querier's Query Interval (i.e., the time between membership queries). *QQIC* uses the same representation as field *RESP CODE*.

The last part of an IGMP query message consists of zero or more sources; field *NUM SOURCES* specifies the number of entries that follow. Each *SOURCE ADDRESS* consists of a 32-bit IP address. The number of sources is zero in a *general query* (i.e., a request from a router for information about all multicast groups in use on the network) and in a *group specific query* (i.e., a request from a router for information about a specified multicast group). For a *group and source specific query*, the message contains a list of one or more sources; a router uses such a message to request reception status for a combination of the multicast group and any of the specified sources.

15.17 IGMP Membership Report Message Format

The second type of message used with IGMPv3 is a *membership report* that hosts use to pass participation status to a router. Figure 15.10 illustrates the format. As the figure shows, a membership report message consists of an 8-octet header that specifies the message type and an integer count of group records, *K*, followed by *K group records*. Figure 15.11 illustrates the format of each group record. The format is straightforward. The initial field, labeled *REC TYPE*, allows the sender to specify whether the list of sources in the record corresponds to an *inclusive filter*, an *exclusive filter*, or a change in a previous report (e.g., an additional source to be included or excluded). The field labeled *MULTICAST ADDRESS* specifies the multicast address to which the group record refers, and the field labeled *NUM OF SOURCES* specifies the number of source addresses contained in the group record.

It is important to note that IGMP does not provide all possible messages or facilities. For example, IGMP does not include a mechanism that allows a host to discover the IP address of a group — application software must know the group address before it can use IGMP to join the group. Thus, some applications use permanently assigned group addresses, some allow a manager to configure the address when the software is installed, and others obtain the address dynamically (e.g., from a server). Similarly, IGMPv3 does not provide explicit messages a host can issue to leave a group or to listen for all communication on a group. Instead, to leave a group, a host sends a membership report message that specifies an inclusive filter with an empty IP source address list. To listen to all sources, a host sends a membership report message that specifies an exclusive filter with an empty IP source address list.

0 — 8	8 — 16	16 — 31
TYPE (0x22)	RESERVED	CHECKSUM
RESERVED		NUM GROUP RECORDS (K)
Group Record 1		
Group Record 2		
⋮		
Group Record K		

Figure 15.10 The format of an IGMPv3 *membership report* message.

0 — 8	8 — 16	16 — 31
REC TYPE	ZEROES	NUM OF SOURCES
MULTICAST ADDRESS		
SOURCE ADDRESS 1		
SOURCE ADDRESS 2		
⋮		
SOURCE ADDRESS N		

Figure 15.11 The format of each *group record* within an IGMPv3 *membership report* message.

15.18 IPv6 Multicast Group Membership With MLDv2

IPv6 does not use IGMP. Instead, it defines a *Multicast Listener Discovery Protocol*. The current version is 2, and the protocol is abbreviated *MLDv2*. Despite the changes, IPv4 and IPv6 use essentially the same approach. In fact, the MLDv2 standard states that MLDv2 is merely a translation of IGMP to use IPv6 semantics.

A host uses MLDv2 to inform multicast routers on the local network of the host's group membership(s). As in IGMP, once a host announces membership, a router on the network uses MLDv2 to poll the host periodically to determine whether the host is still a member of the group(s). A set of multicast routers on a given network cooperate to choose one *querier router* that will send periodic queries; if the current querier router fails, another multicast router on the network takes over the responsibility.

MLDv2 defines three types of query messages that routers send: *General Queries*, *Multicast Address Specific Queries*, and *Multicast Address and Source Specific Queries*. As with IGMP, a typical multicast router sends general queries which ask hosts to respond by specifying multicast groups to which they are listening. Figure 15.12 illustrates the format of an MLDv2 query message.

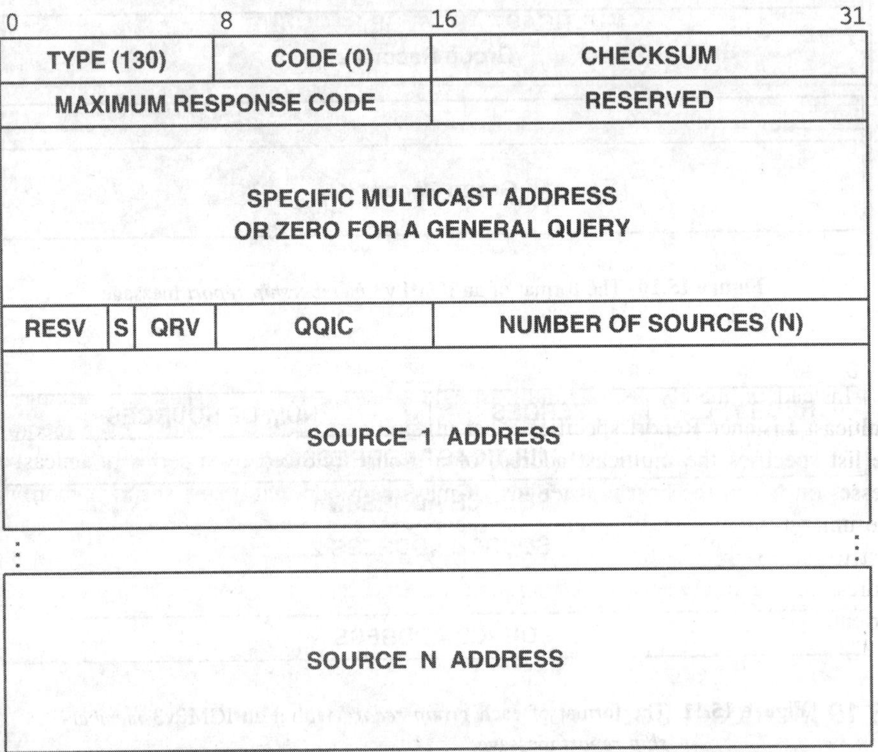

Figure 15.12 The format of an MLDv2 query message. A multicast router sends such messages to determine whether hosts on a network are participating in multicast.

As mentioned earlier, the *QQIC* field specifies a query interval. In a general query, there is no specific multicast address, so the field is set to zero, and because there are no sources, the *NUMBER OF SOURCES* field contains zero and the message contains no *SOURCE ADDRESS* fields.

When a query arrives, a host follows the same steps as in IGMP: the host delays a random time and answers by sending a reply that specifies the multicast addresses to which the host is still listening. The reply consists of a *Multicast Listener Report* message. Figure 15.13 shows the general format.

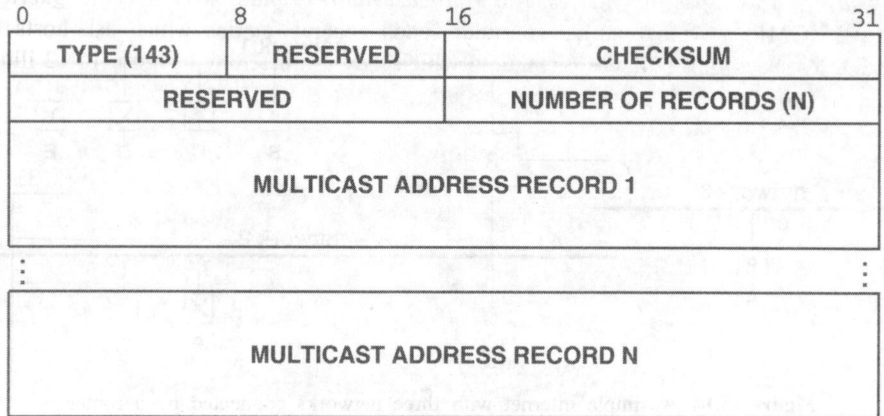

Figure 15.13 The general form of a Multicast Listener Report message.

Instead of merely listing multicast addresses to which the host is listening, the Multicast Listener Report specifies a list of multicast address records. Each record on the list specifies the multicast address of a group followed by a series of unicast addresses on which the host is listening. It may seem odd that a host specifies more than one unicast address because most hosts are singly-homed. Thus, we would expect a host to have only one unicast address. However, IPv6 allows a host to have multiple addresses on a single network. Therefore, the Listener Report allows multiple addresses per entry.

15.19 Multicast Forwarding And Routing Information

Although IP's multicast addressing scheme allows a host to send and receive local multicasts and IGMP or MLDv2 allow a router to keep track of hosts on a local network that are listening to multicast groups, we have not specified how multicast routers exchange group membership information or how the routers ensure that a copy of each multicast datagram reaches all group members.

Interestingly, several protocols have been proposed that allow routers to exchange multicast routing information. However, no single standard has emerged as the leader. In fact, although much effort has been expended, there is no agreement on an overall design — existing protocols differ in their goals and basic approach. Consequently, multicasting is not widely used in the global Internet.

Why is multicast routing so difficult? Why not extend conventional routing schemes to handle multicast? The answer is that multicast routing protocols differ from conventional routing protocols in fundamental ways because multicast forwarding differs from conventional forwarding. To appreciate some of the differences, consider multicast forwarding over the architecture that Figure 15.14 depicts.

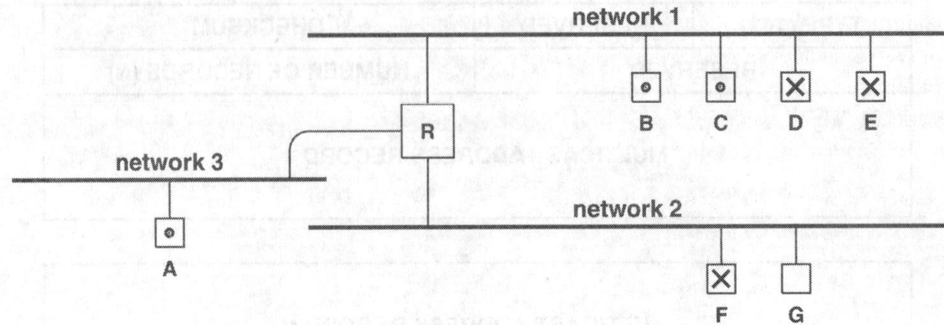

Figure 15.14 A simple internet with three networks connected by a router that illustrates multicast forwarding. Hosts marked with a dot participate in one multicast group, while those marked with an "X" participate in another.

15.19.1 Need For Dynamic Forwarding

Even for the simple topology shown in Figure 15.14, multicast forwarding differs from unicast forwarding. For example, the figure shows two multicast groups: the group denoted by a dot has members *A*, *B*, and *C*, and the group denoted by a cross has members *D*, *E*, and *F*. The dotted group has no members on network *2*. To avoid needless transmissions, router *R* should never send packets intended for the dotted group across network *2*. However, a host can join any group at any time — if the host is the first on its network to join the group, multicast forwarding must be changed to include the network. Thus, we come to an important difference between conventional route propagation and multicast route propagation:

> *Unlike unicast forwarding in which routes change only when the topology changes or equipment fails, multicast routes can change simply because an application program joins or leaves a multicast group.*

15.19.2 Insufficiency Of Destination Forwarding

The example in Figure 15.14 illustrates another aspect of multicast forwarding. If host *F* and host *E* each send a datagram to the cross group, router *R* will receive and forward them. Because both datagrams are directed at the same group, they have the same destination address. However, the correct forwarding actions differ: *R* sends the datagram from *E* to network 2, and sends the datagram from *F* to network 1. Interestingly, when it receives a datagram destinated for the cross group sent by host *A*, the router uses a third action: it forwards two copies, one to network 1 and the other to network 2. Thus, we see the second major difference between conventional forwarding and multicast forwarding:

> *Unlike unicast forwarding, multicast forwarding requires a router to examine more than the destination address.*

15.19.3 Arbitrary Senders

The final feature of multicast forwarding illustrated by Figure 15.14 arises because IP allows an arbitrary host, one that is not necessarily a member of the group, to send a datagram to the group. In the figure, host *G* can send a datagram to the dotted group, even though *G* is not a member of any group and there are no members of the dotted group on *G's* network. More important, as it travels through the internet, the datagram may pass across other networks that have no group members attached. We can summarize:

> *A multicast datagram may originate on a computer that is not part of the multicast group, and may be forwarded across networks that do not have any group members attached.*

15.20 Basic Multicast Forwarding Paradigms

We know from the example above that multicast routers must use more than a destination address when processing a datagram. Exactly what information does a multicast router use when deciding how to forward a datagram? The answer lies in understanding that because a multicast destination represents a set of computers, an optimal forwarding system will reach all members of the set without sending a datagram across a given network twice. Although a single multicast router such as the one in Figure 15.14 can simply avoid sending a datagram back over the interface on which it arrives, using the interface alone will not prevent a datagram from being forwarded among a set of routers that are arranged in a cycle. To avoid such forwarding loops, multicast routers rely on the datagram's source address.

One of the first ideas to emerge for multicast forwarding was a form of broadcasting described earlier. Known as *Reverse Path Forwarding*† (*RPF*), the scheme uses a datagram's source address to prevent the datagram from traveling around a loop repeatedly. To use RPF, a multicast router must have a conventional unicast forwarding table with shortest paths to all destinations. When a datagram arrives, the router extracts the source address, looks it up in its unicast forwarding table, and finds *I*, the interface that leads to the source. If the datagram arrived over interface *I*, the router forwards a copy to each of the other interfaces; otherwise, the router discards the copy.

Because it ensures that a copy of each multicast datagram is sent across every network in an internet, the basic RPF scheme guarantees that every host in a multicast group will receive a copy of each datagram sent to the group. However, RPF alone is not used for multicast forwarding because it wastes network cycles by sending multicast datagrams over networks that neither have group members nor lead to group members.

To avoid propagating multicast datagrams where they are not needed, a modified form of RPF was invented. Known as *Truncated Reverse Path Forwarding* (*TRPF*) or *Truncated Reverse Path Broadcasting* (*TRPB*), the scheme follows the RPF algorithm, but further restricts propagation by avoiding paths that do not lead to group members. To use TRPF, a multicast router needs two pieces of information: a conventional unicast forwarding table and a list of multicast groups reachable through each network interface. When a multicast datagram arrives, the router first applies the RPF rule. If RPF specifies discarding the copy, the router does so. However, if RPF specifies sending the datagram over a particular interface, the router makes an additional check to verify that one or more members of the group designated in the datagram's destination address are reachable via the interface. If no group members are reachable over the interface, the router skips that interface, and continues examining the next one. In fact, we can now understand the origin of the term *truncated* — a router truncates forwarding when no group members lie along the path.

We can summarize:

> *When making a forwarding decision, a multicast router uses both the datagram's source and destination addresses. The basic mechanism is known as Truncated Reverse Path Forwarding (TRPF).*

†Reverse path forwarding is sometimes called *Reverse Path Broadcasting* (*RPB*).

15.21 Consequences Of TRPF

Although TRPF guarantees that each member of a multicast group receives a copy of each datagram sent to the group, it has two surprising consequences. First, because it relies on RPF to prevent loops, TRPF delivers an extra copy of datagrams to some networks just like conventional RPF. Figure 15.15 illustrates how duplicates can arise.

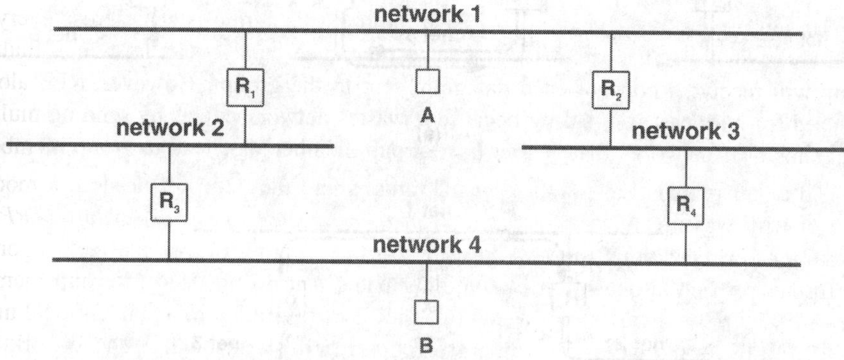

Figure 15.15 A topology that causes an RPF scheme to deliver multiple copies of a datagram to some destinations.

In the figure, when host *A* sends a datagram, routers R_1 and R_2 each receive a copy. Because the datagram arrives over the interface that lies along the shortest path to *A*, R_1 forwards a copy to network *2*, and R_2 forwards a copy to network *3*. When it receives a copy from network *2* (the shortest path to *A*), R_3 forwards the copy to network *4*. Unfortunately, R_4 also forwards a copy to network *4*. Thus, although RPF allows R_3 and R_4 to prevent a loop by discarding the copy that arrives over network *4*, host *B* receives two copies of the datagram.

A second surprising consequence arises because TRPF uses both source and destination addresses when forwarding datagrams: delivery depends on a datagram's source. For example, Figure 15.16 shows how multicast routers forward datagrams from two different sources across a fixed topology.

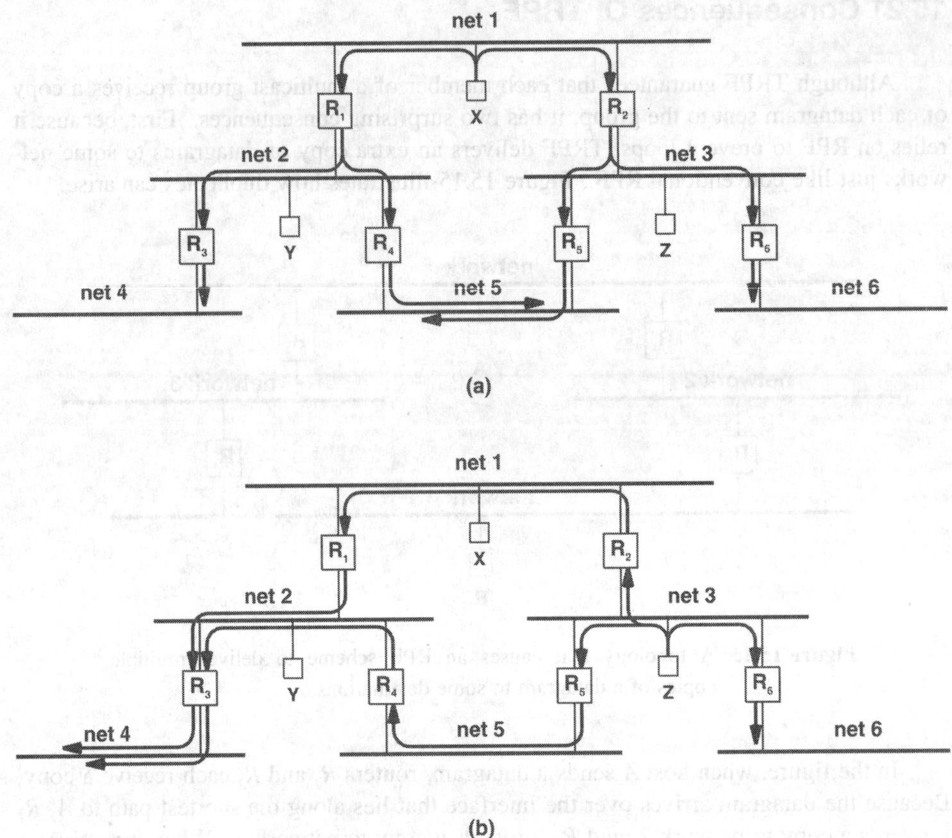

Figure 15.16 Examples of paths a multicast datagram follows under TRPF assuming the source is (a) host *X*, and (b) host *Z*, and the group has a member on each of the networks. The number of copies received depends on the source.

As the figure shows, the source affects both the path a datagram follows to reach a given network as well as the delivery details. For example, in part (a) of Figure 15.16, a transmission by host *X* causes TRPF to deliver two copies of the datagram to network *5*. In part (b), only one copy of a transmission by host *Z* reaches network *5*, but two copies reach networks *2* and *4*.

15.22 Multicast Trees

Researchers use graph theory terminology to describe the set of paths from a given source to all members of a multicast group: the paths define a graph-theoretic *tree*†, which is sometimes called a *forwarding tree* or a *delivery tree*. Each multicast router

†A graph is a tree if it does not contain any cycles (i.e., a router does not appear on more than one path).

corresponds to a *node* in the tree, and a network that connects two routers corresponds to an *edge* in the tree. The source of a datagram is the *root* or *root node* of the tree. Finally, the last router along each of the paths from the source is called a *leaf* router. The terminology is sometimes applied to networks as well — researchers call a network hanging off a leaf router a *leaf network*.

As an example of the terminology, consider Figure 15.16. Part (a) shows a tree with root *X*, and leaves R_3, R_4, R_5, and R_6. Technically, part (b) does not show a tree because router R_3 lies along two paths. Informally, researchers often overlook the details and refer to such graphs as trees.

The graph terminology allows us to express an important principle:

> *A multicast forwarding tree is defined as a set of paths through multicast routers from a source to all members of a multicast group. For a given multicast group, each possible source of datagrams can determine a different forwarding tree.*

One of the immediate consequences of the principle concerns the size of tables used to forward multicast. Unlike conventional unicast forwarding tables, each entry in a multicast table is identified by a pair:

(multicast group, source)

Conceptually, *source* identifies a single host that can send datagrams to the group (i.e., any host in the internet). In practice, keeping a separate entry for each host is unwise because the forwarding trees defined by all hosts on a single network are identical. Thus, to save space, forwarding protocols use a network prefix as a *source*. That is, each router defines one forwarding entry that is used for all hosts on the same IP network.

Aggregating entries by network prefix instead of by host address reduces the table size dramatically. However, multicast forwarding tables can grow much larger than conventional forwarding tables. Unlike a conventional unicast table in which the size is proportional to the number of networks in the underlying internet, a multicast table has size proportional to the product of the number of networks in the internet and the number of multicast groups.

15.23 The Essence Of Multicast Route Propagation

Observant readers may have noticed an inconsistency between the features of IP multicasting and TRPF. We said that TRPF is used instead of conventional RPF to avoid unnecessary traffic: TRPF does not forward a datagram to a network unless that network leads to at least one member of the group. Consequently, a multicast router must have knowledge of group membership. We also said that IP allows any host to join or leave a multicast group at any time, which can result in rapid membership changes. More important, membership does not follow local scope — a host that joins may be far from a multicast router that is forwarding datagrams to the group. So, group membership information must be propagated across the underlying internet.

The issue of dynamic group membership is central to multicast routing; all multicast routing schemes provide a mechanism for propagating membership information as well as a way to use the information when forwarding datagrams. In general, because membership can change rapidly, the information available at a given router is imperfect, so route updates may lag changes. Therefore, a multicast design represents a tradeoff between the overhead of extra routing traffic and inefficient data transmission. On the one hand, if group membership information is not propagated rapidly, multicast routers will not make optimal decisions (i.e., they either forward datagrams across some networks unnecessarily or fail to send datagrams to all group members). On the other hand, a multicast routing scheme that communicates every membership change to every router is doomed because the resulting traffic can overwhelm an internet. Each design chooses a compromise between the two extremes.

15.24 Reverse Path Multicasting

One of the earliest forms of multicast routing was derived from TRPF. Known as *Reverse Path Multicast* (*RPM*), the scheme extends TRPF to make it more dynamic. Three assumptions underlie the design. First, it is more important to ensure that a multicast datagram reaches each member of the group to which it is sent than to eliminate unnecessary transmission. Second, multicast routers each contain a conventional unicast forwarding table that has correct information. Third, multicast routing should improve efficiency when possible (i.e., eliminate needless transmission).

RPM uses a two step process. When it begins, RPM uses the RPF broadcast scheme to send a copy of each datagram across all networks in the internet. Doing so ensures that all group members receive a copy. Simultaneously, RPM proceeds to have multicast routers inform one another about paths that do not lead to group members. Once it learns that no group members lie along a given path, a router stops forwarding along that path.

How do multicast routers learn about the location of group members? As in most multicast routing schemes, RPM propagates membership information bottom-up. The information starts with hosts that choose to join or leave groups. Hosts communicate membership information with their local router by using local protocols IGMP or MLDv2. The local protocols only inform a multicast router about local members on each of its directly-attached networks; the router will not learn about distant group members. As a consequence, a multicast router that attaches a leaf network to the rest of the Internet can decide which multicast datagrams to forward over the leaf network. If a leaf network does not contain members for group G, the router connecting the leaf network to the rest of the Internet will not forward datagrams for group G. As soon as any host on a network joins group G, the leaf router will inform the next router along the path back to the source and will begin forwarding datagrams that arrive destined for group G. Conversely, if all hosts beyond a given router leave group G, the router informs the next router along the path to the source to stop sending datagrams destined for G.

Using graph-theoretic terminology, we say that when a router learns that a group has no members along a path and stops forwarding, it has *pruned* (i.e., removed) the path from the forwarding tree. In fact, RPM is called a *broadcast and prune* strategy because a router broadcasts (using RPF) until it receives information that allows it to prune a path. Researchers also use another term for the RPM algorithm: they say that the system is *data-driven* because a router does not send group membership information to any other routers until datagrams arrive for that group.

In the data-driven model, a multicast router must also handle the case where a host decides to join a particular group after the router has pruned the path for that group. RPM uses a bottom-up approach to accommodate rejoining a group that has been pruned: when a host informs a local multicast router, M_1, that the host wants to rejoin a particular group, M_1 consults its record of the group and obtains the address of the multicast router, M_2, to which it had previously sent a prune request. M_1 sends a new message that undoes the effect of the previous prune and causes datagrams to flow again. Such messages are known as *graft requests*, and the algorithm is said to graft the previously pruned branch back onto the tree.

15.25 Example Multicast Routing Protocols

The IETF has investigated many multicast protocols, including *Distance Vector Multicast Routing Protocol* (*DVMRP*), *Core Based Trees* (*CBT*), and *Protocol Independent Multicast* (*PIM*). Although the protocols have been implemented and vendors have offered some support, none of them has become widely used. The next sections provide a brief description of each protocol.

15.25.1 Distance Vector Multicast Routing Protocol And Tunneling

An early protocol, known as the *Distance Vector Multicast Routing Protocol* (*DVMRP*), allows multicast routers to pass group membership and routing information among themselves. DVMRP resembles the RIP protocol described in Chapter 14, but has been extended for multicast. In essence, the protocol passes information about current multicast group membership and the cost to transfer datagrams between the routers. For each possible (group, source) pair, the routers impose a forwarding tree on top of the physical interconnections. When a router receives a datagram destined for an IP multicast group, it sends a copy of the datagram out over the network links that correspond to branches in the forwarding tree†. DVMPR is implemented by a Unix program named *mrouted* that uses a special *multicast kernel*.

Mrouted uses multicast tunneling to allow sites to forward multicast across the Internet. At each site, a manager configures an *mrouted tunnel* to other sites. The tunnel uses IP-in-IP encapsulation to send multicast. That is, when it receives a multicast da-

†DVMRP changed substantially between version *2* and *3* when it incorporated the RPM algorithm described above.

tagram generated by a local host, *mrouted* encapsulates the datagram in a conventional unicast datagram, and forwards a copy to *mrouted* at each of the other sites. When it receives a unicast datagram through one of its tunnels, *mrouted* extracts the multicast datagram, and then forwards according to its multicast forwarding table.

15.25.2 Core Based Trees (CBT)

The *Core Based Trees* (*CBT*) multicast routing protocol takes another approach to building a multicast forwarding system. CBT avoids broadcasting and allows all sources to share the same forwarding tree whenever possible. To avoid broadcasting, CBT does not forward multicasts along a path until one or more hosts along that path join the multicast group. Thus, CBT reverses the flood-and-prune approach used by DVMRP — instead of forwarding datagrams until negative information has been propagated, CBT does not forward along a path until positive information has been received. We say that instead of using the data-driven paradigm, CBT uses a *demand-driven* paradigm.

The demand-driven paradigm in CBT means that when a host uses IGMP to join a particular group, the local router must inform other routers before datagrams will be forwarded. Which router or routers should be informed? The question is critical in all demand-driven multicast routing schemes. Recall that in a data-driven scheme, a router uses the arrival of data traffic to know where to send routing messages (it propagates routing messages back over networks from which the traffic arrives). However, in a demand-driven scheme, no traffic will arrive for a group until the membership information has been propagated.

CBT uses a combination of static and dynamic algorithms to build a multicast forwarding tree. To make the scheme scalable, CBT divides the underlying internet into *regions*, where the size of a region is determined by network administrators. Within each region, one of the routers is designated as a *core router*, and other routers in the region must either be configured to know the core router for their region or to use a dynamic *discovery mechanism* to find the core router when they boot.

Knowledge of a core router is important because it allows multicast routers in a region to form a *shared tree* for the region. As soon as a host joins a multicast group, a local router, *L*, receives the host request. Router *L* generates a CBT *join request*, which it sends to the core router using conventional unicast forwarding. Each intermediate router along the path to the core router examines the request. As soon as the request reaches a router *R* that is already part of the CBT shared tree, *R* returns an acknowledgement, passes the group membership information on to its parent, and begins forwarding traffic for the new group. As the acknowledgement passes back to the leaf router, intermediate routers examine the message, and configure their multicast forwarding tables to forward datagrams for the group. Thus, router *L* is linked into the forwarding tree at router *R*.

We can summarize:

> *Because CBT uses a demand-driven paradigm, it divides an internet into regions and designates a* core router *for each region; other routers in the region dynamically build a forwarding tree by sending* join requests *to the core.*

15.25.3 Protocol Independent Multicast (PIM)

In reality, PIM consists of two independent protocols that share little beyond the name and basic message header formats: *Protocol Independent Multicast — Dense Mode* (*PIM-DM*) and *Protocol Independent Multicast — Sparse Mode* (*PIM-SM*). The distinction arises because no single protocol works well in all situations. In particular, PIM's dense mode is designed for a LAN environment in which all, or nearly all, networks have hosts listening to each multicast group; whereas, PIM's sparse mode is designed to accommodate a wide area environment in which the members of a given multicast group are spread wide and involve only a small subset of all possible networks.

The term *protocol independence* arises because PIM assumes a traditional unicast forwarding table that contains a shortest path to each destination. Because PIM does not specify how such a table should be built, an arbitrary routing protocol can be used. Thus, we say that PIM operates *independently* from the unicast routing update protocol(s) that a router employs.

To accommodate many listeners, PIM-DM uses a broadcast-and-prune approach in which datagrams are forwarded to all routers using RPF until a router sends an explicit *prune* request. By contrast, PIM's sparse mode can be viewed as an extension of basic concepts from CBT. Sparse mode designates a router, called a *Rendezvous Point* (*RP*), that is the functional equivalent of a CBT core router.

15.26 Reliable Multicast And ACK Implosions

The term *reliable multicast* refers to any system that uses multicast delivery, but also guarantees that all group members receive data in order without any loss, duplication, or corruption. In theory, reliable multicast combines the advantage of a forwarding scheme that is more efficient than broadcast with the benefit of having all data arrive intact. Thus, reliable multicast has great potential benefit and applicability (e.g., a stock exchange could use reliable multicast to deliver stock prices to many destinations).

In practice, reliable multicast is not as general or straightforward as it sounds. First, if a multicast group has multiple senders, the notion of delivering datagrams in sequence becomes meaningless. Second, we have seen that widely used multicast forwarding schemes such as RPF can produce duplication even on small internets. Third, in addition to guarantees that all data will eventually arrive, applications like audio or video expect reliable systems to bound the delay and jitter. Fourth, because reliability requires acknowledgements and a multicast group can have an arbitrary number of members, traditional reliable protocols require a sender to handle an arbitrary number of acknowledgements. Unfortunately, no computer has enough processing power to do so. We refer to the problem as an *ACK implosion*; the problem has become the focus of much research.

To overcome the ACK implosion problem, reliable multicast protocols take a hierarchical approach in which multicasting is restricted to a single source†. Before data is sent, a forwarding tree is established from the source to all group members and *acknowledgement points* must be identified.

An acknowledgement point, which is also known as an *acknowledgement aggregator* or *designated router* (*DR*), consists of a router in the multicast forwarding tree that agrees to cache copies of the data and process acknowledgements from routers or hosts further down the tree. If a retransmission is required, the acknowledgement point obtains a copy from its cache.

Most reliable multicast schemes use negative rather than positive acknowledgements — a receiving host does not respond unless a datagram is lost. To allow a host to detect loss, each datagram must be assigned a unique sequence number. When a gap appears in sequence numbers, a host detects loss and sends a *NACK* to request retransmission of the missing datagram. The NACK propagates along the forwarding tree toward the source until it reaches an acknowledgement point. The acknowledgement point processes the NACK, and retransmits a copy of the lost datagram along the forwarding tree.

How does an acknowledgement point ensure that it has a copy of all datagrams in the sequence? It uses the same scheme as a host. When a datagram arrives, the acknowledgement point checks the sequence number, places a copy in its memory, and then proceeds to propagate the datagram down the forwarding tree. If it finds that a datagram is missing, the acknowledgement point sends a NACK up the tree toward the source. The NACK either reaches another acknowledgement point that has a copy of the datagram (in which case the acknowledgement point transmits a second copy), or the NACK reaches the source (which retransmits the missing datagram).

The choice of a branching topology and acknowledgement points is crucial to the success of a reliable multicast scheme. Without sufficient acknowledgement points, a missing datagram can cause an ACK implosion. In particular, if a given router has many descendants, a lost datagram can cause that router to be overrun with retransmission requests. Unfortunately, automating selection of acknowledgement points has not turned out to be simple. Consequently, many reliable multicast protocols require manual configuration. Thus, reliable multicast is best suited to: services that tend to persist over long periods of time, topologies that do not change rapidly, and situations where intermediate routers agree to serve as acknowledgement points.

Is there an alternative approach to reliability? Some researchers have experimented with protocols that incorporate redundant information to reduce or eliminate retransmission. One scheme sends redundant datagrams. Instead of sending a single copy of each datagram, the source sends *N* copies (typically *2* or *3*). Redundant datagrams work

†Note that a single source does not limit functionality, because the source can agree to forward any message it receives via unicast. Thus, an arbitrary host can send a packet to the source, which then multicasts the packet to the group.

especially well when routers implement a *Random Early Discard* (*RED*) strategy because the probability of more than one copy being discarded is extremely small.

Another approach to redundancy involves *forward error-correcting codes.* Analogous to the error-correcting codes used with audio CDs, the scheme requires a sender to incorporate error-correction information into each datagram in a data stream. If one datagram is lost, the error correcting code contains sufficient redundant information to allow a receiver to reconstruct the missing datagram without requesting a retransmission.

15.27 Summary

IP multicasting is an abstraction of hardware multicasting. It allows delivery of a datagram to an arbitrary subset of computers. Both IPv4 and IPv6 define a set of multicast addresses. IPv6 uses the second octet to represent scope, allowing the scope to be independent of the service. IP multicast uses hardware multicast, if available.

IP multicast groups are dynamic: a host can join or leave a group at any time. For local multicast, hosts only need the ability to send and receive multicast datagrams. For IP multicast that spans multiple networks, multicast routers must propagate group membership information and arrange routing so that each member of a multicast group receives a copy of every datagram sent to the group. The IP multicasting scheme is complicated by the rule that an arbitrary host can send to a multicast group, even if the host is not a member.

Hosts communicate their group membership to multicast routers using IGMP (IPv4) or MLDv2 (IPv6). The protocols are closely related, and have been designed to be efficient and to avoid using excessive network resources.

A variety of protocols have been designed to propagate multicast routing information across an internet. The two basic approaches are data-driven and demand-driven. In either case, the amount of information in a multicast forwarding table is much larger than in a unicast forwarding table because multicasting requires entries for each (group, source) pair.

Not all routers in the global Internet propagate multicast routes or forward multicast traffic. Tunneling can be used to connect multicast *islands* that are separated by parts of an internet that do not support multicast routing. When using a tunnel, a program encapsulates a multicast datagram in a conventional unicast datagram. The receiver extracts and handles the multicast datagram.

Reliable multicast refers to a scheme that uses multicast forwarding but offers reliable delivery semantics. To avoid the ACK implosion problem, reliable multicast designs either use a hierarchy of acknowledgement points or send redundant information.

EXERCISES

15.1 The IPv4 standard suggests using 23 bits of an IP multicast address to form a hardware multicast address. In such a scheme, how many IP multicast addresses map to a single hardware multicast address?

15.2 Answer the question above for IPv6.

15.3 Argue that IP multicast group IDs do not need as many bits as have been allocated. Suppose a group ID used 23 bits and analyze the disadvantages. (Hint: what are the practical limits on the number of groups to which a host can belong and the number of hosts on a single network?)

15.4 IP software must always check the destination addresses on incoming multicast datagrams and discard datagrams if the host is not in the specified multicast group. Explain how the host might receive a multicast destined for a group to which that host is not a member.

15.5 Multicast routers need to know whether a group has members on a given network because the router needs to know which multicast trees to join. Is there any advantage to routers knowing the exact set of hosts on a network that belong to a given multicast group? Explain.

15.6 Find three applications that can benefit from IP multicast.

15.7 The standard says that IP software must arrange to deliver a copy of any *outgoing* multicast datagram to application programs on the same host that belong to the specified multicast group. Does the design make programming easier or more difficult? Explain.

15.8 When the underlying hardware does not support multicast, IP multicast uses hardware broadcast for delivery. How can doing so cause problems? Is there any advantage to using IP multicast over such networks?

15.9 DVMRP was derived from RIP. Read RFC 1075 on DVMRP and compare the two protocols. How much more complex is DVMRP than RIP?

15.10 Version 3 of IGMP and MLDv2 both include a measure of robustness that is intended to accommodate packet loss by allowing transmission of multiple copies of a message. How does the protocol arrive at an estimate of the robustness value needed on a given network?

15.11 Explain why a multi-homed host may need to join a multicast group on one network, but not on another. (Hint: consider an audio teleconference.)

15.12 Suppose an application programmer makes a choice to simplify programming: when joining a multicast group, simply join on each network to which the host attaches. Show that joining on all local interfaces can lead to arbitrary traffic on remote networks.

15.13 Estimate the size of the multicast forwarding table needed to handle multicast of audio from 100 radio stations, if each station has a total of ten million listeners at random locations around the world.

15.14 Consider a cable TV provider using IP technology. Assume each set-top box uses IP and devise a scheme in which the cable provider broadcasts all channels to a neighborhood distribution point and then uses multicast to deliver to residences.

15.15 Argue that only two types of multicast are practical in the Internet: statically configured commercial services that multicast to large numbers of subscribers and dynamically configured services that include a few participants (e.g., family members in three households participating in a single IP phone call).

15.16 Consider reliable multicast achieved through redundant transmission. If a given link has high probability of corruption, is it better to send redundant copies of a datagram or to send one copy that uses forward error-correcting codes? Explain.

15.17 The data-driven multicast routing paradigm works best on local networks that have low delay and excess capacity, while the demand-driven paradigm works best in a wide area environment that has limited capacity and higher delay. Does it make sense to devise a single protocol that combines the two schemes? Why or why not? (Hint: consider MOSPF.)

15.18 Read the PIM-SM protocol specification to find how the protocol defines the notion of *sparse*. Find an example of an internet in which the population of group members is sparse, but for which DVMRP is a better multicast routing protocol.

15.19 Devise a quantitative measure that can be used to decide when PIM-SM should switch from a shared tree to a shortest path tree.

Chapter Contents

16

Label Switching, Flows, And MPLS

16.1 Introduction

Earlier chapters describe IP addressing and describe how hosts and routers use a forwarding table and the longest-prefix match algorithm to look up a next hop and forward datagrams. This chapter considers an alternative approach that avoids the overhead of longest prefix matching. The chapter presents the basic idea of label switching, explains the technology, and describes its use for traffic engineering.

The next chapter continues the discussion by considering software defined networking, and explains how the basic idea of flow labels can be used in a software-defined network.

16.2 Switching Technology

In the 1980s, as the Internet grew in popularity, researchers began to explore ways to increase the performance of packet processing systems. An idea emerged that was eventually adopted by commercial vendors: replace IP's connectionless packet switching approach that requires longest-prefix table lookup with a connection-oriented approach that accommodates a faster lookup algorithm. The general concept, which is known as *label switching*, led vendors to create a networking technology known as *Asynchronous Transfer Mode* (*ATM*). In the 1990s, ATM had a short-lived popularity, but the fad faded.

There were several reasons for ATM's eventual demise. The main reason was economic: Ethernet switches and IP routers were much less expensive than ATM switches, and once the IETF created label switching technologies using conventional IP routers, IT departments did not find compelling reasons for ATM. Once we understand the general concepts, we see how it is possible to implement switching with a conventional router that does not rely on expensive, connection-oriented hardware.

At the heart of switching lies a basic observation about lookup: if there are N items in a forwarding table, a computer requires on average approximately log_2N steps to perform a longest-prefix match. The proponents of label switching point out that hardware can perform an array index in one step. Furthermore, indexing can translate directly into combinatorial hardware, while searching usually involves multiple memory references.

Switching technologies exploit indexing to achieve extremely high-speed forwarding. To do so, each packet carries a small integer known as a *label*. When a packet arrives at a switch, the switch extracts the label and uses the value as an index into the table that specifies the appropriate action. Each switch has a set of output interfaces, and the action usually consists of sending the packet out one of the interfaces. Figure 16.1 illustrates the concept.

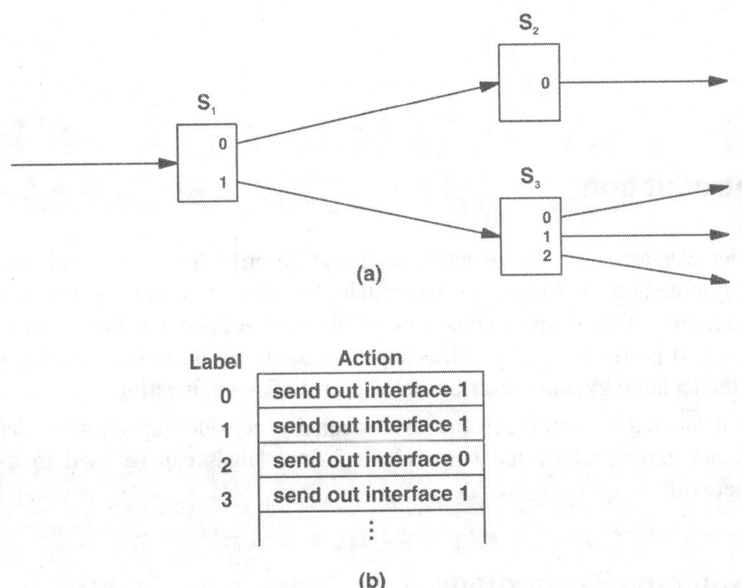

Figure 16.1 Illustration of basic switching with (a) a network of three interconnected switches, and (b) a table from switch S_1.

In the figure, the table entries specify how switch S_1 forwards packets with labels in the range 0 through 3. According to the table, a packet with label *2* will be forwarded out interface *0*, which leads to switch S_2; a packet with a label of *0*, *1*, or *3* will be forwarded over interface *1*, which leads to switch S_3.

16.3 Flows And Flow Setup

The chief drawback of the basic switching scheme described above arises because each label consists of a small integer. How can the scheme be extended to a network that has many destinations? The key to answering the question involves rethinking our assumptions about internets and forwarding:

- Instead of focusing on destinations, focus on packet *flows*.
- Instead of assuming that forwarding tables remain static, imagine a system that can set up or change forwarding tables quickly.

We define a *packet flow* to be a sequence of packets sent from a given source to a given destination. For example, all the packets on a TCP connection constitute a single flow. A flow also might correspond to a VoIP phone call or a longer-term interaction, such as all the packets sent from a router in a company's east-coast office to a router in the company's west-coast office. We can summarize the key idea:

> *Switching technologies use the* flow *abstraction and create forwarding for flows rather than for destinations.*

In terms of packet flows, we will assume a mechanism exists to create entries in switches when a flow is set up and remove entries when a flow terminates. Unlike a conventional internet where forwarding tables remain static, the tables in switches are expected to change frequently. Of course, the system to set up flows needs mechanisms that understand destinations and how to reach them. Thus, flow setup may need to understand conventional forwarding that uses destinations. For now, we will concentrate on the operation of switches, and will postpone the discussion of flow setup until later in the chapter.

16.4 Large Networks, Label Swapping, And Paths

In the simplistic description above, each flow must be assigned a unique label. A packet carries the label assigned to its flow, and at every switch the forwarding mechanism uses the label to select an outgoing interface. Unfortunately, the simplistic scheme does not scale to large networks. Before a unique label can be assigned to a flow, software would need to verify that no other flow anywhere in the internet is using the label. Therefore, before a flow could be established, the setup system would have to communicate with every switch in the internet.

Designers found an ingenious way to solve the problem of scale while preserving the speed of switching. The solution allows the label to be chosen independently for each switch along the path. That is, instead of a unique label for a given flow, a new label can be chosen at each switch along a path. Only one additional mechanism is needed to make independent label selection work: a switch must be able to rewrite the label on packets. The system is known as *label swapping*, *label switching*, or *label rewriting*.

To understand label swapping, we must focus on the *path* a given flow will follow through the network. When label swapping is used, the label on a packet can change as the packet passes from switch to switch. That is, the action a switch performs can include rewriting the label. Figure 16.2 illustrates a path through three switches.

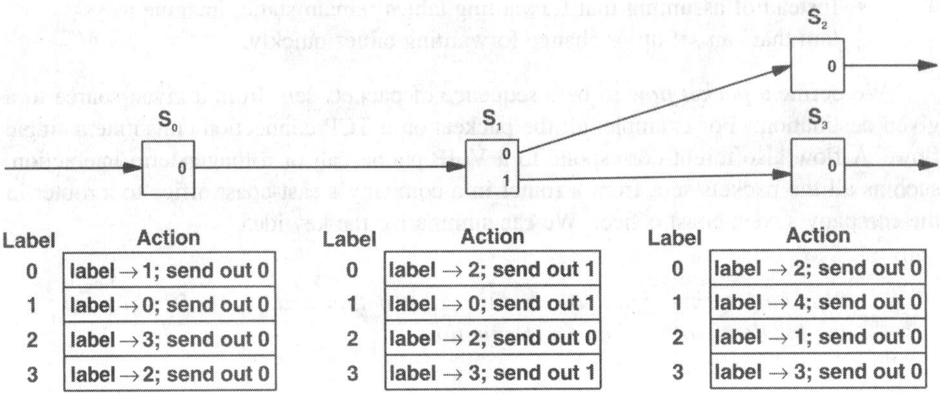

Label	Action
0	label → 1; send out 0
1	label → 0; send out 0
2	label → 3; send out 0
3	label → 2; send out 0

Label	Action
0	label → 2; send out 1
1	label → 0; send out 1
2	label → 2; send out 0
3	label → 3; send out 1

Label	Action
0	label → 2; send out 0
1	label → 4; send out 0
2	label → 1; send out 0
3	label → 3; send out 0

Figure 16.2 Illustration of label swapping, in which the label in a packet can be rewritten by each switch.

In the figure, a packet that enters S_0 with label *1* has the label rewritten before being forwarded. Thus, when switch S_1 receives the packet, the label will be *0*. Similarly, S_1 replaces the label with *2* before sending the packet to S_3. S_3 replace the label with *1*. Label swapping makes it easier to configure a switched network because it allows a manager to define a path through the network without forcing the same label to be used at each point along the path. In fact, a label only needs to be valid across one hop — the two switches that share the physical connection need to agree on the label to be assigned to each flow that crosses the connection.

The point is:

> *Switching uses a connection-oriented approach. To avoid the need for global agreement on the use of labels, the technology allows a manager to define a path of switches without requiring that the same label be used along the entire path.*

16.5 Using Switching With IP

The question arises, can we create a technology that has the advantages of label switching and the advantages of IP's destination-based forwarding? The answer is yes. Although the connection-oriented paradigms used with switching appear to conflict with IP's connectionless paradigm, the two have been combined. There are three advantages:

- Fast forwarding
- Aggregated route information
- Ability to manage aggregate flows

Fast Forwarding. The point is easy to understand: switching allows routers to perform forwarding faster because the router can use indexing in place of forwarding table lookup. Of course, hardware implementations of conventional IP forwarding are extremely fast (i.e., can forward many inputs each operating at 10 Gbps without dropping any packets). So, the choice between switching or forwarding largely depends on the cost.

Aggregated Route Information. Large Tier-1 ISPs at the center of the Internet use switching as a way to avoid having complete routing tables in each of their routers. When a packet first reaches the ISP, an edge router examines the destination address and chooses one of several paths. For example, one path might lead to a peer ISP, a second path might lead to another peer ISP, and a third might lead to a large customer. The packet is assigned a label, and routers on the ISP's backbone use the label to forward the packet. In such cases labels are coarse-grain — the label only specifies the next ISP to which the packet should be sent and not the ultimate destination. Therefore, all traffic going to a given ISP will have the same label. In other words, all packet traveling to the same next hop are aggregated into a single flow.

Ability To Manage Aggregate Flows. ISPs often write *Service Level Agreements* (*SLAs*) regarding traffic that can be sent across a peering point. Usually, such SLAs refer to aggregate traffic (e.g., all traffic forwarded between the two ISPs or all VoIP traffic). Having a label assigned to each aggregate makes it easier to implement mechanisms that measure or enforce the SLA.

16.6 IP Switching Technologies And MPLS

So far, we have described label switching as a general-purpose, connection-oriented network technology. We will now consider how label switching has been combined with Internet technology. Ipsilon Corporation was one of the first companies to produce products that merged IP and switching hardware. In fact, Ipsilon used modified ATM hardware switches, named their technology *IP switching*, and called their devices *IP switches*. Since Ipsilon, other companies have produced a series of designs and names, including *tag switching*, *Layer 3 switching*, and *label switching*. Several of the ideas have been folded into a standard endorsed by the IETF known as *Multi-Protocol Label Switching* (*MPLS*). As the term *multi-protocol* implies, MPLS is designed to carry arbitrary payloads. In practice, MPLS is used almost exclusively to transport IP.

How is MPLS used? The general idea is straightforward: a large ISP (or even a corporation that has a large intranet) uses MPLS at the center of its network, sometimes called an *MPLS core*. Routers near the edge of the ISP's network (i.e., routers that connect to customers) use conventional forwarding; only routers in the core understand MPLS and use switching. In most cases, MPLS is not used to establish paths for individual flows. Instead, the ISP configures semi-permanent MPLS paths across the core that stay in place. For example, at each main entry point to the core, the ISP configures a path to each of the exit points.

Routers near the edge of an ISP's network examine each datagram and choose whether to use one of the MPLS paths or handle the datagram with conventional forwarding. For example, if a customer in one city sends a datagram to another customer in the same city, the edge router can deliver the datagram without crossing the MPLS core. However, if the datagram must travel to a remote location or the datagram requires special handling, an edge router can choose one of the MPLS paths and send the datagram along the path. When it reaches the end of the MPLS path, the datagram arrives at another edge router, which will use conventional forwarding for delivery.

As mentioned earlier, one of the main motivations for using MPLS is the ability to aggregate flows as they cross the ISP's core. However, MPLS allows ISPs to offer special services to individual customers as well. For example, consider a large corporation with offices in New York and San Francisco. Suppose the corporation wants a secure connection between its two sites with performance guarantees. One way to achieve such a connection consists of leasing a digital circuit. Another alternative involves MPLS: an ISP can establish an MPLS path between the two offices, and can configure routers along the path to provide a performance guarantee.

When two major ISPs connect at a peering point, there are two options: they can each maintain a separate MPLS core or they can cooperate to interconnect their MPLS cores. The disadvantage of using separate cores arises when a datagram must traverse both cores. The datagram travels across the first ISP's core to an edge router that removes the label. The datagram then passes to a router in the second ISP, which assigns a new label and forwards the datagram across the second MPLS core. If the two ISPs agree to interconnect their MPLS cores, a label can be assigned once, and the datagram is switched along an MPLS path until it reaches the edge router in the second ISP that removes the label and delivers the datagram. The disadvantage of such an interconnection arises from the need to coordinate — both ISPs must agree on label assignments used across the connection.

16.7 Labels And Label Assignment

We said that an edge router examines each datagram and chooses whether to send the datagram along an MPLS path. Before an edge router can send a datagram across an MPLS core, the datagram must be assigned a label. Because MPLS performs label swapping, the label assigned to a datagram is only the initial label for a path. One can think of the mapping from a datagram to a label as a mathematical function:

$$\text{label} = f(\text{datagram})$$

where *label* is the initial label for one of the MPLS paths that has been set up, and *f* is a function that performs the mapping.

In practice, function *f* does not usually examine the entire datagram. In most instances, *f* only looks at selected header fields. The next chapter describes packet classification in detail.

16.8 Hierarchical Use Of MPLS And A Label Stack

Consider the use of MPLS in an organization where networks are arranged into a two-level hierarchy: an outer region that uses conventional IP forwarding and an inner region that uses MPLS. As we will see, the protocol makes additional levels of hierarchy possible. For example, suppose a corporation has three campuses, with multiple buildings on each campus. The corporation can use conventional forwarding within a building, one level of MPLS to interconnect the buildings within a campus, and a second level of MPLS to interconnect sites. Two levels of hierarchy allows the corporation to choose policies for traffic between sites separately from the policies used between buildings (e.g., the path that traffic travels between buildings is determined by the type of traffic, but all traffic between a pair of sites follows the same path).

To provide for a multi-level hierarchy, MPLS incorporates a *label stack*. That is, instead of attaching a single label to a packet, MPLS allows multiple labels to be attached. At any time, only the top label is used; once the packet finishes traversing a level, the top label is removed and processing continues with the next label.

In the case of our example corporation, it is possible to arrange two MPLS areas — one for traffic traveling between buildings and one for traffic traveling between two sites. Thus, when a datagram travels between two buildings at a given site, the datagram will have one label attached (the label will be removed when the datagram reaches the correct building). If a datagram must travel between sites and then to the correct building at the destination site, the datagram will have two labels attached. The top label will be used to move the datagram between the sites, and will be removed once the datagram reaches the correct site. When the top label is removed, the second label will be used to forward the datagram to the correct building.

16.9 MPLS Encapsulation

Interestingly, MPLS does not require the underlying network to use a connection-oriented paradigm or support label switching. But conventional networks do not provide a way to pass a label along with a packet and the IPv4 datagram header does not provide space to store a label. So, the question arises: how can an MPLS label accompany a datagram across a conventional network? The answer lies in an encapsulation technique: we think of MPLS as a packet format that can encapsulate an arbitrary payload. The primary use is the encapsulation of IPv4 datagrams†. Figure 16.3 illustrates the conceptual encapsulation.

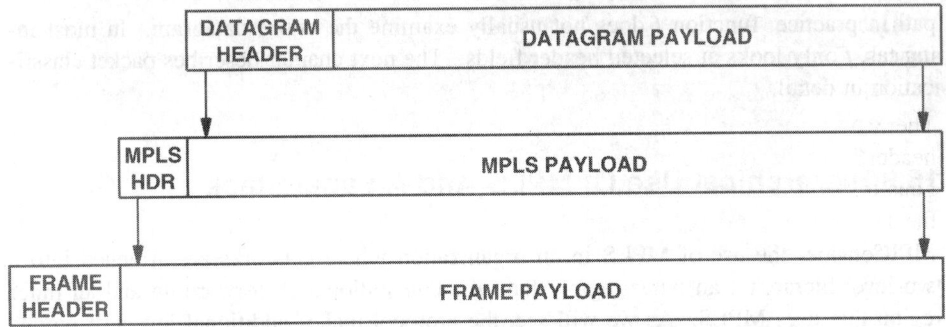

Figure 16.3 The encapsulation used with MPLS to send an IPv4 datagram over a conventional network, such as an Ethernet. An MPLS header is variable size, and depends on the number of entries in the label stack.

As an example, consider using MPLS to send a datagram across an Ethernet. When using MPLS, the Ethernet type field is set to 0x8847 for unicast transmission‡. Thus, there is no ambiguity about the contents of a frame — a receiver can use the frame type to determine whether the frame carries MPLS or a conventional datagram.

An MPLS header is variable length. The header consists of one or more entries, each of which is 32 bits long and specifies a label plus information used to control label processing. Figure 16.4 illustrates the format of an entry in the header.

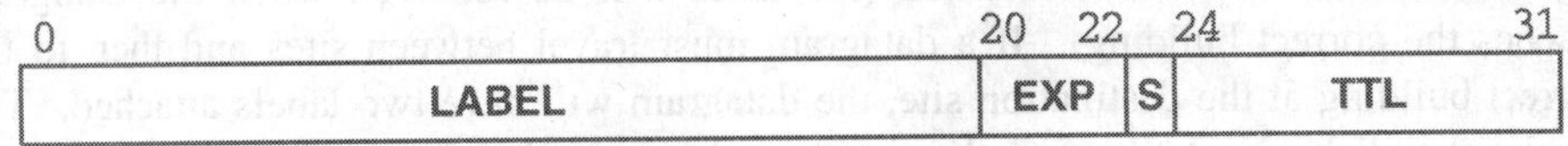

Figure 16.4 Illustration of the fields in an MPLS header entry. An MPLS header consists of one or more of these entries.

†Although MPLS can be used for IPv6, the presence of a flow label in the IPv6 header reduces the need for MPLS.

‡Ethernet type 0x8848 has been assigned for use when MPLS is multicast, but MPLS does not handle multicast well.

As Figure 16.4 indicates, there is no field to specify the overall size of an MPLS header, nor does the header contain a field to specify the type of the payload. To understand why, recall that MPLS is a connection-oriented technology. Before an MPLS frame can be sent across a single link, an entire path must be set up. The label switching router along the path must be configured to know exactly how to process a packet with a given label. Therefore, when the MPLS path is configured, the two sides will agree on the size of the MPLS label stack and the contents of the payload area.

An entry in the MPLS header begins with a *LABEL* field that the receiver uses to process the packet. If the receiver is an intermediate hop along an MPLS path, the receiver performs label switching and continues. If the receiver lies at the boundary between two levels in an MPLS hierarchy, the receiver will remove the first label on the stack and use the next label. When the packet reaches the final hop along an MPLS path, the receiver will remove the final MPLS header and use conventional IP forwarding tables to handle the encapsulated datagram.

The field labeled *EXP* in an MPLS header entry is reserved for experimental use. The *S* bit is set to 1 to denote the bottom of the stack (i.e., the last entry in an MPLS header); in other entries, the *S* bit is 0. Finally, the *TTL* field (*Time To Live*) is analogous to the TTL field in an IPv4 datagram header: each switch along the path that uses the label to forward the packet decrements the TTL value. If the TTL reaches zero, MPLS discards the packet. Thus, MPLS prevents a packet from cycling forever, even if a manager misconfigures switches and accidentally creates a forwarding loop.

16.10 Label Semantics

Note that an MPLS label is 20 bits wide. In theory, an MPLS configuration can use all 20 bits of the label to accommodate up to 2^{20} simultaneous flows (i.e., 1,048,576 flows). In practice, however, MPLS installations seldom use a large number of flows because a manager is usually required to authorize and configure each switched path.

The description of switching above explains that a label is used as an index into an array. Indeed, some switching implementations, especially hardware implementations, do use a label as an index. However, MPLS does not require that each label correspond to an array index. Instead, MPLS implementations allow a label to be an arbitrary 20-bit integer. When it receives an incoming packet, an MPLS router extracts the label and performs a lookup. Typically, the lookup mechanism uses a *hashing* algorithm, which means the lookup is approximately as fast as an array index†.

Allowing arbitrary values in labels makes it possible for managers to choose labels that make monitoring and debugging easier. For example, if there are three main paths through a corporate network, each path can be assigned a prefix 0, 1, or 2, and the prefix can be used at each hop along the path. If a problem occurs and a network manager captures packets, having bits in the label that identify a path makes it easier to associate the packet with a path.

†On average, hashing only requires one probe to find the correct entry in a table if the load factor of the table is low.

16.11 Label Switching Router

A router that implements MPLS is known as a *Label Switching Router* (*LSR*). Typically, an LSR consists of a conventional router that has been augmented with software (and possibly hardware) to handle MPLS. Conceptually, MPLS processing and conventional datagram processing are completely separate. When a packet arrives, the LSR uses the frame type to decide how to process the packet, as Figure 16.5 illustrates.

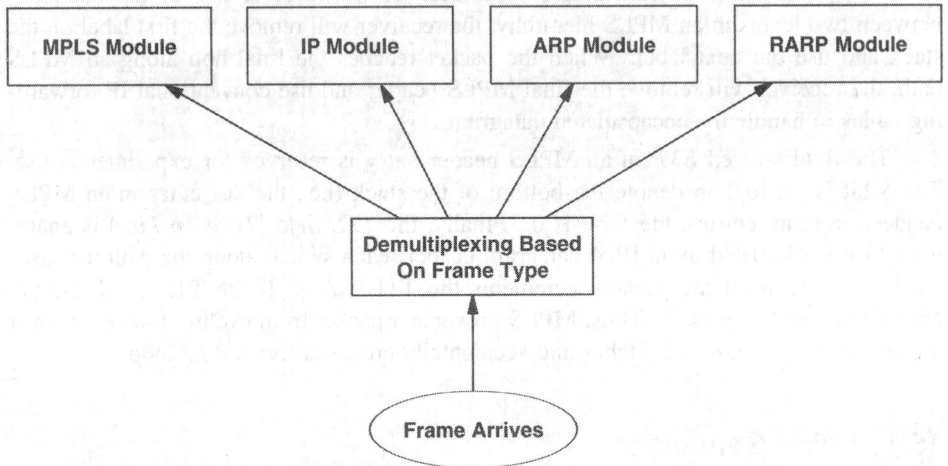

Figure 16.5 Frame demultiplexing in an LSR that handles both MPLS and conventional IP forwarding.

In practice, having both MPLS and IP capability in a single LSR allows the router to serve as the interface between a non-MPLS internet and an MPLS core. That is, an LSR can accept a datagram from a conventional network, classify the datagram to assign an initial MPLS label, and forward the datagram over an MPLS path. Similarly, the LSR can accept a packet over an MPLS path, remove the label, and forward the datagram over a conventional network. The two functions are known as *MPLS ingress* and *MPLS egress*.

The table inside an LSR that specifies an action for each label is known as a *Next Hop Label Forwarding Table*, and each entry in the table is called a *Next Hop Label Forwarding Entry* (*NHLFE*). Each NHLFE specifies two items, and may specify three more:

- Next hop information (e.g., the outgoing interface)

- The operation to be performed

- The encapsulation to use (optional)
- How to encode the label (optional)
- Other information needed to handle the packet (optional)

An NHLFE contains an operation field that specifies whether the packet is crossing a transition to or from one level of the MPLS hierarchy to another, or merely being switched along a path within a single level. The possibilities are:

- Replace the label at the top of the stack with a specified new label, and continue to forward via MPLS at the current level of the hierarchy.
- Pop the label stack to exit one level of MPLS hierarchy. Either use the next label on the stack to forward the datagram, or use conventional forwarding if the final label was removed.
- Replace the label on the top of the stack with a specified new label, and then push one or more new labels on the stack to increase the level(s) of MPLS hierarchy.

16.12 Control Processing And Label Distribution

The discussion above has focused on *data path* processing (i.e., forwarding packets). In addition, engineers who defined MPLS considered mechanisms for a *control path*. Control path processing refers to configuration and management — control path protocols make it easy for a manager to create or manage a path through an MPLS core, which is known as a *label switched path* (*LSP*).

The primary functionality provided by a control path protocol is automatic selection of labels. That is, the protocols allow a manager to establish an MPLS path by specifying where the path should go without manually configuring the labels to use at each LSR along the path. The protocols allow pairs of LSRs along the path to choose an unused label for the link between a pair, and fill in NHLFE information for the new path so the labels can be swapped at each hop.

The process of choosing labels along a path is known as *label distribution*. Two protocols have been created to perform label distribution for MPLS: the *Label Distribution Protocol* (*LDP*), which is sometimes referred to as *MPLS-LDP*, and the *Constraint-based Routing LDP* (*CR-LDP*). Label distribution handles the task of insuring that labels are assigned consistently; the constraint-based routing extension of LDP handles the task of building paths along routes that match a set of administrative constraints. In addition, existing protocols such as *OSPF*, *BGP*, and *RSVP* have also been extended to provide label distribution. Although it recognizes the need for a label distribution protocol, the IETF working group that developed MPLS has not specified any of the protocols as the required standard.

16.13 MPLS And Fragmentation

Observant readers may have realized that there is a potential problem with MPLS and fragmentation. In fact, MPLS and IP fragmentation interact in two ways. First, we said that when it sends a datagram over a label switched path, MPLS adds a header of at least four octets. Doing so can have an interesting consequence, especially in a case where the underlying networks have the same MTU. For example, consider an ingress LSR that connects an Ethernet using conventional IP forwarding to an MPLS core that uses label switching. If a datagram arrives over a non-MPLS path with size exactly equal to the Ethernet MTU, adding a 32-bit MPLS header will make the resulting payload exceed the Ethernet MTU. As a result, the ingress LSR must fragment the original datagram, add the MPLS header to each fragment, and transmit two packets across the MPLS core instead of one.

A second interaction between MPLS and fragmentation occurs when an ingress LSR receives IP fragments instead of a complete datagram. When the datagram exits the MPLS core, a router may need to examine TCP or UDP port numbers as well as IP addresses to decide how to process the packet. Unfortunately, only the first fragment of a datagram contains the transport protocol header. Thus, an ingress LSR must either collect fragments and reassemble the datagram or rely only on the IP source and destination addresses. A large ISP that uses MPLS has two choices. On the one hand, the ISP can require customers to use a smaller MTU than the network allows (e.g., an Ethernet MTU of 1492 octets leaves room for two MPLS header entries without any significant decrease in overall throughput). On the other hand, an ISP can simply decide to prohibit the use of MPLS with fragments. That is, in cases where the egress router must examine transport layer fields, the ingress router examines each datagram and drops any datagram that is too large to send over an MPLS path without fragmentation.

16.14 Mesh Topology And Traffic Engineering

Interestingly, many ISPs who use MPLS follow a straightforward approach: they define a *full mesh* of MPLS paths. That is, if the ISP has *K* sites and peers with *J* other ISPs, the ISP defines an MPLS path for each possible pair of points. As a result, traffic moving between any pair of sites travels over a single MPLS path between the sites. A beneficial side effect of defining separate paths arises from the ability to measure (or control) the traffic traveling from one site to another. For example, by watching a single MPLS connection, an ISP can determine how much traffic travels from one of its sites across a peering connection to another ISP.

Some sites extend the idea of a full mesh by defining multiple paths between each pair of sites to accommodate various types of traffic. For example, an MPLS path with minimum hops might be reserved for VoIP, which needs minimum delay, while a longer path might be used for other traffic, such as email and web traffic. Many LSRs provide a mechanism to guarantee a given MPLS path a percentage of the underlying network. Therefore, an ISP can specify that an MPLS path carrying voice traffic always receives *N* percent of the network capacity. MPLS classification makes it possible to use a variety of measures to choose a path for data, including the IP source address as well as the transport protocol port numbers. The point is:

> *Because MPLS classification can use arbitrary fields in a datagram, including the IP source address, the service a datagram receives can depend on the customer sending the datagram as well as the type of data being carried.*

As an alternative to assigning a single MPLS path for each aggregate flow, MPLS allows an ISP to balance traffic between two disjoint paths. Furthermore, to insure high reliability, the ISP can arrange to use the two paths as mutual backups — if one path fails, all traffic can be forwarded along the other path.

We use the term *traffic engineering* to characterize the process of using MPLS to direct traffic along routes that achieve an organization's policies. A manager creates a set of MPLS paths, specifies the LSRs along each path, and designs rules that assign a datagram to one of the paths. Many traffic engineering facilities allows managers to use some of the *Quality of Service* (*QoS*) techniques defined in Chapter 26 to control the rate of traffic on each path. Thus, it is possible to define two MPLS flows over a single physical connection, and use QoS techniques to guarantee that if each flow has traffic to send, 75% of the underlying network capacity is devoted to one flow and the remaining 25% to the other flow.

16.15 Summary

To achieve high speed, switching technologies use indexing rather than longest-prefix lookup. As a consequence, switching follows a connection-oriented paradigm. Because switches along a path can rewrite labels, the label assigned to a flow can change along the path.

The standard for switching IP datagrams, which is known as MPLS, was created by the IETF. When sending a datagram along a label switched path, MPLS prepends a header, creating a stack of one or more labels; subsequent LSRs along the path use the labels to forward the datagram without performing routing table lookups. An ingress LSR classifies each datagram that arrives from a non-MPLS host or router, and an egress LSR can pass datagrams from an MPLS path to a non-MPLS host or router.

EXERCISES

16.1 Consider the IPv6 datagram format described in Chapter 7. What mechanism relates directly to MPLS?

16.2 Read about MPLS. Should MPLS accommodate Layer 2 forwarding (i.e., bridging) as well as optimized IP forwarding? Why or why not?

16.3 If all traffic from host X will traverse a two-level MPLS hierarchy, what action could be taken to ensure that no fragmentation will occur?

16.4 Read more about the Label Distribution Protocol, LDP, and the Constraint-based Routing extension. What are the possible constraints that can be used?

16.5 If a router at your site supports MPLS, enable MPLS switching and measure the performance improvement over conventional routing table lookup. (Hint: be sure to measure many packets to a given destination to avoid having measurements affected by the cost of handling the initial packet.)

16.6 Is it possible to conduct an experiment to determine whether your ISP uses MPLS? (Assume it is possible to transmit arbitrary packets.)

16.7 Cisco Systems, Inc. offers a switching technology known as *Multi-Layer Switching* (*MLS*). Read about MLS. In what ways does MLS differ from MPLS?

16.8 If your site has a VLAN switch that offers MLS service, enable the service and test what happens if one sends a valid Ethernet frame that contains an incorrect IP datagram. Should a Layer 2 switch examine IP headers? Why or why not?

16.9 Assume that it is possible to obtain a copy of all frames that travel across an Ethernet. How do you know whether a given frame is MPLS? If you encounter an MPLS frame, how can you determine the size of the MPLS header?

Chapter Contents

17

Packet Classification

17.1 Introduction

Earlier chapters describe traditional packet processing systems and explain two fundamental concepts. First, we saw how each layer of protocol software in a host or router uses a type field in a protocol header for demultiplexing. The type field in a frame is used to select a Layer 3 module to handle the frame, the type field in an IP header is used to select a transport layer protocol module, and so on. Second, we saw how IP performs datagram forwarding by looking up a destination address to select a next-hop.

This chapter takes an entirely different view of packet processing than previous chapters. In place of demultiplexing, we will consider a technique known as *classification*. Instead of assuming that a packet proceeds through a protocol stack one layer at a time, we will examine a technique that crosses layers.

Packet classification is pertinent to three topics covered in other chapters. First, the previous chapter describes MPLS, and we will see that routers use classification when choosing an MPLS path over which to send a datagram. Second, earlier chapters describe Ethernet switches, and we will learn that switches use classification instead of demultiplexing. Finally, Chapter 28 will complete our discussion of classification by introducing the important topic of *Software Defined Networking* (*SDN*). We will see that classification forms the basis of SDN technologies, and understand how a software-defined network subsumes concepts from MPLS as well as concepts from Ethernet switches.

17.2 Motivation For Classification

To understand the motivation for classification, consider a router with protocol software arranged in a traditional layered stack, as Figure 17.1 illustrates.

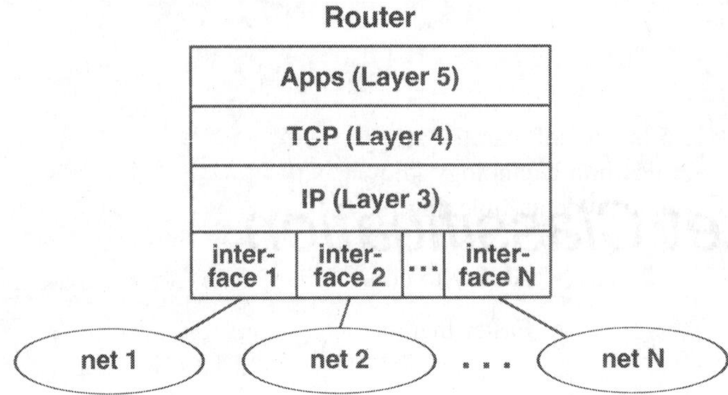

Figure 17.1 The protocol stack in a traditional router with layers involved in forwarding a transit datagram highlighted.

As the figure indicates, datagram forwarding usually only requires protocols up through Layer 3. Packet processing relies on *demultiplexing* at each layer of the protocol stack. When a frame arrives, protocol software looks at the type field to learn about the contents of the frame payload. If the frame carries an IP datagram, the payload is sent to the IP protocol module for processing. IP uses the destination address to select a next-hop address. If the datagram is in *transit* (i.e., passing through the router on its way to a destination), IP forwards the datagram by sending it back out one of the interfaces. A datagram only reaches TCP if the datagram is destined for the router itself.

To understand why traditional layering does not solve all problems, consider MPLS processing as described in the previous chapter. In particular, consider a router at the border between a traditional internet and an MPLS core. Such a router must accept packets that arrive from the traditional internet and choose an MPLS path over which to send the packet. Why is layering pertinent to path selection? In many cases, network managers use transport layer protocol port numbers when choosing a path. For example, suppose a manager wants to send all web traffic down a specific MPLS path. All the web traffic will use TCP port 80, which means that the selection must examine TCP port numbers.

Unfortunately, in a traditional demultiplexing scheme, a datagram does not reach the transport layer unless the datagram is destined for the router itself. Therefore, protocol software must be reorganized to handle MPLS path selection. We can summarize:

> *A traditional protocol stack is insufficient for the task of MPLS path selection, because path selection often involves transport layer information and a traditional stack will not send transit datagrams to the transport layer.*

17.3 Classification Instead Of Demultiplexing

How should protocol software be structured to handle tasks like MPLS path selection? The answer lies in a technology known as *classification*. A classification system differs from conventional demultiplexing in two ways:

- Ability to cross multiple layers
- Faster than demultiplexing

To understand classification, imagine a packet that has been received at a router and placed in memory. Recall that encapsulation means that the packet will have a set of contiguous protocol headers at the beginning. For example, Figure 17.2 illustrates the headers in a TCP packet (e.g., a request sent to a web server) that has arrived over an Ethernet.

Ethernet header	IP header	TCP header	. . . TCP Payload . . .

Figure 17.2 The arrangement of protocol header fields in a TCP packet.

Given a packet in memory, how can we quickly determine whether the packet is destined for the Web? A simplistic approach simply looks at one field in the headers: the TCP destination port number. However, it could be that the packet isn't a TCP packet at all. Maybe the frame is carrying ARP instead of IP. Or maybe the frame does indeed contain an IP datagram, but instead of TCP, the transport layer protocol is UDP. To make certain that it is destined for the Web, software needs to verify each of the headers: the frame contains an IP datagram, the IP datagram contains a TCP segment, and the TCP segment is destined for the Web.

Instead of parsing protocol headers, think of the packet as an array of octets in memory. As an example, consider IPv4†. To be an IPv4 datagram, the Ethernet type field (located in array positions 12 through 13) must contain *0x0800*. The IPv4 protocol field, located at position 23 must contain *6* (the protocol number for TCP). The destination port field in the TCP header must contain *80*. To know the exact position of the TCP header, we must know the size of the IP header. Therefore, we check the header length octet of the IPv4 header. If the octet contains *0x45*, the TCP destination port number will be found in array positions 36 through 37.

†We use IPv4 to keep the examples small; although the concepts apply to IPv6, extension headers complicate the details.

As another example, consider *Voice over IP* (*VoIP*) traffic that uses the Real-Time Transport Protocol (*RTP*). Because RTP is not assigned a specific UDP port, vendors employ a heuristic to determine whether a given packet carries RTP traffic: check the Ethernet and IP headers to verify that a packet carries UDP, and then examine the octets at a known offset in the RTP message to verify that the value in the packet matches the value expected by a known codec.

Observe that all the checks described in the preceding paragraphs only require array lookup. That is, the lookup mechanism merely checks to verify that location *X* contains value *Y*, location *Z* contains value *W*, and so on — the mechanism does not need to understand any of the protocol headers or the meaning of octets. Furthermore, observe that the lookup scheme crosses multiple layers of the protocol stack.

We use the term *classifier* to describe a mechanism that uses the lookup approach described above, and we say that the result is a packet *classification*. In practice, a classification mechanism usually takes a list of classification *rules* and applies them until a match is found. For example, a manager might specify three rules: send all web traffic to MPLS path *1*, send all FTP traffic to MPLS path *2*, and send all VPN traffic to MPLS path *3*.

17.4 Layering When Classification Is Used

If classification crosses protocol layers, how does it relate to our earlier layering diagrams? We think of a classification layer as an extra layer that has been squeezed between the Network Interface layer and IP. Once a packet arrives, the packet passes from the Network Interface module to the classification layer. All packets proceed to the classifier; no demultiplexing occurs before classification. If any of the classification rules match the packet, the classification layer follows the rule. Otherwise, the packet proceeds up the traditional protocol stack. For example, Figure 17.3 illustrates layering when classification is used to send some packets across MPLS paths.

Interestingly, the classification layer can subsume the first level of demultiplexing. That is, instead of only classifying packets for MPLS paths, the classifier can be configured with additional rules that check the type field in a frame for IP, ARP, RARP, and so on.

17.5 Classification Hardware And Network Switches

The description above describes a classification mechanism that is implemented in software — an extra layer is added to a software protocol stack that classifies frames once they arrive at a router. Classification is also implemented in hardware. In particular, Ethernet switches and other packet processing hardware devices contain classification hardware that allows packet forwarding to proceed at high speed. The next sections explain hardware classification mechanisms. Chapter 28 continues the discussion by showing how Software Defined Networking technologies use the classification mechanisms in switches to achieve traffic engineering at high speed.

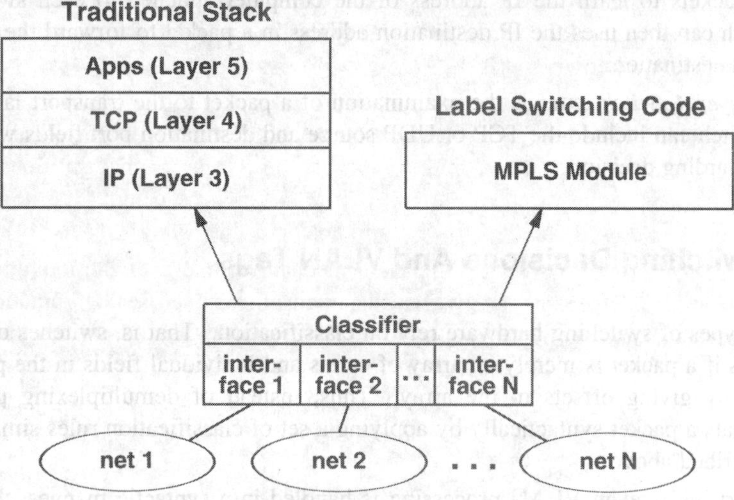

Figure 17.3 Layering when a router uses classification to select MPLS paths.

We think of network devices, such as switches, as being divided into broad categories by the level of protocol headers they examine and the consequent level of functionality they provide:

- Layer 2 switching
- Layer 2 VLAN switching
- Layer 3 switching
- Layer 4 switching

Chapter 2 describes Layer 2 switches. In essence, such a switch examines the MAC source address in each incoming frame to learn the MAC address of the computer that is attached to each port. Once a switch learns the MAC addresses of all the attached computers, the switch can use the destination MAC address in each frame to make a forwarding decision. If the frame is unicast, the switch only sends one copy of the frame on the port to which the specified computer is attached. For a frame destined to the broadcast or a multicast address, the switch delivers a copy of the frame to all ports.

A *VLAN switch* permits the manager to assign each port to a specific VLAN. VLAN switches extend forwarding in one minor way: instead of sending broadcasts and multicasts to all ports on the switch, a VLAN switch consults the VLAN configuration and only sends to ports on the same VLAN as the source.

A *Layer 3 switch* acts like a combination of a VLAN switch and a router. Instead of only using the Ethernet header when forwarding a frame, the switch can look at fields in the IP header. In particular, the switch watches the source IP address in incoming packets to learn the IP address of the computer attached to each switch port. The switch can then uses the IP destination address in a packet to forward the packet to its correct destination.

A *Layer 4 switch* extends the examination of a packet to the transport layer. That is, the switch can include the TCP or UDP source and destination port fields when making a forwarding decision.

17.6 Switching Decisions And VLAN Tags

All types of switching hardware rely on classification. That is, switches operate on packets as if a packet is merely an array of octets and individual fields in the packet are specified by giving offsets in the array. Thus, instead of demultiplexing packets, a switch treats a packet syntactically by applying a set of classification rules similar to the rules described above.

Surprisingly, even VLAN processing is handled in a syntactic manner. Instead of merely keeping VLAN information in a separate data structure that holds meta information, the switch inserts an extra field in an incoming packet and places the VLAN number of the packet in the extra field. Because it is just another field, the classifier can reference the VLAN number just like any other header field.

We use the term *VLAN tag* to refer to the extra field inserted in a packet. The tag contains the VLAN number that the manager assigned to the port over which the frame arrived. For Ethernet, IEEE standard *802.1Q* specifies placing the VLAN tag field after the MAC source address field. Figure 17.4 illustrates the format.

Destination Address	Source Address	VLAN Tag	Frame Type	Frame Payload (Data)
6 octets	6 octets	4 octets	2 octets	46–1500 octets . . .

Figure 17.4 Illustration of an IEEE 802.1Q VLAN tag field inserted in an Ethernet frame after the frame arrives at a VLAN switch.

A VLAN tag is only used internally — once the switch has selected an output port and is ready to transmit the frame, the tag is removed. Thus, when computers attached to a switch send and receive frames, the frames do not contain a VLAN tag.

An exception can be made to the rule: a manager can configure one or more ports on a switch to leave VLAN tags in frames when sending the frame. The purpose is to allow two or more switches to be configured to operate as a single, large switch. That is, the switches can share a set of VLANs — a manager can configure each VLAN to include ports on one or both of the switches.

17.7 Classification Hardware

We can think of hardware in a switch as being divided into three main components: a classifier, a set of units that perform actions, and a management component that controls the overall operation. Figure 17.5 illustrates the overall organization and the flow of packets.

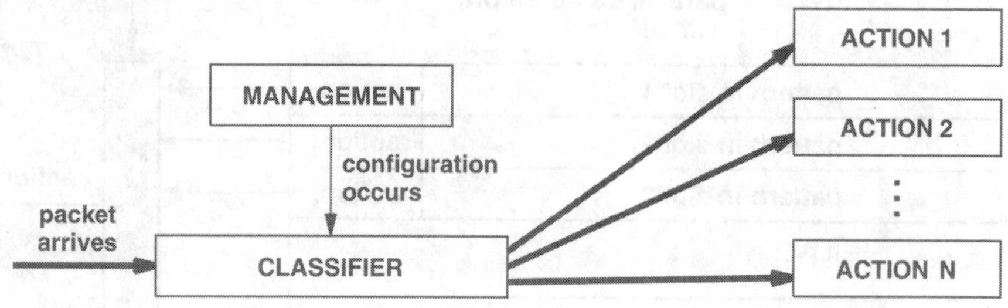

Figure 17.5 The conceptual organization of hardware in a switch.

As the figure indicates, the classifier provides the high-speed data path that packets follow. A packet arrives, and the classifier uses the rules that have been configured to choose an action. The management module usually consists of a general-purpose processor that runs management software. A network manager can interact with the management module to configure the switch, in which case the management module can create or modify the set of rules the classifier follows.

As with MPLS classification, a switch must be able to handle two types of traffic: transit traffic and traffic destined for the switch itself. For example, to provide management or routing functions, a switch may have a local TCP/IP protocol stack, and packets destined for the switch must be passed to the local stack. Therefore, one of the actions a classifier takes may be *pass packet to the local stack for demultiplexing*.

17.8 High-Speed Classification And TCAM

Modern switches can allow each interface to operate at 10 Gbps. At 10 Gbps, a frame only takes 1.2 microseconds to arrive, and a switch usually has many interfaces. A conventional processor cannot handle classification at such speeds. So the question arises: how does a hardware classifier achieve high speed? The answer lies in a hardware technology known as *Ternary Content Addressable Memory (TCAM)*.

TCAM uses parallelism to achieve high speed — instead of testing one field of a packet at a given time, TCAM checks all fields simultaneously. Furthermore, TCAM performs multiple checks at the same time. To understand how TCAM works, think of a packet as a string of bits. We imagine TCAM hardware as having two parts: one part holds the bits from a packet and the other part is an array of values that will be compared to the packet. Entries in the array are known as *slots*. Figure 17.6 illustrates the idea.

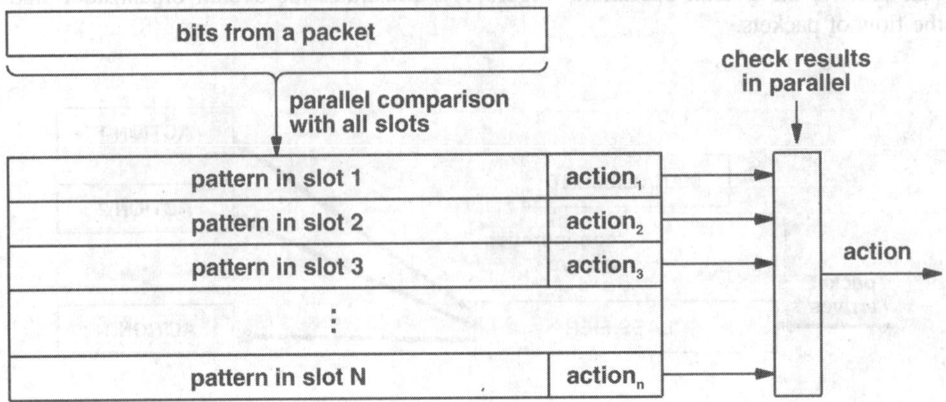

Figure 17.6 The conceptual organization of a high-speed hardware classifier that uses TCAM technology.

In the figure, each slot contains two parts. The first part consists of hardware that compares the bits from the packet to the pattern stored in the slot. The second part stores a value that specifies an action to be taken if the pattern matches the packet. If a match occurs, the slot hardware passes the action to the component that checks all the results and announces an answer.

One of the most important details concerns the way TCAM handles multiple matches. In essence, the output circuitry selects one match and ignores the others. That is, if multiple slots each pass an action to the output circuit, the circuit only accepts one and passes the action as the output of the classification. For example, the hardware may choose the lowest slot that matches. In any case, the *action* that the TCAM announces corresponds to the action from one of the matching slots.

The figure indicates that a slot holds a *pattern* rather than an exact value. Instead of merely comparing each bit in the pattern to the corresponding bit in the packet, the hardware performs a pattern match. The adjective *ternary* is used because each bit position in a pattern can have three possible values: a one, a zero, or a "don't care." When a slot compares its pattern to the packet, the hardware only checks the one and zero bits in the pattern — the hardware ignores pattern bits that contain "don't care." Thus, a pattern can specify exact values for some fields in a packet header and omit other fields.

To understand TCAM pattern matching, consider a pattern that identifies IP packets. Identifying such packets is easy because an Ethernet frame that carries an IP datagram will have the value 0x0800 in the Ethernet type field. Furthermore, the type field occupies a fixed position in the frame: bits 96 through 111. Thus, we can create a pattern that starts with 96 'don't care" bits (to cover the Ethernet destination and source MAC addresses) followed by sixteen bits with the binary value 0000100000000000 (the binary equivalent of 0x0800) to cover the type field. All remaining bit positions in the pattern will be "don't care." Figure 17.7 illustrates the pattern and example packets.

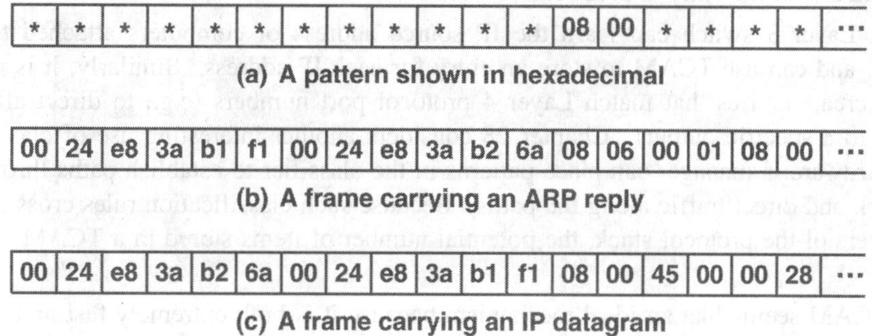

Figure 17.7 (a) A pattern in a TCAM with asterisks indicating "don't care", (b) an ARP packet that does not match the pattern, and (c) an IP datagram that matches the pattern.

Although a TCAM hardware slot has one position for each bit, the figure does not display individual bits. Instead, each box corresponds to one octet, and the value in a box is a hexadecimal value that corresponds to eight bits. We use hexadecimal simply because binary strings are too long to fit comfortably onto a printed page.

17.9 The Size Of A TCAM

A question arises: how large is a TCAM? The question can be divided into two important aspects:

- The number of bits in a slot
- The total number of slots

Bits per slot. The number of bits per slot depends on the type of Ethernet switch. A basic switch uses the destination MAC address to classify a packet. Therefore, the TCAM in a basic switch only needs 48 bit positions. A VLAN switch needs 128 bit positions to cover the VLAN tag as Figure 17.4 illustrates†. A Layer 3 switch must have sufficient bit positions to cover the IP header as well as the Ethernet header.

Total slots. The total number of TCAM slots determines the maximum number of patterns a switch can hold. The TCAM in a typical switch has 32,000 entries. When a switch learns the MAC address of a computer that has been plugged into a port, the switch can store a pattern for the address. For example, if a computer with MAC ad-

†Figure 17.4 can be found on page 374.

dress X is plugged into port 29, the switch can create a pattern in which destination address bits match X and the action is *send packet to output port 29*.

A switch can also use patterns to control broadcasting. When a manager configures a VLAN, the switch can add an entry for the VLAN broadcast. For example, if a manager configures VLAN 9, an entry can be added in which the destination address bits are all 1s (i.e., the Ethernet broadcast address) and the VLAN tag is 9. The action associated with the entry is *broadcast on VLAN 9*.

A Layer 3 switch can learn the IP source address of computers attached to the switch, and can use TCAM to store an entry for each IP address. Similarly, it is possible to create entries that match Layer 4 protocol port numbers (e.g., to direct all web traffic to a specific output). Chapter 28 considers another interesting use of classification hardware: a manager can place patterns in the classifier to establish paths through a network and direct traffic along the paths. Because such classification rules cross multiple layers of the protocol stack, the potential number of items stored in a TCAM can be large.

TCAM seems like an ideal mechanism because it is both extremely fast and versatile. However, TCAM has a significant drawback: cost. In addition, because it operates in parallel, TCAM consumes much more energy than conventional memory. Therefore, designers minimize the amount of TCAM to keep costs and power consumption low.

17.10 Classification-Enabled Generalized Forwarding

Perhaps, the most significant advantage of a classification mechanism arises from the generalizations it enables. Because classification examines arbitrary fields in a packet before any demultiplexing occurs, cross-layer combinations are possible. For example, classification can specify that all packets from a given MAC address should be forwarded to a specific output port regardless of the packet type or the packet contents. In addition, classification can make forwarding decisions depend on the source address in a packet as well as the destination. An ISP can use source addresses to distinguish among customers. For example, an ISP can forward all packets with IP source address X along one path while forwarding packets with IP source address Y along another path, even if all the packets have the same destination address.

ISPs use the generality that classification offers to handle traffic engineering that is not usually available in a conventional protocol stack. In particular, classification allows ISPs to offer tiered services. An ISP can arrange to use both the type of traffic and the amount a customer pays when classifying packets. Once the packet has been classified, all packets with the same classification can be forwarded along the appropriate path.

17.11 Summary

Classification is a fundamental performance optimization that allows a packet processing system to cross layers of the protocol stack without demultiplexing. A classifier treats each packet as an array of bits and checks the contents of fields at specific locations in the array.

Classification is used with MPLS as well as in Ethernet switches. Most Ethernet switches implement classification in hardware; a hardware technology known as TCAM uses parallelism to perform classification at extremely high speed.

EXERCISES

17.1 Read about Ethernet switches and find the size of TCAM used.

17.2 If your site employs MPLS, make a list of the classification rules that are used and state the purpose of each.

17.3 If a Layer 2 switch has *P* ports that connect to computers, what is the maximum number of MAC destination addresses the switch needs to place in its classifier? Be careful because the answer is not obvious.

17.4 Write classification rules that send all VoIP traffic down MPLS path 1, web traffic down MPLS path 2, *ssh* traffic down MPLS path 3, and all other traffic down MPLS path 4.

17.5 A manager wants to send all multicast traffic down MPLS path 17 and all other traffic down MPLS path 18. What is the simplest set of classification rules that can be used?

17.6 Does your answer to the previous question change if a site uses both IPv4 and IPv6?

17.7 The text asserts that classification is needed to process packets that arrive at 10 Gbps because an Ethernet frame only takes 1.2 microseconds to arrive. How many bits are in the payload of such a frame?

17.8 In the previous problem, how many instructions can a high-speed processor execute in 1.2 microseconds?

17.9 On most networks, the smallest packets contain a TCP ACK traveling in an IPv4 datagram. How long does it take for such a frame to arrive?

Chapter Contents

18

Mobility And Mobile IP

18.1 Introduction

Previous chapters describe the IP addressing and forwarding schemes used with stationary computers and an IP addressing and forwarding scheme that uses network-based addressing.

This chapter considers technology that allows a portable computer to move from one network to another. We will see that the extension can work with wired or wireless networks, has versions that apply to IPv4 or IPv6, and retains backward compatibility with existing internet routing.

18.2 Mobility, Addressing, And Routing

In the broadest sense, the term *mobile computing* refers to a system that allows computers to move from one location to another. Although wireless technologies allow rapid and easy mobility, wireless access is not required — a traveler might carry a laptop computer and connect to a remote wired network (e.g., in a hotel).

The IP addressing scheme, which was designed and optimized for stationary hosts, makes mobility difficult. A prefix of each host address identifies the network to which the host attaches, and routers use the prefix to forward datagrams to the correct network for final delivery. As a result, moving a host to a new network requires one of two possible changes:

- The host's address must change.
- Datagram forwarding must change.

18.3 Mobility Via Host Address Change

The approach of changing a host's IP address is widely used in the global Internet and works well for slow, semi-permanent mobility. For example, consider a user who carries a computer to a coffee shop and stays for a while sipping coffee while using the shop's Wi-Fi connection. Or consider a traveler who carries a computer to a hotel room, works at the hotel for two days, and then returns home. As we will see in Chapter 22, such mobility is enabled with *dynamic address assignment*. In particular, IPv4 hosts use the DHCP protocol to obtain an IP address, and IPv6 hosts use the IPv6 Neighbor Discovery protocol to generate and verify a unique address.

Most operating systems perform address assignment automatically without informing the user. There are two conditions that trigger dynamic address acquisition. First, when it boots, an IPv4 host always runs DHCP and an IPv6 host generates a unicast address and validates uniqueness. Second, an operating system reassigns an address when it detects the loss and then reacquisition of network connectivity. Thus, if a portable computer remains running while it is moved from one Wi-Fi hotspot to another, the operating system will detect disconnection from the first Wi-Fi network and reconnection to the second.

Although it works well for casual users, changing a host's address has disadvantages. An address change breaks all ongoing transport layer connections. For example, a transport connection is used to watch a streaming video or to use a VPN. In each case, changing a host's IP address breaks all transport layer connections and causes the operating system to inform applications that are using the connections. An application can recover from connection loss by informing the user or by restarting the connection automatically. Even if an application restarts a connection, restarting may take time, which means a user may notice a disruption in service.

If a host offers network services (i.e., runs servers), changing an IP address has more severe consequences. Typically, each application that runs a service must be restarted. Furthermore, computers that run services are usually assigned a domain name. Thus, when the computer's IP address changes, the host's DNS entry must also be updated†. Of course, an arbitrary computer is not permitted to change a DNS entry, which means additional infrastructure is needed to authenticate DNS updates.

The point is:

> *Although dynamic address assignment enables a basic form of mobility that allows a user to move a host from one network to another, changing a host's address has the disadvantage of breaking transport layer connections.*

†Chapter 23 explains the *Domain Name System* (*DNS*).

18.4 Mobility Via Changes In Datagram Forwarding

Can we allow a host to retain its original IP address when it moves to a new network? In theory, the answer is yes — all we need to do is change forwarding tables in routers throughout the Internet so datagrams destined for the host will be forwarded to the new network. We could even create network hardware that detects the presence of new IP addresses and informs the routing system about their presence.

Unfortunately, the simplistic scheme described above is impractical because host-specific routing does not scale to the size of the global Internet. Internet routing only works because routing protocols exchange information about networks rather than hosts and because networks are stationary. That is, the total size of routing information is limited and the information is relatively static. If routing protocols are used to handle hosts instead of networks, the amount of routing traffic becomes overwhelming, even if only a small fraction of hosts change location each day. The point is:

> *We cannot use host-specific routing to handle mobility because the global Internet does not have sufficient capacity to propagate host-specific routes that change frequently.*

18.5 The Mobile IP Technology

The IETF devised a technology to permit IP mobility; versions are available for both IPv4 and IPv6. Officially named *IP mobility support* and popularly called *mobile IP*†, the technology provides a compromise. Mobile IP has the advantages of not changing a host's IP address and not requiring host-specific routing, but the disadvantage that datagram forwarding can be inefficient. The general characteristics include:

- *Transparency.* Mobility is transparent to applications, transport layer protocols, and routers. In particular, a TCP connection can survive a change in location. The only proviso is that if the transition takes a long time (i.e., a host remains disconnected from all networks for a while), the connection cannot be used during the transition. The reason is that TCP will timeout the connection after two maximum segment lifetimes.

- *Backward Compatibility.* A host using mobile IPv4 can interoperate with stationary hosts that run conventional IPv4 software as well as with other mobile IPv4 hosts. Similarly, a host using mobile IPv6 can interoperate with stationary hosts that use IPv6 or other mobile IPv6 hosts. That is, a mobile host uses the same IP address scheme as a stationary host.

- *Scalability.* The solution permits mobility across the global Internet.

- *Security.* Mobile IP can ensure that all messages are authenticated (i.e., to prevent an arbitrary computer from impersonating a mobile host).

†When it is necessary to distinguish, we use the terms *mobile IPv4* and *mobile IPv6*

- *Macro Mobility.* Rather than attempting to handle continuous, high-speed movement, such as a cell phone in a car, mobile IP focuses on the problem of long-duration moves (e.g., a user who takes a portable device on a business trip).

18.6 Overview Of Mobile IP Operation

How can mobile IP allow a host to retain its address without requiring routers to learn host-specific routes? Mobile IP solves the problem by allowing a host to hold two addresses simultaneously: a permanent and fixed *primary address* that applications use, and a *secondary address* that is temporary and associated with a particular network to which the host is attached. A temporary address is only valid for one location; when it moves to another location, a mobile host must obtain a new temporary address.

A mobile host is assumed to have a permanent *home* in the Internet, and a mobile host's primary address is the address that the host has been assigned on its home network. Furthermore, to support mobility, a host's home network must include a special network system known as a *home agent.* Typically, home agent software runs in a conventional router, but that is not strictly necessary. In essence, a home agent agrees to intercept each datagram that arrives for the host's permanent address and forward the datagram to the host's current location (later sections discuss details).

How does a home agent know the current location of a mobile host? After it moves to a *foreign* network, a mobile host must obtain a secondary (i.e., temporary) address, and must then contact its home agent to inform the agent about the current location. We say that the mobile host *registers* a secondary address with its home agent.

The secondary address is only valid while a mobile host remains at a given location. If the host moves again, it must obtain a new secondary address for the new location and inform the home agent of the change. Finally, when a mobile host returns home, it must contact the home agent to *deregister*, meaning that the agent will stop intercepting datagrams. In fact, a mobile host can choose to deregister before it returns home (e.g., when it leaves a remote location).

18.7 Overhead And Frequency Of Change

We said that mobile IP technology is designed to support *macro mobility.* In particular, mobile IP is not intended for the continuous, high-speed network change associated with a smart phone being used in a car as it moves down a highway. Thus, we think of a traveler using mobile IP once they reach a new destination rather than at each point along the trip.

The reason that mobile IP does not support rapid changes should be obvious: overhead. Networks in the Internet do not monitor devices or track their movements. Most important, network systems do not coordinate to perform hand-off. Instead, each mobile device must monitor its network connection and detect when it has moved from one network to another. When it does detect a change, the mobile device must communicate across the foreign network to request a secondary address for the network. Once it has obtained a secondary address, the mobile device must communicate with its home agent to register the address and establish forwarding. Note that a mobile device can be arbitrarily far from its home network, which means that registration may involve communication across arbitrary distance. The point is:

> *Because it requires considerable overhead after each change, mobile IP is intended for situations in which a host moves infrequently and remains at a given location for a relatively long period of time (e.g., hours or days).*

The details of addressing, registration, and forwarding will become clear as we understand the technology. We first consider mobility for IPv4, which illustrates the basic concepts, and then consider why so much additional complexity is needed to support mobile IPv6†.

18.8 Mobile IPv4 Addressing

When using IPv4, a mobile host's primary or *home address* is a conventional IPv4 address that is assigned and administered as usual. Applications on a mobile host always use the primary address; they remain unaware of any other address. The host's secondary address, which is also known as a *care-of address*, is a temporary address that is used only by the mobile IP software on the host. A care-of address is only valid for a given foreign network.

Mobile IPv4 supports two types of care-of addresses that differ in the method by which the address is obtained and in the way datagram forwarding occurs:

- Co-located
- Foreign Agent

IPv4 Co-located Care-of Address. A co-located address allows a mobile computer to handle all forwarding and datagram tunneling without any assistance from hosts or routers on the foreign network. In fact, from the point of view of systems on the foreign network, the mobile host appears to be a conventional host that follows the normal pattern of obtaining a local address, using the address, and then relinquishing the address. The temporary address is assigned via DHCP like any other address.

The chief advantage of a co-located address arises from its universal applicability. Because the mobile host handles all registration and communication details, no additional facilities are required on the foreign network. Thus, a mobile host can use co-located care-of addressing on an arbitrary network, including a conventional Wi-Fi hotspot, such as those found in a coffee shop.

†The standard for IPv6 mobility, RFC 6275, comprises 169 pages, defines many message types, and gives many rules for protocol operation.

There are two disadvantages of the co-located approach. First, co-location requires extra software on a mobile host. Second, the foreign network cannot distinguish a host that uses mobile IP from an arbitrary visitor. We will see that the inability to identify a host as using mobile IP can impact forwarding.

IPv4 Foreign Agent Care-of Address. The second type of temporary address allows a foreign network to know whether a host is using mobile IP because a system on the foreign network participates in all forwarding. The system is known as a *foreign agent*, and a temporary address used with the scheme is known as a *foreign agent care-of address*. To use the foreign agent approach, a mobile host does not obtain a local address itself. In particular, a mobile host does *not* use DHCP. Instead, when a mobile host arrives at a foreign site, the mobile host uses a discovery protocol to obtain the identity of a foreign agent. The mobile host then communicates with the agent to learn the care-of address to use. Surprisingly, a foreign agent does not need to assign each mobile host a unique address. Instead, when using a foreign agent, the care-of address is the agent's IPv4 address. The agent then delivers incoming datagrams to the correct visiting mobile host.

18.9 IPv4 Foreign Agent Discovery

The process of IPv4 *foreign agent discovery* uses the ICMP *router discovery* mechanism in which each router periodically sends an ICMP *router advertisement* message, and allows a host to send an ICMP *router solicitation* to prompt for an advertisement†. A router that acts as a foreign agent appends a *mobility agent extension*‡ to each message; the extension specifies the network prefix, which a mobile host uses to determine that it has moved to a new network. Interestingly, mobility extensions do not use a separate ICMP message type. Instead, a mobile extension is present if the datagram length specified in the IP header is greater than the length specified in the ICMP router discovery message. Figure 18.1 illustrates the extension format.

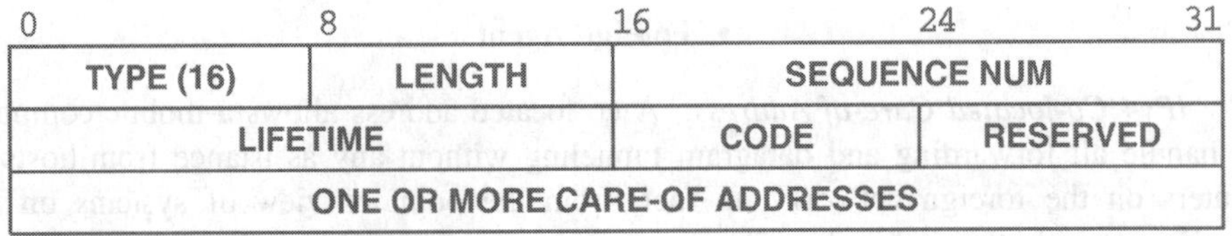

Figure 18.1 The format of an IPv4 *mobility agent advertisement extension* message when sent by a foreign agent. The extension is appended to an ICMP router advertisement.

Each extension message begins with a 1-octet *TYPE* field followed by a 1-octet *LENGTH* field. The *LENGTH* field specifies the size of the extension message in octets, excluding the *TYPE* and *LENGTH* octets. The *LIFETIME* field specifies the max-

†A mobile host can also multicast to the *all agents group* (*224.0.0.11*).

‡A mobility agent also appends a *prefix extension* to each message.

imum amount of time in seconds that the agent is willing to accept registration requests, with all 1s indicating *infinity*. Field *SEQUENCE NUM* specifies a sequence number for the message to allow a recipient to determine when a message is lost, and the last field lists the address of at least one foreign agent. Each bit in the *CODE* field defines a specific feature of the agent as listed in Figure 18.2.

Bit	Meaning
7	Registration with an agent is required even when using a co-located care-of address
6	The agent is busy and is not accepting registrations
5	Agent functions as a home agent
4	Agent functions as a foreign agent
3	Agent uses minimal encapsulation
2	Agent uses GRE-style encapsulation
1	Unused (must be zero)
0	Agent supports reversed tunneling

Figure 18.2 Bits of the *CODE* field of an IPv4 mobility agent advertisement, with bit 0 being the least-significant bit of the octet.

As the figure indicates, bit *2* and bit *3* specify the encapsulation used when a mobile host communicates with the foreign agent. *Minimal encapsulation* is a standard for IP-in-IP tunneling that abbreviates fields from the original header to save space. *Generic Route Encapsulation* (*GRE*) is a standard that allows an arbitrary protocol to be encapsulated; IP-in-IP is one particular case.

18.10 IPv4 Registration

Before it can receive datagrams at a foreign location, a mobile host must be registered with its home agent. If it is using a foreign agent care-of address, the mobile host must be registered with a foreign agent. The *registration* protocol allows a host to:

- Register with an agent on the foreign network, if needed
- Register with its home agent to request forwarding
- Renew a registration that is due to expire
- Deregister after returning home

If it obtains a co-located care-of address, a mobile host performs registration directly; the co-located care-of address is used in all communication with the mobile's home agent. If it obtains a foreign agent care-of address, a mobile host allows the foreign agent to register with the home agent on the host's behalf.

18.11 IPv4 Registration Message Format

All registration messages are sent via UDP; agents use port 434. A registration message begins with a set of fixed-size fields followed by variable-length *extensions*. Each request is required to contain a *mobile-home authentication extension* that allows the home agent to verify the mobile's identity. Figure 18.3 illustrates the message format.

0 — 8	8 — 16	16 — 31
TYPE (1 or 3)	FLAGS/CODE	LIFETIME
HOME ADDRESS		
HOME AGENT		
CARE-OF-ADDRESS (request only)		
IDENTIFICATION		
EXTENSIONS . . .		

Figure 18.3 The format of an IPv4 *mobile IP registration request* or *mobile IP reply* message.

The *TYPE* field specifies whether the message is a request (*1*) or a reply (*3*). The *LIFETIME* field specifies the number of seconds the registration is valid (a zero requests immediate deregistration, and all 1s specifies an infinite lifetime). The *HOME ADDRESS*, *HOME AGENT*, and *CARE-OF ADDRESS* fields specify the two IP addresses of the mobile and the address of its home agent, and the *IDENTIFICATION* field contains a 64-bit number generated by the mobile that is used to match requests with incoming replies and to prevent the mobile from accepting old messages. Bits of the *FLAGS/CODE* field are used as a result code in a registration reply message and to specify forwarding details in a registration request, such as whether the registration corresponds to an additional (i.e., new) address request and the encapsulation that the agent should use when forwarding datagrams to the mobile.

18.12 Communication With An IPv4 Foreign Agent

We said that a foreign agent can assign one of its IPv4 addresses for use as a care-of address. The consequence is that the mobile will not have a unique address on the foreign network. The question becomes: how can a foreign agent and a mobile host communicate over a network if the mobile does not have a valid IP address on the network? Communication requires relaxing the rules for IP addressing and using an alternative scheme for address binding: when a mobile host sends to a foreign agent, the mobile is allowed to use its home address as an IP source address, and when a foreign agent sends a datagram to a mobile, the agent is allowed to use the mobile's home address as an IP destination address. To avoid sending an invalid ARP request, a foreign agent records the mobile's hardware address when the first request arrives and uses the hardware address to send a reply. Thus, although it does not use ARP, the foreign agent can send datagrams to a mobile via hardware unicast. We can summarize:

> *If a mobile does not have a unique foreign address, a foreign agent must use the mobile's home address for communication. Instead of relying on ARP for address binding, the agent records the mobile's hardware address when a request arrives and uses the recorded information to supply the necessary binding.*

18.13 IPv6 Mobility Support

Experience with mobile IPv4 and the design of the IPv6 protocol led the IETF to make significant changes between mobile IPv4 and mobile IPv6. The IETF intended to integrate mobility support more tightly into the protocol, compensate for some of the problems and weaknesses that had been discovered with mobile IPv4, and stimulate use. The differences can be characterized as follows:

- IPv6 does not use a foreign agent or a foreign agent care-of address. Instead, an IPv6 mobile host uses a co-located care-of address and handles all communication with a home agent directly.
- Because it permits a host to have multiple IP addresses, IPv6 makes it easy for a mobile host to have a home address and a co-located care-of address simultaneously.
- Because IPv6 does not broadcast a request to discover a home agent, an IPv6 host only receives a response from one agent. (IPv4 can receive responses from each agent on the home network.)
- Unlike communication between a mobile IPv4 host and a foreign agent, mobile IPv6 does not depend on link-layer forwarding.
- As we will see later, the IPv6 routing extension header makes forwarding to an IPv6 mobile host more efficient than forwarding to an IPv4 mobile host.
- An IPv6 mobile host does not need a foreign agent because the host can generate a local address and communicate with a router on the foreign network.

18.14 Datagram Transmission, Reception, And Tunneling

Once it has registered, a mobile host on a foreign network can communicate with an arbitrary computer, *X*. There are two possibilities. In the simplest case, the mobile host creates and sends an outgoing datagram that has computer *X*'s IP address in the destination address field and the mobile's home address in the IP source address field. The outgoing datagram follows a shortest path from the mobile host to destination *X*.

Technically, using a home address as a source address violates the TCP/IP standards because a datagram will be transmitted by a host on network *N*, and the IP source address in the datagram will not match the IP prefix for network *N*. If a network manager chooses to apply strict rules, the manager may configure routers to prohibit transmissions where the source address does not match the local network. How can such restrictions be overcome? Mobile IPv4 uses a two-step technique known as *tunneling*. In essence, the mobile host uses tunneling to send an outgoing datagram back to its home agent, and the home agent transmits the datagram as if the mobile host were located on the home network.

To use tunneling, a mobile host encapsulates an outgoing datagram, D_1, in another datagram, D_2. The source address on D_2 is the mobile's care-of address and the destination is the address of the mobile's home agent. When it receives a tunneled datagram, the home agent extracts the inner datagram, D_1, and forwards D_1 to its destination. Both steps use valid addresses. The transmission from the mobile host to the home agent has a source address on the foreign network. The inner datagram, which travels from the home agent to destination *X*, has a source address on the home network.

For mobile IPv4, a reply will not follow the shortest path directly to the mobile. Instead, a reply will always travel to the mobile's home network first. The home agent, which has learned the mobile's location from the registration, intercepts the reply and uses tunneling to deliver the reply to the mobile. That is, when it receives a datagram destined for a mobile host, a home agent also uses tunneling — it encapsulates the reply in another datagram, D_3, uses the mobile's care-of address as the destination for D_3, and sends the encapsulated datagram to the mobile. Figure 18.4 illustrates the path of a reply from a computer, *D*, to a mobile host, *M*.

We can summarize:

> *Because a mobile uses its home address as a source address when communicating with an arbitrary destination, each IPv4 reply is forwarded to the mobile's home network, where an agent intercepts the datagram, encapsulates it in another datagram, and forwards it either directly to the mobile or to the foreign agent the mobile is using.*

Mobile IPv6 uses an interesting optimization to avoid inefficient routes. Before it communicates with a destination *D*, a mobile host informs its home agent. The host then includes a mobility header in datagrams it sends. Destination *D* can communicate with the home agent, verify the mobile host's current location, and use an IPv6 route header to direct the datagram to the mobile host's current location.

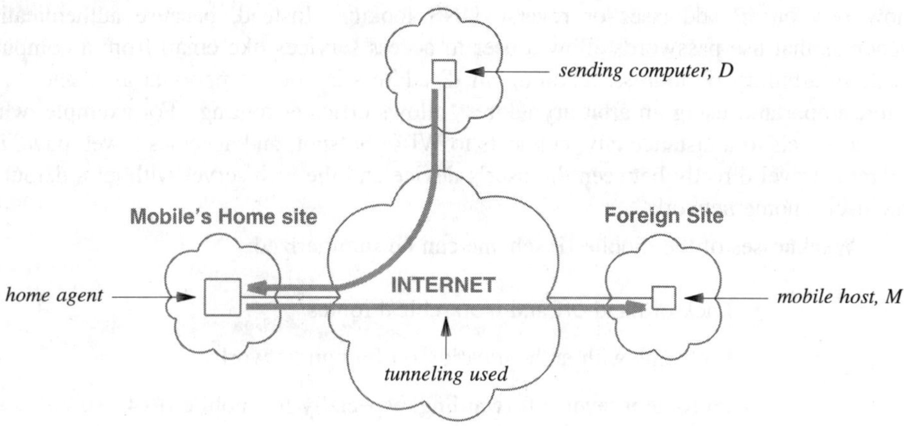

Figure 18.4 The path a reply takes from computer D to mobile host M when the mobile host is connected to a foreign network.

Of course, the exchanges among a mobile host, home agent, and destination must be secure. Furthermore, an exchange must occur for each destination. Therefore, the entire procedure entails considerable overhead, and is only suitable for situations in which a mobile remains attached to a given foreign network for an extended time and communicates with a given destination extensively. The point is:

> *To optimize reply forwarding, IPv6 makes it possible for a destination to learn a mobile host's current location and send datagrams directly to the mobile without going through a home agent; because route optimization requires several message exchanges, it is only useful for mobiles that move infrequently and tend to communicate with a given destination extensively.*

18.15 Assessment Of IP Mobility And Unsolved Problems

Despite the best intentions of the IETF, mobile IP has not been an overwhelming success. One reason for the lack of interest has arisen from a shift in the type of mobility that users enjoy. When IP mobility was envisioned, mobility was limited to bulky laptop computers — a user could transport a laptop computer to a remote site and then use the computer. Now, many mobile users have smart phones that allow continuous, online mobility.

Two more influences have further conspired to discourage the use of mobile IP. First, VPN technology (covered in the next chapter) was invented. A VPN allows a remote device to retain a home address and have complete access to its home network *as if the remote device is attached directly to its home network.* Second, few applications now rely on IP addresses or reverse DNS lookup. Instead, because authentication schemes that use passwords allow a user to access services like email from a computer with an arbitrary IP address, retaining an IP address is not as important as it once was. More important: using an arbitrary address allows efficient routing. For example, when a user travels to a distance city, connects to Wi-Fi hotspot, and accesses a web page, datagrams travel directly between the user's device and the web server without a detour to the user's home network.

Weaknesses of the mobile IP scheme can be summarized:

- Lack of hand-off and hierarchical routes
- Problems with authentication on foreign networks
- Inefficient reverse forwarding, especially for mobile IPv4
- Duplicate address detection in mobile IPv6
- Communication with hosts on the mobile's home network

The next sections consider each of these topics in more detail.

18.15.1 Lack Of Hand-Off And Hierarchical Routes

When they thought of mobility, the designers envisioned portable computers being used in remote locations. Consequently, mobile IP does not behave like a cellular system. It does not have facilities for high-speed hand-off among local cell towers, nor does it provide a system of hierarchical routing that could restrict the scope of route changes during migration from an access network to an adjacent access network.

18.15.2 Problems With Authentication On Foreign Networks

Although some foreign networks permit unrestricted access, many do not. In particular, networks often require a user to authenticate themselves before access will be granted. For example, a hotel might require a guest to enter a room number and last name before the guest is granted access. Typically, authentication requires the user to obtain an IP address and then use the address to launch a web browser. The hotel intercepts the web request, and displays an authentication page for the user. Once authentication has been completed, the user's device is granted access to the global Internet.

Mobile IP cannot handle web-based access authentication for two reasons. First, mobile IP always begins by registering with a home agent. A remote network that requires authentication will not forward packets to the home agent until authentication completes. Second, mobile IP specifies that applications must always use the mobile host's home address. Thus, even if the user launches a web browser, the browser will attempt to use an IP address from the home network, and the authentication mechanism will reject the connection.

18.15.3 Inefficient Reverse Forwarding, Especially For Mobile IPv4

As we have seen, a reply sent to an IPv4 mobile host will always be forwarded to the mobile's home network first and then to the mobile's current location. The problem is especially severe because computer communication exhibits *spatial locality of reference* — a mobile host visiting a foreign network tends to communicate with computers on the foreign network. To understand why spatial locality is a problem, consider Figure 18.5.

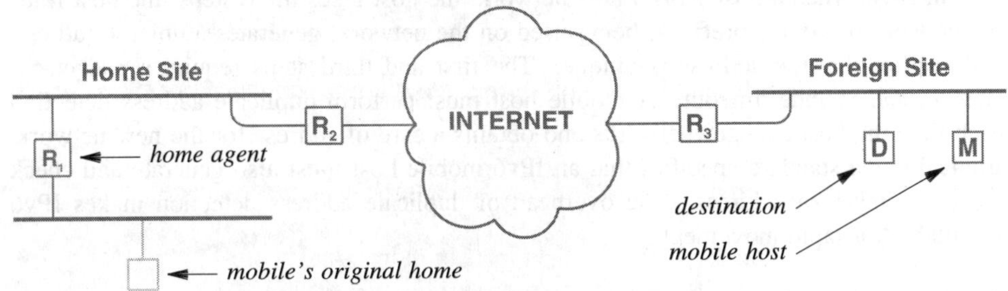

Figure 18.5 A topology in which mobile IPv4 routing is incredibly inefficient. When a mobile host, *M*, communicates with a local destination, *D*, replies from *D* travel across the Internet to the mobile's home agent, R_1, and then back to the mobile host.

In the figure, mobile *M* has moved from its home network to a foreign network. The mobile has registered with its home agent, router R_1, and the home agent has agreed to forward datagrams. When the mobile host communicates with destination *D*, which is located at the same site as the mobile, replies sent from *D* to *M* follow a path through R_3, across the Internet to the mobile's home network, and are then tunneled back across the Internet to the mobile host. That is, a datagram sent between two adjacent computers crosses the Internet twice. Because crossing the Internet can take orders of magnitude longer than local delivery, the situation described above is sometimes called the *two-crossing problem*. If destination *D* is not on the same network as the mobile, a slightly less severe version of the problem occurs which is known as *triangle forwarding* or *dog-leg forwarding*.

If a site knows that a given mobile host will visit for a long time and expects the mobile host to interact with local computers, the network manager can install host-specific routes to avoid inefficient forwarding. Each router at the site must have a host-specific route for the visiting mobile host. The disadvantage of such an arrangement arises from the lack of automated updates: when the mobile host leaves the site, the manager must manually remove the host-specific routes or the host will be unreachable from computers at the site. We can summarize:

> *Mobile IP introduces a routing inefficiency known as the two-crossing problem that occurs when a visiting mobile communicates with a computer at or near the foreign site. Each datagram sent to the mobile travels across the Internet to the mobile's home agent which then forwards the datagram back to the foreign site. Eliminating the inefficiency requires propagation of a host-specific route.*

18.15.4 Duplicate Address Detection In Mobile IPv6

In IPv6, when a host joins a new network, the host takes three steps: the host finds the network prefix (or prefixes) being used on the network, generates a unicast address, and verifies that the address is unique. The first and third steps require a packet exchange, and include timeout. A mobile host must perform duplicate address detection each time the host changes networks and obtains a care-of address for the new network. Ironically, the standard specifies that an IPv6 mobile host must also generate and check a unique link-local address. The overhead of duplicate address detection makes IPv6 unsuitable for rapid movement.

18.15.5 Communication With Hosts On The Mobile's Home Network

Another interesting problem arises when a computer on the mobile's home network attempts to communicate with a mobile that is visiting a foreign network. We said that when a mobile computer is currently away from home, its home agent intercepts all datagrams that arrive at the home site destined for the mobile. Intercepting datagrams that arrive at the site is relatively straightforward: a network manager chooses to run home agent software on the router that connects the home site to the rest of the Internet.

A special case arises, however, when a host on a mobile's home network sends a datagram to the mobile. Because IP specifies direct delivery over the local network, the sender will not forward the datagram through a router. Instead, an IPv4 sender will use ARP to find the mobile's hardware address, and an IPv6 host will use neighbor discovery. In either case, the host will encapsulate the datagram in a frame and transmit the frame directly to the mobile.

If a mobile has moved to a foreign network, hosts and routers on the home network cannot send datagrams directly to the mobile. Therefore, the home agent must arrange to capture and forward all datagrams destined for the mobile, including those sent by local hosts. An IPv4 home agent uses a form of *proxy ARP* to handle local interception: whenever a computer on the home network ARPs for an IPv4 mobile host that has moved to a foreign network, the home agent answers the ARP request and supplies its own hardware address. That is, local IPv4 hosts are tricked into forwarding any datagram destined for the mobile to the home agent; the home agent can then forward the datagram to the mobile on the foreign network.

For IPv6, local transmission poses a greater problem that requires additional protocol support. In particular, computers on an IPv6 network use the Neighbor Discovery Protocol (NDP) to know which neighbors are present. If a mobile leaves the home network, other computers using NDP will quickly declare that the mobile is unreachable†. Therefore, mobile IP must arrange a way that hosts on the home network can be informed when a mobile host has moved to another location.

To solve the problem, mobile IPv6 modifies neighbor discovery. In essence, a home agent acts as a *proxy* when a mobile is away. The home agent informs computers on the local network that a specific host is mobile. If they encounter datagrams intended for the mobile host, other computers on the home network forward the datagrams accordingly. When the mobile returns home, the forwarding must be removed.

18.16 Alternative Identifier-Locator Separation Technologies

The fundamental problem a designer faces when adding mobility support to IP arises from a fundamental principle of IP addressing: the prefix in an IP address ties the address to a specific network. That is, an IP address serves as a *locator*. The advantage of a locator lies in an efficient routing system that forwards each datagram to the correct destination network. The disadvantage of a locator arises from its inability to accommodate movement: if the location changes, the address must change. Ethernet MAC addressing illustrates the alternative: an Ethernet address is a globally-unique value, but does not contain any information about where the computer is located. That is, an address serves as a unique *identifier*. The disadvantage of using an identifier arises from routing inefficiency: host-specific routes are needed.

How can one design an addressing scheme that combines the advantages of both locators and identifiers? We have seen the fundamental idea: a host address needs two conceptual parts. The first part is a globally-unique identifier that never changes and the second is a locator that changes when the host moves to a new network. In mobile IP, the two conceptual pieces are represented by two independent IP addresses. That is a host stores two addresses, and uses its home address as an identifier and its care-of address as a locator.

Several proposals have been created to formalize the idea of an *identifier-locator pair*. The approaches differ in the size of the two items, the way values are assigned, whether the two parts are viewed as bit fields in a single large address or as two separate items, and whether both parts are visible to applications. For example, Cisco Systems defined the *Locator/ID Separation Protocol* (*LISP*), which uses a pair of IP addresses similar to the way mobile IP uses addresses. The IETF has defined a protocol named *TRansparent Interconnection of Lots of Links* (*TRILL*) that extends the idea of learning bridges to mobility in a wide area internet.

†Chapter 22 discusses NDP, which is sometimes written *IPv6-ND* to emphasize that the protocol is an integral part of IPv6.

18.17 Summary

Mobile IP allows a computer to move from one network to another without changing its IP address and without requiring routers to propagate a host-specific route. When it moves from its original home network to a foreign network, a mobile computer must obtain an additional, temporary address known as a care-of address. Applications use the mobile's original, home address; the care-of address is only used by underlying network software to enable forwarding and delivery across the foreign network.

Once it detects that it has moved, an IPv4 mobile either obtains a co-located care-of address or discovers a foreign mobility agent and requests the foreign agent to assign a care-of address. An IPv6 mobile can generate a co-located care-of address without needing a foreign agent. After obtaining a care-of address, the mobile registers with its home agent (either directly or indirectly through the foreign agent), and requests that the agent forward datagrams.

Once registration is complete, a mobile can use its home address to communicate with an arbitrary computer on the Internet. Datagrams sent by the mobile are forwarded directly to the specified destination. Reply routing can be inefficient because a datagram sent to the mobile will be forwarded to the mobile's home network where it is intercepted by the home agent, encapsulated in IP, and then tunneled to the mobile.

The scheme for mobile IP was designed for slow movement, such as visiting a hotel. When applied to devices that move rapidly, mobile IP has severe drawbacks and has not been widely adopted.

EXERCISES

18.1 Compare the encapsulation schemes in RFCs 2003 and 2004. What are the advantages and disadvantages of each?

18.2 Read the mobile IP specification carefully. How frequently must a router send a mobility agent advertisement? Why?

18.3 Consult the mobile IP specification. When a foreign agent forwards a registration request to a mobile's home agent, which protocol ports are used? Why?

18.4 The specification for mobile IP allows a single router to function as both a home agent for a network and a foreign agent that supports visitors on the network. What are the advantages and disadvantages of using a single router for both functions?

18.5 Read the specification for mobile IPv6. How many separate message formats are defined?

18.6 Suppose a cell phone provider adopts mobile IPv6 for use with their phones. Compute the number of packets sent when a phone passes from one network to another.

18.7 Extend the previous exercise. If N active cell phone users drive along a highway at 60 MPH and each must switch from one cell tower to another within a 1500 foot area halfway between two cell towers, estimate the network capacity needed to handle the messages mobile IPv6 generates to relocate phones from one cell tower to another.

18.8 Read the specifications for mobile IPv4 and mobile IPv6 to determine how a mobile host joins a multicast group. How are multicast datagrams routed to the mobile in each case? Which approach is more efficient? Explain.

18.9 Compare mobile IPv4 and mobile IPv6 to Cisco's LISP protocol. What are the differences in functionality?

18.10 Compare mobile IPv4 and mobile IPv6 to the TRILL protocol. What does TRILL offer?

18.11 Read about hand-off protocols used in a cellular network. Can similar protocols be used with IP? Why or why not?

18.12 Consider the applications you use. Do any of the applications require you to retain an IP address (i.e., does your personal Internet device need a permanent home address)? Explain.

Chapter Contents

19

Network Virtualization: VPNs, NATs, And Overlays

19.1 Introduction

Previous chapters describe an internet as a single-level abstraction that consists of networks interconnected by routers. This chapter considers an alternative — a two-level internet architecture that virtualizes the Internet. The first level consists of a conventional internet that provides universal connectivity. An organization uses the underlying connectivity to build a second level that conforms to the needs of the organization.

The chapter examines three technologies that employ virtualization. One technology permits a corporation to connect multiple sites across the global Internet, or to allow an employee to use the global Internet to access the corporate network from an arbitrary remote location while keeping all communication confidential. A second form allows a site to provide global Internet access for many hosts while only using a single globally-valid IP address. A third technology allows an organization to create an arbitrary network topology on top of the Internet topology.

19.2 Virtualization

We use the term *virtualization* to describe an abstraction that is used to hide implementation details and provide high-level functionality. In general, virtualization mechanisms use an underlying mechanism that does not include the necessary desired functionality.

We have already seen technologies and protocols that provide a level of network virtualization. For example, a VLAN Ethernet switch allows a manager to configure the switch to act like a set of independent Ethernet switches. TCP provides the abstraction of a reliable, end-to-end connection. In each case, however, the service is an illusion — the underlying mechanism does not offer the service that the virtualization creates. TCP, for example, builds reliable, connection-oriented delivery over an unreliable connectionless transport.

This chapter shows that several forms of network virtualization are useful as well as popular. We will consider the motivation and uses of virtualizations as well as the mechanisms used to create each form. Chapter 28 continues the discussion by considering a technology that can be used to create virtual paths through an internet.

19.3 Virtual Private Networks (VPNs)

Packet switching used in the global Internet has the advantage of low cost, but the disadvantage that packets from multiple users travel across a given network. As a result, the global Internet cannot guarantee that communication conducted over the Internet remains *private*. In particular, if an organization comprises multiple sites, the contents of datagrams that travel across the Internet between the sites can be viewed by outsiders because they pass across networks owned by outsiders (i.e., ISPs).

When thinking about privacy, network managers often classify networks into a two-level architecture that distinguishes between networks that are *internal* to an organization and networks that are *external*. Because the organization can control the internal networks it owns, the organization can make guarantees about how data is routed and prevent it from becoming visible to others. Thus, internal networks can guarantee privacy, while external networks cannot.

If an organization has multiple sites, how can the organization guarantee privacy for traffic sent among the sites? The easiest approach consists of building a completely isolated network that is owned and operated by the organization. We use the term *private network* or *private intranet* for such a network. Because a private network uses leased digital circuits to interconnect sites and because the phone companies guarantee that no outsiders have access to such circuits, all data remains private as it travels from one site to another.

Unfortunately, a completely private intranet may not suffice for two reasons. First, most organizations need access to the global Internet (e.g., to contact customers and suppliers). Second, leased digital circuits are expensive. Consequently, many organizations seek alternatives that offer lower cost. One approach uses a form of virtualization that Chapter 16 discusses: MPLS. An MPLS connection may cost significantly less than a leased digital circuit of the same capacity.

Despite being less expensive than a digital circuit, an MPLS path is much more expensive than a traditional Internet connection. Thus, the choice is clear: lowest cost can be achieved by sending traffic over the global Internet, and the greatest privacy can be achieved by dedicated connections. The question arises: is it possible to achieve a high degree of privacy and the low cost of conventional Internet connections? Phrased another way, one can ask:

> *How can an organization that uses the global Internet to connect its sites guarantee that all communication is kept private?*

The answer lies in a technology known as a *Virtual Private Network* (*VPN*). The idea of a VPN is straightforward: send datagrams across the global Internet but encrypt the contents. The term *private* arises because the use of encryption means that communication between any pair of computers remains concealed from outsiders. The term *virtual* arises because a VPN does not require dedicated leased circuits to connect one site to another. Figure 19.1 illustrates the concept.

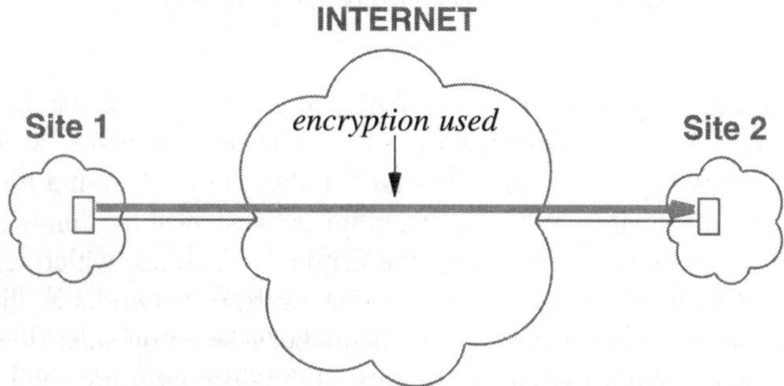

Figure 19.1 Illustration of a VPN that uses encryption when sending data across the global Internet between two routers at two sites of an organization.

19.4 VPN Tunneling And IP-in-IP Encapsulation

A technique mentioned in the previous chapter plays an important role in VPN technology: *tunneling*. A VPN uses tunneling for the same reason as mobile IP: to send a datagram across the Internet between two sites. Why not just forward the datagram normally? The answer lies in increased privacy (i.e., confidentiality). Encrypting the payload in a datagram does not guarantee absolute privacy because an outsider can use the IP source and destination fields, the datagram type field, and the frequency and volume of traffic to guess who is communicating. A VPN encrypts an entire datagram, including the IP header. In fact, to hide information from outsiders, some VPNs pad all datagrams with extra octets before encrypting them, which means an outsider cannot use the length of the datagram to deduce the type of communication. The consequence is that encryption means the datagram header cannot be used for forwarding.

Most VPNs use *IP-in-IP tunneling*. That is, the original datagram is encrypted, and the result is placed in the payload section of another datagram for transmission. Figure 19.2 illustrates the encapsulation.

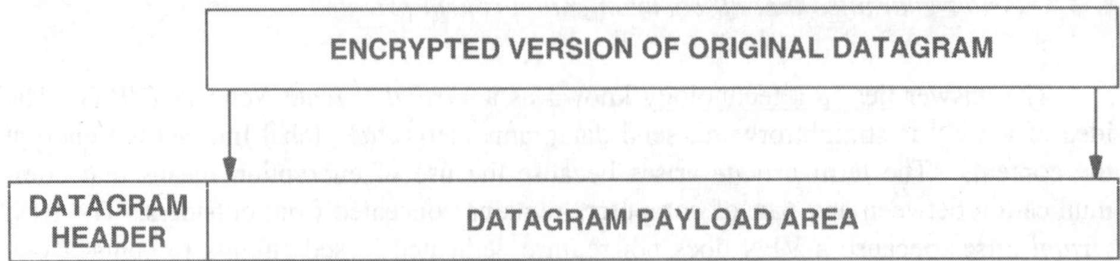

Figure 19.2 Illustration of IP-in-IP encapsulation used with a VPN. The original datagram is encrypted before being sent.

An organization may have many computers at each site. For maximal privacy, individual computers do not participate in a VPN. Instead, a manager arranges forwarding so that datagrams sent across the VPN tunnel always travel from a router at one site to a router at the other site. When a datagram arrives over the tunnel, the receiving router decrypts the payload to reproduce the original datagram, which it then forwards within the site. Although the datagrams traverse arbitrary networks as they pass across the Internet, outsiders cannot decode the contents because an outsider does not have the encryption key. Furthermore, even the identity of the original source and ultimate destination are hidden, because the header of the original datagram is encrypted. Thus, only two addresses in the outer datagram header are visible: the source address is the IP address of the router at one end of a tunnel, and the destination address is the IP address of the router at the other end of the tunnel. Consequently, an outsider cannot deduce which computers at the two sites are communicating.

To summarize:

> *Although a VPN sends data across the global Internet, outsiders cannot deduce which computers at the two sites are communicating or what data they are exchanging.*

19.5 VPN Addressing And Forwarding

The easiest way to understand VPN addressing and routing is to think of each VPN tunnel as a replacement for a leased circuit between two routers. As usual, the forwarding table in each of the two routers contains entries for destinations inside the organization. The forwarding table also contains a network interface that corresponds to the VPN tunnel, and datagrams sent to another site are directed across the tunnel. Figure 19.3 illustrates the idea by showing networks at two sites and the forwarding table for a router that handles VPN tunneling. Although the example uses IPv4, the same approach can be used for IPv6.

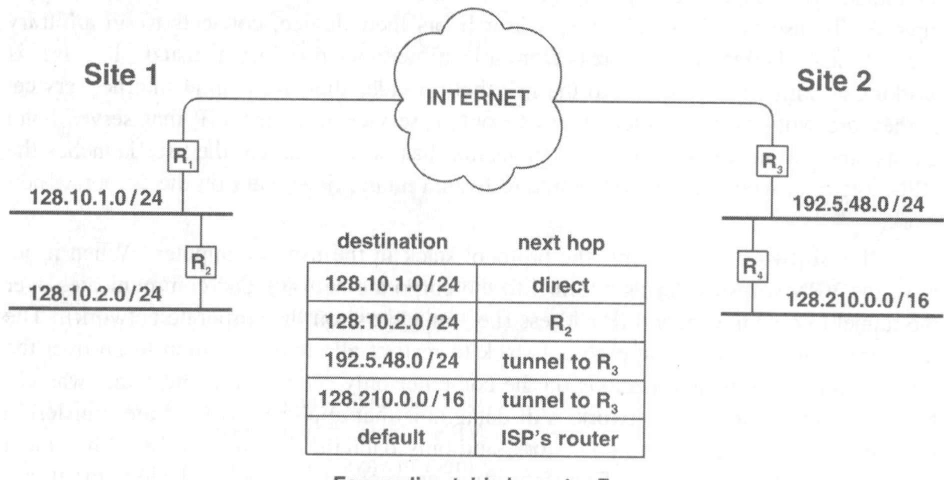

destination	next hop
128.10.1.0 / 24	direct
128.10.2.0 / 24	R_2
192.5.48.0 / 24	tunnel to R_3
128.210.0.0 / 16	tunnel to R_3
default	ISP's router

Figure 19.3 A VPN that spans two sites and R_1's forwarding table with a VPN tunnel from R_1 to R_3 configured like a point-to-point circuit.

The figure shows a default entry in R_1's forwarding table with an ISP as the next hop. The idea is that computers at site 1 can access computers at site 2 or computers on the global Internet. The tunnel is only used for site-to-site access; other datagrams are forwarded to the ISP.

As an example of forwarding in a VPN, consider a datagram sent from a computer on network *128.10.2.0* to a computer on network *128.210.0.0*. The sending host forwards the datagram to R_2, which forwards it to R_1. According to the forwarding table in R_1, the datagram must be sent across the tunnel to R_3. Therefore, R_1 encrypts the datagram, encapsulates the result in the payload area of an outer datagram with destination R_3. R_1 then forwards the outer datagram through the local ISP and across the Internet. The datagram arrives at R_3, which recognizes it as tunneled from R_1. R_3 decrypts the payload to produce the original datagram, looks up the destination in its forwarding table, and forwards the datagram to R_4 for delivery.

19.6 Extending VPN Technology To Individual Hosts

Many corporations use VPN technology to permit employees to work from remote locations. The employee is given VPN software that runs on a mobile device (e.g., a laptop). To use the VPN software, a user boots their device, connects to an arbitrary network, and obtains an IP address from a local network provider as usual. If a user is working at home, they connect to the ISP that provides their residential Internet service. If they are working in a hotel, they can obtain service from the ISP that serves hotel guests, and so on. Once a network connection has been obtained, the user launches the VPN software, which is pre-configured to form a tunnel to a router on the corporate network.

VPN software reconfigures the protocol stack in the user's computer. When it begins, the VPN software forms a tunnel to the corporate network and communicates over the tunnel to obtain a second IP address (i.e., an address on the corporate network). The software then configures the protocol stack to restrict all communication to go over the VPN tunnel. That is, applications on the computer only see the IP address that was obtained from the corporate network. All datagrams that applications send are transferred over the tunnel to the corporate network, and only datagrams coming in from the tunnel are delivered to applications. Therefore, from an application's point of view, the user's computer appears to be attached directly to the corporate network.

To insure that communication is confidential, all datagrams traveling across the tunnel are encrypted. However, there is a potential security flaw: unlike a router, a laptop can be stolen easily. If the VPN software can handle encryption and decryption, an outsider who steals the laptop would be able to obtain access to the corporate network. Therefore, VPN software issued to users usually requires a password. The password is combined with the time-of-day to generate a one-time encryption key that is used for a single session. Without the correct VPN password, a stolen laptop cannot be used to gain access to the corporate network.

19.7 Using A VPN With Private IP Addresses

Interestingly, although a VPN uses the global Internet when communicating between sites, the technology makes it possible to create a private intranet that does not provide global Internet connectivity for hosts on the corporate network. To see how, imagine assigning hosts non-routable addresses (e.g., an IPv6 site-specific address or an IPv4 private address). One router at each site is assigned a globally-valid IP address, and the router is configured to form a VPN tunnel to the router at the other site. Figure 19.4 illustrates the concept.

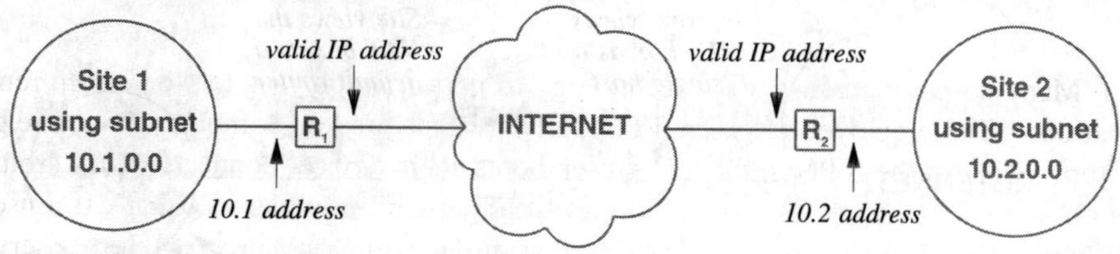

Figure 19.4 Example of a VPN that interconnects two sites over the global Internet while computers at each site use non-routable (i.e., private) addresses.

In the figure, the organization has chosen to use the non-routable IPv4 prefix *10.0.0.0/8* (a prefix that has been reserved for use in a private network). Site 1 uses subnet 10.1.0.0/16, while site 2 uses subnet 10.2.0.0/16. Only two globally valid IP addresses are needed to make a VPN possible. One is assigned to the connection from router R_1 to the Internet, and the other is assigned to the connection from R_2 to the Internet. The two sites may be far apart and may obtain service from two independent ISPs, which means that the two globally-valid addresses may be unrelated. Routers and hosts within each site use the private address space; only the two routers that participate in VPN tunneling need to know about or use globally-valid IP addresses.

19.8 Network Address Translation (NAT)

The previous sections describe a form of virtualization that allows an organization to connect sites across the global Internet while keeping all communication confidential. This section considers a technology that inverts the virtualization by providing IP-level access between hosts at a site and the global Internet, without requiring each host at the site to have a globally-valid IP address. Known as *Network Address Translation* (*NAT*), the technology has become extremely popular for both consumers and small businesses. For example, *wireless routers* used in homes employ NAT.

The idea behind NAT is straightforward. A site places a *NAT device*, informally called a *NAT box*†, between network(s) at the site and the rest of the Internet as Figure 19.5 illustrates.

†Although the name implies that NAT requires special-purpose hardware, it is possible to run NAT software on a general-purpose computer (e.g., a PC).

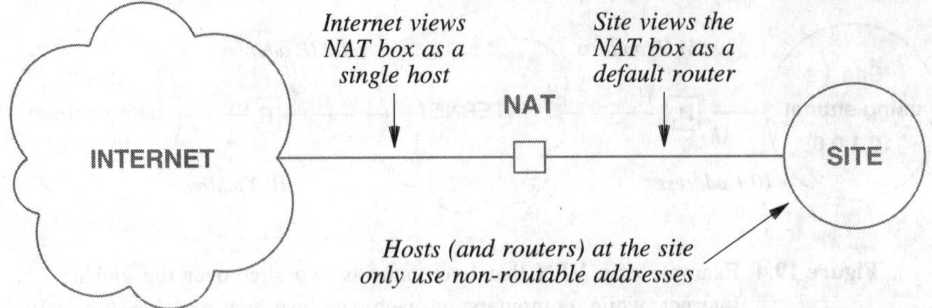

Figure 19.5 Illustration of a NAT box that allows a site to use non-routable IP addresses.

From the point of view of hosts at the site, the NAT box appears to be a router that connects to the Internet. That is, forwarding at the site is set up to direct outgoing datagrams to the NAT box. From the point of an ISP that provides service to the site, the NAT box appears to be a single host. That is, the NAT box obtains a single, globally-valid IP address, and appears to use the address to send and receive datagrams.

The key to NAT technology arises because NAT *translates* (i.e., changes) datagrams that travel in either direction. When a host at the site sends a datagram to a destination on the Internet, NAT places information about the outgoing datagram (including a record of the original sender) in a table, changes fields in the header, and sends the modified datagram to its destination. In particular, NAT changes the source IP address to make it appear that the datagram came from the NAT box. Thus, if a site on the Internet that receives a datagram replies, the reply will be sent to the NAT box. When it receives a datagram from the Internet, the NAT box consults its table, finds the original sender, changes fields in the header, and forwards the datagram. In particular, NAT changes the IP destination address to the private address that the host at the site is using.

Because both outgoing and incoming datagrams travel through the NAT box, NAT software can fool both hosts behind the NAT box and arbitrary hosts in the Internet. When a host in the Internet receives datagrams from the site, the datagrams appear to have originated at the NAT box. When a host behind the NAT box obtains an IP address, the address is non-routable (or site-local). However, the host can use the non-routable source address when sending and receiving datagrams with an arbitrary Internet host.

The chief advantage of NAT arises from its combination of generality and transparency. NAT is more general than a set of application gateways because it allows an arbitrary internal host to access an arbitrary service on a computer in the global Internet. NAT is transparent because hosts at the site run completely standard protocol software. To summarize:

Network Address Translation (NAT) technology provides transparent IP-level access to the Internet for a host that has a private, non-routable IP address.

19.9 NAT Translation Table Creation

Our overview of NAT glosses over a few details because it does not specify how a NAT box knows which internal host should receive a datagram that arrives from the Internet. We said that NAT maintains a translation table and uses the table when forwarding to a host. What information does NAT place in the translation table and when are table entries created?

The most widely used form of NAT† stores six items in its translation table:

- *Internal IP*. The non-routable IP address used by an internal computer.
- *Internal Port*. The protocol port number used by an internal computer.
- *External IP*. The IP address of an external computer located somewhere in the Internet.
- *External Port*. The protocol port number used by an external computer.
- *Payload Type*. The transport protocol type (e.g., TCP, UDP, or ICMP).
- *NAT Port*. The protocol port number used by a NAT box (to avoid situations in which two internal computers choose the same port number).

When a datagram arrives from the Internet, NAT searches the table. If the IP source address in the datagram matches *External IP*, the source protocol port number matches *NAT Port*, and the datagram type matches *Payload Type*, NAT uses the table entry. NAT replaces the datagram's destination IP address (which is always the address of the NAT box itself) with *Internal IP*, replaces the destination protocol port number with *Internal Port*, and sends the datagram to the internal host.

Of course, a table entry must be created before a datagram arrives from the Internet; otherwise, NAT has no way to identify the correct internal host to which the datagram should be forwarded. How and when is the table initialized? The above description implies that outgoing datagrams are always used to create table entries. Although we have described the most widely used form of NAT, others exist. The possibilities include:

---

†Technically, the version of NAT described here is *Network Address and Port Translation* (*NAPT*).

- *Manual Initialization.* A manager configures the translation table manually before any communication occurs.

- *Outgoing Datagrams.* The table is built as a side-effect of an internal host sending a datagram. NAT uses the outgoing datagram to create a translation table entry that records the source and destination addresses.

- *Incoming Name Lookups.* The table is built as a side-effect of handling domain name lookups. When a host on the Internet looks up the domain name of an internal host†, the DNS software sends the address of the NAT box as the answer and creates an entry in the NAT translation table to forward to the correct internal host.

Each initialization technique has advantages and disadvantages. Manual initialization provides permanent mappings that allow arbitrary hosts in the Internet to reach services at the site. Using an outgoing datagram to initialize the table has the advantage of making outgoing communication completely automatic, but has the disadvantage of not allowing outsiders to initiate communication. Using incoming domain name lookups accommodates communication initiated from outside, but requires modifying the domain name software.

As we said above, most implementations of NAT use outgoing datagrams to initialize the table; the strategy is especially popular for wireless routers used at Wi-Fi hot spots. The router can be connected directly to an ISP, exactly like a host. For example, the wireless router can be plugged into the DSL or cable modem the ISP supplies. The wireless router then offers Wi-Fi radio connections. When a mobile host connects via Wi-Fi, NAT software running in the wireless router assigns the mobile host a private, non-routable IP address and assigns its address as a default router address. A mobile host can communicate with any host on the Internet merely by sending datagrams to the wireless router over the Wi-Fi network. Figure 19.6 illustrates the architecture.

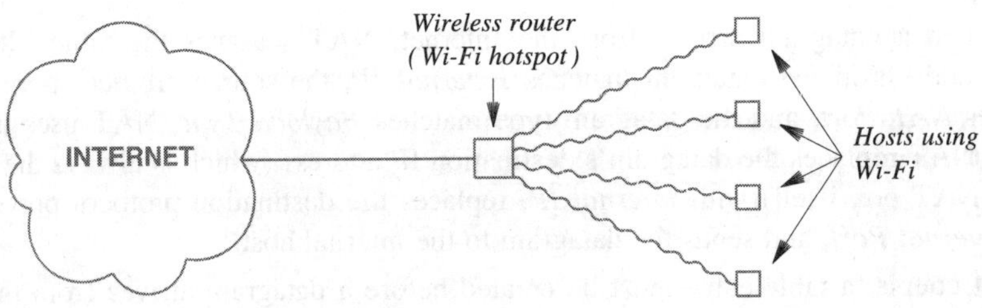

Figure 19.6 The use of NAT by a wireless router. Each host is assigned a private IP address.

†Chapter 23 describes how the *Domain Name System* (*DNS*) operates.

A wireless router must assign an IP address to a host whenever the host connects. For example, if a host uses IPv4, the router might assign the first host *192.168.0.1*, the second *192.168.0.2*, and so on. When a host sends a datagram to a destination on the Internet, the host forwards the datagram over the Wi-Fi network, and the wireless router applies the outgoing NAT mapping before sending the datagram over the Internet. Similarly, when a reply arrives from the Internet, the wireless router applies the incoming NAT translation and forwards the datagram over the Wi-Fi network to the correct host.

19.10 Variant Of NAT

Many variants of NAT exist, and many names have been used to describe the variants. So far, we have described *symmetric NAT* that allows an arbitrary host at the site to contact an arbitrary protocol port on a host in the Internet. Many of the proposed variants focus on running servers behind a NAT box to allow external Internet hosts to initiate communication (i.e., packets can arrive before a host at the site sends a packet). For example, a variant known as *port restricted cone NAT* uses one outgoing packet to establish an external port, and then sends all packets that arrive at the port to the internal host. Thus, if internal host H_1 sends a packet from source port X and the NAT box maps it to external port Y, all incoming packets destined for port Y will be directed to port X on H_1, no matter which host in the Internet sends the packets.

19.11 An Example Of NAT Translation

An example will clarify NAT translation. Recall that the version of NAT we have discussed is called NAPT because it translates protocol ports as well as IP addresses. Figure 19.7 illustrates the contents of an IPv4 translation table used with NAPT when four computers at a site have created six TCP connections to external sites on the Internet.

Internal IP Address	Internal Port	External IP Address	External Port	NAT Port	Payload Type
192.168.0.5	38023	128.10.19.20	80	41003	tcp
192.168.0.1	41007	128.10.19.20	80	41010	tcp
192.168.0.6	56600	207.200.75.200	80	41012	tcp
192.168.0.6	56612	128.10.18.3	25	41016	tcp
192.168.0.5	41025	128.10.19.20	25	41009	tcp
192.168.0.3	38023	128.210.1.5	80	41007	tcp

Figure 19.7 An example of a translation table used by NAPT. The table includes port numbers as well as IPv4 addresses.

The figure illustrates three interesting cases: a single host at the site has formed connections to two hosts on the Internet, two hosts at the site have each formed a connection to the same web server on the Internet, and two hosts at the site are using the same source port number simultaneously.

In the figure, each entry corresponds to a TCP connection. Internet host *192.168.0.6* has formed two connections to external hosts, one to a web server (port 80) on external host *207.200.75.200* and the other to an email server (port 25) on external host *128.10.18.3*. Two internal hosts, *192.168.0.5* and *192.168.0.1*, are both accessing protocol port *80* on external computer *128.10.19.20*. Because each host at the site is free to choose a source port number, uniqueness cannot be guaranteed. In the example, TCP connections from *192.168.0.5* and *192.168.0.3* both have source port *38023*. Thus, to avoid potential conflicts, NAT assigns a unique NAT port to each communication that is used on the Internet. Furthermore, a *NAT port* is unrelated to the source port that a sending host chooses. Thus, the connection from host *192.168.0.1* can use port *41007*, and the NAT box can use port *41007* for a completely different connection.

Recall that TCP identifies each connection with a 4-tuple that represents the IP address and protocol port number of each endpoint. For example, the first two entries in the table correspond to TCP connections with the following 4-tuples:

(192.168.0.5, 38023, 128.10.19.20, 80)
(192.168.0.1, 41007, 128.10.19.20, 80)

However, when computer *128.10.19.20* in the Internet receives datagrams, the NAT box will have translated the source address, which means the same two connections will have the following 4-tuples:

(G, 41003, 128.10.19.20, 80)
(G, 41010, 128.10.19.20, 80)

where *G* is the globally valid address of the NAT box.

The primary advantage of NAPT lies in the generality it achieves with a single globally valid IP address; the primary disadvantage arises because it restricts communication to TCP, UDP, and ICMP†. Because almost all applications use TCP or UDP, NAPT is transparent. A computer at the site can use arbitrary source port numbers, and can access multiple external computers simultaneously. Meanwhile, multiple computers at the site can access the same port on a given external computer simultaneously without interference. To summarize:

> *Although several variants of NAT exist, the NAPT form is the most popular because it translates protocol port numbers as well as IP addresses.*

†The next section explains that a NAT box translates and forwards some ICMP messages, and handles other messages locally.

19.12 Interaction Between NAT And ICMP

Although we have described NAT as operating on IP addresses and protocol port numbers, the address translation can affect other parts of a packet. For example, consider ICMP. To maintain the illusion of transparency, NAT must understand and change the contents of an ICMP message. For example, suppose an internal host uses *ping* to test reachability of a destination on the Internet. The host expects to receive an ICMP *echo reply* for each ICMP *echo request* message it sends. Thus, NAT must forward incoming echo replies to the correct host. However, NAT does not forward all ICMP messages that arrive from the Internet (e.g., if routes in the NAT box are incorrect, an ICMP message must be processed locally). Thus, when an ICMP message arrives from the Internet, NAT must first determine whether the message should be handled locally or sent to an internal host.

Before forwarding to an internal host, NAT must translate the entire ICMP message. To understand the need for ICMP translation, consider an ICMP *destination unreachable* message. The message contains the header from a datagram, *D*, that caused the error. Unfortunately, NAT translated addresses before sending *D*, so the source address in *D* is the globally-valid address of the NAT box rather than the address of the internal host. Thus, before forwarding the ICMP message back to the internal host, NAT must open the ICMP message and translate the addresses in *D* so they appear in exactly the form that the internal host used. After making the change, NAT must recompute the checksum in *D*, the checksum in the ICMP header, and the checksum in the outer datagram header.

19.13 Interaction Between NAT And Applications

Although ICMP complicates NAT, providing transparency to some application protocols requires substantial effort. In general, NAT will not work with any application that sends IP addresses or protocol ports as data. In particular, the *File Transfer Protocol* (*FTP*), which is used to download large files, establishes a control connection between the client and server, and then forms a new TCP connection for each file transfer. As part of the protocol, one side obtains a protocol port on the local machine, converts the number to ASCII, and sends the result across the control connection to the other side. The other side then forms a TCP connection to the specified port. Consider what happens when communication between the two sides passes through a NAT box. A host behind the NAT box can form a control connection. However, if the host obtains a local port and passes the information to the other side, NAT will not expect packets to arrive and will discard them. Therefore, FTP can only work if NAT monitors the contents of the control connection, selects a port number, and changes the data stream to reflect the new number.

Many implementations of NAT recognize popular application protocols, including FTP, and make the necessary change in the data stream. As an alternative, variants of applications have been created that avoid passing such information in the data stream (i.e., avoid making connections in the reverse direction). For example a version of FTP that does not require the server to connect back to the client is known as *passive FTP*. Application programmers must be aware of NAT, and to make their applications totally general, they should avoid passing addresses or port numbers in the data stream. To summarize:

> *NAT affects ICMP and application protocols; except for a few standard applications like FTP, an application protocol that passes IP addresses or protocol port numbers as data will not operate correctly across NAT.*

Changing items in a data stream increases the complexity of NAPT in two ways. First, it means that NAPT must have detailed knowledge of each application that transfers such information. Second, if the port numbers are represented in ASCII, as is the case with FTP, changing the value can change the number of octets transferred. Inserting even one additional octet into a TCP connection is difficult because each octet in the stream has a sequence number. A sender does not know that additional data has been inserted, and continues to assign sequence numbers without the additional data. When it receives additional data, the receiver will generate acknowledgements that account for the data. Thus, after it inserts additional data, NAT must use a technique known as *TCP splicing* to translate the sequence numbers in each outgoing segment and in each incoming acknowledgement.

19.14 NAT In The Presence Of Fragmentation

The above description of NAT has made an important assumption about IP: a NAT system receives complete IP datagrams and not fragments. What happens if a datagram is fragmented? IP addresses are not a problem because each fragment contains the IP addresses of the source and destination hosts. Unfortunately, fragmentation has a significant consequence for NAPT (the most widely used variant of NAT). As Figure 19.7 shows, NAPT table lookup uses protocol port numbers from the transport header as well as IP addresses from the IP header. Unfortunately, port numbers are not present in all fragments because only the first fragment of a datagram carries the transport protocol header. Thus, before it can perform the lookup, a NAPT system must receive and examine the first fragment of the datagram. IP semantics further complicate NAT because fragments can arrive out-of-order. Therefore, the fragment carrying the transport header may not arrive before other fragments.

A NAPT system can follow one of two designs: the system can save the fragments and attempt to reassemble the datagram, or the system can discard fragments and only process complete datagrams. Neither option is desirable. Reassembly requires state information, which means the system cannot scale to high speed or large numbers of flows (and is susceptible to malicious attack). Discarding fragments means the system will not process arbitrary traffic. In practice, only those NAPT systems that are designed for slow-speed networks choose to reassemble; many systems reject fragmented datagrams.

19.15 Conceptual Address Domains

We have described NAT as a technology that can be used to connect a private network to the global Internet. In fact, NAT can be used to interconnect any two *address domains*. Thus, NAT can be used between two corporations that each have a private network using address 10.0.0.0. More important, NAT can be used at two levels: between a customer's private address domain and an ISP's private address domain as well as between the ISP's address domain and the global Internet. Finally, NAT can be combined with VPN technology to form a hybrid architecture in which private addresses are used within the organization, and NAT is used to provide connectivity between each site and the global Internet.

As an example of multiple levels of NAT, consider an individual who works at home from several computers which are connected to a LAN. The individual can assign private addresses to the computers at home, and use NAT between the home network and the corporate intranet. The corporation can also assign private addresses and use NAT between its intranet and the global Internet.

19.16 Linux, Windows, And Mac Versions Of NAT

In addition to stand-alone devices, such as wireless routers, software implementations of NAT exist that allow a conventional computer to perform NAT functions. For example, Microsoft uses the name *Internet Connection Sharing* for NAT software that users can configure; additional software is available for Windows servers. Several versions of NAT have been created for the Linux operating system. In particular, *iptables* and *IP Masquerade* both implement NAT. In general, NAT software consists of a combination: application tools that allow a user to configure NAT and kernel support for packet rewriting and firewalling. Most NAT software supports multiple variants. For example, because it offers stateful packet inspection, *iptables* can be configured to handle basic NAT or NAPT.

19.17 Overlay Networks

The theme of this chapter is virtualization: using technologies that provide abstract services to a subset of computers that mimic the service provided by dedicated hardware. For example, VPN technology allows users to connect their computers to a distant network *as if* there were a direct connection. NAT technology allows a set of computers with private addresses to communicate with arbitrary destinations on the Internet *as if* each computer in the set had a globally-valid IP address. Can we extend virtualization further? Yes. We will see that it is possible to create a virtual network that connects an arbitrarily large set of hosts across many sites and allows the hosts to communicate *as if* they all attached to a single hardware network.

How might an overlay network be useful? We already discussed a prime example when we considered VPNs: security. Suppose a corporation has six sites and wants to create a corporate intranet. The corporation would like to guarantee that communication among sites is kept confidential. VPN technology allows the corporation to configure routers at each site to use the Internet in place of individual links and encrypt datagrams that flow across the virtual links.

Overlay networking extends virtualization in two ways. First, instead of individual links, overlay technology can be used to create an entire network. Second, instead of creating a virtual internet, overlay technology can be used to create a virtual layer 2 network.

To understand how an overlay network operates, imagine our example corporation with six sites. As with a VPN, the corporation configures one or more routers at each site to tunnel datagrams to other sites. More important, the corporation can impose an arbitrary routing topology and arbitrary traffic policies. For example, if the corporation observes that video traffic sent directly from site 1 to site 4 experiences high delays, overlay routing can be arranged as if there is a direct link between each pair of sites except for 1 and 4. Alternatively, if sites 1 – 3 are on the east coast and sites 4 – 6 are on the west coast, the corporation might arrange the overlay network to emulate three long-distance links. Figure 19.8 illustrates the two possible routing topologies.

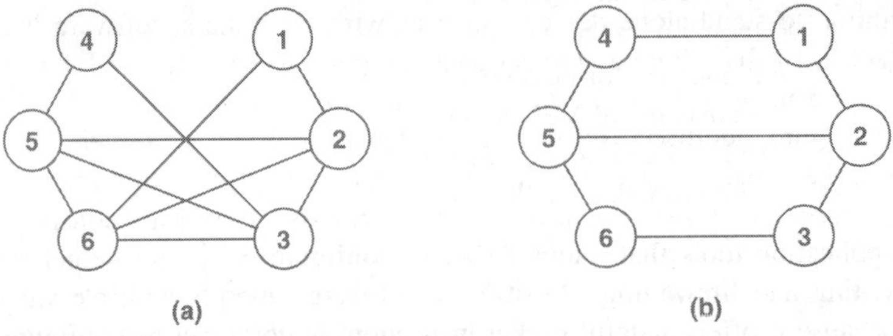

Figure 19.8 Example of two possible topologies that can be achieved with overlay technology.

It is important to understand that the topologies shown in the figure are virtual, not real. In practice, there are no links. Instead, all sites connect to the Internet and use the Internet to deliver datagrams. Thus, only the overlay configuration in Figure 19.8(a) can prevent site 1 from sending datagrams directly to site 4.

19.18 Multiple Simultaneous Overlays

The topologies in Figure 19.8 may seem somewhat pointless. After all, if all sites connect to the global Internet, datagrams can be forwarded directly to the correct destination site. However, an organization may have reasons for preferring one topology over another. To understand, suppose that the organization has established routing policies for subgroups. For example, a policy may require that all financial traffic must be isolated from customer traffic or that computers in the legal department at each site must be on a private network that is isolated from the Internet.

The two key ideas behind overlay technologies are:

- Operation within a site
- Simultaneous operation of many overlays

Operation within a site. Although we have described the overlays for wide-area topologies that connect sites, overlay technology extends to hosts and routers within a site. Thus, it is possible to create a separate overlay network that connects computers owned by the financial department and another overlay that connects the computers owned by the legal department.

Simultaneous operation of many overlays. The second key idea in overlay technology is the simultaneous operation of multiple overlays. That is, several overlay networks can co-exist (i.e., operate at the same time), making it possible for an organization to create multiple virtual networks that only meet at specific interconnection points. In our example, computers in the legal department can be completely isolated from other computers.

Chapter 28 continues the discussion of virtualization and overlay networks. The chapter combines the concepts of VPN and overlay networking presented in this chapter with the concepts of classification and switching discussed in Chapter 17. We will see that the result is a technology that can be used to configure virtual paths.

19.19 Summary

Virtualization technologies allow us to create artificial networks with desirable properties by imposing constraints on conventional Internet communication. We examined three virtualization technologies: VPN, NAT, and overlay networks.

Although a private network guarantees confidentiality, the cost can be high. *Virtual Private Network* (*VPN*) technology offers a lower-cost alternative by which an organization can use the global Internet to interconnect multiple sites and use encryption to guarantee that intersite traffic remains confidential. Like a traditional private network, a VPN can either be completely isolated (in which case hosts are assigned private addresses) or a hybrid architecture that allows hosts to communicate with destinations on the global Internet.

Network Address Translation provides transparent IP-level access to the global Internet from a host that has a private address. NAT is especially popular with wireless routers used in Wi-Fi hot spots. NAT translates (i.e., rewrites) datagrams that travel from a host at the site to the Internet or back from the Internet to a host at the site. Although several variants of NAT exist, the most popular is known as *Network And Port Translation* (*NAPT*). In addition to rewriting IP addresses, NAPT rewrites transport-level protocol port numbers, which provides complete generality and permits arbitrary applications running on arbitrary computers at the site to access services on the Internet simultaneously.

Overlay networking technologies allow an organization to define a network among multiple sites as if the sites were connected by leased digital circuits. The overlay defines possible interconnections among sites. With an overlay, conventional routing protocols can be used to find routes along the overlay paths.

EXERCISES

19.1 Under what circumstances will a VPN transfer substantially more packets than conventional IP when sending the same data across the Internet? (Hint: think about encapsulation.)

19.2 Software implementations of NAT that are used to provide remote employees access to an organization's intranet often reduce the network MTU that is reported to local applications. Explain why.

19.3 Look up the definition of *cone* as applied to NAT. When is a NAT system considered to be full cone?

19.4 NAT translates both source and destination IP addresses. Which addresses are translated on datagrams that arrive from the Internet?

19.5 Consider an ICMP host unreachable message sent through two NAT boxes that interconnect three address domains. How many address translations will occur? How many translations of protocol port numbers will occur?

19.6 Imagine that we decide to create a new Internet parallel to the existing Internet that allocates addresses from the same address space. Can NAT technology be used to connect the two arbitrarily large Internets that use the same address space? If so, explain how. If not, explain why not.

19.7 Is NAT completely transparent to a host? To answer the question, try to find a sequence of packets that a host can transmit to determine whether it is located behind a NAT box.

19.8 What are the advantages of combining NAT technology with VPN technology? The disadvantages?

19.9 Configure NAT on a Linux system between a private address domain and the Internet. Which well-known services work correctly and which do not?

19.10 Read about a variant of NAT called *twice NAT* that allows communication to be initiated from either side of the NAT box at any time. How does twice NAT ensure that translations are consistent? If two instances of twice NAT are used to interconnect three address domains, is the result completely transparent to all hosts?

19.11 Draw a diagram of the protocol layering used with an overlay network.

19.12 Overlay technology can be used with Layer 2 as well as Layer 3. Design a system that uses an overlay to form a large Ethernet VLAN that includes multiple sites.

Chapter Contents

20

Client-Server Model Of Interaction

20.1 Introduction

Previous chapters present the details of TCP/IP technology, including the protocols that provide basic services and protocols that routers use to propagate routing information. Now that we understand the basic technology, we turn to the question of how application programs profit from the cooperative use of the TCP/IP protocols and the global Internet. While the example applications are both practical and interesting, they do not form the main emphasis because no Internet application lasts forever. New applications are created and old applications fade. Therefore, our focus rests on the patterns of interaction among communicating application programs.

The primary pattern of interaction among applications that use a network is known as the *client-server* paradigm. Client-server interaction forms the basis of network communication, and provides the foundation for application services. Various high-level extensions to the client-server model have been created, including *peer-to-peer* networking and *map-reduce* processing. Despite marketing hype, the extensions do not replace client-server interactions. Instead, the new models merely suggest new ways to organize large distributed systems — at the lowest level, they rely on client-server interactions.

This chapter considers the basic client-sever model; later chapters describe its use in specific applications. Volume 3 expands the discussion by explaining in detail how applications, such as web servers, use processes and threads.

20.2 The Client-Server Model

A *server* is an application program that offers a service over a network. A server accepts an incoming request, forms a response, and returns the result to the requester. For the simplest services, each request arrives in a single datagram and the server returns a response in another datagram.

An executing program becomes a *client* when it sends a request to a server and waits for a response. Because the client-server model is a convenient and natural extension of interprocess communication used on a single machine, it is easy for programmers to build programs that use the model to interact.

Servers can perform simple or complex tasks. For example, a *time-of-day server* merely returns the current time whenever a client sends the server a packet. A *web server* receives requests from browsers to fetch copies of web pages; the server returns the requested page for each request.

We said that a server is an application program. In fact, a server is a running application, which is usually called a *process*. The advantage of implementing servers as application programs is a server can execute on any computing system that supports TCP/IP communication. As the load on a server increases, the server can be run on a faster CPU. Technologies exist that allow a server to be replicated on multiple physical computers to increase reliability or performance — incoming requests are spread among the computers running the server to reduce the load. If a computer's primary purpose is support of a particular server program, the term "server" may be applied to the computer as well as to the server program. Thus, one hears statements such as "machine *A* is our web server."

20.3 A Trivial Example: UDP Echo Server

The simplest form of client-server interaction uses datagram delivery to convey messages from a client to a server and back. For example, Figure 20.1 illustrates the interaction in a *UDP echo server*. A UDP *echo server* is started first and must be running before the client sends a request. The server specifies that it will use the port reserved for the UDP *echo* service, UDP port 7. The server then enters an infinite loop that has three steps:

(1) Wait for a datagram to arrive at the UDP echo port

(2) Reverse the source and destination addresses† (including source and destination IP addresses as well as UDP port numbers)

(3) Return the resulting datagram to its original sender

Once it is running, the server application program can supply the echo service. At some sites in the Internet, an application becomes a client of the UDP echo service by sending a datagram.

†One of the exercises suggests considering this step in more detail.

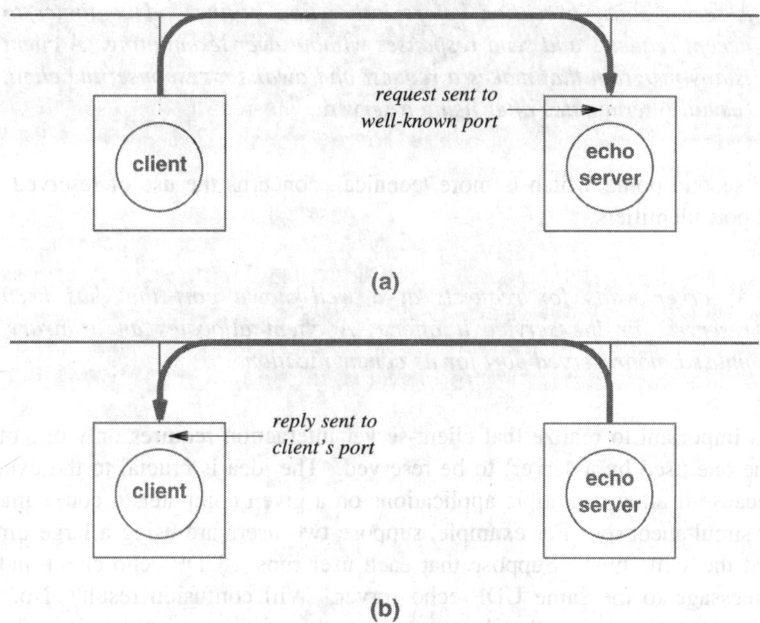

Figure 20.1 The UDP echo service as an example of the client-server model. In (a), the client sends a request to the server's IP address and UDP port. In (b), the server returns a response.

Who would use an echo service? It is not a service that the average user finds interesting. However, programmers who design, implement, measure, or modify network protocol software, or network managers who test routes and debug communication problems, often use echo servers in testing. For example, an echo service can be used to determine if it is possible to reach a remote machine. Furthermore, a client will receive back exactly the same data as it sent. A client can check the data in a reply to determine whether datagrams are being corrupted in transit.

A major distinction between clients and servers arises from their use of protocol port numbers. A server uses the well-known port number associated with the service it offers. A client knows that a UDP echo server will use port 7 because the standards reserve port 7 for the echo service. However, a client does not use a well-known port. Instead, a client obtains an unused UDP protocol port from its local operating system, and uses the port number as the source port when sending a UDP message. The client waits for a reply, and the server uses the source port in incoming messages to send a reply back to the correct client.

The UDP echo service illustrates two important points that are generally true about client-server interaction. The first concerns the difference between the lifetime of servers and clients:

> *A server starts execution before interaction begins and continues to accept requests and send responses without ever terminating. A client is any program that makes a request and awaits a response; the client (usually) terminates after using a server.*

The second point, which is more technical, concerns the use of reserved and non-reserved port identifiers:

> *A server waits for requests at a well-known port that has been reserved for the service it offers. A client allocates an arbitrary, unused, nonreserved port for its communication.*

It is important to realize that client-server interaction requires only one of the two ports (the one used by a server) to be reserved. The idea is crucial to the overall paradigm because it allows multiple applications on a given computer to communicate with a server simultaneously. For example, suppose two users are using a large timesharing system at the same time. Suppose that each user runs a UDP echo client and they all send a message to the same UDP echo server. Will confusion result? No. Because each client obtains a unique local port number, there is never ambiguity in the server's replies.

20.4 Time And Date Service

The echo server is extremely simple, and little code is required to implement either the server or client side (provided that the operating system offers a reasonable way to access the underlying UDP/IP protocols). Our second example, a time server, is equally trivial. However, the example shows that even trivial applications can be useful, and the time service raises the question of data representation.

A time server solves the problem of automatically setting a computer's time-of-day clock. When it boots, a computer contacts a time-of-day server and uses the reply to set its local clock. If additional accuracy is needed, a computer can contact a time server periodically.

20.4.1 Data Representation And Network Standard Byte Order

How should time be represented? One useful representation stores the time and date in a single integer by giving a count of seconds after an epoch date. The TCP/IP protocols define the epoch date to be January 1, 1900, and store the time in a 32-bit integer. The representation accommodates all dates for a few decades in the future; by the time a 32-bit integer is exhausted, most computers are expected to have 64-bit integer capability.

Simply specifying that a value will be stored as a 32-bit integer is insufficient because the representation of integers varies among computers. Most application protocol designers follow the same approach as the TCP/IP protocols: integers are represented in *network standard byte order*. That is, before sending a message, the sending application translates each integer from the local machine's byte order to network byte order, and upon receiving a message, the receiving application translates each integer from network byte order to the local host byte order. Thus, two computers with different integer representations can exchange integers without ambiguity.

Most applications also follow the TCP/IP standards when choosing their standard for network byte order: they use *big endian* representation. In big endian order, the most significant byte of the integer comes first, followed by the next most significant byte, and so on. It may seem that using a network standard byte order introduces extra overhead or that the choice of big endian order is inefficient. However, experience has shown that the overhead involved in translating between local byte order and network byte order is trivial compared to the other costs of message processing. Furthermore, using a single, well-known byte order standard prevents many problems and ambiguities.

20.4.2 Time Server Interaction

The interaction between a client and a time server illustrates an interesting twist on client-server interaction. A time service operates much like an echo service. The server begins first, and waits to be contacted. However, the time protocol does not define a request message. Instead, the time server uses the arrival of a UDP message to trigger a response. That is, a time server assumes *any* arriving UDP message, independent of the message size or contents, is a request for the current time. Therefore, the server responds to each incoming message by sending a reply that contains the current time in a 32-bit integer. Figure 20.2 illustrates the interaction.

We can summarize:

> *Sending an arbitrary datagram to a time server is equivalent to making a request for the current time; the server responds by returning a UDP message that contains the current time in network standard byte order.*

20.5 Sequential And Concurrent Servers

The examples above illustrate basic sequential servers (i.e., a server that processes one request at a time). After accepting a request, a sequential server sends a reply before waiting for another request to arrive. The idea of sequential servers raises an important question about protocol software: what happens if a subsequent request arrives while a server is busy handling a previous request?

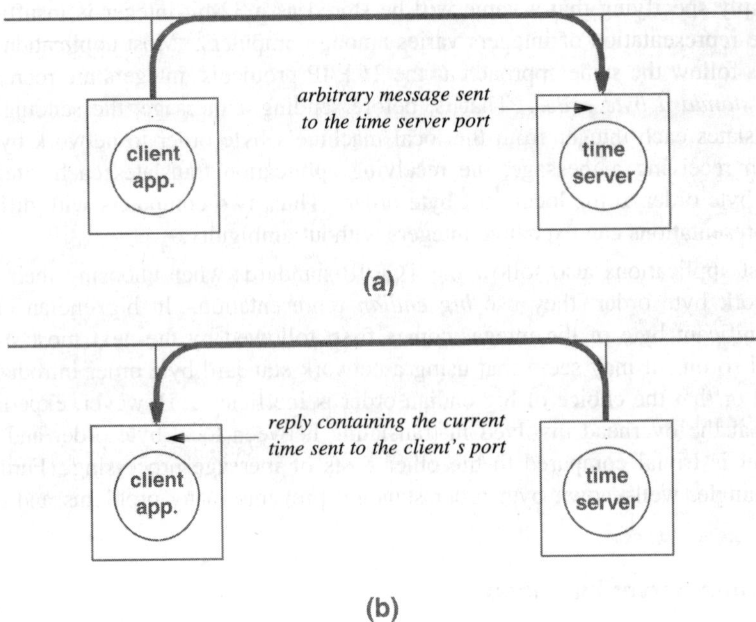

Figure 20.2 Illustration of the interaction used with a time server. The protocol does not define a request message because an arbitrary UDP datagram will trigger a reply.

For our trivial examples, the question is irrelevant. For servers, such as a video download server, in which a single request can take minutes or hours to honor, the question becomes important. In general, servers must be engineered to meet the expected demand. Two techniques can be used to accommodate many requests:

- Incoming requests can be placed in a queue
- A server can satisfy multiple requests concurrently

Request queuing. If a sequential server is busy processing a request when a subsequent request arrives, the server cannot place the incoming request in a queue. Unfortunately, packets tend to arrive in bursts, which means that multiple requests can arrive in rapid succession. To handle bursts, protocol software is designed to provide a queue for each application. Because queueing is merely intended to handle bursts, typical queue sizes are extremely small (e.g., some operating systems limit a queue to five or fewer entries). Therefore, queueing only suffices for applications where the expected processing time is negligible.

Concurrent servers. To handle multiple simultaneous requests, most production servers are *concurrent*. A concurrent server can handle multiple requests "at the same time." We use the term *concurrent* rather than *simultaneous* to emphasize that all clients share the underlying computational and network resources. A concurrent server can handle an arbitrarily large set of clients at a given time, but the service each client receives degrades proportional to the number of clients.

To understand why concurrency is important, imagine what would happen with a sequential server if a client requests a video download over an extremely slow network. No other client requests would be honored. With a concurrent design, however, a server will honor other requests while it continues to send packets over the slow connection.

The key to a concurrent server lies in the operating system abstraction of a *concurrent process* and the ability to create processes dynamically. Figure 20.3 gives the basic steps a concurrent server follows.

Open port

The server opens the well-known port at which it can be reached.

Wait for client

The server waits for the next client request to arrive.

Start copy

The server starts an independent, concurrent copy of itself to handle the request (i.e., a concurrent process or thread). The copy handles one request and then terminates.

Continue

The original server returns to the *wait* step, and continues accepting new requests while the newly created copy handles the previous request concurrently.

Figure 20.3 The steps a concurrent server takes that allow the server to handle multiple requests at the same time.

20.6 Server Complexity

The chief advantage of a concurrent server is the ability to handle requests promptly: a request that arrives later does not need to wait for requests that started earlier to complete. The chief disadvantage is complexity: a concurrent server is more difficult to construct.

In addition to the complexity that results because servers handle requests concurrently, complexity also arises because servers must enforce authorization and protection rules. Because they read system files, keep logs, and access protected data, server applications usually need to execute with highest privilege. A privileged program must be designed carefully because the operating system will not restrict a server program if it attempts to access an arbitrary user's files, access an arbitrary database, or send an arbitrary packet. Thus, servers cannot blindly honor requests from other sites. Instead, each server takes responsibility for enforcing the system access and protection policies. For example, a file server must examine a request and decide whether the client is authorized to access the specified file.

Finally, servers are complex to design and implement because a server must protect itself against malformed requests or requests that will cause the server application to abort. Often, it is difficult to foresee potential problems. For example, one project at Purdue University designed a file server that allowed student operating systems to access files on a UNIX timesharing system. Students discovered that requesting the server to open a file named */dev/tty* caused the server to abort because in UNIX the name refers to the control terminal a program is using. However, because it was launched at startup, the file server had no control terminal. Therefore, an attempt to open the control terminal caused the operating system to abort the server process.

We can summarize our discussion of servers:

> *Servers are usually more difficult to build than clients. Although they can be implemented with application programs, servers must enforce all the access and protection policies of the computer system on which they run, and must protect themselves against possible errors.*

20.7 Broadcasting Requests

So far, all our examples of client-server interaction require the client to know the complete server address. In some cases, however, a client does not know the server's address. For example, when it boots, a computer can use DHCP to obtain an address, but the client does not know the address of a server†. Instead, the client broadcasts its request.

The point is:

> *For protocols where the client does not know the location of a server, the client-server paradigm permits client programs to broadcast requests.*

20.8 Client-Server Alternatives And Extensions

We said that client-server interaction is the basis for almost all Internet communication. However, the question arises: what variations are possible? Three general approaches are used:

†Chapter 22 examines DHCP.

- Proxy caching
- Prefetching
- Peer-to-peer access

Proxy caching. We said that the conventional client-server paradigm requires an application to become a client and contact a server whenever it needs information from the server. However, latency can be a problem, especially in cases were the server is far from the client. If requests are likely to be repeated, caching can improve the performance of client-server interaction by reducing latency and lowering network traffic. For example, consider a set of employees in a corporation with access to the Web. If one employee finds a web page useful or interesting, the employee is likely to pass the URL to a few friends who then view the page and pass the URL to other friends. Thus, a given web page may be accessed a dozen times. With a conventional client-server approach, each access requires the page to be fetched from the server.

To improve performance, a corporation can install a *proxy web cache*. When it receives a request, the proxy cache looks on its disk to see if the requested item is available. If not, the proxy contacts the appropriate web server to obtain the item, places a copy on disk, and returns a copy to the browser that made the request. Because the proxy can satisfy each subsequent request from its local disk, the web server is only contacted once.

Of course, clients must agree to use the proxy or the approach will not work. That is, each user must configure their web browser to contact the proxy for requests (most web browsers have a setting that uses a proxy). Individuals have strong motivation for using a proxy because the proxy does not inject significant overhead and may improve performance considerably.

Other examples of client-server caching exist. For example, the ARP protocol presented in Chapter 6 also follows the client-server model. ARP uses a cache to avoid repeatedly requesting the MAC address of a neighbor. If ARP did not use a cache, network traffic would double.

Prefetching. Although it improves performance, caching does not change the essence of client-server interaction — information is fetched only when the first client makes a request. That is, an application executes until it needs information and then acts as a client to obtain the information. Taking a demand-driven view of the world is natural and arises from experience. Caching helps alleviate the cost of obtaining information by lowering the retrieval cost for subsequent fetches, but does not reduce the cost of the first fetch.

How can we lower retrieval cost for an initial request? The answer lies in *prefetching* — arrange to collect and store information *before* any particular program requests it. Prefetching reduces the latency for the initial request. More important, precollecting information means that a client can obtain an answer even if the network is temporarily disconnected or congested when the client makes a request.

An early Unix program named *ruptime* illustrates the idea of prefetching that is now used in many data center management systems. The *ruptime* program provided the

CPU load of all computers on the local network. A ruptime client always operated instantly because the information was prefetched by a background application. Each computer on the network would broadcast its current load periodically, and the background programs collected announcements sent by other computers. Pre-collecting performance information is important because an overloaded computer cannot respond to a request quickly.

Precollection has two disadvantages. First, precollection uses processor and network resources even if no client will access the data being collected. In our performance example, each machine must participate by broadcasting its status and collecting broadcasts from other machines. If only a few machines participate in the broadcast, precollection costs will be insignificant. In a large data center cluster that includes hundreds of machines, the broadcast traffic generated by precollection can impose significant load on the network. Thus, precollection is usually reserved for special cases where the processing cost and network overhead can be limited.

Peer-to-peer access. The third variation of client-server interaction is known as *peer-to-peer networking* (*P2P*). P2P was popularized by file sharing applications that allow users to exchange files, such as MP3 files containing music or videos.

The idea behind the peer-to-peer approach is straightforward: instead of having a single server, arrange to give many servers a copy of each file and allow a user to download from the nearest server. The same idea is used by *Content Distribution Network* (*CDN*) technologies, such as the one pioneered by Akami. However, peer-to-peer networking adds an interesting twist: instead of special server computers, a peer-to-peer system relies on users' computers. That is, in exchange for file access, a user agrees to allow their computer to be used like a server. When a client makes a request, the peer-to-peer system knows the set of users who have downloaded a copy and selects one that will provide fastest access for the new request. Some peer-to-peer file systems start downloads from a handful of locations, and then use the download that proceeds the fastest. Other peer-to-peer systems divide files into chunks and arrange for a chunk of the file to be downloaded from one location while other chunks are downloaded from other locations. In any case, once a user has downloaded an item (i.e., a complete file or a chunk of the file), the user's computer becomes a potential source of the item for other users to download.

20.9 Summary

Many modern applications use computer networks and the Internet to communicate. The primary pattern of use is known as client-server interaction. A server process waits for a request, performs actions based on the request, and returns a reply. A client program formulates a request, sends the request to a server, and awaits a reply. Some clients send requests directly, while others broadcast requests; broadcasting is especially useful when an application does not know the address of a server.

We examined a few trivial examples of clients and servers, such as a time-of-day service and a UDP echo service. The time-of-day service illustrates the importance of network standard byte order, and also shows that a service does not need to define a request format.

Although trivial services use a sequential approach, most production servers permit concurrent processing. Because it creates a separate process to handle each request, a concurrent server does not require a client to wait for previous requests to be served. Concurrency is especially important for services, such as video download, in which it can take minutes or hours to satisfy a single request.

We considered alternatives and extensions to the client-server paradigm, including caching, prefetching, and peer-to-peer interactions. Each technique can increase performance, depending on the pattern of repeated requests and the time required to access data.

EXERCISES

20.1 Build a UDP echo client that sends a datagram to a specified echo server, awaits a reply, and compares it to the original message.

20.2 Carefully consider how a UDP echo server forms a reply. Under what conditions is it *incorrect* to create new IP addresses by reversing the source and destination IP addresses?

20.3 Although most servers are implemented by separate application programs, an ICMP echo server is usually built into the protocol software in the operating system. What are the advantages and disadvantages of having an application program (user process) per server?

20.4 Suppose you do not know the IP address of a local host computer that runs a UDP echo server, but you know that it responds to requests sent to port 7. Is there an IP address you can use to reach the server? Explain.

20.5 Build a UDP client for the Internet time service, and demonstrate that it works correctly.

20.6 Can a server run on the same physical host computer as a client? Explain.

20.7 Consider a data center cluster with 200 computers. If each computer broadcasts its current load every 5 seconds and each message contains 240 octets of information (plus associated headers), how much network capacity is used by the broadcasts?

20.8 What servers are running on computers at your site? If you do not have access to system configuration files that list the servers started for a given computer, see if your system has a command that prints a list of open TCP and UDP ports (e.g., the UNIX *netstat* command).

20.9 Some servers allow a manager to implement graceful shutdown or restart. What is the advantage of graceful server shutdown?

20.10 Suppose a concurrent server follows the algorithm given in Figure 20.3 (on page 425). What vulnerability does such a server exhibit?

Chapter Contents

21

The Socket API

21.1 Introduction

Earlier chapters discuss the principles and concepts that underlie the TCP/IP protocols, and the previous chapter considers the client-server paradigm that applications use to communicate over a TCP/IP internet. The chapters omit an important detail: they do not specify the exact interface that application programs use to interact with protocol software. This chapter completes the discussion by consider an *Application Program Interface* (*API*) that has become a de facto standard for the Internet. The chapter describes the overall approach taken, and reviews enough of the functions in the API to explain an example. We gloss over many details and focus on understanding the basics; doing so will help us appreciate the code needed for a trivial client-server application. Volume 3 expands the discussion by showing more details and larger examples of client and server applications that use the API.

There are two reasons we postponed the discussion of APIs until this chapter. First, the TCP/IP standards do not specify the exact interface that applications use to access network services; the details depend on the operating system. Second, it is important to distinguish between the functionality that protocols provide and the functionality that is made available through a specific interface. For example, TCP is designed to handle an extreme case where two endpoints each try to form a TCP connection simultaneously. However, none of the widely-used APIs ever permitted such a case.

21.2 Versions Of The Socket API

We will examine the *socket API*, which is informally called *sockets*. The socket interface was originally created as part of the BSD Unix operating system. Versions of sockets appear in more recent BSD systems, Linux, and Mac OS X; Microsoft adapted a version of sockets known as *Windows Sockets*† for their operating systems.

The chapter provides an overview of the socket API that applies to all systems and shows a basic example that follows the BSD style. Readers who want further details and examples for a specific version of the API are referred to Volume 3 of the text, which comes in versions for BSD, Linux, and Windows sockets.

21.3 The UNIX I/O Paradigm And Network I/O

Developed in the late 1960s and early 1970s, the UNIX operating system was originally designed as a timesharing system for single processor computers. It is a process-oriented operating system in which each application program executes as a user level process. An application program interacts with the operating system by making *system calls*. From the programmer's point of view, a system call looks and behaves exactly like other function calls. A system call can take arguments and can return one or more results. Arguments can be data values (e.g., integers) or pointers to objects in the application program (e.g., a buffer to be filled with characters).

Derived from those in Multics and earlier systems, the UNIX input and output (I/O) primitives follow a paradigm sometimes referred to as *open-close-read-write*. Before an application can perform I/O operations, it calls *open* to specify the file or device to be used. The call to *open* returns a small integer *file descriptor*‡ that the application uses to perform I/O operations. Once it has opened a file (or device), an application invokes *read* or *write* operations to transfer data. A call has arguments that specify the descriptor to use, the address of a buffer, and the number of bytes to transfer. After all transfer operations are complete, the user process calls *close* to inform the operating system that it has finished using the file or device.

21.4 Adding Network I/O to UNIX

The group adding network protocols to BSD UNIX made two design decisions. The first design decision arose from the rich functionality of network protocols. Because network protocols offer many more possibilities than conventional devices and files, interaction between applications and network protocols needed to specify new functions. For example, a protocol interface must allow programmers to create both server code (that awaits connections passively) as well as client code (that forms connections actively). In addition, an application program that sends a datagram may wish to specify the destination address along with each datagram instead of binding the destination address to the socket. To handle all cases, the designers chose to abandon the

†Programmers often use the term *WINSOCK* to refer to Windows Sockets.

‡The term "file descriptor" arises because in UNIX devices are mapped into the file system.

traditional UNIX open-close-read-write paradigm and add several new system calls. The design increased the complexity of the I/O interface substantially, but was necessary.

The second design decision arose because many protocols existed, and it was not obvious that TCP/IP would be so successful. Therefore, designers attempted to build a general mechanism to accommodate all protocols. For example, the generality makes it possible for the operating system to include software for other protocol suites as well as TCP/IP and to allow an application program to use one or more of the protocol suites at a given time. As a consequence, an application program cannot merely supply a binary value and expect the protocols to interpret the value as an IP address. Instead, an application must specify the type of the address (i.e., the address family) explicitly. The generality has paid off for IPv6 — instead of redesigning the socket interface, engineers merely needed to add options for IPv6 addresses.

21.5 The Socket Abstraction And Socket Operations

The basis for network I/O in the socket API centers on an operating system abstraction known as the *socket*. We think of a socket as a mechanism that provides an application with a descriptor that can be used for network communication. Sockets are dynamic — an application program requests a socket when one is needed and releases the socket when it has finished performing I/O.

Sockets do share one thing with other I/O — a socket is given a descriptor just like an open file. In most systems, a single set of descriptors are used. Thus, descriptors 5 and 7 might correspond to an open file, and descriptor 6 might correspond to a socket for a TCP connection.

21.5.1 Creating A Socket

The *socket* function creates a socket on demand. The function takes three integer arguments and returns an integer descriptor:

descriptor = socket(pfam, type, protocol)

Argument *pfam* specifies the protocol family to be used with the socket (i.e., it specifies how to interpret addresses). The most important families are IP version 4 (*PF_INET*†) and IP version 6 (*PF_INET6*).

Argument *type* specifies the type of communication desired. Possible types include a reliable stream delivery service (*SOCK_STREAM*), a connectionless datagram delivery service (*SOCK_DGRAM*), and a raw type (*SOCK_RAW*) that allows privileged programs to access special protocols or network interfaces.

Because a single protocol family can have multiple protocols that provide the same type of communication, the *socket* call has a third argument that can be used to select a

†Upper case terms used throughout the examples are the names of symbolic constants that programmers use with the socket API.

specific protocol; if the protocol family only contains one protocol of a given *type* (e.g., only TCP supplies a *SOCK_STREAM* service for IPv4 and IPv6), the third argument can be set to 0.

21.5.2 Socket Inheritance And Termination

In UNIX systems, the *fork* and *exec* system calls are used to create a process running a specific application program. In most systems, when a new process is created, the newly created process inherits access to all open sockets. A concurrent server uses socket inheritance to create a new process to handle each new client.

Both the old and the new process share access rights to existing descriptors. Therefore, both can access the socket for a given client. Thus, it is the responsibility of the programmer to ensure that the two processes use the shared socket meaningfully.

When a process finishes using a socket it calls *close*. *Close* has the form:

close(descriptor)

where argument *descriptor* specifies the descriptor of a socket to close. When a process terminates for any reason, the system closes all sockets that remain open. Internally, a call to *close* decrements the reference count for a socket and destroys the socket if the count reaches zero.

21.5.3 Specifying A Local Address

Initially, a socket is created without any association to local or destination addresses. For the TCP/IP protocols, this means that a new socket does not begin with local or remote IP addresses or protocol port numbers. Client programs do not care about the local address they use, and are willing to allow the protocol software to fill in the computer's IP address and choose a port number. However, server processes that operate at a well-known port must be able to specify the port to the system. Once a socket has been created, a server uses the *bind* function to establish a local address for the socket†. *Bind* has the following form:

bind(descriptor, localaddr, addrlen)

Argument *descriptor* is the integer descriptor of the socket to be bound. Argument *localaddr* is a structure that specifies the local endpoint to which the socket should be bound, and argument *addrlen* is an integer that specifies the length of the structure measured in bytes. Instead of giving the endpoint merely as a sequence of bytes, the designers chose to define a structure. Figure 21.1 illustrates the *sockaddr_in* structure used for IPv4 endpoints.

†If a client does not call *bind*, the operating system assigns a port number automatically; typically, port numbers are assigned sequentially.

Figure 21.1 The *sockaddr_in* structure used when passing an IPv4 endpoint to a socket function.

The structure begins with a 16-bit *ADDRESS FAMILY* field that identifies the protocol suite to which the address belongs; each protocol family defines the layout of the remainder of the structure. The value *2* in the *ADDRESS FAMILY* field indicates that the structure is used for IPv4, and therefore, the remainder of the structure consists of a 16-bit protocol port number and a 32-bit IPv4 address. When passed as an argument, the structure must be cast to a generic structure, *sockaddr*.

For IPv6 addresses, an application may need to supply two additional pieces of information: an identifier for an IPv6 flow or the scope of an address (e.g., link-local, site-local, or global). Figure 21.2 illustrates the *sockaddr_in6* structure used to represent an IPv6 endpoint.

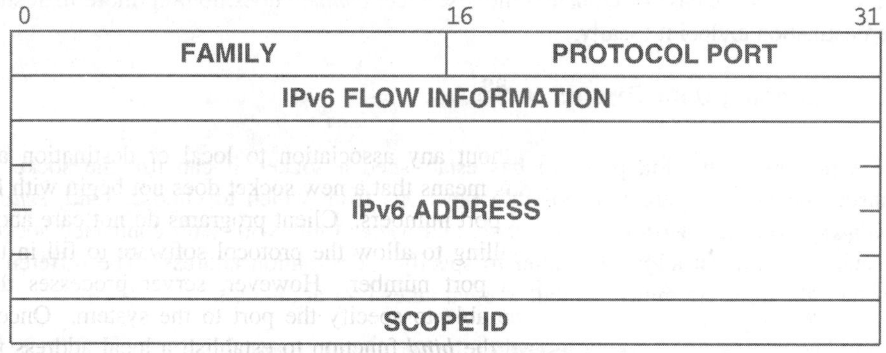

Figure 21.2 The *sockaddr_in6* structure used when passing an IPv6 endpoint to a socket function.

Although it is possible to specify arbitrary values in the address structure when calling *bind*, not all possible bindings are valid. For example, the caller might request a local protocol port that is already in use by another program, or it might request an invalid IP address. In such cases, the *bind* call fails and returns an error code.

21.5.4 Connecting A Socket To A Destination Endpoint

Initially, a socket is created in the *unconnected state*, which means that the socket is not associated with any remote destination. The function *connect* binds a permanent remote endpoint to a socket, placing it in the *connected state*. An application program must call *connect* to establish a connection before it can transfer data through a reliable stream socket. Sockets used with connectionless datagram services do not need to be connected before they are used, but doing so makes it possible to transfer data without specifying the destination each time.

The *connect* function has the form:

connect(descriptor, destaddr, addrlen)

Argument *descriptor* is the integer descriptor of the socket to connect. Argument *destaddr* is a socket address structure that specifies the destination address to which the socket should be bound. Argument *addrlen* specifies the length of the destination address measured in bytes.

The semantics of *connect* depend on the underlying protocol. Selecting the reliable stream delivery service in the PF_INET or PF_INET6 families means choosing TCP. In such cases, *connect* builds a TCP connection with the destination and returns an error if it cannot. In the case of connectionless service, *connect* does nothing more than store the destination endpoint locally.

21.5.5 Sending Data Through A Socket

Once an application program has established a socket, it can use the socket to transmit data. There are five possible functions from which to choose: *send*, *sendto*, *sendmsg*, *write*, and *writev*. *Send*, *write*, and *writev* only work with connected sockets because they do not allow the caller to specify a destination address. The differences between the three are minor. A call to *send* takes four arguments:

send(descriptor, buffer, length, flags)

Argument *descriptor* is an integer socket descriptor, argument *buffer* contains the address of the data to be sent, argument *length* specifies the number of bytes to send, and argument *flags* controls the transmission. One value for *flags* allows the sender to specify that the data should be sent out-of-band (e.g., TCP urgent data). A call to *send* blocks until the data can be transferred (e.g., it blocks if internal system buffers for the socket are full). Another value for *flags* allows the caller to request that the message be sent without using the local forwarding table. The intention is to allow the caller to take control of forwarding, making it possible to write network debugging software. Of course, not all sockets support all requests from arbitrary programs. Some requests require a program to have special privileges; other requests are simply not supported on all sockets. Like most system calls, *send* returns an error code to the application calling it, allowing the programmer to know if the operation succeeded.

21.5.6 Receiving Data Through A Socket

Analogous to the five different output operations, the socket API offers five functions that a process can use to receive data through a socket: *read*, *readv*, *recv*, *recvfrom*, and *recvmsg*. The input operations *recv* and *read* can only be used when the socket is connected. *Recv* has the form:

recv(descriptor, buffer, length, flags)

Argument *descriptor* specifies a socket descriptor from which data should be received. Argument *buffer* specifies the address in memory into which the message should be placed, argument *length* specifies the length of the buffer area, and argument *flags* allows the caller to control the reception. Among the possible values for the *flags* argument is one that allows the caller to look ahead by extracting a copy of the next incoming message without removing the message from the socket.

To form a reply, a UDP server needs to obtain more than the contents of the UDP payload — it must also obtain the sender's IP address and protocol port number. To do so, it uses the socket function *recvfrom*. A call has the form:

recvfrom(descriptor, buffer, length, flags, fromaddr, fromlen)

The two additional arguments, *fromaddr* and *fromlen*, are pointers to a socket address structure and an integer. The operating system records the sender's endpoint information in location *fromaddr* and the length of the endpoint information in location *fromlen*. When sending a reply, a UDP server can pass the endpoint information to function *sendto*. Thus, forming a reply is straightforward.

21.5.7 Obtaining Local And Remote Socket Endpoint Information

We said that newly created processes inherit the set of open sockets from the process that created them. Sometimes, a newly created process needs to extract the remote endpoint address from a socket that has been inherited. In addition, because the operating system fills in the local endpoint information automatically, a process may need to determine the local endpoint address that is used for a socket. Two functions provide such information: *getpeername* and *getsockname* (despite the function names, both handle what we think of as endpoint addresses, not domain names).

A process calls *getpeername* to determine the endpoint of a peer (i.e., the remote application to which a socket connects). The call has the form:

getpeername(descriptor, destaddr, addrlen)

Argument *descriptor* specifies the socket for which the destination endpoint is desired. Argument *destaddr* is a pointer to a structure of type *sockaddr* (see Figures 21.1 and 21.2) that will receive the endpoint information. Finally, argument *addrlen* is a pointer to an integer that will receive the length of the endpoint structure. *Getpeername* only works with connected sockets.

Function *getsockname* returns the local endpoint associated with a socket. A call has the form:

getsockname(descriptor, localaddr, addrlen)

As expected, argument *descriptor* specifies the socket for which the local endpoint is desired. Argument *localaddr* is a pointer to a structure of type *sockaddr* that will contain the endpoint, and argument *addrlen* is a pointer to an integer that will contain the length of the endpoint structure.

21.6 Obtaining And Setting Socket Options

In addition to binding a socket to a local endpoint or connecting it to a destination endpoint, the need arises for a mechanism that permits application programs to control the socket. For example, when using protocols that employ timeout and retransmission, the application program may want to obtain or set the timeout parameters. The application may also want to control the allocation of buffer space, determine if the socket allows transmission of broadcast, or control processing of out-of-band data. Rather than add new functions for each new control operation, the designers decided to build a single mechanism. The mechanism has two operations: *getsockopt* and *setsockopt*.

Function *getsockopt* allows the application to request information about the socket. A caller specifies the socket, the option of interest, and a location at which to store the requested information. The operating system examines its internal data structures for the socket, and passes the requested information to the caller. The call has the form:

getsockopt(descriptor, level, optionid, optionval, length)

Argument *descriptor* specifies the socket for which information is needed. Argument *level* identifies whether the operation applies to the socket itself or to the underlying protocols being used. Argument *optionid* specifies a single option to which the request applies. The pair of arguments *optionval* and *length* specify two pointers. The first gives the address of a buffer into which the system places the requested value, and the second gives the address of an integer into which the system places the length of the option value.

Function *setsockopt* allows an application program to set a socket option using the set of values obtained with *getsockopt*. The caller specifies a socket for which the option should be set, the option to be changed, and a value for the option. The call to *setsockopt* has the form:

setsockopt(descriptor, level, optionid, optionval, length)

where the arguments are like those for *getsockopt*, except that the *length* argument is an integer that specifies the number of bytes in the option being passed to the system. The caller must supply a legal value for the option as well as a correct length for that value. Of course, not all options apply to all sockets. The correctness and semantics of individual requests depend on the current state of the socket and the underlying protocols being used.

21.6.1 Specifying A Queue Length For A Server

We said that the operating system maintains a queue of incoming requests. A queue is especially important for sequential servers, but may also be needed to handle packet bursts for concurrent servers. One of the options that applies to sockets is used so frequently that a separate function has been dedicated to it: setting the queue length.

Socket function *listen* allows servers to prepare a socket for incoming connections. In terms of the underlying protocols, *listen* puts the socket in a passive mode ready to accept connections. Only servers use *listen*. In addition to placing a protocol in passive mode, *listen* contains an argument that configures the size of a queue for incoming requests. A call has the form:

```
listen(descriptor, qlength)
```

Argument *descriptor* gives the descriptor of a socket that should be prepared for use by a server, and argument *qlength* specifies the length of the request queue for that socket. After the call, the system will enqueue up to *qlength* requests for connections. If the queue is full when a request arrives, the operating system will refuse the connection by discarding the request. *Listen* applies only to sockets that have selected reliable stream delivery service.

21.7 How A Server Accepts TCP Connections

As we have seen, a server process uses the functions *socket*, *bind*, and *listen* to create a socket, bind it to a well-known protocol port, and specify a queue length for connection requests. Note that the call to *bind* associates the socket with a well-known protocol port, but that the socket is not connected to a specific remote destination. In fact, the remote destination must specify a *wildcard*, allowing the socket to receive connection requests from an arbitrary client.

Once a socket has been established, the server needs to wait for a connection. To do so, the server calls function *accept*. A call to *accept* blocks until a new connection request arrives. The call has the form:

```
newsock = accept(descriptor, addr, addrlen)
```

Argument *descriptor* specifies the descriptor of the socket on which to wait. Argument *addr* is a pointer to a structure of type *sockaddr*, and *addrlen* is a pointer to an integer.

When a request arrives, the system fills in argument *addr* with the endpoint information of the client that made the request, and sets *addrlen* to the length of the endpoint structure. Finally, the system creates a new socket that has its destination connected to the requesting client, and returns the new socket descriptor to the caller. The original socket still has a wildcard remote destination, and it still remains open. Thus, the original server can continue to accept additional requests at the original socket.

When a connection request arrives, the call to *accept* returns. The server can either handle the request itself or use the concurrent approach. If it handles the request itself, the server sends a reply, closes the new socket, and then calls *accept* to obtain the next connection request. In the concurrent approach, after the call to *accept* returns, the server creates a new process to handle the request (in UNIX terminology, it *forks a child process* to handle the request). The child process inherits a copy of the new socket, so it can proceed to service the request. When it finishes, the child closes the socket and terminates. Meanwhile, the original server process closes its copy of the new socket (after starting the child), and continues to call *accept* to obtain the next connection request.

The concurrent design for servers may seem confusing because multiple processes will be using the same local protocol port number. The key to understanding the mechanism lies in the way underlying protocols treat protocol ports. Recall that in TCP, a pair of endpoints define a connection. Thus, it does not matter how many processes use a given local protocol port number as long as they connect to different destinations. In the case of a concurrent server, there is one process per client and one additional process that accepts connections. The socket that the original server process uses has a wildcard for the remote destination, allowing an arbitrary remote site to form a new connection. When *accept* returns a new socket, the socket will have a specific remote endpoint. When a TCP segment arrives, the protocol software will send the segment to the socket that is already connected to the segment's source. If no such socket exists, the segment will be sent to the socket that has a wildcard for its remote destination. Because the socket with a wildcard remote destination does not have an open connection, it will only honor a TCP segment that requests a new connection (i.e., a SYN segment); all others will be discarded.

21.8 Servers That Handle Multiple Services

The socket API provides another interesting possibility for server design because it allows a single process to wait for connections on multiple sockets. The system call that makes the design possible is called *select*, and it applies to I/O in general, not just to communication over sockets†. A call to *select* has the form:

```
nready = select(ndesc, indesc, outdesc, excdesc, timeout)
```

In general, a call to *select* blocks waiting for one of a set of file descriptors to become ready. Argument *ndesc* specifies how many descriptors should be examined (the

†The version of *select* in Windows Sockets applies only to socket descriptors.

descriptors checked are always *0* through *ndesc*-1). Argument *indesc* is a pointer to a bit mask that specifies the file descriptors to check for input, argument *outdesc* is a pointer to a bit mask that specifies the file descriptors to check for output, and argument *excdesc* is a pointer to a bit mask that specifies the file descriptors to check for exception conditions. Finally, if argument *timeout* is nonzero, it is the address of an integer that specifies how long to wait for a connection before returning to the caller. A zero value for timeout forces the call to block until a descriptor becomes ready. Because the *timeout* argument contains the address of the timeout integer and not the integer itself, a process can also request zero delay by passing the address of an integer that contains zero (i.e., a process can poll to see if I/O is ready).

A call to *select* returns the number of descriptors from the specified set that are ready for I/O. It also changes the bit masks specified by *indesc*, *outdesc*, and *excdesc* to inform the application which of the selected file descriptors are ready. Thus, before calling *select*, the caller must turn on those bits that correspond to descriptors to be checked. Following the call, all bits that remain set to *1* correspond to a ready file descriptor.

To communicate over more than one socket, a process first creates all the sockets it needs, and then uses *select* to determine which socket becomes ready for I/O first. Once it finds a socket is ready, the process uses the input or output functions defined above to communicate.

21.9 Obtaining And Setting The Host Name

Although IP uses a destination address when delivering datagrams, user and application programs use a *name* to refer to a computer. For computers on the Internet, a computer's name is derived from the Domain Name System described in Chapter 23. The *gethostname* function allows an application to obtain the local computer's name. A related function, *sethostname*, allows a manager to set the host name to a given string. *Gethostname* has the form:

```
gethostname(name, length)
```

Argument *name* gives the address of an array of bytes where the name is to be stored, and argument *length* is an integer that specifies the maximum length of a name (i.e., the size of the *name* array). The function returns the length of the name that is retrieved. To set the host name, a privileged application calls:

```
sethostname(name, length)
```

where argument *name* gives the address of an array in which a name has been stored, and argument *length* is an integer that gives the length of the name.

21.10 Library Functions Related To Sockets

In addition to the functions described previously, the socket API offers a large set of functions that perform useful tasks related to networking. Because they do not interact directly with protocol software, many of the additional socket functions are implemented as library routines. Figure 21.3 illustrates the difference between system calls and library routines.

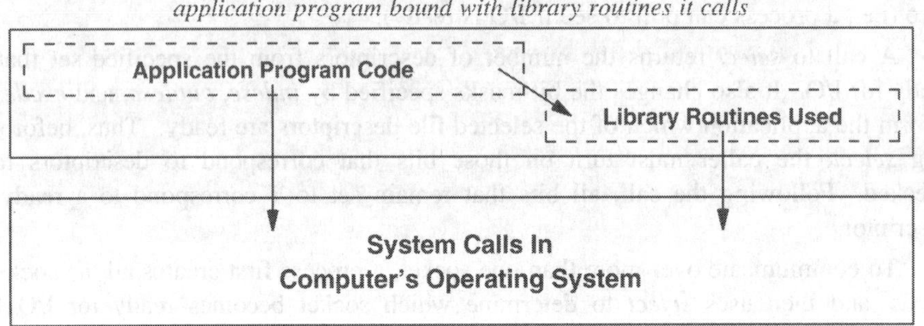

Figure 21.3 Illustration of the difference between library routines, which are bound into an application program, and system calls, which are part of the operating system.

As the figure shows, a system call passes control directly to the computer's operating system. Calling a library function passes control to a copy of the function that has been incorporated into the application. An application can make a system call directly or can invoke library functions that (usually) make a system call.

Many of the socket library functions provide database services that allow a process to determine the names of machines and network services, protocol port numbers, and other related information. For example, one set of library routines provides access to the database of network services. We think of entries in the services database as 3-tuples:

(service_name, protocol, protocol_port_number)

where *service_name* is a string that gives the name of the service, *protocol* is a transport protocol that is used to access the service, and *protocol_port_number* is the port number to use. For example, the UDP echo service described in Chapter 20 has an entry:

("echo", "udp", 7)

The next sections examine examples of library routines, explaining their purposes and providing information about how they are used. We will see that sets of socket library functions often follow the same pattern. Each set allows the application to: establish communication with the database (which can be a file on the local computer or a remote server), obtain entries one at a time, and terminate use. The routines used for the three operations are named *setXent*, *getXent*, and *endXent*, where *X* is the name of the database. For example, the library routines for the host database are named *sethostent*, *gethostent*, and *endhostent*. The sections that describe the routines summarize the calls without repeating the details of their use.

21.11 Network Byte Order And Conversion Routines

Recall that machines differ in the way they store integer quantities and that the TCP/IP protocols define a network standard byte order that is independent of any computer. The socket API provides four macros that convert between the local machine byte order and the network standard byte order. To make programs portable, they must be written to call the conversion routines every time they copy an integer value from the local machine to a network packet or when they copy a value from a network packet to the local machine.

All four conversion routines are functions that take a value as an argument and return a new value with the bytes rearranged. For example, to convert a short (2-byte) integer from network byte order to the local host byte order, a programmer calls *ntohs* (network to host short). The format is:

localshort = ntohs(netshort)

Argument *netshort* is a 2-byte (16-bit) integer in network standard byte order and the result, *localshort*, is the same integer in local host byte order.

The C programming language calls 4-byte (32 bit) integers *longs*. Function *ntohl* (network to host long) converts a 4-byte long from network standard byte order to local host byte order. Programs invoke *ntohl* as a function, supplying a long integer in network byte order as an argument:

locallong = ntohl(netlong)

Two analogous functions allow the programmer to convert from local host byte order to network standard byte order. Function *htons* converts a 2-byte (short) integer in the host's local byte order to a 2-byte integer in network standard byte order. Programs invoke *htons* as a function:

netshort = htons(localshort)

The final conversion routine, *htonl*, converts a 4-byte integer to network standard byte order. Like the others, *htonl* is a function:

netlong = htonl(locallong)

21.12 IP Address Manipulation Routines

Because many programs translate between 32-bit IPv4 addresses and the corresponding dotted decimal notation or between 128-bit IPv6 addresses and colon-hex notation, the socket library includes utility routines that perform the translations. For example, function *inet_aton* translates from dotted decimal format to a 32-bit IPv4 address in network byte order. A call has the form:

error_code = inet_aton(string, address)

where argument *string* gives the address of an ASCII string that contains the IPv4 address expressed in dotted decimal format, and *address* is a pointer to a 32-bit integer into which the binary value is placed. The dotted decimal form can have one to four segments of digits separated by periods (dots). If all four appear, each segment corresponds to a single octet of the resulting 32-bit integer. If fewer than four appear, the last segment is expanded to fill remaining octets of the address.

Function *inet_ntoa* performs the inverse of *inet_aton* by mapping a 32-bit IPv4 address to an ASCII string in dotted decimal format. It has the form:

str = inet_ntoa(internetaddr)

where argument *internetaddr* is a 32-bit IPv4 address in network byte order, and *str* is the address of the resulting ASCII version.

21.13 Accessing The Domain Name System

A set of five library functions constitute the interface to the *Domain Name System*† (*DNS*). Application programs that call the library functions become clients of the Domain Name System. That is, when an application calls a library function to obtain information, the library function forms a query, sends the query to a domain name server, and awaits an answer. Once the answer arrives, the library function returns the information to the application that made the call. Because many options exist, the library functions have only a few basic arguments. They rely on a global structure, *res*, to hold additional arguments. For example, one field in *res* enables debugging messages, while another field controls whether the application specifies using UDP or TCP for queries. Most fields in *res* begin with reasonable defaults, so socket library functions can often be used without changing *res*.

A program calls *res_init* before calling other functions. The call takes no arguments:

res_init()

Res_init stores the name of a domain name server in global structure *res*, making the system ready to contact the server.

†Chapter 23 considers the Domain Name System in detail.

Function *res_mkquery* forms a domain name query and places the query in a buffer in memory. The form of the call is:

res_mkquery(op, dname, class, type, data, datalen, newrr, buffer, buflen)

The first seven arguments correspond directly to the fields of a domain name query. Argument *op* specifies the requested operation, *dname* gives the address of a character array that contains a domain name, *class* is an integer that gives the class of the query, *type* is an integer that gives the type of the query, *data* gives the address of an array of data to be included in the query, and *datalen* is an integer that gives the length of the data. In addition to the library functions, the socket API provides application programs with definitions of symbolic constants for important values. Thus, programmers can use the Domain Name System without understanding the details of the protocol. The last two arguments, *buffer* and *buflen*, specify the address of an area into which the query should be placed and the integer length of the buffer area, respectively. In the current implementation, argument *newrr* is unused.

Once a program has formed a query, it calls *res_send* to send it to a name server and obtain a response. The form is:

res_send(buffer, buflen, answer, anslen)

Argument *buffer* is a pointer to memory that holds the message to be sent (presumably, the application called function *res_mkquery* to form the message). Argument *buflen* is an integer that specifies the length. Argument *answer* gives the address in memory into which a response should be written, and integer argument *anslen* specifies the length of the answer area.

In addition to functions that make and send queries, the socket library contains two functions that translate domain names between conventional ASCII and the compressed format used in queries. Function *dn_expand* expands a compressed domain name into a full ASCII version. It has the form:

dn_expand(msg, eom, compressed, full, fullen)

Argument *msg* gives the address of a domain name message that contains the name to be expanded, with *eom* specifying the end-of-message limit beyond which the expansion cannot go. Argument *compressed* is a pointer to the first byte of the compressed name. Argument *full* is a pointer to an array into which the expanded name should be written, and argument *fullen* is an integer that specifies the length of the array.

Generating a compressed name is more complex than expanding a compressed name because compression involves eliminating common suffixes. When compressing names, the client must keep a record of suffixes that have appeared previously. Function *dn_comp* compresses a full domain name by comparing suffixes to a list of previously used suffixes and eliminating the longest possible suffix. A call has the form:

dn_comp(full, compressed, cmprlen, prevptrs, lastptr)

Argument *full* gives the address of a full domain name. Argument *compressed* points to an array of bytes that will hold the compressed name, with argument *cmprlen* specifying the length of the array. The argument *prevptrs* is the address of an array of pointers to previously compressed suffixes in the current message, with *lastptr* pointing to the end of the array. Normally, *dn_comp* compresses the name and updates *prevptrs* and *lastptr* if a new suffix has been used.

Function *dn_comp* can also be used to translate a domain name from ASCII to the internal form without compression (i.e., without removing suffixes). To do so, a process invokes *dn_comp* with the *prevptrs* argument set to *NULL* (i.e., zero).

21.14 Obtaining Information About Hosts

Library functions exist that allow an application to retrieve information about a host given either its domain name or its IP address. The library functions make the application a client of the Domain Name System: they send a request to a domain name server and wait for a response. For example, function *gethostbyname* takes a domain name and returns a pointer to a structure of information for the specified host. A call takes the form:

```
ptr = gethostbyname(namestr)
```

Argument *namestr* is a pointer to a character string that contains a domain name for the host. The value returned, *ptr*, points to a structure that contains the following information: the official host name, a list of aliases that have been registered for the host, the host address type (i.e., IPv4, IPv6, or some other type), the length of an address, and a list of one or more addresses for the host. More details can be found in the UNIX Programmer's Manual.

Function *gethostbyaddr* produces the same information as *gethostbyname*. The difference between the two functions is that *gethostbyaddr* accepts a host address as an argument:

```
ptr = gethostbyaddr(addr, len, type)
```

Argument *addr* is a pointer to a sequence of bytes that contain a host address. Argument *len* is an integer that gives the length of the address, and argument *type* is an integer that specifies the type of the address (e.g., that it is an IPv6 address).

As mentioned earlier, functions *sethostent*, *gethostent*, and *endhostent* provide sequential access to the host database — an application can open the database, extract entries sequentially, and then close the database.

21.15 Obtaining Information About Networks

The socket library also includes functions that allow an application to access a database of networks. Function *getnetbyname* obtains and formats the contents of an entry from the database given the domain name of a network. A call has the form:

ptr = getnetbyname(name)

where argument *name* is a pointer to a string that contains the name of the network for which information is desired. The value returned is a pointer to a structure that contains fields for the official name of the network, a list of registered aliases, an integer address type (i.e., IPv4, IPv6, or some other type), and the address prefix used with the network (i.e., the network portion of an IP address with the host portion set to zero).

21.16 Obtaining Information About Protocols

Five library functions provide access to the database of protocols available on a machine. Each protocol has an official name, registered aliases, and an official protocol number. Function *getprotobyname* allows a caller to obtain information about a protocol given its name:

ptr = getprotobyname(name)

Argument *name* is a pointer to an ASCII string that contains the name of the protocol for which information is desired. The function returns a pointer to a structure that has fields for the official protocol name, a list of aliases, and a unique integer value assigned to the protocol.

Function *getprotobynumber* allows a process to search for protocol information using the protocol number as a key:

ptr = getprotobynumber(number)

Finally, functions *getprotoent*, *setprotoent*, and *endprotoent* provide sequential access to the protocol database.

21.17 Obtaining Information About Network Services

Recall from Chapters 10 and 11 that some UDP and TCP protocol port numbers are reserved for well-known services. For example, TCP port *37* is reserved for the *time* protocol described in the previous chapter. The entry in the services database specifies the service name, *time*, a protocol, (e.g., *TCP*), and the protocol port number *37*. Five library functions exist that obtain information about services and the protocol ports they use.

Function *getservbyname* is the most important because it maps a named service onto a port number:

ptr = getservbyname(name, proto)

Argument *name* specifies the address of a string that contains the name of the desired service, and argument *proto* is a string that gives the name of the protocol with which the service is to be used. Typically, protocols are limited to TCP and UDP. The value returned is a pointer to a structure that contains fields for the name of the service, a list of aliases, an identification of the protocol with which the service is used, and an integer protocol port number assigned for that service.

Function *getservbyport* allows the caller to obtain an entry from the services database given the port number assigned to it. A call has the form:

ptr = getservbyport(port, proto)

Argument *port* is the integer protocol port number assigned to the service, and argument *proto* specifies the protocol for which the service is desired. As with other databases, an application can access the services database sequentially using *setservent*, *getservent*, and *endservent*.

21.18 An Example Client

The following example C program illustrates how an application uses the socket API to access TCP/IP protocols. The client forms a TCP connection to a server, sends the lines of text a user enters, and displays the server's response to each.

```
/************************************************************************/
/*                                                                      */
/* Program:      Client to test the example echo server                 */
/*                                                                      */
/* Method:       Form a TCP connection to the echo server and repeatedly */
/*               read a line of text, send the text to the server and   */
/*               receive the same text back from the server.            */
/*                                                                      */
/* Use:          client [-p port] host                                  */
/*                                                                      */
/*               where port is a TCP port number or name, and host is   */
/*               the name or IP address of the server's host            */
/*                                                                      */
/* Author:       Barry Shein, bxs@TheWorld.com, 3/1/2013                */
/*                                                                      */
/************************************************************************/
```

```
#include <stdio.h>
#include <unistd.h>
#include <stdlib.h>
#include <getopt.h>
#include <string.h>
#include <stdarg.h>
#include <sys/types.h>
#include <errno.h>
#include <fcntl.h>
#include <time.h>

#ifdef USE_READLINE
#include <readline/readline.h>
#include <readline/history.h>
#endif /* USE_READLINE */

#include <sys/socket.h>
#include <netdb.h>
#include <netinet/in.h>

static  char    *prog;            /* ptr to program name (for messages)   */
#define DEFAULT_PORT    "9000"    /* must match server default port       */

/* Define process exit codes */

#define EX_OK           0         /* Normal termination                   */
#define EX_ARGFAIL      1         /* Incorrect arguments                  */
#define EX_SYSERR       2         /* Error in system call                 */

/* Log - display an error or informational message for the user */

static void Log(char *fmt,...) {
    va_list ap;

    va_start(ap,fmt);
    (void)vfprintf(stderr,fmt,ap);
    va_end(ap);
}

/* Fatal - display a fatal error message to the user and then exit */

static void Fatal(int exval,char *fmt,...) {
    va_list ap;

    va_start(ap,fmt);
```

```
    (void)vfprintf(stderr,fmt,ap);
    va_end(ap);
    exit(exval);
}

/* getLine - get one line of input from keyboard */

static char *getLine(char *prompt) {
#ifdef USE_READLINE
    return(readline(prompt));
#else /* !USE_READLINE */

    (void)fputs(prompt,stdout); /* display the prompt */
    fflush(stdout);

    /* read one line from the keyboard return NULL */
    if(fgets(buf,sizeof(buf),stdin) == NULL)
        return(NULL);
    else {
        char *p;

        /* emulate readline() and strip NEWLINE */
        if((p = strrchr(buf,'\n')) != NULL)
            *p = '\0';
        return(strdup(buf)); /* readline returns allocated buffer */
    }
#endif /* !USE_READLINE */
}

/* initClient - initialize and create a connection to the server */

static int initClient(char *host,char *port) {
    struct addrinfo hints;
    struct addrinfo *result, *rp;
    int s;

    memset(&hints,0,sizeof(hints));
    hints.ai_family = AF_UNSPEC;      /* use IPv4 or IPv6     */
    hints.ai_socktype = SOCK_STREAM; /* stream socket (TCP) */

    /* Get address of server host */
    if((s = getaddrinfo(host,port,&hints,&result)) != 0)
        Fatal(EX_SYSERR,"%s: getaddrinfo: %s\n",prog,gai_strerror(s));

    /* try each address corresponding to name */
```

```
    for(rp=result; rp != NULL; rp = rp->ai_next) {
        int sock, ret;            /* socket descriptor and return value  */
        char hostnum[NI_MAXHOST];         /* host name                   */

        /* Get numeric address of the host for message */
        if((ret = getnameinfo(rp->ai_addr,rp->ai_addrlen,hostnum,
                        sizeof(hostnum), NULL,0,NI_NUMERICHOST)) != 0) {
            Log("%s: getnameinfo: %s\n",prog,gai_strerror(ret));
        } else {
            (void)printf("Trying %s...",hostnum);
            fflush(stdout);
        }

        /* Get a new socket */

        if((sock =
            socket(rp->ai_family,rp->ai_socktype,rp->ai_protocol)) < 0) {
            if((rp->ai_family == AF_INET6) && (errno == EAFNOSUPPORT))
                Log("\nsocket: no IPv6 support on this host\n");
            else
                Log("\nsocket: %s\n",strerror(errno));
            continue;
        }

        /* try to connect the new socket to the server */

        if(connect(sock,rp->ai_addr,rp->ai_addrlen) < 0) {
            Log("connect: %s\n",strerror(errno));
            (void)shutdown(sock,SHUT_RDWR);
            continue;
        } else { /* success */
            (void)printf("connected to %s\n",host);
            return(sock);
            break;
        }
    }
    Fatal(EX_ARGFAIL,"%s: could not connect to host %s\n",prog,host);
    return(-1);    /* never reached, but this suppresses warning */
}

/* runClient - read from keyboard, send to server, echo response */

static void runClient(int sock) {
    FILE *sfp;
    char *input;
```

```
    /* create a buffered stream for socket */
    if((sfp = fdopen(sock,"r+")) == NULL) {
        (void)shutdown(sock,SHUT_RDWR);
        Fatal(EX_SYSERR,"%s: couldn't create buffered sock.\n",prog);
    }
    setlinebuf(sfp);

    (void)printf("\nWelcome to %s: period newline exits\n\n",prog);

    /* read keyboard... */
    while(((input=getLine("> ")) != NULL) && (strcmp(input,".") != 0)) {
        char buf[BUFSIZ];

        (void)fprintf(sfp,"%s\n",input);          /* write to socket */
        free(input);
        if(fgets(buf,sizeof(buf),sfp) == NULL) {    /* get response */
            Log("%s: lost connection\n",prog);
            break;
        } else
            (void)printf("response: %s",buf); /* echo server resp.        */
    }
}

/* doneClient - finish: close socket */

static void doneClient(int sock) {
    if(sock >= 0)
        if(shutdown(sock,SHUT_RDWR) != 0)
            Log("%s: shutdown error: %s\n",strerror(errno));
    Log("client connection closed\n");
}

/* Usage - helpful command line message */

static void Usage(void) {
    (void)printf("Usage: %s [-p port] host\n",prog);
    exit(EX_OK);
}

/* main - parse command line and start client */

int main(int argc,char **argv) {
    int c;
    char *host = NULL;
```

```
    char *port = DEFAULT_PORT;
    int sock;

    prog = strrchr(*argv,'/') ? strrchr(*argv,'/')+1 : *argv;

    while((c = getopt(argc,argv,"hp:")) != EOF)
        switch(c) {
          case 'p':
            port = optarg;
            break;
          case 'h':
            default:
            Usage();
        }
    if(optind < argc) {
        host = argv[optind++];
        if (optind != argc) {
            Log("%s: too many command line args\n",prog);
            Usage();
        }
    } else {
        Log("%s: missing host arg\n",prog);
        Usage();
    }
    sock = initClient(host,port); /* call will exit on error or failure */
    runClient(sock);
    doneClient(sock);
    exit(EX_OK);
}
```

21.19 An Example Server

The example server code is only slightly more complex than the client code. The overall operation is straightforward: the server is iterative. The server begins by specifying a port to use, and then waits for connections. The server accepts an incoming TCP connection, runs a service, and waits for the next connection. The service used is a trivial echo service: the server reads incoming lines of text and sends each line back to the client unchanged. The client must terminate the connection.

The server will allow a client to use either IPv4 or IPv6 (assuming IPv6 is available). Even on systems where the protocol stack is not configured for IPv6, the code assumes that *include* files are available for programs to use.

```
/***********************************************************************/
/*                                                                     */
/* Program:     Server that offers a text echo service via TCP on     */
/*              IPv4 or IPv6                                           */
/*                                                                     */
/* Method:      Repeatedly accept a TCP connection, echo lines of text */
/*              until the client closes the connection, and go on to   */
/*              wait for the next connection.                          */
/*                                                                     */
/* Use:         server [-p port]                                       */
/*                                                                     */
/*              where port is a TCP port number or name               */
/*                                                                     */
/* Author:      Barry Shein, bxs@TheWorld.com, 3/1/2013               */
/*                                                                     */
/***********************************************************************/
#include <stdio.h>
#include <unistd.h>
#include <stdlib.h>
#include <getopt.h>
#include <string.h>
#include <stdarg.h>
#include <sys/types.h>
#include <errno.h>
#include <signal.h>
#include <setjmp.h>
#include <sys/socket.h>
#include <netdb.h>
#include <netinet/in.h>

static  char    *prog;          /* ptr to program name (for messages)   */

/* This is arbitrary but should be unprivileged (>1024) */
#define DEFAULT_PORT    "9000"  /* must match client default port      */

/* Define process exit codes */

#define EX_OK           0       /* Normal termination                   */
#define EX_ARGFAIL      1       /* Incorrect arguments                  */
#define EX_SYSERR       2       /* Error in system call                 */
#define EX_NOMEM        3       /* Cannot allocate memory               */

/* Server structure used to pass information internally */

typedef struct {
```

```
    int     sock;                   /* socket descriptor              */
    char    *port_name;             /* ptr to name of port being used */
    int     port_number;            /* integer value for port         */
    FILE    *ferr;                  /* stdio handle for error messages */
} _Server, *Server;

/* Log - display an error or informational message for the user */

static void Log(Server srv, char *fmt,...) {
    va_list ap;

    va_start(ap,fmt);
    (void)vfprintf(srv->ferr,fmt,ap);
    va_end(ap);
}

/* Fatal - display a fatal error message to the user and then exit */

static void Fatal(Server srv,int exval,char *fmt,...) {
    va_list ap;
    va_start(ap,fmt);
    (void)vfprintf(srv->ferr,fmt,ap);
    va_end(ap);
    exit(exval);
}

/* newServer - Create a new server object */

static Server newServer(void) {
    Server srv;

    /* Allocate memory for new server, exit on error */

    if((srv = (Server)calloc(1,sizeof(*srv))) == NULL) {
        (void)fprintf(stderr,"%s",strerror(errno));
        exit(EX_NOMEM);
    } else {
        srv->ferr = stderr; /* initialize log output */
        return(srv);
    }
}

/* freeServer - free memory associated with instance of a server struct */

static void freeServer(Server srv) {
```

```
    if(srv->port_name != NULL)
        free(srv->port_name);
    free(srv);
}

/* initServer - Initialize instance of a server struct */

static Server initServer(char *port) {
    Server srv;
    char *protocol = "tcp";
    struct protoent *pp;
    struct servent *sport;
    char *ep;
    extern const struct in6_addr in6addr_any;
    struct sockaddr_storage sa;
    int sopt = 0;
    extern int errno;

    srv = newServer();                  /* exits on failure           */
    srv->port_name = strdup(port);      /* save port name they passed */

    /* Look up protocol number for "tcp" */

    if((pp = getprotobyname(protocol)) == NULL)
        Fatal(srv,EX_ARGFAIL,"initServer: %s\n",strerror(errno));

    /* First see if port number is a string of digits, such as "9000", */
    /* and then see if it is a name such as "echo" (see /etc/services)  */

    if(((srv->port_number=strtol(srv->port_name,&ep,0))>0) && (*ep=='\0'))
        srv->port_number = htons(srv->port_number);
    else if((sport = getservbyname(srv->port_name,protocol)) == NULL)
        Fatal(srv,EX_ARGFAIL,"initServer: bad port '%s'\n",srv->port_name);
    else
        srv->port_number = sport->s_port; /* Success */

    /* Get a new IPv4 or IPv6 socket and prepare it for bind() */

    (void)memset(&sa,0,sizeof(sa));
    if((srv->sock = socket(AF_INET6,SOCK_STREAM,pp->p_proto)) < 0) {
        if(errno == EAFNOSUPPORT) { /* No IPv6 on this system; use IPv4 */
            if((srv->sock = socket(AF_INET,SOCK_STREAM,pp->p_proto)) < 0)
                Fatal(srv,EX_SYSERR,"initServer: socket: %s\n",
                                                        strerror(errno));

            else {
```

```
                struct sockaddr_in *sa4 = (struct sockaddr_in *)&sa;
                sa4->sin_family = AF_INET;
                sa4->sin_port = srv->port_number;
                sa4->sin_addr.s_addr = INADDR_ANY;
            }
        }
    } else { /* IPv6 supported */
        struct sockaddr_in6 *sa6 = (struct sockaddr_in6 *)&sa;
        /* Set the socket option IPV6_V6ONLY to zero (off) so we         */
        /* will listen for both IPv6 and IPv4 incoming connections.     */
        if(setsockopt(srv->sock,IPPROTO_IPV6,IPV6_V6ONLY,&sopt,
                                                    sizeof(sopt)) < 0)
            Fatal(srv,EX_SYSERR,"initServer: setsockopt: %s\n",
                                                    strerror(errno));
        sa6->sin6_family = AF_INET6;
        sa6->sin6_port = srv->port_number;
        sa6->sin6_addr = in6addr_any; /* Listen to any iface & addr     */
    }

    /* Bind the new socket to the service */

    if(bind(srv->sock,(const struct sockaddr *)&sa,sizeof(sa)) < 0)
        Fatal(srv,EX_SYSERR,"initServer: bind: %s\n",strerror(errno));
    /* Set the maximum number of waiting incoming connections */
    if(listen(srv->sock,SOMAXCONN) < 0)
        Fatal(srv,EX_SYSERR,"initServer: listen: %s\n",strerror(errno));
    return(srv);
}

/* runServer - Run the server & iteratively accept incoming connections */

static void runServer(Server srv) {
    while(1) {  /* Iterate forever (unti the user aborts the process)   */
        int s;

        /* sockaddr_storage is large enough to hold either IPv6 or      */
        /*      IPv4 socket information, as defined by system.          */

        struct sockaddr_storage addr;
        socklen_t addrlen = sizeof(addr);
        struct sockaddr *sap = (struct sockaddr *)&addr;

        /* accept will block waiting for a new incoming connection */
        memset(&addr,0,sizeof(addr));
        if((s = accept(srv->sock,sap,&addrlen)) >= 0) {
```

```
        char host[NI_MAXHOST];
        char service[NI_MAXSERV];
        FILE *sfp;

        /* Get information about the new client */

/*NOTUSED   if(getpeername(s,sap,&addrlen) != 0) {
            Log(srv,"getpeername: %s\n",strerror(errno));
            (void)shutdown(s,SHUT_RDWR);
            continue;
        } else END_NOTUSED*/ if(getnameinfo(sap,addrlen, host,
                    sizeof(host), service,sizeof(service),0) != 0) {
            Log(srv,"getnameinfo: %s\n",strerror(errno));
            (void)shutdown(s,SHUT_RDWR);
            continue;
        }
        Log(srv,"accept: host=%s port=%s\n",host,service);

        /* create a buffered stream for new socket */

        if((sfp = fdopen(s,"r+")) == NULL) {
            Log(srv,"fdopen: error creating buffered stream?\n");
            (void)shutdown(s,SHUT_RDWR);
            continue;
        } else {     /* A valid connection has been accepted */
            char buf[BUFSIZ];

            /* loop, reading input and responding with char count */
            setlinebuf(sfp);
            while(fgets(buf,sizeof(buf),sfp) != NULL) {
                Log(srv,"client: %s",buf);
                (void)fprintf(sfp,"got %zd chars\n",strlen(buf));
            }
            Log(srv,"client closed connection\n");
            if(shutdown(s,SHUT_RDWR) != 0)
                Log(srv,"%s: shutdown error: %s\n",strerror(errno));
                (void)fclose(sfp);  /* free any memory associated   */
                                    /* with stdio file pointer sfp  */
        }
      }
    }
}

/* doneServer - user aborted process, so close server socket and Log   */
```

```
static void doneServer(Server srv) {
    if(shutdown(srv->sock,SHUT_RDWR) != 0)
        Log(srv,"%s: shutdown error: %s\n",strerror(errno));
    freeServer(srv);
    Log(srv,"\n%s: shut down\n\n",prog);
}

/* Handle server shutdown when various signals occur */

static jmp_buf sigenv;
static void onSignal(int signo) {
    longjmp(sigenv,signo); /* send back signal num if anyone cares */
}

/* Usage - Print a message informing the user about args, and then exit */

static void Usage(void) {
    (void)printf("Usage: %s [-p tcp_port]\n",prog);
    exit(EX_OK);
}

/* main - main program: parse arguments and then start the server */

int main(int argc,char **argv) {
    Server srv;
    char *port = DEFAULT_PORT;  /* default protocol port to use */
    int c;

    prog = strrchr(*argv,'/') ? strrchr(*argv,'/')+1 : *argv;

    /* Parse argument */

    while((c = getopt(argc,argv,"hp:")) != EOF)
        switch(c) {
        case 'p': /* port name or number from command line */
            port = optarg;
            break;
        case 'h': /* help, falls through... */
            default:  /* unrecognized command arg */
            Usage();
        }

    srv = initServer(port); /* this call exits on error */

    if(setjmp(sigenv) > 0) {
```

```
        doneServer(srv);      /* to here on signal */
        exit(EX_OK);
    } else {
        signal(SIGHUP,onSignal);
        signal(SIGINT,onSignal);
        signal(SIGTERM,onSignal);
    }

    Log(srv,"\n%s: Initialized, waiting for incoming connections\n\n",prog);
    runServer(srv);
    return(EX_OK); /* suppresses compile warning */
}
```

21.20 Summary

Although the TCP/IP standards do not define the exact interface between an application program and TCP/IP protocols, the socket API has become a de facto standard used by vendors such as Microsoft and Apple as well as in Linux. Sockets adopted the UNIX open-close-read-write paradigm, and added many new functions. A server application must create a socket, bind addresses to the socket, accept incoming connections or messages, and send replies. A client must create a socket, connect the socket to a remote endpoint, and then communicate. When an application finishes using a socket, the application must close the socket. In addition to the socket system calls, the socket API includes many library routines that help programmers create and manipulate IP addresses, convert integers between the local machine format and network standard byte order, and search for information such as host addresses.

We examined example code for a client and server that illustrated the use of the socket API for a basic textual echo service. In addition to many details related to the use of sockets, the example code is complicated because it is written to use either IPv4 or IPv6, with IPv6 being given preference.

EXERCISES

21.1 Download the example client and server from *comerbooks.com* and run them on your local system.

21.2 Build a simple server that accepts multiple concurrent TCP connections. To test your server, have the process that handles a connection print a short message, delay a random time, print another message, and exit.

21.3 When is the *listen* call important?

21.4 What functions does your local system provide to access the Domain Name System?

21.5 Devise a server that uses a single Linux process (i.e., a single thread of execution), but handles multiple concurrent TCP connections. (Hint: think of *select*.)

21.6 Read about alternatives to the socket interface, such as the *Transport Library Interface* (*TLI*) and compare them to sockets. What are the major conceptual differences?

21.7 Each operating system limits the number of sockets a given program can use at any time. How many sockets can a program create on your local system?

21.8 Can the socket/file descriptor mechanism and associated *read* and *write* operations be considered a form of object-oriented design? Explain why or why not.

21.9 Consider an alternative API design that provides an interface for each layer of protocol software (e.g., the API allows an application program to send and receive raw frames without using IP, or to send and receive IP datagrams without using UDP or TCP). What are the advantages of having such an interface? The disadvantages?

21.10 A client and server can both run on the same computer and use a TCP socket to communicate. Explain how it is possible to build a client and server that can communicate on a single machine without learning the host's IP address.

21.11 Experiment with the sample server in this chapter to see if you can generate TCP connections sufficiently fast to exceed the backlog the server specifies. Do you expect incoming connection requests to exceed the backlog faster if the server operates on a computer that has one core than on a computer that has four cores? Explain.

21.12 Some of the functions in the original socket API are now irrelevant. Make a list of socket functions that are no longer useful.

21.13 Read more about IPv6 address scope. If a server binds a socket to an address with link-local scope, which computers can contact the server?

21.14 If a programmer wants to create a server that can be reached either via IPv4 or IPv6, what socket functions should the programmer use and how should addresses be specified?

Chapter Contents

22

Bootstrap And Autoconfiguration (DHCP, NDP, IPv6-ND)

22.1 Introduction

Earlier chapters explain how TCP/IP protocols operate in the steady state. The chapters assume hosts and routers are running and the protocol software has been configured and initialized. This chapter examines system startup and discusses the steps a system takes to initialize the protocol stack. Interestingly, the chapter explains that many systems use the client-server paradigm as part of their bootstrap procedure. In particular, the chapter considers a host computer attached to a TCP/IP internet. It explains how the computer can obtain an IPv4 or IPv6 address and the associated information, including an address mask, network prefix, and the addresses of a default router and a name server. The chapter describes the protocols a host can use to obtain the necessary information. Such automatic initialization is important because it permits a user to connect a computer to the Internet without understanding the details of addresses, masks, routers, or how to configure protocol software. The chapter concludes with a discussion of IPv6 Neighbor Discovery, which handles tasks such as address binding in addition to configuration.

The bootstrapping procedures described here are surprising because they use IP to transfer messages. It might seem impossible to use IP before a computer has learned its own IP address. We will see, however, that the special IP addresses described earlier make such communication possible.

22.2 History Of IPv4 Bootstrapping

As Chapter 6 describes, the RARP protocol was initially developed to permit a host computer to obtain its IPv4 address. Later, a more general protocol named *BOOTstrap Protocol* (*BOOTP*) replaced RARP. Finally, the *Dynamic Host Configuration Protocol* (*DHCP*) was developed as an extension of BOOTP†. Because DHCP was derived from BOOTP, our description of basics applies broadly to both. To simplify the discussion, we will focus primarily on DHCP.

Because it uses UDP and IP, DHCP can be implemented by an application program. Like other application protocols, DHCP follows the client-server paradigm. In the simplest cases, DHCP requires only a single packet exchange in which a host computer sends a packet to request bootstrap information and a server responds by sending a single packet that specifies items needed at startup, including the computer's IPv4 address, the IPv4 address of a default router, and the IPv4 address of a domain name server. DHCP also includes a vendor-specific *option* in the reply that allows a vendor to send additional information used only for their computers‡.

22.3 Using IP To Determine An IP Address

We said that DHCP uses UDP to carry messages and that UDP messages are encapsulated in IP datagrams for delivery. To understand how a computer can send DHCP in an IP datagram before the computer learns its IP address, recall from Chapter 5 that there are several special-case IPv4 addresses. In particular, when used as a destination address, the IPv4 address consisting of all *1*s (255.255.255.255) specifies limited broadcast. IP software can accept and broadcast datagrams that specify the limited broadcast address even before the software has discovered its local IP address information. The point is:

> *An application program can use the limited broadcast IPv4 address to force IP software to broadcast a datagram on the local network before the IP software on the host has discovered its IP address.*

Suppose client machine *A* wants to use DHCP to find bootstrap information (including its IPv4 address) and suppose *B* is the server on the same physical net that will answer the request. Because it does not know *B*'s IPv4 address or the IP prefix for the network, *A* must broadcast its initial DHCP request using the IPv4 limited broadcast address. Can *B* send a directed reply? No, it cannot, even though *B* knows *A*'s IPv4 address. To see why, consider what happens if an application on *B* attempts to send a datagram using *A*'s IP address. After routing the datagram, IP software on *B* will pass the datagram to the network interface software. The interface software must map the next-hop IPv4 address to a corresponding hardware address. If the network interface uses ARP as described in Chapter 6, ARP will fail — *A* has not yet received the DHCP

†Defining DHCP as an extension of BOOTP enabled DHCP to be deployed without replacing existing BOOTP relay agents.

‡As we will see, the term *options* is somewhat misleading because DHCP uses an options field to carry much of the bootstrap information.

reply, so *A* does not recognize its IP address. Therefore, *A* cannot answer *B*'s ARP request. As a consequence, *B* has only two alternatives: *B* can broadcast the reply back to *A*, or *B* can extract *A*'s MAC address from the frame that carried the request and use the MAC address to send a directed reply. Most protocol stacks do not permit an application to create and send an arbitrary Layer 2 frame. Thus, one technique consists of extracting *A*'s MAC address from the request packet and adding the entry to the local ARP cache for *A*. Once the entry has been placed in the ARP cache, outgoing packets will be sent to *A* (until the entry expires).

22.4 DHCP Retransmission And Randomization

DHCP places all responsibility for reliable communication on the client. We know that because UDP uses IP for delivery, messages can be delayed, lost, delivered out of order, or duplicated. Furthermore, because IP does not provide a checksum for data, the UDP datagram could arrive with some bits corrupted. To guard against corruption, DHCP requires that UDP have the checksum turned on. The DHCP standard also specifies that requests and replies should be sent with the *do not fragment* bit set to accommodate clients that have too little memory to reassemble datagrams. Finally, to handle duplicates, DHCP is constructed to allow multiple replies; the protocol only accepts and processes the first reply†.

To handle datagram loss, DHCP uses the conventional technique of *timeout and retransmission*. When it transmits a request, the client starts a timer. If no reply arrives before the timer expires, the client must retransmit the request. Of course, after a power failure all machines on a network will reboot simultaneously, possibly overrunning the DHCP server(s) with simultaneous requests. Similarly, if all clients use exactly the same retransmission timeout, many or all of them can attempt to retransmit simultaneously. To avoid simultaneous actions, the DHCP specification recommends adding a random delay. In addition to choosing an initial timeout between *0* and *4* seconds at random, the specification recommends doubling the timer after each retransmission. After the timer reaches a large value, *60* seconds, the client does not increase the timer, but continues to use randomization. Doubling the timeout after each retransmission keeps DHCP from adding excessive traffic to a congested network; the randomization helps avoid simultaneous transmissions.

22.5 DHCP Message Format

To keep an implementation as simple as possible, DHCP messages have fixed-length fields, and replies have the same format as requests. Although we said that clients and servers are programs, the DHCP protocol uses the terms loosely, referring to the machine that sends a DHCP request as the *client* and any machine that sends a reply as a *server*. Figure 22.1 shows the DHCP message format.

†Although the standard allows a client to wait for replies from multiple servers, most implementations accept and process the first reply.

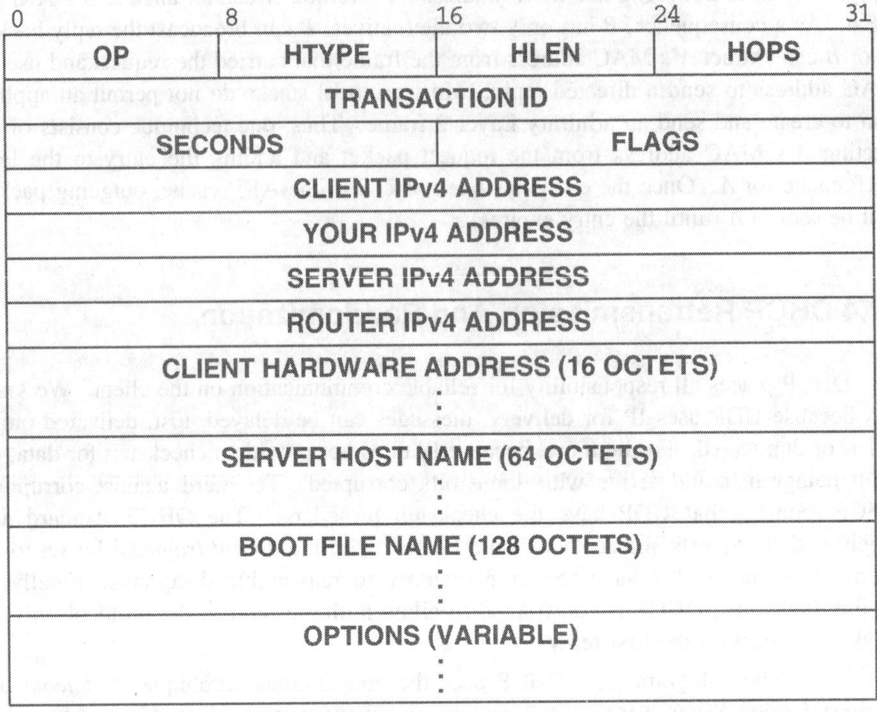

Figure 22.1 The format of a DHCP message. The protocol uses fixed fields to keep the DHCP software small enough to fit into ROM.

Field *OP* specifies whether the message is a request (*1*) or a reply (*2*). As in ARP, fields *HTYPE* and *HLEN* specify the network hardware type and length of the hardware address (e.g., Ethernet has type *1* and address length *6*)†. The client places *0* in the *HOPS* field. If it receives the request and decides to pass the request on to another machine (e.g., to allow bootstrapping across multiple routers), the DHCP server increments the *HOPS* count. The *TRANSACTION ID* field contains an integer that clients use to match responses with requests. The *SECONDS* field reports the number of seconds since the client started to boot.

The *CLIENT IPv4 ADDRESS* field and all fields following it contain the most important information. To allow the greatest flexibility, clients fill in as much information as they know and leave remaining fields set to zero. For example, if a client knows the name or address of a specific server from which it wants information, it can fill in the *SERVER IPv4 ADDRESS* or *SERVER HOST NAME* field. If these fields are nonzero, only the server with matching name/address will answer the request; if they are zero, any server that receives the request will reply.

DHCP can be used from a client that already knows its IPv4 address (i.e., to obtain other information). A client that knows its IP address places it in the *CLIENT IPv4*

†Values for the *HTYPE* field are assigned by the IETF.

ADDRESS field; other clients use zero. If the client's IP address is zero in the request, a server returns the client's IP address in the *YOUR IPv4 ADDRESS* field.

The 16-bit *FLAGS* field allows control of the request and response. As Figure 22.2 shows, only the high-order bit of the *FLAGS* field has been assigned a meaning.

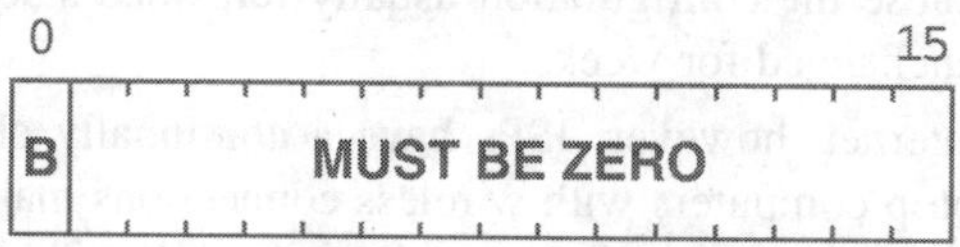

Figure 22.2 The format of the 16-bit *FLAGS* field in a DHCP message. The leftmost bit is interpreted as a broadcast request; all others bits must be set to zero.

A client uses the high-order bit in the *FLAGS* field to control whether the server sends the response via unicast or broadcast. To understand why a client might choose a broadcast response, recall that while it communicates with a DHCP server, a client does not yet have an IP address, which means the client cannot answer ARP queries. Thus, to ensure that the client can receive messages sent by a DHCP server, a client can request that the server send responses using IP broadcast, which corresponds to hardware broadcast. The rules for datagram processing allow IP to discard any datagram that arrives via hardware unicast if the destination address does not match the computer's address. However, IP is required to accept and handle any datagram sent to the IP broadcast address.

Interestingly, DHCP does not provide space in the message to download a specific memory image for an embedded system. Instead, DHCP provides a *BOOT FILE NAME* field that a small diskless system can use. The client can use the field to supply a generic name like "unix," which means, "I want to boot the UNIX operating system for this machine." The DHCP server consults its configuration database to map the generic name into a specific file name that contains the memory image appropriate for the client hardware, and returns the fully qualified file name in its reply. Of course, the configuration database also allows completely automatic bootstrapping, in which the client places zeros in the *BOOT FILE NAME* field and DHCP selects a memory image for the machine. The client then uses a standard file transfer protocol such as TFTP to obtain the image. The advantage of the approach is that a diskless client can use a generic name without encoding a specific file, and the network manager can change the location of a boot image without changing the ROM in embedded systems.

Items in the *OPTIONS* area all use a *Type-Length-Value* (*TLV*) style encoding — each item contains a *type* octet, a *length* octet, and ends with a *value* of the specified length. Two options are especially significant: an IPv4 subnet mask for the local network and an IPv4 address of a default router.

22.6 The Need For Dynamic Configuration

Early bootstrap protocols operated in a relatively static environment in which each host had a permanent network connection. A manager created a configuration file that specified a set of parameters for each host, including an IP address. The file did not change frequently because the configuration usually remained stable. Typically, a configuration continued unchanged for weeks.

In the modern Internet, however, ISPs have a continually changing set of customers, and portable laptop computers with wireless connections make it possible to move a computer from one location to another quickly and easily. To handle automated address assignment, DHCP allows a computer to obtain an IP address quickly and dynamically. That is, when configuring a DHCP server, a manager supplies a set of IPv4 addresses. Whenever a new computer connects to the network, the new computer contacts the server and requests an address. The server chooses one of the addresses from the set that the manager specified, and allocates the address to the computer.

To be completely general, DHCP allows three types of address assignment:

- Static
- Automatic
- Dynamic

A manager chooses how DHCP will respond for each network and for each host. Like its predecessor BOOTP, DHCP allows *static* configuration in which a manager manually configures a specific address for a given computer. DHCP also permits a form of *automatic* address configuration in which a manager allows the DHCP server to assign a permanent address to a computer when the computer first attaches to the network. Finally, DHCP permits *dynamic* address configuration in which a server "loans" an address to a computer for a limited time. Dynamic address assignment is the most powerful and novel aspect of DHCP.

A DHCP server uses the identity of a client and a configuration file to decide how to proceed. When a client contacts a DHCP server, the client sends an identifier, usually the client's hardware address. The server uses the client's identifier (and the network over which the request arrives) to determine how to assign the client an IP address. Thus, a manager has complete control over how addresses are assigned. A server can be configured to assign an IPv4 address to one computer statically, while allowing other computers to obtain addresses automatically or dynamically. To summarize:

> *DHCP permits a computer to obtain all the information needed to communicate on a given network (including an IPv4 address, subnet mask, and the address of a default router) when the computer boots.*

22.7 DHCP Leases And Dynamic Address Assignment

DHCP's dynamic address assignment is temporary. We say that a DHCP server *leases* an address to a client for a finite period of time. The server specifies the lease period when it allocates the address. During the lease period, the server will not lease the same address to another client. At the end of the lease period, the client must renew the lease or stop using the address.

How long should a DHCP lease last? The optimal time for a lease depends on the particular network and the needs of a particular host. For example, to guarantee that addresses can be recycled quickly, computers on a network used by students in a university laboratory can have a short lease period (e.g., one hour). By contrast, a corporate network might use a lease period of one day or one week. An ISP might make the duration of a lease depend on a customer's contract. To accommodate all possible environments, DHCP does not specify a fixed constant for the lease period. Instead, the protocol allows a client to request a specific lease period, and allows a server to inform the client of the lease period it grants. Thus, a manager can decide how long each server should allocate an address to a client. In the extreme, DHCP reserves a value for *infinity* to permit a lease to last arbitrarily long (i.e., to make a permanent address assignment).

22.8 Multiple Addresses And Relays

A multi-homed computer connects to more than one network. When such a computer boots, it may need to obtain configuration information for each of its interfaces. As we have seen, a DHCP message only provides the computer with one IPv4 address and only provides information (e.g., the subnet mask) for one network. The DHCP design means a computer with multiple interfaces must handle each interface separately. Thus, although we describe DHCP as if a computer needs only one address, the reader must remember that each interface of a multi-homed computer needs its own address. If a multi-homed host chooses to send requests on multiple interfaces, the DHCP client software for each interface may be at a different point in the protocol.

DHCP uses the notion of a *relay agent* to permit a computer to contact a server on a nonlocal network. When a relay agent, typically a router, receives a broadcast request from a client, it forwards the request to a DHCP server and returns a reply that is sent from the DHCP server to the host. Relay agents can complicate multi-homed configuration because a server may receive multiple requests from the same computer. Although DHCP uses the term *client identifier*, we assume that a multi-homed client sends a different identifier for each interface (e.g., a unique hardware address for each interface). Thus, a server will always be able to distinguish among requests from a multi-homed host, even when the server receives such requests via a relay agent.

22.9 DHCP Address Acquisition States

When it uses DHCP to obtain an IPv4 address, a client is in one of six states. The state transition diagram in Figure 22.3 shows events and messages that cause a client to change state.

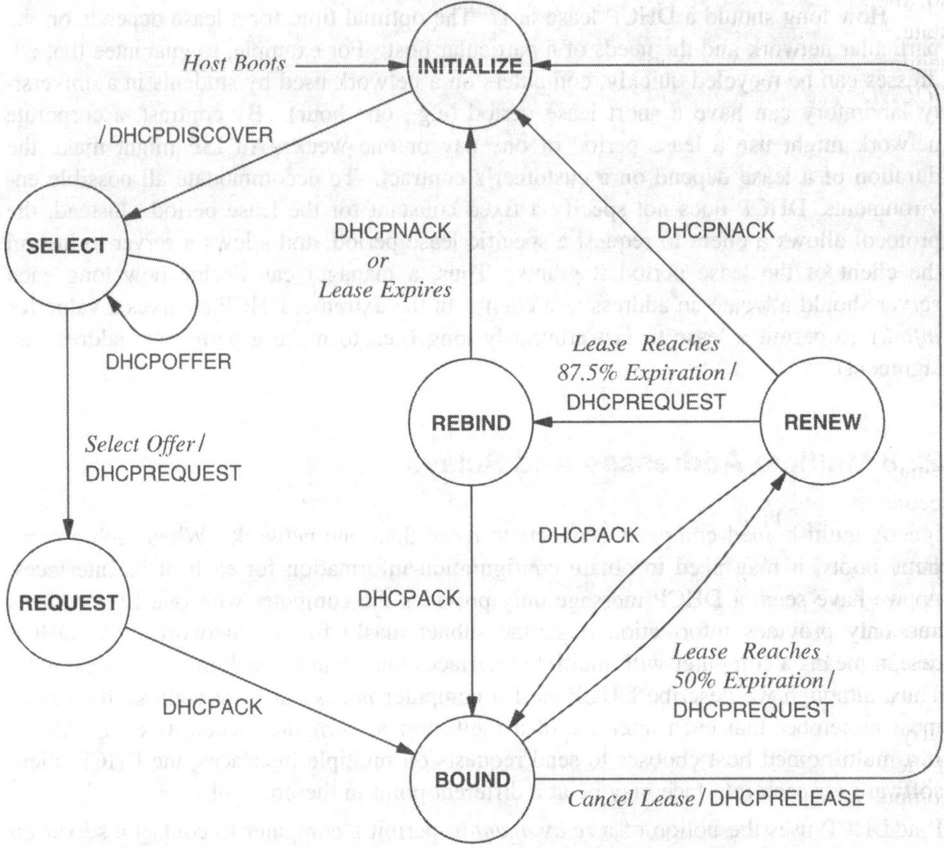

Figure 22.3 The six main states of a DHCP client and transitions among them. Each label on a transition lists the incoming message or event that causes the transmission, followed by a slash and the message the client sends.

When it first boots, a DHCP client enters the *INITIALIZE* state. To start acquiring an IPv4 address, the client first contacts all DHCP servers in the local net. To do so, the client broadcasts a *DHCPDISCOVER* message and moves to the state labeled *SELECT*. Because the protocol is an extension of BOOTP, the client sends the *DHCPDISCOVER* message in a UDP datagram with the destination port set to the

BOOTP port (i.e., port *67*). All DHCP servers on the local net receive the message, and those servers that have been programmed to respond to the particular client send a *DHCPOFFER* message. Thus, a client may receive zero or more responses.

While in state *SELECT*, the client collects *DHCPOFFER* responses from DHCP servers. Each offer contains configuration information for the client along with an IPv4 address that the server is offering to lease to the client. The client must choose one of the responses (e.g., the first to arrive), and negotiate with the server for a lease. To do so, the client sends the server a *DHCPREQUEST* message and enters the *REQUEST* state. To acknowledge receipt of the request and start the lease, the server responds by sending a *DHCPACK*. Arrival of the acknowledgement causes the client to move to the *BOUND* state, where the client proceeds to use the address. To summarize:

> *To use DHCP, a host becomes a client by broadcasting a message to all servers on the local network. The host then collects offers from servers, selects one of the offers, and verifies acceptance with the server.*

22.10 Early Lease Termination

We think of the *BOUND* state as the normal state of operation; a client typically remains in the *BOUND* state while it uses the IP address it has acquired. If a client has secondary storage (e.g., a local disk), the client can store the IPv4 address it was assigned, and request the same address when it restarts again. In some cases, however, a client in the *BOUND* state may discover it no longer needs an IP address. For example, suppose a user attaches a laptop computer to a network, uses DHCP to acquire an IP address, and then uses the computer to read electronic mail. The protocol specifies that a lease must last a minimum of one hour, which may be longer than the user needs.

When an address is no longer needed, DHCP allows a client to terminate the lease early without waiting for the lease to expire. Early termination is especially important if the number of IP addresses a server has available is much smaller than the number of computers that attach to the network. If each client terminates its lease as soon as the IP address is no longer needed, the server will be able to assign the address to another client.

To terminate a lease early, a client sends a *DHCPRELEASE* message to the server. Releasing an address is a final action that prevents the client from using the address further. Thus, after transmitting the release message, the client must not send any other datagrams that use the address. In terms of the state transition diagram of Figure 22.3, a host that sends a *DHCPRELEASE* leaves the *BOUND* state, and must start at the *INITIALIZE* state again before it can use IP.

22.11 Lease Renewal States

We said that when it acquires an address, a DHCP client moves to the *BOUND* state. Upon entering the *BOUND* state, the client sets three timers that control lease renewal, rebinding, and expiration. A DHCP server can specify explicit values for the timers when it allocates an address to the client; if the server does not specify timer values, the client uses defaults. The default value for the first timer is one-half of the total lease time. When the first timer expires, the client must attempt to renew its lease. To request a renewal, the client sends a *DHCPREQUEST* message to the server from which the lease was obtained. The client then moves to the *RENEW* state to await a response. The *DHCPREQUEST* contains the IP address the client is currently using, and asks the server to extend the lease on the address. As in the initial lease negotiation, a client can request a period for the extension, but the server ultimately controls the renewal. A server can respond to a client's renewal request in one of two ways: it can instruct the client to stop using the address or it can approve continued use. If it approves, the server sends a *DHCPACK*, which causes the client to return to the *BOUND* state and continue using the address. The *DHCPACK* can also contain new values for the client's timers. If a server rejects continued use, the server sends a *DHCPNACK* (negative acknowledgement), which causes the client to stop using the address immediately and return to the *INITIALIZE* state.

After sending a *DHCPREQUEST* message that requests an extension on its lease, a client remains in state *RENEW* awaiting a response. If no response arrives, the server that granted the lease is either down or unreachable. To handle the situation, DHCP relies on a second timer, which was set when the client entered the *BOUND* state. The second timer expires after *87.5%* of the lease period, and causes the client to move from state *RENEW* to state *REBIND*. When making the transition, the client assumes the old DHCP server is unavailable, and begins broadcasting a *DHCPREQUEST* message to any server on the local net. Any server configured to provide service to the client can respond positively (i.e., to extend the lease), or negatively (i.e. to deny further use of the IP address). If it receives a positive response, the client returns to the *BOUND* state, and resets the two timers. If it receives a negative response, the client must move to the *INITIALIZE* state, must immediately stop using the IP address, and must acquire a new IP address before it can continue to use IP.

After moving to the *REBIND* state, a client will have asked the original server plus all servers on the local net for a lease extension. In the rare case that a client does not receive a response from any server before its third timer expires, the lease expires. The client must stop using the IP address, must move back to the *INITIALIZE* state, and must acquire a new address.

22.12 DHCP Options And Message Type

Surprisingly, DHCP does not allocate fixed fields in the message header for the message type or lease information. Instead, DHCP retains the BOOTP message format and uses the *OPTIONS* field to identify the message as DHCP. Figure 22.4 illustrates the *DHCP message type* option that specifies the DHCP message being sent.

0	8	16 23
CODE (53)	LENGTH (1)	TYPE (1 - 8)

TYPE FIELD	Corresponding DHCP Message Type
1	DHCPDISCOVER
2	DHCPOFFER
3	DHCPREQUEST
4	DHCPDECLINE
5	DHCPACK
6	DHCPNACK
7	DHCPRELEASE
8	DHCPINFORM

Figure 22.4 The format of a DHCP option used to specify the DHCP message type with a list of the possible values for the third octet.

Over 200 *OPTIONS* have been defined for use in a DHCP reply; each has a type and length field that together determine the size of the option. The assignments are somewhat haphazard because vendors used values that were initially reserved. As it assigned codes, the IETF decided to avoid conflicts by avoiding codes that the vendors were using. Figure 22.5 lists a few of the possible options.

Item Type	Item Code	Length Octet	Contents of Value
Subnet mask	1	4	Subnet mask to use
Routers	3	N	IPv4 addresses of N/4 routers
DNS Servers	6	N	IPv4 addresses of N/4 servers
Hostname	12	N	N bytes of client host name
Boot Size	13	2	2-octet integer size of boot file
Default IP TTL	23	1	Value for datagram TTL
NTP Servers (time)	42	N	IPv4 addresses of N/4 servers
Mail Servers (SMTP)	69	N	IPv4 addresses of N/4 servers
Web Servers	72	N	IPv4 addresses of N/4 servers

Figure 22.5 Examples of *OPTIONS* that can be present in an IPv4 DHCP reply†.

†Because each IPv4 address occupies 4 octets, a field of N octets holds N/4 IPv4 addresses.

22.13 DHCP Option Overload

Fields *SERVER HOST NAME* and *BOOT FILE NAME* in the DHCP message header each occupy many octets. If a given message does not contain information in either of those fields, the space is wasted. To allow a DHCP server to use the two fields for other options, DHCP defines an *Option Overload* option. When present, the overload option tells a receiver to ignore the usual meaning of the *SERVER HOST NAME* and *BOOT FILE NAME* fields, and look for options in the fields instead.

22.14 DHCP And Domain Names

Although it can allocate an IP address to a computer on demand, DHCP does not completely automate all the procedures required to attach a permanent host to an internet. In particular, the DHCP protocol does not specify any interaction with the Domain Name System (DNS)†. Thus, unless an additional mechanism is used, the binding between a host name and the IP address DHCP assigns the host will remain independent.

Despite the lack of a standard, some DHCP servers do indeed interact with DNS when they assign an address. For example, Unix systems such as Linux or BSD arrange for DHCP to coordinate with the DNS software, which is known as *named bind*‡ or simply *bind*. Similarly, the Microsoft DHCP software coordinates with the Microsoft DNS software to ensure a host that is assigned a DHCP address also has a domain name. The coordination mechanisms also work in reverse to ensure that when a DHCP lease is revoked, a DHCP server notifies DNS to revoke the corresponding name.

22.15 Managed And Unmanaged Configuration

There are two broad approaches to configuration of network devices that have consequences for both the network infrastructure and configuration protocols.

- Managed
- Unmanaged

Managed. A *managed* system requires network operators to install and configure servers. When a computer joins a network, the computer contacts a configuration server to obtain information about addressing, routing, and other services. Although it is difficult to envision managed services in the abstract, our discussion of DHCP makes the concept clear because DHCP is often used as a canonical example of managed configuration.

Unmanaged. An *unmanaged* system does not require a network manager to assign addresses nor does it require configuration servers. Instead, when a computer joins a network the computer generates a unique address, and then uses the address to com-

†Chapter 23 considers the Domain Name System in detail.

‡The term *named* is short for *name daemon*.

municate. The original *AppleTalk* protocol illustrates an unmanaged system: when it joined a network, a computer used a random number generator to choose an address, and then broadcast a message to verify that the address was not already in use. If another computer was already using the address, a new random value was selected until a unique address was found. No other configuration was needed because services were reached by broadcasting requests.

Each approach to configuration has advantages and disadvantages. An unmanaged network has the advantages of not requiring humans to configure and operate a set of servers. Thus, computers and other devices (e.g., printers) can attach and communicate automatically. Unfortunately, the unmanaged approach also has disadvantages. Random address assignment can lead to conflicts if a computer is temporarily disconnected or busy when a new computer joins and chooses the same address. Furthermore, as the network size increases, the use of broadcast becomes a problem — an unmanaged approach can work across a single network, but not across the global Internet.

A managed approach has the chief advantage of giving each network owner complete control over the computers and devices that attach to the network. Network managers usually prefer the managed approach because a knowledgeable staff is required for other tasks and a configuration server can be run on hardware with other servers.

22.16 Managed And Unmanaged Configuration For IPv6

When IPv6 was first envisioned, the designers thought about a special case: two IPv6 hosts that connect without any servers on their network. For example, consider two IPv6 mobile devices that have Wi-Fi capability. The designers thought it should be possible for the devices to communicate directly without requiring a base station and without requiring a server to hand out addresses. Consequently, the designers adopted an unmanaged approach in which address assignment is automated. They use the term *IPv6 stateless autoconfiguration* to describe the IPv6 address allocation scheme. Whenever a host joins an unmanaged network, the host employs stateless autoconfiguration to generate an IPv6 address and begin communication. Thus, stateless autoconfiguration means hosts can communicate without requiring a server to hand out addresses.

Many managers objected to stateless autoconfiguration. Network operators who manage large commercial ISP networks were especially disappointed. Because they manage for-profit services that charge customers for network connections, the operators wanted control over which hosts connect to their network (i.e., to exclude non-customers). In particular, the operators wanted a managed service that would give them control over address assignment.

In terms of managed address assignment services, DHCP is widely accepted as the industry standard. Network operators like DHCP because it gives an operator precise control over how addresses are assigned. In particular, a manager can choose the assignment policy on a host-by-host basis by pre-assigning a fixed IP address to a given host or allowing the host to obtain an address from a pool automatically.

22.17 IPv6 Configuration Options And Potential Conflicts

To satisfy network operators who want a managed solution and individuals who want to be able to create ad-hoc networks, the IETF decided to endorse two approaches to IPv6 address configuration:

- Managed via DHCPv6
- Unmanaged via stateless autoconfiguration

Managed via DHCPv6. A new version of DHCP has been created for IPv6. Named *DHCPv6*, the new version is conceptually similar to the original DHCP. Like the original, for example, the new version requires a server to be available for each network and requires a host to contact the server to obtain an IP address. However, because IPv6 does not support broadcast, a host cannot use broadcast to reach a DHCPv6 server the same way an IPv4 host broadcasts a DHCP request. Instead, IPv6 allows a host to generate a link-local address and use link-local multicast, which is effectively the same as an IPv4 limited broadcast.

Unfortunately, DHCPv6 is substantially more complex than DHCP. Like most of IPv6, DHCPv6 tries to accommodate all possibilities. DHCPv6 completely changes the format of messages and adds several new message types that give additional functionality. For example, the specification allows *prefix delegation* in which a server delegates a set of prefixes to another server (e.g., to a home router for assignment to devices in the home). Some of the increased complexity arises from the IPv6 provision that allows a host to use multiple network prefixes on a given interface. Other complexity arises because DHCPv6 allows for authentication. The result is that the RFC that defines DHCPv6 is over twice the size of the RFC that defines DHCP†.

Unmanaged via stateless autoconfiguration. We said that in IPv6, stateless autoconfiguration refers to the method of address creation for an unmanaged link. Stateless autoconfiguration relies on the IPv6 *Neighbor Discovery Protocol* (*NDP*) described in the next section. We will see that NDP provides much more functionality than managed address configuration. However, when comparing NDP to DHCPv6 we only need to consider the basics: without using a configuration server, a host can generate an IPv6 address and verify that the address is unique (i.e., no other node on the network is using the same address).

The use of two approaches for IPv6 configuration leads to questions. Is one approach preferred over another? Can a given host use both approaches? If both are used and the resulting IPv6 addresses differ, should the host retain the two IPv6 addresses or should one address be discontinued? The standards do not specify preferences or how to handle address conflicts. Instead, the standards merely provide two alternative technologies. We can summarize:

> *IPv6 standards include schemes for managed and unmanaged address assignment. The standards do not specify which is preferred or how to handle situations where conflicts arise.*

†Direct comparison of the RFCs for DHCP and DHCPv6 is somewhat unfair because the DHCPv6 specification includes some of the options.

22.18 IPv6 Neighbor Discovery Protocol (NDP)

IPv6's *Neighbor Discovery Protocol* (*NDP* or *IPv6-ND*) includes low-level functionality such as Layer 2 address resolution and host redirect messages. Therefore, it may seem that NDP belongs in early chapters of the text. However, the discussion has been delayed until this chapter because NDP also includes functionality from higher-layer protocols. Specifically, NDP provides a mechanism for address configuration.

NDP operates at Layer 3 by using ICMPv6 messages. The following lists the major functions that NDP provides:

- *Router Discovery*: a host can identify the set of routers on a given link
- *Next-hop Routes*: a host can find the next-hop router for a given destination
- *Neighbor Discovery*: a node can identify the set of nodes on a given link
- *Neighbor Unreachability Detection (NUD)*: a node monitors its neighbors continuously to learn when a neighbor becomes unreachable
- *Address Prefix Discovery*: a host can learn the network prefix(es) being used on a link
- *Configuration Parameter Discovery*: a host can determine parameters, such as the MTU used on a given link
- *Stateless Autoconfiguration*: a host can generate an address for use on a link
- *Duplicate Address Detection (DAD)*: a node can determine whether an address it generates is already in use
- *Address Resolution*: a node can map an IPv6 address to an equivalent MAC address
- *DNS Server Discovery*: a node can find the set of DNS servers on a link
- *Redirect*: a router can inform a node about a preferred first-hop router.

To achieve the above, NDP defines five ICMPv6 message types:

- Router Solicitation
- Router Advertisement
- Neighbor Solicitation
- Neighbor Advertisement
- Redirect

Instead of defining a unique message type for each of the functions described above, NDP uses a combination of the five ICMPv6 message types to achieve each function. The following sections discuss each of the five message types.

22.19 ICMPv6 Router Solicitation Message

A host sends a *Router Solicitation* message to prompt routers to respond. Figure 22.6 illustrates the format of a Router Solicitation.

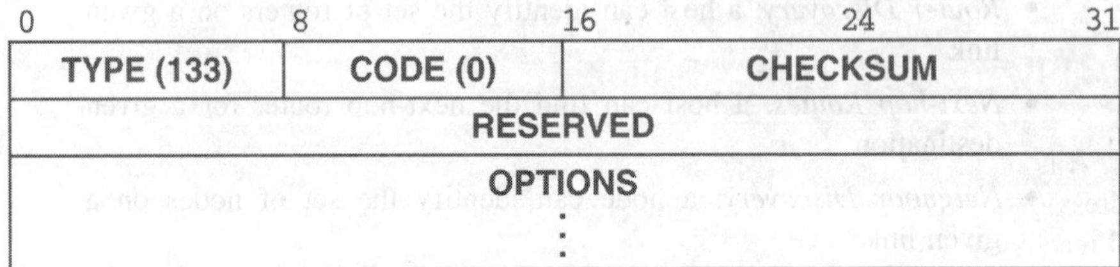

Figure 22.6 The format of an ICMPv6 Router Solicitation Message.

If a node already knows its IP address, the *OPTIONS* field contains the node's MAC address (called a *link layer address* in IPv6).

22.20 ICMPv6 Router Advertisement Message

A router sends a *Router Advertisement* message periodically or when prompted by a Router Solicitation. The message allows a router to announce its presence on the network and its availability as a node through which off-link traffic can be forwarded. Figure 22.7 illustrates the format of a Router Advertisement.

0	8			16	24	31
TYPE (134)	CODE (0)			CHECKSUM		
CUR. HOP LIMIT	M	O	RESERVED	ROUTER LIFETIME		
REACHABLE TIME						
RETRANSMIT TIME						
OPTIONS ⋮						

Figure 22.7 The format of an ICMPv6 Router Advertisement message.

The *CUR. HOP LIMIT* specifies a value that the should be used as the *HOP LIMIT* in each outgoing datagram, the *M* bit specifies whether the network is using managed address assignment (i.e., DHCPv6), and the *O* bit specifies whether other configuration information is available via DHCPv6. If the router can be used as a default router, the *ROUTER LIFETIME* field gives the amount of time the router can be used in seconds. Field *REACHABLE TIME* specifies how long (in milliseconds) a neighbor remains reachable after the neighbor has responded, and field *RETRANSMIT TIME* specifies how frequently to retransmit Neighbor Solicitation messages. Possible options include the senders MAC address, the MTU used on the link, and a list of one or more IPv6 prefixes used on the link.

22.21 ICMPv6 Neighbor Solicitation Message

A node sends a *Neighbor Solicitation* message for two reasons: to obtain the MAC address of a neighbor (the IPv6 equivalent of ARP) and to test whether a neighbor is still reachable. Figure 22.8 illustrates the format of a Neighbor Solicitation.

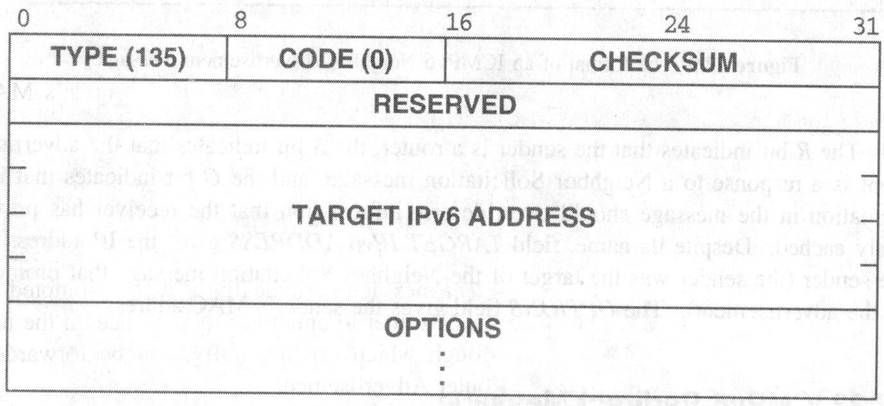

Figure 22.8 The format of an ICMPv6 Neighbor Solicitation message.

Field *TARGET IPv6 ADDRESS* gives the IP address of a neighbor for which a MAC address is needed. If the sender already has an IP address, the *OPTIONS* field includes the sender's MAC address so the receiver knows the sender's IP-to-MAC address binding.

22.22 ICMPv6 Neighbor Advertisement Message

A node sends a *Neighbor Advertisement* message in response to a Neighbor Solicitation message or to propagate reachability. Figure 22.9 illustrates the format of a Neighbor Advertisement.

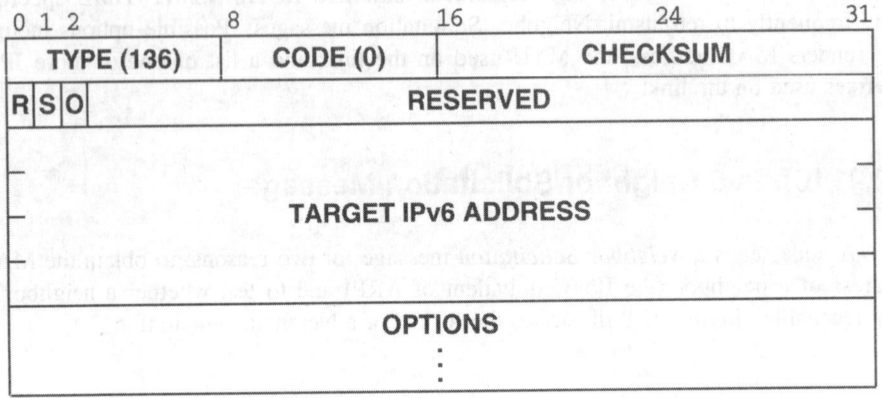

Figure 22.9 The format of an ICMPv6 Neighbor Advertisement message.

The *R* bit indicates that the sender is a router, the *S* bit indicates that the advertisement is a response to a Neighbor Solicitation message, and the *O* bit indicates that information in the message should override any information that the receiver has previously cached. Despite its name, field *TARGET IPv6 ADDRESS* gives the IP address of the sender (the sender was the target of the Neighbor Solicitation message that prompted the advertisement). The *OPTIONS* field gives the sender's MAC address.

22.23 ICMPv6 Redirect Message

A router sends a *Redirect* message for exactly the same reason an IPv4 router sends an ICMP redirect: to request a host to change its first hop for a specific destination. Figure 22.10 illustrates the format of a Redirect message.

As expected, a Redirect message specifies two IPv6 addresses: a destination and the address of a first hop to use. Typically, a Redirect message is prompted when a router receives a datagram from a host on a directly-connected link and the router finds that the destination is reached through another router on the same link. When a host receives a Redirect, the host must change its forwarding table to use the specified *FIRST HOP IPv6 ADDRESS* for future datagrams sent to the *DESTINATION IPv6 ADDRESS*.

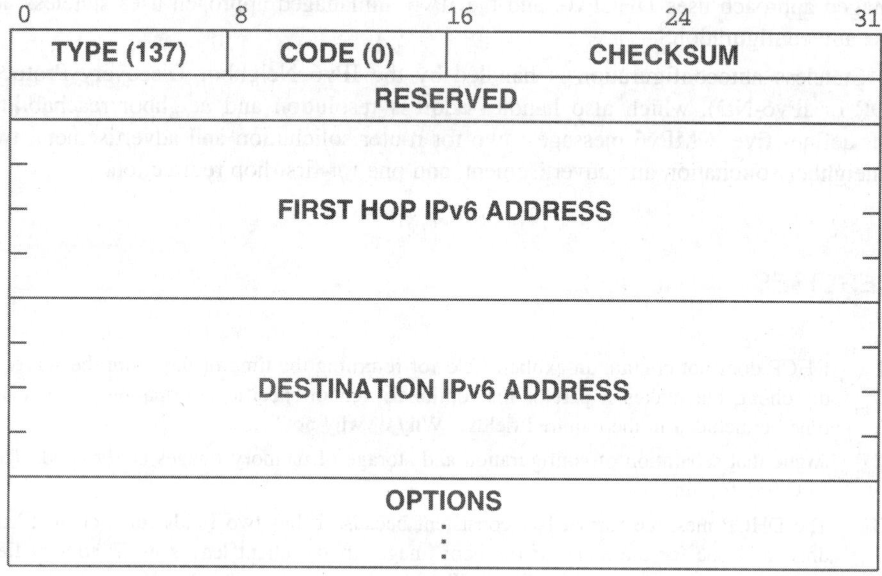

Figure 22.10 The format of an ICMPv6 Redirect message.

22.24 Summary

The Dynamic Host Configuration Protocol allows an IPv4 computer to obtain information at startup, including an IP address, the address of a default router, and the address of a domain name server. DHCP permits a server to allocate IP addresses automatically or dynamically. Dynamic allocation is necessary for environments such as a wireless network where computers can attach and detach quickly.

To use DHCP, a computer becomes a client. The computer broadcasts a request for DHCP servers, selects one of the offers it receives, and exchanges messages with the server to obtain a lease on the advertised IPv4 address. A relay agent can forward DHCP requests on behalf of the client, which means a site can have a single DHCP server handle address assignment for multiple subnets.

When a client obtains an IPv4 address from DHCP, the client starts three timers. After the first timer expires, the client attempts to renew its lease. If a second timer expires before renewal completes, the client attempts to rebind its address from any available DHCP server. If the final timer expires before a lease has been renewed, the client stops using the address and returns to the initial state to acquire a new address. A finite state machine specifies lease acquisition and renewal.

We say that DHCP provides managed address assignment; the alternative is an unmanaged system in which each computer chooses an address and verifies that the address is unique. IPv6 offers both managed and unmanaged assignment. The IPv6 managed approach uses DHCPv6, and the IPv6 unmanaged approach uses stateless address autoconfiguration.

Stateless autoconfiguration is handled by the IPv6 Neighbor Discovery Protocol (NDP or IPv6-ND), which also handles address resolution and neighbor reachability. NDP defines five ICMPv6 messages: two for router solicitation and advertisement, two for neighbor solicitation and advertisement, and one for first-hop redirection.

EXERCISES

22.1 DHCP does not contain an explicit field for returning the time of day from the server to the client, but makes it part of the (optional) vendor-specific information. Should the time be included in the required fields? Why or why not?

22.2 Argue that separation of configuration and storage of memory images is *not* good. (See RFC 951 for hints.)

22.3 The DHCP message format is inconsistent because it has two fields for a client IP address and one for the name of the boot image. If the client leaves its IP address field empty, the server returns the client's IP address in the second field. If the client leaves the boot file name field empty, the server *replaces* it with an explicit name. Why?

22.4 Read the standard to find out how clients and servers use the *HOPS* field in a DHCP message.

22.5 When a DHCP client receives a reply via hardware broadcast, how does it know whether the reply is intended for another DHCP client on the same physical net?

22.6 When a machine obtains its subnet mask with DHCP instead of ICMP, it places less load on *other* host computers. Explain.

22.7 Read the standard to find out how a DHCP client and server can agree on a lease duration without having synchronized clocks.

22.8 Consider a host that has a disk and uses DHCP to obtain an IP address. If the host stores its address on the disk along with the date the lease expires and then reboots within the lease period, can it use the address? Why or why not?

22.9 DHCP mandates a minimum address lease of one hour. Can you imagine a situation in which DHCP's minimum lease causes inconvenience? Explain.

22.10 Read the RFC to find out how DHCP specifies renewal and rebinding timers. Should a server ever set one without the other? Why or why not?

22.11 The state transition diagram for DHCP does not show retransmission. Read the standard to find out how many times a client should retransmit a request.

22.12 Can DHCP guarantee that a client is not "spoofing" (i.e., can DHCP guarantee that it will not send configuration information for host *A* to host *B*)? Why or why not?

22.13 DHCP specifies that a client must be prepared to handle at least *312* octets of options. How did the number *312* arise?

22.14 Can a computer that uses DHCP to obtain an IPv4 address run a server? If so, how does a client reach the server?

22.15 Suppose an IPv6 computer attaches to a network that does not have any routers. How does the IPv6 node know that it should use stateless autoconfiguration to obtain an IPv6 address?

22.16 Extend the previous question: if an IPv6 node attaches to a network that does have a router, how does the node know whether to use stateless autoconfiguration?

22.17 If an IPv6 node uses stateless autoconfiguration, can the node run a server? Explain.

Chapter Contents

23

The Domain Name System (DNS)

23.1 Introduction

The protocols described in earlier chapters use binary values called Internet Protocol addresses (IP addresses) to identify hosts and routers. Although such addresses provide a convenient, compact representation for specifying the source and destination in datagrams sent across an internet, users prefer to assign machines pronounceable, easily remembered names.

This chapter considers a scheme for assigning meaningful high-level names to a large set of machines, and discusses a mechanism that maps between high-level machine names and binary IP addresses. It considers both the translation from high-level names to IP addresses and the translation from IP addresses to high-level machine names. The naming scheme is interesting for two reasons. First, it has been used to assign machine names throughout the Internet. Second, because it uses a geographically distributed set of servers to map names to addresses, the implementation of the name mapping mechanism provides a large scale example of the client-server paradigm described in Chapter 20.

23.2 Names For Computers

The earliest computer systems forced users to understand numeric addresses for objects like system tables and peripheral devices. Timesharing systems advanced computing by allowing users to invent meaningful symbolic names for both physical objects (e.g., peripheral devices) and abstract objects (e.g., files). A similar pattern has emerged in computer networking. Early systems supported point-to-point connections between computers and used low-level MAC addresses to specify computers. Internetworking introduced universal addressing as well as protocol software to map universal addresses into low-level MAC addresses. Because the Internet contains millions of machines, users need meaningful, symbolic names to identify specific computers that they use.

Early computer names reflected the small environment in which they were chosen. It was quite common for a site with a handful of machines to choose names based on the machines' purposes. For example, machines often had names like *accounting*, *development*, and *production*. Users find such names preferable to cumbersome hardware addresses.

Although the distinction between *address* and *name* is intuitively appealing, it is artificial. Any *name* is merely an identifier that consists of a sequence of characters chosen from a finite alphabet. Names are only useful if the system can efficiently map them to the object they denote. Thus, we think of an IP address as a *low-level name*, and we say that users prefer *high-level names* for computers.

The form of high-level names is important because it determines how names are translated to low-level names or bound to objects, as well as how name assignments are authorized. With only a few machines, choosing high-level names is easy — each administrator can choose an arbitrary name and verify that the name is not in use in the local environment. For example, when its main departmental computer was connected to the Internet in 1980, the Computer Science department at Purdue University chose the name *purdue* to identify the connected machine. At the time, the list of potential conflicts contained only a few dozen names. By mid 1986, the official list of hosts on the Internet contained 3100 officially registered names and 6500 official aliases. Although the list was growing rapidly in the 1980s, most sites had additional machines (typically, personal computers) that were unregistered. In the current Internet, with hundreds of millions of machines, choosing symbolic names is much more difficult.

23.3 Flat Namespace

The original set of machine names used throughout the Internet formed a *flat namespace*, in which each name consisted of a sequence of characters without any further structure. In the original scheme, a central site, the *Network Information Center* (*NIC*), administered the namespace and determined whether a new name was appropriate (i.e., it prohibited obscene names or new names that conflicted with existing names).

The chief advantage of a flat namespace is that names are convenient and short; the chief disadvantage is that a flat namespace cannot generalize to large sets of machines for both technical and administrative reasons. First, because names are drawn from a single set of identifiers, the potential for conflict increases as the number of sites increases. Second, because authority for adding new names must rest at a single site, the administrative workload at that central site also increases with the number of sites. To understand the severity of the problem, imagine a central authority trying to handle the current Internet where a new computer appears approximately ten times per second. Third, because the name-to-address bindings change frequently, the cost of maintaining correct copies of the entire list at each site is high and increases as the number of sites increases. Alternatively, if the name database resides at a single site, network traffic to that site increases with the number of sites.

23.4 Hierarchical Names

How can a naming system accommodate a large, rapidly expanding set of names without requiring a central site to administer it? The answer lies in decentralizing the naming mechanism by delegating authority for parts of the namespace and distributing responsibility for the mapping between names and addresses. The Internet uses such a scheme. Before examining the details, we will consider the motivation and intuition behind it.

The partitioning of a namespace must be defined in a way that supports efficient name mapping and guarantees autonomous control of name assignment. Optimizing only for efficient mapping can lead to solutions that retain a flat namespace and reduce traffic by dividing the names among multiple mapping machines. Optimizing only for administrative ease can lead to solutions that make delegation of authority easy but name mapping expensive or complex.

To understand how the namespace should be divided, consider the internal structure of large organizations. At the top, a chief executive has overall responsibility. Because the chief executive cannot oversee everything, the organization may be partitioned into divisions, with an executive in charge of each division. The chief executive grants each division autonomy within specified limits. More to the point, the executive in charge of a particular division can hire or fire employees, assign offices, and delegate authority, without obtaining direct permission from the chief executive.

Besides making it easy to delegate authority, the hierarchy of a large organization introduces autonomous operation. For example, when an office worker needs information like the telephone number of a new employee, he or she begins by asking local clerical workers (who may contact clerical workers in other divisions). The point is that although authority always passes down the corporate hierarchy, information can flow across the hierarchy from one office to another.

23.5 Delegation Of Authority For Names

A hierarchical naming scheme works like the management of a large organization. The namespace is *partitioned* at the top level, and authority for names in subdivisions is passed to designated agents. For example, one might choose to partition the namespace based on *site name* and to delegate to each site responsibility for maintaining names within its partition. The topmost level of the hierarchy divides the namespace and delegates authority for each division; it need not be bothered by changes within a division.

The syntax of hierarchically assigned names often reflects the hierarchical delegation of authority used to assign them. As an example, consider a namespace with names of the form:

local.*site*

where *site* is the site name authorized by the central authority, *local* is the part of a name controlled by the site, and the period† character is a delimiter used to separate them. When the topmost authority approves adding a new site, *X*, it adds *X* to the list of valid sites and delegates to site *X* authority for all names that end in .*X*.

23.6 Subset Authority

In a hierarchical namespace, authority may be further subdivided at each level. In our example of partition by sites, the site itself may consist of several administrative groups, and the site authority may choose to subdivide its namespace among the groups. The idea is to keep subdividing the namespace until each subdivision is small enough to be manageable.

Syntactically, subdividing the namespace introduces another partition of the name. For example, adding a *group* subdivision to names already partitioned by site produces the following name syntax:

local.*group*.*site*

Because the topmost level delegates authority, group names do not have to agree among all sites. A university site might choose group names like *engineering*, *science*, and *arts*, while a corporate site might choose group names like *production*, *accounting*, and *personnel*.

The U.S. telephone system provides another example of a hierarchical naming syntax. The 10 digits of a phone number have been partitioned into a 3-digit *area code*, 3-digit *exchange*, and 4-digit *subscriber number* within the exchange. Each exchange has authority for assigning subscriber numbers within its piece of the namespace. Although it is possible to group arbitrary subscribers into exchanges and to group arbitrary exchanges into area codes, the assignment of telephone numbers is not capricious; the numbers are carefully chosen to make it easy to route phone calls across the telephone network.

†In domain names, the period delimiter is pronounced "dot."

The telephone example is important because it illustrates a key distinction between the hierarchical naming scheme used in a TCP/IP internet and other hierarchies: partitioning the set of machines owned by an organization along lines of authority does not necessarily imply partitioning by physical location. For example, it could be that at some university, a single building houses the mathematics department as well as the computer science department. It might even turn out that although the machines from these two groups fall under completely separate administrative domains, they connect to the same physical network. It also may happen that a single group owns machines on several physical networks. For these reasons, the TCP/IP naming scheme allows arbitrary delegation of authority for the hierarchical namespace without regard to physical connections. The concept can be summarized:

In the Internet, hierarchical machine names are assigned according to the structure of organizations that obtain authority for parts of the namespace, not necessarily according to the structure of the physical network interconnections.

Of course, at many sites the organizational hierarchy corresponds with the structure of physical network interconnections. For example, suppose the computers in a given department all connect to the same network. If the department is assigned part of the naming hierarchy, all machines with names in that part of the hierarchy will also connect to a single physical network.

23.7 Internet Domain Names

The *Domain Name System* (*DNS*) is the system that provides name to address mapping for the Internet. DNS has two conceptually independent aspects. The first is abstract: it specifies the name syntax and rules for delegating authority over names. The second is concrete: it specifies the implementation of a distributed computing system that efficiently maps names to addresses. This section considers the name syntax, and later sections examine the implementation.

The Domain Name System uses a hierarchical naming scheme known as *domain names*. As in our earlier examples, a domain name consists of a sequence of subnames separated by a delimiter character, the dot. In our examples, we said that individual sections of the name might represent sites or groups, but DNS simply calls each section a *label*. Thus, the domain name:

cs.purdue.edu

contains three labels: *cs, purdue*, and *edu*. Any suffix of a label in a domain name is also called a *domain*. In the above example, the lowest-level domain is *cs.purdue.edu*, (the domain name for the Computer Science department at Purdue University), the second level domain is *purdue.edu* (the domain name for Purdue University), and the top-level domain is *edu* (the domain name for educational institutions). As the example shows, domain names are written with the local label first and the top domain last. As we will see, writing them in this order makes it possible to compress messages that contain multiple domain names.

23.8 Top-Level Domains

Figure 23.1 lists examples of the global top-level domain names currently in use.

Domain Name	Meaning
aero	Air transport industry
arpa	Infrastructure domain
asia	Regional domain for Asia
biz	Businesses
cat	Catalan language and cultural
com	Commercial organization
coop	Cooperative associations
edu	Educational institution (4-year)
gov	United States government
info	Information
int	International treaty organizations
jobs	Human resource management
mil	United States military
museum	Museums
name	Individuals
net	Major network support centers
org	Organizations other than those above
pro	Credentialed professionals
travel	Travel industry
xxx	Internet pornography
country code	Each country (geographic scheme)

Figure 23.1 The top-level domains assigned in the Internet and their meanings. Although labels are shown in lower case, domain name comparisons are insensitive to case, so *COM* is equivalent to *com*.

The *Internet Corporation for Assigned Names and Numbers* (*ICANN*), which assigns names, has struggled with the question of how many top-level domains are needed and what names should be allowed. The 2-letter country code scheme, once thought to be permanent, is subject to political changes. For example, when Germany reunified, the top-level domain *dd* that had been assigned to East Germany was made obsolete.

An internationalization mechanism has been invented to permit names in other character sets. Thus, the figure only gives a snapshot that may change as new top-level names are approved and become active.

Conceptually, the top-level names permit two different naming hierarchies: geographic and organizational. The geographic scheme divides the universe of machines by country. Machines in the United States fall under the top-level domain *us*; when a foreign country wants to register machines in the Domain Name System, the central authority assigns the country a new top-level domain with the country's international standard 2-letter identifier as its label. The authority for the US domain has chosen to divide it into one second-level domain per state. For example, the domain for the state of Virginia is:

va.us

As an alternative to the geographic hierarchy, the top-level domains allow organizations to be grouped by organizational type. When an organization wants to participate in the Domain Name System, it chooses how it wishes to be registered and requests approval. A *domain name registrar* reviews the application and assigns the organization a subdomain† under one of the existing top-level domains. The owner of a given top-level domain can decide what to allow and how to further partition the namespace. For example, in the United Kingdom, which has the two-letter country code *uk*, universities and other academic institutions are registered under domain *ac.uk*.

An example will help clarify the relationship between the naming hierarchy and authority for names. A machine named *xinu* in the Computer Science department at Purdue University has the official domain name:

xinu.cs.purdue.edu

The machine name was approved and registered by the local network manager in the Computer Science department. The department manager had previously obtained authority for the subdomain *cs.purdue.edu* from a university network authority, who had obtained permission to manage the subdomain *purdue.edu* from the Internet authority. The Internet authority retains control of the *edu* domain, so new universities can only be added with its permission. Similarly, the university network manager at Purdue University retains authority for the *purdue.edu* subdomain, so new third-level domains may only be added with the manager's permission.

Figure 23.2 illustrates a small part of the Internet domain name hierarchy. As the figure shows, IBM corporation, a commercial organization, registered as *ibm.com*, Purdue University registered as *purdue.edu*, and the National Science Foundation, a government agency, registered as *nsf.gov*. In contrast, the Corporation for National Research Initiatives chose to register under the geographic hierarchy as *cnri.reston.va.us*.

†The standard does not define the term *subdomain*. We have chosen to use the term because its analogy to *subset* helps clarify the relationship among domains.

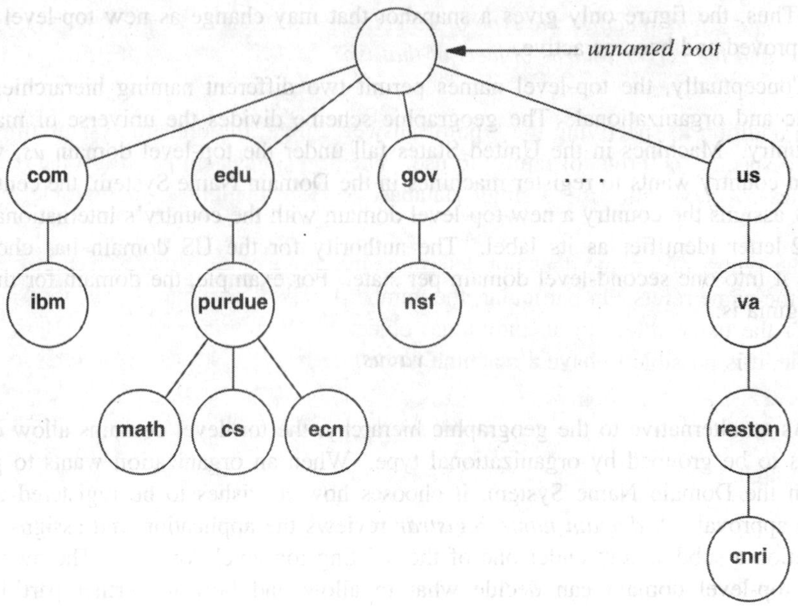

Figure 23.2 A small part of the Internet domain name hierarchy (tree). In practice, the tree is broad and flat; most host entries appear by the fifth level.

23.9 Name Syntax And Type

The Domain Name System is quite general because it allows multiple naming hierarchies to be embedded in one system. In addition, the system can hold various types of mappings. For example, a given name can be the name of a host computer that has an IPv4 address, a host computer that has an IPv6 address, a mail server, and so on. Interestingly, the syntax of names does not indicate the type.

To permit a client to distinguish among multiple types of entries in the system, each named item stored is assigned a *type* that specifies whether it is the address of a computer, a mailbox, a user, and so on. When a client asks the domain system to resolve a name, it must specify the type of answer desired. For example, when an electronic mail application uses the domain system to resolve a name, it specifies that the answer should be the address of a *mail exchanger*. When a browser resolves a domain name for a web site, the browser must specify that it seeks the IP address of the server computer. Interestingly, a given name can map to multiple items. When resolving a name, the answer received depends on the type specified in the query. Thus, if a user sends email to someone at `x.com` and types `x.com` into a browser, the two actions may result in contacting two entirely different computers. We can summarize the key point:

> *A given name may map to more than one item in the domain system. The client specifies the type of object desired when resolving a name, and the server returns objects of that type.*

In addition to specifying the type of answer sought, the domain system allows the client to specify the protocol family to use. The domain system partitions the entire set of names by *class*, allowing a single database to store mappings for multiple protocol suites†.

The syntax of a name does not determine the protocol class or the type of object to which the name refers. In particular, the number of labels in a name does not determine whether the name refers to an individual object (machine) or a domain. Thus, in our example, it is possible to have a machine named

gwen.purdue.edu

even though

cs.purdue.edu

names a subdomain. We can summarize this important point:

> *One cannot distinguish the names of subdomains from the names of individual objects or the type of an object using only the domain name syntax.*

23.10 Mapping Domain Names To Addresses

In addition to the rules for name syntax and delegation of authority, the domain name scheme includes an efficient, reliable, general purpose, distributed system for mapping names to addresses. The system is distributed in the technical sense, meaning that a set of servers operating at multiple sites cooperatively solve the mapping problem. It is efficient in the sense that most names can be mapped locally; only a few require internet traffic. It is general purpose because it is not restricted to computer names (although we will use that example for now). Finally, it is reliable in that no single server failure will prevent the system from operating correctly.

The domain mechanism for mapping names to addresses consists of independent, cooperative systems called *name servers*. A name server is a server program that supplies name-to-address translation, mapping from domain names to IP addresses. Often, server software executes on a dedicated processor, and the machine itself is called the name server. The client software, called a *name resolver*, may contact one or more name servers when translating a name.

†In practice, few domain servers use multiple protocol suites.

The easiest way to understand how domain servers work is to imagine them arranged in a tree structure that corresponds to the naming hierarchy, as Figure 23.3 illustrates. The root of the tree is a server that recognizes the top-level domains and knows which server resolves each domain. Given a name to resolve, the root can choose the correct server for that name. At the next level, a set of name servers each provide answers for one top-level domain (e.g., *edu*). A server at this level knows which servers can resolve each of the subdomains under its domain. At the third level of the tree, name servers provide answers for subdomains (e.g., *purdue* under *edu*). The conceptual tree continues with one server at each level for which a subdomain has been defined.

Links in the conceptual tree do not indicate physical network connections. Instead, they show which other name servers a given server knows and contacts. The servers themselves may be located at arbitrary locations on an internet. Thus, the tree of servers is an abstraction that uses an internet for communication.

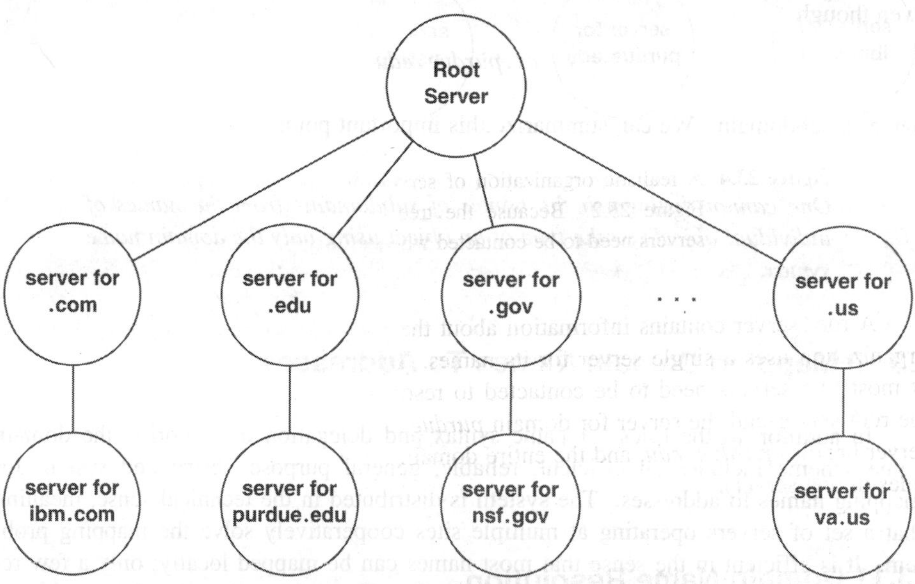

Figure 23.3 The conceptual arrangement of domain name servers in a tree that corresponds to the naming hierarchy. In theory, each server knows the addresses of all lower-level servers for all subdomains within the domain it handles.

If servers in the domain system worked exactly as our simplistic model suggests, the relationship between connectivity and authorization would be quite simple. When authority was granted for a subdomain, the organization requesting it would need to establish a domain name server for that subdomain and link it into the tree.

In practice, the relationship between the naming hierarchy and the tree of servers is not as simple as our model implies. The tree of servers has few levels because a single physical server can contain all of the information for large parts of the naming hierarchy. In particular, organizations often collect information from all of their subdomains into a single server. Figure 23.4 shows a more realistic organization of servers for the naming hierarchy of Figure 23.2.

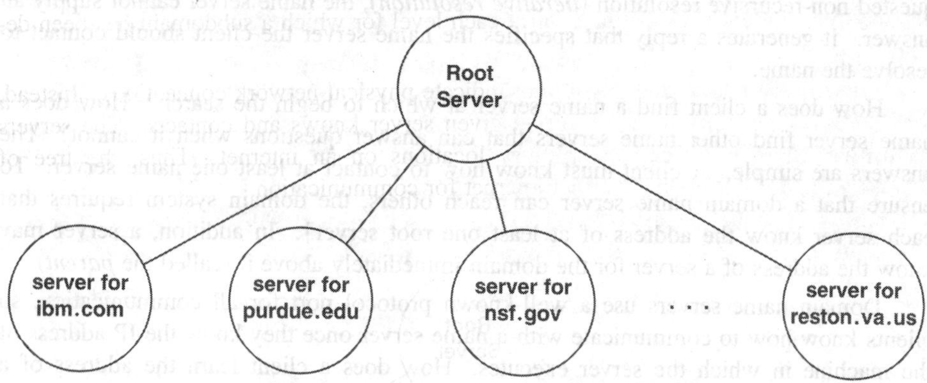

Figure 23.4 A realistic organization of servers for the naming hierarchy of Figure 23.2. Because the tree is broad and flat, only a few servers need to be contacted when resolving a name.

A root server contains information about the root and top-level domains, and each organization uses a single server for its names. Because the tree of servers is shallow, at most two servers need to be contacted to resolve a name like *xinu.cs.purdue.edu*: the root server and the server for domain *purdue.edu* (i.e., the root server knows which server handles *purdue.edu*, and the entire domain information for Purdue University resides in one server).

23.11 Domain Name Resolution

Although the conceptual tree makes understanding the relationship between servers easy, it hides several subtle details. Looking at the name resolution algorithm will help explain them. Conceptually, domain name resolution proceeds top-down, starting with the root name server and proceeding to servers located at the leaves of the tree. There are two ways to use the Domain Name System: by contacting name servers one at a time or asking the name server system to perform the complete translation. In either case, the client software forms a domain name query that contains the name to be resolved, a declaration of the class of the name, the type of answer desired, and a code that specifies whether the name server should translate the name completely. The client sends the query to a name server for resolution.

When a domain name server receives a query, it checks to see if the name lies in the subdomain for which it is an authority. If so, it translates the name to an address according to its database, and appends an answer to the query before sending it back to the client. If the name server cannot resolve the name completely, it checks to see what type of interaction the client specified. If the client requested complete translation (*recursive resolution*, in domain name terminology), the server contacts a domain name server that can resolve the name and returns the answer to the client. If the client requested non-recursive resolution (*iterative resolution*), the name server cannot supply an answer. It generates a reply that specifies the name server the client should contact to resolve the name.

How does a client find a name server at which to begin the search? How does a name server find other name servers that can answer questions when it cannot? The answers are simple. A client must know how to contact at least one name server. To ensure that a domain name server can reach others, the domain system requires that each server know the address of at least one root server†. In addition, a server may know the address of a server for the domain immediately above it (called the *parent*).

Domain name servers use a well-known protocol port for all communication, so clients know how to communicate with a name server once they know the IP address of the machine in which the server executes. How does a client learn the address of a name server? Many systems obtain the address of a domain server automatically as part of the bootstrap process‡. For example, bootstrap protocols such as IPv4's DHCP and IPv6's NDP or DHCPv6 can supply a name server address. Of course, other approaches are possible. For example, the address of a name server can be bound into application programs at compile time. Alternatively, the address can be stored in a file on secondary storage.

23.12 Efficient Translation

Although it may seem natural to resolve queries by working down the tree of name servers, doing so can lead to inefficiencies for three reasons. First, because most name resolution refers to local names, tracing a path through the hierarchy to contact the local authority would be inefficient. Second, if each name resolution always started by contacting the top level of the hierarchy, the machine at that point would become overloaded. Third, failure of machines at the top levels of the hierarchy would prevent name resolution, even if the local authority could resolve the name. The telephone number hierarchy mentioned earlier helps explain. Although telephone numbers are assigned hierarchically, they are resolved in a bottom-up fashion. Because the majority of telephone calls are local, they can be resolved by the local exchange without searching the hierarchy. Furthermore, calls within a given area code can be resolved without contacting sites outside the area code. When applied to domain names, these ideas lead to a two-step name resolution mechanism that preserves the administrative hierarchy but permits efficient translation.

†For reliability, there are multiple servers for each node in the domain server tree; the root server is further replicated to provide load balancing.

‡See Chapter 22 for a discussion of bootstrapping protocols.

In the two-step name resolution process, resolution begins with the local name server. If the local server cannot resolve a name, the query must then be sent to another server in the domain system. The following is a key idea:

A client always contacts a local domain name server first.

23.13 Caching: The Key To Efficiency

If a resolver sends each nonlocal query to a root server, the cost of lookup for nonlocal names can be extremely high. Even if queries go directly to the server that has authority for the name, name lookup can present a heavy load to the Internet. Thus, to improve the overall performance of a name server system, it is necessary to lower the cost of lookup for nonlocal names.

Internet name servers use *caching* to make resolution efficient. Each server maintains a cache of answers to recent lookups as well as a record of where the answer was obtained. When a client asks the server to resolve a name, the server first checks to see if it has authority for the name according to the standard procedure. If not, the server checks its cache to see if the name has been resolved recently. Servers report cached information to clients, but mark it as a *nonauthoritative* binding and give the domain name of the server, *S*, from which they obtained the binding. The local server also sends along additional information that tells the client the binding between *S* and an IP address. Therefore, clients receive answers quickly, but the information may be out-of-date. Because efficiency is important, a client will accept the nonauthoritative answer and proceed.

Caching works well in the Domain Name System because name to address bindings change infrequently. However, they do change. If servers cached information the first time it was requested and never updated an entry, entries in the cache could become *stale* (i.e., incorrect). To keep the cache correct, servers only save cached information while the information is valid — once an item becomes stale, a server removes the item from the cache. After an entry has been removed from its cache, a server must go back to the authoritative source and obtain the binding to satisfy subsequent requests.

The key to DNS success arises because a server does not apply a single fixed timeout to all entries. Instead, DNS allows the authority for an entry to configure its timeout. That is, whenever an authority responds to a request, the authority includes a *Time To Live* (*TTL*) value in the response that specifies how long the binding will remain valid. Thus, authorities can reduce network overhead by specifying long timeouts for entries that they expect to remain unchanged, while specifying short timeouts for entries that they expect to change.

Caching is important in hosts as well as in local name servers. Most resolver software caches DNS entries in the host. Thus, if a user looks up the same name repeatedly, subsequent lookups can be resolved from the local cache without using the network.

23.14 Domain Name System Message Format

Looking at the details of messages exchanged between clients and domain name servers will help clarify how the system operates from the view of a typical application program. We assume that a user invokes an application program and supplies the name of a destination machine with which the application must communicate. Before it can use protocols like TCP or UDP to communicate with the specified machine, the application program must find the machine's IP address. It passes the domain name to a local resolver and requests an IP address. The local resolver checks its cache, and returns the answer if one is present. If the local resolver does not have an answer, it formats a message and sends it to a name server (i.e., the local resolver becomes a client). Although our example only involves one name, the message format allows a client to ask multiple questions in a single message. Each question consists of a domain name for which the client seeks an IP address, a specification of the query class (i.e., *internet*), and the type of object desired (e.g., *address*). The name server responds by returning a similar message that contains answers to the questions for which the server has bindings. If the name server cannot answer all questions, the response will contain information about other name servers that the client can contact to obtain the answers.

Responses also contain information about the name servers that are authorities for the replies and the IP addresses of those servers. Figure 23.5 shows the message format.

0	16 31
IDENTIFICATION	PARAMETER
NUMBER OF QUESTIONS	NUMBER OF ANSWERS
NUMBER OF AUTHORITY	NUMBER OF ADDITIONAL
QUESTION SECTION ...	
ANSWER SECTION ...	
AUTHORITY SECTION ...	
ADDITIONAL INFORMATION SECTION ...	

Figure 23.5 Domain name server message format. The *QUESTION*, *ANSWER*, *AUTHORITY*, and *ADDITIONAL INFORMATION* sections are variable length.

As the figure shows, each message begins with a fixed header. The header contains a unique *IDENTIFICATION* field that the client uses to match responses to queries, and a *PARAMETER* field that specifies the operation requested and a response code. Figure 23.6 gives the interpretation of bits in the *PARAMETER* field.

Bit of PARAMETER field	Meaning
0	Operation: 0 Query 1 Response
1-4	Query Type: 0 Standard 1 Inverse 2 Server status request 4 Notify 5 Update
5	Set if answer authoritative
6	Set if message truncated
7	Set if recursion desired
8	Set if recursion available
9	Set if data is authenticated
10	Set if checking is disabled
11	Reserved
12-15	Response Type: 0 No error 1 Format error in query 2 Server failure 3 Name does not exist 5 Refused 6 Name exists when it should not 7 RR set exists 8 RR set that should exist does not 9 Server not authoritative for the zone 10 Name not contained in zone

Figure 23.6 The meaning of bits of the *PARAMETER* field in a DNS server message. Bits are numbered left to right starting at 0.

In Figure 23.5, the fields labeled *NUMBER OF* each give a count of entries in the corresponding sections that occur later in the message. For example, the field labeled *NUMBER OF QUESTIONS* gives the count of entries that appear in the *QUESTION SECTION* of the message.

The *QUESTION SECTION* contains queries for which answers are desired. The client fills in only the question section; the server returns the questions and answers in its response. Each question consists of a *QUERY DOMAIN NAME* field followed by *QUERY TYPE* and *QUERY CLASS* fields, as Figure 23.7 shows.

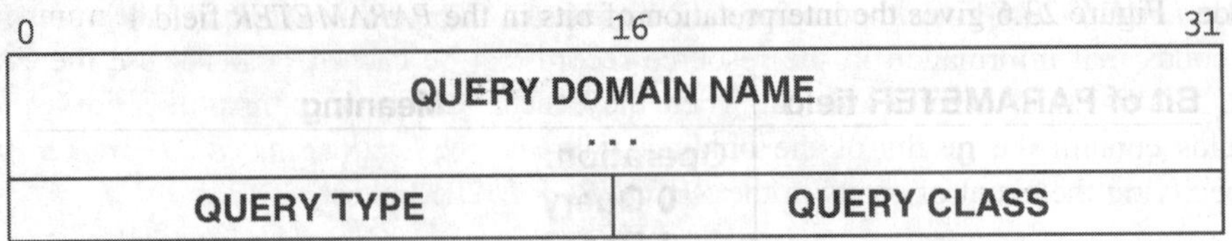

Figure 23.7 The format of entries in the *QUESTION SECTION* of a domain name server message. The domain name is variable length. A client fills in the questions; a server returns the questions along with answers.

Although the *QUERY DOMAIN NAME* field has variable length, we will see in the next section that the internal representation of domain names makes it possible for the receiver to know the exact length. The *QUERY TYPE* field encodes the type of the question (e.g., whether the question refers to a machine name or a mail address). The *QUERY CLASS* field allows domain names to be used for arbitrary objects because official Internet names are only one possible class. It should be noted that although the diagram in Figure 23.7 follows our convention of showing formats in 32-bit multiples, the *QUERY DOMAIN NAME* field may contain an arbitrary number of octets. No padding is used. Therefore, messages sent to or from domain name servers may contain an odd number of octets.

In a domain name server message, each of the *ANSWER SECTION*, *AUTHORITY SECTION*, and *ADDITIONAL INFORMATION SECTION* fields consists of a set of *resource records* that describe domain names and mappings. Each resource record describes one name. Figure 23.8 shows the format of a resource record.

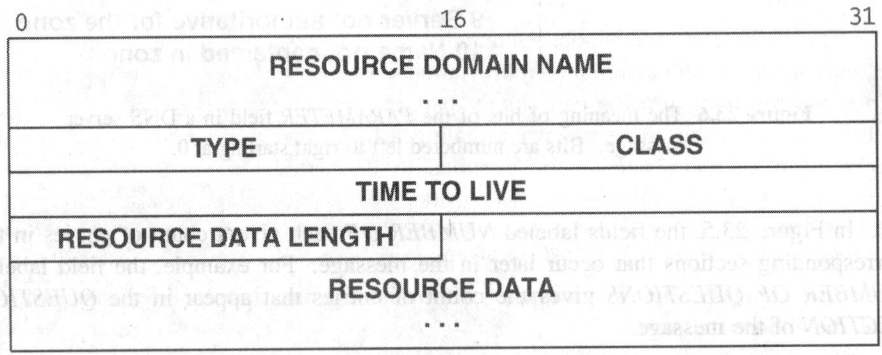

Figure 23.8 The format of a resource record used in later sections of messages returned by domain name servers.

The *RESOURCE DOMAIN NAME* field contains the domain name to which this resource record refers. It may be an arbitrary length. The *TYPE* field specifies the type of the data included in the resource record; the *CLASS* field specifies the data's class. The *TIME TO LIVE* field contains a 32-bit integer. The integer specifies the number of seconds that information in the resource record can be cached. Clients use the *TIME TO LIVE* value to set a timeout when they cache the resource record. The last two fields contain the results of the binding, with the *RESOURCE DATA LENGTH* field specifying the count of octets in the *RESOURCE DATA* field.

23.15 Compressed Name Format

When represented in a message, domain names are stored as a sequence of labels. Each label begins with an octet that specifies its length. Thus, the receiver reconstructs a domain name by repeatedly reading a 1-octet length, *n*, and then reading a label *n* octets long. A length octet containing zero marks the end of the name.

Domain name servers often return multiple answers to a query, and in many cases, suffixes of the domain overlap. To conserve space in a reply packet, a name server compresses names by storing only one copy of each domain name. When extracting a domain name from a message, the client software must check each segment of the name to see whether it consists of a literal string (in the format of a 1-octet count followed by the characters that make up the name) or a pointer to a literal string. When it encounters a pointer, the client must follow the pointer to find the remainder of the name.

Pointers always occur at the beginning of segments and are encoded in the count byte. If the top two bits of the 8-bit segment count field are 1s, the client must take the next 14 bits as an integer pointer. If the top two bits are zero, the next 6 bits specify the number of characters in the label.

23.16 Abbreviation Of Domain Names

The U.S. telephone number hierarchy illustrates another useful feature of local resolution, *name abbreviation*. Abbreviation provides a method of shortening names when the resolving process can supply part of the name automatically. Normally, a subscriber omits the area code when dialing a local telephone number. The resulting digits form an abbreviated name assumed to lie within the same area code as the subscriber's phone. Abbreviation also works well for machine names. Given a name like *xyz*, the resolving process can assume it lies in the same local authority as the machine on which it is being resolved. Thus, the resolver can supply missing parts of the name automatically. For example, within the Computer Science department at Purdue, the abbreviated name:

xinu

is equivalent to the full domain name:

xinu.cs.purdue.edu

Most client software implements abbreviations with a *domain name suffix list*. The local network manager configures a list of possible suffixes to be appended to names during lookup. When a resolver encounters a name, it steps through the list, appending each suffix and looking up the resulting name. For example, the suffix list for the Computer Science department at Purdue includes:

.cs.purdue.edu
.purdue.edu
null

Thus, a local resolver first appends *cs.purdue.edu* to the name *xinu*. If that lookup fails, the resolver appends *purdue.edu* onto the name and tries again. The last suffix in the example list is the null string, meaning that if all other lookups fail, the resolver will attempt to look up the name with no suffix. Managers can use the suffix list to make abbreviation convenient or to restrict application programs to local names.

We said that the client takes responsibility for the expansion of such abbreviations, but it should be emphasized that such abbreviations are not part of the Domain Name System itself. The domain system only allows lookup of a fully specified domain name. As a consequence, programs that depend on abbreviations may not work correctly outside the environment in which they were built. We can summarize:

The Domain Name System only maps full domain names into addresses; abbreviations are not part of the DNS itself, but are introduced by client software to make local names convenient for users.

23.17 Inverse Mappings

We said that the Domain Name System can provide mappings other than a computer name to an IP address. *Inverse queries* allow the client to ask a server to map in the opposite direction by taking an answer and generating the question that would produce that answer. Of course, not all answers have a unique question. Even when they do, a server may not be able to provide it. Although inverse queries have been part of the domain system since it was first specified, they are generally not used because there is often no way to find the server that can resolve the query without searching the entire set of servers.

23.18 Pointer Queries

One form of inverse mapping is an authentication mechanism that a server uses to verify that a client is authorized to access the service: the server maps the client's IP address to a domain name. For example, a server at corporation *example.com* might be configured to provide the service only to clients from the same corporation. When a client contacts the server, the server maps the client's IP address to an equivalent domain name and verifies that the name ends in *example.com* before granting access. Reverse lookup is so important that the domain system supports a special domain and a special form of question called a *pointer query* to provide the service. In a pointer query, the question presented to a domain name server specifies an IP address encoded as a printable string in the form of a domain name (i.e., a textual representation of digits separated by periods). A pointer query requests the name server to return the correct domain name for the machine with the specified IP address.

Pointer queries are not difficult to generate. Consider IPv4. When we think of an IPv4 address written in dotted-decimal form, it has the following format:

aaa.*bbb*.*ccc*.*ddd*

To form a pointer query, the client rearranges the dotted decimal representation of the address into a string of the form:

ddd.*ccc*.*bbb*.*aaa*.*in-addr*.*arpa*

The new form is a name in the special *in-addr*.*arpa* domain†.

IPv6 is more complex and results in much longer names. To form a pointer query, a client represents the IPv6 address as a series of nibbles (i.e., 4-bit quantities), writes each nibble in hexadecimal, reverses the order and appends *ip6.arpa*. For example, the IPv6 address:

2001:18e8:0808:0000:0000:00d0:b75d:19f9

is represented as:

9.f.9.1.d.5.7.b.0.d.0.0.0.0.0.0.0.0.0.0.8.0.8.0.8.e.8.1.1.0.0.2.ip6.arpa

Because the local name server is not usually the authority for the domains *arpa*, *in-addr*.*arpa*, or *ip6*.*arpa*, the local name server will need to contact other name servers to complete the resolution. To make the resolution of pointer queries efficient, the Internet root domain servers maintain a database of valid IP addresses along with information about domain name servers that can resolve each address group.

†The octets of the IP address must be reversed when forming a domain name because IP addresses have the most significant octets first, while domain names have the least-significant octets first.

23.19 Object Types And Resource Record Contents

We have mentioned that the Domain Name System can be used for translating a domain name to a mail exchanger address as well as for translating a host name to an IP address. The domain system is quite general in that it can be used for arbitrary hierarchical names. For example, one might decide to store the names of available computational services along with a mapping from each name to the telephone number to call to find out about the corresponding service. Or one might store names of protocol products along with a mapping to the names and addresses of vendors that offer such products.

Recall that the domain system accommodates a variety of mappings by including a *type* in each resource record. When sending a request, a client must specify the type in its query†; servers specify the data type in all resource records they return. The type determines the contents of the resource record according to the table in Figure 23.9.

Type	Meaning	Contents
A	IPv4 Host Address	32-bit IPv4 address
AAAA	IPv6 Host Address	128-bit IPv6 address
CNAME	Canonical Name	Canonical domain name for an alias
HINFO	CPU & OS	Name of CPU and operating system
MINFO	Mailbox Info	Information about a mailbox or mail list
MX	Mail Exchanger	16-bit preference and name of host that acts as mail exchanger for the domain
NS	Name Server	Name of authoritative server for domain
PTR	Pointer	Domain name (like a symbolic link)
SOA	Start of Authority	Multiple fields that specify which parts of the naming hierarchy a server implements
TXT	Arbitrary text	Uninterpreted string of ASCII text

Figure 23.9 A few examples of DNS resource record types. More than fifty types have been defined.

Most data is of type *A* or *AAAA*, meaning that it consists of the name of a host attached to the Internet along with the host's IP address. The second most useful domain type, *MX*, is assigned to names used for electronic mail exchangers. It allows a site to specify multiple hosts that are each capable of accepting mail. When sending electronic mail, the user specifies an electronic mail address in the form *user@domain-part*. The mail system uses the domain system to resolve *domain-part* with query type *MX*. The domain system returns a set of resource records that each contain a preference field and a host's domain name. The mail system steps through the set from highest preference to lowest (lower numbers mean higher preference). For each *MX* resource record, the

†Queries can specify a few additional types (e.g., there is a query type that requests all resource records).

mailer extracts the domain name and uses a type *A* or type *AAAA* query to resolve that name to an IP address. It then tries to contact the host and deliver mail. If the host is unavailable, the mailer will continue trying other hosts on the list.

To make lookup efficient, a server always returns additional bindings that it knows in the *ADDITIONAL INFORMATION SECTION* of a response. In the case of *MX* records, a domain server can use the *ADDITIONAL INFORMATION SECTION* to return type *A* or *AAAA* resource records for domain names reported in the *ANSWER SECTION*. Doing so substantially reduces the number of queries a mailer sends to its domain server.

23.20 Obtaining Authority For A Subdomain

Before an institution is granted authority for an official second-level domain, it must agree to operate a domain name server that meets Internet standards. Of course, a domain name server must obey the protocol standards that specify message formats and the rules for responding to requests. The server must also know the addresses of servers that handle each subdomain (if any exist) as well as the address of at least one root server. In the current Internet, each enterprise does not need to operate its own name server. Instead, companies exist that, for an annual fee, run domain name servers on behalf of others. In fact, such companies compete for business: they offer a variety of related services, such as verifying that a domain name is available, registering the name with the regional registries, and registering inverse mappings via pointer queries.

23.21 Server Operation And Replication

In practice, the domain system is much more complex than we have outlined. In most cases, a single physical server can handle more than one part of the naming hierarchy. For example, a single name server at Purdue University once handled both the second-level domain *purdue.edu* as well as the geographic domain *laf.in.us*. A subtree of names managed by a given name server forms a *zone of authority*, and the protocols provide for *zone download* where a client can obtain a copy of the entire set of names and resource records from a server. Another practical complication arises because servers must be able to handle many requests, even though some requests take a long time to resolve. Usually, servers support concurrent activity, allowing work to proceed on later requests while earlier ones are being processed. Handling requests concurrently is especially important when the server receives a recursive request that forces it to send the request on to another server for resolution.

Server operation is also complicated because the Internet authority requires that the information in every domain name server be replicated. Information must appear in at least two servers that do not operate on the same computer. In practice, the requirements are quite stringent: the servers must have no single common point of failure. Avoiding common points of failure means that the two name servers cannot both attach to the same network; they cannot even obtain electrical power from the same source. Thus, to meet the requirements, a site must find at least one other site that agrees to operate a backup name server. Of course, at any point in the tree of servers, a name server must know how to locate both the primary and backup name servers for subdomains, and the server must direct queries to a backup name server if the primary name server is unavailable.

23.22 Dynamic DNS Update And Notification

Our discussions of NAT in Chapter 19 and DHCP in Chapter 22 both mention the need for interaction with DNS. In the case of a NAT box that obtains a dynamic address from an ISP, a server can only be placed behind the NAT box if the domain name server and the NAT system coordinate. In the case of DHCP, when a host obtains a dynamic address, the DNS server for the host must be updated with the host's current address. To handle the situations described above and to permit multiple parties to share administration (e.g., to allow multiple registrars to jointly manage a top-level domain), the IETF developed a technology known as *Dynamic DNS*.

There are two aspects of Dynamic DNS: *update* and *notification*. As the name implies, Dynamic DNS update permits changes to be made dynamically to the information that a DNS server stores. Thus, when it assigns an IP address to a host, a DHCP server can use the dynamic update mechanism to inform the DNS server about the assignment. Notification messages solve the problem of propagating changes. In particular, observe that because DNS uses backup servers, changes made in the primary server must be propagated to each backup. When a dynamic change occurs, the primary server sends a notification message to the backup servers, which allows each backup server to request an update of the zone information. Because it avoids sending copies unnecessarily, notification takes less bandwidth than merely using a small timeout for updates.

23.23 DNS Security Extensions (DNSSEC)

Because it is among the most important aspects of Internet infrastructure, the Domain Name System is often cited as a critical mechanism that should be protected. In particular, if a host is giving incorrect answers to DNS queries, application software or users can be fooled into believing imposter web sites or revealing confidential information. To help protect DNS, the IETF has invented a technology known as *DNS Security* (*DNSSEC*).

The primary services provided by DNSSEC include *authentication* of the message origin and *integrity* of the data. That is, when it uses DNSSEC, a host can verify a DNS message did indeed originate at an authoritative DNS server (i.e., the server responsible for the name in the query) and that the data in the message arrived without being changed. Furthermore, DNSSEC can authenticate negative answers — a host can obtain an authenticated message that states a particular domain name does not exist.

Despite offering authentication and integrity, DNSSEC does not solve all problems. In particular, DNSSEC does not provide confidentiality, nor does it fend off denial-of-service attacks. The former means that even if a host uses DNSSEC, an outside observer snooping on a network will be able to know which names the host looks up (i.e., the observer may be able to guess why a given business is being contacted). The inability to fend off denial-of-service attacks means that even if a host and server both use DNSSEC, there is no guarantee that messages sent between them will be received.

To provide authentication and data integrity, DNSSEC uses a digital signature mechanism — in addition to the requested information, a reply from a DNSSEC server contains a digital signature that allows the receiver to verify that the contents of the message were not changed. One of the most interesting aspects of DNSSEC arises from the way the digital signature mechanism is administered. Like many security mechanisms, the DNSSEC mechanism uses *public key encryption* technology. The interesting twist is that to distribute public keys, DNSSEC uses the Domain Name System. That is, a new type has been defined that allows a name to map to a public key. Each server contains the public keys for zones further down the hierarchy (e.g., the server for *.com* contains the public key for *example.com*). To guarantee security for the entire system, the public key for the top level of the hierarchy (i.e., the key for a root server) must be manually configured into a resolver.

23.24 Multicast DNS And Service Discovery

Because the Domain Name System permits arbitrary record types to be added, several groups have created names for objects other than computers. One particular use stands out. Known as *multicast DNS* (*mDNS*), the service is intended for networks that do not have dedicated DNS servers. For example, consider a pair of smart phones that have Wi-Fi interfaces.

Instead of using a DNS server, mDNS uses IP multicast. Suppose host *A* needs to know the IP address of host *B*. Host *A* multicasts its request. All hosts participating in mDNS receive the multicast, and host *B* multicasts its reply. In addition, a host that participates in mDNS caches mDNS replies, which means that the binding can be satisfied from the cache.

In addition to domain name resolution, mDNS has been extended to handle *DNS Service Discovery* (*DNS-SD*). The basic idea is straightforward: create service names in the DNS hierarchy using the *.local* suffix, and use mDNS to look up the name. Thus, a smart phone can use DNS-SD to discover other cell phones in the area that are willing to participate in a given application. The phones only need to agree on a name for the service.

The chief disadvantage of using mDNS for service discovery arises from the traffic generated. Instead of two smart phones, imagine a set of *N* smart phones. Each advertises itself as offering a service and then waits to be synced with a variety of applications. Now imagine the situation where *N* is large and the phones are using a flat (i.e., non-routed) open wireless network, such as a Wi-Fi hotspot in a coffee shop on a busy street in a city. Each phone that connects sends a multicast for the services it offers, and others respond by connecting. Unless *N* is small, the traffic can dominate the network.

23.25 Summary

Hierarchical naming systems allow delegation of authority for names, making it possible to accommodate an arbitrarily large set of names without overwhelming a central site with administrative duties. Although name resolution is separate from delegation of authority, it is possible to create hierarchical naming systems in which resolution is an efficient process that starts at the local server, even though delegation of authority always flows from the top of the hierarchy downward.

We examined the Internet's Domain Name System (DNS) and saw that it offers a hierarchical naming scheme. DNS uses distributed lookup in which domain name servers map each domain name to an IP address or mail exchanger address. Clients begin by trying to resolve names locally. When the local server cannot resolve the name, the client must choose to work through the tree of name servers iteratively or request the local name server to do it recursively. Finally, we saw that the Domain Name System supports a variety of bindings including bindings from IPv4 or IPv6 addresses to high-level names.

DNSSEC provides a mechanism that can be used to secure DNS; it authenticates replies and guarantees the integrity of the answers. DNSSEC uses public-key encryption, and arranges to use DNS to distribute the set of public keys.

Multicast DNS (mDNS) allows two hosts on an isolated network to obtain the IP address of hosts on the network without relying on a DNS server. An extension to mDNS, DNS-SD, provides general service discovery. A smart phone can use DNS-SD to discover other smart phones in its vicinity that are willing to participate in a given application service. The chief disadvantage of mDNS and DNS-SD arises from the traffic generated when a network contains many nodes.

EXERCISES

23.1 The name of a computer should never be bound into an operating system at compile time. Explain why.

23.2 Would you prefer to use a computer that obtained its name from a remote file or from a configuration server? Why?

23.3 Why does each name server know the IP address of its parent instead of the domain name of its parent?

23.4 Devise a naming scheme that tolerates changes to the naming hierarchy. As an example, consider two large companies that each have an independent naming hierarchy, and suppose the companies merge. Can you arrange to have all previous names still work correctly?

23.5 Read the standard and find out how the Domain Name System uses *SOA* records. What is the motivation for *SOA*?

23.6 The Internet Domain Name System can also accommodate mailbox names. Find out how.

23.7 The standard suggests that when a program needs to find the domain name associated with an IP address, it should send an inverse query to the local server first and use domain *in-addr.arpa* or *ip6.arpa* only if that fails. Why?

23.8 How would you accommodate abbreviations in a domain naming scheme? As an example, show two sites that are both registered under *.edu* and a top level server. Explain how each site would treat each type of abbreviation.

23.9 Obtain the official description of the Domain Name System and build a client program. Look up the name *xinu.cs.purdue.edu*.

23.10 Extend the exercise above to include a pointer query. Try looking up the domain name for address *128.10.19.20*.

23.11 Find a copy of the *dig* application, and use it to look up the names in the two previous exercises.

23.12 If we extended the domain name syntax to include a dot after the top-level domain, names and abbreviations would be unambiguous. What are the advantages and disadvantages of the extension?

23.13 Read the RFCs on the Domain Name System. What are the maximum and minimum possible values a DNS server can store in the *TIME-TO-LIVE* field of a resource record? What is the motivation for the choices?

23.14 Should the Domain Name System permit partial match queries (i.e., a wildcard as part of a name)? Why or why not?

23.15 The Computer Science department at Purdue University chose to place the following type *A* resource record entry in its domain name server:

```
localhost.cs.purdue.edu     127.0.0.1
```

Explain what will happen if a remote site tries to *ping* a machine with domain name *localhost.cs.purdue.edu*.

Chapter Contents

24

Electronic Mail (SMTP, POP, IMAP, MIME)

24.1 Introduction

This chapter continues our exploration of internetworking by considering electronic mail services and the protocols that support mail transfer and access. The chapter describes how a mail system is organized, explains how mail system software uses the client-server paradigm to transfer each message, and describes message representation. We will see that email illustrates several key ideas in application protocol design.

24.2 Electronic Mail

An *electronic mail* (*email*) system allows users to transfer memos across the Internet. Email is a widely-used application service that offers a fast, convenient method of transferring information, accommodates small notes or large files, and allows communication between individuals or among a group.

Email differs fundamentally from most other uses of networks because a mail system must provide for instances when the remote destination is temporarily unreachable. To handle delayed delivery, mail systems use a technique known as *spooling*. When a user sends an email message, the user's local system places a copy in its private storage (called a spool†) along with identification of the sender, recipient, destination machine, and time of deposit. The system then initiates the transfer to the remote machine as a background activity, allowing the sender to proceed with other computational activities. Figure 24.1 illustrates the concept.

†A mail spool area is sometimes called a *mail queue* even though the term is technically inaccurate.

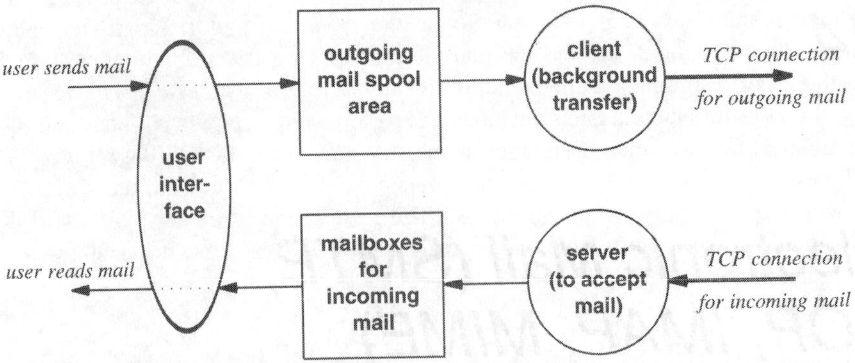

Figure 24.1 Conceptual components of an electronic mail system. The user invokes a mail interface application to deposit or retrieve mail; all transfers occur in the background.

The background mail transfer process becomes a client that uses the Domain Name System to map the destination machine name to an IP address. The client then attempts to form a TCP connection to the mail server on the destination machine. If the connection succeeds, the client transfers a copy of the message to the remote server, which stores a copy of the message temporarily. Once the client and server agree that the transfer is complete, the client removes the local copy and the server moves its copy to the user's mailbox. If the client cannot form a TCP connection or if the connection fails, the client records the time of the attempt and terminates. The sending email system sweeps through the spool area periodically, typically once every 30 minutes, checking for undelivered mail. Whenever it finds a message or whenever a user deposits new outgoing mail, the background process attempts delivery. If it finds that a mail message cannot be delivered after a few hours, the mail software informs the sender; after an extended time (e.g., 3 days), the mail software usually returns the message to the sender.

24.3 Mailbox Names And Aliases

There are three important ideas hidden in our simplistic description of mail delivery. First, users specify each recipient by giving a text string that contains two items separated by an at-sign:

user @ *domain-name*

where *domain-name* is the domain name of a mail destination† to which the mail should be delivered, and *user* is the name of a mailbox on that machine. For example, the author's electronic mail address is:

comer* @ *purdue* . *edu

†Technically, the domain name specifies a *mail exchanger*, not a host.

Second, the names used in such specifications are independent of other names assigned to machines. Typically, a mailbox is the same as a user's login id, and a computer's domain name is used as the mail destination. However, many other designs are possible. For example, a mailbox can designate a position such as *department-head*. Because the Domain Name System includes a separate query type for mail destinations, it is possible to decouple mail destination names from the usual domain names assigned to machines. Thus, mail sent to a user at *example.com* may go to a different machine than a *ping* request sent to the same name. Third, our simplistic diagram fails to account for *mail forwarding*, in which some mail that arrives on a given machine is forwarded to another computer.

24.4 Alias Expansion And Mail Forwarding

Most email servers provide *mail forwarding* software that employs a *mail alias expansion* mechanism. A forwarder allows each incoming message to be sent to one or more destinations. Typically, a forwarder uses a database of mail aliases to map an incoming recipient address into a set of addresses, *S*, and then forwards a copy to each address in *S*.

Because they can be many-to-one or one-to-many, alias mappings increase mail system functionality and convenience substantially. A single user can have multiple mail identifiers, or a group can have a single mail alias. In the latter case, the set of recipients associated with an identifier is called an *electronic mailing list*. Figure 24.2 illustrates the components of a mail system that supports mail aliases and list expansion.

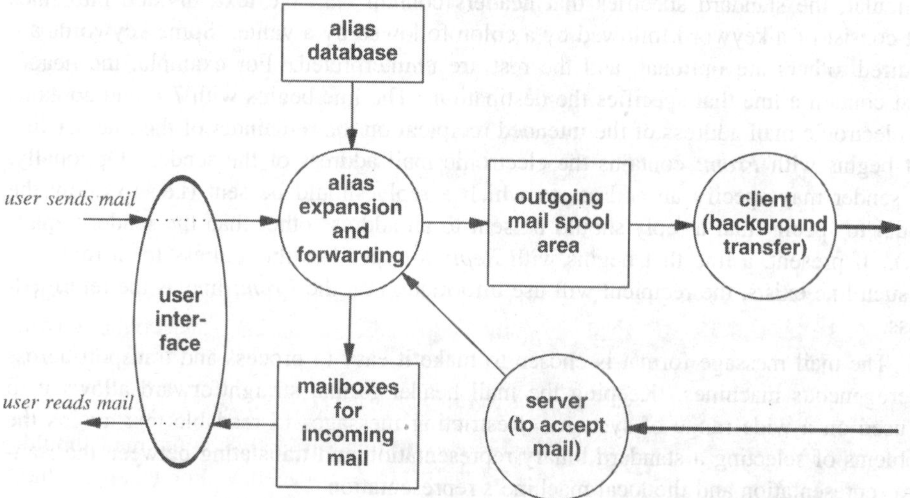

Figure 24.2 An extension of the mail system in Figure 24.1 that supports mail aliases and forwarding. Each incoming and outgoing message passes through the alias expansion mechanism.

As the figure shows, an incoming and outgoing mail message passes through the mail forwarder that expands aliases. Thus, if the alias database specifies that mail address *x* maps to replacement *y*, alias expansion will rewrite destination address *x*, changing it to *y*. The alias expansion program then determines whether *y* specifies a local or remote address, so it knows whether to place the message in the local user's mailbox or send it to the outgoing mail queue.

Mail alias expansion can be dangerous. Suppose two sites establish conflicting aliases. For example, assume the alias database at site *A* maps mail address *x* into mail address *y* @ *B*, and the alias database at site *B* maps mail address *y* into address *x* @ *A*. Any mail message sent to address *x* at site *A* will be forwarded to site *B*, then back to A, and so on†.

24.5 TCP/IP Standards For Electronic Mail Service

Recall that the goal of the TCP/IP protocol suite design is to provide for interoperability across the widest range of computer systems and networks. To extend the interoperability of electronic mail, TCP/IP divides its mail standards into two sets. One standard, given in RFC 2822, specifies the syntactic format used for mail messages‡; the other standard specifies the details of electronic mail exchange between two computers.

According to RFC 2822, a mail message is represented as text and is divided into two parts, a header and a body, which are separated by a blank line. The standard for mail messages specifies the exact format of mail headers as well as the semantic interpretation of each header field; it leaves the format of the body up to the sender. In particular, the standard specifies that headers contain readable text, divided into lines that consist of a keyword followed by a colon followed by a value. Some keywords are required, others are optional, and the rest are uninterpreted. For example, the header must contain a line that specifies the destination. The line begins with *To:* and contains the electronic mail address of the intended recipient on the remainder of the line. A line that begins with *From:* contains the electronic mail address of the sender. Optionally, the sender may specify an address to which a reply should be sent (i.e., to allow the sender to specify that a reply should be sent to an address other than the sender's mailbox). If present, a line that begins with *Reply-to:* specifies the address for a reply. If no such line exists, the recipient will use information on the *From:* line as the return address.

The mail message format is chosen to make it easy to process and transport across heterogeneous machines. Keeping the mail header format straightforward allows it to be used on a wide range of systems. Restricting messages to readable text avoids the problems of selecting a standard binary representation and translating between the standard representation and the local machine's representation.

---

†In practice, most mail forwarders terminate messages after the number of exchanges reaches a predetermined threshold.

‡The original standard was specified in RFC 822; the IETF delayed issuing the replacement until RFC 2822 to make the numbers correlate.

24.6 Simple Mail Transfer Protocol (SMTP)

In addition to message formats, the TCP/IP protocol suite specifies a standard for the exchange of mail between machines. That is, the standard specifies the exact format of messages a client on one machine uses to transfer mail to a server on another. The standard transfer protocol is known as the *Simple Mail Transfer Protocol* (*SMTP*). As the name implies, SMTP is simpler than the earlier *Mail Transfer Protocol* (*MTP*). The SMTP protocol focuses specifically on how the underlying mail delivery system passes messages across an internet from one machine to another. It does not specify how the mail system accepts mail from a user or how the user interface presents the user with incoming mail. Also, SMTP does not specify how mail is stored or how frequently the mail system attempts to send messages.

SMTP is surprisingly straightforward. Communication follows a design that is prevalent in many application-layer protocols: all communication between a client and a server consists of readable ASCII text. Each line begins with a command name, which can be an abbreviated name or 3-digit number; the remaining text on the line either gives arguments for the command or text that humans use to debug mail software. Although SMTP rigidly defines the command format, humans can easily read a transcript of interactions between a mail client and a server because each command appears on a separate line. Initially, the client establishes a reliable stream connection to the server and waits for the server to send a *220 READY FOR MAIL* message. (If the server is overloaded, it may delay sending the *220* command temporarily.) Upon receipt of the *220* command, the client sends a *HELO*† command (if the client supports the extensions defined in RFC 2821, the client sends an alternative, *EHLO*). The end of a line marks the end of a command. The server responds to a *HELO* by identifying itself. Once communication has been established, the client can transmit one or more mail messages and then terminate the connection. The server must acknowledge each command. A client can abort the entire connection or abort the current message transfer.

A message transfer begins with a *MAIL* command that gives the sender identification as well as a *FROM:* field that contains the address to which errors should be reported. A server prepares its data structures to receive a new mail message, and replies to a *MAIL* command by sending the response *250*. Response *250* means that all is well and the client should proceed. The full response consists of the text *250 OK*.

After a successful *MAIL* command, the client issues a series of *RCPT* commands that identify recipients of the mail message. The server must acknowledge each *RCPT* command by sending *250 OK* or by sending the error message *550 No such user here*.

After all *RCPT* commands have been acknowledged, the client issues a *DATA* command. In essence, a *DATA* command informs the server that the client is ready to transfer the body of a mail message. The server responds with message *354 Start mail input*, and specifies the sequence of characters used to terminate the mail message. The termination sequence consists of 5 characters: carriage return, line feed, period, carriage return, and line feed‡.

---

†*HELO* is an abbreviation for "hello."

‡SMTP uses *CR-LF* (carriage return followed by line feed) to terminate a line, and forbids the body of a mail message to have a period on a line by itself.

An example will clarify the communication in an SMTP exchange. Suppose user *Smith* at host *Alpha.edu* sends a message to users *Jones*, *Green*, and *Brown* at host *Beta.gov*. The SMTP client software on host *Alpha.edu* contacts the SMTP server software on host *Beta.gov*, and begins the exchange shown in Figure 24.3.

```
S: 220 Beta.gov Simple Mail Transfer Service Ready
C: HELO Alpha.edu
S: 250 Beta.gov

C: MAIL FROM:<Smith@Alpha.edu>
S: 250 OK

C: RCPT TO:<Jones@Beta.gov>
S: 250 OK

C: RCPT TO:<Green@Beta.gov>
S: 550 No such user here

C: RCPT TO:<Brown@Beta.gov>
S: 250 OK

C: DATA
S: 354 Start mail input; end with <CR><LF>.<CR><LF>
C: ...sends body of mail message...
C: ...continues for as many lines as message contains
C: <CR><LF>.<CR><LF>
S: 250 OK

C: QUIT
S: 221 Beta.gov Service closing transmission channel
```

Figure 24.3 Example of an SMTP transfer from Alpha.edu to Beta.gov during which recipient Green is not recognized. Lines that begin with "C:" are transmitted by the client (Alpha), and lines that begin "S:" are transmitted by the server.

In the example, the server rejects recipient *Green* because it does not recognize the name as a valid mail destination (i.e., *Green* is neither a user nor a mailing list). The SMTP protocol does not specify the details of how a client handles such errors — the client must decide. Although a client can abort the delivery if an error occurs, most clients do not. Instead, a client continues delivery to all valid recipients and then reports problems to the original sender. Usually, the client reports errors using electronic mail. The error message contains a summary of the error as well as the header of the mail message that caused the problem.

Once it has finished sending all mail messages, a client issues a *QUIT* command. The server responds with command *221*, which means it agrees to terminate. Both sides then close the TCP connection gracefully.

SMTP is much more complex than we have outlined here. For example, if a user has moved, the server may know the user's new mailbox address. SMTP allows the server to inform the client about the new address so the client can use the address in future correspondence. When informing the client about a new address, the server may choose to forward the mail that triggered the message, or it may request that the client take the responsibility for forwarding. In addition, SMTP includes *Transport Layer Security* (*TLS*) extensions that allow an SMTP session to be encrypted.

24.7 Mail Retrieval And Mailbox Manipulation Protocols

The SMTP transfer scheme described above implies that a server must remain ready to accept email at all times. The scenario works well if the server runs on a computer that has a permanent Internet connection, but it does not work well for a device that has intermittent connectivity (e.g., a smart phone that is often powered down or otherwise unavailable). It makes no sense for a device with intermittent connectivity to run an email server because the server will only be available while the user's device is connected — all other attempts to contact the server will fail, and email sent to the user will remain undelivered. The question arises: how can a user without a permanent connection receive email?

The answer to the question lies in a two-stage delivery process. In the first stage, each user is assigned a mailbox on a computer that is always on and has a permanent Internet connection. The computer runs a conventional SMTP server, which remains ready to accept email. In the second stage, the user connects to the Internet and runs a protocol that retrieves messages from the permanent mailbox. Figure 24.4 illustrates the idea.

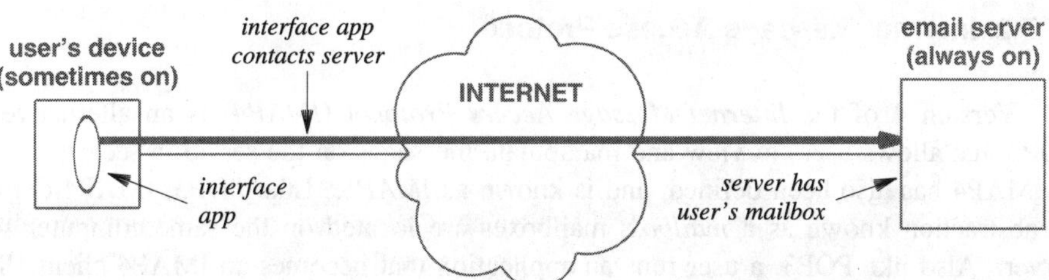

Figure 24.4 Illustration of email access when the email server and user's mailbox are not located on the user's computer.

A variety of techniques have been used to permit a user's mailbox to reside on a remote computer. For example, many ISPs that offer email service provide a web-based interface to email. That is, a user launches a web browser and connects to a special web page that displays email. Companies like Microsoft offer proprietary mechanisms that allow an organization to have a single email server that users can access remotely.

Remote access was pioneered by the IETF, which defined two protocols that allow a remote application to access mail in a permanent mailbox that is stored on a server. Although they have similar functionality, the protocols take opposite approaches: one allows the user to download a copy of messages, and the other allows a user to view and manipulate messages on the server. The next two sections describe the two protocols.

24.7.1 Post Office Protocol

The most popular protocol used to transfer email messages from a permanent remote mailbox to a local computer or portable device is known as version 3 of the *Post Office Protocol* (*POP3*); a secure version of the protocol is known as *POP3S*. The user invokes a POP3 client application, which creates a TCP connection to a POP3 server on the mailbox computer. The user first sends a *login* and a *password* to authenticate the session. Once authentication has been accepted, the client sends commands to retrieve a copy of one or more messages and to delete the messages from the permanent mailbox. The messages are stored and transferred as text files in the standard format specified by RFC 2822.

Note that the computer with the permanent mailbox must run two servers — an SMTP server and a POP3 server. The SMTP server accepts mail sent to a user and places each incoming message in the user's mailbox. The POP3 server allows a user to examine each message in their mailbox, save a copy on the local computer, and delete the message from the mailbox on the server. To ensure correct operation, the two servers must coordinate use of the mailbox so that if a message arrives via SMTP while a user is extracting messages via POP3, the mailbox is left in a valid state.

24.7.2 Internet Message Access Protocol

Version 4 of the *Internet Message Access Protocol* (*IMAP4*) is an alternative to POP3 that allows users to view and manipulate messages on the server; a secure version of IMAP4 has also been defined, and is known as *IMAPS*. Like POP3, IMAP4 defines an abstraction known as a *mailbox*; mailboxes are located on the same computer as a server. Also like POP3, a user runs an application that becomes an IMAP4 client. The application contacts the server to view and manipulate messages. Unlike POP3, however, IMAP4 allows a user to access mail messages from multiple locations (e.g., from work and from home), and ensures that all copies are synchronized and consistent.

IMAP4 also provides extended functionality for message retrieval and processing. A user can obtain information about a message or examine header fields without retrieving the entire message. In addition, a user can search for a specified string and retrieve portions of a message. Partial retrieval is especially useful for slow-speed connections because it means a user does not need to download useless information.

24.8 The MIME Extensions For Non-ASCII Data

The Internet standards for email were created when email messages consisted of text. Users liked email, but wanted a way to send *attachments* (i.e., data files) along with an email message. Consequently, the IETF created *Multipurpose Internet Mail Extensions* (*MIME*) to permit transmission of non-ASCII data items through email. MIME does not change or replace protocols such as SMTP, POP3, and IMAP4. Instead, MIME allows arbitrary data to be encoded in ASCII and then transmitted in a standard email message. To accommodate arbitrary data types and representations, each MIME message includes information that tells the recipient the type of the data and the encoding used. MIME information resides in the RFC 2822 mail header — the MIME header lines specify the MIME version, the data type, and the encoding that was used to convert the data to ASCII. Most users never see the MIME encoding because a typical mail reader application removes or hides such details.

Figure 24.5 illustrates a MIME message that contains a photograph in standard *JPEG*† representation. The JPEG image has been converted to a 7-bit ASCII representation using the *base64* encoding.

```
From: bill@acollege.edu
To: john@example.com
MIME-Version: 1.0
Content-Type: image/jpeg
Content-Transfer-Encoding: base64
```

...data for the image goes here...

Figure 24.5 An example of the header in a MIME message. Header lines identify the type of the data as well as the encoding used.

In the figure, the header line *MIME-Version:* declares that the message was composed using version *1.0* of the MIME protocol. The *Content-Type:* declaration specifies that the data is a JPEG image, and the *Content-Transfer-Encoding:* header declares that *base64* encoding was used to convert the image to ASCII.

The base64 encoding is analogous to hexadecimal because it allows arbitrary binary values to be represented using printable characters. Instead of sixteen characters, base64 uses sixty-four, which makes the resulting file smaller. Base64 was chosen to provide sixty-four ASCII characters that have the same representation across various versions of ISO English character sets‡. Thus, a receiver can be guaranteed that the image extracted from the encoded data is exactly the same as the original image.

---

†JPEG is the *Joint Picture Encoding Group* standard used for digital pictures.

‡The characters consist of 26 uppercase letters, 26 lowercase letters, ten digits, the plus sign, and the slash character.

If one were to examine the data actually transferred, it would appear to be a nonsense stream of characters. For example, Figure 24.6 shows the first few lines from a jpeg image that has been encoded in Base64 for transmission with MIME.


```
/9j/4AAQSkZJRgABAQEAYABgAAD/4QBERXhpZgAATU0AKgAAAAgAA0AAAAMAAAABAAAAAEABAAEA
AAABAAAAAEACAAIAAAAKAAAAMgAAAAB0d21tZy5jb20A/9sAQwANCQoLCggNCwsLDw4NEBQhFRQS
EhQoHR4YITAqMjEvKi4tNDtLQDQ4RzktLkJZQkdOUFRVVDM/XWNcUmJLU1RR/9sAQwEODw8UERQn
FRUnUTYuNlFRUVFRUVFRUVFRUVFRUVFRUVFRUVFRUVFRUVFRUVFRUVFRUVFRUVFRUVFRUVFRUVFR
/8AAEQgAgACAAwEiAAIRAQMRAf/EAB8AAAEFAQEBAQEBAAAAAAAAAAABAgMEBQYHCAkKC//EALUQ
AAIBAwMCBAMFBQQEAAABfQECAwAEEQUSITFBBhNRYQcicRQygZGhCCNCscEVUtHwJDNicoIJChYX
```


Figure 24.6 Example of the base64 encoding used with MIME. The lines are taken from a large jpeg file.

To view the image in a figure, a receiver's mail application must first convert from *base64* encoding back to binary and then run an application that displays a JPEG image on the user's screen. In most email systems, the conversion is performed automatically; a user sees icons or actual files that have been attached to an email message.

How does a mail interface application know how to handle each attachment? The MIME standard specifies that a *Content-Type* declaration must contain two identifiers, a *content type* and a *subtype*, separated by a slash. In Figure 24.5, *image* is the content type, and *jpeg* is the subtype.

The MIME standard defines seven basic content types, the valid subtypes for each, and transfer encodings. For example, although an *image* must be of subtype *jpeg* or *gif*; content type *text* cannot use either subtype. In addition to the standard types and subtypes, MIME permits a sender and receiver to define private content types†. Figure 24.7 lists the seven basic content types.

Content Type	Used When Data In the Message Is
text	Textual (e.g. a document).
image	A still photograph or computer-generated image
audio	A sound recording
video	A video recording that includes motion
application	Raw data for a program
multipart	Multiple messages that each have a separate content type and encoding
message	An entire email message (e.g., a memo that has been forwarded) or an external reference to a message (e.g., an FTP server and file name)

Figure 24.7 The seven basic types that can appear in a MIME *Content-Type* declaration and their meanings.

†To avoid potential name conflicts, the standard requires that names chosen for private content types each begin with the two-character string *X-*.

24.9 MIME Multipart Messages

The MIME multipart content type is useful because it adds considerable flexibility. The standard defines four possible subtypes for a multipart message; each provides important functionality. Subtype *mixed* allows a single message to contain multiple, independent submessages that each can have an independent type and encoding. Mixed multipart messages make it possible to include text, graphics, and audio in a single message, or to send a memo with additional data segments attached, similar to *enclosures* included with a business letter. Subtype *alternative* allows a single message to include multiple representations of the same data. Alternative multipart messages are useful when sending a memo to many recipients who do not all use the same hardware facilities or application software. For example, one can send a document as both plain ASCII text and in formatted form, allowing recipients who have computers with graphic capabilities to select the formatted form for viewing†. Subtype *parallel* permits a single message to include subparts that are to be displayed together (e.g., video and audio subparts must be played simultaneously). Finally, subtype *digest* permits a single message to contain a set of other messages (e.g., a collection of the email messages from a discussion).

Figure 24.8 illustrates an email message that contains two parts. The first is a message in plain text and the second is an image.

```
From: bill@acollege.edu
To: john@example.com
MIME-Version: 1.0
Content-Type: Multipart/Mixed; Boundary=StartOfNextPart
--StartOfNextPart
Content-Type: text/plain
Content-Transfer-Encoding: 7bit
John,
   Here is the photo of our research lab that I promised
to send you.  You can see the equipment you donated.

Thanks again,
Bill

--StartOfNextPart
Content-Type: image/gif
Content-Transfer-Encoding: base64
        ...data for the image...
```

Figure 24.8 An example of a MIME mixed multipart message. Each part of the message has an independent content type and subtype.

†Many email systems use the *alternative* MIME subtype to send a message in both ASCII and HTML formats.

Figure 24.8 illustrates a few details of MIME. For example, each header line can contain parameters of the form $X = Y$ after basic declarations. The keyword *Boundary*= following the multipart content type declaration in the header defines the string used to separate parts of the message. In the example, the sender has selected the string *StartOfNextPart* to serve as the boundary. Declarations of the content type and transfer encoding for a submessage, if included, immediately follow the boundary line. In the example, the second submessage is declared to be a *Graphics Interchange Format* (*GIF*) image.

24.10 Summary

Electronic mail is among the most widely available application services on the Internet. Like most TCP/IP services, email follows the client-server paradigm. A mail system buffers outgoing and incoming messages, allowing the transfer from client and server to occur in background.

The TCP/IP protocol suite provides two separate standards that specify the mail message format and mail transfer details. The mail message format, defined in RFC *2822*, uses a blank line to separate a message header and the body. The Simple Mail Transfer Protocol (SMTP) defines how a mail system on one machine transfers mail to a server on another. Version 3 of the Post Office Protocol (POP3) and version 4 of the Internet Message Access Protocol (IMAP4) specify how a user can retrieve the contents of a mailbox; they allow a user to have a permanent mailbox on a computer with continuous Internet connectivity and to access the contents from a computer with intermittent connectivity.

The Multipurpose Internet Mail Extensions (MIME) provides a mechanism that allows arbitrary data to be transferred using SMTP. MIME adds lines to the header of an email message to define the type of the data and the encoding used. MIME's mixed multipart type permits a single message to contain multiple data types.

EXERCISES

24.1 Find out if your computing system allows you to invoke SMTP directly.

24.2 Build an SMTP client and use it to transfer a mail message.

24.3 See if you can send mail through a mail forwarder back to yourself.

24.4 Make a list of mail address formats that your site handles, and write a set of rules for parsing them.

24.5 Find out how a Linux system can be configured to act as a mail forwarder.

24.6 Find out how often your local mail system attempts delivery, and how long it will continue before giving up.

24.7 Some mail systems allow users to direct incoming mail to a program instead of storing it in a mailbox. Build a program that accepts your incoming mail, places your mail in a file, and then sends a reply to tell the sender you are on vacation.

24.8 Read the SMTP standard carefully. Then use TELNET to connect to the SMTP port on a remote machine and type the commands to ask the remote SMTP server to expand a mail alias. Verify that the server returns the correct expansion.

24.9 A user receives mail in which the *To:* field specifies the string *important-people*. The mail was sent from a computer on which the alias *important-people* includes no valid mailbox identifiers. Read the SMTP specification carefully to see how such a situation is possible.

24.10 POP3 separates message retrieval and deletion by allowing a user to retrieve and view a message without deleting it from the permanent mailbox. What are the advantages and disadvantages of such separation?

24.11 Read about POP3. How does the *TOP* command operate, and why is it useful?

24.12 Read about IMAP4. How does IMAP4 guarantee consistency when multiple concurrent clients access a given mailbox at the same time?

24.13 Read the MIME RFCs carefully. What servers can be specified in a MIME external reference?

24.14 If you use a smartphone with a limit on the number of data bytes received each month, would you prefer POP3 or IMAP4? Explain.

24.15 To disguise the recipients, spam messages often list *Undisclosed Recipients* in the *To:* field. Does your email interface allow you to send a message to a user that shows up in the user's mailbox as being sent to *Undisclosed Recipients*? Explain.

Chapter Contents

25

World Wide Web (HTTP)

25.1 Introduction

This chapter continues the discussion of applications that use TCP/IP technology by focusing on the application that has had the most impact: the *World Wide Web* (the *Web*). After a brief overview of concepts, the chapter examines the primary protocol used to transfer a web page between a server and a web browser. The discussion covers caching as well as the basic transfer mechanism.

25.2 Importance Of The Web

During the early history of the Internet, data transfers using the *File Transfer Protocol* (*FTP*) accounted for approximately one third of Internet traffic, more than any other application. From its inception in the early 1990s, however, the Web has had a high growth rate. By 1995, web traffic overtook FTP to become the largest consumer of Internet backbone bandwidth, and has remained the leading application.

The impact of the Web cannot be understood from traffic statistics alone. More people know about and use the Web than any other Internet application. In fact, for many users, the Internet and the Web are indistinguishable.

25.3 Architectural Components

Conceptually, the Web consists of a large set of documents, called *web pages*, that are accessible to Internet users. Each web page is classified as a *hypermedia* document. The prefix *hyper* is used because a document can contain *selectable links* that refer to other documents, and the suffix *media* is used to indicate that a web document can contain items other than text (e.g., graphics images).

Two main building blocks are used to implement the Web on top of the global Internet: a *web browser* and a *web server.* A browser consists of an application program that a user invokes to access and display a web page. A browser becomes a client that contacts the appropriate web server to obtain a copy of a specified page. Because a given server can manage more than one web page, a browser must specify the exact page when making a request.

The data representation standard used for a web page depends on its contents. For example, standard graphics representations such as *Graphics Interchange Format* (*GIF*) or *Joint Picture Encoding Group* (*JPEG*) can be used for a page that contains a single graphics image. Pages that contain a mixture of text and other items are represented using the *HyperText Markup Language* (*HTML*). An HTML document consists of a file that contains text along with embedded commands, called *tags*, that give guidelines for display. A tag is enclosed in less-than and greater-than symbols; some tags come in pairs that apply to all items between the pair. For example, the two commands *<CENTER>* and *</CENTER>* cause items between the commands to be centered in the browser's window.

25.4 Uniform Resource Locators

Each web page is assigned a unique name that is used to identify it. The name, which is called a *Uniform Resource Locator* (*URL*)†, begins with a specification of the *scheme* used to access the page. In effect, the scheme specifies the transfer protocol; the format of the remainder of the URL depends on the scheme. For example, a URL that follows the *http scheme* has the following form‡:

http: // *hostname [:port] / path [;parameters] [? query]*

where italic denotes an item to be supplied and brackets denote an optional item. For now, it is sufficient to understand that the *hostname* string specifies the domain name, dotted decimal IPv4 address, or colon hex IPv6 address of the computer on which the server for the page operates, *:port* is an optional protocol port number needed only in cases where the server does not use the well-known web port (*80*), *path* is a string that identifies one particular document on the server, *;parameters* is an optional string that specifies additional parameters supplied by the client, and *?query* is an optional string used when the browser sends a question. A user is unlikely ever to see or use the optional parts directly. Instead, URLs that a user enters contain only a *hostname* and *path*.

---

†A URL is a specific type of the more general *Uniform Resource Identifier* (*URI*).

‡Some of the literature refers to the initial string, *http:*, as a *pragma*.

For example, the URL:

http://www.cs.purdue.edu/people/comer/

specifies the author's web page at Purdue University. The server operates on computer *www.cs.purdue.edu*, and the document is named */people/comer/*.

The protocol standards distinguish between the *absolute* form of a URL, illustrated above, and a *relative* form. A relative URL, which is seldom seen by a user, is only meaningful after communication has been established with a specific web server. For example, when communicating with server *www.cs.purdue.edu*, only the string */people/comer/* is needed to specify the document named by the absolute URL above. We can summarize:

> *Each web page is assigned a unique identifier known as a Uniform Resource Locator (URL). The absolute form of a URL contains a full specification; a relative form that omits the address of the server is only useful when the server is implicitly known.*

25.5 An Example HTML Document

An example will illustrate how a URL is produced from a *selectable link* in a document. For each selectable link, a document contains a pair of values: an item to be displayed on the screen and a URL to follow if the user selects the item. In HTML, a pair of tags *<A>* and *</A>*, which are known as an *anchor*, define a selectable link; a URL is added to the first tag, and items to be displayed are placed between the two tags. For example, the following HTML document contains a selectable link:

```
<HTML>
    The author of this text is
    <A HREF="http://www.cs.purdue.edu/people/comer">
    Douglas Comer.</A>
</HTML>
```

When the document is displayed, a single line of text appears on the screen:

The author of this text is Douglas Comer.

The browser underlines the phrase *Douglas Comer* to indicate that it corresponds to a selectable link. Internally, the browser stores the URL from the *<A>* tag, which it follows when the user selects the link.

25.6 Hypertext Transfer Protocol

The protocol used for communication between a browser and a web server or between intermediate machines and web servers is known as the *HyperText Transfer Protocol* (*HTTP*). HTTP has the following set of characteristics:

- *Application Layer.* HTTP operates at the application layer. It assumes a reliable, connection-oriented transport protocol such as TCP, but does not provide reliability or retransmission itself.
- *Request/Response.* Once a transport session has been established, one side (usually a browser) must send an HTTP request to which the other side responds.
- *Stateless.* Each HTTP request is self-contained; the server does not keep a history of previous requests or previous sessions.
- *Bi-Directional Transfer.* In most cases, a browser requests a web page, and the server transfers a copy to the browser. HTTP also allows transfer from a browser to a server (e.g., when a user supplies data).
- *Capability Negotiation.* HTTP allows browsers and servers to negotiate details such as the character set to be used during transfers. A sender can specify the capabilities it offers, and a receiver can specify the capabilities it accepts.
- *Support For Caching.* To improve response time, a browser caches a copy of each web page it retrieves. If a user requests a page again, the browser can interrogate the server to determine whether the contents of the page has changed since the copy was cached.
- *Support For Intermediaries.* HTTP allows a machine along the path between a browser and a server to act as a *proxy server* that caches web pages and answers a browser's request from its cache.

25.7 HTTP GET Request

In the simplest case, a browser contacts a web server directly to obtain a page. The browser begins with a URL, extracts the hostname section, uses DNS to map the name into an equivalent IP address, and uses the resulting IP address to form a TCP connection to the web server. Once the TCP connection is in place, the browser and web server use HTTP to communicate; the browser sends a request to retrieve a specific page, and the server responds by sending a copy of the page.

A browser sends an HTTP *GET* command to request a web page from a server†. The request consists of a single line of text that begins with the keyword *GET* and is

†The standard uses the object-oriented term *method* instead of *command*.

followed by a URL and an HTTP version number. For example, to retrieve the web page in the example above from server *www.cs.purdue.edu*, a browser can send the following request with an absolute URL:

GET http://www.cs.purdue.edu/people/comer/ HTTP/1.1

Once a TCP connection is in place, there is no need to send an absolute URL — the following relative URL will retrieve the same page:

GET /people/comer/ HTTP/1.1

To summarize:

> *The Hypertext Transfer Protocol (HTTP) is used between a browser and a web server. The browser sends a GET request to which a server responds by sending the requested page.*

25.8 Error Messages

How should a web server respond when it receives an illegal request? In most cases, the request has been sent by a browser, and the browser will attempt to display whatever the server returns. Consequently, servers usually generate error messages in valid HTML. For example, one server generates the following error message as a response whenever the server cannot honor a request:

```
<HTML>
    <HEAD> <TITLE>400 Bad Request</TITLE>
    </HEAD>
    <BODY>
        <H1>Error In Request</H1> Your browser sent a request
        that this server could not understand.
    </BODY>
</HTML>
```

The browser uses the *head* of the document (i.e., the items between <HEAD> and </HEAD>) internally, and only shows the *body* of the document to the user. The pair of tags <H1> and </H1> causes the browser to display *Error In Request* as a heading (i.e., large and bold), resulting in two lines of output on the user's screen:

Error In Request

Your browser sent a request that this server could not understand.

25.9 Persistent Connections

The first version of HTTP uses a paradigm of one TCP connection per data transfer. A client opens a TCP connection and sends a *GET* request. The server sends a copy of the requested page and closes the connection. The paradigm has the advantage of being unambiguous — the client merely reads until an *end of file* condition is encountered, and then closes its end of the connection.

Version 1.1 of HTTP changes the basic paradigm in a fundamental way: instead of using a TCP connection per transfer, version 1.1 adopts a *persistent connection* approach as the default. That is, once a client opens a TCP connection to a particular web server, the client leaves the connection in place during multiple requests and responses. When either a client or server is ready to close the connection, it informs the other side, and the connection is closed.

The chief advantage of persistent connections lies in reduced overhead — fewer TCP connections means lower response latency, less overhead on the underlying networks, less memory used for buffers, and less use of CPU time. A browser using a persistent connection can further optimize by *pipelining* requests (i.e., send requests back-to-back without waiting for a response). Pipelining is especially attractive in situations where multiple images must be retrieved for a given web page, and the underlying internet has both high throughput and long delay.

The chief disadvantage of using a persistent connection lies in the need to identify the beginning and end of each item sent over the connection. There are two possible techniques to handle the situation: either send a length followed by the item, or send a *sentinel value* after the item to mark the end. HTTP cannot reserve a sentinel value because the items transmitted include graphics images that can contain arbitrary sequences of octets. Thus, to avoid ambiguity between sentinel values and data, HTTP uses the approach of sending a length followed by an item of that size.

25.10 Data Length And Program Output

It may be inconvenient or even impossible for a web server to know the length of a web page before sending the page. To understand why, one must know that many web pages are generated upon request. That is, the server uses a technology such as the *Common Gateway Interface* (*CGI*) that allows a computer program running on the server machine to create a web page. When a request arrives that corresponds to a CGI-generated page, the web server runs the appropriate CGI program, and sends the output from the program back to the client as a response. Dynamic web page generation allows the creation of information that is current (e.g., a list of the current scores in sporting events or a list of sites that match a search term), but the server may not know the exact data size in advance. Furthermore, saving the data to a file before sending it is undesirable for two reasons: it uses resources at the web server and delays transmission. Thus, to provide for dynamic web pages, the HTTP standard specifies that if the server does not know the length of a page *a priori*, the server can inform the browser that it will close the connection after transmitting the page. To summarize:

> *To allow a TCP connection to persist through multiple requests and responses, HTTP sends a length before each response. If it does not know the length, a server informs the client, sends the response, and then closes the connection.*

25.11 Length Encoding And Headers

What representation should a server use to send length information? Interestingly, HTTP borrows the basic format from email, using the same format specified in RFC 2822 for email messages and MIME Extensions†. Like a standard RFC 2822 email message, each HTTP transmission contains a header, a blank line, and the document being sent. Furthermore, each line in the header contains a keyword, a colon, and information. Figure 25.1 lists a few of the possible HTTP headers and their meaning.

Header	Meaning
Content-Length:	Size of document in octets
Content-Type:	Type of the document
Content-Encoding:	Encoding used for document
Content-Language:	Language(s) used in document

Figure 25.1 Examples headers that can appear before a document. The *Content-Type:* and *Content-Encoding:* headers are taken directly from MIME.

As an example, consider Figure 25.2 which shows a few of the headers that are used when a short HTML document (34 characters) is transferred across a persistent TCP connection.

```
Content-Length:   34
Content-Language: en
Content-Encoding: ascii

<HTML> A trivial example. </HTML>
```

Figure 25.2 An illustration of an HTTP transfer with header lines used to specify attributes, a blank line, and the document itself. A *Content-Length:* header is required if the connection is persistent.

†See the previous chapter for a discussion of email and MIME.

In addition to the headers listed in Figure 25.1, HTTP includes a wide variety of headers that allow a browser and server to exchange meta information. For example, if a server does not know the length of a page, the server closes the connection after sending the document. However, the server does not act without warning — the server informs the browser to expect a close. To do so, the server includes a *Connection:* header before the document in place of a *Content-Length:* header:

Connection: close

When it receives a connection header, the browser knows that the server intends to close the connection after the transfer; the browser is forbidden from sending further requests. The next sections describe the purposes of other HTTP headers.

25.12 Negotiation

In addition to specifying details about a document being sent, HTTP uses headers to permit a client and server to *negotiate* capabilities. The set of negotiable capabilities includes a wide variety of characteristics about the connection (e.g., whether access is authenticated), representation (e.g., whether graphics images in JPEG format are acceptable or which types of compression can be used), content (e.g., whether text files must be in English), and control (e.g., the length of time a page remains valid).

There are two basic types of negotiation: *server-driven* and *agent-driven* (i.e., browser-driven). Server-driven negotiation begins with a request from a browser. The request specifies a list of preferences along with the URL of the desired document. The server selects, from among the available representations, one that satisfies the browser's preferences. If multiple documents satisfy the browser's preferences, the server uses a local policy to select one. For example, if a document is stored in multiple languages and a request specifies a preference for English, the server will send the English version.

Agent-driven negotiation means that a browser uses a two-step process to perform the selection. First, the browser sends a request to the server to ask what is available. The server returns a list of possibilities. The browser selects one of the possibilities, and sends a second request to obtain the document. The disadvantage of agent-driven negotiation is that it requires two server interactions; the advantage is that a browser retains control over the choice.

A browser uses an HTTP *Accept:* header to specify which media or representations are acceptable. The header lists names of formats with a preference value assigned to each. For example,

```
Accept: text/html, text/plain; q=0.5, text/x-dvi; q=0.8
```

specifies that the browser is willing to accept the *text/html* media type, but if the type does not exist, the browser will accept *text/x-dvi*, and if that does not exist, *text/plain*.

The numeric values associated with the second and third entry can be thought of as a *preference level*, where no value is equivalent to $q=1$, and a value of $q=0$ means the type is unacceptable. For media types where "quality" is meaningful (e.g., audio), the value of q can be interpreted as a willingness to accept a given media type if it is the best available after other forms are reduced in quality by q percent.

A variety of *Accept* headers exist that correspond to the *Content* headers described earlier. For example, a browser can send any of the following:

```
Accept-Encoding:
Accept-Charset:
Accept-Language:
```

to specify which encodings, character sets, and languages the browser is willing to accept.

We can summarize the discussion about negotiation:

> *HTTP uses MIME-like headers to carry meta information. Both browsers and servers send headers that allow them to negotiate agreement on the document representation and encoding to be used.*

25.13 Conditional Requests

HTTP allows a sender to make a request *conditional*. That is, when a browser sends a request, it includes a header that qualifies conditions under which the request should be honored. If the specified condition is not met, the server does not return the requested document. Conditional requests allow a browser to optimize retrieval by avoiding unnecessary transfers. One of the most useful conditions uses an *If-Modified-Since:* request — it allows a browser to avoid transferring a document unless it has been updated since a specified date. For example, a browser can include the header:

If-Modified-Since: Mon, 01 Apr 2013 05:00:01 GMT

with a *GET* request to avoid a transfer if the document is older than April 1, 2013.

25.14 Proxy Servers And Caching

Proxy servers are an important part of the web architecture because they provide an optimization that can decrease latency and reduce the load on servers. Two forms of proxy servers exist: *nontransparent* and *transparent*. As the name implies, a *nontransparent* server is visible to a user — the user configures a browser to contact the proxy instead of the original source. A *transparent* proxy does not require any changes to a browser's configuration. Instead, a transparent proxy examines all TCP connections that pass through the proxy, and intercepts any connection to port 80. In either case, a proxy caches web pages and answers subsequent requests for a page from the cache.

HTTP includes explicit support for proxy servers. The protocol specifies exactly how a proxy handles each request, how headers should be interpreted by proxies, how a browser negotiates with a proxy, and how a proxy negotiates with a server. Furthermore, several HTTP headers have been designed specifically for use by proxies. For example, one header allows a proxy to authenticate itself to a server, and another allows each proxy that handles a web page to record its identity so the ultimate recipient receives a list of all intermediate proxies. Finally, HTTP allows a server to control how proxies handle each web page. For example, a server can include the *Max-Forwards:* header in a response to limit the number of proxies that handle a page before it is delivered to a browser. If the server specifies a count of one, as in:

Max-Forwards: 1

at most one proxy can handle the page along the path from the server to the browser. A count of zero prohibits any proxy from handling the page.

25.15 Caching

The goal of caching is improved efficiency: a cache reduces both latency and network traffic by eliminating unnecessary transfers. The most obvious aspect of caching is storage. When a web page is initially accessed, a copy is stored on disk, either by the browser, an intermediate proxy, or both. Subsequent requests for the same page can short-circuit the lookup process and retrieve a copy of the page from the cache instead of the web server.

The central question in all caching schemes concerns timing: how long should an item be kept in a cache? On one hand, keeping a cached copy too long results in the copy becoming *stale*, which means that changes to the original are not reflected in the cached copy. On the other hand, if the cached copy is not kept long enough, inefficiency results because the next request must go back to the server.

HTTP allows a web server to control caching in two ways. First, when it answers a request for a page, a server can specify caching details, including whether the page can be cached at all, whether a proxy can cache the page, the community with which a cached copy can be shared, the time at which the cached copy must expire, and limits on transformations that can be applied to the copy. Second, HTTP allows a browser to force *revalidation* of a page. To do so, the browser sends a request for the page, and uses a header to specify that the maximum *age* (i.e., the time since a copy of the page was stored) cannot be greater than zero. No copy of the page in a cache can be used to satisfy the request because the copy will have a nonzero age. Thus, only the original web server will answer the request. Intermediate proxies along the way will receive a fresh copy for their cache as will the browser that issued the request.

To summarize:

> *Caching is key to the efficient operation of the Web. HTTP allows web servers to control whether and how a page can be cached as well as its lifetime; a browser can force a request for a page to bypass caches and obtain a fresh copy from the server that owns the page.*

25.16 Other HTTP Functionality

Our description of HTTP has focused exclusively on retrieval in which a client, typically a browser, issues a *GET* request to retrieve a copy of a web page from a server. However, HTTP includes facilities that allow more complex interactions between a client and server. In particular, HTTP offers *PUT* and *POST* methods that allow a client to send data to a server. Thus, it is possible to build a script that prompts a user for an ID and password and then transfers the results to the server.

Surprisingly, although it permits transfer in either direction, the underlying HTTP protocol remains stateless (i.e., does not require a persistent transport layer connection to remain in place during an interaction). Thus, additional information is often used to coordinate a series of transfers. For example, in response to an ID and password, a server might send an identifying integer known as a *cookie* that the client returns in successive transfers.

25.17 HTTP, Security, And E-Commerce

Although it defines a mechanism that can be used to access web pages, HTTP does not provide security. Thus, before they make web purchases that require the transfer of information such as a credit card number, users need assurance that the transaction is safe. There are two issues: confidentiality of the data being transferred and authentication of the web site offering items for sale. As we will see in Chapter 29, encryption is used to ensure confidentiality. In addition, a certificate mechanism can be used to authenticate the merchant.

A security technology has been devised for use with web transactions. Known as *HTTP over SSL* (*HTTPS*), the technology runs HTTP over the Secure Socket Layer (*SSL*) protocol. HTTPS solves both security issues related to e-commerce: because they are encrypted, data transfers are confidential, and because SSL uses a certificate tree, a merchant is authenticated.

25.18 Summary

The World Wide Web consists of hypermedia documents stored on a set of web servers and accessed by browsers. Each document is assigned a URL that uniquely identifies it; the URL specifies the protocol used to retrieve the document, the location of the server, and the path to the document on that server.

The HyperText Markup Language, HTML, allows a document to contain text along with embedded commands that control formatting. HTML also allows a document to contain links to other documents.

A browser and server use the HyperText Transfer Protocol, HTTP, to transfer information. HTTP is an application-level protocol with explicit support for negotiation, proxy servers, caching, and persistent connections. A related technology known as HTTPS uses SSL to provide secure HTTP communication.

EXERCISES

25.1 Read the standard for URLs. What does it mean when a pound sign (#) is followed by a string at the end of a URL?

25.2 Extend the previous exercise. Is it legal to send the pound sign suffix on a URL to a web server? Why or why not?

25.3 How does a browser distinguish between a document that contains HTML and a document that contains arbitrary text? To find out, experiment by using a browser to read from a file. Does the browser use the name of the file or the contents to decide how to interpret the file?

25.4 What is the purpose of an HTTP *TRACE* command?

25.5 What is the difference between an HTTP *PUT* command and an HTTP *POST* command? When is each useful?

25.6 When is an HTTP *Keep-Alive* header used?

25.7 Can an arbitrary web server function as a proxy? To find out, choose an arbitrary web server and configure your browser to use it as a proxy. Do the results surprise you?

25.8 Download and install the Squid transparent proxy cache. What networking facilities in the OS does Squid use to cache web pages?

25.9 Read about HTTP's *must-revalidate* cache control directive. Give an example of a web page that would use such a directive.

25.10 Suppose you work for a company that configures your laptop computer always to use the company's proxy web server. Explain what happens if you travel and connect to the Internet at a hotel.

25.11 If a browser does not send an HTTP *Content-Length:* header before a request, how does a server respond?

25.12 Read more about HTTPS and explain the impact of HTTPS on caching. Under what circumstances can a proxy cache web pages when using HTTPS?

25.13 Read the HTTP specification carefully. Can HTTP be used for streaming video? Explain why or why not.

25.14 Consider a denial-of-service attack on a web server in which a perpetrator arranges to have many clients form a connection to the server and repeatedly send requests for non-existent web pages. How can such an attack be prevented?

25.15 Because many web pages include ads, most web pages contain at least some dynamic content (i.e., content that is generated when the page is fetched). How should a web designer arrange such pages to maximize caching effectiveness?

Chapter Contents

26

Voice And Video Over IP (RTP, RSVP, QoS)

26.1 Introduction

Previous chapters consider applications that transfer email messages and data files. This chapter focuses on the transfer of real-time data, such as voice and video over an IP network. In addition to discussing the protocols used to transport such data, the chapter considers two broader issues. First, it examines protocols and technologies used for commercial IP telephone service. Second, it examines the question of how routers in an IP network can guarantee sufficient quality of service to provide high-quality video and audio reproduction.

26.2 Digitizing And Encoding

Before voice or video can be sent over a packet network, hardware known as a *coder/decoder* (*codec*) must be used to convert the analog signal to digital form. The most common type of codec, a *waveform coder*, measures the amplitude of the input signal at regular intervals and converts each sample into a digital value (i.e., an integer)†. At the receiving side, a codec accepts a sequence of integers as input and creates a continuous analog signal that matches the digital values.

Several digital encoding standards exist, with the main tradeoff being between quality of reproduction and the size of digital representation. For example, the conventional telephone system uses the *Pulse Code Modulation* (*PCM*) standard that specifies taking an 8-bit sample every 125 μ seconds (i.e., 8000 times per second). As a result, a

†An alternative known as a *voice coder/decoder* (*vocodec*) recognizes and encodes human speech rather than general waveforms.

digitized telephone call produces data at a rate of 64 Kbps. The PCM encoding produces a surprising amount of output — storing an uncompressed 128-second audio clip requires one megabyte of memory.

There are three ways to reduce the amount of data generated by digital encoding: take fewer samples per second, use fewer bits to encode each sample, or use a digital compression scheme to reduce the size of the resulting output. Various systems exist that use one or more of the techniques, making it possible to find products that produce encoded audio at a rate of only 2.2 Kbps. However, each technique has disadvantages. The chief disadvantage of taking fewer samples or using fewer bits to encode a sample is lower quality audio — the system cannot reproduce as large a range of sound frequencies. The chief disadvantage of compression is delay — digitized output must be held while it is compressed. Furthermore, because greater reduction in size requires more processing, the best compression either requires a fast CPU or introduces longer delay. Thus, compression is most useful when delay is unimportant (e.g., when the output from a codec is being stored in a file).

26.3 Audio And Video Transmission And Reproduction

Many audio and video applications are classified as *real-time* because they require timely transmission and delivery†. For example, interactive telephone calls and streaming videos are classified as real-time because audio and video must be delivered without significant delay or users find the result unsatisfactory. Timely transfer means more than low delay because the resulting signal is unintelligible unless it is presented in exactly the same order as the original and with exactly the same timing. Thus, if a sending system takes a sample every 125 μ seconds. A receiving system must convert digital values to analog at exactly the same rate as they were sampled.

How can a network guarantee that the stream is delivered at exactly the same rate that the sender used? The original U.S. telephone system introduced one answer: an *isochronous* architecture. Isochronous design means that the entire system, including the digital circuits, must be engineered to deliver output with exactly the same timing as was used to generate input. Thus, an isochronous system with multiple paths between any two points must be engineered so all paths have exactly the same delay.

TCP/IP technology and the global Internet are not isochronous. We have seen that datagrams can be duplicated, delayed, or arrive out of order. Variance in delay, known as *jitter*, is especially pervasive in IP networks. To allow meaningful transmission and reproduction of digitized signals across a network with IP semantics, additional protocol support is required. To handle datagram duplication and out-of-order delivery, each transmission must contain a sequence number. To handle jitter, each transmission must contain a *timestamp* that tells the receiver at which time the data in the packet should be played back. Separating sequence and timing information allows a receiver to reconstruct the signal accurately, independent of how the packets arrive. Such timing information is especially critical when a datagram is lost or if the sender stops encoding dur-

†Timeliness is more important than reliability; there is no time for retransmission — data that does not arrive in time must be skipped.

ing periods of silence; it allows the receiver to pause during playback the amount of time specified by the timestamps. To summarize:

> *Because an IP internet is not isochronous, additional protocol support is required to deliver real-time data such as audio and video. In addition to basic sequence information that allows detection of duplicate or reordered packets, each packet must carry a separate timestamp that tells the receiver the exact time at which the data in the packet should be played.*

26.4 Jitter And Playback Delay

How can a receiver recreate a signal accurately if the network introduces jitter? The receiver must implement a *playback buffer*† as Figure 26.1 illustrates.

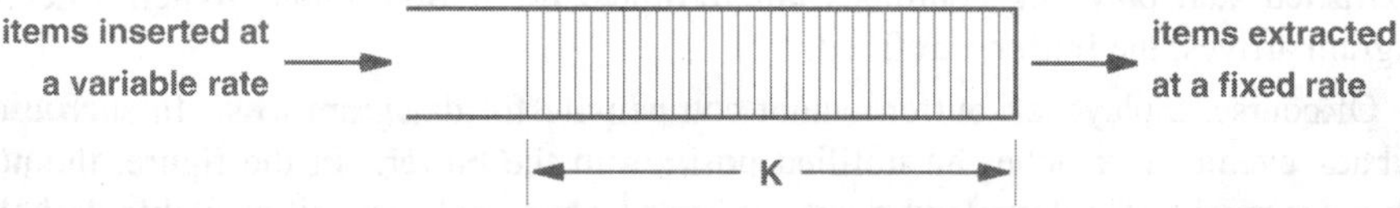

Figure 26.1 The conceptual organization of a playback buffer that compensates for jitter. The buffer holds K time units of data.

When a session begins, the receiver delays playback and places incoming data in the buffer. When data in the buffer reaches a predetermined threshold, known as the *playback point*, output begins. The playback point, labeled K in the figure, is measured in time units of data to be played. Thus, playback begins when a receiver has accumulated K time units of data.

Applications that play streaming audio or video usually present users with a graphical representation of playback buffering. Typically, the display consists of a horizontal bar that represents the time required to display the object. For example, if a user plays the video for a 30-minute television show, the display represents time from zero to 30 minutes. At any time, shading is used to divide the bar into three segments. A segment on the left shows the amount of the video that has been played, the next segment shows the amount of the unplayed video that has been downloaded, and the third segment shows the amount of the video that must still be downloaded. We use the term *playback point* to refer to the point in the video currently being displayed and the term *download point* to refer to the amount of the video currently downloaded. Figure 26.2 shows how a playback display might appear to a user with the segments labeled.

†A playback buffer is also called a *jitter buffer*.

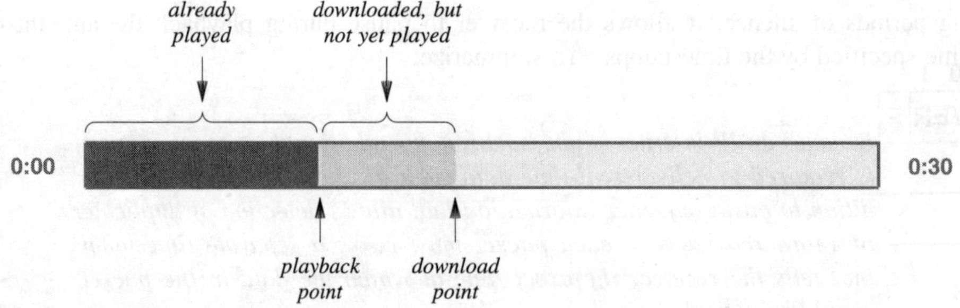

Figure 26.2 Illustration of a display that shows playback buffering for a 30-minute streaming video with segments and points labeled.

As playback proceeds, datagrams continue to arrive. If there is no jitter, new data will arrive at exactly the same rate old data is being extracted and played, meaning the buffer will always contain exactly K time units of unplayed data. If a datagram experiences a small delay, playback is unaffected. The buffer size decreases steadily as data is extracted, and playback continues uninterrupted for K time units. When a delayed datagram arrives, the buffer is refilled.

Of course, a playback buffer cannot compensate for datagram loss. In such cases, playback eventually reaches an unfilled position in the buffer. In the figure, the playback point reaches the download point. When playback exhausts all available data, output must pause for a time period corresponding to the missing data.

The choice of K is a compromise between loss and delay†. If K is too small, a small amount of jitter causes the system to exhaust the playback buffer before the data arrives. If K is too large, the system remains immune to jitter, but the extra delay, when added to the transmission delay in the network, may be noticeable to users. Despite the disadvantages, most applications that send real-time data across an IP internet depend on playback buffering as the primary solution for jitter.

26.5 Real-time Transport Protocol (RTP)

The protocol used to transmit digitized audio or video signals over an IP internet is known as the *Real-time Transport Protocol* (*RTP*). Interestingly, RTP does not contain mechanisms that ensure packets traverse an internet in a timely manner; such guarantees, if they exist, must be made by the underlying system. Instead, RTP provides two key facilities: a sequence number in each packet that allows a receiver to detect out-of-order delivery or loss, and a timestamp that allows a receiver to control playback.

Because RTP is designed to carry a wide variety of real-time data, including both audio and video, RTP does not enforce a specific encoding for data. Instead, each packet begins with a header; initial fields in the header specify how to interpret remaining header fields and how to interpret the payload. Figure 26.3 illustrates the format of RTP's header.

†Although network loss and jitter can be used to determine a value for K dynamically, many playback buffering schemes use a constant.

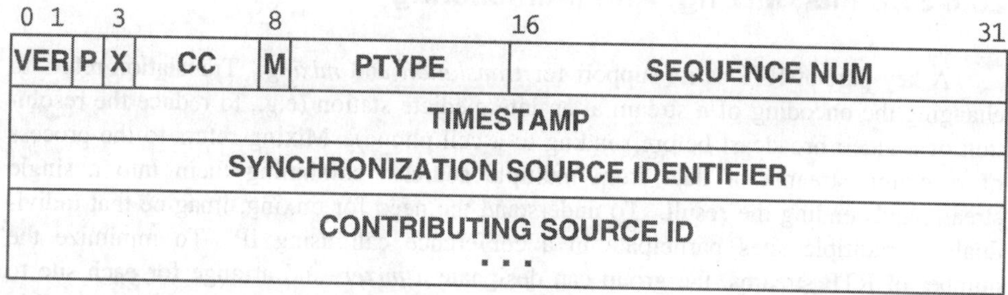

Figure 26.3 Illustration of the header used with RTP. Each message begins with this header; the exact interpretation of remaining fields in the message depends on the payload type, *PTYPE*.

As the figure shows, each packet begins with a two-bit RTP version number in field *VER*; the current version is *2*. The *P* bit specifies whether zero padding follows the payload; it is used with encryption that requires data to be allocated in fixed-size blocks. Some applications define an optional header extension to be placed between the header shown above and the payload. If the application type allows an extension, the *X* bit is used to specify whether the extension is present in the packet. The four-bit *CC* field contains a count of contributing source IDs in the header. Interpretation of the *M* (*marker*) bit depends on the application; it is used by applications that need to mark points in the data stream (e.g., the beginning of each frame when sending video). The seven-bit *PTYPE* field specifies the payload type being sent in the message; interpretation of remaining fields in the header and payload depends on the value in *PTYPE*. The sixteen-bit *SEQUENCE NUM* field contains a sequence number for the packet. The first sequence number in a particular session is chosen at random.

The payload type affects the interpretation of the *TIMESTAMP* field. Conceptually, a *timestamp* is a 32-bit value that gives the time at which the first octet of digitized data was sampled, with the initial timestamp for a session chosen at random. The standard specifies that the timestamp is incremented continuously, even during periods when no signal is detected and no values are sent, but the standard does not specify the exact granularity. Instead, the granularity is determined by the payload type, which means that each application can choose a clock granularity that allows a receiver to position items in the output with accuracy appropriate to the application. For example, if a stream of audio data is being transmitted over RTP, a logical timestamp granularity of one clock tick per sample might be appropriate†. Thus, an audio timestamp might have a granularity of one tick for each 125 μ seconds. When a stream contains video data, a sample might correspond to one frame. However, a granularity of one tick per frame will be undesirable — a higher granularity will achieve smoother playback.

The separation of sequence number and timestamp is important for cases where a sample spans multiple packets. In particular, the standard allows the timestamps in two packets to be identical in the case where two packets contain data that was sampled at the same time.

†The *TIMESTAMP* is sometimes referred to as a *MEDIA TIMESTAMP* to emphasize that its granularity depends on the type of signal being measured.

26.6 Streams, Mixing, And Multicasting

A key part of RTP is its support for *translation* and *mixing*. Translation refers to changing the encoding of a stream at an intermediate station (e.g., to reduce the resolution of a video broadcast before sending to a cell phone). Mixing refers to the process of receiving streams of data from multiple sources, combining them into a single stream, and sending the result. To understand the need for mixing, imagine that individuals at multiple sites participate in a conference call using IP. To minimize the number of RTP streams, the group can designate a *mixer*, and arrange for each site to establish an RTP session to the mixer. The mixer combines the audio streams (possibly by converting them back to analog and resampling the resulting signal), and sends the result as a single digital stream.

Fields in the RTP header support mixing by indicating that mixing has occurred and identifying the sources of data. The field in Figure 26.3 labeled *SYNCHRONIZATION SOURCE IDENTIFIER* specifies the source of a stream. Each source must choose a unique 32-bit identifier; the protocol includes a mechanism for resolving conflicts if they arise. When a mixer combines multiple streams, the mixer becomes the synchronization source for the new stream. Information about the original sources is not lost, however, because the mixer uses the variable-size *CONTRIBUTING SOURCE ID* field to provide the synchronization IDs of streams that were mixed together. The four-bit *CC* field gives a count of contributing sources, which means that a maximum of 15 sources can be listed.

RTP is designed to work with IP multicasting, and mixing is especially attractive in a multicast environment. To understand why, imagine a teleconference that includes many participants. Unicasting requires a station to send a copy of each outgoing RTP packet to each participant. With multicasting, however, a station only needs to send one copy of the packet, which will be delivered to all participants. Furthermore, if mixing is used, all sources can unicast to a mixer, which combines them into a single stream before multicasting. Thus, the combination of mixing and multicast results in substantially fewer datagrams being delivered to each participating host.

26.7 RTP Encapsulation

Its name implies that RTP is a transport level protocol. Indeed, if it functioned like a conventional transport protocol, RTP would require each message to be encapsulated directly in an IP datagram. In fact, the name is a misnomer because RTP does not function like a transport protocol†. That is, direct encapsulation of RTP messages in IP datagrams does not occur in practice. Instead, RTP runs over UDP, meaning that each RTP message is encapsulated in a UDP datagram. The chief advantage of using UDP is concurrency — a single computer can have multiple applications using RTP without interference.

Unlike many of the application protocols we have seen, RTP does not use a reserved UDP port number. Instead, a port is allocated for use with each session, and the remote application must be informed about the port number. By convention, RTP

†The name *Real-time Transfer Protocol* would have been more appropriate.

chooses an even numbered UDP port; the following section explains that a companion protocol, RTCP, uses the next sequential port number.

26.8 RTP Control Protocol (RTCP)

Our description of real-time transmission has focused on the protocol mechanisms that allow a sender to associate a timestamp with real-time data and allow a receiver to reproduce the content. Another aspect of real-time transmission is equally important: monitoring of the underlying network during the session and providing *out-of-band* communication between the endpoints. Such a mechanism is especially important in cases where adaptive coding schemes are used. For example, an application might choose a lower-bandwidth encoding when the underlying network becomes congested, or a receiver might vary the size of its playback buffer when network delay or jitter changes. Finally, an out-of-band mechanism can be used to send information in parallel with the real-time data (e.g., captions to accompany a video stream).

A companion protocol and integral part of RTP, known as the *RTP Control Protocol* (*RTCP*), provides the needed control functionality. RTCP allows senders and receivers to transmit a series of reports to one another that contain additional information about the data being transferred and the performance of the network. RTCP messages are encapsulated in UDP for transmission†, and are sent using a port number one greater than the port number of the RTP stream to which they pertain.

26.9 RTCP Operation

Figure 26.4 lists the five basic message types RTCP uses to allow senders and receivers to exchange information about a session.

Type	Meaning
200	Sender report
201	Receiver report
202	Source description message
203	Bye message
204	Application specific message

Figure 26.4 The five RTCP message types. Each message begins with a fixed header that identifies the type.

The last two messages on the list are easiest to understand. A sender transmits a *bye* message when shutting down a stream and an *application specific* message to define a new message type. For example, to send closed-caption information along with a video stream, an application might choose to define a new RTCP message type.

---

†Because some messages are short, the standard allows multiple RTCP messages to be combined into a single UDP datagram for transmission.

Receivers periodically transmit *receiver report* messages that inform the source about conditions of reception. Receiver report messages are important for two reasons. First, the messages allow each receiver participating in a session, as well as a sender, to learn about reception conditions of other receivers. Second, the messages allow receivers to adapt their rate of reporting to avoid using excessive bandwidth and overwhelming the sender. The adaptive scheme guarantees that the total control traffic will remain less than 5% of the real-time data traffic and that receiver reports generate less than 75% of the control traffic. Each receiver report identifies one or more synchronization sources, and contains a separate section for each source. A section specifies the highest sequence number packet received from the source, the cumulative and percentage packet loss experienced, the time since the last RTCP sender report arrived from the source, and the interarrival jitter.

Senders periodically transmit a *sender report* message that provides an absolute timestamp. To understand the need for a timestamp, recall that RTP allows each stream to choose a granularity for its timestamp and that the first timestamp is chosen at random. The absolute timestamp in a sender report is essential because it provides the only mechanism a receiver has to *synchronize* multiple streams. In particular, because RTP requires a separate stream for each media type, the transmission of video and accompanying audio requires two streams. The absolute timestamp information allows a receiver to play the two streams simultaneously.

In addition to the periodic sender report messages, senders also transmit *source description* messages that provide general information about the user who owns or controls the source. Each message contains one section for each outgoing RTP stream; the contents are intended for humans to read. For example, the only required field consists of a *canonical name* for the stream owner, a character string in the form:

user @ host

where *host* is either the domain name of the computer or its IP address in dotted decimal or hex colon form, and *user* is a login name. Optional fields in the source description contain further details such as the user's email address (which may differ from the canonical name), telephone number, the geographic location of the site, the application program or tool used to create the stream, or other textual notes about the source.

26.10 IP Telephony And Signaling

One aspect of real-time transmission stands out as especially important: the use of IP as the foundation for telephone service. Known as *IP telephony* or *Voice over IP* (*VoIP*), the approach is now employed by many telephone companies. The question arises: what additional technologies are needed before VoIP can completely replace the existing isochronous telephone system? Although no simple answer exists, three basic components are needed. First, we have seen that a protocol like RTP is required when transferring real-time data across an IP internet. The protocol labels each sample with a timestamp that allows a receiver to recreate an analog output signal that exactly matches the original input signal. Second, a mechanism is needed to establish and terminate telephone calls. Third, researchers are investigating ways an IP internet can be made to function like an isochronous network.

The telephone industry uses the term *signaling* to refer to the process of establishing a telephone call. Specifically, the signaling mechanism used in the conventional *Public Switched Telephone Network* (*PSTN*) is *Signaling System 7* (*SS7*); SS7 performs call routing before audio is sent. Given a phone number, SS7 forms a circuit through the network, rings the designated telephone, and connects the circuit when the phone is answered. SS7 also handles details such as call forwarding and error conditions such as the destination phone being busy.

Before IP can be used to make phone calls, signaling functionality must be available. Furthermore, to enable adoption by the phone companies, the signaling system used by IP telephony must be compatible with extant telephone signaling — it must be possible for the IP telephony system to interoperate with the conventional phone system at all levels. Thus, it must be possible to translate between the signaling used with IP and SS7, just as it must be possible to translate between the voice encoding used with IP and standard PCM encoding. As a consequence, the two signaling mechanisms will have equivalent functionality.

The general approach to interoperability uses a *gateway* between the IP phone system and the conventional phone system. A call can be initiated on either side of the gateway. When a signaling request arrives, the gateway translates and forwards the request; the gateway must also translate and forward the response. Finally, after signaling is complete and a call has been established, the gateway must forward voice in both directions, translating from the encoding used on one side to the encoding used on the other.

Two groups have proposed standards for IP telephony. The ITU has defined a suite of protocols known as *H.323*, and the IETF has proposed a signaling protocol known as the *Session Initiation Protocol* (*SIP*). The next sections summarize the two approaches.

26.10.1 H.323 Standards

The ITU originally created H.323 to allow the transmission of voice over local area network technologies. The standard has been extended to allow transmission of voice over IP internets, and telephone companies have adopted it. H.323 is not a single protocol. Instead, it specifies how multiple protocols can be combined to form a functional IP telephony system. For example, in addition to gateways, H.323 defines devices known as *gatekeepers* that each provide a contact point for telephones using IP. To obtain permission to place outgoing calls and enable the phone system to direct incoming calls to the correct destination, each IP telephone must register with a gatekeeper. H.323 includes the necessary registration protocols.

In addition to specifying a protocol for the transmission of real-time voice and video, the H.323 framework provides protocols that specify how participants transfer and share data. Of particular significance is data sharing related to a real-time teleconference. For example, a pair of users engaged in an audio-video conference can also share an on-screen whiteboard, send still images, or exchange copies of documents.

Figure 26.5 lists the four major protocols that form the building blocks of H.323.

Protocol	Purpose
H.225.0	Signaling used to establish a call
H.245	Control and feedback during the call
RTP	Real-time data transfer (sequence and timing)
T.120	Exchange of data associated with a call

Figure 26.5 The four basic protocols that H.323 uses for IP telephony.

Taken together, the suite of H.323 protocols covers all aspects of IP telephony, including phone registration, signaling, real-time data encoding and transfer (both voice and video), and control.

Figure 26.6 illustrates relationships among the protocols that constitute H.323. As the figure shows, the entire suite ultimately depends on UDP and TCP running over IP.

<table>
<tr><td colspan="2">audio / video applications</td><td colspan="4">signaling and control</td><td>data applications</td></tr>
<tr><td>video codec</td><td>audio codec</td><td rowspan="2">RTCP</td><td rowspan="2">H.225.0 Registr.</td><td rowspan="2">H.225.0 Signaling</td><td rowspan="2">H.245 Control</td><td rowspan="2">T.120 Data</td></tr>
<tr><td colspan="2">RTP</td></tr>
<tr><td colspan="4">UDP</td><td colspan="3">TCP</td></tr>
<tr><td colspan="7">IP</td></tr>
</table>

Figure 26.6 Relationships among major protocols that constitute the ITU's H.323 IP telephony standard. Protocols that are omitted handle details such as security and FAX transmission.

26.10.2 Session Initiation Protocol (SIP)

The IETF has proposed an alternative to H.323, called the *Session Initiation Protocol* (*SIP*), that only covers signaling; SIP does not recommend specific codecs nor does it require the use of RTP for real-time transfer. Thus, SIP does not provide all the functionality of H.323.

SIP uses client-server interaction, with servers being divided into two types. A *user agent server* runs in a SIP telephone. Each user agent server is assigned an identifier (e.g., *user @ site*), and can receive incoming calls. The second type of server is an *intermediate server* that is placed between two SIP telephones to handle tasks such as call set up and call forwarding. An intermediate server can function as a *proxy server* that can forward an incoming call request to the next proxy server along the path or to the called phone. An intermediate server can also function as a *redirect server* that tells a caller how to reach the requested destination.

To provide information about a call, SIP relies on a companion protocol, the *Session Description Protocol* (*SDP*). SDP is especially important in a conference call because it permits participants to join and leave a call dynamically. SDP also specifies details such as the media encoding, protocol port numbers, and multicast address.

26.11 Quality Of Service Controversy

The term *Quality of Service* (*QoS*) refers to statistical performance guarantees that a network system can make regarding loss, delay, throughput, and jitter. An isochronous network that is engineered to meet strict performance bounds is said to provide QoS guarantees, while a packet switched network that uses best effort delivery is said to provide no QoS guarantee. Is guaranteed QoS needed for real-time transfer of voice and video over IP? If so, how should it be implemented? A major controversy surrounds the two questions. On one hand, engineers who designed the telephone system insist that toll-quality voice reproduction requires the underlying system to provide QoS guarantees about delay and loss for each phone call. On the other hand, engineers who designed IP insist that the Internet works reasonably well without QoS guarantees and that adding per-flow QoS is infeasible because routers will make the system both expensive and slow.

The QoS controversy has produced many proposals, implementations, and experiments. Although it operates without QoS, the Internet is already used to send audio and video. Commercial providers offer IP telephone services, and telephone companies around the world are switching to IP. Many efforts to provide QoS have been unsuccessful. For example, *Asynchronous Transfer Mode* (*ATM*), which was created by telephone companies as an alternative to the Internet, has almost disappeared. ATM attempted to provide QoS guarantees for each individual connection (i.e., each *flow*). After an effort known as *Integrated Services* (*IntServ*) investigated defining per-flow quality of service, the IETF changed direction and adopted a conservative *Differentiated Services* (*DiffServ*) approach that divides traffic into separate classes. The differentiated services scheme, which sacrifices fine grain control for less complex forwarding, is sometimes called a *Class of Service* (*CoS*) approach.

26.12 QoS, Utilization, And Capacity

The debate over QoS is reminiscent of earlier debates on resource allocation, such as those waged over operating system policies for memory allocation and processor scheduling. In the earlier debates, proponents argued that improved resource allocation would optimize the overall throughput of a computing system, thereby giving users better service. The argument has intuitive appeal, and much research was conducted. Unfortunately, none of the processor and memory management schemes worked well in practice. Users remained dissatisfied. After decades, however, computing did improve and users were happy with the results. What changed? Processors became much faster and memories became much larger. Instead of relying on scheduling algorithms to find the best way to share a slow processor among many computations, the hardware became so fast that a processor could keep up with the required computation.

The analogy with networking is strong. Proponents of QoS are making the same argument about network resources. They assert that if network resources are scheduled effectively (i.e., the network gives some packets priority over others), users will be happy. The premise is especially attractive to network operators because, if true, it will allow them to sell upgraded service with the existing underlying infrastructure. Unfortunately, experience with networking reveals:

When a network has sufficient resources for all traffic, QoS constraints are unnecessary; when traffic exceeds network capacity, no QoS system can satisfy all users' demands.

The central issue is utilization. On the one hand, a network with 1% utilization does not need QoS because no packet is ever blocked. On the other hand, a network where utilization exceeds 100% of capacity will fail under any QoS. Nevertheless, proponents of QoS mechanisms assert that sophisticated QoS mechanisms should be able to achieve two goals. First, by dividing the existing resources among more users, QoS will make the system more fair. Second, by shaping the traffic from each user, QoS allows the network to run at higher utilization without danger of collapse.

One of the major reasons complicated QoS mechanisms have not been widely adopted arises from increases in the performance of networks. Network capacity has increased dramatically during the past thirty years, and will continue to increase in the foreseeable future. As long as rapid performance increases allow capacity to exceed demand, QoS mechanisms merely constitute unnecessary overhead. However, if demand rises more rapidly than capacity, QoS may become an economic issue — by associating higher prices with higher levels of service, ISPs can use cost to ration capacity (and reap higher profits because no increase in infrastructure will be required).

26.13 Emergency Services And Preemption

Are there valid reasons to prioritize traffic? Of course. For example, if network management traffic has low priority, a manager may be unable to diagnose the source of congestion or take steps to correct the problem. Similarly, consider a network that handles VoIP telephone service. On such a network, emergency calls (to 911 in the U.S.) should not be blocked waiting for normal traffic. Thus, packets that carry voice samples from an emergency call should have priority.

It may seem that the examples provide a strong argument for a QoS mechanism that understands the purpose of each flow. As a later section explains, a per-flow mechanism is not needed. Emergency calls and network management traffic can be handled by a system that has only two or three levels of priority. More important, a QoS mechanism that only guarantees a percentage of the underlying network capacity may not work if the capacity is reduced. For example, consider a QoS system that reserves 1% of the network capacity for management traffic. In normal situations, 1% may be more than sufficient. However, consider what happens if a network hardware failure begins to corrupt a few bits in packets randomly. The QoS guarantee means that after a network management packet is sent, ninety-nine other packets will be sent before another network management packet is sent (e.g., a retransmission). Thus, the time between successive network management packets is long. If successive management packets are corrupted, the time required to diagnose the problem can be long.

What is needed to handle cases like the one above is not a typical QoS system, but an absolute priority scheme. In particular, we need a mechanism that allows emergency traffic to *preempt* the network. Under a preemption policy, emergency traffic is granted highest priority, which means that if a packet carrying emergency traffic arrives, the packet is sent immediately without waiting for other traffic.

26.14 IntServ And Resource Reservation

Two decades ago, the IETF began to consider the question of resource allocation. Specifically, the IETF began with the question: if QoS is needed, how can an IP network provide it? At the time, many groups argued for fine-grain QoS, which led the IETF to a program of research called *Integrated Services* (*IntServ*). The IntServ approach has two parts. Before data is transferred, the endpoints must specify the resources needed, and all routers along the path between the endpoints must agree to supply the resources; the procedure can be viewed as a form of *signaling*. Second, as datagrams traverse the flow, routers need to monitor and control traffic forwarding. Monitoring, sometimes called *traffic policing*, is needed to ensure that the traffic sent on a flow does not exceed the specified bounds.

QoS guarantees are especially difficult in a packet switching network because traffic is often *bursty*. For example, a flow that specifies an average throughput of 1 Mbps may have 2 Mbps of traffic for ten milliseconds followed by no traffic for ten milliseconds. Although the router must contend with a flood of packets for ten milliseconds, the flow still meets the required average. To control queueing and forwarding, a router that offers QoS usually implements a mechanism to handle packet bursts. The idea, which is known as *traffic shaping*, is to smooth each burst. To smooth bursts, a router temporarily queues incoming datagrams and then sends them at a steady rate of 1 Mbps.

26.14.1 Resource ReSerVation Protocol (RSVP)

As part of the IntServ work, the IETF developed two protocols to provide QoS: the *Resource ReSerVation Protocol* (*RSVP*) to reserve resources and the *Common Open Policy Services* (*COPS*)† protocol to enforce constraints. Both protocols require changes to the basic Internet infrastructure — all routers must agree to reserve resources (e.g., link capacity) for each flow between a pair of endpoints.

RSVP handles reservation requests and replies. It is not a route propagation protocol, nor does it enforce policies once a flow has been established. Instead, RSVP operates before any data is sent. To initiate an end-to-end flow, an endpoint first sends an RSVP *path* message to determine the path to the destination; the datagram carrying the message uses a *router alert* option (IPv4) or a special hop-by-hop header (IPv6) to guarantee that routers examine the message. After it receives a reply to its path message, the endpoint sends an RSVP *request* message to reserve resources for the flow. The request specifies the QoS bounds desired; each router that forwards the request along to the destination must agree to reserve the resources the request specifies. If any router along the path denies the request, the router uses RSVP to send a negative reply back to the source. If all systems along the path agree to honor the request, RSVP returns a positive reply.

Each RSVP flow is *simplex* (i.e., unidirectional). If a pair of communicating applications requires QoS guarantees in two directions, each endpoint must use RSVP to request a flow. Because RSVP uses existing forwarding, there is no guarantee that the two flows will pass through the same routers, nor does approval of a flow in one direction imply approval in the other. We can summarize:

> *An endpoint uses RSVP to request a simplex flow through an IP internet with specified QoS bounds. If each router along the path agrees to honor the request, the flow is approved; otherwise, the flow is denied. If a pair of applications needs QoS in two directions, each endpoint must use RSVP to request a separate flow.*

26.14.2 IntServ Enforcement (COPS)

When an RSVP request arrives, a router must consider two aspects: feasibility (i.e., whether the router has the resources necessary to satisfy the request) and policy (i.e., whether the request lies within policy constraints). Feasibility is a local decision — a router can decide how to manage the bandwidth, memory, and processing power that is

†The name *COPS* is meant as a humorous reference to traffic police.

available. However, policy enforcement requires global cooperation — all routers must agree to the same set of policies.

To implement global policies, the IETF architecture uses a two-level model with client-server interaction between the levels. When a router receives an RSVP request, it becomes a client that consults a server known as a *Policy Decision Point* (*PDP*) to determine whether the request meets policy constraints. The PDP does not handle traffic; it merely evaluates requests to see if they satisfy global policies. If a PDP approves a request, the router must operate as a *Policy Enforcement Point* (*PEP*) to ensure traffic adheres to the approved policy.

The COPS protocol defines the client-server interaction between a router and a PDP (or between a router and a local PDP if an organization has multiple levels of policy servers). Although COPS defines its own message header, the underlying format shares many details with RSVP. In particular, COPS uses the same format as RSVP for individual items in a *request* message. Thus, when a router receives an RSVP request, it can extract items related to policy, place them in a COPS message, and send the result to a PDP.

26.15 DiffServ And Per-Hop Behavior

After much work on RSVP and IntServ, the IETF decided to pursue an entirely different approach: instead of looking for technologies that provide QoS for each individual flow, the new work focuses on groups of flows. That is, a small set of categories is created, and each flow is assigned to one of the categories. The result is DiffServ†, which differs from IntServ in two significant ways. First, instead of specifying resources needed for an individual flow, DiffServ allocates service to a *class* (i.e., a set of flows that match a specified set of parameters). Second, unlike the RSVP scheme in which a reservation is made end-to-end, DiffServ allows each node along the path to define the service that a given class will receive. For example, a router can choose to divide bandwidth so that the DiffServ class known as *Expedited Forwarding* (*EF*) receives 50% of the bandwidth and the remaining 50% is divided among the classes that are known as *Assured Forwarding* (*AF*). The next router along the path can choose to give the EF class 90% of the bandwidth and divide the AF classes among the remaining 10%. We use the phrase *per-hop behavior* to describe the approach and to point out that DiffServ does not provide end-to-end guarantees.

26.16 Traffic Scheduling

To implement any form of QoS, a router needs to assign priorities to outgoing traffic and choose which packet to send at a given time. The process of selecting from among a set of packets is known as *traffic scheduling*, and the mechanism is called a *traffic scheduler*. There are four aspects to consider when constructing a traffic scheduler:

†Chapter 7 describes the DiffServ mechanism and the datagram header field it uses.

- *Fairness.* The scheduler should ensure that the resources (i.e., bandwidth) consumed by a flow fall within the amount assigned to the flow†.
- *Delay.* Packets on a given flow should not be delayed excessively.
- *Adaptability.* If a given flow does not have packets to send, the scheduler should divide the extra bandwidth among other flows proportional to their assigned resources.
- *Computational Overhead.* Because it operates in the fast path, a scheduler must not incur much computational overhead. In particular, theoretical algorithms such as *Generalized Processor Scheduling* (*GPS*) cannot be used.

The most straightforward practical traffic scheduling scheme is named *Weighted Round Robin* (*WRR*) because it assigns each flow a weight and attempts to send data from the flow according to the flow's weight. For example, we can imagine three flows, *A*, *B*, and *C*, with weights 2, 2, and 4, respectively. If all three flows have packets waiting to be sent, the scheduler should send twice as much from flow *C* (weight 4) as from *A* or *B* (each with weight 2).

It may seem that a WRR scheduler could achieve the desired weights by selecting from flows in the following order:

C C A B

That is, the scheduler repeatedly makes selections:

C C A B C C A B C C A B...

The pattern appears to achieve the desired weights because one half of the selections come from flow *C*, one quarter come from *B*, and one quarter come from *A*. Furthermore, the pattern services each queue at regular intervals throughout the sequence, which means that no flow is delayed unnecessarily (i.e., the rate at which packets are sent from a given flow is constant).

Although the sequence above does make the packet rate match the assigned weights, the WRR approach does not achieve the goal of making the data rates match the weights because datagrams are not uniform size. For example, if the average datagram size on flow *C* is half of the average datagram size on flow *A*, selecting flow *C* twice as often as flow *A* will make the data rate of the two flows equal.

To solve the problem, a modified algorithm was invented that accommodates variable-size packets. Known as *Deficit Round Robin* (*DRR*), the algorithm computes weights in terms of total octets sent rather than number of packets. Initially, the algorithm allocates a number of octets to each flow proportional to the bandwidth the flow should receive. When a flow is selected, DRR transmits as many packets as possible without exceeding the allotted number of octets. The algorithm then computes the

†Throughout this section we discuss scheduling among *flows*; the reader should understand that when DiffServ is used, the same techniques are used for traffic scheduling among classes.

remainder (i.e., the difference between the number of octets that was allocated and the size of the packets actually sent), and adds the remainder to the amount that will be sent in the next round. Thus, DRR keeps a running total of the *deficit* that each flow should receive. Even if the deficit gained on a given round is small, the value will grow through multiple rounds until it is large enough to accommodate an extra packet. Thus, over time the proportion of data that DRR sends from a given flow approaches the weighted value for the flow.

Round-robin scheduling algorithms such as WRR and DRR have advantages and disadvantages. The chief advantage arises from efficiency: once weights have been assigned, little computation is required to make a packet selection. In fact, if all packets are the same size and weights are selected as multiples, the weighted selection can be achieved through the use of an array rather than through computation.

Despite the advantages, round-robin algorithms do have drawbacks. First, the delay that a given flow experiences depends on the number of other flows that have traffic to send. In the worst case, a given flow may need to wait while the scheduler sends one or more packets from each of the other flows. Second, because they send a burst of packets from a given queue and then delay while servicing other queues, round robin algorithms can introduce jitter.

26.17 Traffic Policing And Shaping

A *traffic policer* is required to verify that arriving traffic does not exceed its stated statistical profile. Suppose a scheduler allocates 25% of the outgoing bandwidth to a DiffServ class, *Q*. If three incoming flows all map to class *Q*, the flows will compete for the bandwidth allocated to *Q*. If the system does not monitor incoming traffic, one of the flows might take all the bandwidth allocated to class *Q*. So, a policing mechanism protects other flows to insure that each receives its fair share.

Several mechanisms have been proposed for traffic policing. In general, the idea is to slow down traffic to an agreed rate, the *traffic shaping* idea mentioned above. An early traffic shaping mechanism, based on the *leaky bucket* approach, uses a counter to control the packet rate. Conceptually, the algorithm increments the counter periodically; each time a packet arrives, the algorithm decrements the counter. If the counter becomes negative, the incoming flow has exceeded its allocated packet rate.

Using a packet rate to shape traffic does not make sense in the Internet because datagrams vary in size. Thus, more sophisticated policing schemes have been proposed to accommodate variable-size packets. For example, a *token bucket* mechanism extends the approach outlined above by making the counter correspond to bits rather than packets. The counter is incremented periodically in accordance with the desired data rate, and decremented by the number of bits in each arriving packet.

In practice, the policing mechanisms described do not require a timer to periodically update a counter. Instead, each time a packet arrives, the policer examines the clock to determine how much time has elapsed since the flow was processed last, and uses the amount of time to compute an increment for the counter. Computing an increment has less computational overhead, and makes traffic policing more efficient.

26.18 Summary

Real-time data consists of audio or video in which the playback of a sample must match the time at which the sample was captured. A hardware unit known as a codec encodes analog data such as audio in digital form. The telephone standard for digital audio encoding, Pulse Code Modulation (PCM), produces digital values at 64 Kbps; other encodings sacrifice some fidelity to achieve lower bit rates.

RTP is used to transfer real-time data across an IP network. Each RTP message contains two key pieces of information: a sequence number and a media timestamp. A receiver uses the sequence number to place messages in order and detect lost datagrams. A receiver uses a timestamp to determine when to play the encoded values. An associated control protocol, RTCP, is used to supply information about sources and to allow a mixer to combine several streams. To accommodate burstiness and jitter an application that plays real-time data uses a playback buffer and introduces a slight delay before playing an item.

Commercial IP telephone services exist that use VoIP technology; most telephone companies are moving to IP. Two standards have been created for use with IP telephony: the ITU created the H.323 standard and the IETF created SIP.

A debate continues over whether Quality of Service (QoS) guarantees are needed to provide real-time services. Initially, the IETF followed a program known as Integrated Services (IntServ) that explored per-flow QoS. Later, the IETF decided to move to a Differentiated Services (DiffServ) approach that provides QoS among classes of flows rather than individual flows.

Implementation of QoS requires a traffic scheduling mechanism to select packets from outgoing queues and traffic policing to monitor incoming flows. Because it is computationally efficient and handles variable-size packets, the Deficit Round Robin algorithm is among the most practical for traffic scheduling. The leaky bucket algorithm is among the most pragmatic for traffic policing and shaping.

EXERCISES

26.1 Read about the Real-Time Streaming Protocol, RTSP. What are the major differences between RTSP and RTP?

26.2 Find out how the Skype voice telephone service operates. How does it set up a connection?

26.3 Network operators have an adage: you can always buy more bandwidth, but you can't buy lower delay. What does the adage mean?

26.4 If an RTP message arrives with a sequence number far greater than the sequence expected, what does the protocol do? Why?

26.5 Consider a video shot from your cell phone and transferred over the Internet in real time. How much capacity is required? (Hint: what is the resolution of the camera in your cell phone?)

26.6 Consider a conference telephone call that uses RTP to connect N users. Give two possible implementations that could achieve the call.

26.7 A movie usually has two conceptual streams: a video stream and an audio stream. How can RTP be used to transfer a movie?

26.8 Are sequence numbers necessary in RTP, or can a timestamp be used instead? Explain.

26.9 An engineer insists that "SIP is for children; grown-ups all use H.323." What does the engineer mean? Guess the type of company for which the engineer works.

26.10 When VoIP was first introduced, some countries decided to make the technology illegal. Find out why.

26.11 Would you prefer an Internet where QoS was required for all traffic? Why or why not?

26.12 Measure the utilization on your connection to the Internet. If all traffic required QoS reservation, would service be better or worse? Explain.

26.13 Suppose you are asked to set up DiffServ classes for a cable ISP. The ISP's network, which only uses IPv6, must handle: broadcast television channels, voice (i.e., VoIP), movie download, residential Internet service, and streaming video on demand. How do you assign DiffServ classes? Why?

26.14 If the input to a traffic shaper is extremely bursty (i.e., sporadic bursts of packets with fairly long periods of no traffic), the output from the shaper may not be steady. What technique can be used to guarantee smooth output? (Hint: consider a method described in a previous chapter.)

Chapter Contents

27

Network Management (SNMP)

27.1 Introduction

In addition to protocols that provide network level services and application programs that use those services, a subsystem is needed that allows a manager to configure a network, control routing, debug problems, and identify situations in which computers violate policies. We refer to such activities as *network management*. This chapter considers the ideas behind TCP/IP network management, and describes a protocol used for network management.

27.2 The Level Of Management Protocols

When data networks first appeared, designers followed a management approach used in telephone systems by designing special management mechanisms into the network. For example, wide area networks usually defined management messages as part of their link-level protocol. If a packet switch began misbehaving, a network manager could instruct a neighboring packet switch to send it a special *control packet*. An incoming control packet caused the receiver to suspend normal operation and respond to the command in the control packet. A manager could interrogate a packet switch, examine or change routes, test one of the communication interfaces, or reboot the switch. Once the problem was repaired, a manager could instruct the switch to resume normal operations. Because management tools were part of the lowest-level protocol, managers were often able to control switches even if higher-level protocols failed.

Unlike a homogeneous wide area network, the Internet does not have a single link-level protocol. Instead, the Internet consists of multiple physical network types and devices from multiple vendors. As a result, the Internet requires a new network management paradigm that offers three important capabilities. First, a single manager must be able to control many types of devices, including IP routers, bridges, modems, workstations, and printers. Second, because the Internet contains multiple types of networks, the controlled entities will not share a common link-level protocol. Third, the set of machines a manager controls may attach to a variety of networks. In particular, a manager may need to control one or more machines that do not attach to the same physical network as the manager's computer. Thus, it may not be possible for a manager to communicate with machines unless the management software uses protocols that provide end-to-end connectivity across an internet. As a consequence, the network management protocol used with TCP/IP operates above the transport level:

> *In a TCP/IP internet, a manager needs to examine and control hosts, routers, and other network devices. Because such devices attach to arbitrary networks, protocols for network management operate at the application layer and communicate using TCP/IP transport layer protocols.*

Designing network management software to operate at the application level has several advantages. Because the protocols can be designed without regard to the underlying network, one set of protocols can be used for all networks. Because the protocols can be designed without regard to the hardware on the managed device, the same protocols can be used for all managed devices. From a manager's point of view, having a single set of management protocols means uniformity — all routers respond to exactly the same set of commands. Furthermore, because the management software uses IP for communication, a manager can control the routers across an entire TCP/IP internet without having direct attachment to every physical network or router.

Of course, building management software at the application level also has disadvantages. Unless the operating system, IP software, and transport protocol software work correctly, the manager may not be able to contact a router that needs managing. For example, if a router's forwarding table becomes damaged, it may be impossible to correct the table or reboot the machine from a remote site. If the operating system on a router crashes, it will be impossible to reach the application program that implements the internet management protocols, even if the router can still process hardware interrupts and forward packets. When the idea of building network management at the application layer was first proposed, many network engineers declared that the whole approach was flawed. In fact, many network researchers also raised serious objections.

27.3 Architectural Model

Despite the potential disadvantages, having TCP/IP management software operate at the application level has worked well in practice. The most significant advantage of placing network management protocols at a high level becomes apparent when one considers a large internet, where a manager's computer does not need to attach directly to all physical networks that contain managed entities. Figure 27.1 shows an example intranet that helps explain the management architecture.

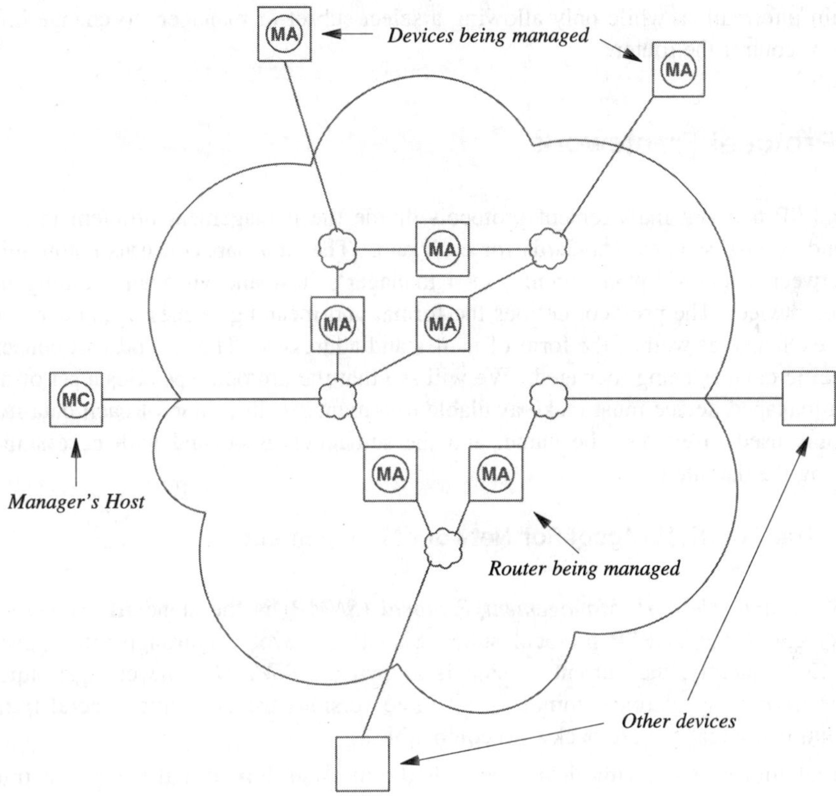

Figure 27.1 Example of network management where a manager invokes management client (MC) software that can contact management agent (MA) software that runs on devices throughout an intranet.

As the figure shows, client software usually runs on the manager's workstation. Each participating managed system, which can be a router or a network device, runs a management server†. In IETF terminology, the management server software is called a *management agent* or merely an *agent*. A manager invokes client software on the local

†We use the term *managed system* to include conventional devices such as routers and desktop computers, as well as specialized devices such as printers and sensors.

host computer and specifies an agent with which it wishes to communicate. After the client connects to the specified agent, the manager can request that the client software send queries to obtain information or send commands that configure and control the managed device.

Of course, not all devices in a large internet fall under a single manager. Most managers only control devices at their local sites; a large site may have multiple managers. Network management software uses an authentication mechanism to ensure only authorized managers can access or control a particular device. Some management protocols support multiple levels of authorization, allowing a manager specific privileges on each device. For example, a specific router might allow several managers to obtain information, while only allowing a select subset of managers to change information or control the router.

27.4 Protocol Framework

TCP/IP network management protocols divide the management problem into two parts and specify separate standards for each part. The first part concerns communication between client software running in a manager's host and an agent running in a managed device. The protocol defines the format and meaning of messages clients and servers exchange as well as the form of names and addresses. The second part concerns the specific devices being managed. We will see that the protocol specifies a set of data items a managed device must make available to a manager, the name of each data item, the syntax used to express the name, and the semantics associated with accessing or modifying the data item.

27.4.1 The TCP/IP Protocol For Network Management

The *Simple Network Management Protocol* (*SNMP*) is the standard for network management in the TCP/IP protocol suite. SNMP has evolved through three generations. Consequently, the current version is known as *SNMPv3*. The changes among versions have been relatively minor — all three versions use the same general framework, and many features are backward compatible.

In addition to specifying details such as the message format and the use of transport protocols, the SNMP standard defines a set of operations and the meaning of each. We will see that the approach is minimalistic — a few operations provide all functionality. We will start by examining SNMP for IPv4; a later section summarizes the changes for IPv6.

27.4.2 A Standard For Managed Information

A device being managed maintains control and status information that a manager can access. For example, a router keeps statistics on the status of its network interfaces along with counts of incoming and outgoing packets, dropped datagrams, and error messages generated. A modem keeps statistics about the number of bits (or characters) sent and received and the status of the carrier (whether the modem at the other end of the connection is responding). Although it allows a manager to access statistics, SNMP does not specify exactly which data can be accessed on which devices. Instead, a separate standard specifies the details for each type of device. Known as a *Management Information Base* (*MIB*), the standard specifies the data items that each managed device must keep, the operations allowed on each data item, and the meaning of the operations. For example, the MIB for IP specifies that the software must keep a count of all octets that arrive over each network interface and that network management software can only read the count.

The MIB for TCP/IP divides management information into many categories. The choice of categories is important because identifiers used to specify items include a code for the category. Figure 27.2 lists a few examples of categories used with IPv4.

MIB category	Includes Information About
system	The host or router operating system
interfaces	Individual network interfaces
at	Address translation (e.g., ARP mappings)
ip	Internet Protocol software version 4
ipv6	Internet Protocol software version 6
icmp	Internet Control Message Protocol software version 4
ipv6Icmp	Internet Control Message Protocol software version 6
tcp	Transmission Control Protocol software
udp	User Datagram Protocol software
ospf	Open Shortest Path First software
bgp	Border Gateway Protocol software
rmon	Remote network monitoring
rip-2	Routing Information Protocol software
dns	Domain name system software

Figure 27.2 Example categories of MIB information. The category is encoded in the identifier used to specify an object.

Keeping the MIB definition independent of the network management protocol has advantages for both vendors and users. A vendor can include SNMP agent software in a product such as a router, with the guarantee that the software will continue to adhere to the standard after new MIB items are defined. A customer can use the same network management client software to manage multiple devices that have slightly different versions of a MIB. Of course, a device that does not have new MIB items cannot provide the information for those items. However, because all managed devices use the same language for communication, each device can parse a query and either provide the requested information or send an error message explaining the requested item is not available.

27.5 Examples of MIB Variables

Early versions of SNMP collected variables together in a single large MIB, with the entire set documented in a single RFC. To avoid having the MIB specification become unwieldy, the IETF decided to allow the publication of many individual MIB documents that each specify a set of MIB variables for a specific type of device. As a result, more than 100 separate MIB documents have been defined as part of the standards process; they specify more than 10,000 individual variables. For example, separate RFCs now exist that specify the MIB variables associated with devices such as: a hardware bridge, an uninterruptible power supply, an Ethernet switch, and a cable modem. In addition, many vendors have defined MIB variables for their specific hardware or software products.

Examining a few of the MIB data items associated with TCP/IP protocols will help clarify the contents. Figure 27.3 lists example MIB variables along with their categories.

Most of the items listed in Figure 27.3 have numeric values — each can be stored in a single integer. However, the MIB also defines more complex structures. For example, the MIB variable *ipRoutingTable* refers to an entire forwarding table†. Additional MIB variables under the table (not listed in the figure) define the contents of a forwarding table entry, and allow the network management protocols to reference an individual entry in the forwarding table, including the prefix, address mask, and next hop fields. Of course, MIB variables present only a logical definition of each data item — the internal data structures a router uses may differ from the MIB definition. When a query arrives, software in the agent on the router is responsible for mapping between the MIB variable references in the query and the internal data structure the router uses to store the information.

27.6 The Structure Of Management Information

In addition to the standards that specify MIB variables and their meanings, a separate standard specifies a set of rules used to define and identify MIB variables. The rules are known as the *Structure of Management Information* (*SMI*) specification. To keep network management protocols simple, the SMI places restrictions on the types of variables allowed in the MIB, specifies the rules for naming MIB variables, and creates rules for defining variable types. For example, the SMI standard includes definitions of the term *Counter* (defining it to be an integer in the range of 0 to $2^{32}-1$) and the term *InetAddress* (defining it to be a string of octets), and specifies that the definition of MIB variables should use the terminology. More important, the rules in the SMI describe how the MIB refers to tables of values (e.g., an IPv4 routing table).

†When the MIB was defined, the terminology *routing table* was used instead of *forwarding table*.

MIB Variable	Meaning
Category system	
sysUpTime	Time since last reboot
Category system	
ifNumber	Number of network interfaces
ifMtu	MTU for an interface (IPv4)
ipv6IfEffectiveMtu	MTU for an interface (IPv6)
Category ip	
ipDefaultTTL	Value IPv4 uses as a TTL
ipv6DefaultHopLimit	Value IPv6 uses as a hop limit
ipInReceives	Number of IPv4 datagrams received
ipv6IfStatsInReceives	Number of IPv6 datagrams received
ipForwDatagrams	Number of IPv4 datagrams forwarded
ipv6IfStatsOutForwDatagrams	Number of IPv6 datagrams forwarded
ipOutNoRoutes	Number of routing failures
ipReasmOKs	Number of datagrams reassembled
ipFragOKs	Number of IPv4 datagrams fragmented
ipv6IfStatsOutFragOKs	Number of IPv6 datagrams fragmented
ipRoutingTable	IPv4 forwarding table
ipv6RouteTable	IPv6 forwarding table
ipv6AddrTable	IPv6 interface address table
ipv6IfStatsTable	IPv6 statistics for each interface
Category icmp	
icmpInEchos	Number of ICMP Echo Requests recvd
Category tcp	
tcpRtoMin	Minimum retransmission time for TCP
tcpMaxConn	Maximum TCP connections allowed
tcpInSegs	Number of segments TCP has received
Category udp	
udpInDatagrams	Number of UDP datagrams received

Figure 27.3 Examples of MIB variables along with their categories.

27.7 Formal Definitions Using ASN.1

The SMI standard specifies that all MIB variables must be defined and referenced using ISO's *Abstract Syntax Notation 1* (*ASN.1*†). ASN.1 is a formal language that has two main features: a notation used in documents that humans read and a compact encoded representation of the same information used in communication protocols. In both cases, the use of a precise and formal notation removes ambiguity from both the representation and meaning. For example, instead of saying that a variable contains an integer value, a protocol designer who uses ASN.1 must state the exact form and range

†ASN.1 is usually pronounced by reading the dot: "A-S-N dot 1".

of each numeric value. Such precision is especially important when implementations include heterogeneous computers that do not all use the same representations for data items.

In addition to specifying the name and contents of each item, ASN.1 defines a set of *Basic Encoding Rules* (*BER*) that specify precisely how to encode both names and data items in a message. Thus, once the documentation of a MIB has been expressed using ASN.1, variables can be translated directly and mechanically into the encoded form used in messages. In summary:

> *The TCP/IP network management protocols use a formal notation called ASN.1 to define names and types for variables in the management information base. The precise notation makes the form and contents of variables unambiguous.*

27.8 Structure And Representation Of MIB Object Names

We said that ASN.1 specifies how to represent both data items and names. However, understanding the names used for MIB variables requires us to know about the underlying namespace. Names for MIB variables are taken from the *object identifier* namespace administered by ISO and ITU. The key idea behind the object identifier namespace is that it provides a namespace in which all possible objects can be designated. The namespace is not restricted to variables used in network management — it includes names for arbitrary objects (e.g., each international protocol standard document has a name).

The object identifier namespace is *absolute* (*global*), meaning that names are structured to make them globally unique. Like most namespaces that are large and absolute, the object identifier namespace is hierarchical. Authority for parts of the namespace is subdivided at each level, allowing individual groups to obtain authority to assign some of the names without consulting a central authority for each assignment†.

Figure 27.4 illustrates pertinent parts of the object identifier hierarchy and shows the position of the *mgmt* and *mib* nodes used by TCP/IP network management protocols. The root of the object identifier hierarchy is unnamed, but has three direct descendants managed by: ISO, ITU, and jointly by ISO and ITU, as the top level of the figure illustrates. Each node in the hierarchy is assigned both a short textual name and a unique integer identifier (humans use the text string to help understand object names; computer software uses the integer to form a compact, encoded representation for use in messages). ISO allocated the *org* subtree for use by other national or international standards organizations (including U.S. standards organizations). The U.S. National Institute for Standards and Technology (NIST)‡ allocated subtree *dod* under *org* for the U.S. Department of Defense. Finally, the IAB petitioned the Department of Defense to allocate an *internet* subtree in the namespace and then to allocate four subtrees, including *mgmt*. The *mib* subtree was allocated under *mgmt*.

†Chapter 23 explains how authority is delegated in a hierarchical namespace.

‡NIST was formerly the National Bureau of Standards.

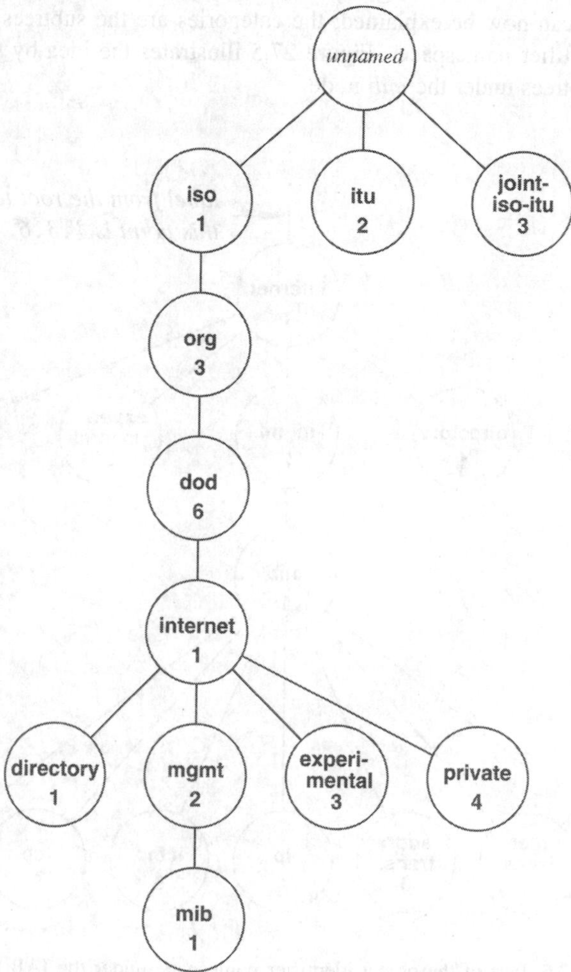

Figure 27.4 Part of the hierarchical object identifier namespace used to name MIB variables. An object's name begins with a path through the hierarchy.

The name of an object in the hierarchy is the sequence of labels on the nodes along a path from the root to the object. The sequence is written with periods separating the individual components. When expressed for humans to read, textual names are used. When names are sent in messages, numeric values are used instead. For example, the string *1.3.6.1.2.1* denotes the node labeled *mib*. Because they fall under the MIB node. all MIB variables have names beginning with the prefix *1.3.6.1.2.1*.

Earlier we said that the MIB groups variables into categories. The exact meaning of the categories can now be explained: the categories are the subtrees of the *mib* node of the object identifier namespace. Figure 27.5 illustrates the idea by showing the first few nodes for subtrees under the *mib* node.

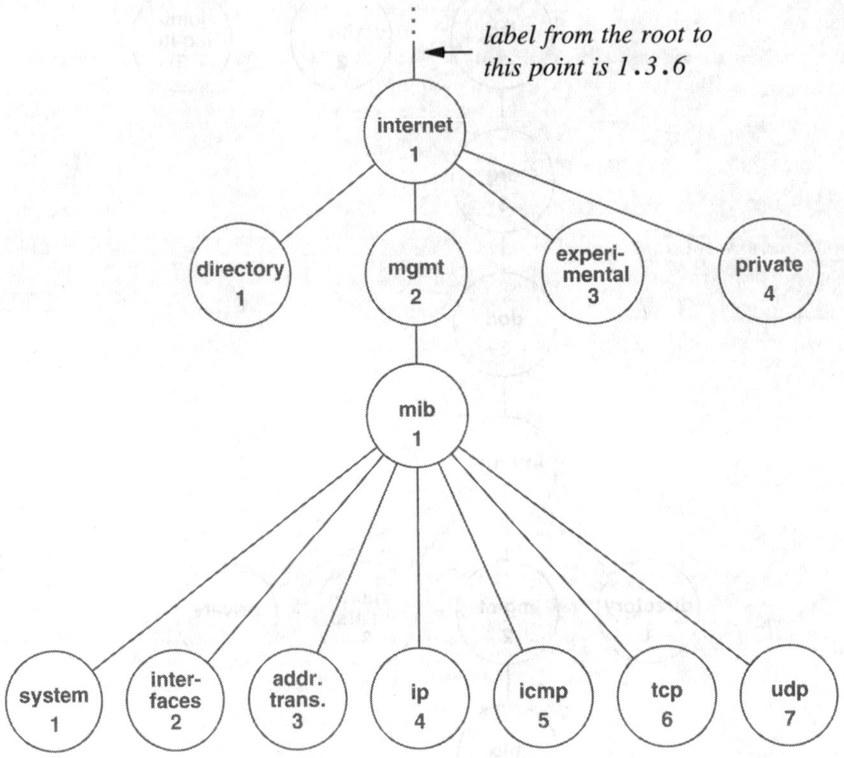

Figure 27.5 Part of the object identifier namespace under the IAB *mib* node. Each subtree corresponds to one of the categories of MIB variables.

Two examples will make the naming syntax clear. Figure 27.5 shows that the category labeled *ip* has been assigned the numeric value *4*. Thus, the names of all MIB variables corresponding to IP have an identifier that begins with the prefix *1.3.6.1.2.1.4*. If one wanted to write out the textual labels instead of the numeric representation, the name would be:

iso.org.dod.internet.mgmt.mib.ip

A MIB variable named *ipInReceives* has been assigned numeric identifier *3* under the *ip* node in the namespace, so its name is:

iso . org . dod . internet . mgmt . mib . ip . ipInReceives

and the corresponding numeric representation is:

1 . 3 . 6 . 1 . 2 . 1 . 4 . 3

When network management protocols use names of MIB variables in messages, each name has a suffix appended. For simple variables, the suffix *0* refers to the instance of the variable with that name. So, when it appears in a message sent to a router, the numeric representation of *ipInReceives* is:

1 . 3 . 6 . 1 . 2 . 1 . 4 . 3 . 0

which refers to the instance of *ipInReceives* on that router. Note that there is no way to guess the numeric value or suffix assigned to a variable. One must consult the published standards to find which numeric values have been assigned to each object type. Thus, programs that provide mappings between the textual forms and underlying numeric values do so entirely by consulting tables of equivalences — there is no closed-form computation that performs the transformation.

As a second, more complex example, consider the MIB variable *ipAddrTable*, which contains a list of the IPv4 addresses for each network interface. The variable exists in the namespace as a subtree under *ip*, and has been assigned the numeric value *20*. Therefore, a reference to it has the prefix:

iso . org . dod . internet . mgmt . mib . ip . ipAddrTable

with a numeric equivalent:

1 . 3 . 6 . 1 . 2 . 1 . 4 . 20

In programming language terms, we think of the IP address table as a one-dimensional array, where each element of the array consists of a structure (record) that contains five items: an IP address, the integer index of an interface corresponding to the entry, an IP subnet mask, an IP broadcast address, and an integer that specifies the maximum datagram size that the router will reassemble. Of course, it is unlikely that a router has such an array in memory. The router may keep this information in many variables or may need to follow pointers to find it. However, the MIB provides a name for the array as if it existed, and allows network management software on individual routers to map table references into appropriate internal variables. The point is:

> *Although they appear to specify details about data structures, MIB standards do not dictate the implementation. Instead, MIB definitions provide a uniform, virtual interface that managers use to access data; an agent must translate between the virtual items in a MIB and the internal implementation.*

Using ASN.1 style notation, we can define *ipAddrTable*:

```
ipAddrTable ::= SEQUENCE OF IpAddrEntry
```

where *SEQUENCE* and *OF* are keywords that define an ipAddrTable to be a one-dimensional array of *IpAddrEntry*s. Each entry in the array is defined to consist of five fields (the definition assumes that *IpAddress* has already been defined).

```
IpAddrEntry ::= SEQUENCE {
    ipAdEntAddr
        IpAddress,
    ipAdEntIfIndex
        INTEGER,
    ipAdEntNetMask
        IpAddress,
    ipAdEntBcastAddr
        IpAddress,
    ipAdEntReasmMaxSize
        INTEGER (0..65535)
}
```

Further definitions must be given to assign numeric values to *ipAddrEntry* and to each item in the *IpAddrEntry* sequence. For example, the definition:

```
ipAddrEntry { ipAddrTable 1 }
```

specifies that an *ipAddrEntry* is under *ipAddrTable* and has numeric value *1*. Similarly, the definition:

```
ipAdEntNetMask { ipAddrEntry 3 }
```

assigns *ipAdEntNetMask* numeric value *3* under *ipAddrEntry*.

We said that *ipAddrTable* is like a one-dimensional array. However, there is a significant difference in the way programmers use arrays and the way network management software uses tables in the MIB. Programmers think of an array as a set of elements that have an index used to select a specific element. For example, the programmer might write *xyz[3]* to select the third element from array *xyz*. ASN.1 syntax does not use integer indices. Instead, MIB tables append a suffix onto the name to select a specific element in the table. For our example of an IP address table, the standard specifies that the suffix used to select an item consists of an IP address. Syntactically, the IP address (in dotted decimal notation) is concatenated onto the end of the object name to form the reference. Thus, to specify the network mask field in the IP address table entry corresponding to address `128.10.2.3`, one uses the name:

iso.org.dod.internet.mgmt.mib.ip.ipAddrTable.ipAddrEntry.ipAdEntNetMask.128.10.2.3 which, in numeric form, becomes:

1.3.6.1.2.1.4.20.1.3.128.10.2.3

Although concatenating an index to the end of a name may seem awkward, it provides a powerful tool that allows clients to search tables without knowing the number of items or the type of data used as an index. A later section shows how network management protocols use this feature to step through a table one element at a time.

27.9 MIB Changes And Additions For IPv6

IPv6 changes the MIB slightly. Instead of using current MIB variables that correspond to IP (e.g., a count of all IP datagrams that have arrived), the IETF decided to use separate variables for IPv6. Thus, new names were defined for IPv6 and the previously-defined MIB variables for IP now refer only to IPv4. Similarly, a new category has been established for ICMPv6.

Part of the motivation for a new MIB structure arises because IPv6 did not merely change the size of addresses. Instead, IPv6 changes the way addresses are assigned. In particular, IPv6 allows multiple IP prefixes to be assigned to a given interface simultaneously. Therefore, the IPv6 MIB must be structured in a way that creates a table (i.e., an array) of entries that hold addresses. Similarly, because IPv6 uses Neighbor Discovery instead of ARP, an IPv6 table gives IP-to-MAC address bindings. Figure 27.6 lists the tables used with IPv6 and explains the purpose of each.

Table	Purpose
ipv6IfTable	Information about IPv6 interfaces
ipv6IfStatsTable	Traffic statistics for each interface
ipv6AddrPrefixTable	IPv6 prefixes for each interface
ipv6AddrTable	IPv6 addresses for each interface
ipv6RouteTable	The IPv6 (unicast) forwarding table
ipv6NetToMediaTable	IPv6 address-to-physical address

Figure 27.6 The six major MIB tables introduced for IPv6 and a description of their contents.

27.10 Simple Network Management Protocol

Network management protocols specify communication between a network management application running on the manager's computer and a network management agent (i.e., server) executing on a managed device. In addition to defining the form and meaning of messages exchanged and the representation of names and values in those messages, network management protocols also define administrative relationships among routers being managed. That is, they provide for authentication of managers.

One might expect network management protocols to contain many commands. Some early protocols, for example, supported commands that allowed the manager to: *reboot* the system, *add* or *delete* routes, *disable* or *enable* a particular network interface, and *remove* cached address bindings. The main disadvantage of building management protocols around commands arises from the resulting complexity. For example, the command to delete a routing table entry differs from the command to disable an interface. As a result, the protocol must be changed to accommodate new functionality.

SNMP takes an interesting alternative approach to network management. Instead of defining a large set of commands, SNMP casts all operations in a *fetch-store paradigm*†. Conceptually, SNMP contains only two commands that allow a manager to fetch a value from a data item or store a value into a data item. All other operations are defined as side-effects of these two operations. For example, although SNMP does not have an explicit *reboot* operation, system reboot is defined by declaring a MIB variable that gives *the time until the next reboot*, allowing a manager to assign the variable a value. If the manager assigns the value zero, the device will be rebooted instantly (i.e., the assignment acts like a *reboot* command).

The chief advantages of using a fetch-store paradigm are stability, simplicity, and flexibility. SNMP is especially stable because its definition remains fixed, even though new data items are added to the MIB and new operations are defined as side-effects of storing into those items. SNMP is simple to implement, understand, and debug because it avoids the complexity of having special cases for each command. Finally, SNMP is especially flexible because it can accommodate arbitrary functionality in an elegant framework.

From a manager's point of view, of course, SNMP remains hidden. The user interface to network management software can phrase operations as imperative commands (e.g., *reboot*). Thus, there is little visible difference between the way a manager uses SNMP and other network management protocols. In fact, vendors sell network management software that offers a graphical user interface. Such software displays diagrams of network connectivity, and uses a point-and-click style of interaction.

In practice, SNMP offers more than fetch and store operations. Figure 27.7 lists the eight operations. In practice, only some of them are essential. For example, operations *get-request* and *set-request* provide the basic fetch and store operations. After a device receives a message and performs the operation, the device sends a *response*. A single *get-request* or *set-request* message can specify operations on multiple MIB variables. SNMP specifies that operations must be *atomic*, meaning that the agent must either perform all operations in a message or none of them. In particular, if a *set-request* specifies multiple assignments and any of the items are in error, no assignments will be made.

†Readers familiar with hardware architecture will observe that the I/O bus on a typical computer also casts all operations into a fetch-store paradigm.

Command	Meaning
get-request	Fetch a value from a specific variable
get-next-request	Fetch a value without knowing its exact name
get-bulk-request	Fetch a large volume of data (e.g., a table)
response	A response to any of the above requests
set-request	Store a value in a specific variable
inform-request	Reference to third-part data (e.g., for a proxy)
snmpv2-trap	Reply triggered by an event
report	Undefined at present

Figure 27.7 The set of possible SNMP operations. *Get-next-request* allows the manager to iterate through a table of items.

We said that SNMP follows a request-response paradigm in which a manager issues a command and the managed device responds. In fact, SNMP allows an exception: a manager can configure a device to send *snmpv2-trap* messages asynchronously. For example, an SNMP server can be configured to send an *snmpv2-trap* message to the manager whenever one of its attached networks becomes unreachable (i.e., an interface goes down). Similarly, a device can be configured to send an *snmpv2-trap* message whenever one of the counters exceeds a predefined threshold.

27.10.1 Searching Tables Using Names

Recall that ASN.1 does not provide mechanisms for declaring arrays or indexing them in the usual sense. However, it is possible to denote individual elements of a table by appending a suffix to the object identifier for the table. Unfortunately, a client program may wish to examine entries in a table for which it does not know all valid suffixes. The *get-next-request* operation handles the problem by allowing a manager to iterate through a table without knowing how many items the table contains. The rules are quite simple. When sending a *get-next-request*, the client supplies a prefix of a valid object identifier, *P*. The agent examines the set of object identifiers for all variables it controls, and sends a response for the variable that occurs immediately *after* prefix *P* in lexicographic order. That is, the agent must know the ASN.1 names of all variables and be able to select the first variable with an object identifier lexicographically greater than *P*. The mechanism allows a manager to iterate through all entries in a table without knowing the identifiers for individual items. Each table has a name. When storing an item in a table, SNMP creates a name that begins with the name of the table and has a suffix that identifies a particular object in the table. The idea of assigning a name to each table is key: the name does not correspond to a variable, but allows a client to form a *get-next request* by specifying the name of the table. Assuming the table is non-empty, the managed device will return the value of the first element in the table. Once the first item in the table has been retrieved, the client can use the name of the first item in a subsequent *get-next* request to retrieve the second item, and so on. The iteration continues until the device returns an item with a name that does not match the table prefix (i.e., one item beyond the end of the table).

Consider an example search. Recall that *ipAddrTable* uses IP addresses to identify entries in the table. A client that does not know which IP addresses are in the table on a given router cannot form a complete object identifier. However, the client can still use the *get-next-request* operation to search the table by sending the prefix:

iso . org . dod . internet . mgmt . mib . ip . ipAddrTable . ipAddrEntry . ipAdEntNetMask

which, in numeric form, is:

1 . 3 . 6 . 1 . 2 . 1 . 4 . 20 . 1 . 3

The server returns the network mask field of the first entry in *ipAddrTable*. The client uses the full object identifier returned by the server to request the next item in the table.

27.11 SNMP Message Format

Unlike most TCP/IP protocols, SNMP messages do not have fixed fields. Instead, they use the standard ASN.1 encoding. Thus, a message can be difficult for humans to decode and understand. After examining the SNMP message definition in ASN.1 notation, we will review the ASN.1 encoding scheme briefly, and see an example of an encoded SNMP message.

Figure 27.8 shows how an SNMP message can be described with an ASN.1-style grammar. In general, each item in the grammar consists of a descriptive name followed by a declaration of the item's type. For example, an item such as:

msgVersion INTEGER (0..2147483647)

declares the name *msgVersion* to be a nonnegative integer less than or equal to 2147483647.

```
SNMPv3Message ::=
    SEQUENCE {
        msgVersion INTEGER (0..2147483647),
        -- note: version number 3 is used for SNMPv3
        msgGlobalData HeaderData,
        msgSecurityParameters OCTET STRING,
        msgData ScopedPduData
    }
```

Figure 27.8 The SNMP message format in ASN.1-style notation. Text following two consecutive dashes is a comment.

As the figure shows, each SNMP message consists of four main parts: an integer that identifies the protocol *version*, additional header data, a set of security parameters, and a data area that carries the payload. A precise definition must be supplied for each of the terms used. For example, Figure 27.9 illustrates how the contents of the *Header-Data* section can be specified.

```
HeaderData ::= SEQUENCE {
  msgID  INTEGER (0..2147483647),
    -- used to match responses with requests
  msgMaxSize  INTEGER (484..2147483647),
    -- maximum size reply the sender can accept
  msgFlags  OCTET STRING (SIZE(1)),
    -- Individual flag bits specify message characteristics
    -- bit 7 authorization used
    -- bit 6 privacy used
    -- bit 5 reportability (i.e., a response needed)
  msgSecurityModel  INTEGER (1..2147483647)
    -- determines exact format of security parameters that follow
}
```

Figure 27.9 The definition of the *HeaderData* area in an SNMP message.

The data area in an SNMP message is divided into *Protocol Data Units* (*PDUs*). Each PDU consists of a request (sent by client) or a response (sent by an agent). SNMPv3 allows each PDU to be sent as plain text or to be encrypted for confidentiality. Thus, the grammar specifies a *CHOICE*. In programming language terminology, the concept is known as a *discriminated union.*

```
ScopedPduData ::= CHOICE {
  plaintext  ScopedPDU,
  encryptedPDU  OCTET STRING  -- encrypted ScopedPDU value
}
```

An encrypted PDU begins with an identifier of the *engine*† that produced it. The engine ID is followed by the name of the context and the octets of the encrypted message.

```
ScopedPDU ::= SEQUENCE {
  contextEngineID  OCTET STRING,
  contextName  OCTET STRING,
  data  ANY                -- e.g., a PDU as defined below
}
```

The item labeled *data* in the *ScopedPDU* definition has a type *ANY* because field *contextName* defines the exact details of the item. The SNMPv3 Message Processing Model (*v3MP*) specifies that the data must consist of one of the SNMP PDUs as Figure 27.10 illustrates:

†SNMPv3 distinguishes between an *application* that uses the service SNMP supplies and an *engine*, which is the underlying software that transmits requests and receives responses.

```
PDU ::=
    CHOICE {
        get-request
            GetRequest-PDU,
        get-next-request
            GetNextRequest-PDU,
        get-bulk-request
            GetBulkRequest-PDU,
        response
            Response-PDU,
        set-request
            SetRequest-PDU,
        inform-request
            InformRequest-PDU,
        snmpV2-trap
            SNMPv2-Trap-PDU,
        report
            Report-PDU,
    }
```

Figure 27.10 The ASN.1 definitions of an SNMP PDU. The syntax for each request type must be specified further.

The definition specifies that each PDU consists of one of eight types. To complete the definition of an SNMP message, the standard must further specify the syntax of the eight individual types. For example, Figure 27.11 shows the definition of a *get-request*.

```
GetRequest-PDU ::= [0]
    IMPLICIT SEQUENCE {
        request-id
            Integer32,
        error-status
            INTEGER (0..18),
        error-index
            INTEGER (0..max-bindings),
        variable-bindings
            VarBindList
    }
```

Figure 27.11 The ASN.1 definition of a *get-request* message. Formally, the message is defined to be a *GetRequest-PDU*.

Further definitions in the standard specify the remaining undefined terms. Both *error-status* and *error-index* are single octet integers which contain the value zero in a request. If an error occurs, the values sent in a response identify the cause of the error. Finally, *VarBindList* contains a list of object identifiers for which the client seeks values. In ASN.1 terms, the definitions specify that *VarBindList* is a sequence of pairs of object name and value. ASN.1 represents the pairs as a sequence of two items. Thus, in the simplest possible request, *VarBindList* is a sequence of two items: a name and a *null*.

27.12 An Example Encoded SNMP Message

The encoded form of ASN.1 uses variable-length fields to represent items. In general, each field begins with a header that specifies the type of an object and its length in bytes. For example, each *SEQUENCE* begins with an octet containing the value 30 (hexadecimal); the next octet specifies the number of following octets that constitute the sequence.

Figure 27.12 contains an example SNMP message that illustrates how values are encoded into octets. The message is a *get-request* that specifies data item *sysDescr* (numeric object identifier *1.3.6.1.2.1.1.1.0*). Because the example shows an actual message, it includes many details that have not been discussed. In particular, the message contains a *msgSecurityParameters* section; the example message uses the *UsmSecurityParameters* form of security parameters. It should be possible, however, to correlate other sections of the message with the definitions above.

As Figure 27.12 shows, the message starts with a code for *SEQUENCE* which has a length of 103 octets†. The first item in the sequence is a 1-octet integer that specifies the protocol *version*; the value *3* indicates that this is an SNMPv3 message. Successive fields define a message ID and the maximum message size the sender can accept in a reply. Security information, including the name of the user (*ComerBook*) follows the message header.

The *GetRequest-PDU* occupies the tail of the message. The sequence labeled *ScopedPDU* specifies a context in which to interpret the remainder of the message. The octet *A0* specifies the operation as a *get-Request*. Bit five of *A0* indicates a nonprimitive data type, and the high-order bit means the interpretation of the octet is *context specific*. That is, the hexadecimal value *A0* only specifies a *GetRequest-PDU* when used in context; it is not a universally reserved value. Following the *A0* request octet, the length octet specifies the request is *26* octets long. The length of the *request-ID* is *2* octets; the *error-status* and *error-index* fields are each one octet. Finally, the *VarBindList* sequence of pairs contains one binding, a single object identifier bound to a *null* value. The identifier is encoded as expected except that the first two numeric labels are combined into a single octet.

†Sequence items occur frequently in an SNMP message because SNMP uses *SEQUENCE* instead of conventional programming language constructs like *array* or *struct*.

```
   30      67         02         01       03
SEQUENCE len=103 INTEGER  len=1     vers=3

   30      0D         02         01         2A
SEQUENCE len=13 INTEGER  len=1    msgID=42

   02        02         08        00
INTEGER  len=2    maxmsgsize=2048

   04        01         04
  string  len=1   msgFlags=0x04 (bits mean noAuth, noPriv, reportable)

   02        01         03
INTEGER  len=1   used-based security

   04        25        30          23
  string  len=37 SEQUENCE len=35 UsmSecurityParameters

   04        0C        00          00          00          63          00          00          00
  string  len=12 msgAuthoritativeEngineID ...

   A1        C0         93          8E          23
engine is at IP address 192.147.142.35, port 161

   02        01         00
INTEGER  len=1   msgAuthoritativeEngineBoots=0

   02        01         00
INTEGER  len=1   msgAuthoritativeEngineTime=0

   04        09            43          6F          6D          65          72          42          6F
  string  len=9          -----msgUserName value is "ComerBook"-------------

   6F        6B
--------------

   04        00
  string  len=0    msgAuthenticationParameters (none)

   04        00
  string  len=0   msgPrivacyParameters (none)

   30        2C
SEQUENCE len=44  ScopedPDU

   04        0C          00          00          00          63          00          00
  string  len=12       ------------------contextEngineID-------

   00        A1          c0          93          8E          23
  --------------------------------------------------------

   04        00
  string  len=0   contextName = "" (default)
```

```
CONTEXT [0] IMPLICIT SEQUENCE

  A0        1A
 getreq. len=26

  02        02        4D        C6
 INTEGER len=2    request-id = 19910

  02        01        00
 INTEGER len=1 error-status = noError(0)

  02        01        00
 INTEGER len=1 error-index=0

  30        0E
SEQUENCE  len=14 VarBindList

  30        0C
SEQUENCE  len=12 VarBind

  06                       08
 OBJECT IDENTIFIER name   len=8

  2B        06        01        02        01        01        01        00
 1.3   .    6    .    1    .    2    .    1    .    1    .    1    .    0 (sysDescr.0)

  05        00
 null     len=0 (no value specified)
```

Figure 27.12 An example of an encoded SNMPv3 *get-request* for data item *sysDescr* with octets shown in hexadecimal and a comment explaining their meaning below. Related octets have been grouped onto lines; they are contiguous in the message.

27.13 Security In SNMPv3

Version 3 of SNMP represents an evolution that follows and extends the basic framework of earlier versions. The primary changes arise in the areas of security and administration. The goals were twofold. First, SNMPv3 is designed to have both general and flexible security policies, making it possible for the interactions between a manager and managed devices to adhere to the security policies an organization specifies. Second, the system is designed to make administration of security easy.

To achieve generality and flexibility, SNMPv3 includes facilities for several aspects of security, and allows each to be configured independently. For example, SNMPv3 supports *message authentication* to ensure that instructions originate from a valid manager, *privacy* to ensure that no one can read messages as they pass between a manager's station and a managed device, and *authorization* and *view-based access con-*

trol to ensure that only authorized managers access particular items. To make the security system easy to configure or change, SNMPv3 allows *remote configuration*, meaning that an authorized manager can change the configuration of the security items listed above without being physically present at the device.

27.14 Summary

Network management protocols allow a manager to monitor and control network devices, such as hosts and routers. A network management client executes on a manager's workstation and can contact one or more servers, called agents, running on the managed devices. Because an internet consists of heterogeneous machines and networks, TCP/IP management software executes as application programs and uses a transport protocol (e.g., UDP) for communication between clients and servers.

The standard TCP/IP network management protocol is SNMP, the Simple Network Management Protocol. SNMP defines a low-level management protocol that provides two conceptual operations: fetch a value from a variable or store a value into a variable. In SNMP, most other operations occur as side-effects of changing values in variables. SNMP defines the format of messages that travel between a manager's computer and a managed entity.

A set of companion standards to SNMP define the set of variables that a managed entity maintains. The set of variables constitute a Management Information Base (MIB). MIB variables are described using ASN.1, a formal language that provides a concise encoded form as well as a precise human-readable notation for names and objects. ASN.1 uses a hierarchical namespace to guarantee that all MIB names are globally unique while still allowing subgroups to assign parts of the namespace.

EXERCISES

27.1 Capture an SNMP packet with a network analyzer and decode the fields.

27.2 Read the standard to find out how ASN.1 encodes the first two numeric values from an object identifier in a single octet. What is the motivation for the encoding?

27.3 Suppose the MIB designers need to define a variable that corresponds to a two-dimensional array. Explain how ASN.1 notation can accommodate references to such a variable.

27.4 What are the advantages and disadvantages of defining globally unique ASN.1 names for MIB variables?

27.5 Consult the standards and match each field in Figure 27.12 with a corresponding ASN.1 definition.

27.6 If you have SNMP client code available, try using it to read MIB variables in a local router. What is the advantage of allowing arbitrary managers to read variables in all routers? The disadvantage?

27.7 Read the MIB specification to find the definition of variable *ipRoutingTable* that corresponds to an IPv4 routing table. Design a program that will use SNMP to contact multiple routers and see if any entries in their forwarding tables cause a routing loop. Exactly what ASN.1 names should such a program generate?

27.8 Extend the previous exercise to perform the same task for IPv6.

27.9 Consider the implementation of an SNMP agent. Does it make sense to arrange MIB variables in memory exactly the way SNMP describes them? Why or why not?

27.10 Argue that SNMP is a misnomer because SNMP is not "simple."

27.11 Read about the IPsec security standard described in Chapter 29. If an organization uses IPsec, are the security features of SNMPv3 also necessary? Why or why not?

27.12 Does it make sense to use SNMP to manage all devices? Why or why not? (Hint: consider a simple hardware device such as a DSL modem.)

Chapter Contents

28

Software Defined Networking (SDN, OpenFlow)

28.1 Introduction

Previous chapters describe the fundamental communication paradigm offered by IP and used in the global Internet: a best-effort packet delivery service. The communication system consists of routers that use the destination address of each datagram to decide how to forward the datagram toward its destination.

This chapter considers an alternative: a communication system that can direct traffic along paths prescribed by network managers, according to a wide variety of criteria. The chapter briefly considers the motivation for the new approach and a few potential uses. It then explores the use of extant hardware, and examines one particular technology managers can use to specify paths. We will see that the approach presented here is not completely new. Instead, it combines many ideas from previous chapters, including MPLS (Chapter 16), packet classification (Chapter 17), Ethernet switching (Chapter 2), and network virtualization (Chapter 19).

28.2 Routes, Paths, And Connections

The basic IP forwarding paradigm can be characterized as *egalitarian* in the sense that all traffic from a given source to a given destination follows the same path. Moreover, once any datagram reaches a router, forwarding proceeds by using the datagram's destination and is independent of the datagram's source or contents. That is, a forwarding table in a router only contains one entry for a given destination.

As see have seen, several variations have been created. For example, Chapter 15 introduces the concept of tunneling and Chapter 16 discusses MPLS, which allows an edge router to consider individual packets and choose a path along which to send each packet. Specifically, we saw how a datagram can be encapsulated in an MPLS header. and how intermediate routers use the information in the encapsulating header rather than the datagram's destination address when making forwarding decisions.

28.3 Traffic Engineering And Control Of Path Selection

Recall from Chapter 16 that a major motivation for MPLS arises from the desire of network operators to perform *traffic engineering*. That is, instead of sending all traffic for a destination along a single path, a network manager may want to choose paths based on the type of the traffic, the priority assigned to datagrams, the amount each sender has paid, or other economic considerations. In essence, traffic engineering moves from a system where routing protocols make decisions to a system where network operators have control of the paths datagrams follow. An operator can specify how each individual datagram is mapped into one of the pre-defined MPLS paths appropriate for the datagram. Note that the MPLS path selected for a given datagram may not be a shortest path through intermediate routers. More important, MPLS networks usually guarantee that all the datagrams from a given flow are mapped to the same MPLS path. The point is:

> *Traffic engineering technologies move from a paradigm where routing protocols find shortest paths that all datagrams must follow to a system where a network manager can control the path for each individual flow.*

28.4 Connection-Oriented Networks And Routing Overlays

Two broad approaches have been used to provide per-flow control in a communication system:

- Use a connection-oriented network infrastructure
- Impose routing overlays on a packet-switched infrastructure

Connection-Oriented Networks. A connection-oriented network sets up an independent forwarding path for each flow. Various connection-oriented network technologies have been created (e.g., X.25 and ATM). Although details vary, each technology follows the same generic approach: before an application can send data, the application must contact the network to request a connection be established. The network can chooses a specific path for each connection. After using the connection to communicate, the application again contacts the network to request that the connection be terminated.

Because each use requires a new end-to-end connection, a connection-oriented network gives a manager control over path selection and forwarding. Typically, a manager configures a set of policies at each switch in the network. Connection setup requires each switch along a path to agree to the connection. When a connection request arrives at a switch, the switch consults the policies to determine whether and how to satisfy the request.

Routing Overlay Technologies. A routing overlay consists of a forwarding system that imposes a virtual network topology and then uses existing internet forwarding to deliver packets among nodes in the virtual topology. In essence, the routing overlay creates a set of tunnels. From the point of view of routing protocols, each tunnel acts like a point-to-point network connection between routers. Thus, routing protocols only find paths across the tunnels, which means that forwarding will be constrained to the virtual topology.

Chapter 19 discusses the general idea of overlay networks and other chapters provide specific examples. Chapter 18 discusses how mobile IP uses tunneling to forward datagrams to a mobile that is temporarily away from home, and Chapter 16 describes the use of overlays in label switching technologies, such as MPLS.

Both connection-oriented networking and overlay technologies have advantages and disadvantages. A connection-oriented network can be implemented in hardware, which means it can use high-speed hardware-based classification and label switching mechanisms. Therefore, a connection-oriented network can scale to higher network data rates. Because they are created by software, overlays are flexible and easy to change. Furthermore, if sites are connected by the global Internet, an arbitrary overlay topology can be imposed or changed quickly. More important, a set of topologies can be imposed simultaneously, which allows traffic to be segregated onto multiple virtual networks.

In addition to requiring processing overhead, overlays can result in inefficient routing. To understand why, observe that the overlay abstraction hides the architecture and costs of the underlying network. For example, suppose a company configures overlay tunnels among six sites and each tunnel goes across the global Internet between sites. The company can use an estimate of the Internet costs to configure artificial routing metrics that direct traffic along preferred routes. However, the Internet routing system and the overlay routing system operate independently. If the routing cost of an underlying network increases, the overlay system will not learn of the change. Consequently, overlay forwarding will continue to follow the original path. The point is:

> *Although connection-oriented networks and overlay routing technologies can each give network managers control over traffic, each approach has some disadvantages.*

28.5 SDN: A New Hybrid Approach

The question arises: can we combine connection-oriented networking technologies and routing overlay technologies to overcome their individual weaknesses and enjoy the strengths of both approaches? For specialized cases, the answer is yes. The combination, which is known as *Software Defined Networking* (*SDN*), uses the following ideas:

- To avoid the overhead that arises from performing classification in software, use high-speed classification hardware.
- To avoid the bottleneck that results from performing packet forwarding in software, use high-speed forwarding hardware.
- To give managers reliability and enable traffic engineering, avoid using routing protocols to set the routes for all traffic and instead allow managers to specify how to handle each case.
- To scale to the size of the Internet, allow management applications rather than humans to configure and control the network devices.

The next sections examine each of the basic ideas and then describe a specific technology that incorporates them.

28.6 Separation Of Data And Control

Conceptually, a network device, such as a router or switch, can be divided into two parts: mechanisms that permit managers to configure and control the device and mechanisms that handle packets. To capture the dichotomy, we use the terms *control plane* and *data plane*. The data plane handles all packet processing and forwarding. The control plane provides a management interface. Figure 28.1 illustrates the conceptual division.

As the figure indicates, the connections over which packets arrive and depart have much higher capacity than the management connection used for control. We use the terms *data path* to refer to the high-capacity path for packet traffic and *control path* to refer to the lower-capacity path a manager uses to control the device.

Unfortunately, when they create network devices, vendors usually follow a highly integrated approach in which the device's control plane and data plane are tightly coupled. The device exports a management interface that allows a manager to control specific functions. For example, a vendor's interface on a VLAN switch allows a manager to specify a set of VLANs and associate a given port with one of the VLANs. Similarly, a vendor's interface on a router allows a manager to fill in forwarding table entries. However, a manager cannot configure specific classification rules or control how individual packets are handled.

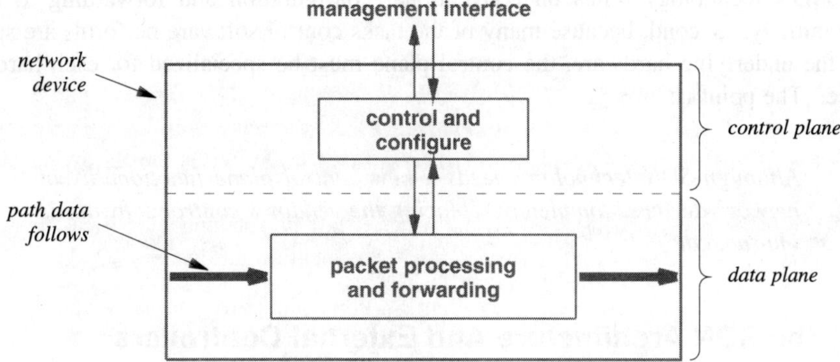

Figure 28.1 Illustration of the two conceptual parts of a network device: the control and data planes.

To achieve a hybrid solution, we must find a way to separate the data plane and control plane. That is, we need a way to replace the vendor's control plane system with a customized version. Our new control system must have direct access to the data plane hardware, and must be able to configure packet processing and forwarding. Figure 28.2 illustrates the concept: a new control system added to a network device.

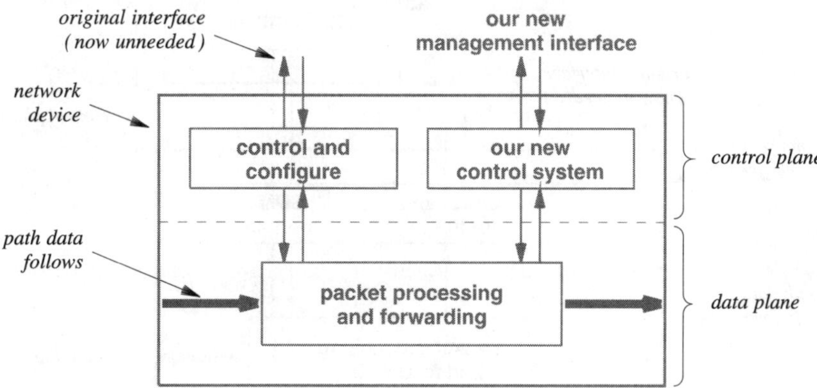

Figure 28.2 The conceptual organization of a device with a new control system replacing the vendor's system.

In theory, it might be possible to install a new control system in a network device without adding more hardware. To understand why, observe that most control systems are implemented in software: an embedded processor executes the control program from ROM. Thus, the control system can be changed by loading new software into the ROM. In practice, replacing the vendor's control software is untenable for two reasons.

First, SDN technology relies on conventional configuration and forwarding to be in place initially. Second, because many of the tasks control software performs are specific to the underlying hardware, the control plane must be specialized for each hardware device. The point is:

> *Although SDN technology needs a new control plane functionality in network devices, completely replacing the vendor's control software is impractical.*

28.7 The SDN Architecture And External Controllers

The approach that has been adopted for SDN separates control software from the underlying network devices. Instead of completely rewriting the vendors' control software, SDN uses an augmentation approach: SDN software runs in an external system and a small module is added to the device that allows the external SDN system to configure the underlying hardware. The external system, usually a conventional PC, is called a *controller*. Figure 28.3 illustrates the architecture.

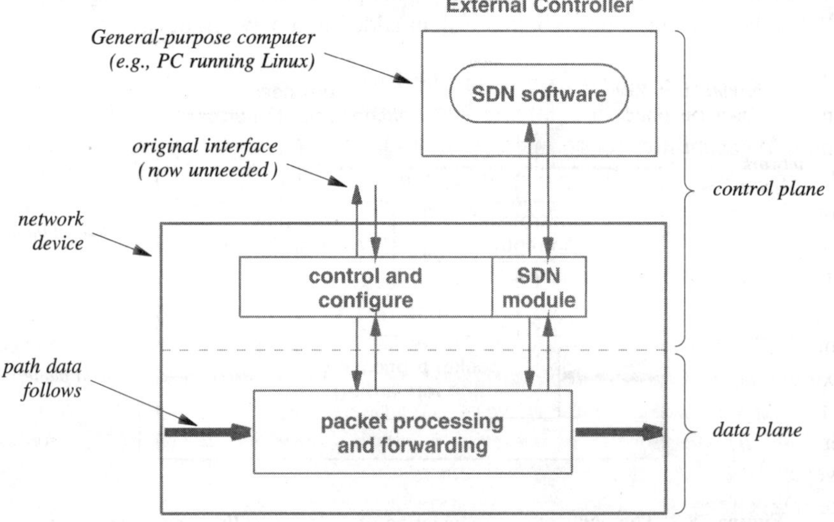

Figure 28.3 The basic SDN architecture with an external controller configuring classification and forwarding hardware in a network device.

As the figure shows, adding an external controller extends control plane functionality outside the device. A new *SDN module* must be added to the control plane of a device to permit the external controller to configure the data plane. The figure shows the SDN module as small because the code does not contain intelligence nor does it provide a conventional management interface. Instead, the SDN module merely accepts low-level commands from the external controller and passes each command through to the data plane processing unit. The point is that an SDN module is minimalistic — it contains substantially less complexity and functionality than a typical control plane mechanism.

By moving complex control-plane functions to an external controller, the SDN approach gives managers more control. A manager can configure whatever classification and forwarding rules the SDN software allows, even if they differ from conventional VLAN or IP subnet rules allowed by the vendor's software. We will see that a manager can choose how to classify and forward each individual packet. In essence, SDN uses the data classification and forwarding hardware in a network device, but ignores the control plane that the vendor supplies. The idea can be summarized:

> *The SDN approach separates control plane processing from data plane processing by moving control functions into an external controller. Because it issues low-level commands that configure the data plane of the device, an external controller can offer a manager more control than the vendor's control-plane software.*

28.8 SDN Across Multiple Devices

The description above focuses on the basic mechanism by explaining how SDN technology can be used to configure and control a single network device. To provide meaningful capabilities for an internet, the technology must be extended to multiple network devices (e.g., all the devices in a campus intranet or in an ISP's network). The important idea is that we want all the controllers to be connected to a network, which will enable management application software running on the controllers to communicate and coordinate across the entire set of devices.

Two fundamental questions concern an overall architecture: how many controllers are needed, and how should they be interconnected? As one might imagine, the number of external controllers required depends on the type of network devices being controlled and the SDN software. If the network devices are small (e.g., modems) and the computer used as a controller is powerful, a single controller can handle many devices. However, if a given device requires the control system to handle many exceptions or make frequent changes to the configuration, a controller may only be able to handle one network device. For now, we will assume that each network device has a dedicated controller; later sections consider an extension where a controller can handle multiple devices.

In terms of communication among controllers, we will imagine that a separate management network exists to connect the set of controllers. Controllers use the management network to communicate with one another, which means that we can create management application software that runs on the controllers and coordinates across the entire set of devices. To permit a human manager to set policies and perform other management tasks, we will assume that the management network also includes a manager's computer. Figure 28.4 illustrates an idealized version of a management network that interconnects controllers.

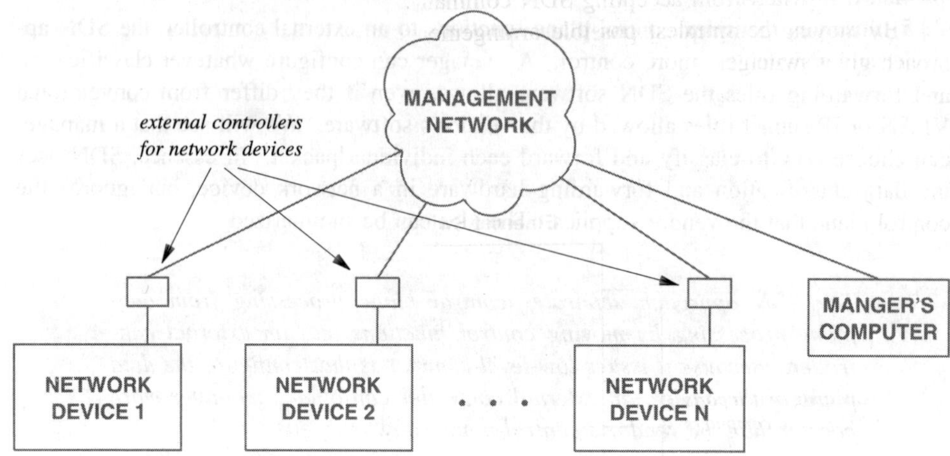

Figure 28.4 An idealized interconnection of SDN controllers on a separate management network. Management applications on the controllers use the management network to coordinate with one another.

Because it only shows a management network, the figure omits an important piece of the architecture: the data networks that are being controlled. Without seeing any of the data networks, it may be difficult to understand why controllers need to be connected. The answer is that the network devices being controlled share data networks. For example, suppose device 1 and device 2 are both VLAN switches that have a direct data connection. Further suppose that the two switches are co-located in a large university lab where they connect a set of computers. If a manager configures a VLAN for the lab, the VLAN must span both switches and the configurations must be coordinated. When the SDN approach is used, management applications running in the two controllers must coordinate; to do so, the management applications communicate over the management network.

28.9 Implementing SDN With Conventional Switches

Perhaps the most interesting aspect of SDN technology arises from the integration of the management and the data network. SDN adopts the same approach as SNMP: management traffic travels over the same wires as data traffic†. That is, rather than use a physically separate network, the management system uses the network that is being managed.

†Chapter 27 covers SNMP and explains how management traffic runs over the data network that is being managed.

To understand the SDN paradigm, consider the physical connection between an Ethernet switch and the SDN controller for the switch. Instead of using a specialized hardware interface, the controller can connect to a standard Ethernet port on the switch. Of course, the switch must be configured to recognize the controller as privileged to prevent the switch from accepting SDN commands from an arbitrary computer. Figure 28.5 illustrates the simplest possible arrangement: a direct connection between a controller and a switch.

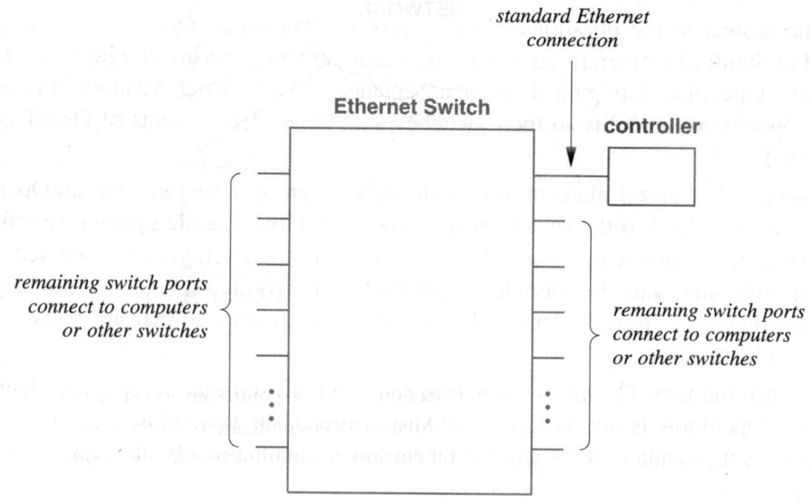

Figure 28.5 The connection between an Ethernet switch and the SDN controller for the switch.

The idea can be generalized. Observe that most intranets contain multiple switches. If we imagine a conventional intranet, Layer 2 and Layer 3 forwarding in the switches is arranged in a way that allows a controller connected to a switch to communicate with other switches. For example, each switch will be assigned an IP address and forwarding will be configured so a computer can send an IP datagram to any switch. SDN assumes such a configuration has been put in place before SDN software takes control. Thus, a controller can use IP to reach any network device. In essence, the management network in Figure 28.4 is a virtual overlay on a conventional intranet rather than a separate physical network. As with SNMP, managers and management applications using SDN must be careful to preserve connectivity in the management overlay — incorrect changes to forwarding rules can leave a controller unable to communicate with one or more switches.

28.10 OpenFlow Technology

Several questions arise. Exactly what configuration and control capabilities should a switch offer to an external SDN controller? When sending an SDN request to the switch, what format should a controller use? How can a switch distinguish between SDN requests intended for the switch itself and other packets that the controller is sending (e.g., packets sent to other controllers)? In short, what protocol should be used between a controller and a switch?

The answer to the questions lies in a protocol known as *OpenFlow*†. Originally created at Stanford University as a way for researchers to experiment with new network protocols, OpenFlow has gained wider acceptance. Many switch vendors have agreed to add OpenFlow capability to their switches, and larger deployments of OpenFlow are being used.

Because the control-plane in most switches runs an operating system, an OpenFlow module can be added to the switch easily. The OpenFlow module operates exactly like the *SDN module* shown in Figure 28.3‡ — most of the intelligence is located in the external controller, and the module in the switch merely acts as an intermediary that translates messages from the external controller into commands that are passed to the data plane hardware.

We use the term *OpenFlow switch* to refer to a switch that accepts the OpenFlow protocol. OpenFlow is not an IETF standard. Instead, the *OpenFlow Switch Specification*, the central standard document for OpenFlow, is maintained by the *OpenFlow Consortium*:

OpenFlowSwitch.org

OpenFlow provides a technology for network virtualization. An OpenFlow switch can be configured to handle both specialized network traffic (including nonstandard experimental protocols) and production network traffic simultaneously. OpenFlow permits multiple traffic types to co-exist without interference. We will see that the presence of a production network is crucial to OpenFlow because the production network permits a controller to communicate with a switch. More important, even if a switch has conventional forwarding rules, OpenFlow can establish exceptions. For example, if the normal forwarding rules send traffic for IP destination *X* to a given switch port, OpenFlow allows an administrator to specify that IP traffic for *X* that originates from IP source *Y* should be forwarded to another switch port.

28.11 OpenFlow Basics

There are two versions of the OpenFlow protocol. A whitepaper written in 2008 describes the basic idea and specifies how a basic OpenFlow switch operates. The OpenFlow specification, released in version 1.1, expands the model, fills in protocol details, and includes additional functionality. Our investigation of OpenFlow begins by

†The web site *http://www.openflow.org/wk/index.php/OpenFlow_Tutorial* contains a tutorial, and *www.opennetworking.org* has OpenFlow standards documents.

‡Figure 28.3 can be found on page 588.

examining the overall concept; later sections continue the discussion by describing the expanded model and more advanced features. In both the basic and advanced versions, OpenFlow specifies three aspects of the technology:

- The communication used between a controller and a switch
- The set of items that can be configured and controlled in a switch
- The format of messages a controller and switch use to communicate

Communication. OpenFlow specifies that a controller and switch use TCP to communicate. Furthermore, OpenFlow specifies that communication should occur over a secure communication channel. Although a TCP connection is permitted, the use of SSL (described in Chapter 29) is recommended as a way to guarantee confidentiality of all communication. It is important to remember that OpenFlow does not require a direct physical connection between a controller and a network device. Instead, OpenFlow assumes that a stable production network will remain in place and that a controller will always be able to use the production network to communicate with the network device(s) that are being controlled. The use of TCP over SSL means a single controller can establish communication with multiple network devices even if the controller does not have a physical connection to each device.

Items That Can Be Configured. OpenFlow specifies that a Type 0 OpenFlow switch (a minimum configuration) has a *Flow Table* that implements classification† and forwarding. The classification part of a Flow Table holds a set of patterns that are matched against packets. In most switches, pattern matching is implemented with TCAM hardware, but OpenFlow allows a vendor to choose an implementation. In addition to a pattern, each entry in the Flow Table is assumed to contain an *action* that specifies how to process a packet that matches the pattern and *statistics* related to the entry. The statistics include a count of packets that match the entry, a count of octets in packets that match the entry, and a timestamp that specifies the last time the entry was matched. Statistics can be accessed by an OpenFlow controller, and are useful for making decisions about traffic engineering.

Format Of Messages. A later section describes the format of messages used with version 1.1 of OpenFlow; for now, it is sufficient to know that the specification defines the exact message format and a representation for data items. For example, OpenFlow specifies that integers are sent in big endian order.

28.12 Specific Fields In An OpenFlow Pattern

Recall from Chapter 17 that classification mechanisms specify combinations of bits in packet headers. Thus, it is possible to specify values for arbitrary header fields. To save costs, some switches only provide classification hardware for specific cases (e.g., the VLAN tag field and IP addresses, but not transport layer headers). To accommodate switches that do not offer arbitrary pattern matching, OpenFlow defines a minimal

†See Chapter 17 for a discussion of classification.

set of requirements for a Type 0 switch. Figure 28.6 lists the fields that an OpenFlow switch must be able to match.

Field	Meaning
In Port	Switch port over which the packet arrived
Ether src	48-bit Ethernet source address
Ether dst	48-bit Ethernet destination address
Ether Type	16-bit Ethernet type field
VLAN id	12-bit VLAN tag in the packet
IPv4 src	32-bit IPv4 source address
IPv4 dst	32-bit IPv4 destination address
IPv4 Proto	8-bit IPv4 protocol field
TCP/UDP/SCTP src	16-bit TCP/UDP/SCTP source port
TCP/UDP/SCTP dst	16-bit TCP/UDP/SCTP destination port

Figure 28.6 Fields in packet headers that can be used for classification in a Type 0 OpenFlow switch.

Readers may be surprised to see that many of the fields in Figure 28.6 are related to conventional protocols. That is, the fields allow OpenFlow to match TCP traffic running over IPv4 and Ethernet. Does the set of fields limit experiments? Yes: the fields mean that a Type 0 OpenFlow switch cannot specify special forwarding for *ping* traffic, nor can it distinguish between ARP requests and replies. However, even a Type 0 OpenFlow switch allows experimenters to use an unassigned Ethernet type or to establish special forwarding for all traffic that arrives over a given switch port. Thus, many experiments are possible.

28.13 Actions That OpenFlow Can Take

As Figure 28.7 lists, a Type 0 OpenFlow switch defines three basic actions that can be associated with a classification pattern.

Action	Effect
1	Forward the packet to a given switch port or a specified set of switch ports.
2	Encapsulate the packet and send to the external controller for processing.
3	Drop (discard) the packet without any further processing.

Figure 28.7 Possible actions a Type 0 OpenFlow switch can take when a packet matches one of the classification rules.

Action 1 is the most common case. When a switch is booted, the vendor's control software configures the switch with forwarding rules such that every packet that arrives at the switch will be forwarded. Thus, in most instances, OpenFlow only has to configure exceptions. The idea of forwarding to a set of switch ports is used to implement broadcast and multicast.

Action 2 is intended to permit an external controller to handle packets for which no forwarding has been established. For example, consider how OpenFlow can be used to establish per-flow forwarding. OpenFlow begins by specifying Action 2 as a default for all TCP traffic. When the first packet of a new TCP connection arrives, the switch follows Action 2 by encapsulating the packet and forwarding the result to the external controller. The controller can choose a path for the TCP flow, configure a classification rule in the switch, and then forward the packet to the switch for further processing (i.e., to be forwarded according to the new classification rule). All subsequent packets on the TCP connection follow the new classification rule.

Action 3 is intended to allow OpenFlow to handle problems, such as a denial-of-service attack or excessive broadcast from a given host. When a problem is detected, the external controller can identify the source and configure Action 3 for the source, which causes the switch to drop all packets from the source.

We said that in addition to experimental forwarding, an OpenFlow switch also supports a production network. The question arises: how does the switch handle production traffic? There are two possibilities: special VLANs are configured for OpenFlow and production traffic occurs on other VLANs, or OpenFlow includes a fourth action that causes a packet to be forwarded according to the rules configured for the production network. OpenFlow allows either approach.

28.14 OpenFlow Extensions And Additions

Version 1.1 of the OpenFlow specification extends the basic model and adds considerable functionality. Additions can be classified into five categories:

- Multiple Flow Tables that are arranged in a pipeline
- Additional packet header fields available for matching
- A field used to pass information along the pipeline
- New actions that provide significant functionality
- A Group Table that allows a set of actions to be performed

A Pipeline of Flow Tables. In version 1.1, the underlying model of a switch was changed. Instead of a single Flow Table, an OpenFlow switch is assumed to have one or more Flow Tables arranged in a pipeline. Matching always begins with the first Flow Table in the pipeline. As before, each entry in a Flow Table specifies an action. One possible action specifies that processing should continue by jumping to the ith Flow

Table, where *i* is farther along the pipeline. A jump can never specify a previous Flow Table — each jump must move forward, which means there can never be a loop. When the packet reaches a Flow Table that does not specify a jump, the switch performs one or more actions, such as forwarding the packet.

Additional Packet Header Fields. Version 1.1 includes new protocols and the header fields that correspond to each. MPLS is a significant new protocol because it means OpenFlow can be used to configure MPLS paths. Figure 28.8 lists the fields available for use with classification (called *match fields* in the specification).

Field	Meaning
Ingress Port	Switch port over which the packet arrived
Metadata	64-bit field of metadata used in the pipeline
Ether src	48-bit Ethernet source address
Ether dst	48-bit Ethernet destination address
Ether Type	16-bit Ethernet type field
VLAN id	12-bit VLAN tag in the packet
VLAN priority	3-bit VLAN priority number
MPLS label	20-bit MPLS label
MPLS class	3-bit MPLS traffic class
IPv4 src	32-bit IPv4 source address
IPv4 dst	32-bit IPv4 destination address
IPv4 Proto	8-bit IPv4 protocol field
ARP opcode	8-bit ARP opcode
IPv4 tos	8-bit IPv4 Type of Service bits
TCP/UDP/SCTP src	16-bit TCP/UDP/SCTP source port
TCP/UDP/SCTP dst	16-bit TCP/UDP/SCTP destination port
ICMP type	8-bit ICMP type field
ICMP code	8-bit ICMP code field

Figure 28.8 Fields available for use with Version 1.1 of OpenFlow.

As the figure shows, OpenFlow is not completely general because it does not permit matching on all possible header fields. More important, OpenFlow does not always permit a controller to exploit the underlying switch hardware. To see why, recall from Chapter 17 that the classification mechanism in many switches allows matching to occur on arbitrary bit fields. Emerging versions of OpenFlow are expected to take advantage of the capability; instead of specifying well-known header fields, a controller can specify each classification pattern as a triple:

(bit_offset, length, pattern)

where *bit_offset* specifies an arbitrary bit position in a packet, *length* specifies the size of a bit field starting at the specified offset, and *pattern* is a bit string of *length* bits that is to be matched.

Intra-pipeline Communication. The field labeled *Metadata* in Figure 28.8 is not part of the packet. Instead, the field is intended for use within the pipeline. For example, one stage of the pipeline might compute a next-hop IPv4 address that it needs to pass to a later stage of the pipeline along with the packet. OpenFlow does not specify the contents of the *Metadata* field — the pipeline must be arranged so that successive stages of the pipeline know the contents and format of information that is passed.

New Actions. In Version 1.1, actions are not performed immediately when a match occurs. Instead, a set of actions *to be performed* is accumulated as a packet proceeds along the pipeline. Each stage of the pipeline can add or remove actions from the set. When the packet reaches a pipeline stage that does not specify a jump to another stage (i.e., the final stage of the pipeline), OpenFlow performs all the actions that have accumulated. OpenFlow requires that the action set contain an *output* action that specifies the ultimate disposition of the packet (e.g., the output port over which to forward).

In addition to changing the way actions are performed, Version 1.1 defines a set of required actions that every OpenFlow switch must support and a long list of optional actions that are recommended, but not required. For example, the specification includes actions that manipulate the TTL in a datagram header. Another action allows OpenFlow to forward a packet to the switch's local protocol stack. Many of the new actions are intended to support MPLS. In particular, a switch may need to receive an incoming IP datagram, encapsulate the datagram in an MPLS shim header, place the result in an Ethernet frame, and forward the resulting frame. Similarly, a switch may need to de-encapsulate a datagram when an MPLS packet arrives so the datagram can be forwarded without the MPLS shim header. Finally, because Version 1.1 includes QoS queueing, actions have been defined that allow a switch to place a packet on a particular queue.

A Group Table. A Group Table adds flexibility to the forwarding paradigm, and handles several cases. For example, an entry in a Group Table can specify how to forward packets, and multiple classification rules can direct flows to the entry. Alternatively, an entry in a Group Table can specify forwarding to *any* switch port in a specified set. Selection is performed in a device-specific manner (e.g., the switch computes a hash of header fields and uses the value to select one of the specified ports). The idea is that a set of switch ports that all connect to the same next hop can act like a single high-capacity connection.

Each Group Table entry contains four items: a 32-bit *identifier* that uniquely identifies the group, a *type*, a set of *counters* that collect statistics, and a set of *Action Buckets* that each specify an action. Figure 28.9 lists the possible group types.

A fast fail-over type provides a limited form of conditional execution in which a controller can configure a set of buckets that each specify a forwarding action. Each bucket is associated with a *liveness test*. For example, the switch might monitor output ports and declare a port is no longer live if a carrier is lost (e.g., the device is unplugged). Once a particular bucket is no longer live, a fast fail-over selection will skip the bucket and try an alternative. The idea is to avoid the delay that would be entailed if each loss of liveness caused the switch to inform the external controller and the external controller had to reconfigure the forwarding.

Type	Meaning
all	Execute all Action Buckets for the group (e.g., to handle broadcast)
select	Execute one Action Bucket (e.g., using a hash or round-robin algorithm for selection)
indirect	Execute the only Action Bucket defined for the group (designed to allow multiple Flow Table entries to point to a single group)
fast fail-over	Execute the first live Action Bucket (or drop the packet if no bucket is live)

Figure 28.9 The four OpenFlow group types and the meaning of each.

28.15 OpenFlow Messages

An OpenFlow message begins with a fixed-size header that comprises sixteen octets. Figure 28.10 illustrates the message format.

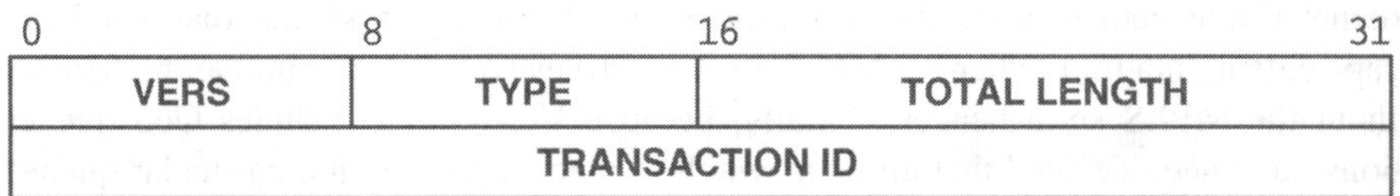

Figure 28.10 The fixed-size header used for every OpenFlow message.

Field *VERS* is a version number (e.g., the value 0x02 specifies version 2). The *TYPE* field specifies the type of the message that follows. OpenFlow defines twenty-four message types. The *TOTAL LENGTH* field specifies the total length of the message, including the header, measured in octets. The *TRANSACTION ID* is a unique value that allows the controller to match replies with requests.

The format of the rest of the message beyond the header is determined by the message type. Although an examination of all message formats is beyond the scope of our overview, it should be noted that there are several categories of messages: controller-to-switch, asynchronous (the switch informs the controller when an event has occurred), and symmetric (e.g., an echo request and response). The reader is referred to the OpenFlow Specification for further information.

28.16 Uses Of OpenFlow

How can OpenFlow be used? OpenFlow allows a manager to configure forwarding as a function of source, destination, and type fields in a packet header. Thus, many configurations are possible. A few examples will illustrate some of the possibilities:

- Experimental protocol used between two hosts
- Layer 2 VLAN that crosses a wide area
- Source-based IP forwarding
- On-demand VPN connection between two sites

Because OpenFlow can use the Ethernet type field when making forwarding decisions, forwarding can allow two hosts to exchange Ethernet packets that use a nonstandard Layer 3 protocol. OpenFlow can also recognize the VLAN ID assigned to packets, and can use VLAN IDs to create a VLAN that spans a pair of switches across a wide area. Unlike conventional Ethernet or IP forwarding, OpenFlow can examine the source address fields in a packet, and the combination of source and destination addresses can be used when choosing a route. Thus, traffic to a given destination from source host *A* can be sent along a different path than traffic from source host *B*. As a final example, consider a VPN tunnel. Because Version 1.1 allows encapsulation, OpenFlow can create a VPN tunnel when the first packet of a TCP connection appears.

The list is not exhaustive because many arrangements are possible. However, the key to understanding OpenFlow does not lie in thinking about configurations or forwarding rules. Instead, the important point is that OpenFlow allows experimenters to build custom network management software that can coordinate the actions of multiple controllers. Thus, OpenFlow can be used to make multiple switches act in a consistent manner.

28.17 OpenFlow: Excitement, Hype, And Limitations

The research community has embraced OpenFlow with wild enthusiasm. Many university researchers have been eager to adopt and try OpenFlow. Those who do not have access to switch hardware are conducting experiments on software emulators. Entire research meetings and conferences are devoted to papers and presentations on OpenFlow. Startup companies are being formed. In the excitement, many of the claims tend toward hyperbole. One researcher proudly announced that OpenFlow would “break the chains” that are holding us to vendor-supplied network management.

Despite the hype, we have seen that OpenFlow does not completely fulfill the SDN goal of making all devices completely configurable. Instead, OpenFlow selects a small subset of possible devices, functions, and capabilities. The next paragraphs highlight a few limitations.

Limited Devices. OpenFlow does not allow a manager to control arbitrary devices. Although it has been used with a handful of devices, such as access points, the primary work on OpenFlow has been directed toward switches.

Ethernet Only. As we have seen, Version 1.1 of the OpenFlow specification focuses on Ethernet frames. In particular, OpenFlow defines pattern matches for fields in Ethernet frame headers, but not for other frames. Although Ethernet is widespread, no comprehensive system is complete without Wi-Fi or the framing used on digital circuits.

IPv4 Focus. Originally, Version 1.1 of OpenFlow focused exclusively on IPv4 and the associated support protocols, such as ARP and ICMP. The specification was later extended to include matching for IPv6 and its associated protocols (e.g., Neighbor Discovery). The focus on IPv4 was especially surprising given the original purpose of OpenFlow: to encourage research. Emerging versions include support for more protocols, including IPv6.

Given the limitations, many network vendors have taken a sober view of OpenFlow. They point out that the lack of generality limits OpenFlow's applicability. However, many switch vendors have agreed to add an OpenFlow module to their products. Consequently, the excitement surrounding OpenFlow remains high.

28.18 Software Defined Radio (SDR)

The basic idea in Software Defined Networking — separation of data and control planes — has also been applied to wireless networking. The result is known as *Software Defined Radio* (*SDR*). One of the key components in SDR is a flexible radio device (i.e., a chip). Unlike a conventional design in which details such as the frequency to use and the signal modulation are hard-wired into the equipment, an SDR radio allows the details to be specified while the radio is operating. More important, the configuration can be changed easily, and the radio can handle multiple frequencies at the same time. Thus, it is possible to configure the radio device to move from one frequency to another (frequency hopping) or use two frequencies at the same time. A pair of SDR radios can scan a set of frequencies, find a frequency not in use, and agree to use it.

One obvious use of a configurable radio chip is that a vendor can use the same chip in multiple products and simply configure each one according to the needs of the product. However, the chief advantage of SDR arises because a radio system can be created that allows application software to configure the chip dynamically. That is, application software running on a radio device can sense the frequencies being used, and then adjust the chip accordingly. Thus, two SDR devices can find ways to communicate that maximize throughput and minimize interference with other radios.

One of the limitations of SDR technology arises from the limitations of antennas. In SDN, configuration merely chooses paths for packets, but SDR deals with Layer 1 parameters. When the frequency changes, the antenna needed to transmit or receive electromagnetic radiation also changes. Experimental SDR designs have used a variety of techniques, including limiting frequencies to a specific range, using multiple antennas that each cover a set of frequencies, and using antennas in a new way that can add the radiation from multiple small antennas to achieve the same capability as one larger antenna.

28.19 Summary

Software Defined Networking separates control plane processing from data plane processing and moves control processing to an external controller (e.g., a PC). In essence, intelligence is located in the external controller; a minimalistic module in a network device accepts requests from the controller and configures the device's data plane accordingly.

The primary SDN technology is known as OpenFlow. OpenFlow, which was designed to permit researchers to experiment with new protocols and network management applications, uses the classification and forwarding mechanisms in the data plane of an Ethernet switch. The original whitepaper describes a basic version of OpenFlow that handles Ethernet, IPv4, and TCP; Version 1.1 of the OpenFlow specification extends the model to have a pipeline of Flow Tables, many new actions and messages, and a Group Table that allows multiple output ports to operate as a parallel bundle and fast fail-over. Although the research community is enthusiastic, vendors point out OpenFlow's limitations.

EXERCISES

28.1 If your organization uses an SDN technology, find out why.

28.2 A pipeline of Flow Tables can be implemented by using metadata and iteratively searching a single table. Show that any packet processing that can be achieved by a pipeline can also be handled by iterative lookup.

28.3 Read the OpenFlow specification carefully. How would you use OpenFlow to create a conventional IP forwarding table?

28.4 Suppose two researchers who have host computers attached to an OpenFlow switch want to experiment with a nonstandard Layer 3 protocol. What are the possible ways to configure the switch to support the experiment? What are the advantages and disadvantages of each?

28.5 Take the tutorial on the OpenFlow web site and learn how OpenFlow handles ARP.

28.6 Read the OpenFlow specification carefully. Can a set of controllers be arranged in a hierarchy? If so, what is the reason? If not, why not?

28.7 What is the purpose of the *indirect* type in a Group Table entry?

28.8 As a packet travels along an OpenFlow pipeline, each stage in the pipeline can record one or more actions to be taken on the packet or can remove one or more actions that were specified in previous stages. Find an example where removing an action is useful.

28.9 OpenFlow includes a *LOCAL* action that delivers a packet to the switch's local protocol stack, and a *NORMAL* action that causes the packet to be forwarded according to the traditional forwarding rules in the switch. If traditional forwarding includes delivery to the switch's stack, why are both actions needed?

28.10 Does Version 1.1 of OpenFlow allow a Flow Table entry to check the Type-Of-Service (TOS) bits in an IP header? Does Version 1.1 allow an action that sets the TOS bits? Explain.

28.11 Consult the *Open Networking Foundation* web site:

www.opennetworking.org

to find the latest version of the OpenFlow protocol specification. List the most significant new features that have been added.

Chapter Contents

29

Internet Security And Firewall Design (IPsec, SSL)

29.1 Introduction

Security in an internet environment is both important and difficult. It is important because information has significant value — information can be bought and sold directly or used indirectly to create valuable artifacts. Security in an internet is difficult because security involves understanding when and how participating users, computers, services, and networks can trust one another, as well as understanding the technical details of network hardware and protocols. A single weakness can compromise the security of an entire network. More important, because TCP/IP supports a wide diversity of users, services, and networks, and an internet can span many political and organizational boundaries, participating individuals and organizations may not agree on a level of trust or policies for handling data.

This chapter considers two fundamental techniques that form the basis for internet security: perimeter security and encryption. Perimeter security allows an organization to determine the services and networks it will make available to outsiders and the extent to which outsiders can use resources. Encryption handles most other aspects of security. We begin by reviewing a few basic concepts and terminology.

29.2 Protecting Resources

The terms *network security* and *information security* refer in a broad sense to confidence that information and services available on a network are authentic and cannot be accessed by unauthorized users. Security implies safety, including assurance of data integrity, freedom from unauthorized access of computational resources, freedom from snooping or wiretapping, and freedom from disruption of service. Of course, just as no physical property is absolutely secure against crime, no network is completely secure. Organizations make an effort to secure networks for the same reason they make an effort to secure buildings and offices: basic security measures can discourage crime by making it significantly more difficult.

Providing security for information requires protecting both physical and abstract resources. Physical resources include passive storage devices such as disks as well as active devices such as users' computers and smart phones. In a network environment, physical security extends to the cables, switches, and routers that form the network infrastructure. Indeed, although it is seldom mentioned, physical security often plays an integral role in an overall security plan. Good physical security can eliminate sabotage (e.g., disabling a router to cause packets to be forwarded through an alternative, less secure path).

Protecting an abstract resource such as information is usually more difficult than providing physical security because information is elusive. Information security encompasses many aspects of protection:

- *Data Integrity.* A secure system must protect information from unauthorized change.
- *Data Availability.* The system must guarantee that outsiders cannot prevent legitimate access to data (e.g., any outsider should not be able to block customers from accessing a web site).
- *Privacy Or Confidentiality.* The system must prevent outsiders from making copies of data as it passes across a network or understanding the contents if copies are made.
- *Authorization.* Although physical security often classifies people and resources into broad categories, (e.g., all nonemployees are forbidden from using a particular hallway), security for information usually needs to be more restrictive (e.g., some parts of an employee's record are available only to the personnel office, others are available only to the employee's boss, and others are available to the payroll office).
- *Authentication.* The system must allow two communicating entities to validate each other's identity.
- *Replay Avoidance.* To prevent outsiders from capturing copies of packets and using them later, the system must prevent a retransmitted copy of a packet from being accepted.

29.3 Information Policy

Before an organization can enforce network security, the organization must assess risks and develop a clear policy regarding information access and protection. The policy specifies who will be granted access to each piece of information, the rules an individual must follow in disseminating the information to others, and a statement of how the organization will react to violations.

An information policy begins with people because:

> *Humans are usually the most susceptible point in any security scheme. A worker who is malicious, careless, or unaware of an organization's information policy can compromise the best security.*

29.4 Internet Security

Internet security is difficult because datagrams traveling from source to destination often pass across many intermediate networks and through routers that are not owned or controlled by either the sender or the recipient. Thus, because datagrams can be intercepted or compromised, the contents cannot be trusted. As an example, consider a server that attempts to use *source authentication* to verify that requests originated from valid customers. Source authentication requires the server to examine the source IP address on each incoming datagram, and only accept requests from computers on an authorized list. Because it can be broken easily, source authentication is classified as *weak*. In particular, an intermediate router can watch traffic traveling to and from the server, and record the IP address of a valid customer. Later, the intermediate router can manufacture a request that has the same source address (and intercept the reply). The point is:

> *An authorization scheme that uses a remote machine's IP address to authenticate its identity does not suffice in an unsecure internet. An imposter who gains control of an intermediate router can obtain access by impersonating an authorized client.*

Stronger authentication requires *encryption*. Careful choices of an encryption algorithm and associated keys can make it virtually impossible for intermediate machines to decode messages or manufacture messages that are valid.

29.5 IP Security (IPsec)

The IETF has devised a set of protocols that provide secure Internet communication. Collectively known as *IPsec* (short for *IP security*), the protocols offer authentication and privacy services at the IP layer, and can be used with both IPv4 and IPv6. More important, instead of completely specifying the functionality or the encryption algorithm to be used, the IETF chose to make the system both flexible and extensible. For example, an application that employs IPsec can choose whether to use an authentication facility that validates the sender or to use an encryption facility that also ensures the payload will remain confidential. The choices can be asymmetric in each direction (e.g., one endpoint can choose to use authentication when sending datagrams and the other endpoint can choose to send datagrams without authentication). Furthermore, IPsec does not restrict senders to a specific encryption or authentication algorithm. Instead, IPsec provides a general framework that allows each pair of communicating endpoints to choose algorithms and parameters, such as the size of a key. To guarantee interoperability, IPsec does include a basic set of encryption algorithms that all implementations must recognize. The point is:

> *IPsec is not a single security protocol. Instead, IPsec provides a set of security algorithms plus a general framework that allows a pair of communicating entities to use whichever algorithms provide security appropriate for the communication.*

29.6 IPsec Authentication Header

IPsec follows the basic approach that has been adopted for IPv6: a separate *Authentication Header* (*AH*) carries authentication information. Interestingly, IPsec applies the same approach to IPv4. That is, instead of modifying the IPv4 header, IPsec inserts an extra header in the datagram. We think of inserting a header because authentication can be added as a last step, after the datagram has been created. Figure 29.1 illustrates an authentication header being inserted into a datagram that has carries TCP.

As the figure shows, IPsec inserts the authentication header immediately after the original IP header, but before the transport header. For IPv4, IPsec modifies the *PROTOCOL* field in the IP header to specify that the payload is authentication; for IPv6, IPsec uses the *NEXT HEADER* field. In either case, the value *51* indicates that the item following the IP header is an authentication header.

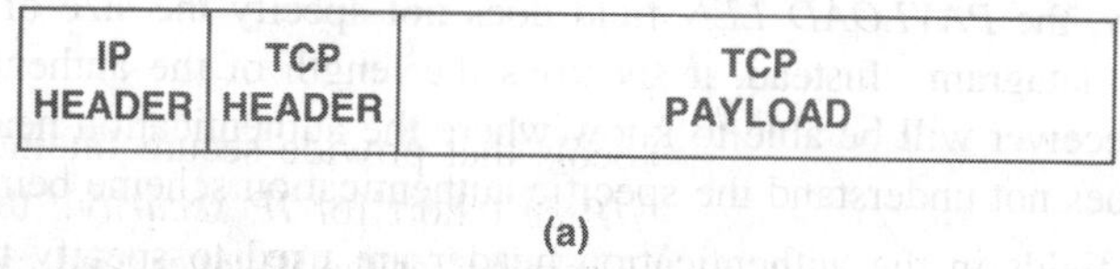

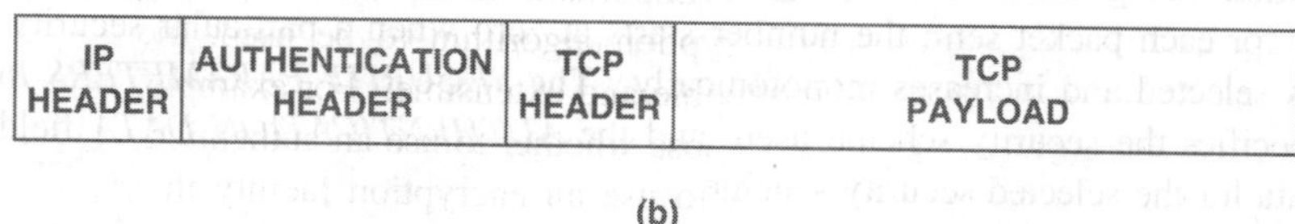

Figure 29.1 Illustration of (a) an IP datagram, and (b) the same datagram after an IPsec authentication header has been inserted. The approach is used for both IPv4 and IPv6.

An authentication header is not a fixed size. Instead, the header begins with a set of fixed-size fields that describe the security information being carried followed by a variable-size area that depends on the type of authentication being used. Figure 29.2 illustrates the authentication header format.

0	8	16	31
NEXT HEADER	PAYLOAD LEN	RESERVED	
SECURITY PARAMETERS INDEX			
SEQUENCE NUMBER			
AUTHENTICATION DATA (VARIABLE) . . .			

Figure 29.2 The IPsec authentication header format. The same format is used with IPv4 and IPv6.

How does a receiver determine the type of information carried in the datagram? The authentication header has its own *NEXT HEADER* field that specifies the type — IPsec records the original *PROTOCOL* value in the *NEXT HEADER* field of the authentication header. When a datagram arrives, the receiver uses security information from the authentication header to verify the sender, and uses the *NEXT HEADER* field in the authentication header to further demultiplex the datagram.

The idea of inserting an extra header and the concept of a *NEXT HEADER* field in each header were originally designed for use with IPv6. When IPsec was retro-fitted from IPv6 into IPv4, the designers chose to retain the general approach even though it does not follow the usual IPv4 paradigm.

Interestingly, the *PAYLOAD LEN* field does not specify the size of the final payload area in the datagram. Instead, it specifies the length of the authentication header itself. Thus, a receiver will be able to know where the authentication header ends, even if the receiver does not understand the specific authentication scheme being used.

Remaining fields in the authentication header are used to specify the type of authentication being used. Field *SEQUENCE NUMBER* contains a unique sequence number for each packet sent; the number starts at zero when a particular security algorithm is selected and increases monotonically. The *SECURITY PARAMETERS INDEX* field specifies the security scheme used, and the *AUTHENTICATION DATA* field contains data for the selected security scheme.

29.7 Security Association

To understand the reason for using a security parameters index, observe that a security scheme defines many possible variations. For example, the security scheme includes an authentication algorithm, a key (or keys) that the algorithm uses, a lifetime over which the key will remain valid, a lifetime over which the destination agrees to use the algorithm, and a list of source addresses that are authorized to use the scheme. Further observe that the information cannot fit into the header.

To save space in the header, IPsec arranges for each receiver to collect all the details about a security scheme into an abstraction known as a *security association* (*SA*). Each SA is given a number, known as a *security parameters index*, through which the SA is known. Before a sender can use IPsec to communicate with a receiver, the sender and receiver must agree on an index value for a particular SA. The sender then places the index value in the field *SECURITY PARAMETERS INDEX* of each outgoing datagram.

Index values are not globally specified. Instead, each destination creates as many SAs as it needs, and assigns an index value to each. The destination can specify a lifetime for each SA, and can reuse index values once an SA becomes invalid. Consequently, the security parameters index cannot be interpreted without consulting the destination (e.g., the index *1* can have entirely different meanings to two destinations). To summarize:

> *A destination uses the security parameters index to identify the security association for a packet. The values are not global; a combination of destination address and security parameters index is needed to identify each SA.*

29.8 IPsec Encapsulating Security Payload

To handle confidentiality as well as authentication, IPsec uses an *Encapsulating Security Payload* (*ESP*), which is more complex than an authentication header. Instead of inserting an extra header, ESP requires a sender to replace the IP payload with an encrypted version of the payload. A receiver decrypts the payload and recreates the original datagram.

As with authentication, IPsec sets the *NEXT HEADER* (IPv6) or *PROTOCOL* (IPv4) field in the IP header to indicate that ESP has been used. The value chosen is *50*. An ESP header has a *NEXT HEADER* field that specifies the type of the original payload. Figure 29.3 illustrates how ESP modifies a datagram.

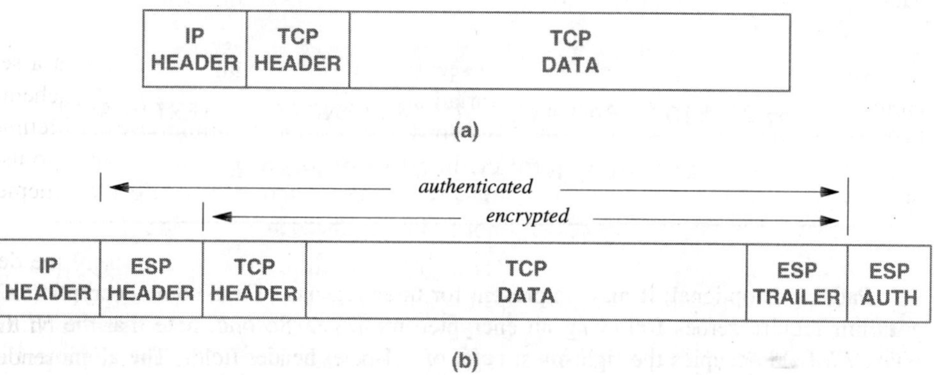

Figure 29.3 (a) A datagram, and (b) the same datagram using IPsec Encapsulating Security Payload. Intermediate routers can only interpret unencrypted fields.

As the figure shows, ESP adds three additional areas to the datagram. An *ESP HEADER* immediately follows the IP header and precedes the encrypted payload. An *ESP TRAILER* is encrypted along with the payload. Finally a variable-size *ESP AUTH* field follows the encrypted section. Why is authentication present? The idea is that ESP is not an alternative to authentication, but should be an addition. Thus, authentication is a required part of ESP.

Although it accurately represents the use of IPsec with IPv4, Figure 29.3 overlooks an important concept in IPv6: multiple headers. In the simplest case, an IPv6 datagram might be structured exactly as in the figure, with an IPv6 base header followed by a TCP header and TCP payload. However, the set of optional IPv6 headers include hop-by-hop headers that are processed by intermediate routers. For example, the datagram might contain a source route header that specifies a set of intermediate points along a path to the destination. If ESP encrypts the entire datagram following the IPv6 base header, hop-by-hop information would be unavailable to routers. Therefore, ESP is only applied to items that follow the hop-by-hop headers.

The ESP headers use many of the same fields found in the authentication header, but rearrange their order. For example, an *ESP HEADER* consists of 8 octets that identify the security parameters index and a sequence number.

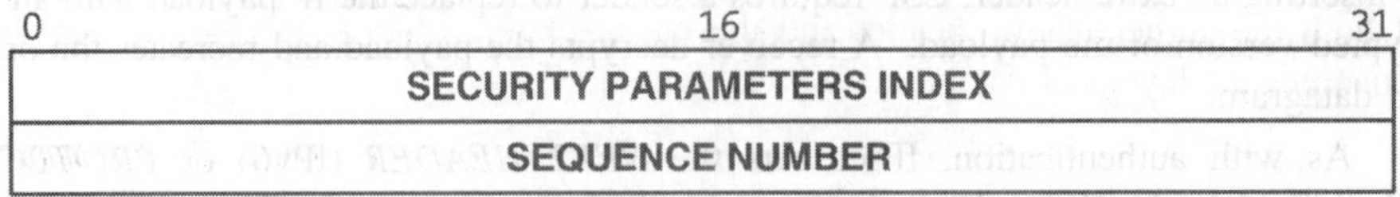

The *ESP TRAILER* consists of optional padding, a padding length field, *PAD LENGTH*, and a *NEXT HEADER* field that is followed by a variable amount of authentication data.

0 – 255 OCTETS OF PADDING (bits 0–15)	PAD LENGTH (bits 16–23)	NEXT HEADER (bits 24–31)
ESP AUTHENTICATION DATA (VARIABLE) . . .		

Padding is optional; it may be present for three reasons. First, some decryption algorithms require zeroes following an encrypted message. Second, note that the *NEXT HEADER* field occupies the right-most octet of a 4-octet header field. The alignment is important because IPsec requires the authentication data that follows the trailer to be aligned at the start of a 4-octet boundary. Thus, padding may be needed to ensure alignment. Third, some sites may choose to add random amounts of padding to each datagram so eavesdroppers at intermediate points along the path cannot use the size of a datagram to guess its purpose.

29.9 Authentication And Mutable Header Fields

The IPsec authentication mechanism is designed to ensure that an arriving datagram is identical to the datagram sent by the source. However, such a guarantee is impossible to make. To understand why, recall that IP is classified as a machine-to-machine layer because the layering principle only applies across one hop. In particular, each intermediate router decrements the hop-limit (IPv6) or time-to-live (IPv4) field and recomputes the checksum.

IPsec uses the term *mutable fields* to refer to IP header fields that are changed in transit. To prevent such changes causing authentication errors, IPsec specifically omits mutable fields from the authentication computation. Thus, when a datagram arrives, IPsec only authenticates immutable fields (e.g., the source address and protocol type).

29.10 IPsec Tunneling

Recall from Chapter 19 that VPN technology uses encryption along with IP-in-IP tunneling to keep inter-site transfers confidential. IPsec is specifically designed to accommodate an encrypted tunnel. In particular, the standard defines tunneled versions of both the authentication header and the encapsulating security payload. Figure 29.4 illustrates the layout of datagrams in tunneling mode.

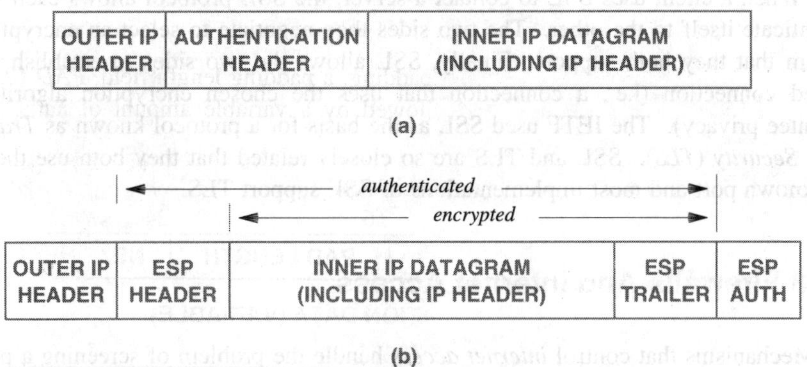

Figure 29.4 Illustration of IPsec tunneling mode for (a) an authenticated datagram and (b) an encapsulated security payload. The entire inner datagram is protected.

29.11 Required Security Algorithms

IPsec defines a minimal set of security algorithms that are mandatory (i.e., that all implementations must supply). In each case, the standard defines specific uses. Figure 29.5 lists the required security algorithms.

Authentication

HMAC with MD5	RFC 2403
HMAC with SHA-1	RFC 2404

Encapsulating Security Payload

DES in CBC mode	RFC 2405
HMAC with MD5	RFC 2403
HMAC with SHA-1	RFC 2404
Null Authentication	
Null Encryption	

Figure 29.5 The security algorithms that are mandatory for IPsec.

29.12 Secure Socket Layer (SSL and TLS)

By the mid 1990s when it became evident that security was important for Internet commerce, several groups proposed security mechanisms for use with the Web. Although not formally adopted by the IETF, one of the proposals has become a de facto standard.

Known as the *Secure Sockets Layer* (*SSL*), the technology was originally developed by Netscape, Inc. As the name implies, SSL resides at the same layer as the socket API. When a client uses SSL to contact a server, the SSL protocol allows each side to authenticate itself to the other. The two sides then negotiate to select an encryption algorithm that they both support. Finally, SSL allows the two sides to establish an encrypted connection (i.e., a connection that uses the chosen encryption algorithm to guarantee privacy). The IETF used SSL as the basis for a protocol known as *Transport Layer Security* (*TLS*). SSL and TLS are so closely related that they both use the same well-known port and most implementations of SSL support TLS.

29.13 Firewalls And Internet Access

Mechanisms that control *internet access* handle the problem of screening a particular network or an organization from unwanted communication. Such mechanisms can help prevent outsiders from: obtaining information, changing information, or disrupting communication on an organization's intranet. Successful access control requires a careful combination of restrictions on network topology, intermediate information staging, and packet filters.

A single technique, known as an *internet firewall*†, has emerged as the basis for internet access control. An organization places a firewall on its connection to the global Internet (or to any untrusted external site). A firewall partitions an internet into two regions, referred to informally as the *inside* and *outside*.

29.14 Multiple Connections And Weakest Links

Although the concept seems simple, details complicate firewall construction. First, an organization's intranet can have multiple external connections. The organization must form a *security perimeter* by installing a firewall on each external connection. To guarantee that the perimeter is effective, all firewalls must be configured to use exactly the same access restrictions. Otherwise, it may be possible to circumvent the restrictions imposed by one firewall by entering the organization's internet through another‡. We can summarize:

†The term *firewall* is derived from building architecture in which a firewall is a thick, fireproof partition that makes a section of a building impenetrable to fire.

‡The well-known idea that security is only as strong as the weakest point has been termed the *weakest link axiom* in reference to the adage that a chain is only as strong as its weakest link.

> *An organization that has multiple external connections must install a firewall on each external connection and must coordinate all firewalls. Failure to restrict access identically on all firewalls can leave the organization vulnerable.*

29.15 Firewall Implementation And Packet Filters

How should a firewall be implemented? In theory, a firewall simply blocks all unauthorized communication between computers in the organization and computers outside the organization. In practice, the details depend on the network technology, the capacity of the connection, the traffic load, and the organization's policies. No single solution works for all organizations — firewall systems are designed to be configurable. Informally called a *packet filter*, the mechanism requires the manager to specify how the firewall should dispose of each datagram. For example, the manager might choose to filter (i.e., block) all datagrams that come from one source and allow those from another, or a manager might choose to block all datagrams destined for some TCP ports and allow datagrams destined for others.

To operate at network speeds, a packet filter needs hardware and software optimized for the task. Many commercial routers include hardware for high-speed packet filtering. Once a manager configures the firewall rules, the filter operates at wire speed, discarding unwanted packets without delaying valid packets.

Because TCP/IP does not dictate a standard for packet filters, each network vendor is free to choose the capabilities of their packet filter as well as the interface a manager uses to configure the filter. Some firewall systems offer a graphical interface. For example, the firewall might run a web server that displays web pages with configuration options. A manager can use a conventional web browser to access the server and specify a configuration. Other firewall systems use a command-line interface.

If a router offers firewall functionality, the interface usually permits a manager to configure separate filter rules for each interface. Having a separate specification for each interface is important because one interface of a router may connect to an external network (e.g., an ISP), while other interfaces connect to internal networks. Thus, the rules for which packets to reject vary between interfaces.

29.16 Firewall Rules And The 5-Tuple

Many firewall rules focus on the five fields found in protocol headers that are sufficient to identify a TCP connection. In the industry, the set is known as the *5-tuple*. Figure 29.6 lists the fields.

IPsrc	IP source address
IPdst	IP destination address
Proto	Transport protocol type (e.g., TCP or UDP)
srcPort	Source port number for transport protocol
dstPort	Destination port number for transport protocol

Figure 29.6 Header fields that make up the 5-tuple. The five fields are sufficient to identify an individual TCP connection.

Because it refers to IP datagrams, the 5-tuple does not include a Layer 2 type field. That is, we tacitly assume the Layer 2 frame specified the packet to be an IP datagram.

A firewall packet filter usually allows a manager to specify arbitrary combinations of fields in the 5-tuple, and may provide additional possibilities. Figure 29.7 illustrates an example filter specification that refers to fields of the 5-tuple.

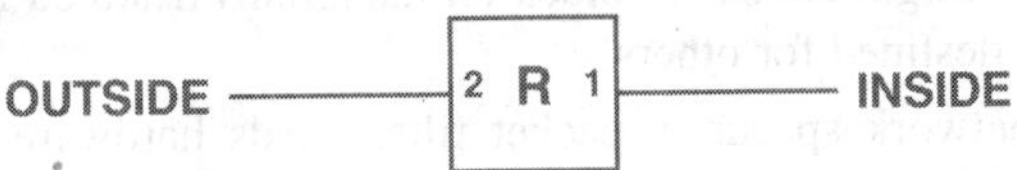

Arrival Interface	IPsrc	IPdst	Proto	srcPort	dstPort
2	*	*	TCP	*	21
2	*	*	TCP	*	23
1	128.5.0.0/16	*	TCP	*	25
2	*	*	UDP	*	43
2	*	*	UDP	*	69
2	*	*	TCP	*	79

Figure 29.7 A router with two interfaces and an example datagram filter specification.

In the figure, a manager has chosen to block incoming datagrams destined for FTP (TCP port *21*), TELNET (TCP port *23*), WHOIS (UDP port *43*), TFTP (UDP port *69*), and FINGER (TCP port *79*). In addition, the filter blocks outgoing datagrams that originate from any host with an address that matches the IPv4 prefix *128.5.0.0/16* and a destination of a remote email server (TCP port *25*).

29.17 Security And Packet Filter Specification

Although the example filter configuration in Figure 29.7 specifies a small list of services to be blocked, such an approach does not work well for an effective firewall. There are three reasons.

1. The number of well-known ports is large and growing rapidly. Thus, listing each service requires a manager to update the list continually. Unfortunately, an error of omission can leave the firewall vulnerable.
2. Second, much of the traffic on an internet does not travel to or from a well-known port. In addition to programmers who can choose port numbers for their private client-server applications, services like *Remote Procedure Call* (*RPC*) and file sharing applications assign ports dynamically.
3. Third, listing ports of well-known services leaves the firewall vulnerable to *tunneling*. Tunneling can circumvent security if a host on the inside agrees to accept encapsulated datagrams from an outsider, removes one layer of encapsulation, and forwards the datagram to the service that would otherwise be restricted by the firewall. The problem is significant because malware that is inadvertently installed on a user's computer can exploit weaknesses in the firewall.

How can a firewall use a packet filter effectively? The answer lies in reversing the filter configuration: instead of specifying which datagrams should be blocked, a firewall should be configured to block all datagrams except those that the manager admits. That is, a manager must specify the hosts and protocol ports for which external communication has been approved. By default, all communication is prohibited. Before enabling any port, a manager must examine the organization's information policy carefully and determine that the policy allows the communication. In practice, the packet filters in many commercial products allow a manager to specify a set of datagrams to admit instead of a set of datagrams to block. We can summarize:

> *To be effective, a firewall that uses datagram filtering should restrict access to all IP sources, IP destinations, protocols, and protocol ports except those computers, networks, and services the organization explicitly decides to make available externally. A packet filter that allows a manager to specify which datagrams to admit instead of which datagrams to block can make such restrictions easy to specify.*

29.18 The Consequence Of Restricted Access For Clients

It may seem that our simplistic rule of blocking all datagrams that arrive for an unknown protocol port will solve many security problems by preventing outsiders from accessing arbitrary servers in the organization. Such a firewall has an interesting consequence: it also prevents an arbitrary computer inside the firewall from becoming a client that accesses a service outside the firewall. To understand why, recall that although each server operates at a well-known port, a client does not. When a client application begins, the application requests the operating system to assign a protocol port number that is neither among the well-known ports nor currently in use on the client's computer. When it begins to communicate with a server outside the organization, the client generates one or more datagrams and sends them to the server. Each outgoing datagram has the client's protocol port as the source port and the server's well-known protocol port as the destination port. Assuming the external server has been approved, the firewall will not block datagrams as they leave. When it generates a response, however, the server reverses the protocol ports, which means the client's port becomes the destination port. When a response reaches the firewall, the firewall rules will block the packet because no rule has been created to approve the destination port. Thus, we can see an important idea:

> *If an organization's firewall restricts incoming datagrams except for ports that correspond to services the organization makes available externally, an arbitrary application inside the organization cannot become a client of a server outside the organization.*

29.19 Stateful Firewalls

How can arbitrary clients within the organization be allowed to access services on the Internet without admitting incoming datagrams that are destined to arbitrary protocol ports? The answer lies in a technique known as a *stateful firewall*. In essence, the firewall monitors all outgoing datagrams and adapts the filter rules accordingly to accommodate replies.

As an example of a stateful firewall, suppose a client on the inside of an organization forms a TCP connection to a web server. If the client has source IP address I_1 and source TCP port P_1 and connects to a web server at port 80 with IP address I_2, the outgoing SYN segment that initiates the connection will pass through the firewall, which records the 5-tuple:

$$(I_1, I_2, TCP, P_1, 80)$$

When the server returns a SYN+ACK, the firewall will match the two endpoints to the tuple that was stored, and the incoming segment will be admitted.

Interestingly, a stateful firewall does not permit clients inside the organization to initiate connections to arbitrary destinations. Instead, the actions of a stateful firewall are still controlled by a set of packet filter rules. Thus, a firewall administrator can still choose whether to permit or deny transit for a given packet. In the case of a packet that is allowed to pass through the firewall, the filter rule can further specify whether to record state information that will permit a reply to be returned.

How should state be managed in a stateful firewall? There are two broad approaches: a firewall can use *soft state* by setting a timer that removes inactive state information after a timeout period, or *connection monitoring* in which the firewall watches packets on the flow and removes state information when the flow terminates (e.g., when a FIN is received on a TCP connection). Even if a stateful firewall attempts to monitor connections, soft state is usually a backup to handle cases such as a UDP flow that does not have explicit termination.

29.20 Content Protection And Proxies

The security mechanisms described above focus on access. Another aspect of security focuses on content. We know, for example, that an imported file or email message can contain a virus. In general, such problems can only be eliminated by a system that examines incoming content.

One approach, known as *Deep Packet Inspection* (*DPI*), examines the payload of incoming packets. Although it can catch some problems, DPI cannot always handle situations where content is divided into many packets and the packets arrive out of order. Thus, alternatives have been invented that extract the content from a connection and then examine the result before allowing it to pass into the organization.

A mechanism that examines content acts as an *application proxy*. For example, an organization can run an HTTP proxy that intercepts each outgoing request, obtains a copy of the requested item, and scans the copy. If the copy is found to be free from a virus, the proxy forwards the copy to the client. If the copy contains a virus, the client is sent an error message. Note that an application proxy can be *transparent* (i.e., except for a delay, the client does not realize a proxy has intercepted a request) or *nontransparent* (i.e., the client must be configured to use a specific proxy).

Although many organizations use a stateful firewall to protect the organization against random probes from the outside, fewer check content. Thus, it is typical to find an organization that is immune to arbitrary attacks from the outside, but is still plagued with email viruses and trojan horse problems when an unsuspecting employee imports a program that can breach a firewall by forming an outgoing connection.

29.21 Monitoring And Logging

Monitoring is one of the most important aspects of a firewall design. A network manager who is responsible for a firewall needs to be aware of attempts to bypass security. A list of failed penetration attempts can provide a manager clues about the attacker, such as an IP address or a pattern of times at which attempts are made. Thus, a firewall must report incidents.

Firewall monitoring can be *active* or *passive*. In active monitoring, a firewall notifies a manager whenever an incident occurs. The chief advantage of active monitoring is speed — a manager is notified quickly whenever a potential problem arises. The chief disadvantage is that active monitors often produce so much information that a manager cannot comprehend it or notice problems. Thus, many managers prefer passive monitoring, or a combination of passive monitoring with a few high-risk incidents reported by an active monitor.

In passive monitoring, a firewall logs a record of each incident in a file on disk. A passive monitor usually records information about normal traffic (e.g., simple statistics) as well as datagrams that are filtered. A manager can access the log at any time; most managers use a computer program. The chief advantage of passive monitoring arises from its record of events — a manager can consult the log to observe trends and when a security problem does occur, review the history of events that led to the problem. More important, a manager can analyze the log periodically (e.g., daily) to determine whether attempts to access the organization increase or decrease over time.

29.22 Summary

Security problems arise because an internet can connect organizations that do not have mutual trust. Several technologies are available to help ensure that information remains secure when being sent across an internet. The Secure Sockets Layer (SSL) protocol adds encryption and authentication to the socket API. IPsec allows a user to choose between two basic schemes: one that provides authentication of the datagram and one that provides authentication plus privacy. IPsec modifies a datagram either by inserting an Authentication Header or by using an Encapsulating Security Payload, which inserts a header and trailer and encrypts the data being sent. IPsec provides a general framework that allows each pair of communicating entities to choose an encryption algorithm. Because security is often used with tunneling (e.g., in a VPN), IPsec defines a secure tunnel mode.

The firewall mechanism is used to control internet access. An organization places a firewall at each external connection to guarantee that the organization's intranet remains free from unauthorized traffic. A firewall contains a packet filter that an administrator must configure to specify which packets can pass in each direction. A stateful firewall can be configured so the firewall automatically allows reply packets once an outgoing connection has been established.

EXERCISES

29.1 Read the description of a packet filter for a commercially available router. What features does it offer?

29.2 Collect a log of all traffic entering your site. Analyze the log to determine the percentage of traffic that arrives from or is destined to a well-known protocol port. Do the results surprise you?

29.3 If encryption software is available on your computer, measure the time required to encrypt a 10 Gbyte file, transfer it to another computer, and decrypt it. Compare the result to the time required for the transfer if no encryption is used.

29.4 Survey users at your site to determine if they send sensitive information in email. Are users aware that messages are transferred in plain text, and that anyone watching network traffic can see the contents of an email message?

29.5 Can a firewall be combined with NAT? What are the consequences?

29.6 The military only releases information to those who "need to know." Will such a scheme work for all information in your organization? Why or why not?

29.7 Give two reasons why the group of people who administer an organization's security policies should be separate from the group of people who administer the organization's computer and network systems.

29.8 Some organizations use firewalls to isolate groups of users internally. Give examples of ways that internal firewalls can improve network performance and examples of ways internal firewalls can degrade network performance.

29.9 If your organization uses IPsec, find out which algorithms are being used. What is the key size?

29.10 Can IPsec be used with NAT? Explain.

Chapter Contents

30

Connected Embedded Systems (The Internet of Things)

30.1 Introduction

Early chapters describe the principles, protocols, and architecture behind TCP/IP and the global Internet. Later chapters focus on application protocols and paradigms that applications use to communicate over an internet. Most Internet applications, which include email, web browsing, music download, chat programs, and even network management, have one thing in common: a human initiates communication. Indeed, the early Internet has been described as focused on providing communication mechanisms that humans use.

This chapter focuses on a major new area that is emerging as part of the Internet: communication among intelligent embedded systems. The idea is that computing systems can be embedded in many devices, and the systems will be able to communicate with other devices. Of course, some of the embedded devices will provide data for humans to view and use, so human interaction is included. However, the major emphasis will be on systems that can interact with their environment, rather than on conventional computers that store data and run applications. Researchers and professionals working on the topic have coined the terms *Internet of Things*† (*IoT*) and *Machine to Machine* (*M2M*) *applications* to capture the idea.

The chapter begins by presenting examples of intelligent embedded systems and the way they use communication. It then discusses one particular technology in detail: a protocol stack for a wireless network that is intended for smart grid applications. The use of IPv6 and some of the consequences of the IPv6 design are of particular relevance to the discussion.

†Despite sounding awkward, the phrase *Internet of Things* appears to be widely accepted. However, one vendor's marketing department uses a variation: the *Internet of Everything*.

30.2 Sensing, Monitoring, And Control

We use the term *embedded system* to refer to a computational system that is an integral part of another mechanism or device. The chief difference between an embedded system and a conventional computer system arises from their external connections. A conventional computer system deals with information: the computer can store, access, and manipulate data. In contrast, an embedded system can *sense* and *control* the physical world around it.

As an example, consider a thermostat used to control a heating and air conditioning system. A modern thermostat (called a "smart thermostat") constitutes an embedded system: the thermostat contains an embedded processor that runs software to perform all functions. A user can configure the thermostat to use the time of day to change settings. The thermostat has connections to a variety of sensors that might include: an indoor temperature sensor, an outdoor temperature sensor, a sensor that detects airflow (i.e., whether the fan is operating), and a sensor connected to push buttons that allow a user to set the desired temperature. More advanced systems have sensors for the relative humidity of the air. In addition, the thermostat has connections to controls that allow the processor to turn the heater or air conditioner on or off, regulate the speed of the fan, and control humidifier and dehumidifier functions.

Most computer users are already familiar with embedded systems. For example, a printer connected to a computer incorporates an embedded system. When a computer sends a document to the printer, the printer's embedded system controls the motors and mechanisms in the printer, causing them to feed sheets of paper through the printer, move the ink jet mechanism, and spray drops of ink. The printer also contains sensors that can detect a paper jam or low ink supplies.

General Electric, the largest industrial company in the U.S., is going much further than items for the consumer market. G.E. produces aircraft engines, power plant turbines, locomotives for railroads, medical imaging equipment, and heavy-duty machinery that transports people, heats homes, and powers factories. Using the phrase *industrial Internet*, G.E. has launched a major initiative to incorporate communicating embedded systems in both its factories and its products.

30.3 Power Conservation And Energy Harvesting

Some embedded systems, such as the embedded control system in a printer, attach to a reliable source of continual power. However, many embedded systems rely on temporary power, and are designed to conserve energy. For example, cell phones run on batteries and environmental sensors located in remote locations (e.g., a desert) may use photocells.

As a special case, some embedded systems are designed to *harvest energy* from the environment around them. For example, a sensor in the ocean might use the motion of waves to generate power, and a sensor near a hot spring might use thermal energy. Energy harvesting even includes the kinetic energy that humans generate merely by opening a door or flipping a light switch. An embedded system that uses harvested energy may need to operate periodically — the system might need to accumulate energy until a sufficient charge is available (e.g., to run a radio transmitter).

30.4 A World Of Intelligent Embedded Devices

To understand the Internet of Things, we have to imagine that embedded systems will be everywhere: houses, office buildings, vehicles, shopping malls, and on street corners. Consider vehicles as an example. In addition to embedded systems that provide information, entertainment, and navigation, each car will have an embedded system that finds the distance to surrounding cars, senses objects in the road, and warns of changes in the pavement (e.g., a slight drop or bump due to construction). Embedded systems will be able to sense lanes and warn the driver if the car drifts out of its lane or when traffic congestion lies ahead. If the system is intelligent, it can monitor other cars and apply the brakes if necessary. Furthermore, an intelligent system can identify the driver (e.g., via facial recognition), monitor the individual's driving habits, and adjust reaction times accordingly.

In office buildings, embedded systems can sense the presence of individuals and adjust lights and heating or cooling accordingly. The system can also change the heating and cooling systems when windows are open. More important, by adding intelligence to embedded systems, the system will be able to learn patterns. For example, if an employee moves in and out of their office frequently during the work day, the system can learn not to turn off the heat until the employee is absent for a longer time. Similarly, if an employee tends to work late, the system will learn the pattern and control the office accordingly. Thus, if an employee with flexible hours goes home at three o'clock each day, an intelligent system can learn the pattern and shut down lighting and heating early.

30.5 The Importance of Communication

Why is emphasis shifting to intelligent embedded systems that can communicate? There are many advantages: communication allows control, coordination, and transfer of data. Small embedded systems can achieve much more by working together with nearby embedded systems or by accessing remote information.

As an example, consider a set of sensors used to assess the stress on bridges. Measuring stress is important in understanding how much traffic a bridge can carry safely. Stress measurements can indicate when reinforcement is warranted or if the bridge should be replaced. To measure stress, engineers place small battery-powered sensors at various points along the bridge. Without communication, each sensor must store measurements along with a timestamp. Periodically, engineers collect the stored data and reset the sensor to collect more. If each sensor includes a radio, the set of sensors can form a wireless network. Network communication allows the sensors to coordinate so they take each reading simultaneously. It also allows the sensors to send the results to a common collection point, possibly at a location far from the bridge. Although collecting readings electronically is much more convenient than a manual method, the most important aspect of communication is the new functionality it enables. In the case of sensors, uploading data in real time makes it possible to detect dangerous situations and divert traffic before a disaster occurs.

As a second example of communication, consider *smart meters* used by utility companies. The traditional approach used to assess usage consists of placing a meter outside each customer's location and sending a person to record the meter reading each month. A smart meter incorporates wireless communication, which means the utility company can read the meter from a remote location. Even if the wireless network only reaches to the street, the meter can be read from a passing vehicle, which lowers the cost of reading meters dramatically.

30.6 Example: Electronic Ads In Shopping Malls

Many shopping malls now have large video display panels that show ads. The ads change continuously — stores in the mall pay a fee to show fixed images or full-motion videos of their products. They also advertise discounts and feature special short-term promotions (e.g., for the next 30 minutes if you buy product *Y* at store *X* and mention this ad, you will receive a second one free). Communication is needed to download ads dynamically because the content and schedules can change at any time — management needs the ability to control which ad is displayed on a given screen and how long the ad remains visible.

Where is the controller that management uses located, and what networking technology is needed to connect the controller to the individual displays? The answer is interesting and a bit surprising: each display contains a TCP/IP protocol stack and a connection to the global Internet. There are two reasons. First, an Internet connection allows the controller to be located anywhere. In particular, the mall can outsource IT functions by placing the controller "in the cloud." More important, having an Internet connection means that the content does not need to reside on the same physical host as the controller.

Allowing content to be separate from the controller is important because many stores in a mall are part of a national (or international) chain. For example, *Apple Computer* may have stores in many malls. Individual stores do not produce promotional videos. Instead, the parent company creates all advertising and makes it available to individual stores. The video content for ads resides on the parent company's server. Having Internet access means the controller only needs to specify a schedule of items to display along with the URL of each item. Because they each have Internet access, the display systems can download a copy of each item they have been assigned to show (possibly through a local cache to improve performance).

30.7 Collecting Data From Embedded Systems

The shopping mall example illustrates another important capability of networked systems: the ability to collect data. Although it is not obvious to customers, some of the displays in shopping malls are equipped with a camera, and the software is programmed to operate the camera. When someone approaches the display, the system uses the camera to detect their presence and apply facial recognition algorithms. Once faces have been identified, the system uses facial features (e.g., the distance between the eyes) to analyze the individual. With high accuracy, software in the embedded system is able to tell whether the individual in front of the camera is male or female as well as their approximate age. Instead of merely following a predetermined schedule of ads to display, the system can use the characteristics of the individual to choose an appropriate ad. Thus, a middle-aged male might be shown an ad for a sports car instead of an ad for a dress.

Although a camera can be used to select ads, the system can also use a camera to gather and report data about the interaction. For example, the system can upload statistics about how many people watched a given ad, their sex and age, and how long the person or group remained in front of the display. Grocery stores are using the same approach: they are installing cameras with embedded processing capability over freezers and at other locations in the store. The cameras record whether customers stop to look at a given product display, how long each person stands still and looks, and how many customers finally select a product or merely move on. In each case, the information is uploaded to a server for analysis†.

To summarize:

> *Adding communication capability to an intelligent embedded system allows information to flow in two directions: data can be downloaded to control the actions of the system, and the system can upload data gathered from sensors.*

30.8 Wireless Networking And IEEE 802.15.4

Many of our examples use wireless networking technology. Wireless networks work extremely well for environmental sensors that are deployed across a wide area (e.g., sensors on a bridge or earthquake sensors deployed for miles around a fault). However, wireless networking is also used for semi-permanent deployments in a small area. For example, using wireless networking on the electronic displays in malls means that a display unit can be moved without installing a new network connection. The units are large and heavy, which means that the installation is semi-permanent (i.e., the display remains stationary for weeks). The use of wireless makes relocation much easier than a wired network.

†The examples presented here are not mere speculations — these systems exist and are being deployed.

What wireless networking technologies should be used to connect an intelligent embedded system? The answer depends on several factors, including the geographic distance between nodes of the network, desired data rates, and the power to be used. Power is especially important for two reasons. First, many embedded sensor systems run on battery power. To maximize battery life, the power consumption must be minimized (we note that, among other things, reducing overall power utilization may mean reducing the amount of power used by the radio transmitter, and may mean reducing the memory or processor speed). Second, even if the embedded system has a source of power, it may be necessary to limit the signal strength to avoid interfering with other devices or other transmissions.

Several low-power wireless networking technologies have been standardized, including the well-known *blue-tooth* technology. For our example, we will use a low-power personal-area network technology defined by the IEEE standard 802.15.4. The IEEE standard specifies the physical and MAC layers of the network, and other groups have defined upper-layer protocols for use on the network. Various versions of 802.15.4 have been produced; they differ in the frequency bands and modulation techniques used. For our purposes, it is only necessary to understand that the data rate is relatively low (a maximum of 250 Kbps), the MTU is extremely small (127 octets), and the distance limited (a maximum of 10 meters with a conventional antenna and power from a battery). The next sections consider an application of 802.15.4 wireless technology and upper layers of a protocol stack.

30.9 A Mesh Network For Smart Grid Sensors

One application of 802.15.4 wireless technology arises from an effort to add intelligent computer management to the electrical power distribution system. Known as *Smart Grid*, the overall plan includes placing sensors in all devices that use electricity. In addition to large systems, such as those used for heating and cooling, the designers envision sensors in kitchen appliances (e.g., ovens, refrigerators, dishwashers, and even toasters), computer systems, and entertainment systems (e.g., televisions and stereos). The utility companies want to charge more during peak hours, and the sensors will communicate with the utility company to find out about pricing and warn users when prices are high. Alternatively, the sensors will be capable of disabling certain uses during peak hours.

The most obvious design for a system of sensors consists of placing a base station in each residence and using a wireless technology that allows the base station to communicate with each sensor. The approach is known as a *hub-and-spoke* topology. As we have seen, 802.11 (Wi-Fi) technologies use a hub-and-spoke approach. However, such a design does not work well for all situations. In particular, metal pipes and other obstructions that interfere with wireless signals can make it impossible to reach all locations from a single point, especially for portable appliances that can be moved from one room to another. Therefore, the designers envision an adaptive system in which the set of sensor nodes automatically forms a *self-organized mesh network* (usually abbreviated as *mesh*). Each node in the mesh performs two tasks: communication for the appliance to which it attaches and forwarding for other nodes.

Each residence will contain a *border router* that connects sensor nodes in the residence to the outside world. When a node boots, it joins the mesh and tries to establish a connection to the border router. If it can reach the border router, the node communicates directly with the border router. If it cannot reach the border router directly, the node searches for a nearby neighbor node that does have a path to the border router. In essence, the neighbor agrees to act like a router that forwards packets.

If multiple neighbors have a path to the border router, a node applies a selection algorithm to choose one. The selection algorithm can take into account several metrics, including quality of the radio signal (i.e., the level of interference), latency, link capacity, and capacity of intermediate forwarding nodes. Once a node has a path to the border router, it informs neighbors and agrees to forward their packets. Thus, if it is possible to create a network that gives each node connectivity, the nodes will form a mesh network automatically. To summarize:

> *Rather than using a single, powerful base station that can reach the sensor in each electrical applicance, a system is being designed in which a set of sensor nodes self-organizes to form a mesh network; each node in the mesh agrees to forward packets for other nodes.*

30.10 A Forwarding Tree For a Sensor Mesh

Our description makes the selection of paths in a mesh seem trivial. In fact, a mesh offers many possible paths. Furthermore, the distinction between routing (choosing paths among networks) and forwarding (choosing paths within a network) is blurred because we can think of each radio link like a network. More important, connectivity is pair-wise among nodes. The routing aggregation that occurs from an IP prefix does not apply because a mesh does not function like a single network to which all nodes attach. If mesh nodes are mobile, forwarding must change dynamically. Despite the potential complexity of mesh routing, we need to find a solution that works for basic cases. Therefore, we will assume a static mesh topology, and only consider forwarding between the border router and individual nodes.

If each sensor node chooses one way to reach the border router, the forwarding paths in the network form a *tree* (i.e., a graph with no cycles). Figure 30.1 illustrates a set of nodes and one possible forwarding tree. As the figure indicates, a border router is usually larger than other nodes in the network (i.e., has more processing power and memory). We will see that a border router is expected to run servers that provide services to the mesh as a whole.

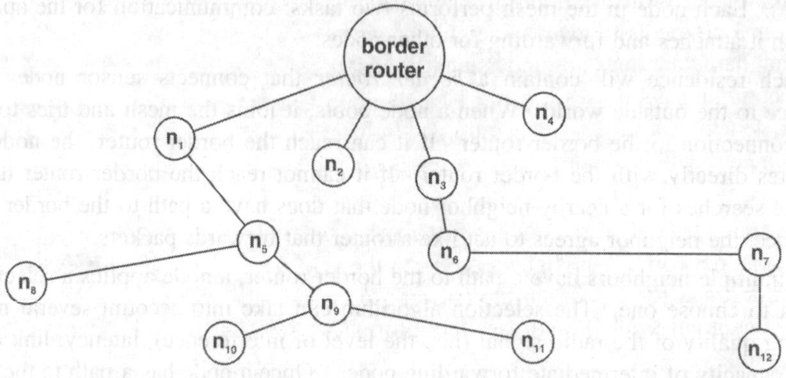

Figure 30.1 An example forwarding tree imposed on a set of sensor nodes. A tree results if each node chooses one path to the border router.

30.11 Using Layer 2 And Layer 3 Protocols In A Mesh

Recall from Chapter 4 that two approaches have been devised to create a forwarding tree across a mesh:

- Mesh-under: forwarding uses Layer 2 protocols
- Route-over: forwarding uses Layer 3 protocols

In either approach, when a node enters the mesh, the node must choose how to link itself into the tree. There are two steps. In the first step, a node must find the set of neighboring nodes that can be reached directly and asses the quality of the radio signal for each neighbor. In the second step, the node must choose either to communicate with the border router directly or to use one of the neighbors when forwarding packets. Note that the quality of a signal is of key importance — even if a node can reach the border router directly, the node may choose an indirect path if the signal quality of the direct connection is sufficiently low.

Mesh-under. With the *mesh-under* approach, which is favored by IEEE, a node uses Layer 2 protocols to form a forwarding tree. The idea is similar to the bridge and spanning tree protocols used for Ethernet. For example, a node uses a Layer 2 broadcast to discover which neighbors are within radio range. Each neighbor responds, which allows the pair to learn that they can reach each other and the signal quality. The border router also uses Layer 2 broadcast to advertise itself. Nodes in the mesh pass along information about which nodes they can reach. Eventually, each node in the mesh is aware of other nodes and how to reach them, as well as how to forward broadcast packets. Thus, given the Layer 2 address of the border router, nodes in the mesh will know how to forward packets (i.e., they will have formed a forwarding tree).

Route-over. With the *route-over* approach, which is favored by the IETF, a node uses Layer 3 protocols to identify neighbors and form a forwarding tree. Of course, the underlying hardware does not understand IP addresses or the IP datagram format. Thus, Layer 3 communication uses Layer 2 packets. For example, consider finding neighbors. Software generates a Layer 3 datagram with a local broadcast address, and the datagram is sent via hardware broadcast.

In terms of an IP protocol stack, the major difference between mesh-under and route-over arises in IP forwarding. The mesh-under approach treats the entire set of nodes as one network. IP assigns a prefix to the network and IP forwarding causes any datagram destined for a node on the network to be passed to the interface. Layer 2 accepts the datagram from IP and uses the information that has been gathered to forward the datagram.

The route-over approach makes IP aware that some nodes on the network are reachable directly and others are not. In IPv6 terminology, we say that a node is either *on link* or *off link*. To handle nodes that are not directly reachable, IP uses *source routing*. That is, IP must understand the topology of the mesh and be able to specify a path (e.g., go to node 9, then node 5, then node 1, and finally to the border router). The next sections describe the ZigBee protocol stack that uses the route-over approach and assesses some of the problems that arise.

30.12 The ZigBee IPv6 Protocol Stack

The ZigBee Alliance and the IETF are exploring the use of IPv6 in a mesh design that follows the route-over approach. Figure 30.2 lists three IETF working groups related to the ZigBee effort.

Name	Purpose
6lowpan	IP-over-802.15.4 shim layer
roll	RPL routing protocol for mesh networks
coap	Lightweight RESTful protocol for constrained devices

Figure 30.2 IETF working groups related to the ZigBee effort.

The basic idea of the ZigBee route-over design is to use IPv6 when possible and introduce modifications as needed. A protocol has been created to compress IPv6 datagrams and send them over an 802.15.4 radio link. A modified form of IPv6 *Neighbor Discovery* is used to find the IP addresses of directly-reachable neighbors, and a protocol has been invented to allow neighbors to exchange characteristics. In addition, a new routing protocol is used to gather information about connectivity throughout the mesh. Finally, an IPv6 source route header is used to forward each datagram hop-by-hop across the mesh. The next sections describe some of the basic protocols.

30.12.1 IPv6 Over Low Power Wireless Networks (6LoWPAN)

The 6LoWPAN effort (IPv6 over Low-power Wireless Personal Area Networks) defines the transmission of IPv6 over a 802.15.4 radio link. The primary problem is a conflict between the IPv6 requirement for an MTU of at least 1280 octets and the 802.15.4 protocol that species a maximum of 127 octets. In fact, if AES-CCM-128 encryption is used, the available payload size is reduced to 81 octets. To send an IPv6 datagram over such a link, 6LoWPAN introduces an extra shim layer that performs compression and transmission. The shim layer accepts an outgoing IPv6 datagram, compresses the header, divides the datagram into a series of pieces we will call *fraglets*, and sends each fraglet in a separate packet. On the receiving side, the 6LoWPAN shim layer accepts incoming fraglets, recombines them into a single datagram, decompresses the header, and passes the result to the IP layer. Thus, IPv6 is configured to send and receive complete datagrams.

Note that 6LoWPAN does not use conventional IPv6 fragmentation. There are two reasons. First, 6LoWPAN only needs to operate over a single link. Thus, the protocol is much simpler because all the fraglets of a datagram must arrive in order. Second, IPv6 fragmentation cannot handle an MTU of 127 octets.

30.12.2 6LoWPAN Neighbor Discovery (6LoWPAN-ND)

As we have seen, *IPv6 Neighbor Discovery* (*IPv6-ND*) includes duplicate address detection. A fundamental assumption is that each IPv6 prefix maps to a broadcast domain; a node can use a broadcast transmission to reach all other nodes that share the prefix. In a mesh network, however, a broadcast may only reach some of the nodes in the mesh. We say that some nodes are *off link*. As a result, conventional duplicate address detection, which assumes all nodes are reachable via broadcast or multicast, will not work correctly.

6LoWPAN-ND defines several changes and optimizations of IPv6-ND that are intended specifically for lossy, low-power wireless networks. In general, 6LoWPAN-ND avoids all mechanisms that flood packets across the mesh. Instead of requiring each node to perform duplicate address detection, 6LoWPAN-ND uses a *registration* approach in which a node in the mesh can register its address with software that runs on the border router. Each node registers its address, and software on the border router flags any duplicates (recall that a border router has the processing power and memory needed to handle network-wide services, such as address registration). Finally, 6LoWPAN-ND allows nodes to *sleep* (i.e., go into stasis state to conserve power). When the node reawakens, it renews its address registration.

30.12.3 Mesh Link Establishment (MLE)

IPv6 is designed with the assumption that links have been configured before IP software runs. In particular, the radio connection between two nodes cannot be assessed by sending a packet in one direction: a two-way exchange is needed. Furthermore, IPv6 expects exchanges to be authenticated, which means that links must already be in place. To allow an IPv6 route-over mesh, a lower-level protocol is required that pairs of nodes can use to test and configure the links between them.

ZigBee uses the *Mesh Link Establishment* (*MLE*) protocol for link configuration. MLE allows two nodes to assess the quality of the signal during packet transmission, exchange configuration information (including address information), and choose a type of security for the link. In addition, MLE can assess multiple links that lead to the border router, and choose one to use.

30.13 Forwarding In A ZigBee Route-Over Mesh

Perhaps the most serious consequence of using IPv6 to implement a route-over mesh arises from the requirement for source routing. We know that some nodes of the network will be on link (i.e., directly reachable), but others will be off link (i.e., only reachable indirectly). Therefore, IP must use more than the network prefix to decide how to forward a datagram. There are two ways to handle the problem: *storing mode* and *nonstoring mode*.

Storing mode. As the term *storing* implies, each node in the network stores a significant amount of information. In particular, each node learns and stores the topology of the entire network (i.e., which pairs of nodes can communicate). When it needs to send a datagram, the IP software consults the stored information to obtain a path through the mesh to the destination. The sender places the path in a source route header and sends the datagram.

Non-storing mode. In non-storing mode, each node in the network only learns two things: the set of directly-reachable neighbors and the identify of one neighbor that leads to the border router. However, the border router (which is presumed to have significantly more memory and processor capability than individual nodes) learns the complete topology of the network. When a node has a datagram to send, the node forwards the datagram to the border router. The border router, which knows the topology, uses source routing to send the datagram to its destination.

Non-storing mode may seem to waste network resources because a datagram sent from one node to another first goes to the border router and then to its destination. However, non-storing mode has been selected to permit individual nodes to be extremely small (have limited memory). Although networks are expected to have only a few nodes (perhaps two dozen), the size is important. Even if a network contains only a few nodes, mesh nodes will not have memory sufficient to store forwarding tables for the entire mesh; for a larger mesh, storing mode implies that each node must store extremely large tables. Using non-storing mode means each node in the network only needs to keep the following items in memory:

- A list of all directly-reachable neighbors, including the MAC address of each

- The identity of the neighbor that has been chosen as the path to the border router.

30.13.1 Routing Protocol For Low-Power And Lossy Networks (RPL)

The IETF has defined a protocol that can be used with IPv6 in a route-over mesh network. Known as *Routing Protocol For Low-Power And Lossy Networks* (*RPL*), the protocol allows nodes to advertise direct connections and to learn about connections. In non-storing mode, RPL propagates connection information "upward" to the border router. The border router runs a special version of RPL software that gathers the information, which means that it learns the topology of the entire mesh.

Once it learns the topology, the border router computes a forwarding tree. Instead of a tree and an undirected graph, RPL makes each link directed and the direction is toward the root (i.e., toward the border router). Thus, RPL calls the graph of the mesh topology a *Destination-Oriented Directed Acyclic Graph* (*DODAG*). Figure 30.3 illustrates the DODAG form of the tree from Figure 30.1†.

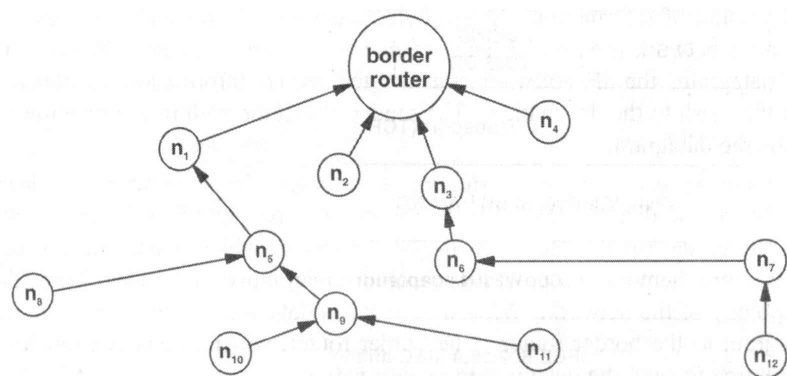

Figure 30.3 The DODAG RPL defines for the tree in Figure 30.1.

The DODAG representation is merely a detail of the protocol. When a border router needs to send a datagram to one of the nodes, the source route used in the header will list nodes down the tree (i.e., in the reverse of the arrows in the figure).

RPL separates nodes in the tree into three types: *root* (the border router acts as the root of the DODAG), *leaf* (i.e., a node that has only one connection), and *intermediate* (a node that has at least two connections and forwards datagrams). Because intermediate nodes forward packets, the ZigBee standards use the term *ZigBee IP router*, abbreviated *ZIP router*. Leaf nodes do not run RPL. Instead, each leaf node connects to a ZIP

---

†Figure 30.1 can be found on page 630.

router, which handles all forwarding responsibilities for the leaf node. That is, a ZIP router informs the border router about each leaf node to which it connects.

RPL is much more complex than indicated here. For example, RPL can also be used with storing mode; messages must specify the mode being used. In addition, RPL has the ability to distribute information down the tree. For example, it is possible to use RPL to inform nodes about IP prefixes being used.

30.13.2 Other Protocols In The ZigBee Specification

Besides the major protocols defined above, the ZigBee specification includes many other protocols. ZigBee uses IPv6 and ICMPv6, TCP, UDP, *Protocol for carrying Authentication for Network Access* (*PANA*), *multicast DNS* (*mDNS*), *DNS Service Discovery* (*DNS-SD*), and *Transport Layer Security* (*TLS*), which is used in conjunction with PANA, EAP, and EAP-TLS for authentication. Finally, applications that conform to the *Smart Energy Profile 2.0* can use HTTP. Figure 30.4 summarizes the major protocols.

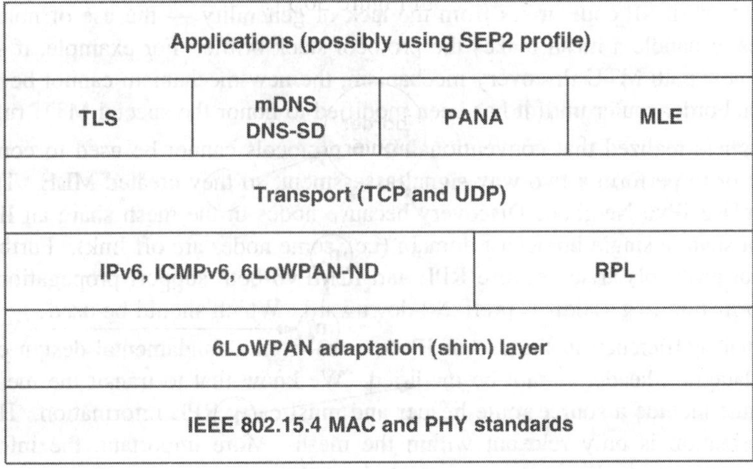

Figure 30.4 The layer of major protocols used in a ZigBee mesh network.

30.14 Assessment Of Using IPv6 Route-Over For A Mesh

Many questions arise about the route-over approach and the use of IPv6 for a mesh of low-power sensor nodes. Is a route-over design better than a mesh-under design? How much additional protocol overhead is needed for route-over? Will a route-over implementation require more memory than a mesh-under implementation? If so, how much more? Does it make sense to use IPv6 in a mesh network that has an extremely small MTU and extremely slow links? If RPL uses non-storing mode, what is the overhead in terms of additional packet forwarding? How much of IPv6 and the IPv6 support protocols must change to make them operate in the mesh environment?

We have already seen that the IPv6 specification prohibits using IPv6 over a network with an MTU smaller than 1280. Thus, a 6LoWPAN shim layer is needed to allow IPv6 to use a technology that has an MTU of only 127 (less than 127 if an authentication header is used). A further complication with small MTU arises because 802.15.4 networks can be lossy. Although the 6LoWPAN specification recognizes lossy behavior, it relies on the use of fraglets, which means that the probability of datagram loss (or delay for retransmission) will be much higher than the probability of loss for a single packet.

Another problem related to MTU arises because a border router must forward datagrams that arrive from outside the mesh. The IPv6 standard specifies a minimum link MTU of 1280. Suppose the border router advertises an MTU of 1280 on external links. When a datagram arrives from the outside, the datagram must be further encapsulated before transmission across the mesh. Unfortunately, the additional header increases the datagram size to $1280+\delta$, which makes it larger than the 6LoWPAN MTU of 1280. One solution defines the 6LoWPAN MTU to be $1280+\delta$, but requires the border router to enforce an MTU of 1280 for external sources. The disadvantage of embedding special restrictions in IP code arises from the lack of generality — the use of nonstandard techniques to handle a mesh makes the protocol stack brittle. For example, if someone invents a new path MTU discovery mechanism, the new mechanism cannot be integrated into the border router until it has been modified to honor the special MTU rules.

Designers realized that conventional IPv6 protocols cannot be used to configure a radio link or to perform a two-way signal assessment, so they created MLE. They also had to replace IPv6 Neighbor Discovery because nodes in the mesh share an IP prefix, but do not share a single broadcast domain (i.e., some nodes are off link). Further questions about protocols arise because RPL and ICMPv6 both support propagation of network information (e.g., address prefixes) downward. Which should be used?

A final inefficiency in the use of IPv6 arises from a fundamental design decision: an IPv6 datagram header cannot be modified. We know that to transit the mesh, a datagram must include a source route header and must carry RPL information. However, such information is only relevant within the mesh. More important, the information cannot be sent outside the mesh because the datagram might pass across another ZigBee mesh — the extra headers must be removed to avoid being misinterpreted. Similarly, if a datagram passes from the outside into the mesh, the appropriate headers must be added. As a consequence of the IPv6 design, headers cannot be changed. Therefore, the only option is encapsulation: each IPv6 datagram sent across the mesh must be encapsulated in an outer IPv6 datagram that has the appropriate headers. In normal networks, IP-in-IP encapsulation adds a small overhead. For an 802.15.4 network, however, the extra header is huge relative to the MTU. As a result, the overhead increases significantly. To summarize:

> *Although it is possible to use a route-over paradigm and IPv6 for a ZigBee mesh, doing so means inventing many alternative protocols and incurs significant overhead.*

30.15 Summary

The early Internet focused on connecting users to remote resources. A new trend focuses on an Internet of Things, in which intelligent embedded systems that sense and control their environment use Internet technology to communicate. Examples include sensors in vehicles, residences, office buildings, shopping malls, and on civil infrastructure.

A consortium of vendors known as the ZigBee Alliance is exploring the use of IEEE 802.15.4 wireless network technology with a mesh of Smart Grid sensors. A ZigBee network has a border router that connects to the outside; other nodes in the mesh self-organize to connect and establish forwarding.

In terms of protocols, the ZigBee Alliance is working with the IETF on a route-over approach that uses IPv6. In principle, a route-over system uses Layer 3 forwarding. In practice, IPv6 and the associated support protocols are insufficient for a low-power, lossy wireless mesh technology that has a small MTU and a low data rate. Consequently, work has focused on replacing many parts of IPv6, adding a shim layer to accommodate small MTU, and inventing a new mesh routing protocol. Even with the changes, the design of IPv6 introduces many inefficiencies.

EXERCISES

30.1 Suppose your car had an embedded system that could recognize your face and configure the car accordingly. What parameters would you choose to set?

30.2 One of the first uses of connected embedded systems arose from cash registers. When a consumer makes a purchase, the cash register identifies the consumer (e.g., from a frequent-shopper ID or a credit card) and sends details of the purchase back to a server. Find examples of other connected embedded systems that consumers use.

30.3 Cameras are being placed in supermarkets to monitor shoppers' habits. If the store also installs cameras at check-out counters, it may be possible to learn the identity of individuals. What are the consequences for privacy?

30.4 If you had to design protocols for a mesh network, would you choose mesh-under or route-over? Justify your choice.

30.5 If applications assume an MTU of 1280 and an original IPv6 datagram must be encapsulated in an outer IPv6 datagram, how many fraglets must be sent to transmit the datagram?

30.6 Assume a datagram is divided into K fraglets and the probability of losing a given fraglet is p $(0 \leq p \leq 1)$. What is the probability that the datagram will be lost?

30.7 What are the advantages of using IPv6 as the basis for an Internet of Things? What are the disadvantages?

30.8 Consider the choice of paths in a mesh network. One possible metric chooses a path with fewest hops. Explain why a hop count metric does not always work well in a mesh network.

30.9 The work on a ZigBee stack resulted in yet another routing protocol, RPL. Why was a new protocol invented instead of using existing routing protocols (e.g., RIP, OSPF)?

30.10 Compare the 6LoWPAN-ND model of address registration with the use of DHCP for address assignment. What are the differences? Under what circumstances is one preferable?

Appendix 1

Glossary Of Internetworking Terms And Abbreviations

TCP/IP Terminology

Like most large undertakings, TCP/IP and the Internet have created their own language. A curious blend of networking jargon, protocol names, and abbreviations, the terminology is both difficult to learn and difficult to remember. To outsiders, discussions among the cognoscenti sound like meaningless babble laced with acronyms at every possible opportunity. Even after a moderate amount of exposure, readers may find that specific terms are difficult to understand. The problem is compounded because some terminology is loosely defined, the volume is overwhelming, and various subgroups have attempted to redefine terms from time to time.

This glossary helps solve the problem by providing short definitions for terms used by the protocols and throughout the Internet. The glossary is not intended as a tutorial for beginners. Instead, we focus on providing a concise reference to make it easy for those who are generally knowledgeable about networking to look up the meaning of specific terms or acronyms quickly. Readers will find it substantially more useful as a reference after they have studied the text than before.

A Glossary of Terms and Abbreviations In Alphabetical Order

10/100/1000 hardware

A term applied to Ethernet hardware that negotiates whether to operate at 10 Mbps, 100 Mbps, or 1 Gbps.

1000Base-T, 1000Base-X

The technical names for Gigabit Ethernet over twisted pair and optical fiber.

10GigE

The name used for Ethernet that operates at 10 Gbps.

127.0.0.1

The IP *loopback* address used for testing. Packets sent to this address are processed by the local protocol software without ever being sent across a network.

1280 (MTU)

The minimum datagram size all IPv6 hosts and routers must handle.

2822 mail

The standard format for electronic mail messages (from RFC 2822).

3-way handshake

The technique used in TCP to start or terminate a connection reliably.

5-layer reference model

The protocol layering model used by TCP/IP. See *7-layer reference model.*

5-tuple

A reference to the five fields needed to identify a TCP connection: source and destination IP addresses, source and destination protocol ports, and the payload type.

576 (MTU)

The minimum datagram size all IPv4 hosts and routers must handle.

6LoWPAN

A standard used to send IPv6 across low-power wireless networks.

7-layer reference model

An older protocol layering model created by ISO. See *5-layer reference model.*

802.11

A prefix for IEEE standards that specify wireless networking. Specific standards include 802.11a, 802.11b, 802.11g, 802.11i, and 802.11n.

802.15.4

An IEEE standard for a low-power wireless network technology.

802.3

The IEEE standard for Ethernet.

ABR

Either *Available Bit Rate*, an ATM designation for service that does not guarantee a rate, or *Area Border Router*, an OSPF designation for a router that communicates with another area.

ACK

Abbreviation for *acknowledgement.*

acknowledgement

A response sent by a receiver to indicate successful reception. Typically, an acknowledgement is sent when a packet arrives.

active open

The operation that a client performs to establish a TCP connection with a server at a known address.

adaptive retransmission

The scheme TCP uses to make the retransmission timer track changes in the round-trip time.

address

An integer value used to identify a particular computer. Each packet sent to the computer contains the address.

address binding

Synonym for address resolution.

address mask

A binary value with 1 bits indicating the network prefix and 0 bits indicating the host suffix. In IPv4, an address mask is 32 bits long; in IPv6, an address mask is 128 bits long.

address resolution

Conversion of a protocol address into a corresponding hardware (MAC) address (e.g., conversion of an IP address into an Ethernet address). See *ARP* and *IPv6-ND*.

ADSL
(*Asymmetric Digital Subscriber Line*) A popular technology for simultaneously sending data over the same wires used for telephone service.

AFRINIC
See *registry*.

agent
In network management, an agent is the server software that runs on a network device that is being managed.

AH
(*Authentication Header*) A header used by IPsec to guarantee the authenticity of a datagram's source.

AIMD
(*Additive Increase Multiplicative Decrease*) A reference to TCP's congestion control mechanism in which the congestion window decreases rapidly and increases slowly.

all routers group
The well-known IP multicast group that includes all routers on the local network.

all systems group
The well-known IP multicast group that includes all hosts and routers on the local network.

anonymous FTP
An FTP session that uses login name *anonymous* to access public files. A server that permits anonymous FTP often allows the password *guest*.

anonymous network
A synonym for *unnumbered network*.

ANSI
(*American National Standards Institute*) An organization that defines U.S. standards for the information processing industry.

anycast
An address form introduced with IPv6 in which a datagram sent to the address can be routed to any of a set of computers. An *anycast address* was originally called a *cluster address*.

API
(*Application Program Interface*) The specification of the interface an application uses. The socket API is the most popular for Internet communication.

APNIC

See *registry*.

area

In OSPF, a group of routers that exchange routing information.

area manager

A person in charge of an IETF area. The set of area managers form the IESG.

ARIN

See *registry*.

ARP

(*Address Resolution Protocol*) The protocol used to dynamically bind an IPv4 address to a hardware (MAC) address. ARP is used across a single physical network and is limited to networks that support hardware broadcast.

ARPA

(*Advanced Research Projects Agency*) The government agency that funded the ARPANET, and later, the global Internet. ARPA is also known as *DARPA*.

ARPANET

A pioneering long haul network funded by ARPA and built by BBN. It served from 1969 through 1990 as the basis for early networking research and as a central backbone during development of the Internet. The ARPANET consisted of individual packet switching nodes interconnected by leased lines.

AS

(*Autonomous System*) A collection of routers and networks that fall under one administrative entity and cooperate closely to propagate network reachability (and routing) information among themselves using an interior gateway protocol of their choice. Routers within an autonomous system have a high degree of trust. Before two autonomous systems can communicate, one router in each system sends reachability information to a router in the other.

ASN.1

(*Abstract Syntax Notation.1*) The ISO presentation standard protocol used by SNMP to represent messages.

ATM

(*Asynchronous Transfer Mode*) A connection-oriented network technology that uses small, fixed-size cells at the lowest layer.

authority zone

A part of the domain name hierarchy in which a single name server is the authority.

autonomous system
See *AS*.

base header
The required header found at the beginning of each IPv6 datagram.

base64
An encoding used with MIME to send non-textual data such as a binary file through email.

baseband
Characteristic of any network technology like Ethernet in which all stations share access to the medium. Compare to *broadband*.

BCP
(*Best Current Practice*) A label given to a subset of RFCs that contain recommendations from the IETF about the use, configuration, and deployment of internet technologies.

Bellman-Ford
A synonym for *distance-vector*.

best-effort delivery
Characteristic of network technologies that do not provide reliability at link levels. IP works well over best-effort delivery hardware because IP does not assume that the underlying network provides reliability. The UDP protocol provides best-effort delivery service to application programs.

BGP
(*Border Gateway Protocol*) The major exterior gateway protocol used in the Internet. Four major versions of BGP have appeared, with BGP-4 being the current.

big endian
A format for storage or transmission of binary data in which the most-significant byte (bit) comes first. The TCP/IP standard network byte order is big endian. Compare to *little endian*.

binary exponential backoff
A technique used to control network contention or congestion quickly. A sender doubles the amount of time it waits between each successive retransmission.

bind
The name of popular commercial DNS software that originally was derived from software in BSD Unix.

bps

(*bits per second*) A measure of the rate of data transmission.

bridge

A device that connects two or more networks and forwards frames among them. Bridges differ from routers because bridges use physical addresses, while routers use IP addresses.

broadband

Characteristic of a network technology that multiplexes multiple, independent network carriers onto a single cable (usually using frequency division multiplexing). Compare to *baseband*.

broadcast

A packet delivery system that delivers a copy of a given packet to all hosts that attach to it is said to *broadcast* the packet. Broadcast can be implemented with hardware (e.g., as in Ethernet) or software (e.g., IP broadcasting in the presence of subnets). See *multicast* and *unicast*.

broadcast and prune

A technique used in data-driven multicast forwarding in which routers forward each datagram to each network until they learn that the network has no group members.

BSD UNIX

(*Berkeley Software Distribution UNIX*) A version of the UNIX operating system modified at U.C. Berkeley to contain TCP/IP protocols.

buffer bloat

A term used to criticize vendors who use incredibly large packet buffers, even in small devices (e.g., a cable modem or a wireless router). Large buffers can cause long delays that impact real-time communication.

care-of address

A temporary IP address used by a mobile while visiting a foreign network.

category 5 cable

The standard for wiring used with twisted pair Ethernet. Variants include *Cat5*, *Cat5e*, and *Cat6*, which each provide more speed than the previous category.

CBT

(*Core Based Trees*) A demand-driven multicast routing protocol that builds shared forwarding trees.

CCITT

(*Consultative Committee on International Telephony and Telegraphy*) The former name of the ITU.

cell

A small, fixed-size packet. An ATM cell contains 48 octets of data and 5 octets of header.

CGI

(*Common Gateway Interface*) A technology a server uses to create a web page dynamically when the request arrives.

checksum

A small integer value sent with a packet and used to detect errors that can result when a packet is transmitted from one machine to another.

CIDR

(*Classless Inter-Domain Routing*) The standard that specifies the details of both classless addressing and an associated routing scheme.

CL network

See *connectionless service.*

class of address

In classful addressing, the class of an address determines the location of the boundary between network prefix and host suffix.

classful addressing

The original IPv4 addressing scheme in which host addresses were divided into three classes: A, B, and C.

classless addressing

An extension of the original IPv4 addressing scheme that ignores the original class boundaries to make better use of the address space.

client-server

The model of interaction in a distributed system in which a client program on one computer sends a request to a server program on another computer and awaits a response.

closed window

A situation in TCP where a receiver has sent a window advertisement of size zero because no additional buffer space is available. When space becomes available, the receiver opens the window again.

CO

See *connection-oriented service.*

codec
(*coder/decoder*) A hardware device used to convert between an analog audio signal and a stream of digital values.

congestion
A situation in which traffic (temporarily) exceeds the capacity of networks or routers.

connection
An abstraction provided by protocol software. TCP provides a connection from one application program to another.

connection-oriented service
Characteristic of the service offered by any networking technology in which communicating parties first establish communication and then send data. TCP provides connection-oriented service as does ATM hardware.

connectionless service
Characteristic of the service offered by any networking technology in which each message or packet identifies the destination and is handled independently. Both IP and UDP provide connectionless service.

COPS
(*Common Open Policy Service*) A protocol used with RSVP to verify whether a request meets policy constraints.

CoS
(*Class of Service*) The designation assigned to a packet that determines its priority and how it is routed.

count to infinity
An informal name for the *slow convergence* problem.

CR-LF
(*Carriage Return - Line Feed*) The two-character sequence used to terminate each line of text in application layer protocols such as TELNET and SMTP.

CRC
(*Cyclic Redundancy Code*) A small, integer value sent with a packet that is used to detect transmission errors. Also see *checksum.*

CSMA/CA
(*Carrier Sense Multiple Access with Collision Avoidance*) A characteristic of network hardware that operates by allowing multiple stations to contend for access to a transmission medium by listening to see if the medium is idle and by sending a short reservation message to inform other stations before transmitting data. 802.11 wireless networks use CSMA/CA.

CSMA/CD
(*Carrier Sense Multiple Access with Collision Detection*) The original access control scheme used with Ethernet and now replaced with Ethernet switching.

CSU/DSU
(*Channel Service Unit/Data Service Unit*) An electronic device that connects a computer or router to a digital circuit leased by the telephone company. Although the device fills two roles, it usually consists of a single physical piece of hardware.

cumulative acknowledgement
The acknowledgement scheme used by TCP in which an acknowledgement reports the point in a stream at which data has been received successfully. See *SACK*.

DARPA
(*Defense Advanced Research Projects Agency*) The government agency that funded the ARPANET, and later, the global Internet. DARPA is also known as *ARPA*.

datagram
See *IP datagram.*

DCE
(*Data Communications Equipment*) Equipment in the network, as opposed to user's equipment that attaches to the network. See *DTE*.

default free zone
The core of the Internet in which default routing is prohibited.

default route
A single entry in a list of routes that covers all destinations which are not included explicitly. The routing tables in most routers and hosts contain an entry for a default route.

delay
One of the two primary measures of a network. Delay refers to the difference between the time a bit of data is injected into a network and the time the bit exits.

delayed acknowledgement
A heuristic employed by a receiving TCP to avoid silly window syndrome.

demultiplex

To separate from a common input into several outputs. Demultiplexing occurs at each layer of the protocol stack. See *multiplex*.

DHCP

(*Dynamic Host Configuration Protocol*) A protocol that a host uses to obtain configuration information including an IP address, the address of a router, and the address of a domain name server.

DiffServ

(*Differentiated Services*) The definition used for type-of-service in an IP datagram. DiffServ uses six bits in the IP header.

dig

An application program used by network managers to query the Domain Name System.

directed broadcast address

An IPv4 address that specifies all hosts on a specific network. Use of directed broadcast is discouraged.

distance-vector

A class of routing update protocols in which each participating router sends its neighbors a list of networks it can reach and the distance to each network. See *link-state*.

DNS

(*Domain Name System*) The system used to map human-readable machine names into IP addresses. DNS uses a hierarchy of servers.

DNS-SD

(*Domain Name System Service Discovery*) A protocol that uses mDNS to find a service.

DNSSEC

(*Domain Name System SECurity*) A set of security extensions for the Domain Name System.

domain name

A name consisting of a sequence of labels separated by periods (dots). Each computer in the Internet is assigned a unique domain name.

Domain Name System

See *DNS*.

dotted decimal notation

A syntactic form used to represent 32-bit binary integers. Four 8-bit values are written in base 10 with periods (dots) separating them.

dotted hex notation

A syntactic form used to represent binary values that consists of hexadecimal values for each 8-bit quantity with dots separating them.

dotted quad notation

A syntactic form used to represent binary values that consists of hexadecimal values for each 16-bit quantity with dots separating them.

DPI

(*Deep Packet Inspection*) A security mechanism that considers items that lie in the payload area of a packet as well as the header.

DRR

(*Deficit Round Robin*) An algorithm used for traffic shaping.

DSL

(*Digital Subscriber Line*) A set of technologies used to provide high-speed data service over the copper wires that connect between telephone offices and local residences or businesses.

DTE

(*Data Terminal Equipment*) Equipment that attaches to a network, as opposed to equipment that forms the network. Also see *DCE*.

DVMRP

(*Distance Vector Multicast Routing Protocol*) A protocol used to propagate multicast routes.

E.164

An address format specified by ITU.

echo request and reply

A type of message that is used to test network connectivity. The *ping* program uses ICMP echo request and reply messages.

ECN

(*Explicit Congestion Notification*) A mechanism that allows a router to inform end systems when a packet encounters congestion.

EF

(*Expedited Forwarding*) A DiffServ class for high-priority packets.

EGP
(*Exterior Gateway Protocol*) A term applied to any protocol used by a router in one autonomous system to advertise network reachability to a router in another autonomous system. BGP-4 is currently the most widely used exterior gateway protocol.

encapsulation
The technique used by layered protocols in which a lower-level protocol accepts a message from a higher-level protocol and places it in the data portion of the low-level packet.

end-to-end
Characteristic of any mechanism that provides communication from the original source to the final destination. Protocols like TCP are classified as end-to-end.

epoch date
A point in history chosen as the date from which time is measured. TCP/IP uses January 1, 1900, Universal Time (formerly called Greenwich Mean Time) as its epoch date.

ESP
(*Encapsulating Security Payload*) A packet format used by IPsec to send encrypted information.

Ethernet
A popular local area network technology originally invented at the Xerox Corporation's Palo Alto Research Center. Ethernet is a best-effort delivery system that uses CSMA/CD technology.

EUI-64
A 64-bit IEEE Layer 2 addressing standard.

exponential backoff
See *binary exponential backoff*.

extension header
Any of the optional IPv6 headers that follows the base header.

Exterior Gateway Protocol
See *EGP*.

eXternal Data Representation
See *XDR*.

extra hop problem
An error condition in which communication is possible, but each datagram takes an extra, unnecessary trip across a network.

fair queueing

A well-known technique for traffic scheduling that is used in routers. See *WRR*.

FDM

(*Frequency Division Multiplexing*) The method of passing multiple, independent signals across a single medium by assigning each a unique carrier frequency. Hardware to combine signals is called a multiplexor; hardware to separate them is called a demultiplexor. Also see *TDM*.

FIB

(*Forwarding Information Base*) The data collected by routing protocols and used to build a forwarding table.

file server

An application program that provides remote clients with access to files. The term is also used for the computer that runs the file server application.

FIN

A type of TCP segment. To close a connection, each side must send a FIN.

firewall

A mechanism placed between an organization's internal intranet and the Internet to provide security.

fixed-length subnetting

A subnet address assignment scheme in which all physical nets in an organization use the same mask. The alternative is *variable-length subnetting*.

flat namespace

Characteristic of any naming scheme in which object names are selected from a single set of strings (e.g., street names in a typical city).

flow

A term used to characterize a sequence of packets sent from a source to a destination. Some networking technologies define a separate flow for each pair of communicating applications, while others define a single flow to include all packets between a pair of hosts. See *5-tuple*.

flow control

Control exerted by a receiver, typically in a transport protocol, to limit the rate at which a sender transfers data.

Ford-Fulkerson algorithm

A synonym for the distance-vector algorithm that refers to the researchers who discovered it.

forwarding

The process of accepting an incoming packet, looking up a next hop in a routing table, and sending the packet on to the next hop.

forwarding loop

An error condition in which a cycle of routers each has the next router in the cycle as the shortest path to a given destination. Also known as a *routing loop*.

fragment extension header

An optional header used by IPv6 to mark a datagram as a fragment.

fragmentation

The process of dividing an IP datagram into smaller pieces. A router fragments a datagram when the network MTU is smaller than the datagram; the ultimate destination reassembles fragments.

frame

A term for a Layer 2 packet derived from early protocols that added special start-of-frame and end-of-frame markers when transmitting a packet.

Frame Relay

The name of an older connection-oriented network technology offered by telephone companies.

FTP

(*File Transfer Protocol*) A standard application layer protocol for file transfer.

full duplex

Characteristic of a technology that allows simultaneous transfer of data in two directions.

FYI

(*For Your Information*) A subset of the RFCs that contain tutorials or general information about topics related to TCP/IP or the connected Internet.

gated

(*gateway daemon*) A program that runs on a router and interconnects multiple routing protocols, often an IGP and an EGP.

gateway

Any mechanism that connects two or more heterogeneous systems and translates among them. Originally, researchers used the term *IP gateway*; vendors adopted *IP router*.

Gbps
(*Giga bits per second*) A measure of the rate of data transmission equal to 10^9 bits per second. Also see *Kbps* and *Mbps*.

GigE
(*Gigabit Ethernet*) An Ethernet technology that operates at 1 Gbps.

graceful shutdown
A protocol mechanism that allows two communicating parties to agree to terminate communication without confusion even if underlying packets are lost, delayed, or duplicated. TCP uses a 3-way handshake to guarantee graceful shutdown.

GRE
(*Generic Routing Encapsulation*) A scheme for encapsulating information in IP that includes IP-in-IP as one possibility.

H.323
An ITU recommendation for a suite of protocols used for IP telephony.

half duplex
Characteristic of a technology that only permits data transmission in one direction at a time. Compare to *full duplex*.

hardware address
An address used by a physical network (e.g., Ethernet uses a 48-bit hardware address). Synonyms include *physical address* and *MAC address*.

header
Information at the beginning of a packet or message that describes the contents and specifies a destination.

HELO
The command on the initial exchange of the SMTP protocol.

hierarchical addressing
An addressing scheme in which an address can be subdivided into parts that each identify successively finer granularity. IPv4 and IPv6 both use a two-level hierarchy in which the first part of an address identifies a network and the second part identifies a particular host on that network. Subnetting can be used to introduce additional levels of addressing hierarchy.

historic
An IETF classification used to discourage the use of a protocol. In essence, a protocol that is declared historic is obsolete.

hold down

A short, fixed time period following a change to a routing table during which no further changes are accepted. Hold down helps avoid forwarding loops.

hop count

A measure of distance between two points in the Internet. A hop count of *n* means that *n* networks separate the source and destination.

hop limit

The IPv6 name for the datagram header field that IPv4 originally called *time to live*. Now applied to IPv4 as well. The hop limit prevents datagrams from following a forwarding loop forever.

hop-by-hop

A reference to processing that is performed at each router (as opposed to end-to-end). IPv6 classifies some extension headers as hop-by-hop

host

The TCP/IP term for an end-user computer system. In addition to desktop systems, hosts include devices such as printers, laptops, and small embedded systems. Compare to *IP router*.

host requirements

RFC documents that specify revisions and updates of many TCP/IP protocols. See *router requirements*.

host-specific route

An entry in a routing table that refers to a single host computer as opposed to routes that refer to a network, an IP subnet, or a default.

HTML

(*HyperText Markup Language*) The standard document format used for web pages.

HTTP

(*HyperText Transfer Protocol*) The protocol used to transfer web documents from a server to a browser.

HTTPS

(*HyperText Transfer Protocol with Security*) A secure version of HTTP.

IAB

(*Internet Architecture Board*) A group of people in the IETF who set policy and direction for TCP/IP protocols. The IAB was originally known as the *Internet Activities Board*. See *IETF*.

IANA

(*Internet Assigned Numbers Authority*) The group responsible for assigning values used in protocols.

ICANN

(*Internet Corporation For Assigned Names and Numbers*) A group responsible for setting policy and coordinating registries that assign IP addresses.

ICMP

(*Internet Control Message Protocol*) An integral part of the Internet Protocol (IP) that handles error and control messages (e.g., *ping*). Routers and hosts use ICMP to send reports of problems about datagrams back to the original source that sent the datagram.

ICMPv6

(*Internet Control Message Protocol version 6*) The version of ICMP that has been defined for use with IPv6.

identifier-locator split

The idea that to support mobility, an IP address must be divided into a piece that identifies a node and a piece that specifies where the node is presently located.

IEEE

(*Institute of Electrical and Electronic Engineers*) A professional society that publishes standards for many Local Area networks, such as Ethernet.

IESG

(*Internet Engineering Steering Group*) A committee consisting of the IETF chairperson and the area managers that charters working groups and approves RFCs.

IETF

(*Internet Engineering Task Force*) A group of people under the IAB who work on the design and engineering of TCP/IP and the global Internet. The IETF is divided into areas, which are further subdivided into working groups.

IGMP

(*Internet Group Management Protocol*) A protocol that hosts use to keep local routers apprised of their membership in multicast groups. IGMPv3 refers to the current version (3).

IGP

(*Interior Gateway Protocol*) The generic term applied to any protocol used to propagate network reachability and routing information within an autonomous system.

IMAP
(*Internet Message Access Protocol*) A protocol used to transfer email messages between a user's mailbox and an agent that the user runs to read email. A secure version is named IMAPS. See *SMTP*.

inter-autonomous system routing
A synonym for exterior routing. See *BGP* and *CIDR*.

inter-domain routing
A synonym for exterior routing. See *BGP* and *CIDR*.

Interior Gateway Protocol
See *IGP*.

International Organization for Standardization
See *ISO*.

International Telecommunications Union
See *ITU*.

Internet
A collection of data networks around the world that are interconnected by routers and use TCP/IP protocols to function as a single, large, virtual network.

Internet address
See *IP address*.

Internet draft
A draft document generated by the IETF; if approved, the document will become an RFC.

Internet of Things
A reference to a shift from early Internet applications that provided communication for humans to new services that connect embedded systems, such as sensors.

Internet Protocol
See *IP*.

interoperability
The ability of software and hardware on multiple machines from multiple vendors to communicate efficiently, reliably, and meaningfully.

intranet
A private corporate network consisting of hosts, routers, and networks that use TCP/IP technology. Most corporate intranets connect to the Internet.

IntServ

(*Integrated Services*) The original effort to add QoS to TCP/IP. See *DiffServ*.

IP

(*Internet Protocol*) The protocol in the TCP/IP suite that defines the connectionless, best-effort packet delivery service that forms the basis for the Internet. The term can refer to version 4 or 6 (IPv4 or IPv6).

IP address

A binary number assigned to each host in the Internet. An IPv4 address is 32 bits long; an IPv6 address is 128 bits.

IP datagram

The basic unit of information passed across a TCP/IP internet analogous to a hardware packet. Each datagram contains the addresses of the original sender and ultimate destination.

IP gateway

The term originally used for *IP router*.

IP multicast

An addressing and forwarding scheme that allows transmission of IP datagrams to a subset of hosts. The Internet currently does not have extensive facilities to handle IP multicast.

IP router

A special purpose network system that connects two or more (possibly heterogeneous) networks and passes IP traffic between them.

IP switching

Originally, a high-speed IP forwarding technology developed by Ipsilon Corporation, now generally used in reference to any of several similar technologies.

IP telephony

A telephone system that uses IP to transport digitized voice. See *VoIP*.

IP-in-IP

The encapsulation of one IP datagram inside another for transmission through a tunnel. IP-in-IP is used with VPNs and IPv6.

IPng

(*Internet Protocol — the next generation*) An older term used for *IPv6*.

IPsec

(*IP security*) A security standard used with either IPv4 or IPv6 to allow a sender to authenticate or encrypt a datagram.

IPv4

(*Internet Protocol version 4*) A reference to the original version of IP defined in 1978 and used as the basis for the global Internet. IPv4 is being replaced by IPv6.

IPv6

(*Internet Protocol version 6*) A reference to the version of IP defined in the 1990s as a successor to IPv4.

IPv6 migration

A reference to the change from an IPv4 Internet to an IPv6 Internet. Several strategies have been proposed, including the use of dual stacks (each computer runs both IPv4 and IPv6) and translation (a device at the boundary between an IPv4 network and an IPv6 network sends the payload from one type of datagram in a datagram of the other type).

IPv6-ND

(*IPv6 Neighbor Discovery*) A support protocol that an IPv6 node uses to identify other nodes attached to the same network and learn their MAC addresses. See *ARP*.

IRTF

(*Internet Research Task Force*) A relatively inactive group parallel to the IETF.

IS-IS

(*Intermediate System to Intermediate System*) A routing protocol designed for OSI, but later modified for use with TCP/IP.

ISO

(*International Organization for Standardization*) An international body that drafts, discusses, proposes, and specifies standards for network protocols. ISO is best known for its 7-layer reference model that describes the conceptual organization of protocols.

isochronous

Characteristic of a network system that does not introduce jitter. The conventional telephone system is isochronous.

ISP

(*Internet Service Provider*) Any organization that sells Internet access, either permanent connectivity or dialup access.

ITU

(*International Telecommunication Union*) An international organization that sets standards for interconnection of telephone equipment.

IXP
(*Internet eXchange Point*) A physical location at which ISPs connect. See *NAP* and *peering agreement*.

jitter
A term used to describe unwanted variance in delay caused when one packet in a sequence must be delayed more than another. Jitter can result when routers in a packet switching network experience congestion.

Karn's Algorithm
An algorithm that allows transport protocols to distinguish between valid and invalid round-trip time samples, and thus, improve round-trip estimations.

Kbps
(*Kilo bits per second*) A measure of the rate of data transmission equal to 10^3 bits per second. Also see *Gbps* and *Mbps*.

keepalive
A small message sent periodically between two communicating entities to ensure that network connectivity remains intact and that both sides are still responding.

LACNIC
See *registry*.

LAN
(*Local Area Network*) Any physical network technology designed to span short distances (up to a few thousand meters). See *WAN*.

Layer 1
A reference to the lowest layer in a layering model. Layer 1 includes physical connections and voltages on wires.

Layer 2
A reference to the second lowest layer in a layering model. Layer 2 includes frame format and addressing.

Layer 3
A reference to the IP layer that provides internetworking.

Layer 4
A reference to the transport layer that includes TCP and UDP.

link-state
A class of routing update protocols in which each participating router broadcasts status messages and each router uses Dijkstra's SPF algorithm to compute shortest routes to each destination. See *distance-vector*.

link-status

A synonym for *link-state*.

link-local address

An address used with IPv6 that has significance only on a single network.

LIS

(*Logical IP Subnet*) A term used when IP runs over ATM to describe a virtual network that has a single IP prefix.

little endian

A format for storage or transmission of binary data in which the least-significant byte (bit) comes first. See *big endian*.

logical subnet

See *LIS*.

long haul network

Older term for *WAN*.

longest-prefix match

See *LPM*.

loopback address

A network address used for testing that causes outgoing packets to be delivered to the local machine. IP uses 127.0.0.0/8 as the loopback prefix, so 127.0.0.1 is a loopback address.

LPM

(*Longest-Prefix Match*) The technique used when searching a routing table that chooses an entry with the largest prefix that matches the target address.

LSP

(*Label Switched Path*) A path through a series of LSRs that run MPLS.

LSR

(*Loose Source Route* also *Label Switching Router*) Loose Source Route is an IP option that contains a list of router addresses that the datagram must visit in order. The datagram may also be forwarded to additional intermediate stops. A Label Switching Router is a router that has facilities to forward MPLS traffic. Usually, such a router also handles conventional IP forwarding, and can be configured to transfer packets between MPLS and conventional IP. A Label Switching Router uses labels instead of addresses when forwarding datagrams. See *SSR* and *MPLS*.

MABR
(*Multicast Area Border Router*) The MOSPF term for a multicast router that exchanges routing information with another area.

MAC
(*Media Access Control*) A general reference to the low-level hardware protocols used to access a particular network. The term *MAC address* is often used as a synonym for *physical address*.

mail exchanger
A computer that accepts email. DNS has a separate lookup type for mail exchangers.

Management Information Base
See *MIB*.

mask
See *address mask*.

maximum transfer unit
See *MTU*.

MBONE
(*Multicast backBONE*) A cooperative agreement among sites to forward multicast datagrams across the Internet by use of IP tunneling.

Mbps
(*Millions of bits per second*) A measure of the rate of data transmission equal to 10^6 bits per second. Also see *Gbps* and *Kbps*.

mDNS
(*multicast DNS*) A mechanism that uses IP multicast to allow a host to find another host's IP address or the addresses of hosts that offer a service.

mesh network
A type of network in which a set of nodes establishes point-to-point links between pairs of nodes and agrees to forward packets on behalf of other nodes. A mesh is typically used for a wireless network.

mesh-under
An approach to building mesh networks that uses Layer 2 protocols to forward packets. See *route-over*.

MIB
(*Management Information Base*) The set of variables (database) that a system running an SNMP agent maintains. Managers can fetch or store into MIB variables.

MIME

(*Multipurpose Internet Mail Extensions*) A standard used to encode data such as images as printable ASCII text for transmission through email.

MLS

(Multi-Layer Switching) An IP switching technology offered by Cisco Systems.

mobile IP

A technology developed by the IETF to permit a computer to travel to a new site while retaining its original IP address.

MOSPF

(*Multicast Open Shortest Path First*) Multicast extensions to the OSPF routing protocol.

MPLS

(*Multi-Protocol Label Switching*) A technology that uses high-speed switching hardware to carry IP datagrams. MPLS is derived from IP switching.

mrouted

(*multicast route daemon*) A program used with a protocol stack that supports IP multicast to establish multicast forwarding.

MSL

(*Maximum Segment Lifetime*) The longest time a datagram can survive in the Internet. Protocols use the MSL to guarantee a bound on the time duplicate packets can survive.

MSS

(*Maximum Segment Size*) A value negotiated when using TCP that specifies the largest amount of data that can be transmitted in one segment.

MTU

(*Maximum Transmission Unit*) The largest amount of data that can be transferred across a given physical network in a single packet.

multi-homed host

A TCP/IP host that has connections to two or more physical networks.

multicast

A technique that allows copies of a single packet to be passed to a selected subset of all possible destinations. Some hardware (e.g., Ethernet) supports multicast. See *broadcast* and *unicast*.

multiplex

To combine data from several sources into a single stream in such a way that it can be separated again later. See *demultiplex*.

multiplicative decrease

A technique used by TCP to reduce transmission when congestion occurs. The size of the effective window is reduced by half each time a segment is lost.

MX record

(*Mail eXchanger record*) A type of DNS record used to store the address of a mail server for a given domain.

NACK

(*Negative ACKnowledgment*) A message returned to deny a request.

Nagle algorithm

A self-clocking heuristic that clumps outgoing data to improve throughput and avoid silly window syndrome.

name resolution

The process of mapping a name into a corresponding address. The Domain Name System provides a mechanism for naming computers in which programs use remote name servers to resolve a machine name into an IP address.

NAP

(*Network Access Point*) A physical location where ISPs interconnect networks. Also see *IXP*.

NAPT

(*Network Address and Port Translation*) The most popular form of NAT in which protocol port numbers and IP addresses are used in the translation.

NAT

(*Network Address Translation*) A technology that allows hosts using private addresses to communicate with an arbitrary destination on the Internet.

net 10 address

A general reference to a nonroutable address (i.e., one that is reserved for use in an intranet and not used on the Internet).

network byte order

The TCP/IP standard for transmission of integers that specifies the most significant byte appears first (big endian).

network management

See *MIB* and *SNMP*.

Next Header
A field used in IPv6 to specify the type of the item that follows.

next-hop forwarding
The paradigm used in the Internet where each router only knows how to forward a packet one hop.

NFS
(*Network File System*) A protocol that uses UDP to allow a set of cooperating computers to access each other's file systems.

NIC
(*Network Interface Card*) A hardware device that plugs into the bus on a computer and connects the computer to a network.

NOC
(*Network Operations Center*) Originally, the organization at BBN that monitored and controlled several networks that formed part of the Internet. Now, used for any organization that manages a network.

nonroutable address
Any address using a prefix reserved for use in intranets. Routers in the Internet will not forward datagrams that contain a nonroutable address. See *net 10 address*.

NVT
(*Network Virtual Terminal*) The character-oriented protocol used by TELNET.

OC series standards
A series of standards for the transmission of data over optical fiber. For example, OC-48 has a bit rate of approximately 2.5 gigabits per second.

octet
An 8-bit unit of data. Although engineers frequently use the term *byte* as a synonym for octet, a byte can be smaller or larger than 8 bits.

off link
Two IPv6 nodes that share a prefix but are not directly connected. Most often, the term refers to a mesh network. See *on link*.

on link
Two IPv6 nodes that share a prefix and are directly connected. See *off link*.

one-armed router
An IP router that understands two addressing domains, but only has one physical network connection. Also called a *one-armed firewall*.

OpenFlow
A protocol used to implement Software Defined Networking. See *SDN*.

OSPF
(*Open Shortest Path First*) A link-state routing protocol designed by the IETF.

OUI
(*Organizationally Unique Identifier*) Part of an address assigned to an organization that manufactures network hardware; the organization assigns a unique address to each device by using its OUI plus a suffix number.

out-of-band data
Data sent outside the normal delivery path, often used to carry abnormal or error indicators (e.g., TCP's *urgent data*).

P2P
(*Peer to Peer*) A paradigm applications use to propagate information quickly, in which each client agrees to act as a server and make information available to other clients.

packet
A small unit of data sent across a packet switching network.

packet filter
A mechanism in a router that can be configured to reject some types of packets and admit others. Packet filters are used to create a security firewall.

PAR
(*Positive Acknowledgement with Retransmission*) The paradigm protocols use to achieve reliable data transport.

passive open
The operation that a server performs to wait at a known port for a TCP connection.

path MTU
The minimum MTU along a path from the source to destination (i.e., the size of the largest datagram that can be sent along the path without fragmentation).

PCM
(*Pulse Code Modulation*) A standard for voice encoding used in digital telephony that produces 8000 8-bit samples per second.

PDU
(*Protocol Data Unit* also *Packet Data Unit*) An ISO term for packet that was adopted for use with SNMP messages.

peering agreement

A cooperative agreement between two ISPs to exchange both reachability information and data packets. In addition to peering at IXPs, large ISPs often have private peering agreements.

perimeter security

A network security mechanism that places a firewall at each connection between a site and outside networks.

physical address

A synonym for *MAC address* or *hardware address.*

PIM-DM

(*Protocol Independent Multicast Dense Mode*) A multicast routing protocol.

PIM-SM

(*Protocol Independent Multicast Sparse Mode*) A multicast routing protocol that uses an approach similar to CBT.

ping

(*Packet InterNet Groper*) The name of a program used with TCP/IP internets to test reachability of destinations by sending them an ICMP echo request and waiting for a reply. The term is now used like a verb as in, "please *ping* host *A* to see if it is alive."

playback point

The minimum amount of data required in a jitter buffer before playback can begin.

PoE

(*Power over Ethernet*) A technology used with IP telephones to supply power over the same cable used for an Ethernet connection.

point-to-point network

Any network technology that connects exactly two machines (e.g., a leased circuit or dialup connection).

poison reverse

A heuristic used by distance-vector protocols such as RIP to avoid forwarding loops.

POP

(*Post Office Protocol*) A protocol used to access and extract email from a mailbox. The current version is POP3, and a secure version is named POP3S.

port

See *protocol port.*

POS
(*Packet Over SONET*) The method used to send packets over a SONET network.

positive acknowledgement
Synonym for *acknowledgement*.

POTS
(*Plain Old Telephone Service*) A reference to the standard voice telephone system.

PPP
(*Point to Point Protocol*) A protocol for framing when sending IP datagrams across a serial line.

PPPoE
A version of the Point to Point Protocol used over Ethernet.

promiscuous mode
A feature of network interface hardware that allows a computer to receive all packets on the network.

protocol
A formal description of message formats and the rules two or more machines must follow to exchange messages.

protocol port
TCP/IP transport protocols use the protocol port abstraction to distinguish among multiple applications within a given host computer. TCP and UDP use small integers as port numbers.

provider prefix
An addressing scheme in which an ISP owns a network prefix and assigns each customer addresses that begin with the prefix.

provisioned service
A service that is configured manually.

proxy
Any device or system that acts in place of another (e.g., a proxy web server acts in place of another web server).

proxy ARP
The technique in which one machine, usually a router, answers ARP requests intended for another by supplying its own physical address. Proxy ARP allows multiple networks to share a single IP prefix.

pseudo-header

Additional information used in a TCP or UDP checksum computation, but not present in the UDP datagram or TCP segment. A pseudo-header includes source and destination IP addresses.

PSTN

(*Public Switched Telephone Network*) The standard voice telephone system.

public key encryption

An encryption technique that generates encryption keys in pairs. One of the pair must be kept secret, and one is published.

push

The operation an application performs on a TCP connection to force data to be sent immediately. A bit in the segment header marks pushed data.

PVC

(*Permanent Virtual Circuit*) The type of ATM virtual circuit established by an administrator rather than by software in a computer. See *SVC*.

QoS

(*Quality of Service*) Bounds on the loss, delay, jitter, and minimum throughput that a network guarantees to deliver.

RARP

(*Reverse ARP*) An old protocol used to obtain an IPv4 address; now being used in data centers to inform a switch about virtual machine migration.

RDP

(*Remote Desktop Protocol*) A protocol defined by Microsoft that provides a remote desktop capability for their operating systems.

reachability

A destination is *reachable* from a given source if a route exists from the source to the destination.

reassembly

The process of collecting all the fragments of an IP datagram and using them to create a copy of the original datagram. The ultimate destination performs reassembly.

RED

(*Random Early Detection*) A technique routers use instead of tail-drop to manage buffers when memory begins to fill. See *tail-drop*.

redirect

An ICMP message sent from a router to a host on a local network to instruct the host to change a route.

reference model

A description of how layered protocols fit together. TCP/IP uses a 5-layer reference model; earlier protocols used the ISO 7-layer reference model.

registry

An organization authorized to assign blocks of IP addresses. The registries include: AFRINIC, APNIC, ARIN, LACNIC, and RIPE.

reliable transfer

Characteristic of a mechanism that guarantees to deliver data without loss, without corruption, without duplication, and in the same order as it was sent, or to inform the sender that delivery is impossible.

replay

An error situation in which packets from a previous session are erroneously accepted as part of a later session.

reserved address

A synonym for *nonroutable address*.

reset (TCP)

A segment sent by TCP in response to an error condition such as a malformed incoming segment or an incoming segment for which the receiver has no record of a connection.

resolution

See *address resolution*

RFC

(*Request For Comments*) The name of a series of documents that contain surveys, measurements, ideas, techniques, and observations, as well as proposed and accepted TCP/IP protocol standards. RFCs are available on-line.

RIP

(*Routing Information Protocol*) A protocol used to propagate routing information inside an autonomous system.

RIPE

See *registry*.

round trip time

See *RTT*.

route
The path that network traffic takes from source to destination.

route aggregation
The technique used by routing protocols to combine multiple destinations that have the same next hop into a single entry.

route-over
An approach to building mesh networks that uses Layer 3 protocols to forward packets. See *mesh-under.*

routed
(*route daemon*) A UNIX program that implements the RIP protocol. Pronounced "route-d."

router
See *IP router*.

router requirements
A document that contains updates to TCP/IP protocols used in routers. See *host requirements.*

routing loop
An error condition in which a cycle of routers each has the next router in the cycle as the shortest path to a given destination. Also known as a *forwarding loop*.

RPC
(*Remote Procedure Call*) A technology in which a program invokes services across a network by making modified procedure calls.

RPF
(*Reverse Path Forwarding*) A technique used to propagate broadcast packets that ensures there are no forwarding loops. IP uses reverse path forwarding to propagate subnet broadcast and multicast datagrams.

RPM
(*Reverse Path Multicast*) A general approach to multicasting that uses the TRPB algorithm.

RST
(*ReSeT*) An abbreviation for a TCP *reset* segment.

RSVP
(*Resource ReserVation Protocol*) The protocol that allows an endpoint to request a flow with specific QoS; each router along the path to the destination must agree to approve the request.

RTCP

(*RTP Control Protocol*) The companion protocol to RTP used to control a session.

RTO

(*Round-trip Time-Out*) The time a protocol waits before retransmitting a packet. See *RTT*.

RTP

(*Real-time Transport Protocol*) The primary protocol used to transfer real-time data such as voice and video over the Internet.

RTT

(*Round Trip Time*) The total time taken for a single packet or datagram to leave one computer, reach another, and return.

SA

(*Security Association*) Used with IPsec to denote a binding between a set of security parameters and an identifier carried in a datagram header. A host chooses SA bindings; they are not globally standardized. See *SPI*.

SACK

(*Selective ACKnowledgement*) An optional addition to the TCP acknowledgement mechanism that allows a receiver to specify which segments have been received. Compare with *cumulative acknowledgement*.

scoped address

A term used with IPv6 to refer to an address that is limited to a link, a site, or an organization.

scp

(*secure copy program*) A program that operates like the Unix copy command, *cp*, except that *scp* can transfer files from one computer to another and use encryption to keep the transfer secure.

SDN

(*Software Defined Networking*) The separation of the control plane from the data plane of a network device to permit an external controller to specify forwarding.

SDR

(*Software Defined Radio*) An approach analogous to SDN that allows software to set radio characteristics, such as frequency and modulation.

Security Association

See SA.

segment
The unit of transfer used by TCP.

selective acknowledgement
See *SACK*.

self clocking
Characteristic of any system that operates periodically without requiring an external clock (e.g., uses the arrival of a packet to trigger an action).

server
An application program that supplies service to clients over a network.

shortest path first
See *SPF*.

signaling
A telephony term that refers to protocols which establish a circuit.

silly window syndrome
A condition that can arise in TCP in which the receiver repeatedly advertises a small window and the sender repeatedly sends a small segment to fill it.

SIP
(*Session Initiation Protocol*) A protocol devised by the IETF for signaling in IP telephony.

sliding window
Characteristic of a protocol that allows a sender to transmit more than one packet of data before receiving an acknowledgement. The number of outstanding packets or bytes is known as the window size; increasing the window size improves throughput.

slow convergence
A problem in distance-vector protocols in which two or more routers form a forwarding loop that persists until the routing protocols increment the distance to infinity.

slow start
A congestion avoidance scheme in TCP in which TCP increases its window size as ACKs arrive.

SMTP
(*Simple Mail Transfer Protocol*) The TCP/IP standard protocol for transferring electronic mail messages from one machine to another.

SNAP
(*SubNetwork Attachment Point*) An IEEE standard for a small header placed in the data area of a frame to specify the data type.

SNMP
(*Simple Network Management Protocol*) A protocol used to manage devices such as hosts, routers, and printers. Also see *MIB*.

SOA
(*Start Of Authority*) A keyword used with DNS to denote the beginning of the records for which a particular server is the authority.

socket API
The definition of an interface between application programs and TCP/IP software.

soft state
A technique in which a receiver times out information rather than depending on the sender to maintain it.

Software Defined Networking
See *SDN*.

Software Defined Radio
See *SDR*.

source quench
An ICMP message sent back to the source when datagrams overrun a router.

source route
A route that is determined by the source and specified as a list of specific intermediate routers the packet should visit. See *LSR* and *SSR*.

SPF
(*Shortest Path First*) A class of routing update protocols that uses Dijkstra's algorithm to compute shortest paths. See *link-state*.

SPI
(*Security Parameters Index*) The identifier IPsec uses to specify the *Security Association* (*SA*) that should be used to process a datagram.

split horizon
A heuristic used by distance-vector protocols such as RIP to avoid forwarding loops.

SS7
(*Signaling System 7*) The conventional telephone system standard used for signaling.

ssh
(*secure shell*) An alternative to TELNET that uses encryption to keep sessions confidential.

SSL
(*Secure Sockets Layer*) A de facto standard for secure communication originally created by Netscape, Inc.

SSR
(*Strict Source Route*) An IPv4 option that contains a list of router addresses that the datagram must visit in order. See *LSR*.

standard byte order
See *network byte order*.

STD
(*STanDard*) The designation used to classify a particular RFC as describing a standard protocol.

store-and-forward
The paradigm used by packet switching systems in which an incoming packet is stored in memory until it can be forwarded on toward its destination.

subnet addressing
An extension of the IP addressing scheme that allows a site to use a single IP network address for multiple physical networks.

subnet mask
See *address mask*.

SubNetwork Attachment Point
See *SNAP*.

supernet addressing
Another name for *CIDR*.

SVC
(*Switched Virtual Circuit*) The type of ATM virtual circuit established when needed by software rather than by an administrator.

SWS
See *silly window syndrome*.

SYN
(*SYNchronizing segment*) The first segment sent by the TCP protocol, it is used to synchronize the two ends of a connection in preparation for opening a connection.

tail-drop

A policy routers use to manage buffers by discarding all packets that arrive after memory is full. See *RED*.

TCP

(*Transmission Control Protocol*) The TCP/IP standard transport layer protocol that provides the reliable, full duplex, stream service on which many application protocols depend.

TCP splicing

A technique in which an intermediate system rewrites TCP segments to map from one sequence space to another. The technique is used in systems that establish two TCP connections and then map one into the other so neither endpoint is aware of the splice.

TCP/IP Internet Protocol Suite

The official name of the TCP/IP protocols.

TDM

(*Time Division Multiplexing*) A technique used to multiplex multiple signals onto a single hardware transmission channel by allowing each signal to use the channel for a short time before going on to the next one. See *FDM*.

TELNET

An early TCP/IP standard protocol for remote terminal access sometimes used by network managers to control network devices.

TFTP

(*Trivial File Transfer Protocol*) A TCP/IP standard protocol for file transfer with minimal capability and minimal overhead.

three-way handshake

The 3-segment exchange TCP uses to reliably start or gracefully terminate a connection.

TLV encoding

Any representation format that encodes each item with three fields: a type, a length, and a value.

TOS

(*Type Of Service*) A reference to the original interpretation of the field in an IPv4 header that allows the sender to specify the type of service desired. Now replaced by *DiffServ*.

traceroute

A program that uses successively larger TTL values and ICMP error messages to determine intermediate hops along the path to a destination.

traffic class

A reference to a set of services available in the *DiffServ* interpretation.

traffic policing

Checking to ensure that incoming traffic adheres to preestablished bounds.

traffic shaping

Ensuring that outgoing traffic adheres to a specified rate.

triggered updates

A heuristic used with distance-vector protocols such as RIP to send an update as soon as routes change without waiting for the next update cycle.

TRPB

(*Truncated Reverse Path Broadcast*) A technique used in data-driven multicasting to forward multicast datagrams.

TRPF

(*Truncated Reverse Path Forwarding*) A synonym for *TRPB*.

TTL

(*Time To Live*) A value in the IPv4 header used to ensure that a datagram does not remain in the Internet forever, even if routes are incorrectly configured. Now interpreted as a *hop limit*.

tunneling

A technique in which a packet is encapsulated in a high-level protocol for transmission. Tunneling is used for VPNs. See *IP-in-IP*.

twisted pair Ethernet

Ethernet wiring scheme that uses twisted pair cable. See *GigE* and *category 5 cable*.

type of service routing

A routing scheme in which the choice of path depends on the characteristics of the network needed by the flow as well as the shortest path to the destination.

UDP

(*User Datagram Protocol*) A transport protocol that allows an application program on one machine to send a datagram to an application program on another.

unicast

An address that specifies forwarding a packet to a single destination. See *broadcast* and *multicast*.

unnumbered network

A technique for conserving IP network prefixes in which a point-to-point connection between two routers is not assigned a prefix.

unreliable delivery

Characteristic of a mechanism that does not guarantee to deliver data without loss, corruption, duplication, or in the same order as it was sent. See *best-effort delivery*.

urgent data

A facility that TCP uses to send data out of band.

URL

(*Uniform Resource Locator*) A syntactic form that specifies an item and a protocol used to access the item.

variable-length subnetting

A subnet address assignment scheme in which each physical net in an organization can have a different mask. See *fixed-length subnetting*.

VC

(*Virtual Circuit*) A path through a network from one application to another that is used to send data.

vector-distance

Now called *distance-vector*.

VLAN

(*Virtual Local Area Network*) A set of ports on an Ethernet switch that are configured by the network manager to be part of a single broadcast domain.

VLSM

(*Variable Length Subnet Mask*) The mask used with *variable-length subnetting*.

VoIP

(*Voice over IP*) Technology that allows voice telephone calls to be carried over the Internet. See *IP telephony*.

VPN

(*Virtual Private Network*) A technology that connects two or more separate sites over the Internet, but allows them to function as if they were a single, private network.

WAN

(*Wide Area Network*) Any physical network technology that spans large geographic distances. See *LAN* and *long haul network*.

well-known port

A protocol port number used by TCP or UDP that is preassigned to a specific service (e.g., email).

Wi-Fi

A marketing term vendors use to sell IEEE 802.11 wireless network products.

Wi-MAX

A marketing term vendors use to sell IEEE 802.16 wireless network products.

window

See *sliding window*.

window advertisement

A value used by TCP to allow a receiver to tell a sender the size of an available buffer.

Windows Sockets Interface

A variant of the socket API developed by Microsoft that is also called *WINSOCK*.

working group

A committee in the IETF working on a particular protocol or design issue.

World Wide Web

The large hypermedia service available on the Internet that allows a user to browse information.

WRR

(*Weighted Round-Robin*) A packet scheduling mechanism used to accept packets from multiple queues and send them across a single transmission channel. WRR allows each queue to be given a guaranteed percentage of the channel bandwidth.

WWW

See *World Wide Web*.

X-Window System

A software system developed at MIT for presenting and managing output on bit-mapped displays.

XDR

(*eXternal Data Representation*) The standard for a machine-independent data representation. To use XDR, a sender translates from the local machine representation to the standard external representation and a receiver translates from the external representation to the local machine representation.

zero window

See *closed window*.

ZigBee

An alliance of vendors that is standardizing protocols for use with a wireless mesh network of sensors.

zone of authority

Term used in the Domain Name System to refer to the group of names for which a given name server is an authority.

Index

B

D

Q

R